THE TRANSFORMATION OF NIGERIA

THE TRANSFORMATION OF NIGERIA:

Essays in Honor of Toyin Falola

Edited by
Adebayo Oyebade

Africa World Press, Inc.

P.O. Box 1892
Trenton, NJ 08607

P.O. Box 48
Asmara, ERITREA

Africa World Press, Inc.

P.O. Box 1892
Trenton, NJ 08607

P.O. Box 48
Asmara, ERITREA

Copyright © 2002 Adebayo Oyebade
First Printing 2002

All rights reserved. No part of this publication may be reproduced, stored in a retrieval system or transmitted in any form or by any means electronic, mechanical, photocopying, recording or otherwise without the prior written permission of the publisher.

Cover design: Ashraful Haque

Library of Congress Cataloging-in-Publication Data

The transformation of Nigeria : essays in honor of Toyin Falola / edited by Adebayo Oyebade.
   p. cm.
Includes bibliographical references and index.
  ISBN 0-86543-997-4 -- ISBN 0-86543-998-2 (pbk.)
 1. Nigeria--History. I. Falola, Toyin. II. Oyebade, Adebayo.
  DT515.57 .T73 2002
  966.9--dc21
                         2001007103

CONTENTS

Preface ix

PART A: EDUCATION, POLITICS, AND LAW

1. Exploring Uncharted Frontiers in African Studies: Toyin Falola and His Works
   Funso Afolayan 3

2. Colonial State and Education in Benin Division, 1897-1959
   Uyilawa Usuanlele 47

3. Constitution-Making and the Nigerian Identity, 1914-1960
   Ebere Nwaubani 73

4. The Collapse of Nigeria's Federal System of Government
   Akanmu G. Adebayo 113

5. Reluctant Democracy: The State, the Opposition, and the Crisis of Political Transition, 1985-1993
   Adebayo Oyebade 137

6. Intellectual Property Law and Prospects for Development
   Adebambo Adewopo — 167

PART B: ECONOMY AND SOCIETY

7. Politicization of Merchant Capital during Decolonization: European Business in Nigeria, 1948-1951
   G. Ugo Nwokeji — 183

8. State Policy, Agricultural Transformation and Decline in Eastern Nigeria, 1960-1970
   Chima J. Korieh — 223

9. Devaluation and Economic Crisis: A Political Economy Analysis
   J. I. Dibua — 261

10. State-Corporation Relationship: Impact on Management Practice
    Nimi Wariboko — 289

11. Economic Bases for Political Development
    Michael Anda — 329

PART C: GENDER AND ETHNICITY

12. Breaking Ethnic Barriers and Urban Interethnic Conflicts: The Gender Imperative
    Gloria I. Chuku — 359

13. More than Farmers' Wives: Yoruba Women and
    Cash Crop Production, c. 1920-1957
    Olatunji Ojo 383

14. Nationalism, Ethnicity, and National
    Integration: An Analysis of Political History
    Julius O. Adekunle 405

15. Political Ethnicity in Western Nigeria:
    Chieftaincy, Communal Identities, and Party Politics
    Olufemi Vaughan 435

16. The Evolution of an Ethnic Identity:
    The Owan of Mid-Western Nigeria
    Onaiwu W. Ogbomo 463

PART D: LANGUAGE, CULTURE, AND ART

17. The Mata Kharibu Model and Its Oppositions:
    Conflicts and Transformations in Cultural Valuation
    Oyekan Owomoyela 483

18. Understanding the Nigerian State:
    Popular Culture and the Struggle for Meaning
    O. B. Lawuyi 511

19. The Poet as Historian: Form and Discourse
    in Contemporary Nigerian Poetry
    Yinka Agbetuyi 531

20. From Nigeria to Benin: Introducing the Ìdaacha
    Dialect of Yoruba
    Désiré Baloubi 559

21. Orality as Scripture: Verses and Supplications in Yoruba Religion
    Abdul-Rasheed Na'Allah   585

22. Apprenticeship and Continuity in Traditional Yoruba Art
    Christopher O. Adejumo   599

Notes on Contributors   613

Index   619

PREFACE

This book is divided into four broad parts designed to explore the salient elements in the transformation of Nigeria, all of which are areas covered by the scholarship of Toyin Falola. Part A contains chapters that deal with education, law, and various issues of political development. In Part B, the chapters discuss key aspects of the economy and society. Part C contains discourses on gender and ethnicity, while the themes of Part D are language, cultures, and art. Together, these chapters constitute a scholarly interpretation of the thematic issues that have defined Nigeria in the last hundred years.

This book is offered as the first tribute to recognize and honor the immense contribution of Toyin Falola to the development of historical scholarship on Africa in general and Nigeria in particular. Toyin Falola requires no elaborate introduction given his stature in academia as a distinguished Africanist and a leading historian of Nigeria.

Falola's enduring legacy in the development of academic African history is unquestionable. Academic historiography owes its evolution and early development to the pioneering efforts of scholars such as Kenneth Dike, J. F. Ade Ajayi, Adu Boahen, and others. It was the task of the pioneer scholars during the era of decolonization and the immediate post-independence period to establish the validity of African history as a true intellectual enterprise. By the 1970s this task was achieved, attested to not only by an impressive body of published works on Africa, but also by university programs that boasted of a wide range of undergraduate and graduate courses in African history. By the early 1980s, a new generation of African academic historians was taking the baton from the pioneering scholars. Toyin Falola belongs to this second generation of scholars whose unique contribution to academic history is to expand the horizon of the discipline through teaching, and particularly through research into new historical terrain. Falola quickly established himself as a leading figure in the new historical school. His truly remarkable professional career reveals his immense contribution to the new African historiography. He has been a recipient of many awards and honors from institutions in Africa, Europe, Australia, and North America. He has held numerous leadership positions in professional bodies and served on the editorial boards of more than a dozen journals. He is the editor of various monograph series such as the Greenwood Series on the Culture and Customs of Africa; the Africa World Press's Classic Authors of Text and Authors on Africa; and the much-acclaimed University of Rochester Studies in Africa and the Diaspora.

Falola's scholarly productivity is phenomenal: over twenty books, authored or co-authored; another twenty edited or coedited books; journal articles, book chapters, and reviews, in excess of two hundred. Not many scholars of our time can lay claim to such an extraordinary contribution to scholarship of the first order. Falola's legacy to the development of African history is also measured by his active involvement in the training of a younger generation of historians. In a career that has spanned nearly a quarter of a century, Falola has taught scores of students, supervised many theses and dissertations on diverse historical themes, and won major teaching awards. Many of his former students have gone on to successful academic careers as historians, and are already making their mark in the discipline. Many who had the benefit of studying under him still enjoy his undying interest in assisting former students in the development of their professional careers.

Although Falola has written on a wide variety of African themes, his most significant contribution has been to Nigerian historical studies. He has a passion for Nigeria, with an ambition to cover all the leading issues and find answers to the problems of underdevelopment. He has written a seminal work on Ibadan, the city of his birth, in addition to contributing many important studies on the Yoruba. His works not only cut across historical periods, ranging from precolonial to contemporary times, they also explore a broad range of issues: politics, economy, religion, culture, and historiography. His prolific scholarship on Nigerian studies makes it appropriate, then, that this first festschrift should focus on Nigeria.

I am grateful to the contributors to this book. They are colleagues, friends, and former students of Falola. Limitation of space did not allow for the inclusion of many more scholars who indicated an interest in the idea of the festschrift, but they will certainly be included in a second tribute. The authors of the chapters are drawn from three continents—Africa, Europe, and North America. They also come from diverse disciplines, and so they bring to their subject different perspectives and approaches to understanding Nigeria. Nigeria is an important country, not just in African terms, but in global terms as well. Despite its recent history of economic downturn and unenviable pariah status in the international community, it is a country that is not easily ignored. Its history has been a roller coaster ride. The dawn of a new democratic political dispensation (one that will hopefully endure), and the opening of a new millennium perhaps offer a good historical juncture from which to take a critical look at the transformation in the Nigerian state.

Adebayo Oyebade
Tennessee State University

PART A

EDUCATION, POLITICS, AND LAW

1

EXPLORING UNCHARTED FRONTIERS IN AFRICAN STUDIES: TOYIN FALOLA AND HIS WORKS

Funso Afolayan

INTRODUCTION

One late afternoon, in 1983, at a University of Ife History Department seminar, at which the current writer (then a graduate student) was present, Toyin Falola opened his seminar presentation on Ibadan with a statement that would rebound with far-reaching consequences for the new and unknown scholar as well as for Yoruba and Nigerian history. First he affirmed what was already well-known and unquestioned:

> Nearly all the writers on Ibadan history have commented on the ease with which strangers were accommodated and the opportunities opened to them to achieve fame, wealth and success at Ibadan.[1]

Thereafter, and here comes the clincher, he asserted that these views, widely held and given academic credence by leading Yoruba historians, most notably Bolanle Awe and Banji Akintoye, "are partly correct and partly misleading."[2] Before his audience could take in the full implications of his statement, he went on to argue:

> It is correct to say that Ibadan welcomed people from other places, and tried as much as possible to integrate them into the society. It is, however, misleading to assert that the strangers had equal and limitless opportunities, like the indigenes, to land, wealth and power.[3]

Using extant sources, old and new, oral and written, Falola employed data and statistics to controvert what was then an established cliché among scholars: that Ibadan society gave strangers and indigenes equal opportunities to obtain wealth and power. Instead, he showed how the Oyo-Ibadan group dominated the politics as well as the economy of the new mega-city state of Ibadan throughout the nineteenth century. Settlers from other Yoruba groups, such as the Ijebu, Egba, Igbomina, Ekiti, Ijesa, and others who flocked to Ibadan in search of fame, power, and wealth, were deliberately and systematically excluded from power by the Oyo-Yoruba group who held all the key political offices and controlled much of the wealth. Thus, Falola concluded that contrary to the widely accepted thesis of Awe, Akintoye, and others before them, discrimination on the basis of birth and place of origin was a common and important feature of the Ibadan political economy in the nineteenth century. Focused on the most studied period of Yoruba history, Falola's counter-hegemonic thesis would re-echo far and wide and the writing of Yoruba history would never be the same again.

But beside its historical and historiographical significance, the disturbing political implication of Falola's new and daring thesis was clear: those looking towards, and indeed espousing, Ibadan as a model of nation-building and multigroup integration in the contemporary struggle of African countries, such as Nigeria, to forge new and united nations out of conglomerations of ethnic and linguistic nationalities are advised to either look elsewhere or begin to seriously modify their propositions. Within weeks, the *Journal of African History*, the most prestigious periodical in the field, accepted the seminar paper for publication. Falola became an instant celebrity; a scholar to watch and full of promise. In the years to come, he would not fail to live up to that expectation. The bold and incisive style, the readiness to question old and established views, and the originality and creativeness of imagination that signaled his debut in the field of African scholarship in 1983 would remain his trademarks for the rest of his academic career. This chapter is an attempt to assess the nature of Falola's contributions to Yoruba, Nigerian and African studies.

FALOLA AND THE RECONCEPTUALIZING OF YORUBA HISTORY

Yoruba history was Falola's first love. It was here that he made his first mark and some of his most enduring contributions. By the time Falola began his graduate study in 1977 at the University of Ife, the study of the Yoruba-speaking people had made many strides. Already well-known for their well-developed urban culture, exquisite verbal and sculptural arts, highly organized political institutions, and sophisticated religious and cultural traditions, the Yoruba had attracted considerable attention. Starting with the first Western-educated elite of the late nineteenth and early twentieth centuries, Yoruba authors took steps to document the history of their various communities. With the advent of colonialism and the opportunities it offered for university education, scholars of Yoruba extraction and others were able to indulge their fascination and explore their interests in Yoruba history, through the production of what have become standard academic works. The pioneer in this respect was Saburi Biobaku, with his *Egba and Their Neighbours, 1842-1872*. He was followed by Adeagbo

Akinjogbin, with his *Dahomey and its Neighbours*; Bolanle Awe, with "The Rise of Ibadan"; J.F. Ade Ajayi and Emmanuel Ayandele with their seminal works on the Christian missions; T.G.O. Gbadamosi on the spread of Islam; G. D. Jenkins on Ibadan; O.O. Ayantunga on Ijebu; and A.B. Aderibigbe and Robert S. Smith on the development of Lagos. Among the others who made their mark were Adeniyi Oroge on the institution of slavery; Robin Law on Oyo and the Atlantic slave trade; J. B. Webster and John Peel on new religious movements such as the Aladura; Banji Akintoye and Ade Obayemi on the eastern and northeastern Yoruba groups; and J.A. Atanda and A.I. Asiwaju on the Yoruba experience of European imperialism.[4] It was into this star-studded sea of established and renowned scholars that Falola plunged himself, when he decided to devote the best part of his academic life to the study of the history of the Yoruba.

In 1977, after a thorough review of Yoruba historiography, Falola came to one resounding conclusion: it is a one-sided and distorted history. One-sided because it is a history fashioned within the well-trodden tradition of "bands and trumpets," focused on popular heroes to the nearly complete neglect of the masses. It is distortive because by concentrating solely on military and political issues, it undermines the significance of socioeconomic forces in the formation of Yoruba society. While acknowledging the valuable contributions of earlier scholars, Falola argued that "we cannot continue indefinitely to talk of the Alafin, the Ooni, the Olubadan, the Owa and the Ewi as if the ordinary people without names were insignificant."[5] Heroes and rulers are important, but without their followers they are like bodies without clothes, birds without feathers, and trees without leaves and branches. As the Yoruba say, *Eniyan ni aso mi* ("People are my clothes or covering"). A king without his subjects loses the right to be addressed as a king, while a military general (*Oloogun*) without his soldiers has no one to command and is hardly better than an ordinary soldier. For Falola this was stating the obvious; though it is somewhat surprising that it had taken so long, with a few notable exceptions, for this fact to be acknowledged and addressed.

After rejecting the argument or excuse that the available sources are too scanty and too tenuous to permit a valid study of socioeconomic issues, Falola insisted that a creative use of extant documentary and especially nondocumentary sources should permit a reconstruction of the socioeconomic history of the Yoruba and of other precolonial African societies. The need for such a reconstruction, he argued, is both urgent and necessary if we are to begin to understand the material basis of African social existence. As he aptly puts it, any attempt to study the political organization without taking cognizance of the socioeconomic dimension is a false approach, since economic considerations have been crucial factors in the shaping of political and military activities. He proposed a new historiographical approach to the study of Yoruba history, which will take into consideration all aspects of human endeavors and place the necessary emphasis on the socioeconomic dimension. This approach will enable scholars to grapple with the difficult task of concentrating on the masses, who as the majority occupy the lowest rung of the social ladder, while placing the roles played by the heroes in proper perspective. The usefulness and significance of this approach transcend the confines of Yoruba history and society. As Falola puts it:

> The emphasis on the socio-economic themes would not benefit the Yoruba society alone; it can throw a great deal of light on, and enrich African history as a whole. It will make in-depth studies and analysis possible and this exercise will provide fruitful case studies relevant and necessary for a general understanding of the levels of development, and the similarities and differences in the socio-economic institutions of the various African societies.[6]

To set the pace for this new direction in Yoruba and African studies, Falola chose to research and write the economic history of Ibadan in the nineteenth century. The choice of

Ibadan was not accidental. First, Ibadan was one of the new states founded in Yorubaland in the nineteenth century. By the end of the century, it had developed into the most powerful of the Yoruba states, with hegemonic influence over much of the region. It was at Ibadan, more than at any of the other states, that many of the pre-nineteenth century institutions and structures were transformed. Focusing on Ibadan would permit an understanding of these changes as well as of their impact on Yoruba society. Second, the wide territorial extent of Yorubaland makes an in-depth study methodologically difficult, since one can easily fall into the temptation of making undue generalizations and presenting the basic outline at the expense of local peculiarities. Third, a study of Ibadan economic history would mark a major thematic shift in Nigerian economic history from a focus on trade relations with Europe or on the colonial economy to one concentrating on the domestic economy. Finally, there is a wide variety of sources, oral and written, for the reconstruction of the economic history of Ibadan from its earliest beginnings, through the colonial era, to the present.[7]

Achieving these ends involved, for Falola, a paradigmatic and methodological shift. After exposing the poverty of the traditional economic history approaches, variously referred to as economic theory, econometrics, historiometrics, or "new economic history," he rejected them as being deficient in providing for a thorough study and understanding of the precolonial African economic systems. Economic theories he criticized for being too remote and divorced from real life, while the other disciplines, by abstracting economic from social and political realities, tend to create artificial boundaries and dichotomies at variance with the multidimensional and integrated realities of human existence. While such an approach may be useful for societies where social, religious, and political organizations are peripheral to or distinct from economic ones, the approach is inapplicable to precolonial Yoruba society and many other African societies, in which all the institutions of society, political, social, or religious, are blended with the economy and intermeshed in one inseparable and interconnected ongoing historical process. For the study of such African societies, Falola proposed the adoption of a political economy approach, with its recognition of the importance of change and of time perspectives and its acknowledgment of the interlocking relationship of economic, social, religious, and political institutions as factors of change in every society.

The end product of this effort, *The Political Economy of a Pre-Colonial African State: Ibadan, 1830-1900*, was a major achievement. Methodologically sophisticated and a pioneering work of innovative scholarship, it was the first and is still the most comprehensive economic history of any precolonial Yoruba or Nigerian state ever undertaken. It discussed in great detail, laced with penetrating insights, the economic foundations of Ibadan militarism and society, while bringing into sharp focus the interrelationships between politics and economy in a precolonial African state. The study rejects unequivocally the various myths and misconceptions that had characterized many of the previous attempts by Western scholars to study and describe the structure of the indigenous African economy. Coming from a Eurocentric approach and in an ingenious attempt to locate the root of contemporary socioeconomic underdevelopment in the African past, these scholars misunderstood and thus misrepresented the pre-colonial economic system. They castigated it for its lack of diversification and specialization; its focus on subsistence instead of exports; its lack of market principles; its failure to commoditize land and labor; its lack of credit or banking institutions; the peripheral nature of its market systems and its lack of moneticization; its emphasis on leisure and welfare rather than work and profit; its rudimentary transport system and lack of inventiveness in technology; its communal forms of land ownership and its complex and cumbersome extended family systems. After condemning all the key elements of the indigenous African economy, these scholars dismissed them as "static" and unchanging and as real obstacles to development and modernization. Falola attacked this near unanimous chorus of condemnation and denigration. After a detailed, critical and well-documented examination of the indigenous economy of a major precolonial African state, Ibadan, he brought into proper perspective the errors and misconceptions dominant in the existing studies. He rejected the dominant epistemology, which privileged Europe and Europeans as the major agents of transformation in Africa. The case of Ibadan, he argued, showed that trade with Europe was not the major factor leading to economic development in the nineteenth or even the twentieth-century Yoruba states. While noting that the Ibadan economy was neither static nor backward, he showed that the indigenous system of production and exchange was both efficient and well organized and adequately met the needs of the time. The social organization fitted well with the economic system and was in no way a hindrance to either development or profit making. On the whole, the economy was diversified, moneticized, and dynamic, serviced by a well-developed market and credit facilities. While acknowledging the validity of the point made by western scholars that some of the features of the indigenous economy are no longer relevant today in the light of contemporary experience, he insisted that "their references to such institutions as being obstacles to development 'yesterday, today and tomorrow' betray their ignorance of the working and efficiency of the system in the past. What is bad and obsolete for modern times was not necessarily so for the past."[8] In the same vein, he maintained that the Eurocentric view that changes in the economy inevitably lead toward modernization are both theoretically and empirically wrong. He further argued that the so-called concept of modernization has no universal applicability or validity, since it wrongly assumes that there could be only one direction in social change, exemplified by the European capitalist evolution. Finally, Falola rejected the view that a study of the precolonial African economic system is unnecessary, since the "indigenous" system can not be adapted to meet the needs of modern times and that what Africans needed was to strive to understand and learn to duplicate the history of the growth of the industrial nations of Europe, the Americas, and Asia. This view, according to Falola, is a product of self-delusion. It is false thinking for Africans to believe that they can find answers to their problems of socioeconomic underdevelopment without understanding their own previous endeavors and experiences, at a time when it has virtually become an axiom that the past cannot be divorced from the present. What is needed, Falola concluded,

> is an awareness and a recognition of the capability of every society to transform itself that is being offered here as a lesson for the underdeveloped countries. ...The mode of production is a driving force in history and a society should be able to set its goals and values determined by its own people. To do this, African states would first have to regain economic sovereignty and autonomy. It is in their subordination to the political and economic institutions of the capitalist world and "not in population growth, inertia and traditionalism that the fundamental cause of underdevelopment resides."[9]

The interconnectedness of economic with social and political issues becomes even more apparent through an examination of the Yoruba commercial system. Though many aspects of the precolonial Yoruba economy are yet to be studied, thanks to the pioneering work of Falola, we now know a little about the Yoruba caravan and toll systems. An understanding of commerce in precolonial southwestern Nigeria would be incomplete without a study of the place of caravans, that is, a company of traders traveling together. Complex in organization and in forms, extensive in territorial reach, and diverse in amounts of goods and numbers of participants, caravans constituted the core of the commercial systems; they connected states and communities and mediated social and political relations between groups. Following in the steps and benefiting from the scholarship of Catherine Coquery-Vidrovith, Paul Lovejoy, Adu Boahen, David Birmingham, Claude Meillassoux, Anthony Hopkins, Philip Curtin, Allen Isaacman, and others who had studied African long-distance trade, Falola attempted to integrate the Yoruba data into the existing historiography, while at the same time bringing out the peculiarities of the Yoruba system and its significance in the overall scheme of African trade. Based on the analysis of available data, Falola identified five distinct features of the Yoruba caravan system. First, unlike most other African caravans, Yoruba caravans relied on porters, rather than pack animals. Second, unlike the Hausa, Dyula, and Swahili traders, the Yoruba did not use Islam as a cultural strategy to organize the traders. Instead, traders belonged to different religions. Third, Yoruba caravans were not dominated by traders from certain subgroups or towns, as was the case with the Dyula and the Hausa of West Africa or the Yao and Swahili of East Africa. Fourth, Yoruba caravans were not controlled by powerful families or proprietors like the Wandervba of East Africa, the Sate Feredi of the Diakhanke (of Senegambia) or the Madugu of the Hausa. Trade was carried out on an individual basis. Military escorts were employed to provide security but rarely served as leaders. While rich merchants or others with strong personalities might emerge as leaders of individual caravans, such temporary leaders exercised little authority beside maintaining peace and order and did not interfere in any way with how individual traders or group of traders transacted their business. Finally, Yoruba caravans were peopled largely by women. However, unlike women in other African caravans, these women were traders themselves and not wives, concubines, or dependents of male traders. The implication of this was that since women combined domestic (childrearing) with commercial duties, most could not afford to leave their homes for long periods or travel for long distances, though many did travel frequently within an area. However, women who had passed the age of childbearing, or co-wives, or had access to capital and porters, or could assert themselves and damn the social consequences, did travel for long durations.[10]

A major element of the caravan system was the Yoruba toll system. Writing on this in 1989, Falola noted:

> The Yoruba toll system has not been studied, in spite of its major role in the indigenous economy

and politics. It is common knowledge that the tollgates were prevalent in all Yoruba towns; what is less obvious is that the collection of duties from these gates was well integrated with the organization of trade and that proceeds from tolls were part of the revenues relied upon by the political elite in all Yoruba towns. Neither has the toll system received the attention it deserves in the analysis of the establishment of the colonial economy at the turn of this century.[11]

Focusing on the operation of the toll system in the nineteenth century and on its subsequent abolition by the British at the beginning of the twentieth century, Falola was able to show that the toll system was a significant aspect of Yoruba economy and politics. For the ruling elite, tolls were an integral part of the economic basis of their military and political power. As sources of revenue, tolls were more efficient, more reliable, more lucrative, and easier to collect than others sources such as taxes, death duties, and judicial fees and fines. With regard to British rule, Falola showed that the attitude of British officials to the toll system was a major political issue in their relations with the chiefs, while the issue of what to do with the toll system generated widespread debates and controversies among the Yoruba elite as well as among European traders and officials in Nigeria and in Britain. For the British, bringing the chiefs under control meant striking at the economic basis of their political power, the toll system. Since they could neither regulate nor control the toll system, they decided to abolish it. After a number of failed attempts they succeeded in abolishing the system between 1904 and 1908. The British were able to achieve this end because of the gradualist approach they eventually adopted, the administrative and military power available to them and their ability to generate alternative sources of revenue to support both themselves and pay the chiefs. More importantly, while its impact on the general economy remains uncertain, the abolition of tolls was a major step in the successful constitution of the colonial economy.

Another aspect of the indigenous economy that intrigued Falola is domestic slavery, its operation, practice, and abolition in Yorubaland. His foray into this field began with his examination of power relations and social interactions among Yoruba slaves. Focusing on Ibadan in the nineteenth century, and using oral evidence, especially data gleaned from lineage history, he contended that slaves were not all of the same status. A few became privileged and powerful members of important households, served as royal messengers and governors of conquered provinces, had harems of wives, and owned their own retinues of slaves. These privileged slaves exercised power, first over their own slaves, and second over the slaves of their masters. Falola further argued that contrary to the trend in the literature emphasizing the "mild" and "humane" nature of African domestic slavery vis-à-vis trans-Atlantic slavery, when the chips were down, a slave was always a slave and while the level of ill-treatment and dehumanization never approached anything close to the standards set in the Americas, there were many cases of cruelties and discrimination against slaves in Yorubaland; this challenged the thesis of slavery as a benign institution in pre-colonial Africa. After examining how the privileged slaves interacted with other slaves, not as members of the same servile class, but as masters in their own right, he described in telling detail how the slaves, men and women, rich and poor, acted together to secure integration into the households of their masters, failing which they often acted in concert to obtain their freedom or escape. On the basis of the evidence from Yorubaland, he concluded that contrary to the claims made by many scholars on African slavery:

> It is not true, as some have suggested, that slaves were content with their status to the extent that most regarded their masters as mentors and friends. Slaves were aware of being exploited and united to ameliorate their conditions and, if possible, to es-

cape, even if a class consciousness did not fully develop for reasons which Catherine Coquery-Vidrovitch and Paul Lovejoy have explained in another context.[12]

Writing on the same theme in the *Journal of Religious History*, Falola showed how and why Christian missionaries, especially those of the Anglican Church, were incorrigibly averse to domestic slavery. For the Church Missionary Society (CMS), domestic slavery was the root of many evils. First they argued that it made the abolition of the Atlantic slave trade difficult, since it was it was that trade's major source. In this, as Falola showed, they were mistaken. Domestic slaves, as a rule, were not sold, except as punishment for serious crimes and attempts to escape. In addition, it was the abolition of the Atlantic slave trade that led to the expansion of domestic slavery, as those who could not be sold had to be retained in the domestic sphere. Second, missionaries as well as other European visitors argued that the search for slaves was responsible for most of the wars fought in Yorubaland during the nineteenth century. In this they were also partly wrong. As Falola argued:

> it is true that slaves, indeed hundreds of them, were gained from the numerous nineteenth-century wars. But it is not true that the wars were primarily for the object of obtaining slaves. Political considerations—for example, the ambition to create larger polities and to struggle for independence—were the key underlying factors.[13]

Finally, the missionaries argued that the wars were disruptive and did not allow agricultural and industrial growth. These claims, Falola noted, were not entirely true. First the devastation caused by the wars was exaggerated; disruptions were often temporary and only during periods of actual fighting. The normal activities of trading and farming went on as before, though with added caution and security measures. On the claim that slavery hampered economic growth, Falola argued that the reverse was actually the case, by showing that the expansion in the volume of economic production and distribution in nineteenth-century Yorubaland was due in part to the use of slaves in large numbers as major sources of labor in the extensive farms owned by chiefs, in craft workshops, and in caravans. Acting against this background of misconception and prejudices, the Anglican Church attacked domestic slavery, discouraged slave holding by its converts, and put pressure on the nascent British imperial administration to stamp out the practice. These efforts achieved very little.

According to Falola, there were five major reasons for this failure. The first was that the various missions were not united in their campaigns against domestic slavery. First, while the Anglican Church remained hostile to domestic slavery, most of the other missions were only halfhearted in their opposition. Second, it was difficult to convince most of the converts that an institution such as slavery, which had existed for centuries and had become an integral part of the economic order, was a social evil. Many of these converts who were themselves former slaves also owned slaves and did not hesitate to advice the missionaries not to meddle in such sensitive domestic matters. Third, the larger society did not buy the missionaries' arguments and propaganda against slavery. Local authorities in Yoruba towns such as Ibadan, Abeokuta, and others were quick to warn the missionaries that any interference in the institution of domestic slavery would lead to trouble for everyone. Fourth, the church was also benefiting from the existence of the institution, since many of the early converts were slaves or pawns. As individuals on the margins of the sociopolitical system and often with an acute sense of alienation from local communities, slaves and pawns were more susceptible to the lure of an alien religion that promised equality for everyone in this life and rewards for the oppressed in the world to come. Finally, the Anglican Church itself was divided on the issue. While its directors in London encouraged active abolition efforts, most of its African clergymen were more favorably disposed to the institution, advocating caution and pointing out on several occasions the "humane" and paternalistic nature of Yoruba slavery in comparison to the treatment of slaves in Europe or the Americas.

However, where the missionaries failed, the British colonial officials succeeded. This happened, as Falola pointed out in another essay, not merely because of the British possession and monopoly of force, but rather because of their adoption of a gradualist and pragmatic approach to the institution. Thus, its abolition among the Yoruba was not sudden, while its final end cannot be dated, since no single colonial law or policy brought about its demise. Besides, slavery did not end at the same time in all parts of Yorubaland. In places like Lagos, where the forces of change operated rapidly and colonial laws were easier to implement, slavery witnessed a speedier death; while in other places, more remote from effective colonial control, the institution witnessed a slower death. In the final analysis, beginning in the 1890s and extending over a period of four decades, a combination of social, economic, and political forces brought about the disintegration and end of the institution. Other forms of dependency, such as pawnship (*iwofa*), and new forms of labor relations, such as migrant and wage labor systems, came to replace the dying institution.[14]

For the Yoruba, the nineteenth century was above all a century of warfare. The century opened and closed with warfare. The Yoruba fought a series of wars with their neighbors, but even more consequential were the civil wars fought within Yorubaland, between Yoruba states and groups. The wars led to far-reaching sociopolitical transformations, resulting in the destruction of many states such as the Old Oyo Empire and the establishment of new polities such as Ibadan, Abeokuta, and Ijaiye. Consequently, more than any other period of Yoruba history, the nineteenth century has attracted considerable academic attention. Most of the leading scholars of Yoruba history from Biobaku, Ajayi, Smith, and Ayandele to Awe, Gbadamosi, Akintoye, Oroge, and others made their names writing on aspects of nineteenth-century Yoruba history. Falola's major achievement has been to add an economic dimension to the story. But he has done more than this. In

1968, after a panoramic review of the literature on the nineteenth century, Falola concluded correctly "that the gaps are still many to the extent that what we know of the century is only partial and incomplete."[15] With penetrating insight, he then proceeded to identify and describe the gaps and lapses in existing studies. First he emphasized the need to study the nineteenth-century with a view to establishing its significance in relation to preceding centuries as well as to contemporary society. Then he examined the ways in which the attempt to put the history of the century to different uses had resulted in distortions and reinterpretations, with far-reaching consequences for intergroup and intragroup relations in twentieth-century Yorubaland.

Next, Falola argued that though we have more information on the nineteenth-century wars than on any other aspects of Yoruba history, much about the wars still remains to be studied. We know more about the major wars and the major states and very little about the minor wars between the smaller states. The focus on the new states has led to the neglect of the older ones, making our knowledge of groups like the Egba and the Egbado before the 1830s perfunctory. Other issues ignored in the existing literature include the ethics of war, the roles of youths and women, warfare on rivers and lagoons, and the impact of migrations and large-scale interactions on the spread of the dialects of the Yoruba languages. We also know very little about the much-celebrated war heroes, especially their last days, and their impact on the postwar political activities of their communities.[16] Falola also noted the need to make a distinction (both in theory and in practice) between wars, raids, and brigandage, since everything is erroneously represented in the literature as war. Next Falola identified new issues that should engage historians of the century. The most obvious of these is the need to focus on the history of the frontier communities, especially those to the north and east that had benefited very little from academic research due to the lack of written sources such as missionary and colonial records. Such studies should reveal the nature of the relationship between the communities on the peripheries and their neighbors, Yoruba and non-Yoruba, and should shed light on the boundaries of the Yoruba-speaking people. Beyond the wars and beyond the nineteenth century, why did these frontier communities of the Igbomina, Ekiti, Akoko, Okun-Yoruba, and others remain small and segmentary and why did they not conform to the pattern of political centralization dominant in the central and southwestern parts of Yorubaland? How did the wars affect these frontier communities, especially in relation to the issues of identity formation and the transformation of social institutions? Why, for instance, did these communities resist Islamic penetration in the nineteenth century while welcoming incorporation into the British colonial system in the twentieth century?[17]

On slavery, Falola contended that, in spite of the landmark works by Oroge, "there is as yet no convincing and detailed essay on the changing status of slaves during the century, slavery and class, women and slavery, the ideology of slavery, slave control, and resistance."[18] Other issues that require their historians included pawnship, lineage systems and social differentiation, the state and practice of indigenous religion, secret societies, forms of social vices, crimes, and poverty, expressions of sexual domination such as concubinage and prostitution,[19] the development of technology and science, crafts and industries, and the elaboration of old and new ideas and ideologies of state formation and social and power hegemony. On the role of women, Falola stressed the need to relate the data on the Yoruba to the various feminist theories as well as to the larger context of social and political institutions dominated by men.[20] Noting the limitations of existing methodologies and approaches, Falola concluded his exploration of these uncharted frontiers of Yoruba history by calling on the historians of the Yoruba not to shy away from the models, theories, and concepts of the social sciences, a deficiency in existing studies that had given John Peel the opportunity to correctly castigate the "Ibadan School of History" for ignoring sociology and anthropology or maintaining an unnecessary distance from them.[21]

In the last few years and in consonance with this seminal essay, Falola has maintained an active and innovative agenda of research into Yoruba history. On the wars, as early as 1984, he published, with Dare Oguntomisin, *The Military in Nineteenth Century Yoruba Politics*. Though this volume like others before it suffers from the tendency to privilege the major states over the smaller ones, its publication was a major departure in the study of the Yoruba in the nineteenth century. Previous studies had focused on individual states. This volume was the first to take a pan-Yoruba approach and among the few to underscore the significance of the military in the transformation of states and societies in nineteenth-century Yorubaland. After a comparative analysis of the involvement of the military in Ibadan, Ijaiye, Abeokuta, Oke Odan, and other Yoruba states, the volume concluded that the unprecedented and dominant role of the military in nineteenth-century Yorubaland was a by-product of the perennial state of warfare and insecurity that dominated the century and called into question many of the traditions and institutions of the previous era.[22] This exploration of the role of the military was carried further when Falola again collaborated with Oguntomisin to produce *Yoruba Warlords of the Nineteenth Century*,[23] which successfully grappled with some of the issues raised in Falola's research agenda essay. A pioneering book, written with lucidity and laced with interesting anecdotes and fresh insights, *Yoruba Warlords* examines the life histories of the most distinguished of the Yoruba warriors, focusing on their exploits, mistakes, and contributions as well as their diplomatic strategies and the enduring consequences of their actions. In the same vein, Falola's essay on "Brigandage and Piracy in Nineteenth Century Yorubaland" offered a corrective to the prevailing trend in the literature to confusedly describe all violent encounters between groups as "warfare." After insisting that many of the so-called wars were nothing but brigandage and robberies perpetrated by soldiers in search of material accumulation and sustenance, Falola cautioned scholars to be aware of the attempts in oral traditions to turn brigands into successful war heroes with long praise poems c oriki.[24]

On the question of how the new states solved the enormous problems of building new economies, Falola provided an exploratory discussion in his essay on "The Construction and Destruction of Ijaiye Economy, c. 1832-1862," where he examined the linkage between warfare and the economy, of which the short-lived but powerful military autocracy provided an excellent example.[25] In another essay on Ijaiye, Falola examined how the survivors and refugees from the collapsed states coped with the problems of integration and resettlement.[26] The subject of refugees and resettlement was further explored in another essay coauthored with Oguntomisin, titled, "Refugees in Yorubaland in the Nineteenth Century," where the authors contended that warfare and the consequent dislocation resulted in much cultural synthesis as well as political experimentation in Yorubaland, as new forms of government were evolved to cope with the exigencies of the era. More pertinent is the fact that many of the intergroup and intracommunity hostilities that have continued to plague relations in parts of Yorubaland, as in the incessant and bloody Ife-Modakeke crisis, to mention the most intractable, can be traced to the incomplete and unsuccessful nature of some of the attempts at host-refugee integration in the nineteenth-century.[27] A diplomatic history of the Yoruba is yet to be written. However, in a number of essays, Falola has attempted a conceptual discussion of the role of diplomacy in the nineteenth century Yoruba wars. In an essay on "The Foreign Policy of Ibadan in the Nineteenth Century,"[28] he showed how the army was used to serve the interests of an aggressive state and promote a pro-war approach to diplomacy. In another essay, written with Hakeem Danmole, he examined how diplomacy was used by Ibadan to secure alliances and tilt the balance of power in its favor, in the grim struggle for power and supremacy in nineteenth-century Yorubaland.[29] Finally, in an essay published in 1985, Falola argued that diplomacy proved ineffective as an instrument of conflict resolution in nineteenth-century Yorubaland, because the participants were not genuinely committed to a peaceful resolution; they employed diplomacy only to obscure their selfish pursuit of aggressive military goals such as improving their striking capacity and their access to European weapons.[30]

Beyond the nineteenth century, Falola has carried his exploration of Yoruba history into the twentieth, focusing particularly on the impact of British colonialism on Yoruba politics, economy, and society. This interest has generated a number of notable works. The most significant of these is *Politics and Economy in Ibadan, 1893-1945*. Conceived within the same historiographical tradition that gave birth to *The Political Economy of a Pre-Colonial African State*, the book "extends the frontier of knowledge [of the Yoruba] to the colonial period." However, it does more than this. As Falola points out, most of the "previous studies have chosen larger territories as case studies, thereby ignoring local peculiarities and developments." The work remedies this deficiencies, by focusing on Ibadan, the most populous sub-Saharan African city during the colonial period. Second, the emphasis in the literature has been on the political aspects of the colonial administration, "to the neglect of the social and economic" dimensions. This study, the first of its kind on any of the major Yoruba states, by taking a political economy approach underscored the significance of socioeconomic issues in the development of an African colonial society. Finally, the book represented a departure from most of the previous studies, which had been carried out from the perspective of the British, a perspective "that erroneously attributes much positive impact to the colonial enterprise." Instead, using the experience of Ibadan as a case study, the book argued that British rule "halted the development of indigenous institutions and introduced changes that were not conducive to rapid positive growth and development."[31] As a follow-up to this major work, Falola, in a series of essays, examined the extent and limits of the impact of British domination on the sociopolitical transformation of Yoruba society. He argued that by privileging the "impact of colonialism on chieftaincy institutions," as the main focus of analysis, studies by Atanda, Asiwaju, and others have failed to understand the multidimensional and complex nature of the colonial encounter. Falola argued that just as men and women competed for power and space in the colonial system, values and ideas also competed for recognition and acceptance. He concluded that

> the rejection of values and the authority of the chiefs, the struggles among the chiefs for power and promotion, the debates about the criteria for leadership in the indigenous system, the ambition of a new generation of educated men to become chiefs and acquire prominence in the society, all point to an active, competitive, and dynamic system which cannot be understood just by focusing on the impact of colonialism on chieftaincy institutions, as most studies have done to date.[32]

Falola has also made important contributions to the study of the social history of the Yoruba. Building on the seminal works of Ade Ajayi and Ayandele, on the impact of the Christian missions, Falola pushed the boundaries of our knowledge of Yoruba social history. The most detailed of Falola's contributions is in the area of intellectual history, an aspect that had previously received scant attention from Yoruba scholars, in spite of the availability of considerable data. His book, *Yoruba Gurus: Indigenous Production of Knowledge in Africa*,[33] decried the way in which the intellectual contributions of Africans outside the academy have, over the years, been ignored, slighted or maligned. By examining the life histories, the times, and the intellectual production of prominent Yoruba intelligentsia members without university certificates or connections to the academy, he showed that intellectual contributions need not be divorced from the concerns of local communities or deliberately constructed to promote narrative inequality and distance. The book rejected the academy's tendency of privileging itself to the detriment of other sites of production and voices. After criticizing as manipulative the position of J. F. Ade Ajayi, the doyen of Nigerian historiography, that local histories should "be treated only as sources for analyzing and reconstructing the past,"[34] Falola called on scholars to go beyond the prevalent approach of treating chronicles as *sources*. Instead, he insisted, they should be viewed "as a distinct and viable body of autonomous and respectable knowledge that deserves to be celebrated in its own right."[35] This is a reassuring and positive affirmation of the legitimacy of this form of indigenous historiography. Any historian who has either read or used Samuel Johnson on Oyo or Kemi Morgan on Ibadan will no doubt agree. Nevertheless, Falola's affirmation, while a useful corrective, underestimates or at least ignores the serious limitations and generally tendentious nature of many of these histories. After examining in separate chapters the remarkable success of the works of notable indigenous scholars such as Samuel Johnson and M. C. Adeyemi on the Oyo-Yoruba, Isaac Akinyele and Kemi Morgan on Ibadan, Samuel Ojo Bada on Ilorin, and Theophilus Avoseh on Epe and Badagry, among others, Falola attributed their wide circulation and respectability at the local level to their simplicity, language accessibility, cheapness, and availability. Their often-nationalistic tone, their focus on identity formation, and their cultivation and celebration of culture heroes also helped to ensure their popularity and continuing relevance.

Thereafter Falola turned his searchlight on Nigerian academic historians, among whom he is a distinguished member, but some of whom he sharply criticized for ghost-writing for pay, thus giving "hagiographers" or false authors the opportunity to be justly contemptuous of scholars while unashamedly appropriating intellectual discourse through corruption and debasement of scholarship. Without under-estimating the validity of this criticism, it must however, be noted that intellectual prostitution developed in Nigeria, among grossly underpaid academics, largely as a strategy of survival in the face of deteriorating economic conditions and grinding mass poverty characteristic of Nigeria during the late 1980s and the early 1990s. More problematic, however, is the academy's crisis of relevance vis-à-vis contemporary Nigerian realities. Falola has traced this socio-disconnectedness to the alien nature of Nigerian academic history. It did not grow from an indigenous tradition; it developed as a child of Western historiography. This association, Falola argued, has been both a blessing and a curse. A blessing, because academic history has benefited from the Western historiographical tradition with its easily available tools, methods, and ideas. It is, however, a tragedy because by this association, Nigerian academic history has dissociated itself from the vibrant indigenous tradition. In a characteristically controversial and sharply worded criticism, whose far-reaching implications our limited space will not permit us to examine here, but which historians of non-Western societies should note, Falola concluded:

> Academic history in Nigeria has set itself on a path of self-destruction. It is nothing but a caricature of a Western tradition, failing so far to attain any respectable domestication, unable to give birth to any large body of autonomous theories and ideas, always borrowing, and . . . as yet to connect effectively with a tangible reading public.[36]

FALOLA AND THE HISTORY OF MODERN NIGERIA

Though Falola's most original and most penetrating works have been in the field of Yoruba history, his contributions to the recovery and reconstruction of the history of modern Nigeria are no less significant. As with Yoruba studies, Falola has focused more on social and economic issues than on political ones. Notable among the social issues he has studied are religion, health, pawnship,[37] prostitution, and corruption. On religion, besides journal articles and book chapters, he has authored, coauthored, and coedited a number of notable works. In *Religion and Society in Nigeria*, coedited with Jacob Olupona, Falola and other scholars attempted to grapple with the underlying *problematique* of the fundamental approaches to the study of religion, from structuralism to functionalism, and to the intellectualist school. The book contended with such issues as the best ways to study the role of religion in modern society, the issues to include in or exclude from such a study, and the appropriateness of an eclectic approach that welcomes many views and perspectives. Among the many issues examined within the context of religion are ethnicity, kingship, gender, and the mass media. Others are medicine and healing, economy and capitalism, resistance and self-determination, and ideology and politics. The book argued that religious fanaticism can only be understood within the framework of economic deprivation and political marginalization, though this is inadequate to explain the complicity of the dominant ruling and affluent elite in the generation of religious violence. This is an innovative work, complex in its categorization of the many issues involved, intriguing in its representation of conflicting perspectives, and fascinating in its articulation of problems.[38]

In *Religious Impact on the Nation State: The Nigerian Predicament*, written with Pat Williams, Falola again returned to the issue of religion and politics, arguing that the pluralistic nature of the Nigerian society makes religion a potentially disruptive force in the hands of a parasitic elite seasoned in the art of manipulating religion for political ends. In another essay, Falola argued that the contest for hegemony in troubled economic and political environments have turned both Islam and Christianity into "political ideologies" perpetually seeking strategies, including violence, to dominate political space and impose narrow values.[39] Finally, in *Violence in Nigeria: The Crisis of Religious Politics and Secular Ideologies*,[40] Falola provided the most comprehensive study of religious violence and aggression in Nigeria to date. Drawing together divergent though mutually reinforcing approaches and paradigms from the various humanistic disciplines, the book explores the ways in which the institutionalization of religious violence and the aggressive competition for dominance by adherents of both Islam and Christianity continue to threaten peace as well as the corporate existence of the Nigerian nation. While recognizing the importance of the fundamentalist factor in the generation of religious violence, Falola rejected attempts to privilege any single variable. Instead, he called for the adoption of an eclectic approach that would situate religious violence within the context of the post-independent realities and problems of Nigeria in which violence has become a viable response to social decay, economic deprivation, and political malaise. A product of extensive primary research, painstakingly balanced almost to a fault, controversial and disturbing, though surprisingly exhilarating and engrossing, *Violence in Nigeria* is a splendid achievement. It should become one of Falola's most enduring contributions to modern Nigerian historiography.[41]

On the economy, Falola has also made some notable contributions. In a series of articles and edited and collaborative works, he attempted a reassessment of the economic impact of British colonialism in Nigeria. Issues and themes that had been ignored by earlier scholars did not escape his exploring mind. In "Cassava Starch for Export in Nigeria during the Second World War," he showed, first, how far the imperial government would go in search of resources, second, the creative and innovative response of colonial subjects to new opportunities, and third, the unpredictability of the market in export commodities.[42] In "An Ounce Is Enough," he showed how the efforts of the colonial government to control gold production and export failed, in the face of stiff and covert resistance by indigenous goldsmiths and consumers, who used the availability of a domestic market to subvert the government's attempt to check the "illicit" trade in raw and smelted gold.[43] In "My Friend the Shylock," he used an analysis of the organization of the Yoruba credit systems of *ajo, esusu,* and *iwofa* (pawnship), to argue that indigenous institutions that survived during the colonial era "did so because they were able to 'modernize' themselves by borrowing from alien ideas and practices and by responding to the demands of a 'new' colonial society." As in the case of the gold industry, the efforts of the colonial government to protect debtors and regulate trade, through the enactment of ordinances, failed. Lenders devised ways to continue to charge exorbitant interests, while the poor and the needy, most especially in the rural areas, with no access to modern banking, remained subject to humiliation, harassment, and property seizure.[44] In two insightful articles, Falola argued that even though there were similarities between Lebanese activities in different parts of West Africa, there were significant differences in the way the Lebanese in different countries sought integration into their host societies. He insisted that, contrary to the common assumption in existing literature, the Lebanese were not apolitical. Though they avoided overt and aggressive involvement, they were wise enough to stabilize the political environment in their favor, to court the support of colonial officials and of local chiefs.[45]

In one of the major studies of British imperialism, *Development Planning and Decolonization in Nigeria*, Falola zeroed in on the late colonial period, 1940-1960, when the radicalization of indigenous nationalism and the major shift in colonial thinking effected by World War II engendered optimism and the belief that centralized planning by the state and within the framework of a mixed economy would provide the "big push" that would transform a "traditional" society into a "modern" one.[46] Wonderfully crafted, provocative, and firmly grounded in the historiography of colonialism and development theory, *Development Planning* is the first comprehensive book on the foundations of economic planning in Nigeria. Scholars and others interested in understanding the historical roots of the contemporary crisis of the Nigerian state would do well to pay attention to its detailed but nuanced account of the beginning of the attempts to find an intelligent solution to the seemingly intractable problem of development in Nigeria. The book ended on a positive note, emphasizing that while no one underestimated the enormity of the challenges, most of the economic and social indicators at the time of independence testify to Nigeria's great potential for rapid development.[47]

Less optimistic was *Britain and Nigeria: Exploitation or Development?*[48] In this book, Falola brought together an array of notable Nigerian economic historians and political scientists such as Segun Osoba, O. Njoku, Don Ohadike, Akanmu

Adebayo, and Julius Ihonvbere to reexamine the precise nature of the economic impact of British colonialism. While agreeing that British rule led to the establishment of schools, hospitals, a civil service, an armed force, roads and railways, a new language (English), and a new religion (Christianity), the contributors were unanimous in their view that any claim by the British to have achieved or laid the foundation of concrete development for the benefit of the Nigerian people was illusory. They argued that given the destructive and exploitative goals to which the colonial infrastructure was put, any development that occurred can at best be described as unintended or meant to facilitate the furtherance of colonial exploitation and incorporation. This explains why the major legacies of colonialism have remained the distorted and outward orientation of the Nigerian economy, the absence of a technological and an industrial base, the neocolonial and alienating content of the educational system, the viciousness and unproductive nature of the armed and security forces, all arising from a colonial system that emphasized the interests of the metropolis at the expense of Nigeria and Nigerians. The study concludes that

> the peripheral role and location of the Nigerian formation today in the international division of labour, the existence of a weak and largely unproductive bourgeoisie, the co-existence of modes of production (the pre- and capitalist modes), the existence of an unstable state and the generally low standards of living were the direct consequences of the colonial planning and policies which are being reproduced in the contemporary period.[49]

Similarly, in *Nigeria and the International Capitalist System*, coedited with Julius Ihonvbere, with contributions by Segun Osoba and Akanmu Adebayo, Falola pointed out the limitations of the orthodox approach to the study of foreign policies of underdeveloped countries, and advocated the adoption of a radical, political-economy approach. After an analysis of the connections between the economy and the foreign policy performance of the successive Nigerian regimes from 1960 to the mid-1980s, the book argued that the dependent economy of Nigeria limited what it could do in foreign policy. Its colonial and neocolonial dependence on Euro-American powers for aid and for markets for its major export goods, especially petroleum, created a serious crisis of helplessness in Nigeria's ability to formulate and implement radical policies that might benefit its people, for fear of antagonizing its international benefactors and creditors.[50]

The consequences of a depressed and distorted economy are far-reaching. Among these is the problem of rural neglect, resulting from the practice among Nigerian policy makers, from the colonial era to the present, of concentrating investments in urban areas with the expectation that the benefits of such urban investments would eventually trickle down to the rural areas. In *Rural Development Problems in Nigeria*, co-edited with Samuel Olanrewaju, Falola showed how the Nigerian experience revealed that such a trickle-down-effect rarely happens. Instead, rural-urban dichotomy developed in which all the basic infrastructural facilities, good roads, hospitals, and schools, were concentrated in the urban areas, with the vast majority of rural settlements left with no school, no electricity, no pipe-borne water, and of course no access to telephones or good health care systems. The consequences of this neglect for Nigeria have been particularly crippling, resulting in rural-urban migration, neglect of agriculture, food shortage, and declining export production. For instance, Nigeria, which during the 1960s was the leading exporter of palm oil products in the world, was by the 1980s importing palm oil to satisfy its domestic needs. Similarly, the problems and challenges of transportation are examined in another book edited with Olanrewaju, in which the contributors discussed the yet to be resolved crisis of urban, rural, and public transport development and management. The book ended with a call for further study of the Nigerian transport systems, especially bus and train financing and services, and also road transportation, its special characteristics, the nature of its organization and management, the cost of its maintenance, its pricing policy, its productivity, and its profitability.[51] In *Child Health in Nigeria*, edited with Tola Olu Pearce, Falola examined the impact of a depressed economy on health care delivery, most especially as it relates to the most vulnerable group in the population, children. All the contributors identified a sharp deterioration in the health status of children as a result of the economic crisis that had bedeviled African countries since the 1980s. Old health problems associated with preventable diseases such as malaria, hookworm, and others have reappeared with a vengeance. Other factors such as child abuse, forced or childhood marriages, early childbirth, street hawking by children, proliferation of gangs, street begging by children, child labor, and poor programs for juveniles and disabled children have combined to complicate the problems of child health care in Nigeria.[52] *The Political Economy of Health Care in Africa*, which Falola edited with Dennis Ityavyar, reemphasized the staggering impact of the African economic crisis on the deterioration of health care delivery in various parts of the continent.[53]

Falola has also made his mark in the writing of modern Nigerian political history. The consistent history of political failure, in which the Nigerian ruling elite has distinguished itself since independence in 1960, has received considerable attention from many scholars.[54] Falola's foray into this field began in 1983, with the collapse at the end of that year of the ill-fated Nigerian Second Republic government led by Shehu Shagari. Horrified at the level of mindless corruption, gross mismanagement, blatant abuse of office, and political violence characteristic of this regime, Falola took it upon himself to look into the reasons for its failure. The result was *The Rise and Fall of Nigeria's Second Republic: 1979-84*,[55] written in collaboration with Julius Ihonvbere, whose Marxist imprint on the volume was unmistakable. Taking a Marxist political economy approach, the book criticized Nigerian social science "as it is presently constituted" for its ideological poverty and methodological shallowness. It rejected existing theories of political and economic development as inadequate for explaining the Nigerian crisis, because of their focus on superstructures at the expense of the dynamics and contradictions within substructures. Existing explanations of underdevelopment and political crisis were dismissed as escapist, diversionary, and pro-status quo. Instead, the book called for the adoption of a new approach that would emphasize the specific historical experience of the Nigerian nation, the nature of its state and social relations, the accumulative basis of its dominant classes, its interclass and intraclass contradictions and struggles, and its historically determined location and role within the world capitalist system. Finally, on the failure of what it described as the "terrible, backward, useless and bankrupt [Shagari] government," the book argued that the problem was not just human but systemic:

> The military had assumed that a new constitution, a new anthem and pledge, new states and local governments, indigenization decrees defining spheres of interests and influence, etc., would guarantee stability and accumulation. But these assumptions had not addressed in any manner the systemic contradictions, which have prompted political disintegration and crisis in the past. The Shagari administration was unable, in spite of the human and material resources available to it, to mediate class contradictions and impose a viable hegemony on society.[56]

In *The Military Factor in Nigeria, 1966-1985*,[57] Falola brought the military under critical scrutiny. After surveying the dire and ruinous consequences of twenty-two years of military rule, Falola went as far as to describe the Nigerian military establishment as an "evil empire." Written at the peak of the 1993 election crisis, in which the military under Ibrahim Babangida threw Nigeria into an unnecessary and destructive upheaval, the book is a critique of the diabolical role of the Nigerian military. In his most biting critique of any Nigerian institution, and in words that many of his contemporary scholars would have no difficulty in sharing and applauding, Falola emphasized:

> The Nigerian military is not a fighting force, but a decadent "political party," plagued by a lack of sincere leadership, divided by ethnicity and religion, and permanently committed to the destruction of the country. It has generated the most destabilizing crises for the country, destroyed the economy, undermined the democratic process, and promoted a large-scale use of violence.... Corruption has become institutionalized.... Driven by greed for money and power, the military dominates the Nigerian political scene.... The benefits that the masses of Nigeria should have derived from their oil wealth are denied, mainly because of large-scale mismanagement and fraud.... The Nigerian masses live in a big cage created and nurtured by an army of occupation. They have put their heads in the mouth of a lion, and they either have to free themselves very quickly or get swallowed.[58]

In other essays, written alone or in collaboration with others, Falola showed how a combination of traditional, colonial, and neocolonial power structures instituted corruption as an integral part of the relationships between the rulers and the ruled in Nigeria. Apart from hindering socioeconomic development, such a patrimonial system has had the devastating effect of tying the people to a perpetually unequal system and discouraging revolutionary change.[59]

On the way forward for Nigeria, Falola has made several suggestions. First, he has called for the rejection of the classical federal system as defined by K. C. Wheare and other legal and political theorists.[60] What Nigeria needs, he argued, is a dynamic federal system, which will seek to unite all its nationalities, while recognizing without manipulating its cultural diversity in religion, language, and other aspects of culture. Second, the militarization of the society must end. The military must be depoliticized, sent back to barracks, insulated from partisan politics, and kept under effective civilian authority. Third, Nigeria must develop and adopt norms, values, and a leadership ethos that will ensure the emergence of leaders with national acceptance and endowed with the qualities of courage, honesty, humility, and ability to learn. Fourth, systematic and effective means must be devised through which the common people will be able to elect, guide, monitor, discipline, and remove their leaders. For this to happen, the people must become more articulate and better organized. They must demand good governance and accountability and follow only committed, patriotic, and genuine leadership. Sixth, corruption, which has become an integral part of the governing structures of Nigeria, must be rooted out to ensure that the resources of the nation will be used to promote equitable improvements in the lives of all the people, not just well-connected people. Seventh, for political independence to produce economic independence, Nigeria must break off its dependent and peripheral relationship with the international imperialistic capitalist system, which has kept its economy in shackles and in a rentier and insolvent state. Finally, there is no alternative to democratization and equitable governance, but no one eats democracy. The challenge and the test of a successful democratic order is its ability to deliver the goods, and provide the masses of the people with "freedom, education, food, jobs and shelter."[61]

FALOLA AND AFRICAN HISTORIOGRAPHY

While Falola's most enduring contribution has been in the areas of Yoruba and Nigerian history, he has also made significant contributions at the continental level. In his *African Historiography: Essays in Honour of Jacob Ade Ajayi*, he brought together leading scholars of Africa to make a holistic, albeit controversial, reappraisal of the study of the African past. In the book, E. J. Alagoa discussed the history and the value of the use of oral traditions as sources for the study of the African past, while Paulo Farias examined the reproduction and reception of oral tradition. Adele Afigbo examined the value of colonial historiography as a genre of written and secondary sources. John Peel, Michael Doortmont, and Falola examined a number of methodological issues to suggest new contexts for the understanding of Yoruba historiography. The essays by Felix Ekechi, Ogbu Kalu, Terence Ranger, and Michael Omolewa examined the progress and the limitations of the writings on the activities of the Christian missions and the development of Western education in colonial Africa. The resilience of African institutions and of Islam in the face of internal turmoil and European onslaught received treatment in the essays by Robin Law and Murray Last. The essays by Robert Smith, Paul Lovejoy, Ralph Austin, and Bogumil Jewsiewicki discussed the significance, while sharply criticizing the limited and ill-defined nature of the ideology of the African nationalist historians, of which Ade Ajayi was a leading figure, but they also suggested new methods and approaches to the study of the African past.

As a follow-up to this effort, and in a series of essays, some of which appeared as chapters in the recently published *Oxford History of the British Empire*, Falola carried on this critical reappraisal of nationalist historiography. After articulating its major inspiration as a reaction to colonial historiography, he criticized its characterization of history, its amenability to abuse, its distortion of the colonial era, its elitism, its mythologization of the African past, its obscurantism, and its inability to account for the social changes of the colonial period. Noting the unjustifiable unevenness in the quality and quantity of the African historical literature, he called on Africanist scholars to direct their attention to neglected issues, such as the "histories of agriculture, race relations and commerce, art, material culture, ecology, gender and technology."[62] In the same breath, and against the background of the African celebration of culture heroes, he lamented the frustrating lack of biographies,[63] whether of precolonial, colonial, or postcolonial figures. Finally, he criticized Ade Ajayi's dismissal of colonial rule, calling this a mere episode in African history, as a gross trivialization of the colonial experience, while postulating that the current emphasis on the worth and universalist nature of Western values may generate a revisionist history that may recast European rule as the most significant agency of change in Africa in the twentieth century. Liberating the writing and studying of African history from the shackles of the past is a Herculean task, requiring prodigious and collective efforts. In recognition of this, Falola, in 1995, undertook the task of bringing together an array of scholars of Africa from different disciplines to produce a five-volume history of Africa that will break away from the stereotypes of the past by focusing on the substantive issues of the African past from a genuinely African and rigorously scholarly perspective.[64]

Still on the subject of African nationalism, Falola's recent book, *Nationalism and African Intellectuals*, is a tour de force. A work of imaginative synthesis, comprehensive in scope, controversial in its claims, and penetrating in its analysis, it should generate debates and inspire more scholarly efforts in the years to come. In this book, Falola was not concerned with power politics, but with how nationalism has shaped the production of knowledge and influenced politics in Africa since the nineteenth century. After a review of all the intellectual strands, from pragmatism and traditionalism to negritude, assimilationism, and Afrocentricity, Falola argued that contrary to popular thinking, Africans confronted modernity head-on, with many leading intellectuals working actively to usher it in while using tradition to respond to it. By focusing on nationalist historiography, he succeeded in showing how pioneer university scholars deliberately used history as a strategy of counter-discourse in their assault on colonial bias, domination, and exploitation. The book concluded with a penetrating elucidation of the continuing crisis in African studies, accentuated by the challenges of living in a post-Cold War world in which poverty, dependency, and political instability have combined to marginalize Africa and Africans in world affairs and in intellectual pursuits. Encumbered by the shackles of neocolonialism, institutional decadence, and deteriorating material conditions, the African academy from the mid 1980s began to experience a gradual but devastating season of migration to the more affluent societies of the North and West. Though recognized for their original insights and lauded for their intellect, in their new and foreign abode, African intellectuals live in paradoxical terms, powerful yet powerless, as they continue to grapple, often painfully and traumatically, with the problems of identity politics, cultural alienation, and race relations. Finally, Falola called on African scholars to give more attention to the African Diaspora, the teaching of African languages, the creative pursuit of interdisciplinary collaboration, the positioning of African history as an integral part of world history, and the emphatic reconceptualization of African studies as a striking exemplification of the processes and consequences of globalization that are rapidly transforming our world. Writing in the context of the controversy and bad blood generated by Philip Curtin's article in the *Chronicle of Higher Education* in 1995,[65] Falola warned against a puerile but damaging debate that pose the wrong questions: who owns African studies, and which color should get jobs and grants? "We must not," he continued, "support gatekeepers who close the door to anyone in search of knowledge, truth, and opportunities. Africans deserve the opportunity to know, to tap the knowledge generated by their own people and by others based in different parts of the world. Africans can initiate and pursue their own debates; but others cannot be excluded in a global world. The pursuit of knowledge should not be destroyed by ethnic and racial considerations."[66]

CONCLUSION

Doing justice to the wide range and extensive nature of Falola's scholarly contributions would require more space than possible within the scope of the present publication. An incredible scholar by all standards, Falola is the most extensively published and one of the most prominent Nigerian scholars in the world today. The breadth and the depth of his scholarship are not only impressive but also widely acknowledged. Falola's ability to explore and more importantly master new areas of African historical and cultural studies has become legendary. With 41 books, 70 book chapters, 64 journal articles, 80 book reviews to his name, to say that Falola is a prolific writer is a gross understatement. Among the Yoruba, from whom Falola hails, such scholars are referred to as *oje* or *anjannu eniyan* ("wizards," for want of a better translation), to signify the exceptionally extraordinary nature of their achievements. But even more impressive has been the ranging, perceptive, imaginative, and engaging nature of his scholarship. For Oloruntoyin ("the Almighty God is worthy to be praised"), quantity is as important as quality. He seems to say that a good scholar need not be known only by a single contribution through the production of a *magnus opus*. Since there are many years and many possibilities in a lifetime, why can there not be many seminal contributions in a career spanning a whole lifetime? Being a historian is his profession; writing and publishing are his passions. He has made writing into a way of life, almost an obsession. In his Ife days, he was always the first to arrive on campus, after his early morning run, and long before the administrators, and always the last to leave, late at night, long after everyone else had departed. The current writer still remembers quite vividly Falola surprising him with an invitation to a paid lunch, one week day during the late 1980s, while I was desperately straining to finish a chapter of my doctoral dissertation. My qualification: he had found my car in the parking lot when he arrived for work early that morning before 7 am. I was the first person to beat him to the office in the preceding six months. Those of us very close to him or who had worked with him knew that there is no other secret or magic to his incredibly prodigious output, apart from a deft combination of acute imagination plus hard work, relentless and consistent hard work. Permanently locked up in his office (a more appropriate term would be "book factory") he reappeared only to teach, attend a seminar, or eat lunch. He used to wonder aloud to his friends how a scholar could remain sane for days or even weeks without reading or writing something. For Oloruntoyin, every idea, every thought, every opportunity, every event can be and should be somehow welcomed and translated into yet another writing project. No field or specialization is beyond the reach of his roving and daring mind, hence his forays into health, transportation, religion, and currency, to mention just a few.

Falola's penchant and uncanny aptitude for rereading and reinterpreting sources to reveal hidden and hitherto unperceived meanings and significance ensured the publication of his works in the leading journals in the field, edited by the most distinguished scholars in the profession. Nevertheless, the pace of his work and the rate at which his publications began to appear in quick and dazzling succession were simply too fast and too fantastic to be believable. In the history of academic publishing in Nigeria, no one had proved so consistently and so tirelessly prolific. Falola was a phenomenon.

While this chapter has focused mainly on Falola's publications, it is important to mention that he is selfless in his contributions to the development of the discipline. Many budding scholars have had their careers jump-started through opportunities provided by Falola to contribute to one or more of his many edited volumes. For many of these and for others he has remained a mentor, a model of academic excellence and resourcefulness, as well as a friend and a continuing source of inspiration. A leader in the field of African studies, he has served as editor or member of the editorial board of many leading journals. He is an active and prominent member of several professional associations. While at Ife, along with others he founded the Ife Humanities Society, which over the years developed into a major forum for original and creative Africanist discourse. He has organized many national and international conferences. Above all, he is an indefatigable scholar, a versatile researcher, a prolific writer and an extraordinary teacher, with a consummate passion for the teaching of African history and culture.

NOTES

1. Toyin Falola, "From Hospitality to Hostility: Ibadan and Strangers, 1830-1904," *Journal of African History*, 26, 1985, 51-68. The quotation is taken from page 52.
2. Ibid., 53.
3. Ibid., 53.
4. See S. O. Biobaku, *The Egba and their Neighbours, 1842-1872* (Oxford: Oxford University Press, 1957); I.A. Akinjogbin, *Dahomey and its Neighbours, 1708-1818* (Cambridge: Cambridge University Press, 1967); Bolanle Awe, "The Rise Of Ibadan as a Yoruba Power in the Nineteenth Century," D.Phil. thesis, Oxford University, 1964; J.F.A. Ajayi, *Christian Missions in Nigeria, 1814-1891* (London: Longman, 1965); E..A. Ayandele, *The Missionary Impact on Modern Nigeria* (London: Longman, 1966); T.G.O. Gbadamosi, *The Growth of Islam among the Yoruba* (London: Longman, 1978); G. D. Jenkins, "Politics in Ibadan," Ph.D. thesis, Northwestern University, 1965; O. O. Ayantuga, "Ijebu and its Neighbours, 1851-1941," Ph.D. thesis, University of London, 1965; A.B. Aderibigbe, "The expansion of the Lagos Protectorate," Ph.D. thesis, University of London, 1959; R.S. Smith, *The Lagos Consulate, 1851-1861* (Berkeley and Los Angeles: University of California Press, 1979); A.E. Oroge, "The Institution of Slavery in Yorubaland with Particular Reference to the Nineteenth Century," Ph.D. thesis, University of Birmingham, 1971; Robin Law, *The Oyo Empire c.1600 - c.1836: A West African Imperialism in the Era of the Atlantic Slave Trade* (Oxford: Clarendon Press, 1977); J.B. Webster, *The African Churches among the Yoruba, 1888-1922* (Oxford: Clarendon Press, 1964); J.D.Y. Peel, *Aladura: A Religious Movement Among the Yoruba* (London: Oxford University Press, 1968); S.A. Akintoye, *Revolution and Power Politics in Yorubaland, 1840-1893* (London: Longman, 1971); Ade Obayemi, "The Yoruba and Edo-speaking peoples and their neighbors before 1600," in J.F.A. Ajayi and Michael Crowder, (eds.) *History of West Africa*, Vol. 1, (London: Longman, 1976), 209-240; J.A. Atanda, *The New Oyo Empire: Indirect Rule and Change in Western Nigeria 1894-1934* (London: Longman, 1973); and A.I. Asiwaju, *Western Yorubaland under European Rule 1889-1945* (London: Longman, 1976).
5. Toyin Falola, *The Political Economy of a Precolonial African State: Ibadan, 1830-1900* (Ile-Ife: University of Ife Press, 1984), 5. See also his "Socio Economic Analysis in Yoruba Historiography," *Yoruba: Journal of the Yoruba Studies Association*, 4, 1982.

6. Toyin Falola, *The Political Economy*, 5.
7. Ibid., 6-7.
8. Ibid., 199.
9. Ibid., 204.
10. Toyin Falola, "The Yoruba Caravan System of the Nineteenth Century," *International Journal of African Historical Studies*, 24, 1, 1991, 111-132.
11. Toyin Falola, "The Yoruba Toll System: Its Operation and Abolition," *Journal of African History*, 30, 1989, 69-88. The quotation is taken from page 69.
12. Toyin Falola, "Power Relations and Social Interactions among Ibadan Slaves, 1850-1900," *African Economic History*, 16, 1987, 95-114. The quotation is taken from page 107.
13. Toyin Falola, "Missionaries and Domestic Slavery in Yorubaland in the Nineteenth Century," *Journal of Religious History*, 181-192. The quote is from page 184.
14. Toyin Falola, "Slavery and Pawnship in the Yoruba Economy of the Nineteenth Century," *Slavery and Abolition* (Special Issue on Unfree Labour in the Development of the Atlantic World), 15, 2, August 1994, 221-245; and "The End of Slavery among the Yoruba," *Slavery and Abolition* (Special Issue on Slavery and Colonial Rule in Africa), 19, 2, August 1998, 232-249.
15. Toyin Falola, "A Research Agenda on the Yoruba in the Nineteenth Century," *History in Africa*, 15, 1988, 212. See also his edited collection: *Yoruba Historiography* (Madison: African Studies Program, University of Wisconsin-Madison, 1991).
16. Toyin Falola, "Yoruba Writers and the Construction of Heroes," *History in Africa*, 24, 1997, 157-175.
17. For studies on eastern and northeastern Yoruba frontier groups see G.I. Olomola, "Pre-Colonial Patterns of Inter-State Relations in Eastern Yorubaland," Ph.D. thesis, University of Ife, Ile Ife, 1977; Ade Obayemi, "The Sokoto Jihad and the Okun Yoruba: A Review," *Journal of Historical Society of Nigeria*, 9, 2, 1978, 61-88; and Funso Afolayan, "External Relations and Socio-Political Transformation in Pre-Colonial Igbomina," Ph.D. thesis, Obafemi Awolowo University, Ile Ife, 1991. On western Yoruba groups before the colonial era, the leading authority remains Biodun Adediran, *The Frontier States of Western Yorubaland, 1600-1889* (Ibadan: French Institute for Research in Africa, 1994).
18. Toyin Falola, "Research Agenda on the Yoruba," 221. For recent studies of slavery in Yorubaland see Funso Afolayan, "Slavery, Warfare, and Society in Precolonial Yorubaland: The Witness of

Samuel Johnson," in Toyin Falola, (ed.), *Pioneer, Patriot and Patriarch: Samuel Johnson and the Yoruba People* (Madison: African Studies Program, University of Wisconsin Madison, 1993), 183-196; and Ann O'Hear, *Power Relations in Nigeria: Ilorin Slaves and Their Successors* (Rochester, N. Y.: Rochester University Press, 1997).

19. For an exploratory study of prostitution in Yorubaland, see Toyin Falola, "Prostitution in Ibadan, 1895-1950," *Journal of Business and Social Studies*, New Series, 6, 2, 40-54.

20. On women in Yorubaland see Niara Sudarkasa, *Where Women Work: A Study of Yoruba Women in the Market Place and at Home* (Ann Arbor: University of Michigan Press, 1973); Toyin Falola, "Gender, Business, and Space Control: Yoruba Market Women and Power," in Bessie House-Midamba and Felix K. Ekechi, (eds.), *African Market Women's Economic Power: The Role of Women in African Economic Development* (Westport, Conn: Greenwood Press, 1995), 23-40; Funso Afolayan, "Women and warfare in Yorubaland during the Nineteenth Century," in Toyin Falola, *Warfare and Diplomacy in Precolonial Nigeria* (Madison: African Studies Program, University of Wisconsin, 1992), 78-86. See also the fascinating and provocative study by Oyeronke Oyewumi, *The Invention of Women: Making an African Sense of Western Gender Discourses* (Minneapolis: University of Minnesota Press, 1997), where the author critiqued the misapplication of Western, body-oriented concepts of gender to African societies, and argued that, contrary to the fundamental assumptions of western feminist theory, gender was not socially constructed in old Yoruba society and that age rather than sex determined social organization.

21. Peel, *Ijeshas and Nigerians*, 12-13.

22. Toyin Falola and Dare Oguntomisin, *The Military in Nineteenth Century Yoruba Politics* (Ile Ife: University of Ife Press, 1984).

23. Toyin Falola and G.O. Oguntomisin, *Yoruba Warlords of the Nineteenth Century* (Trenton, NJ.: Africa World Press, 2001).

24. Toyin Falola, "Brigandage and Piracy in 19th Century Yorubaland," *Journal of the Historical Society of Nigeria*, 13, 1-2, Dec. 1985-June 1986, 83-106.

25. Toyin Falola, "The Construction and Destruction of Ijaiye Economy, c. 1832-1862," *Afrika und Ubersee*, 74, 1991, 21-37.

26. Toyin Falola, "The Ijaiye in Diaspora, 1862-1895: Problems of Integration and Resettlement," *Journal of Asian and African Studies*, 22, 1-2, 1987, 67-79.

27. G. O. Oguntomisin and Toyin Falola, "Refugees in Yorubaland in the Nineteenth Century," in *Asian and African Studies, Journal of the Israel Oriental Society*, 21, 2, July 1987, 165-185.
28. Toyin Falola, "The Foreign Policy of Ibadan in the Nineteenth Century," *ODU: A Journal of West African Studies*, 22, 1982.
29. H. O. Danmole and Toyin Falola, "Ibadan-Ilorin Relations in the 19th Century: A Study in Imperial Struggles in Yorubaland," *Trans-African Journal of History*, 14, 1985.
30. Toyin Falola, "The Ibadan Conference of 1855: Yoruba Diplomacy and Conflict Resolution," *Geneve-Afrique*, 23, 2, 1985, 38-56. See also his "Warfare and Trade Relations Between Ibadan and the Ijebu in the Nineteenth Century," in Falola (ed.), *Warfare and Diplomacy in Precolonial Nigeria* (Madison: African Studies Program, University of Wisconsin-Madison, 1992), 26-30.
31. Toyin Falola, *Politics and Economy in Ibadan, 1893-1945*, (Lagos: Modelor Publishers, 1989).
32. Toyin Falola, "Ibadan Power Elite and the Search for Political Order, 1893-1939," *Africa*, (Rome) 47, 3, September 1992, 336-354.
33. Toyin Falola, *Yoruba Gurus: Indigenous Production of Knowledge in Africa* (Trenton, NJ: Africa World Press, Inc., 1999).
34. J. F. Ade Ajayi, "Samuel Johnson and Yoruba Historiography," unpublished paper, 1995, 9. See also Toyin Falola (ed.), *Pioneer, Patriot and Patriarch: Samuel Johnson and the Yoruba People* (Madison: African Studies Program, University of Wisconsin-Madison, 1993)
35. Toyin Falola, *Yoruba Gurus*, 279.
36. Ibid., 280.
37. For Falola's exploratory essay on pawnship in southwestern Nigeria, see "Pawnship in Colonial Southwestern Nigeria," in Falola and Paul Lovejoy, (eds.), *Pawnship in Africa: Debt Bondage in Historical Perspective* (Boulder, Colorado: Westview Press, 1994), 245-266.
38. Jacob Olupona and Toyin Falola (eds.), *Religion and Society in Nigeria: Historical and Sociological Perspectives* (Ibadan: Spectrum Books Limited, 1991). On religious pluralism, see Simeon O. Ilesanmi, *Religious Pluralism and the Nigerian State* (Athens: Ohio University Center for International Studies, 1997), where the author calls for *dialogic politics*, which celebrates pluralism and perceives religious institutions as mediating structures between individual citizens in search of existential meaning and cultural identity, on the one hand, and the impersonal state, on the other.

39. Falola, "Christian Radicalism and Nigerian Politics," in Paul A. Beckett and Crawford Young, *Dilemmas of Democracy in Nigeria* (Rochester, N.Y.: University of Rochester Press, 1997), 265-282. See also Patricia Williams and Toyin Falola, *Religious Impact on the Nation State: The Nigerian Predicament*, (Aldershot, England: Avebury, 1995)
40. Toyin Falola, *Violence in Nigeria: The Crisis of Religious Politics and Secular Ideologies* (Rochester, N.Y.: Rochester University Press, 1998).
41. For a more extended assessment of this book, see the review by Funso Afolayan in *International Journal of African Historical Studies*, 31, 3, 1998, 641-642.
42. Toyin Falola, "Cassava Starch for Export in Nigeria during the Second World War," *African Economic History*, 18, 1989, 73-98.
43. Toyin Falola, "'An Ounce Is Enough': The Gold Industry and the Politics of Control in Colonial Western Nigeria," *African Economic History*, 20, 1992, 27-50.
44. Falola, "'My Friend the Shylock': Money-Lenders and Their Clients in Southwestern Nigeria," *Journal of African History*, 34, 1993, 403-423. The quotation is from page 403. For more on the politics of money among the Yoruba, see Toyin Falola and Akanmu Adebayo, *Culture, Politics and Money among the Yoruba* (New Brunswick, N. J.: Transaction Publishers, 2000).
45. Toyin Falola, "Lebanese Traders in Southwestern Nigeria, 1900-1960," *African Affairs*, vol. 89, October 1990, 523-553; and "The Lebanese in Colonial West Africa," in Ade Ajayi and J.D.Y. Peel (eds.), *People and Empires in African History* (London: Longman, 1992), 121-141.
46. Toyin Falola, *Development Planning and Decolonization in Nigeria* (Gainesville: University Press of Florida, 1996)
47. Ibid., 177.
48. Toyin Falola (ed.), *Britain and Nigeria: Exploitation or Development?* (London: Zed Books Ltd., 1987).
49. Ibid., 217.
50. Toyin Falola and Julius O. Ihonvbere (eds.), *Nigeria and the International Capitalist System* (Boulder, Colorado, and London: Lynne Rienner Publishers, 1988)
51. Toyin Falola and S. Olanrewaju (eds.), *Transport Systems in Nigeria* (Syracuse, N.Y: Foreign and Comparative Studies Program, Syracuse University, 1986), 160.

52. Tola Olu Pearce and Toyin Falola, *Child Health in Nigeria: The Impact of a Depressed Economy*, (Aldershot, England: Avebury, 1994).
53. Toyin Falola and Dennis Ityavyar, *The Political Economy of Health in Africa* (Athens: Ohio University Center for International Studies, 1992).
54. On the crisis of nation building and democratization in Nigeria, see Richard Sklar, *Nigerian Political Parties: Power in an Emergent African Nation* (Princeton: Princeton University Press, 1963); Larry Diamond, *Class, Ethnicity and Democracy in Nigeria: The Failure of the First Republic* (Syracuse, N. Y.: Syracuse University Press, 1988); Richard Joseph, *Democracy and Prebendal Politics in Nigeria: The Rise and Fall of the Second Republic* (Cambridge: Cambridge University Press, 1991); Eghosa E. Osaghae, *Crippled Giant: Nigeria since Independence* (Bloomington: Indiana University Press, 1998).
55. Toyin Falola and Julius Ihonvbere, *The Rise and Fall of Nigeria's Second Republic: 1979-84* (London: Zed Books Ltd., 1985).
56. Ibid., 258
57. Toyin Falola, Adegboyega Ajayi, Akin Alao, and Babatunde Babawale, *The Military Factor in Nigeria, 1966-1985* (Lewiston, N.J.: The Edwin Mellen Press, 1994).
58. Toyin Falola, et al., *The Military Factor in Nigeria*. The quotation is from Falola's introduction to the volume.
59. See Toyin Falola, "Corruption in the Nigerian Public Service, 1945-1960," in John Mukum Mbaku, (ed.), *Corruption and the Crisis of Institutional Reforms in Africa*, (Lewiston: N. Y.: The Edwin Mellen Press, 1998), 137-166; and Andrew J. Clarno and Toyin Falola, "Patriarchy, Patronage, and Power: Corruption in Nigeria," in Mbaku, *Corruption and the Crisis of Institutional Reforms*, 167-192.
60. See K. C. Wheare, *Federal Government* (Oxford: Oxford University Press, 1963), chapter one.
61. See Toyin Falola, "Leadership in Nigeria: Reflections of a Follower," in Falola, *Modern Nigeria: A Tribute to G. O. Olusanya* (Lagos: Modelor Press, 1990), 159-173; Falola and Ihonvbere, *The Rise and Fall of Nigeria's Second Republic*, 235-265; Andrew Clarno and Toyin Falola, "Patriarchy, Patronage and Power: Corruption in Nigeria," 167-193.
62. Toyin Falola, "West Africa," in Robin W. Winks (ed.), *Historiography* [vol. 5 of *The Oxford History of the British Empire*, edited

by Wm. Roger Louis] (Oxford: Oxford University Press, 1999), 498.
63. For an effort in this direction, see his co-edited work: Olasope Oyelaran, Toyin Falola, et al., *Obafemi Awolowo: The End of an Era?* (Ile-Ife: University of Ife Press, 1988).
64. Two of the five volumes have been published; the remaining three are in press. Toyin Falola, (ed.), *Africa, Vol. 1: Peoples and States* (Durham, N. C.: Carolina Academic Press, 2000); *Africa, Vol. 2: Cultures and Societies* (Durham, N. C.: Carolina Academic Press, 2000).
65. Philip Curtin, "Ghettocizing African Studies," *Chronicle of Higher Education*, March 3, 1995.
66. Toyin Falola, *Nationalism and African Intellectuals* (Rochester, N. Y.: University of Rochester Press, 2001).

2

COLONIAL STATE AND EDUCATION IN BENIN DIVISION, 1897-1959

Uyilawa Usuanlele

INTRODUCTION

A reading of colonial intelligence reports and census data of Benin Division shows the people to have been educationally backward in terms of attainment of educational qualifications and employment in the colonial service. According to one intelligence report:

> On the whole the standard of education is low and scanty. In spite of the facilities afforded by the middle school in Benin, no Bini has yet succeeded in attaining the higher flights of education and gracing one of the professions with his presence.[1]

This low educational standard in Benin Division is true when compared to other divisions in Benin Province and Southern Nigeria during the colonial period. The present chapter attempts to provide a basis for understanding this educational backwardness. It does not accept the view that the educational backwardness of the division was caused by the indifference of the people to educational opportunities,[2] or by the personal hostility or indifference of colonial officials to Christian missionary education, as previously claimed.[3] This chapter argues that the colonial state played a crucial role in retarding the educational development and attainment of the people, and that the colonial state's attitude to and role in educational development were influenced by the nature of the economy and society it was developing. The first part of the chapter looks at the nature and character of the colonial state and its economy in relation to the educational needs. The second part focuses on the introduction and growth of colonial Western education and on how the colonial state controlled it.

COLONIAL STATE, COLONIAL ECONOMY, AND EDUCATIONAL NEEDS

Benin Division was carved out of the core area of the Benin Kingdom after the British conquest of the kingdom in 1897. It was incorporated into and subordinated to the colonial state that had been established in the Nigerian area. A colonial state apparatus and bureaucratic organs were established in the division to reorganize and reorientate the economy for the profitable operation of British capitalist enterprise. Because of these essential aims of colonialism, the colonial state was in nature and character interventionist.[4] It was vested with enormous powers which were used to regulate and control social relations (especially labor, taxation, land, and business) so as to ensure the promotion of capitalist enterprise, while at the same time minimizing any threat to its development and profitability for the British economy.

The new colonial capitalist economy, which the colonial state brought into existence, depended at the initial stage on forced and bonded labor. It gradually used the imposition of cash needs to force the populace into producing agricultural raw materials and/or selling their labor to colonial capitalist enterprises.[5] The result was an agricultural raw materials production economy, including private plantations and timber concessions, but dependent largely on peasants and increasingly on migrant labor. This kind of economy, as Majorie Mbilinyi has shown in colonial Tanzania, was not dependent on school-manufactured skills.[6] But in spite of this character of the colonial economy, it still required certain specialized labor skills, training, and efficiency rates that were lacking in the precolonial economy and society. Only a small number of people with these kinds of skill were required for the profitable operations of the colonial economy. Unlike the metropolitan capitalist economy where mass education was necessary for the reproduction of labor power and the maintenance of capitalist relations of production, the education that was introduced to African colonies functioned essentially to produce and pacify a small group of skilled and literate administrative functionaries and workers.[7] Since education is "a function of the society in which it exists,"[8] the functional dissimilarities in education between the metropolitan capita-list countries and the African colonies make it incorrect to use the same concept for both. Hence, to differentiate "Western education" as it obtained in the advanced metropolitan capitalist countries from the type introduced to the African colonies, the latter will be called colonial Western education. This description also includes missionary education, which served similar functions of rationalizing and perpetuating the colonial system and depended on financial and material aid from the colonial state.

Thus, education as a critical ingredient of any economy must be suitably adapted to the needs of that economy. This critical relation between economy and education influenced the introduction of colonial Western education into the colonies. But noneconomic considerations also influenced the type and the quality of education that was sanctioned by the colonial state.

INTRODUCTION, GROWTH, AND STATE CONTROL OF COLONIAL WESTERN EDUCATION, 1897-1960

Three factors influenced the introduction of colonial western education into Benin Division by the colonial state. First, the prejudices of the British against the Benin Kingdom as "barbaric" and "fetish" ridden made the colonial state want to pursue a "civilizing " mission among the people. In the annual report of 1897, Benin was recommended for the establishment of a school to "improve" the people's lot.[9] It was hoped that the Christian missionaries would establish schools and would be assisted by government, but failing which the government would establish a school.[10] The "civilizing" objective was initially taken very seriously by the state and education was seen as the instrument for its achievement.

Second, the precolonial Benin Kingdom bureaucracy and educational system were unsuited to the kind of skills, training, and rate of efficiency necessary for capitalist exploitation and domination of the human and material resources of Benin Division. This problem was initially tackled by simultaneously importing skilled and literate personnel to service the lower echelons of the colonial administration and sending indigenous people out of the division for training in such skills. These solutions were expedient for the establishment and consolidation of colonial domination and exploitation, pending the arrival of Christian missionaries to establish schools. The titleholders were urged to bring out their children for schooling in Calabar. By 1898, they had reluctantly sent only three of their numerous children.[11] They sent only their dependents and slaves, because of their distrust of colonial officials believed to be using schooling in Calabar as a punitive measure against them. The titleholders also feared that their children would be enslaved by Europeans in Calabar.[12] When the pressure on them was increased, they demanded the establishment of schools in Benin City for their children instead. The initial response of the titleholders and the use of imported literate personnel were not in the interest of the colonial state. They constituted dangers and problems for the continuity and practice of the politically expedient and inexpensive administration, which was based on the use of members of the overthrown ruling aristocracy to mediate colonial domination. The problem arose because the acceptability of literate slaves and imported literate personnel in the future mediation of colonial domination would be difficult and expensive to enforce. They lacked the precolonial ideological control and influence over the colonial people on which the mediation of colonial domination depended.

The two immediate and expedient solutions also created politico-financial problems for the colonial state. This was the third factor that influenced the introduction and establishment of colonial western educational institutions in the division. The expensiveness of the immediate solutions conflicted with the colonial state's policy of spending very little on the colonies. The high cost of these solutions is revealed by the fact that the colonial state bore the full cost of the maintenance and education of Benin pupils in Calabar. Also there were the relatively high salaries and wages the colonial state paid to attract imported literate and skilled functionaries and workers.[13] As late as 1914, the governor-general, Lord Frederick Lugard was still battling with these problems when he reported that

> The commercial interests of the country are no less hampered than the government lack of staff, and the merchants say that the greatest boon which at this stage could be conferred on them is a better supply of reliable natives to occupy posts of responsibility, at present filled by subordinate Europeans at a great cost and at a sacrifice of continuity.[14]

Imported functionaries as an "elite class" amongst the colonized people were expected by the colonial state to spend their wages and salaries on the purchases of imported European manufactures. This behavior was expected to be emulated by the mass of colonized people. But these imported literate and skilled functionaries and workers were remitting their salaries and wages home, outside the division and the colonial territory. This had earlier made Consul General Moor frown on the behavior of these imported literate personnel, "who spend as little as possible" in the area to which they were posted.[15]

These problems were worsened by the slow and reluctant response of the Christian missionaries to the invitation to establish schools in the division. The reasons for this kind of response are still not clear. The Roman Catholic Mission (RCM) had acquired a site in Benin City in 1899, but the grant was canceled by the colonial state in 1901.[16] The Church Missionary Society (CMS) had been bedeviled with schisms during this period.[17] A faction of the CMS led and organized personally by Bishop James Johnson had established itself in the division only in 1902, followed by the Southern American Baptists in 1923, the RCM in 1924, the Salvation Army in 1926, and other denominations later on.[18] Though the Muslims had come on the heels of the colonial conquerors as traders, artisans, workers, and so on and established Koranic schools for their wards, it was only in the late 1940s that they started establishing schools that used the Roman script and English as the medium of instruction and taught secular subjects along with Islamic religious knowledge. Like the Christians, they were also bogged down by their sectarian rivalries, manifested in the struggle between the Ahmadiyya and non-Ahmadiyya groups for state recognition. Christian missionary education in the Niger Coast Protectorate area before 1900 was functionally inadequate for the needs of the colonial administration and the trading firms.[19] All these problems made the colonial state introduce colonial Western educational institutions to Benin Division.

In 1901, the colonial state provided materials while the precolonial titleholders mobilized labor for the building and establishment of an elementary school, Government School, Benin City, for a "purely secular education."[20] Moral instructions were introduced into its curriculum only in the late 1910s. Apart from a special class for training government employees, female and industrial craft sections were also added to the school in 1905.[21] It was a day school and the medium of instruction from the beginning was English. Financial support for the school was to be met through a general levy collected from the populace by the precolonial titleholders (hence it was usually mistakenly referred to as "chiefs contribution").[22] Financial support was also obtained through fees paid by some pupils. The educational model that informed the establishment of this school was a British class-structured one in which the elementary school catered for the training of the working-class elements.[23] Though there was no clearly defined policy, a laissez faire situation in education before 1926, as posited by Fafunwa, did not exist.[24] The British colonial state knew and defined what it wanted to achieve with education. The long British experience with colonial education in India, Egypt, Sierra Leone, and the late nineteenth-century Gold Coast and Lagos, which produced political agitators against colonialism, was not a good guide for future educational development in the colonies.[25] Measures were, therefore, taken by the colonial state to ensure that education served rather than subverted its interests. Consequently, educational development had to be controlled. Government School, Benin City, which was established in 1901, was administered by a board composed of official government titleholders (who were employees of the colonial state). This school was to serve the vast Benin City territories with their population scattered over 6,000 square miles. Yet the high commissioner, Sir Ralph Moor, ruled against the establishment of another government school in the area and recommended Christian missionaries to establish schools, which would be assisted if the missionaries changed their methods and subjected themselves to inspection.[26] The limitations of Christian missionary education were well known to Moor. Thus, recommending it for the territories was effectively a means of retarding educational development. Bishop Johnson, who knew the limitations of missionary education, lamented in 1913 that "the lower standards of their [missionary] schools were making them less attractive than the government schools."[27] By 1927, H.T.C. Field, the superintendent of education, Benin City, still observed peoples' preference for the better standards of governments schools and reported that "everywhere there are long waiting lists for admission to government schools."[28] Thus, control over government schools gave the state a great deal of control over colonial Western education in the division.

Colonial Western education as introduced was aimed not only at producing a small crop of clerks, artisans, and progressive capitalist farmers, but also at sociopolitical control. Mbilinyi has rightly described this education as aimed at pacification of the population.[29] As a result this education was limited in standard and directed at certain segments of the society only. It was to be a means of maintaining the existing social order. Hence very early in the administration, Moor declared the limited goals it was intended to achieve:

> I am of the opinion that the education necessary to enable the natives on the completion of same, to take their place as useful members of the community, need not necessarily include the entire secondary course.[30]

Usefulness in the context of Moor's colonial administration obviously meant unquestioned acceptance of the existing order. The experience of anticolonial protestations by the educated elements of the Lagos Colony was not lost on the officials. Sir Moor was against the establishment of a central school for abridged secondary education in Lagos,[31] and went further to recommend that

> The aping of the European destroys the independence of character and initiative of the natives of these territories and certainly during the period of their education, I consider it infinitely preferable to keep them clothed in some suitable native garbs with a view of maintaining their distinctive native character.[32]

His immediate successors did not heed his advice and went ahead to establish the central school, King's College, in Lagos, and even sent Benin pupils there. According to Lieutenant Governor W. Buchanan Smith, the sending of Benin boys to King's College was not a success and he advised its discontinuation.[33] Moor's ideas were not completely jettisoned, as they were to be echoed fifteen years later in the curriculum of the schools. For instance, moral instruction introduced in the state schools in 1916 was to make the pupils "show respect for their chiefs and to be discouraged from throwing off native customs and dress."[34] It should be noted that chiefs and native customs were among the ideological props of Lugardian indirect rule and as such were aimed at mediating colonial domination. While moral and literary education was aimed at pacification, practical subjects were aimed at improving services and meeting the needs of the colonial companies and their metropolitan industries. For instance, according to Lugard's instructions, the school farms where the pupils spent time were

> not to be used for growing yams, beans and co. In usual native fashion . . . school farms can best be used to instruct in the best methods of growing economic plants suitable to the district such as cocoa and para-rubber.[35]

Further, in his memorandum, which was distributed by the provincial commissioner as instructions to district officers, Lugard stated that the goals of rural schools were

> to prepare village boys for their own village life, to give them very literary education and train them in better methods of agriculture and handicrafts which will be useful in their village life.[36]

Though this recommendation was not implemented by the colonial state in Benin Division, the Christian missionaries' educational work in the rural areas of the division fitted into the terms of this recommendation. This was mainly because the missionaries' aims and goals were geared toward evangelization. They were not completely against the existing colonial social order and shared similar views with the colonial state. For instance, in the late nineteenth century, some of the missionaries had expressed their fears about the danger of academic education in the territories.[37] By the 1920s there was still no significant change in their views. The Christian mission synod of 1921 requested in a proposal to the diocesan board that

> The great majority of the population must depend for their livelihood almost entirely on agriculture and the palm oil trade. Such need only a very elementary education that can be provided in village schools, which can be taught by youths who have themselves not progressed very far. They should not teach beyond standard three. Schools of this class should be provided in large numbers and be accessible to all.[38]

The Baptist Mission-initiated Phelps-Stokes Commission report on education in Africa, which was adopted by the colonial state, also recommended rural schools with emphasis on agriculture.[39] The reason for these shared views, aims, and goals till the 1930s was the need to maintain the colonial social order. The missionaries also feared that educated people would "become discontented, unhappy and unwilling to work the land." Though such education, especially of the rural type, can be likened to the English monitor schools which prepared children for working-class life in the metropolis, in the case of the colonies it helped to perpetuate the peasantry. Out of the seventy-one pre-secondary schools in Benin Division in 1936, fifty-seven were in the rural areas, and fifty-four of these were missionary schools. According to Superintendent of Education J. W. A. Thorburn, none of these schools provided instructions above elementary class II, and the general standards of the schools were low, with some exception.[40]

The limited educational aims and goals of the colonial state and the Christian missionaries, coupled with fear of the development of political dissent, influenced colonial state policies, practices, and measures taken against educational development. Measures were largely geared toward control of educational expansion in terms of the social background and numerical strength of recipients as well as the content and quality of the education curriculum.

To this end, after the establishment of a government school in Benin City, in 1901, Moor opposed the suggestion that another government school should be established in the territory.[41] But his successors went ahead to establish government schools in the newly subjugated areas of the territory. However, no more were established in Benin Division, which was the largest division in the Benin Province of the Southern Protectorate.

The reasons for this discrimination against Benin Division in the establishment of government schools are still not clear. But it might not be unconnected with the fear of political agitation, which unemployed educated youths were likely to create. This fear was confirmed quite early in Ishan Division, which had a large number of schools. Resident Dawson demanded the closure of some of the schools because the majority of pupils dropped out at standard 3 or 4, becoming unfit for clerical jobs. Some were "too proud to farm," and many developed "into mere thieves, loafers and agitators."[42] This fear was re-echoed in Benin Division by District Officer R. L. Archer in rejecting Christian missionary agencies' demand for assistance. He argued that "boys with a smattering of English" would not farm or take to craft, and since they could not all be employed as clerks and the like, they became discontented element.[43] Instances abound of colonial state's suppression of the educational aspirations of the people of the division. A 1922 request to the colonial state by the chiefs of Oghada District for provision of teachers and school materials for their hundred pupils, for whom they were ready to provide school buildings and other needs, was turned down on the ground that the state lacked funds.[44] Yet the Benin Native Administration always had surplus revenue. For instance, £1,000 was expended on the presentation of an airplane to the British Imperial Government in 1916 and another £1,000 was invested with the protectorate government in 1917.[45] Benin Division was denied any other government school until 1938 when the Native Authorities were allowed to establish schools. The only government school in Benin City was not only inadequate for the division, but it was reported in 1916 that the teachers lacked adequate knowledge of moral instruction, nature study, geography and history, and the teaching was of no value to the pupil. In 1926 the school was reported to be so poorly staffed that it was unable to admit pupils.[46] Yet this school was supposed to serve the members of the cosmopolitan population of Benin Division and take them to greater heights, which the 1936 intelligence report accused them of failing to achieve.

As already shown, colonial Western education, especially government or state sponsored schools, was aimed at producing clerks or if need be pupils for higher education (at King's College, Lagos) and teachers for government schools (at Government College, Ibadan).[47] It was also aimed at a particular class. In Benin Division, it was aimed at the children of members of the previous ruling aristocracy. Benin City, where the only government school was built, was inhabited largely by members of the aristocracy and their dependents. These titleholders were instructed to recruit pupils for the school and it was natural to expect them to recruit their own children. However, their response was poor. Of about 300 pupils in Government School, Benin City, in 1916 only thirty (of which thirteen were children of the Iyase of Benin) were children of titleholders. A policy of giving special education to the children of chiefs was pursued with fanatical zeal during Lugard's tenure as governor-general of Nigeria. A separate class with boarding facilities was approved for the children of "chiefs" or titleholders in Government School, Benin City, in 1916.[48] The school was to be organized along the lines of English public schools with boarding houses and monitors. It was expected to teach "discipline" and a "command of men," believed to be invaluable for future role as chiefs.[49] Students were also to be taught elements of English and Scottish history, as well as practical education in arts and crafts, reading, writing, simple account keeping, and the geography of the British Empire, Nigeria, and Benin Province.[50] That agriculture and technical subjects like carpentry were excluded from their curriculum meant that they were not being prepared for peasant agricultural or artisanal life. H.C. Moorhouse, secretary to the Southern Provinces, defined clearly the life they were being prepared for when he stated that

> The sons of chiefs should achieve not only literary attainments, but also and primarily the maintenance of discipline, good behaviour and high moral tone. Later when these educated boys return to their homes, they should be able to make themselves leaders of their compatriots and finally become of inestimable value in the better administration of the country.[51]

Products of such schools like the late Oba Akenzua II (King of Benin, 1933-1978) were usually sent on to King's College, Lagos, to complete this special education that prepared them for their future roles.

This colonial Western education, especially its postprimary phase, was largely reserved for members of the former ruling class as a means of perpetuating the precolonial social structure and consolidating the formerly dominant elements as intermediaries between the colonial state and the other sections of the colonized population. This is attested to by the fact that when the Benin Native Authority started awarding scholarships indiscriminately to enable Benin pupils to attend King's College, Lagos, the lieutenant governor, Southern Provinces, Hon. C. W. Alexander, frowned at it. The only Benin scholarship pupil then at King's College, M. E. Omoregha, was withdrawn before he could complete his course.[52] Earlier on, the superintendent of education in Benin Province had requested the district officers to ask the headmasters "only to recommend boys of real ability, *preferably of well known local families*" (my emphasis) for the Native Authority Scholarship selection examination to King's College.[53] This kind of special education can be likened to the British public school for the children of the British upper (ruling class).[54] But in the colonial situation, it was aimed at creating a collaborationist class through educational training and administrative employment, which maintained the aristocracy's advantaged position in the society.

The colonial state also strived to ensure that only the desired type of education and the envisaged quantity of recipients were catered for by its measures and practices in the educational sector. This was easily achieved with the state's control over the Native Administration and the only government school in Benin City. The Christian missions were slow to establish schools in Benin Division, which had only one mission school in 1916, at a time when Asaba and Ishan Divisions had eighteen and two respectively.[57] With the near absence of Christian missionary schools from Benin Division, the colonial state had virtually total control over colonial Western education in the division. For instance, the general levy which enabled children to attend Government School, Benin City, freely, irrespective of class and financial ability was abolished in 1917. The introduction of individual payment of fees in its place forced some of the pupils to withdraw. The school's population was reduced from 327 in 1913 to 310 in 1919 and 246 in 1927.[55] A similar doubling of fees in 1941 was reported to have resulted in the withdrawal of many pupils, especially from Edo College, the only secondary school.[59] In addition, Provincial Commissioner, James Watt, recommended:

> I do not think that [a] school ought to be maintained in any place in which there is not [a] sufficient number of children whose parents are unable and unwilling to pay for education.[56]

Another measure adopted in 1927 to control the increasing demand was the weeding out of pupils, for instance, those labeled as "backward and useless boys," in order to make room for "more promising materials."[57] Thus headmasters were reported as "keeping classes down to reasonable sizes."[58] The weeding out of pupils was at a time when facilities did not exist for the rehabilitation of school dropouts.

The Christian missionaries, expected by the colonial state to provide colonial Western education to other segments of the population, worsened the situation by their negative response. For reasons that are still unclear, their growth in Benin Division was slow and unenthusiastic. Their establishment of schools was particularly slow. Ayandele blamed this on the hostility of the colonial officials toward the Christian missionaries, because they only allowed the missions land grants on a lease rent basis, instead of fee-hold basis used elsewhere in West Africa. Also, they failed to recommend the missionaries to the titleholders.[59] This hostility might have been directed toward the person and likely activities of Bishop Johnson, whose political antecedents were already known in Lagos. Johnson had agitated against the 1897 deposition and deportation of Oba Ovonramwen.[64] The CMS missions established in Benin in 1901 were Johnson's personal enterprise. This probably accounted for the colonial officials' hostile attitude toward the CMS in Benin. Also their activities were resulting in clashes with non-Christians and political heads of communities.[60] Since the colonial officials depended on these political heads for peaceful administration, they sided with them.

But the Johnson-led CMS that established itself in Benin Division lamented that "the smallness of the means at our disposal have made it extremely difficult for us to establish Mission schools in the districts."[61] Between 1902 when the CMS arrived, and about 1923 when other denominations started to enter the division, the CMS had established only one school in Benin City, the St. Matthew's CMS Day School. This was the only Christian mission school in Benin Division at a time when other divisions had numerous mission schools, some of which were being assisted with government funds.

The Benin mission school taught the scriptures, hygiene, English, Yoruba, Bini, geography, signing, and physical drill. The catechist as school manager and the headmaster assisted by one monitor and one pupil teacher catered for seventy pupils in 1919.[62] The arrival of other denominations led to competition in the opening of schools, and a struggle for government financial assistance. The CMS converted its mission stations in the rural areas into schools. The proliferation of these schools was not achieved without attempts at state control. The missionaries were required to obtain the permission of the local chiefs and to notify the resident and the district officer before establishing mission stations in any place.[63] Permission was initially obtained only with difficulty from the local chiefs, whose authority the mission activities tended to undermine. It was not unusual for these mission stations to be closed where missionary activities threatened or breached the peace of the community. This obviously affected the schools as well. The colonial state officials' obsession with law and order made them to usually side with the local chiefs and non-Christian population.

The educational ventures of the Christian missionaries were not free from colonial control measures, despite the relative independence of the missionaries. Where their proliferation and expansion could not be checked, their qualitative development was curtailed. The colonial state directed its control measures at the perpetual financial insolvency of the missionaries and the evangelization aim of their schools. The colonial state's insistence that the mission modify its educational aims, toward the training of "good citizens" and insistence on the submission of their schools to government inspection as a condition for government financial assistance established the basis for state control. These policy measures, which were codified in the 1926 Education Ordinance, empowered the governor, the director of education, and a committee of the Education Board to prohibit the opening of new schools, if the schools could not be efficiently conducted and adequately staffed. This policy was being faithfully implemented in Benin in the 1920s and drew a protest from Bishop Broderick of the Roman Catholic Mission in 1924.[64] It was only after apparent relaxation in the policy that the mission and other private agency schools started to proliferate.

In addition to missionary rivalry, the demand by many rural communities for the establishment of schools by the missions and other agencies encouraged the proliferation. Communities, like Obadan and Oke, which could not attract missionary schools, built their own schools through cooperative societies, while Chief Jackson Obaseki built a private school in Abudu in the 1930s. By 1938, these schools had increased to seventy-eight, of which ten were in Benin City and the rest in the rural areas.[65]

The quality and standards of education especially in the rural areas were very low even as late as 1936. According to a report on these schools in 1938:

> about forty-five percent of these schools have only one teacher who often has to depend upon the collection of fees for salary. The average attendance of non-assisted schools is less than twenty.[66]

The missionary agencies' attempt to secure funding from the colonial state to improve the standards of their schools was largely frustrated by the difficult conditions laid down by the state. These included the employment of certified teachers, the provision of school buildings, games equipment, and scholarships to middle schools.[67] The missions could hardly meet these conditions given the prevalent poverty among the parents of the school children who were largely peasants. Also, there was apathy among these peasants toward the Christian faith, which made it unlikely that they would contribute to the missions' efforts. The missions also lacked the funds to meet the state's conditions on their own. The colonial state officials refused to relax the conditions to enable the missions to receive government financial assistance. According to District Officer R. L. Archer, the mission schools provided inferior education, which did more harm than good, and therefore should not be supported.[68] The missionary agencies' attempt to secure funds from the Benin Native Authority to improve the standards of the rural schools which would qualify them for government assistance, was similarly frustrated. The native authority's grant of only £125 in support of the RCM schools in Benin City, which had 441 pupils in 1930, was stopped. In 1934, the native authority was instructed to secure the lieutenant governor's approval and was told that grants should be requested only in exceptional cases, must be annual, and must be discontinued at the end of each year.[69] As a result of this frustration of the efforts of the missionary agencies, most of their schools remained unimproved and were denied necessary government assistance. Thus while the number of voluntary agency schools increased three-fold from twenty-seven in 1929 to seventy-three in 1938, the number receiving government assistance increased only from three to five in the same period. These five assisted schools were all located in Benin City, while all the rural schools were unassisted.[70] Consequently, a general tendency to leave the village school for those in the city developed. The result of this was over crowding in city schools and reduced attendance in the village school.[71] This development was confirmed by the Senior Education Officer who observed that:

> In 1940 I discovered that large numbers of children from the Benin Districts [rural areas] attended school in the city, living during the week under appalling conditions of accommodation and under nourishment. I was assured on all sides that they came because there were no good schools in the districts. The best method of abating the evil seemed to be to improve the village schools.[72]

On-the-spot assessment in that year also showed that of the 2,772 pupils in Benin City schools in 1940, 734 came from the villages in the division.[73]

To ameliorate the problems of education in the division, the education officers had, since the 1920s, been recommending the utilization of the constant surplus in Benin Native Authority funds. The oba and titleholders as functionaries of the Native Authority showed willingness and enthusiasm toward the development of colonial Western education in the division. But their efforts were as usual frustrated by the colonial state, which rarely approved their initiatives or intended support for educational development. The issues of Benin Native Authority scholarships to King's College, Lagos, and assistance to the RCM schools in Benin City have already been highlighted above. The native authority also tried to solve the problem of idleness and delinquency among unemployed school leavers through the provision of post-primary education facilities. Oba Eweka II's request in 1930 for a secondary school like King's College, funded by the Benin Native Authority and staffed by both Africans and Europeans was turned down on the ground of the lack of a European superintendent to ensure "the right kind of discipline and moral tone."[74] Thus the division was denied secondary education facilities until 1937 when the middle school was converted into a secondary school, Edo College, Benin City. This remained the only government owned post-secondary institution till the establishment of Provincial Teachers Training College, Abudu, in the 1950s. The division remained without another post-secondary institution until 1947 when a private secondary school—Western Boys High School—was established in Benin City.

The artisans' and peasants' response to colonial education was not very different from that of the titleholders. They were initially reluctant to embrace Western colonial education. Till the 1920s, when the missionaries started forcing their way into the rural areas, schools were restricted to Benin City. Apart from the distance from Benin City schools, the fear of the negative social influences of colonial education, and the inability to pay school fees,[75] there was also the general distrust of colonial officials and their policies. This general distrust and resentment were also extended to the missionary agents of both European and African extraction. They were correctly viewed by the people as the same, which was expressed in the saying *A we ghe 'Ebo we we na ghe fada*, literally, "We say look at the white man, and you say look at the reverend father." This saying meant that there was no difference between the colonial officials and missionaries. This attitude toward the missionaries developed into hostility due to the iconoclasm and disregard for precolonial social values which the missionaries encouraged among their converts. This led to censure of missionary agents, conflicts, and the sacking of missionary stations by enraged peasants. The people were further alienated by the hypocrisy of many of the mission agents, who exploited the labor of converts for private ends, involved themselves in illicit sexual affairs with converts (including married women),[76] embezzled church collections, and engaged in tyrannical and oppressive activities.[77] The rivalry between the various missionary bodies further added to the confusion and bewilderment of the mass of the people. But with time, there came a gradual realization that colonial education was a new means of gaining social leverage in colonial society. This realization resulted in the toleration of missionaries for the sake of their schools, and a new wave of migration of rural youths to Benin City to attend schools. Even the introduction of individual payment of school fees in 1916 in state owned schools could not stop the mass demand for and interest in colonial education.

This high demand for colonial Western education reached its peak during the depression years when it was reported that peasants seemed to be realizing the value of education and sending their children to school in large numbers.[78] Missionary infant or "monitor" schools sprang up like mushrooms in the villages. Villages that could not attract missionaries, like Obadan and Oke, took the lead in establishing peasant cooperative society schools for their children.[79] They were soon joined by private individuals who exploited the situation to establish day and night schools. They were mainly aided by the Benin Native Authority, which granted free land to individuals who wished to establish schools. With colonial state policies and measures effectively restricting post-infant school educational facilities to Benin City till the 1940s, the rural-urban migration continued unabated. Instead of improving the educational facilities in the villages as recommended by the senior education officer in 1940,[80] the colonial state increased the school fees by 100 percent in 1941, and this forced many pupils out of school. Less than 1 percent of all pupils remained long enough in school to complete elementary class four.[81] Many could not continue their education, especially secondary education (which was inadequate) and post-secondary education (which was nonexistent) in the division. Only very few pupils who won scholarships or missionary bonded aid were able to continue secondary and post-secondary education outside the division or province or colonial territory.

Rather than the indifference of the people of Benin Division to colonial education as alleged in intelligence reports, it was the colonial state's policies and measures that deliberately discouraged the expansion and development of colonial education and restricted the educational achievements and aspirations of the people. The relatively poor educational achievement and attainment of the people in relation to their neighbors in the protectorate was to result from this controlling role of the colonial state. This was confirmed by F. D. McGrath, district officer in Benin Division, in 1946.

> I have every sympathy with the Native Authority's decision to face risks (and the odium of imposing heavier taxes in a few years time) in overcoming Benin's grave handicap of educational backwardness, by comparison with most other people of the southern provinces. Except for the city schools, the missions have failed, perhaps through no fault of their own; Government has done next to nothing, the Native Authority is right to assume responsibility now.[82]

Though Benin Division's first university graduate (late Hon. Justice Samuel O. Ighodaro) emerged in 1938,[83] he remained the only university graduate till the early 1950s. This unimpressive educational attainment put the division at a disadvantage and was to affect the emergent Benin middle class in their relations with their more educationally advanced neighbors in provincial, regional, and national politics, and especially in employment and appointment to offices. The result was that in spite of the increase in the number of schools provided by the Benin Native Authority and voluntary agencies especially from the 1940s, the educational attainment of the people, especially the indigenes of Benin Division, remained lower than those of other divisions in Benin Province.

CONCLUSION

This chapter has shown that right from the inception of colonial rule, the colonial state had a concern about the education of the people of the division. The needs of the colonial economy and administration for a service class with special skills and the late arrival of missionary agencies influenced colonial education in the division. It was aimed at creating a small class of skilled technical and administrative functionaries, and agricultural raw materials plantation farmers, possibly perpetuating the continued domination of the society by the offspring of members of the overthrown ruling aristocracy. These aims made the colonial state to use various means to control and retard the educational aspirations and development of the people of the division. This affected the quality of the education provided, the numbers of recipients, and the social class and family background of the recipients, in spite of the enthusiasm of the people for education, which developed in the 1910s. This resulted in the poor educational attainment of the people of the division.

NOTES

1. J. A. Macrae-Simpson, "A Political Intelligence Report on the Benin Division of Benin Province, 1936," mimeographed, 2. See also Paula Ben-Amos, "Social Change in the Organization of Wood Carving in Benin City, Nigeria," Ph.D. dissertation, Indiana University, 1971 (Ann Arbor, Michigan University Microfilms) 31.
2. Macrae-Simpson, "A Political Intelligence Report," 2.
3. E. A. Ayandele, *The Missionary Impact on Modern Nigeria 1842-1914: A Political and Social Analysis* (London: Longman Group Ltd., 1977), 157-159.
4. Bill Freund, *The Making of Contemporary Africa: The Development of African Society since 1860* (London: Macmillan Press, 1984), 136.
5. Uyilawa Usuanlele, "State and Class in Benin Division 1897-1959: A History of Colonial Domination and Class Formation," M.A. thesis, Ahmadu Bello University, Zaria, 1988, chapter 4.
6. Majorie Mbilinyi, "African Education during the British Colonial Period, 1919-1961," in M.H.Y. Kaniki (ed.), *Tanzania under Colonial Rule* (London: Longman Group Ltd., 1980), 248.
7. Mbilinyi, "African Education."
8. A. Temu and B. Swai, *Historians and Africanist History: A Critique* (London: Zed Press, 1981), 160.
9. N.A.I. CSO 1/13, Annual Report of Niger Coast protectorate for year 1896-1897, Dispatch no. 159 to Foreign Office, 10 Dec. 1897, 384.
10. Ibid.
11. N.A.I. CSO 1/13, vol. 1, Dispatch no. 15, Annual Report of Niger Coast Protectorate, 1897-1898.
12. Interviews with Chief T.I. Imasogie (aged 92 years), 29 May 1986; Madam Osemwonwa Erebe (aged 81 years), 16 May 1985; and Chief Edokpolo Obakozuwa (aged 85).
13. N.A.I. CSO 1/13, vol. 13, Dispatch no. 260, Annual Report of Niger Coast Protectorate 1899-1900, 500.
14. Quoted in Babs Fafunwa, *A History of Education in Nigeria* (London: George Allen and Unwin, 1982), 113.
15. J.C. Anene, *Southern Nigeria in Transition 1885-1906: Theory and Practice* (Cambridge: Cambridge University Press, 1966), 314.
16. N.A.I. CSO 1/13, vol. 14, Dispatch no. 29, Moor to Colonial Office, 6 Feb. 1901.
17. Ayandele, *The Missionary Impact*, 158.

18. See J.U. Egharevba, *A Short History of Benin* (Ibadan: Ibadan University Press, 1968), 92-93.
19. A. E. Afigbo, "The Background to the Southern Nigeria Education Code of 1903," *Journal of the Historical Society of Nigeria*, 4 (2), June 1968, 206-212.
20. N.A.I. CSO 1/13, vol. 14, Dispatch no. 157.
21. N.A.I. BD 13/2, Quarterly Report of Benin City District, Jan.-Mar. 1905.
23. Mbilinyi, "African Education."
24. Fafunwa, A *History of Education*, 93 and 119.
25. F.O. Ogunlade, "Education and Politics in Colonial Nigeria: The Case of King's College, Lagos (1906-1911)," in *Journal of the Historical Society of Nigeria*, 7 (2), June 1974, 340.
26. N.A.I. CSO 1/13, vol. 14, Dispatch no. 29, Moor to Colonial Office, 6 June 1901, 68.
27. Quoted in Ben-Amos, "social Change," 31.
28. N.A.I. BP 6/1927, H.T.C. Field, Superintendent of Education Benin City, to Resident (BP), 4 Feb. 1928, 24.
29. Mbilinyi, "African Education."
30. N.A.I. CSO 1/13, vol. 14, Dispatch no. 160, enclosure, Moor to Rev. J. Buchanan, 15 June 1901, 480.
31. Ibid.
32. Ibid., 482.
33. Quoted in N.A.I. BP 78/27, B. Bewley, Resident (BP) to DO, 22 Dec. 1931.
34. N.A.I. BP 55/3/1915, Watt to DO, 19 Oct.. 1915.
35. Ibid.
36. Quoted in Ibid., 20 March 1916.
37. Afigbo, "The Background to the Southern Nigeria Education Code," 207.
38. Quoted in Fafunwa, A *History of Education*, 16.
39. Ibid., 119-125.
40. N.A.I. BP 1290, J.W.A. Thorburn, Superintendent of Education, to Resident (BP), 30 July 1936.
41. N.A.I. CSO 1/13, vol. 15, Dispatch no. 157, Moor to Secretary of State for Colonies, 12 June 1901, 470.
42. N.A.I. BP 62/1922, E. Dawson, Resident (BP) to Secretary, Southern Provinces, 11 May 1923.
43. N.A.I. BP 762. Quoted in Extract of Minutes of Meeting of Benin School Committee, 29 Dec. 1929.
44. N.A.I. BP 62/1922, C. N. Cummins, Inspector of Schools (Asaba) to Resident (BP), 6 Oct. 1922, 22.

45. N.A.I. BP 4/2/4, Benin Province Annual Report for Year Ending 31 Dec. 1917, 10.
46. N.A.I. BP 62/1922, D. I. Field, Inspector of Schools, Benin City to Resident (BP), 20 Feb. 1926, 82.
47. Ogunlade, "Education and Politics"; and Annual Report for Nigeria (Lagos: Government Printers, 1937), 3.
48. N.A.I. BP 55/3/1915, Watt to Secretary, Southern Provinces, 16 Sept. 1915.
49. Ibid., Watt to DO, 20 Sept. 1915.
50. Ibid., Watt to Henry Carr, 18 Oct. 1915.
51. Ibid., H.C. Moorhouse, Secretary, Southern Provinces, to Commissioner (BP), 26 Aug. 1915.
52. N.A.I. BP 78/27, B. Bewley, Resident (BP) to DO (BP), 22 Dec. 1931.
53. Ibid., Superintendent of Education (BP) to DO (BP).
54. Mbilinyi, "African Education."
55. *Nigerian Blue Book 1913* (Lagos: Government Press, 1914); N.A.I. BP 66/1919, Education Returns Annual 1919; and N.A.I. BP 6/1927, Educational Returns Annual 1927.
56. N.A.I. BP 553/1915, Watt to Inspector of Schools (Asaba), 28 Jan. 1916.
57. N.A.I. BP 6/1927, Education Annual Returns of Government School, Benin City, 1929.
58. Ibid.
59. E.A. Ayandele, *Holy Johnson: Pioneer of African Nationalism* (London: Frank Cass and Co. Ltd., 1970), 279.
60. N.A.I. BP 433/20, Rev. E. Chuoba and Committee of St. Matthew's Church, Benin City, to DO (BD), 12 March 1923.
61. James Johnson, quoted in Ben-Amos, "Social Change," 31.
62. N.A.I. BP 69-1919, Education returns of St. Matthew's CMS School, Benin City, 1919.
63. N.A.I. BP 1191, H.C. Moorhouse, Lt. Gov. Southeastern Provinces, to Bishop Broderick, Roman Catholic Mission, Asaba, 4 Nov. 1924.
64. Ibid.
65. N.A.I. BP 41, vol. 7, Annual Report of Benin Division, 1938.
66. N.A.I. CSO 26/2, file 14617, vol. 12, Annual Report of Benin Province, 1938.
67. N.A.I. BP 762, F. F. Herbert, Ag. Chief Inspector of Education, (Ibadan) to Superintendent of Education (Benin City), 5 Dec. 1929.

68. Ibid., Extract of Minutes of Meeting of Benin School Committee, 29 Dec. 1929.
69. Ibid., Secretary (Southern Provinces) to Resident (BP), 11 April 1934, and 13 April 1934.
70. N.A.I. BP 41, vol. 7, Annual Report of Benin Division, 1938.
71. N.A.I. BP 1290, J.W.A. Thorburn, Superintendent of Education (BP), to Resident (BP), 30 July 1936.
72. N.A.I. BP 762, Report of Superintendent of Education, Benin Province, quoted in DO (BD) to Resident (BP), 26 March 1945.
73. N.A.I. BP 41, vol. 9, Annual Report of Benin Division, 1940.
74. N.A.I. BP 62/1922, T. N. Lloyd, Superintendent of Education (Benin City), to Chief Inspector of Education (Ibadan), 28 July 1930.
75. Personal communications with Pa Omoigui Oyiawe, the Odionwere of Igue-Iyase (aged about 100 years), 24 April 1986.
76. As late as 1936, the Odionwere of Ugboko opposed the establishment of schools in Ugboko because previous missionary agents had had illicit sexual affairs with his wives. N.A.I. BP 1929, DO (BD) to Resident (BP), 16 Dec. 1936.
77. Missionary agency records are full of reports of these malpractices of their agents. See, for instance, N.A.I. CMS Y2/2, file 15, Report on Benin District, 1922-1933; and N.A.I. R.C.M. BD 3/5, Diocesan letters: Benin City Palaver, 1951-1952.
78. N.A.I CSO 26/2, File 14617, vol. 8. Annual Report of Benin Province, 1933.
79. N.A.I. BP 762, Quoted in DO (BD) to Resident (BP), 26 March 1945.
80. N.A.I. BP 762, Report of Superintendent of Education (BP), quoted in DO (BD), to Resident (BP), 26 March 1945.
81. N.A.I. CSO 26/2, File 14617, vol. 12, Annual Report of Benin Province, 1938.
82. N.A.I. BP 934, F. D. McGrath, DO (BD), to Resident (BP), 8 Oct. 1946.
83. Personal communication with Hon. Justice S. O. Ighodaro (aged 75 years) at his Benin City residence, 30 May 1986.

3

CONSTITUTION-MAKING AND THE NIGERIAN IDENTITY, 1914-1960

Ebere Nwaubani

Nigeria is a British invention, knitted together, above all else, by a spate of constitution-making. I need to quickly add that the ongoing dissolution of nation-states elsewhere[1] suggests that states are necessarily no more than geographic-legal expressions at their inception. They are subsequently given their vibrancy and life through what John Stuart Mill called "a sufficient amount of mutual sympathy among the population."[2] This, essentially, is what nationalism is all about. And this means that the primary prerequisite in the building of a nation-state, as a living and human reality, is psychological commitment, usually generated by a sustained appeal to sybolisms that are basically spiritual, historical, and even psychic. Documents such as the Declaration of Independence and the Constitution, events such as the War of Independence, and symbols such as the flag all combine to serve this purpose for the United States.

The United States experience suggests that a constitution is crucial in generating a feeling of belonging and attachment to a political community in its formative stages as well as mutual empathy or communal identification among the citizenry. In this regard, I recognize that every constitution is supposed to provide a legitimate process for the exercise of public power and a stable order within which political decisions are made. It is, however, also true that the constitution sets the tone for political discourse in the country.

This chapter explores the correlation between constitution-making and the cultivation of a Nigerian identity during the first four and half decades of the country's history. The context for this investigation is that British colonial rule bunched together some 250 nationalities (or ethnic groups) into what became "Nigeria." There is another purpose: by my reckoning, Nigeria has—especially since 1953—stumbled from one major political crisis to another. I therefore hope that this paper will provide some historical context for this endemic crisis. To adequately capture the dynamics involved in this subject matter, I will be looking at both the textual and the practical implications of the constitutions, and in some cases, at aspects of the background to the constitutions.

PRELUDE TO NIGERIA

By the end of 1899, the geographical space today known as Nigeria was under three distinct British administrations: the Colony of Lagos; the Niger Coast Protectorate, exercising jurisdiction from Lagos eastward to the Kamerun (as it was spelt then); and the Niger Territories (practically, the areas flanking the Niger and the Benue and anywhere north of these rivers from which the Royal Niger Company had obtained treaties. The Niger Territories were under the jurisdiction of the company). When, on New Year's Day, 1900, the British government assumed imperial control over all three territories, Lagos retained its crown colony status, complete with a governor, a Legislative Council, a civil service modeled after its British archetype, and a

Supreme Court also patterned on the best traditions of the English high court system; the Niger Coast Protectorate and the portions of the Niger Territories south of Idah became the Protectorate of Southern Nigeria; the rest of the Niger Territories, from Idah northward to the Sokoto Caliphate and Bornu, became the Protectorate of Northern Nigeria. The protectorates were, for all purposes, distinct units of the British Empire, each with its own high commissioner, civil service, and budget. Their boundaries were symbolized by a customs post at Idah. And there was no love lost between the two Nigerias as they "carried their separateness to the point of building competing railway systems."[3] Thus, from the onset, mutual jealousy and rivalry characterized the relations between the British administrators in Nigeria. Nigerians themselves were soon to inherit this antagonism.[4]

In May 1906, the Colony of Lagos and the Protectorate of Southern Nigeria were amalgamated. As Tekena Tamuno and Jeremy White have emphasized, the prime motive of this exercise was economic: Lagos needed funds for large-scale public works like railway and harbor construction. The amalgamation enabled Lagos to draw from the rich vaults of Southern Nigeria.[5] The jurisdiction of the Lagos Legislative Council was extended to cover all of Southern Nigeria; a single civil service was also created. With this exercise, there now existed two distinct British territories in present-day Nigeria: the Colony and Protectorate of Southern Nigeria, and the Protectorate of Northern Nigeria.

THE INVENTION OF NIGERIA

In May 1912, Frederick Lugard, the foundation high commissioner of the Protectorate of Northern Nigeria (1900-1906), was appointed to the joint governorship of both the Colony and Protectorate of Southern Nigeria and the Protectorate of Northern Nigeria. His immediate assignment was to draw up proposals for the amalgamation of the two Nigerias. On the basis of those proposals, the two protectorates (thenceforth known as "Provinces") and the Colony of Lagos were "amalgamated" on New Year's Day, 1914, to form the Colony and Protectorate of Nigeria. The Southern Provinces were headquartered in Enugu, the Northern Provinces in Kaduna.[6]

In many respects, the so-called amalgamation of 1914 was a rickety foundation for the Nigerian nation-state. To begin with, it was informed by British financial imperatives. Lugard himself summarized the "necessity for amalgamation" under two headings: finance and railways. The North, landlocked and poor, was operating at a deficit, which was met by subsidies from the South and grants-in-aid from a reluctant British Treasury. In the period 1906 to 1912, the imperial grants-in-aid to the North averaged £300,000.000 a year; the contribution from the South in the same period averaged £70,000.00 a year.[7] These financial calculations were of particular interest to London. On 27 June 1912, Lewis Harcourt, the secretary of state for the colonies, addressed the House of Commons on a wide of range of issues pertaining to his department. On Nigeria, he reported that "In Southern Nigeria the revenue has increased by £867,000 and the expenditure by £661,000, and there is for the current year an estimated surplus of £2,900,000." By contrast, "Northern Nigeria has up to now been and still is a subsidized Protectorate, but whereas in 1906 the Grant-in-Aid (without any provision for interest on Railway loan) was £315,000, in this current year, after providing for such interest, the Grant-in-Aid asked for is only £156,000." Harcourt hoped that "with the amalgamation of the two Nigerias...we may be able to set a short term to these Grants-in-Aid and at the same time relieve the Treasury from its liabilities and the Protectorate from Treasury control."[8] Lord Hailey was later to note that "As a result of the amalgamation, some of the resources of the South could be made available for the development of the North."[9]

Since the amalgamation was informed by financial expediency rather than issues of broader vision, the sociopolitical particularism of Southern and Northern Nigeria were maintained.[10] In actual fact, the so-called amalgamation meant little more than the unification of the railways, the marine, and the customs departments. The medical, posts and telegraphs, and surveys departments as well as the West African Frontier Force were merely "combined." Except for a common "head" in Lagos, the "combined" departments retained their preexisting Southern and Northern identities and continued to operate as in the pre-amalgamation days. However, the role of the "head" was only advisory; he had no executive authority over the departments.[11] This awkward setup is not surprising since Lugard's guiding principle in amalgamating the Nigerias was, in his own words, "to involve as little dislocation of existing conditions as possible."[12] This, in practice, meant that everything about the provinces, including the supervision of the "combined" departments, was left to the lieutenant governors, who merely referred to Lugard any matter that seemed to affect Nigeria as a whole.

The lieutenant governors of the Provinces and the administrator of Lagos all reported separately to Lugard, with hardly any coordination of their administrations. In effect, "amalgamation" was concentrated in just one person (Lugard) and his office, that of the governor-general. The inadequacies of this political system were complicated by the rudimentary nature of Lugard's supporting staff, his "political secretariat" consisting of his younger brother (Major Edward Lugard), a clerk, and a typist. Of this secretariat, I. M. Okonjo observed that "It developed into an ambulatory administrative organ accompanying Lugard wherever he went."[13] Besides, Lugard failed to create a single roster for the British officials in Nigeria, thereby ensuring that the administrative service remained polarized into two antagonistic South and North camps.[14] Thus, amalgamation did not even lay the groundwork of a Nigerian public administration.

The amalgamation was, in retrospect, a golden opportunity to provide Nigeria with a balanced structural arrangement that would have ensured a harmonious federal system. It is worthy of note that Lugard's contemporaries who advocated the amalgamation of the Nigerias also suggested splitting the resulting territory into more than two units: E. D. Morel, the well-known English trader, proposed four provinces; Charles Temple, lieutenant governor of the North, 1914-1917, called for seven. Lugard opposed these proposals on the grounds that since the two protectorates had developed different laws and different conditions of service for their European and African staffs, the creation of smaller territorial units would inject more confusion into the system. Amalgamation, he insisted, must cause a minimum of dislocation of existing conditions. In addition, he believed that a multiplicity of new governments would mean a large increase in the number of officials who were difficult to recruit.

Lugard's amalgamation was, at least in one respect, retrogressive in the nation-building process: the jurisdiction of the Legislative Council which had hitherto covered all of Southern Nigeria was now restricted to the Lagos Colony.[15] In place of the Legislative Council, he established a "Nigerian Council." Composed of nominees of the governor-general, this council met for a maximum of three days each year, mainly to hear addresses from the governor-general. The restriction of the Legislative Council to Lagos Colony effectively reversed the 1906 amalgamation of the Southern units. In terms of its responsibility and membership,[16] the Nigerian Council lacked the capacity to initiate the process of welding the new country together.

THE 1922 CONSTITUTION

From the beginning of his tenure, Governor Hugh Clifford, who succeeded Lugard, was unsparing in his criticism of the amalgamation. "The scheme drawn up," Clifford contended,

> did not provide for the "amalgamation" of these three units in any sense in which that term is ordinarily used, for "amalgamation" would normally imply some attempt to merge them into a single whole. No such attempt was, in fact, made, and indeed the basic idea of the scheme appears to have been the maintenance of the colony and the two Protectorates as three separate and fully equipped Administrations, bound together principally, if not solely, by the fact that each of these three Administrations was to be immediately responsible to the Governor-General instead of the Secretary of State.[17]

Clifford drew attention to the South-North dualism, enhanced by retaining mutually exclusive secretariats for the two territories. He also complained of the absence of a central secretariat and therefore the absence of a machinery for the coordination of the three administrative units (Lagos, South, and North), stressing that "if the ideal at which we should aim is, as I hold it should be, the eventual evolution not only of an 'amalgamated' but of a *united* Nigeria it is essential that the coordination of administrative work, political and non-political alike, should be directed from a single center."[18]

The 1922 constitution which followed abolished that Lugardian oddity called the Nigerian Council. A Legislative Council for all Nigeria was established for the first time. The Southern and Northern Provinces were to be regarded as a single political unit for fiscal and budgetary purposes: all legislation emanating from the Legislative Council and relating to custom and excise duties as well as the criminal law were made applicable to the North. Otherwise, the council was still precluded from discussing bills "of any description pertaining to the North without the express consent of the Governor."[19] This meant that the governor alone legislated for the Northern Provinces, whose only representatives in the Legislative Council for the next quarter of a century were the lieutenant-governor, the senior residents, and a pair of European businessmen from the Kano Chamber of Commerce and the Jos Chamber of Mines. Thus, the South and the North, though amalgamated in 1914, still remained—except for the British and the businessmen—constitutionally separate. This exclusion of Northern Nigerians, and for so long, from the Legislative Council was a serious omission as it screened them from those influences which shaped the political attitudes of the Southerners.

In addition to the governor, the Legislative Council, under the 1922 constitution, had twenty-six officials, four elected members, and nominated unofficials (who varied in number from thirteen to seventeen). The governor nominated the unofficials at his pleasure; besides six Europeans who represented commercial interests, the rest represented some communities in the South:

(Lagos) Colony Division, Oyo Division, Egba Division, Ijebu Division, Ondo Division, Warri-Benin Division, Igbo Division, Ibibio Division, and Rivers Division (the eastern Niger Delta). These communities were not always represented by indigenes or even Nigerians: Ondo was once represented by a European clergyman.[20] In any case, there was, as Ben Nwabueze has pointed out, "little, if any, contact between the nominated Nigerian members and the communities they were supposed to represent. Within the council, they spoke and acted for themselves and not as representatives of anybody, and they always showed great sympathy towards the government."[21] Of the elected members, three were from Lagos and one from Calabar on a franchise that was limited to adult male British subjects and protected persons who satisfied a residence qualification of twelve months and had a gross annual income of £100. These conditions effectively restricted the franchise to a small segment of the population: out of an estimated population of 40,000 in Lagos and 10,000 in Calabar, only 3,000 and 1,000 respectively qualified to vote.[22]

The Legislative Council, Joan Wheare observed, "kept its limited and somewhat insulated character. The British authorities retained and developed it...to satisfy their own principles."[23] The restriction of the franchise to Lagos and Calabar meant that the council's permissible area of social mobilization was severely limited. Without doubt, an extension of the elective principle to more towns (and certainly Abeokuta, Warri, and Onitsha were well-qualified) would have induced more widespread interest in Lagos and its national politics. This way, the Legislative Council would have served as a psychological medium for generating some shared communal life. As it turned out, barring the Lagos press and elite, the council hardly generated any interest, even in Southern Nigeria.

NIGERIA: TO BE OR NOT TO BE

The 1922 constitution subsisted until 1947. The intervening years witnessed a very intense—indeed, internecine—"battle" among top British officials in Nigeria over the country's political future. Clifford himself embodied this uncertainty. One may note the paradox of his measures: anxious to make the amalgamation a reality, an essential component of his administration was to shift power away from Enugu and Kaduna to Lagos. At the same time, Clifford saw the "native authorities" as holding the key to Nigeria's political evolution. In his widely quoted December 1920 speech, he envisaged each of Nigeria's constituent ethnic groups evolving into a distinctly autonomous unit within the British Empire. Clifford did not even propose a separate Northern Nigeria: subtly seeking to undermine the nineteenth century Fulani empire-building process, he asserted the right of "any of the great Emirates of the North...to maintain that each one of them is, in a very real sense, a nation." He therefore lamented that if it was possible to weld all these groups "into a single homogenous nation—a deadly blow would thereby be struck at the very root of national self-government in Nigeria, which secures to each separate people the right to maintain its identity, its individuality and its nationality."[24]

Clifford's views had their antecedents in those of Charles Temple, who, in 1918, rejected the notion that a "race" could indefinitely "remain subject to another" and thought it inevitable that "they will some day recapture their liberty." Totally discounting the maturation of the nascent central administration established in 1914, he hoped that in a generation or two, the Northern emirates and the Yoruba chiefdoms could attain dominion status and be able to cope with their internal affairs within the British Empire.[25]

Under the guise of indirect rule, the British officials in the North conceived of the emirates as autonomous feudatories. Consequently, during the first two decades of British rule, they advocated that the emirates be accorded the status of semi-independent states. From the mid-1920s onward, the Northern bureaucracy changed focus: it now "continually agitated for distinct and separate development of the north, even up to the point of suggesting that it be cut off from the south."[26] In 1940, Lord Hailey observed that:

> In their [the officials'] view, the Native Administrations, which were to be given a growing measure of

autonomy in the management of their own affairs, would combine to provide the final authority for legislative and executive purposes; they would, in short, become the Government of Northern Nigeria, and Northern Nigeria would remain constitutionally independent of the South.[27]

Richmond Palmer (lieutenant governor of the North, 1925-1930) best embodied this separatist streak.[28] Although the jurisdiction of the Legislative Council was largely limited to the Colony and the Southern Provinces, the lieutenant governor and the five senior residents of the North were also members of the council. But, disapproving of what they regarded as interference by Lagos in Northern affairs, Palmer and his residents stayed away from the Legislative Council, and developed a conference of Northern residents as a substitute. The Colonial Office had to scrap this conference in 1930.[29]

Throughout his tenure, Palmer resisted making laws passed by the Legislative Council applicable to the North, arguing that there were three separate units in Nigeria, which "more and more would require separate legislation for their needs." He hoped that "ultimately, there would have to be a separate federal council for each of the three units as in the Federated Malay States." According to him, the federal councils would consist of the areas east of the Niger, the North, and "the Yoruba country."[30] After an extensive examination of the separatist attitude of the Northern-based officials, Jeremy White held that "Palmer was never ready to accept the full implications of the 1914 Amalgamation and did everything he could to resist those implications. His efforts were directed at getting back to that pre-Amalgamation arrangement, according to which the only nexus between the North and the South was the Governor."[31]

It is worth emphasizing that London was in sync with the Northern officialdom. In February 1926, Palmer requested that the native administrations' share of the revenue derived from direct taxation should be raised from 50 percent to 75 percent. W. G. A. Ormsby-Gore, parliamentary under-secretary of state for the colonies, was delighted with this proposal, because it marked "a yet further important stage in the constitutional future of Nigeria—based on the widening of the sphere of Native Administration activities." Like Clifford, he prophesied that self-government in Nigeria "if it will ever come will be the self-government of the country by the Native Administrations and not by any elected council in Lagos, at least I hope so."[32] Thus, in spite of the amalgamation and the subsequent centralizing policies, there was—right up to the Colonial Office in the 1920s—a great deal of uncertainty regarding Nigeria's political future.

Donald Cameron assumed the governorship of Nigeria in June 1931. It was under his tenure, in 1933, that all the Southern and Northern departments were finally unified. In one of his earliest despatches, Cameron complained of the tendency to regard the Northern Provinces as constituting a unit separate from Southern Nigeria such that a province in the North was regarded as a province of Northern Nigeria and not a province of Nigeria.[33] In 1932, he observed that the idea that the native administrations in the North were to become independent units which were to enter a "United Nigeria" through a federal system had gained ground "during the last six or seven years."[34] He considered this idea untenable since the development of the North as a separate political unit would be a return to a state of affairs that amalgamation was specifically designed to terminate. Second, Cameron was convinced that for geographical reasons, Northern Nigeria could not develop as a self-contained political and economic unit because it must depend on the coast as well as the railways and ports of the South for its international trade.[35]

Cameron appropriately identified the cause of the friction between the Northern officialdom and Lagos to be "the manner in which the doctrine of indirect rule or 'native administration' is being applied in Nigeria, particularly the Northern Provinces." He added that "The root of the evil lies in the conception that a native administration is designed ultimately to administer all the affairs of all the people in a geographical unit."[36] Cameron set himself to confront this problem. The residence of the lieutenant governor in Kaduna used to be called "Government House." Within a month of his assumption of office, Cameron told C. W. Alexander, the lieutenant governor of the North, that "there could be only one Government House in Nigeria" and that the emirs and chiefs were not to be regarded as "rulers."[37]

Addressing northern officials and chiefs in Kaduna in November 1931, Cameron emphasized that "all Provinces and Native Administrations in Nigeria are mutually interdependent units of one great whole." He pledged to support the chiefs by "recognition of the rights and powers" which they held by tradition and custom and to foster and encourage their authority and institutions, not as semi-independent authorities, but "as part of the machinery of the Government of the country."[38] In 1933, Cameron enacted the Native Authority Ordinance, which affirmed that native authorities were local government agents and not semi-independent authorities. In 1934, he published *The Principles of Native Administration and Their Application*, where he talked of the "grave danger" in the absence of any "governing policy as to the political development of the country as a whole." He stressed the need for a coherent policy:

> We must know, in short, where we are going and what are our aims. It is necessary that the Government should form some idea broadly of what the political evolution of Nigeria is likely to be and work towards that end. [39]

Again, he argued:

> at least for geographical and economic reasons—it is not likely that any part of Nigeria will become separate, self-contained political and economic units, and that accordingly wisdom lies in the policy of treating the country as whole, openly and without any mental reservations.[40]

Bernard Bourdillon, who succeeded Cameron, believed that the native authorities "are not autonomous bodies on the lines of units in a federation or local self-governing bodies. . . .they are an integral part of the machinery of Government."[41] Nonetheless, in a March 1938 despatch to the Colonial Office, Bourdillon announced that "It is the essence of that policy [that is, of Native

Administration] that the British Administrative Service should be gradually reduced, its functions being taken over by the Native Administrations... it is therefore in the Executive Service of the Native Administrations that educated Africans should seek employment of a purely administrative nature."[42] This announcement, Lord Hailey noted, "envisaged a future when all administration would be in the hands of native authorities, or of equivalent organizations controlling areas in which native authorities do not exist."[43]

In 1940, Lord Hailey visited Nigeria as part of a trip designed to chart the constitutional future of British dependencies in Africa. His report was a landmark not yet appreciated in Nigerian history. It rejected the notion that the native administrations /authorities constituted the appropriate nucleus and focus for Nigeria's future political development. Lord Hailey concluded that "in any future which we can contemplate, the native authorities should retain the character of agents of Government and be confined to those functions which their place in the organization of native society fits them to perform." He dismissed the idea of a separate and independent legislature for Northern Nigeria, emphasizing that "The economic life of the north is bound up with that of the south." In promoting its parochialism, the Northern bureaucracy had made concerted efforts to fossilize the region's political culture. With this in mind, Lord Hailey immediately added:

> It is true that there is at present no evidence of a demand in the Northern Provinces for representation in a general legislature. But if the north remains for any length of time aloof from the political institutions of the south, there is a danger that the Southern Provinces may so far outstrip the north in political development that southern natives may eventually be in a position to control the interests of the north. It is clear that the north cannot for long continue to maintain itself in political isolation from the south. [44]

In spite of this argument, the Northern bureaucracy remained unwilling to shed its ossified position. Responding to Lord Hailey on the role of native authorities, Theodore Adams (the chief commissioner of the Northern Provinces) advocated a "rulers of protected states" status as in Malaya; he still wanted to promote the autonomous development of the emirates as "Protected States," and believed "the policy of a central African Government incompatible with the Emirate system."[45] With Lord Hailey's report, Bourdillon was now prepared to fend off the anti-Nigerian posture of the Northern-based officials. On Adams' insistence for "rulers of protected states" status, Bourdillon responded: "I can conceive of no greater folly." The governor insisted that the emirs should be encouraged to demand their own "finger in the Nigerian pie."[46] In *Further Memorandum on the Future Political Development of Nigeria* (1942), Bourdillon observed that the Northern-based officials were still not reconciled to a "a central council" sitting in Lagos.

THE 1946 (RICHARDS) CONSTITUTION

Bourdillon's tenure ended in 1943 and he was succeeded by Arthur Richards. Bourdillon had, in 1939, split the South into two: the Eastern and Western Provinces.[47] Building on this structure, the 1946 constitution divided Nigeria into three regions (as the Provinces were now known). Each region, headed by a chief commissioner, had a House of Assembly; the North, in addition, had a House of Chiefs.

In a publication issued to mark Nigeria's attainment of independence, the venerable historian, Kenneth Onwuka Dike, charged the Richards Constitution as "a dividing line in Nigerian constitutional development. Before it the keynote in Nigerian politics was unification, towards the development of a strong centralized state and the realization of a common nationality. . . But with the Richards Constitution, this tendency towards unification was, on the whole arrested." More particularly, Dike criticized the constitution on the grounds that it "carved up the country into three Regions . . . by swinging the pendulum towards regionalism it had let loose emotions and passions that under the old constitution were being gradually canalized in the interests of service to Nigeria as a whole."[48] The evidence does support Dike's charge, which is, by the way, widely shared by Nigerians. ("Regionalism," as Okoi Arikpo observed, "has always been regarded by many Nigerians as one of the worst features" of the 1946 constitution.)[49] Until about the early 1940s, the question—as I have demonstrated—was whether there would even be a Nigeria, as Northern-based British officials campaigned for that territory's secession. The 1946 constitution re-solved this issue: it expanded the scope of the Legislative Council to include Northern (as distinct from Northern-based British) representation for the first time.

In seeking to reconcile the separatism of the Northern-based officials with the implications of the emerging Nigerian nation-state, the 1946 constitution activated the regions as centers of political action, which would link the native administrations with Lagos.[50] Nonetheless, the constitution endorsed a unitary government for Nigeria—it made provision for only one legislature (the Legislative Council) and only one executive (the Executive Council), both in Lagos, for the entire country. True, the constitution established regional Houses of Assembly; but these were merely deliberative and advisory, not legislative, organs. Each could consider only proposed legislation pertaining to the particular region and make recommendations to the Legislative Council. In addition, the regional assemblies served as electoral colleges for the Legislative Council and approved the region's budget.

On Dike's charge that the 1946 constitution "carved up the country into three Regions," Arikpo has since reminded us that although the constitution "gave forceful constitutional validity to the administrative division of the country into three Regions, these divisions existed as far back as 1939, when the Southern Provinces were divided into the Eastern and Western Provinces under the administrative charge of two Chief Commissioners based at Enugu and Ibadan"; that the constitution did not "divide Nigeria into three immutable autonomous Regions," since it also conferred on the governor sufficient discretionary powers to further divide the regions;[51] and that the policy of regionalism was directed more to administrative devolution than to the political separation of Nigerians.[52] Besides, as Bourdillon explained, the regionalization component of the 1946 constitution represented "not the division of one unit into three, but the beginning of the fusion of innumerable small units into three and from these three into one."[53]

At the same time that it added some meaning to Nigerianness, the 1946 constitution revealed the underlying centrifugal tensions among the constituent units. Governor Richards laid his constitutional proposals before the Legislative Council on 5 March 1945. Dissatisfaction with the proposals was most eloquently articulated by the National Convention of Nigeria and the Cameroons (NCNC). Formed only in June 1944, the NCNC—under the leadership of Nnamdi Azikiwe—undertook a vigorous nationwide campaign, followed by a deputation to London in 1947, all aimed at forestalling the implementation of the constitution. In a letter to the *Nigerian Daily Times* (7 May 1947), Abubakar Tafawa Balewa, the Second Member for the North in the Legislative Council, expressed the hostility of the Northern political elite to the NCNC campaign. "Let the South know," Balewa wrote, "that we will never cooperate with that gang of agitators who are not even sure of what they are doing." The attitude of the rump of the Nigerian Youth Movement—essentially, the Yoruba political elite—was no different. The *Daily Times*, owned by British business interests who felt threatened by any anticolonialism, generously allowed Samuel Ladoke Akintola to use its pages to wage a calumnious campaign against the NCNC. Thus, against the background of the Richards constitution, what passed for Nigerian nationalism was taking shape: the fragmented politics of primeval intra-elite hostility.

Against this background, Obafemi Awolowo reflected the reality of the times in an oft-quoted 1947 passage: "Nigeria is not a nation. It is a mere geographical expression. There are no 'Nigerians' in the sense as there are 'English,' 'Welsh,' or 'French.' The word 'Nigerian' is merely a distinctive appellation to distinguish those who live within the boundaries of Nigeria from those who do not." To Awolowo, each of the "various national or ethnic groups" in Nigeria—such as the Hausa, the Igbo, the

Yoruba, the Fulani, the Kanuri, the Ibibio, the Tiv, the Edo, the Nupe, and the Ijaw—"is a nation by itself.... There is as much difference between them as there is between Germans, English, Russians and Turks, for instance."[54] In asserting that "Nigeria is not a nation," Awolowo was implicitly making a distinction between a nation (or ethnic group), such as the Yoruba—with its underlying organic unity—and a state (Nigeria).[55] In fairness, Awolowo was not alone in his dismissiveness of the notion of a Nigerian nation in 1947: in the same year, Balewa held that "Since the amalgamation of the Southern and Northern Provinces in 1914, Nigeria has existed as one country only on paper."[56]

The idea that the nation is the building block of political life reached fruition in nineteenth century Western Europe. The nation in this sense was synonymous with the ethnic group—which meant that cultural homogeneity (a shared historical experience, including ancestry, homeland, language, and religion) and political community tended to coincide. The notion that a nation should consist of a fairly culturally homogenous population is traced to the 18th century German poet and philosopher, Johann Gottfried Herder. Each group, according to Herder, has its own *Volksgeist* or *Nationalgeist*, a distinctive set of customs and a lifestyle, a way of perceiving and behaving—and above all, language. In subscribing to Herder's theoretical disquisition, Awolowo sought to transplant nineteenth century European nationalist ideas to the emerging twentieth century Nigerian "nation-state."

THE 1951 (MACPHERSON) CONSTITUTION

A major nationalist complaint against the 1947 constitution was that it did not involve Nigerian opinion. The next constitution—on the recommendation of a Legislative Council Select Committee—was preceded by extensive discussions beginning at the village level, and continuing through the district and the provincial levels in 1948-1949. Proposals made at the provincial levels were discussed at regional conferences. By October 1949, the regions and the Colony had concluded their conferences.

All the regional conferences and that of the Lagos Colony recommended a federal system based on the three existing regions, and agreed that some of the financial and legislative powers of the central legislature should be delegated to the regional legislatures. There were two broad views on the executive: at both the regional and federal levels, the Eastern, Western, and Lagos conferences wanted full-fledged cabinet or ministerial systems consisting mostly of Nigerians, who would have executive responsibility over their departments. In sharp contrast, the Northern regional conference wanted to retain the existing central Executive Council, whose function was primarily to advise the governor on matters of general policy and on government bills introduced in the central legislature. At the regional level, the North recommended that the chief commissioner should exercise "original executive powers" in all matters on which the regional legislature had legislative competence; that the chief commissioner should be advised by a "Regional Executive Council" of officials and unofficials selected by him at his discretion; that the council should be solely advisory, and that the chief commissioner should not be bound to accept its advice.[57] These differences over executive responsibility masked a deep-seated tension in the political system: the South desired the devolution of some real governmental responsibility by the British; the North was more comfortable with the British keeping the reins of power.

The next stage was the preparation of a statement, based on the regional proposals, by a Drafting Committee.[58] This statement was then considered by a general conference which met in Ibadan on 9-28 January 1950. Since the members of this conference were there as regional representatives, they saw their role primarily in terms of securing the maximum advantages for their respective regions. There were deep differences of opinion over seven issues: the formula for regional representation in the central legislature, the basis of the franchise (direct or indirect; if indirect, how many levels of electoral colleges; universal or not), the principle of revenue allocation, ministerial responsibility, an increase in the number of regions, the advisability of a commission on boundary changes, and whether or not to merge Lagos with the Western Region.[59]

The West asked for a boundary commission to enquire into whether the Yoruba of Ilorin Province and Kabba Division (both in the North) wished to join the Western Region, which was predominantly Yoruba. The North outrightly rejected any such commission and the conference passed the issue over to the governor "to examine and make arrangements for [its] settlement as early as possible." On the central executive, the East, the West, and Lagos Colony argued for the introduction of ministerial responsibility; the North insisted that it was not ready for this development and also won on this matter. On revenue allocation, the North held that each region should receive grants from the central government on a per capita basis for all revenues declared as accruing from a strictly regional source. Again, the East, the West, and Lagos Colony combined to oppose this formula, which would have benefited the North (which insisted that it was more populous). The North and the West favored merging Lagos Colony with the West. With the Igbo increasingly settling in Lagos, the (dominantly Igbo) East countered that only the rural areas of the Colony should become part of the West, while Lagos proper—as the federal capital— should remain a distinct political unit.

The most acrimonious issue was regional representation in the proposed central legislature. The Drafting Committee recommended a membership ratio of 30:22:22 for the North, the East, and the West respectively. Although the East and the West preferred equal representation for all the regions, they both resigned themselves to this ratio. On the other hand, invoking its alleged population superiority, the North remained adamant in its demand for half of the seats in the legislature. So unyielding was the North that the emirs of Katsina and Zaria, at one point, seriously threatened that their region would secede from Nigeria. The conference proposed a central legislature consisting of 45 members from the North, 33 from the East, 33 from the West, 2 from Lagos, and 3 appointed by the governor to represent interests which, in his opinion, were not otherwise adequately represented. This recommendation so incensed the Northern delegates that they abstained from voting on it. They also gave notice that if the North's demand—for half of the seats—was not met, they would dissociate themselves from the other recommendations of the conference.

Given the tension at Ibadan, a number of issues were left unresolved and a Select Committee of the Legislative Council had to be set up to address those issues. The committee proposed to include Lagos with the Western Region; to safeguard the status of Lagos as the capital of Nigeria, it was also proposed a bicameral central legislature; the composition of the lower house was to be based on population while the regions were to have equal representation in the upper chamber.[60] The Legislative Council, in September 1950, decided that a unicameral central legislature should be established and that half of the seats in this legislature should be allocated to the North. As A. H. M. Kirk-Greene has pointed out, this concession to the North "was one that was to dominate the shaping of Nigeria's political culture until the First Republic exploded sixteen years later."[61]

The Nigeria (Constitution) Order in Council, 1951, established a single-chamber central legislature, known as the House of Representatives, and a central executive (the governor advised by a Council of Ministers). The Order in Council also established a legislature and an executive for each region. In the Northern and Western Regions, the legislature comprised two chambers, a House of Chiefs and a House of Assembly; the East had only a House of Assembly. In each region, the executive was the lieutenant governor advised by an Executive Council.

Although it enhanced the powers and status of the regions, the 1951 constitution was quasi-federal, with provisions for a strong central government. The most obvious centralizing features were, of course, the powers of the center over the regions in the legislative and executive fields. To begin with, each regional legislature could legislate on a specified range of matters; the House of Representatives could legislate on all subjects, including those assigned to the regions. Since the constitution placed no limitation on its legislative authority, the center could invade the regional field in order to give effect to central policy or to secure uniformity of legislation on any matter throughout Nigeria.

In addition to its power to legislate on regional subjects, the center was also granted the power to veto regional legislation at the bill stage, for no bill of a regional legislature could be presented for the lieutenant governor's assent until the central executive had seen it and indicated that it did not object to it.[62] The power to object was clearly intended to enable the central executive, when necessary, to exercise a great influence on the legislative policy of the Regions and to secure uniformity of regional legislation on any subject. One other provision further contributed to regional dependence in the legislative field: under section 92, the central legislature could add any matter to the regional legislative list and also remove from the list any matter so added.

In the executive field, the relationship of the Center to the Regions was more or less analogous to what obtained in the legislative field. The executive authority of a Region was coextensive with its legislative authority (section 119). By contrast, the executive authority of the Center, like its legislative authority, was not restricted by the constitution and so extended to those matters in which the Regions had executive authority. The Center and the Regions had concurrent executive powers over specified subjects. However, those powers were not equal, since section 120 provided that the exercise of the executive authority of a Region should not "impede or prejudice" the exercise of the executive authority of the Center. Besides, section 121 empowered the central executive to give directions to a regional executive with respect to the exercise of the executive authority of the Region and the regional executive was required to comply with such directions. The central executive was therefore in a position to shape and coordinate the policies of the three regional Governments on any matter within the legislative and executive competence of the Regions.

In effect, the 1951 constitution enhanced the status of the Regions by providing for regional legislative and executive powers. Nonetheless, it also embodied strong centralizing or unifying features, given that the Center had considerable legislative and executive leverage over the Regions. Paradoxically, the constitution, on a close reading, also provided for some factors which could undermine those centralizing features. The most important in this regard was the manner in which the central organs—the House of Representatives and the Council of Ministers—were to be constituted.

The House of Representatives consisted of a president and 148 members. The members included 136 "Representative Members" elected to the House from among the members of the regional legislative houses: 68 elected from both the House of Chiefs and the House of Assembly of the Northern Region by that Region's Joint Council (a body specifically created for this purpose and consisting of 40 members of each House); 3 elected from among their own number by the members of the Western House of Chiefs; 31 elected from their own number by the members of the Western House of Assembly; and 34 elected from among their own number by the members of the Eastern House of Assembly.

The Council of Ministers consisted of the governor, as the president, six ex officio members, and twelve ministers. Of the ministers, there were four from each Region, chosen from among the representative or elected members of the House of Representatives. The governor appointed the ministers, but only if the appointment had been approved in the Regions according to a set formula: the appointment of a minister from the North and the West required, in both cases, the approval of the particular Region's Joint Council; the appointment of a minister from the East required the approval of the Region's House of Assembly.

These methods of recruitment of members into the House of Representatives and the Council of Ministers had two major implications: they ensured that those so recruited would see themselves more as representatives of their respective Regions; second, they highlighted the importance of the Regions under the constitution and therefore served as a potential check on the Center in terms of the use of its powers of control over the Regions. It may also be noted that although the Center could legislate on subjects in the regional legislative list, central law on those subjects could not automatically prevail over regional law, since section 107 of the Constitution Order provided that where a central law was inconsistent with a regional law, the law which was later in date would prevail. Given the power of the central executive to veto a regional bill, one might argue that the Center was in a stronger position in any legislative struggle; nonetheless, section 107 strengthened the position of the regional legislatures in relation to the central legislature.

From the perspective of cultivating a Nigerian identity, the 1951 constitution had another in-built drawback. Responding to

Northern sensitivities, the constitution failed to provide responsible government at the Center. Ministerial responsibility was, instead, vested in the Council of Ministers as a whole, not in individuals. This meant that members of the council (officials excepted) with portfolios lacked executive control or personal responsibility for the administration of the departments with which they were "concerned."[63] In the absence of any personal responsibility, the council was in no position to engender a sense of collective responsibility or even mutual goodwill. The Council of Ministers was therefore divided into three sharply defined blocks: the East, the North, and the West.[64]

The 1951 constitution was a landmark in one respect: for the first time, Nigerians were offered a meaningful prospect of power in the colonial regime, in the form of legislative powers and "ministerial" positions at both the Center and the regional level. On this account, the constitution induced the birth of the Action Group (AG) led by Obafemi Awolowo, and the Northern Peoples' Congress (NPC) led by Ahmadu Bello, the Sardauna of Sokoto—two political parties inspired by regional and ethnic chauvinism. The NPC was the political expression of essentially primordial Hausa/Fulani interests. Its exceedingly narrow perception of the "national purpose" was no different from that of the AG, an offshoot of Egbe Omo Oduduwa, a Yoruba socio-cultural formation. The NPC was the Hausa/Fulani shield against Southern brashness and domination; the AG was the Yoruba answer to NCNC (read Igbo) hegemony. The primary impulse of both parties was therefore to achieve the exclusion of all others from their home Regions.

The election that followed in late 1951 was a victory for the regionalist forces and ethnic nationalists. Awolowo and the AG came to power in the West; the Sardauna and the NPC secured the North. Elected from Lagos into the Western House of Assembly, Nnamdi Azikiwe, leader of the NCNC, wanted to go to the House of Representatives. But this was not to be: with the regional assemblies serving as electoral colleges to the House, the AG (and therefore Yoruba) dominated Western House was able to frustrate Azikiwe, an Igbo. (My reading of the *Daily Service* of the late 1940s leaves me in no doubt that Azikiwe's fate was decided by ethnic politics.) In the event, Azikiwe found himself in the obscurity of leader of opposition in the Western legislature. The major lesson from this experience was that one's ethnic homeland constituted one's most secure political base.

The 1951 constitution, as I have pointed out, was quasi-federal, in light of the unrestricted authority of the Center and its powers of control over the Regions. Of course, the technicality of a constitution is one thing, the practice another. The constitution could have worked in a unitary fashion or could have fallen into a federal pattern, both depending on Nigerian politicians. In the event, they allowed purely regional interests to define "national" politics, thereby tilting the constitution in a federal direction.

On the whole, the working of the 1951 constitution accelerated the drift towards subgroup (ethnic and Regional) nationalism. The political parties, for example, were tripolarized along regional lines, with each drawing its core support from the largest ethnic group in its core Region. "National" politics in this setting became synonymous with the competing major ethnic interests. Thus, in a political culture that was originally amorphous, no clear meaning of the evolving national community was imported by the leaders and diffused to the mass of the population.

Following Azikiwe's setback in the Western House of Assembly, the NCNC engineered a constitutional crisis in the East aimed at providing Azikiwe with a safe political base. First, the party demanded the resignation of its ministers both in Enugu and in Lagos on the grounds that they were not acting in conformity with the party's policy. The ministers refused unless there was a two-thirds vote against them in a secret ballot as required by the constitution, and despite a vote of 60 to 13 in favor of a motion of "No confidence" in the House of Assembly, they stuck to their guns. Failing to secure the resignation of its ministers, the NCNC-controlled House of Assembly refused to consider government business for three months. The lieutenant governor had to use his reserve powers to authorize expenditure and prevent a breakdown in government business. The constitution had to be amended to allow for the dissolution of the Eastern House of Assembly without disrupting the other regional houses. In the ensuing elections, Azikiwe, who had resigned from the Western House, was easily elected in Onitsha, his hometown, and with that, he assumed the leadership of the government in Enugu. Azikiwe's ascendancy in the East was at the expense of Eyo Ita, the NCNC parliamentary leader, who had been the "Leader of Government Business" in the Eastern Region; this, in turn, produced a splinter group from the NCNC—the National Independence Party, largely drawn from the Ibibio-Efik political elite.[65] Ever since, the relationship between the Igbo and the Ibibio-Efik has remained uneasy at best.

The crisis in the Eastern Region was the first crack in the 1951 constitution. The end of the constitution came with Anthony Enahoro's motion of 31 March 1953 in the House of Representatives: that "this House accepts as a primary political objective the attainment of self-government for Nigeria in 1956." The Sardauna offered an amendment, substituting "as soon as practicable" for the specific date of "1956." Another Northerner, Ibrahim Imam, subsequently moved for an adjournment of the debate on Enahoro's motion, to enable the regional legislatures to discuss it first. The Western members and the majority of the Easterners walked out in protest at this proposal. In an ominous reference to the amalgamation, the Sardauna fumed: "The mistake of 1914 has come to light."[66] Both in Lagos and on their entire rail journey back to Kaduna, the Northern legislators were subjected to vulgar obscenities. The Sardauna later recalled: "This journey just about finished it for us. We were all not only angry at our treatment, but indignant that people who were so full of fine phrases about the unity of Nigeria should set their people against the chosen representatives of another Region. . . What kind of trouble had we let ourselves in for associating with such people."[67]

Alluding to the Northern reluctance to embrace Enahoro's motion, the Sardauna explained:

> we were very conscious indeed that the Northern Region was far behind the others educationally. As things were at the time, if the gates to the departments were to be opened, the Southern Regions had a pool from which they could find suitable people, we had hardly anyone . . . . As things were here, it was a matter of life and death to us. For we were not only educationally back-

ward but we stood at that time far behind the others in material development. If the British Administration had failed to give us the even development that we deserved and for which we craved so much—and they were on the whole a fair administration—what had we to hope from an African Administration, probably in the hands of a hostile party.[68]

As illustrated by Egypt in the nineteenth century, nothing inhibits an Islamic state from "modernizing" along Western lines. But in Northern Nigeria, the British—exploiting the traditional Muslim suspicion of Western secularism—sought to control the content and pace of acculturation. "The policy accepted for some considerable time," Donald Cameron observed, was "that the Moslem administrations [of Northern Nigeria] should be sheltered as far as possible from contact with the world due no doubt to a feeling, however unformulated, that an unreformed feudal autocracy could not be expected to stand up against the natural forces of a Western civilization...a curtain was being drawn between the Native Administrations of the North and the outer world."[69] There was thus an extreme reluctance to introduce Western education in the Islamic North because, according to Charles Temple, indirect rule was incompatible with exposing "young natives" to European habits and customs (including reading and writing in English) and "because practically every young native who has been through a school is divorced from his own people."[70]

By shielding the North from the Westernizing forces that were operating in the South, the British dichotomized Nigeria into two unequal levels of social mobilization, which often led—and continues to lead—to political friction. Although the North, in 1947, claimed to be home to over half of Nigeria's population, only 251 of its children were attending secondary schools—this figure represented a mere 2.5 percent of the total secondary school enrollment in Nigeria at the time.[71] By 1952, only two percent of the total population of the North (of the ages of seven and above) was literate in English as against 17.4 percent in the West and 16 percent in the East.[72] In medical and transportation facilities, the North was equally very far behind the South. The

1951 Hicks-Phillipson Revenue Allocation Commission had to recommend a special grant of £2 million to enable the North to close these gaps.[73] These gaps, especially the educational imbalance, made the Northern elite exceedingly wary of embracing "self-government," which, to them, translated into Southern domination.

Back from Lagos, the Northern politicians resolved to explore secession. In his memoir, the Sardauna recollected that

> Lord Lugard and his Amalgamation were far from popular amongst us at that time. There were agitators in favor of secession; we should set up on our own, we should cease to have anything more to do with Southern people. . . . I must say it looked very tempting.[74]

Secession was decided against on two grounds, neither of which had anything to do with the "national purpose." One was the difficulty of collecting customs duties along a wide land corridor; the other was the unreliability of access to the sea through a neighboring independent country.[75] So, instead, on 23 May 1953, the Northern House of Assembly adopted an "Eight Point Program," which would have turned the central government in Lagos into a customs union.[76]

Meanwhile, the NCNC and the AG "geared up their party machines and newspapers for a country-wide campaign to discredit the Northern legislators. . . as traitors and agents of the British imperialists. For their part the Northerners helped by the attacks of the Southern press. . . had no difficulty in firing anti-Southern feelings" in the North.[77] On 16 May 1953, the bitterness of the parliamentary feud in Lagos and its aftermath took a violent turn in Kano. Incidentally, that was the day an AG team was to arrive in Kano, to begin a tour of the North.

> For four days (from 16 to 19 May) Southerners and Northerners in this bustling commercial capital of the Northern Region were attacking each other, burning and pillaging each other's property, mutilating bodies of victims, and committing the most violent atrocities on

one another in the mass hysteria which gripped the town.[78]

This brutal mob-letting left fifty dead, over two hundred wounded, and a massive destruction of property.[79]

Another casualty of the "self-government" motion was the Council of Ministers. A majority of the council members had decided that ministers should not vote on Enahoro's motion. Unable to abide by this decision, the Western ministers resigned their offices, and made personal statements in the House of Representatives—statements, which the governor later informed the country, had breached the ministerial oath of secrecy. In spite of the exit of the Western ministers, the Council of Ministers still had a quorum and could therefore legally function, but this was politically impracticable.

So, on the heels of Enahoro's motion, South-North relations were wrecked, the Council of Ministers was crippled, and the constitution itself was in total disrepair. The British government was quick to acknowledge these realities. On 21 May 1953, in the aftermath of the massive violence in Kano, Oliver Lyttleton, the secretary of state for the colonies, announced that "Recent events have shown that it is not possible for the three Regions of Nigeria to work together effectively in a federation so closely knit as that provided by the present Constitution." Consequently, "the Constitution will have to be redrawn to provide for greater regional autonomy and for the removal of powers of intervention by the Center in matters which can, without detriment to other Regions, be placed entirely within regional competence."[80]

THE FEDERALIZATION/ REGIONALIZATION OF NIGERIA

A conference of representatives of all the political parties opened in London on 29 July 1953, to devise a new constitution within the broad framework formulated by Lyttleton. The British government refused to fix a date for self-government for Nigeria as a whole, especially since the North held to its principle of "self-government as soon as practicable." To conciliate the East and the

West, the British government accepted that any region that so desired could, in 1956, become self-governing in matters of regional competence, with safeguards against interference in the functioning of the federal government. The conference agreed on federal elections to the House of Representatives, separate from those of the regional Houses of Assembly which had hitherto served as electoral colleges for the central legislature. It was also agreed that the Council of Ministers would consist of nine ministers drawn from the House of Representatives, three from each Region, but without the prior approval of the regional legislatures as under the 1951 constitution. These measures were undoubtedly intended to overcome one of the chief causes of the collapse of the 1951 constitution: the inability of those involved with central government responsibilities to divorce themselves from their regional background and interests. The conference also agreed that those powers not precisely allotted to the federal government should be assigned to the regional governments. In return for this particular consensus, the North dropped its Eight Point Program.[81]

In London, the NCNC-AG alliance, hurriedly formed in the euphoria of Enahoro's motion, collapsed over the question of Lagos: the AG wanted Lagos merged with the West; the NCNC and the NPC wanted it neutralized as a federal territory. Lyttleton broke the deadlock in favor of the NCNC-NPC position. Following this ruling, Awolowo threatened the secession of the West; he backed down only when the British government made it clear that "any attempt to secure the secession of the Western Region from the Federation would be regarded as an act of force" which would be resisted. Subsequently, the AG and the NPC sought, but failed, to insert a clause providing for secession in the constitution.[82]

The conference resumed in Lagos in January 1954. Its report,[83] published a month later, provided for a federation composed of the Eastern, Northern, and Western Regions, as well as the Federal Territory of Lagos. It created a new House of Representatives, whose membership included 184 "Representative Members" composed of 92 from the Northern Region, 42 from the Eastern Region, 42 from the Western Region, 6 from the Southern Cameroons, and 2 from Lagos. The governor of Nigeria was renamed "governor-general," while the lieutenant governors of the regions became "governors."

On the basis of the London and Lagos conferences, the Nigeria (Constitution) Amendment Order in Council, 1954, which went into effect on 1 October 1954, removed the centralizing features of the 1951 constitution. Specific subjects were allocated to the federal government, there was a list of concurrent subjects on which both the federal and regional legislatures could legislate with equal force, all others were exclusively reserved to the regions. This meant that most of the subjects fell exclusively within the scope of the regional legislatures whose legislation was no longer to be submitted to the central executive. There were to be regional high courts and other courts specified by law to interpret and execute all laws enacted by the regional legislature. A federal Supreme Court was created and assigned the duties of interpreting the constitution and hearing appeals from the regional high courts. Each region had its own public service. The marketing boards were also regionalized, which meant that each regional government was to be responsible for the purchasing and marketing of all export commodities produced within the region; and federally collected revenue was to be allocated to the regions primarily on the basis of derivation.

"The 1954 Constitution," as Okoi Arikpo noted, "was the kernel of all further constitutional changes, which culminated in the establishment of the Federal Republic of Nigeria on 1 October 1963. But during the intervening years several amendments were made, some of which intensified the strains which existed between the different communities in the country." Arikpo observed that with the regionalization of the civil service, "the ablest" public servants were recalled from Lagos and other regions to their home regions, thereby denying the "federal service of experienced Nigerians who should at that time have been preparing themselves to take over the burden of running the public service of an independent Nigeria." Similarly, "each of the leaders of the major political parties retired to his Region of origin to become the Regional Premier, while his lieutenants were sent to participate in the Federal Government, and this inevitably tended to make the Federal Government function as an agent of the Regional Governments."[84]

From 1954, the regions, in effect, became the real locale of power. In this way, the constitutional arrangement, as Nwabueze has pointed out, emphasized the country's diversity rather than its unity, and thus "inverted what in an emergent state should be the proper scale of priority."[85] This outcome, Nwabueze adds, derived from "the size of the regions and the powerful interests they represented—these two factors enabled their claims for greater autonomy at the expense of the center."[86] In the same vein, Adebayo Adedeji argues that the regionalization of the marketing boards together with the derivation principle in revenue allocation "gave the regions not only fiscal autonomy, but also financial predominance over the federal government,"[87] which created an attitude of self-sufficiency and intolerance, both of which encouraged the frequent threats of secession.

THE MINORITIES

Each of the regions had a dominant ethnic group as well as "minority" ethnic groups, each status being defined in terms of population (and geography). The Igbo were dominant in the Eastern Region, which also included the Ibibio, the Efik, the Ijaw, and smaller groups in the Ogoja area; the Hausa-Fulani dominated the North, a region which also included the Kanuri, the Tiv, the Igala, the Nupe, the Idoma, the Gwari, and the Yoruba; the Yoruba were dominant in the Western Region, which also included the Edo, the Itsekiri, the Western Igbo, and the Western Ijaw. From 1951, when power gradually passed into Nigerian hands, the political parties that emerged rooted themselves in the regions (the AG in the West, the NCNC in the East, and the NPC in the North) and in the dominant ethnic group in each of the regions. In general, the minority groups were relegated to the background. At its inception, the AG announced itself as a "Western Regional Organization." Nonetheless, the party was, at the time, so concerned with its Yoruba core that it was prepared to discount Lagos (then an NCNC stronghold) and the "Bendel" area.[88] As in the political configuration, the minority areas also suffered in the location of public services and appointment to public positions. On these accounts, some minority groups started, in the early 1950s, to demand their own regions.

The 1953 crisis in the Eastern Region encouraged the Southern Cameroons, which had been part of that region, to intensify its demand for autonomy. The creation of a region for the Southern Cameroons in 1954 fueled demands by several minority groups for their own regions, first at the 1954 Resumed Constitutional Conference. The conference refused to consider those demands on the ground that the creation of more regions was not on the agenda. In 1957, the minority demands could no longer be lightly regarded; a commission had to be set up to deal with the matter. But the British government and the commission, supported by the main Nigerian political actors, saw no need to create more regions.[89] Lugard's original territorial arrangement, sustained by Britain's subsequent stubborn disinclination to create more regions, ensured that the country would operate in the South-North polarity that has been so debilitating in all respects.

CONCLUSION

In retrospect, the extreme decentralization ushered in by the 1914 amalgamation implied that Nigeria's political future was to be in a federal not a unitary direction. The trajectory was, however, not always clear-cut. Thus, Nigeria started off in 1914 more or less in a confederal format; evolved, from the 1920s to 1953, in a unitary mold; and became a federation in 1954.

In view of Nigeria's immense ethnic diversity, federalism, which allows for local autonomy and initiative, is a necessary imperative. However, given the preponderant size of the Northern Region—with roughly four-fifths of the country's land mass and its claim to more than half of the population—the Nigerian system, midwifed by Britain, vitiated a cardinal principle of federalism: that no one constituent unit should be so powerful as to override the will of all the others combined and so bend the center to its desires.

The preponderant size of the North was first given political expression when it was allocated half of the seats in the federal legislature under the 1951 constitution. The 1958 constitutional conference decided to base representation in the legislature on population and no longer on parity between the North and the South. This decision automatically gave the North 174 seats as against 138 for the East, the West, and Lagos combined,[90] and shifted the balance of power in Nigeria decisively in favor of the North—for it meant that by controlling the Northern government, the NPC was simultaneously assured the control of the federal government. It is of significance that until the federal elections of 1964, when it went into an alliance with Akintola's Nigerian National Democratic Party, the NPC never bothered to contest any elections, even indirectly, in the South—and yet its dominance of the federal government remained unassailable. The political crises of the 1960s—the 1962 crisis in the Western Region which culminated in the imprisonment of Awolowo, the bickering over the census figures, the October 1965 Western regional elections and their aftermath, the January 1966 coup, Biafra, and the civil war—all stemmed from Southern frustration at this predominant Northern political advantage.

The period covered here (1914-1960) was the colonial period of Nigeria's history, a period when Britain was the superintendent of Nigeria. To say that Britain undertook no social engineering to convert what started off as an economic and administrative unit into a national reality is superfluous: this goal was never on the colonial agenda. In creating Nigeria, the British were addressing short-term financial goals and this informed the structural framework they instituted. Over the years, the colonialist vision hardly broadened to encompass nation-building. So, in spite of the criticisms targeted at them, I am inclined to spare the Nigerian political elite of the 1950s much blame, for they necessarily had to work within the hopelessly flawed structural framework designed by the British.

The deeper lesson here is that it is too simplistic to assume that the national question can be solely resolved by superstructural constitutional arrangements; the appropriate institutional infrastructure (such as the size and resources of the constituent units) and the human conditions are no less important. History, if it is any guide in this case, teaches that new social allegiances develop over a long period—and often, through complicated processes of social adjustment.

NOTES

1. With the collapse of Stalinist dictatorship, Eastern Europe's nation-states are dissolving in a hot bath of tribalism. Even Scotland now wants to break away from the kingdom it has shared with England and Wales since 1603 (a union that was formalized in 1707). As these states fall apart and boundaries are redrawn almost daily, it is not only the devotees of postmodernist jargon who now accept that political societies are "invented" or "constructed."
2. J. S. Mill, *Considerations on Representative Government* (New York, 1882), 320.
3. Kalu Ezera, *Constitutional Developments in Nigeria* (Cambridge University Press, 1960), 16. Also see E. D. Morel, *Nigeria: Its Peoples and Its Problems* (London, 1911), 194-95.
4. Jeremy J. White, "The Development of Central Administration in Nigeria, 1914-1935," Ph.D. (History) dissertation, University of Ibadan (1970), discusses the rivalries and frictions among the British officials quite extensively. Also see S. O. Okafor, *Indirect Rule: The Development of Central Legislature in Nigeria* (Surrey, England; Ibadan: Thomas Nelson, 1981), chap. 6.
5. Tekena Tamuno, *The Evolution of the Nigerian State: The Southern Phase, 1898-1914* (London: Longman, 1972), 242, 251; White, "The Development of Central Administration in Nigeria," 12. It is instructive that although a proposal to improve Lagos harbor was submitted in 1892, it was not until June 1908 that construction began.
6. For the some of the most critical primary sources on the amalgamation, see A. H. M. Kirk-Greene, *Lugard and the Amalgamation of Nigeria: A Documentary Record* (London: Frank Cass, 1968). My discussion of the amalgamation draws on these sources and on Kirk-Greene's excellent "Introduction."
7. White, "The Development of Central Administration in Nigeria," 13.
8. *The Parliamentary Debates (Official Report) Fifth Series—Vol. 40: House of Commons, 7th Vol. of Session 1912*, 514.
9. Lord Hailey, *Native Administration in the British African Territories, Part III: West Africa* (London: HMSO, 1951), 2.
10. For a more wide-ranging critique, see Tamuno, *The Evolution of the Nigerian State*, chap. 9.

CONSTITUTION-MAKING

11. White, "The Development of Central Administration in Nigeria," 86.
12. F. D. Lugard, *The Dual Mandate in British Tropical Africa* (London: Frank Cass, 1965; first published 1922), 100.
13. I. M. Okonjo, *British Administration in Nigeria, 1900-1950: A Nigerian View* (New York: Nok, 1974), 77. Also see White, "The Development of Central Administration in Nigeria," 56-80; I. F. Nicolson, *The Administration of Nigeria, 1900-1960: Men, Methods, and Myths* (Oxford University Press, 1969), chap. 7.
14. White, "The Development of Central Administration in Nigeria," 120.
15. Lugard based this decision on two reasons: the emirs of Northern Nigeria could not debate in English; and the Southern westernized elite were "unrepresentative" of the masses and the interests of the latter could not be subordinated to the will of an "unrepresentative" authority.
16. Of the council's twenty-eight members, only six were Nigerians. See Nigeria Council Order in Council, 22 November 1913.
17. CO 583/80, Clifford to Milner, 3 December 1919, quoted in White, "The Development of Central Administration in Nigeria," 80.
18. Ibid. Emphasis in the original.
19. *Rules and Orders of the Legislative Council of Nigeria* (Lagos: Government Printer, 1924), Art. 41 (c) and (g).
20. For a discussion of the 1922 Constitution, see Joan Wheare, *The Nigerian Legislative Council* (London: Faber & Faber, 1949), chaps. 2-3.
21. B. O. Nwabueze, *A Constitutional History of Nigeria* (Longman Group Ltd., 1982), 40.
22. Wheare, *The Nigerian Legislative Council*, 56.
23. Ibid., vii.
24. Ibid., 31.
25. Charles L. Temple, *Native Races and their Rulers* (Cape Town: Argus, 1918), 78.
26. I am quoting James S. Coleman, *Nigeria: Background to Nationalism* (Berkeley and Los Angeles: University of California Press, 1958), 47.
27. Lord Hailey, *Native Administration in the British African Territories, Part III*, 4-5.
28. See Okonjo, *British Administration in Nigeria*, chap. 5.
29. Ibid., 151-156.
30. See *Proceedings of the Executive Council Meeting held at the Chief Secretary's Office*, Lagos, 1 December 1928. Available at the National Archives, Ibadan (NAI).
31. White, "The Development of Central Administration in Nigeria," 253.

32. Ibid., 177-178.
33. CO 583/177, Cameron to secretary of state for the colonies, 10 December 1931 (Public Record Office [PRO], London).
34. CO 583/183, Cameron to secretary of state for the colonies, 19 July 1932 (PRO, London).
35. CO 583/177, Cameron to secretary of state for the colonies, 10 December 1931 (PRO, London).
36. CO 583/183, Cameron to Sir Philip Cunliffe-Lister, secretary of state for the colonies, 17 March 1932 (PRO, London).
37. White, "The Development of Central Administration in Nigeria," 267, 270.
38. *Northern Provinces Advisory Council: Record of Proceedings at Full Meetings with Emirs and Chiefs, 1931*, 9. Available at NAI.
39. Ibid.
40. Ibid.
41. Bernard Bourdillon, "Minute on the Apportionment of Revenues and Duties as between the Central Government and the Native Administration" (1939), in A. H. M. Kirk-Greene, *The Principles of Native Administration in Nigeria: Selected Documents, 1900-1947* (London: Oxford University Press, 1965), 232.
42. Quoted in White, "The Development of Central Administration in Nigeria," 329. In all likelihood, the governor was influenced in this regard by Margery Perham, who had described the central administrative service as the "temporary scaffolding round the growing structure of native self-government." See her *Native Administration in Nigeria* (London: Oxford University Press, 1962; first published in 1937), 360-361.
43. File RG/HI, NAI, Lord Hailey, "Confidential Report on Nigeria, 1940-41"; Lord Hailey, *Report on Native Administration and Political Development in British Tropical Africa, 1940-42*, published for the British Crown with an introduction by A. H. M. Kirk-Greene (Nendeln/Liechtenstein: Karus Reprint, 1979), 47.
44. Lord Hailey, *Report on Native Administration and Political Development in British Tropical Africa*, 168-171; also 44-45, 157-158.
45. Adams' memorandum, dated 29 August 1942, was enclosed in CO 847/22/47100/10, Bourdillon to the Colonial Office (PRO, London).
46. CO 847/22/Pt. 1, Bourdillon, "Comments on Lord Hailey's Report on Nigeria," 30 August 1943. Also CO 847/21/47100, Comments by Bourdillon on Hailey's General Report (both in PRO, London).
47. The main reasons for this split were the great distance between Enugu (the capital of the Southern Provinces) and the areas west of the Niger,

that there was hardly any sociocultural affinity between the areas on both sides of the Niger, and the excessive workload of the chief commissioner of the Southern Provinces. See White, "The Development of Central Administration in Nigeria,"323. It is difficult to understand why these same reasons were not found even more applicable to the North, which was more expansive and ethnically more heterogenous than the East and the West combined.

48. K. O. Dike, *100 Years of British Rule in Nigeria* (Lagos: Federal Ministry of Information, 1960), 46-48.
49. Okoi Arikpo, *The Development of Modern Nigeria* (Middlesex, England: Penguin Books, 1967), 51.
50. This framework had been elaborately laid out by Bourdillon in *Further Memo on the Future Political Development of Nigeria* (Lagos: Government Printer, 1942).
51. Section 5 (2) of the Nigeria (Protectorate and Cameroons) Order-in-Council of 1946 provided that "The Governor may by proclamation with the approval of His Majesty signified through a Secretary of State define, and from time to time, vary, the boundaries between any two of such regions for administrative purposes in such manner as he may consider expedient."
52. Arikpo, *The Development of Modern Nigeria*, 51-52.
53. Bernard Bourdillon, "Nigeria's New Constitution," *United Empire*, 37 (1946), 77.
54. Obafemi Awolowo, *Path to Nigerian Freedom* (London: Faber & Faber Ltd., 1947), 47-48. The central argument of this book was that in the movement towards self-rule, the government of the country must be based on a structural framework which conceded an appreciable degree of political autonomy to each ethnic (language) group.
55. For this distinction, see Hugh Seton-Watson, *Nations and States: An Enquiry into the Origins and Politics of Nationalism* (London: Methuen & Co., Ltd., 1977), 1; Sami Zubaida, *Islam, the People and the State: Essays on Political Ideas and Movements in the Middle East* (London: I. B. Tauris, 1989), 121-182.
56. *Legislative Council Debates, 20 March-2 April 1947* (Lagos: Government Printer, 1947), 208.
57. The proceedings and reports of the regional conferences are best followed through contemporary Nigerian newspapers. For a summary, see Arikpo, *The Development of Modern Nigeria*, 65-66.
58. On this, see *Report of the Constitution Drafting Committee on the Constitution* (Lagos: Government Printer, 1950).

59. For the general conference, see *Proceedings of the General Conference on the Review of the Nigerian Constitution* (Lagos: Government Printer, 1950). My discussion of the conference is based on this document.
60. *Report of the Select Committee of the Legislative Council Meeting at Enugu with two Minority Reports, April 1, 1950*. One of the minority reports was by Azikiwe, who criticized the tripartite division of the country as "an artificial creation," which "must inevitably tend towards Balkanization and the existence of chronic minority problems." He suggested the division of the country along the lines of the main ethnic and/or linguistic groups so that each of the groups could exercise "local cultural autonomy."
61. A. H. M. Kirk-Greene, *Crisis and Conflict in Nigeria: A Documentary Sourcebook 1966-1970* (Oxford University Press, 1971), 9.
62. The central executive could object to a bill on the ground that (a) it related to a matter which was not in the regional legislative list, or (b) it was inconsistent with the general interests of Nigeria or with any executive direction given by the center to the region under section 121 of the Constitution Order, or (c) it was inconsistent with the treaty obligations of Nigeria. The effect of an objection was that the bill in question could not be assented to and so could not become law unless the ground for objection was removed by amendment of the bill in the regional legislature in such terms as the central executive required.
63. In addition, the Council of Ministers was to decide all matters of policy and direct executive action, settle any legislation to be laid before the legislature, and formulate Nigeria's annual budget. Individual members of the council with portfolios were to be responsible for initiating discussion on their subjects in the council, and in cooperation with heads of departments, ensure that decisions of the council which related to their departments were carried out. See the despatch from the secretary of state for the colonies to the governor of Nigeria, reproduced in *Nigeria Gazette* (Extra-ordinary), 6 July 1951.
64. Thus, when the first major conflict occurred at the center in 1953, over Anthony Enahoro's motion for self-government, the Council of Ministers—as discussed below—split against itself. On the fictionalization of the council, see Arikpo, *The Development of Modern Nigeria*, 76.
65. See *Debates of the Eastern House of Assembly*, vol. 1 (1953); Arikpo, *The Development of Modern Nigeria*, 76-77; Ezera, *Constitutional Developments in Nigeria*, 156-164; Richard L. Sklar, *Nigerian Political Parties: Power in an Emergent African Nation* (Princeton University Press, 1963), 118-124.

CONSTITUTION-MAKING 111

66. See *House of Representatives, Official Report of Debates* (Lagos), March 31, 1953; Ezera, *Constitutional Developments in Nigeria*, 164-175.
67. Ahmadu Bello, *My Life* (Cambridge University Press, 1962), 135.
68. Ibid., 110-111.
69. Donald Cameron, *Principles of Native Administration and their Application* (Lagos: Government Printer, 13 July 1934), para. 21.
70. Temple, *Native Races and Their Rulers*, 30.
71. Coleman, *Nigeria: Background to Nationalism*, 133.
72. Billy J. Dudley, *Parties and Politics in Northern Nigeria* (London: Frank Cass, 1968), 72.
73. Adebayo Adedeji, *Nigerian Federal Finance* (London: Hutchinson, 1969), 81.
74. Bello, *My Life*, 135.
75. Ibid.
76. The Northern Regional Legislature, House of Assembly, *Official Report of Debates* (Kaduna), May 1953, 30-31.
77. Arikpo, *The Development of Modern Nigeria*, 79.
78. Ibid.
79. *Report on the Kano Disturbances, 16th, 17th, 18th, and 19th May, 1953* (Kaduna: Government Printer, 1953), 10.
80. *Parliamentary Debates (Hansard), Fifth Series—Vol. 515: House of Commons Official Report, Session 1952-53* (London: HMSO, 1953), 2263.
81. Cmd. 8934, *Report by the Conference on the Nigerian Constitution Held in London in July and August, 1953* (London: HMSO, 1953).
82. Ibid.
83. Cmd. 9059, *Report of the Resumed Conference on the Nigerian Constitution held in January and February 1954* (London: HMSO, 1954).
84. Arikpo, *The Development of Modern Nigeria*, 82. Also see Billy Dudley, *An Introduction to Nigerian Government and Politics* (Bloomington: Indiana University Press, 1982), 54.
85. B. O. Nwabueze, *Constitutionalism in the Emergent States* (C. Hurst & Co. Ltd., in association with Nwamife Publishers, 1973), 111.
86. Ibid., 112.
87. Adedeji, *Nigerian Federal Finance*, 108-109.
88. See Sklar, *Nigerian Political Parties*, 96, 105; Obafemi Awolowo, *AWO: The Autobiography of Chief Obafemi Awolowo* (Cambridge University Press, 1960), 213-224.

89. See Cmd. 505, *Report of the Commission Appointed to Enquire Into the Fears of Minorities and the Means of Allaying Them* (London: HMSO, 1958).
90. See Cmd. 569, *Report by the Resumed Nigeria Constitutional Conference Held in London in September and October, 1958* (London: HMSO, 1958). Billy Dudley noted the fact that "while the North was prepared to argue that representation should be based on the principle of 'each to count for one vote and no one to count for more than one,' it did not apply that principle to the adult community in the North itself; women were still to be denied the vote." See his *An Introduction to Nigerian Government and Politics*, 58.

4

THE COLLAPSE OF NIGERIA'S FEDERAL SYSTEM OF GOVERNMENT

Akanmu G. Adebayo

INTRODUCTION

Nigeria's federal system of government is dead. Before we examine the manner in which this occurred, it is important to differentiate between three important terms: the Federal Republic of Nigeria, the federal government of Nigeria, and the federal system of government in Nigeria. "Federal Republic of Nigeria" is the country's official name. It derived partly from the historical process that led in 1954 to the adoption of federalism (as opposed to unitarism) as the country's political system, and partly from the republican status attained by the country in 1963. "Federation of Nigeria" is the older, sometimes preferred, synonym. "Federal Government of Nigeria" (FGN) is the official name of the central government in the federation which also has regional/state and local governments. In times of military rule, "Federal Military Government" (FMG) was preferred to FGN. Usually, the FMG would have an executive council made up of military officers and civilian clients and cronies. In addition, there would be a legislative arm of the FMG called the Armed Forces Ruling Council (AFRC), which rubber-stamped the decrees prepared by the attorney-general on behalf of the dictator. The "federal system of government," on the other hand, is the system of government that the Federal Republic of Nigeria is supposedly ruled by, the system that the FGN and the other two tiers of government are supposed to operate.

The Federal Republic of Nigeria, the country, is alive. The Federal Government of Nigeria has waxed stronger since independence. Until the death of the military dictator, General Sani Abacha, in June 1998, the FMG had become an octopus. Whether it was based in Lagos or Abuja, the FMG had consolidated itself and held the whole country hostage. State and local governments were mere puppets in the hands of the federal government, and state governors were "errand boys," literally, of the president. On the other hand, federalism, on the basis of which the federal government is created and supposedly operates, has collapsed.

This chapter analyzes the slow death of federalism. It examines the factors that have led to the collapse of the federal system of government in Nigeria. It is divided into three parts. The first part defines federalism, and the second traces historically the travails of federalism from its adoption to its demise under Nigeria's innumerable military regimes. The third part evaluates the factors that have slowly weakened the federal system of government and have led to its demise.

DEFINING FEDERALISM

In 1787 a group of American politicians gathered in Philadelphia, and came up with the Constitution of the United States of America. This date and the result of this effort have usually been taken as the beginning of modern federalism. These practical men, later known as the "Founding Fathers" in U.S. history, drew up a new Constitution to replace the Articles of Confederation in the belief that the latter was not working effectively in the specific areas of fostering unity and creating a strong central government. The words "federal" or "federation" did not appear anywhere in this new Constitution, but subsequent elaboration by some of the participants in the conference, notably the federalists, described the document as a federal constitution. This constitution contained a clear-cut division of power between the central and state-local governments. Specific clauses defined the areas of jurisdiction of each level of government, and each level was given complete autonomy in these areas of jurisdiction. Several amendments have been introduced since 1789, but these have strengthened the powers of state governments rather than restricted them. For example, the Tenth Amendment provides that powers not delegated to the federal government (of the United States) by the Constitution, nor prohibited by it to the states, are reserved to the states. These are called the residuary powers.

It was these attributes of the U.S. Constitution that many political theorists have analyzed, concluding that the American system is the best example of federalism. For instance, K. C. Wheare, the British theorist of federalism who was to have considerable influence in the formulation of the principles of Nigerian federalism, develops his definition of federalism around the characteristics of the American system. According to him, federalism is an "association of states which has been formed for certain common purposes, but in which the member states retain a large measure of their original independence."[1] He further describes the federal principle as "the method of dividing powers so that the general and regional governments are each within a sphere, coordinate and independent."

Wheare's formulation dominated political thoughts on federalism for a very long time. In the meantime, these ideas were challenged for their apparent legalism, their emphasis on structure, and their idealistic rather than flexible and dynamic stipulations.[2] One obvious omission from Wheare's conceptualization of federalism is the question of the power and attitudes of political leaders. Major submissions on this have come from Amitai Etzioni.[3] In his view, power politics is a factor to be considered in any process of integration, and federalism is an attempt to come to grips with this problem of power play. Conflict is endemic in any unification process because sociological variables such as ethnicity, race, class, religion, and language all feature in the relationship. The formal division of power between the center and the states, which is the essence of federalism, is the attempt to prevent a single group from dominating the others.

Given the foregoing, Etzioni suggests that federalism belongs to a special class of political systems devised to bring about the unification of political communities while at the same time preserving and encouraging local autonomy (defined in terms of ethnicity, racial affiliation, language, religion, or geographical entity). Although Wheare provided the initial formulation, Etzioni has offered the framework that incorporates the emerging federations in developing countries in the 1950s, such as India and Nigeria, into the fold of federalism.

In Nigeria itself the writings of Chief Obafemi Awolowo, particularly his *Path to Nigerian Freedom*, published in 1947, made a strong case for the adoption of federalism.[4] Of all Nigerian nationalists, Awolowo was the earliest to understand the essence of federalism as the system of government for an independent Nigeria. He had a remarkable understanding of the system both theoretically and in practice. His proposal for creating regions along ethnic lines might be faulted, but he provided a sound argument to support his position. He took the issue further in his subsequent writings.[5]

At the same time, the so-called archetype of federalism, the United States, was undergoing changes. Changes have also occurred in the operation of the federal constitution. These changes moved the Constitution toward big government at the center, but they did not erode the power of the states in enough significant ways to cause alarm. As the federal government got bigger as a result of World Wars I and II and the Depression in between, emphasis came to be placed on Article VI, Section II, of the U.S. Constitution, which states that national laws are "the supreme laws of the land . . .

anything in the Constitution or laws of any state to the contrary notwithstanding."[6] This was one of the tools employed in the period of the Civil Rights Movement to implement civil rights and affirmative action legislations in various states. Wheare could not have anticipated this new emphasis.

Discussions nowadays center on the structure and functions of the "new federalism," by which it is also implied that the "old federalism" is dead. Principal among these discussions is a short monograph published in the 1970s by Michael D. Reagan.[7] In the opening paragraphs of the book, Reagan claimed emphatically that Wheare-type old federalism was dead, for there could be no "nation in which there is no institutionalized final authority."[8] Reagan's formulation is especially fascinating in its itemization of the following attributes of federalism in contemporary U.S. society:

- There is a constitutional division of governmental functions such that each level is autonomous in at least one sphere of action.
- Each government is final and supreme in its constitutionally assigned area.
- Both levels [of government] act directly on the citizens.
- Both levels derive their powers from the sovereign (the people or the Constitution) rather than from one another.
- Therefore, neither can change the relationship unilaterally.
- The regional divisions (or states) exist as of their own right.[9]

How well does Nigeria fare in terms of these attributes of old or new federalism? The answers to this question depend on the period and regime. In 1954-1964, for example, Nigerian federalism shared many of these attributes. Since the Ironsi regime, however, most of the attributes have disappeared. But there is something quite fundamental here. The fact is that theoretical notions assume the establishment of federations through a process called agglomeration: that there already existed communities which decided on their own volition to become one by surrendering to the new central formation parts of the power they used to exercise. The Nigerian federation was created through a process of devolution of power: that is, an already existing central administration decided most grudgingly to give up parts of its powers to the new regional or state governments. One of the first sources of conflict and confusion in Nigeria's federalism, therefore, is the extent to which the federal center was willing to go in the devolution of powers.

Another essential aspect of federalism is the political system that best suits its operation. Wheare holds the view that democracy is best suited for federalism. According to him, dictatorship "with its one-party government and its denial of free election, is incompatible with the working of federal principle. Federalism demands forms of government which have the characteristic usually associated with democracy or free government."[10] Chief Obafemi Awolowo supports this position, but a few Nigerian political scientists have succumbed to the pressure of practicality and they link federalism with any system of government. Representing this group of scholars is L. Adele Jinadu, who asserted that it is irrelevant to assume that military rule, one-party rule, or dictatorships are incompatible with federalism[11]. His position is understandable when one realizes that Jinadu was writing in the euphoria of what has turned out to be the only liberal military government Nigeria has ever produced: the post-war phase of the Gowon regime. I am sure he would like to revise that study in the light of the country's experiences since 1983.

To summarize, federalism, or the federal system of government, is a "form of government whereby political power is divided between a central or national authority and smaller, locally autonomous units such as provinces or states, generally under the terms of a constitution."[12] A federal government, or federation, is formed either through agglomeration or through devolution. In the former, the federation is achieved through the political union of two or more formerly independent states under one sovereign government that does not, in any case, abrogate the individual powers of those states. In the latter, it is formed through the devolution of power by the central government of a hitherto unitary system to the newly formed regional, provincial or state governments. A federation is distinguished from a confederation, which is an alliance of independent countries that retain their respective autonomies, for joint action or cooperation on specific matters of mutual concern. It is also distinguished from a unitary system, in which the central government holds the principal power over administrative units that are virtually agencies of the central government. Federalism thrives best under a liberal, democratic, free government.

THE TRAVAILS OF FEDERALISM IN NIGERIA

From the foregoing, it is clear that Nigeria at present does not measure up to universal standards of federalism. But there was a time when it did, a time when it could answer to the name "Federation of Nigeria" or "Federal Republic of Nigeria." This was the period 1954 through 1964, which I have called the "federal decade" of Nigeria.

It is not the intent of this chapter to delve into the history of the adoption of federalism in Nigeria. Several books on the Nigerian constitutional development have examined this issue. In an article I wrote in the mid-1980s, I have reviewed[13] the different positions taken by eminent scholars from Eme Awa to Ben Nwabueze.[14] The conclusion, in a nutshell, is that the departing British administration saw in federalism the opportunity to bring the different pieces of Nigeria together. On the other hand, a majority of the Nigerian political elites saw in federalism the opportunity to gain and maintain control of their respective regional governments. The creation of the Federation of Nigeria was, therefore, the result of the British "push" and the Nigerian elite's "pull." Both parties were committed to it; even those who had no idea what federalism was soon learned the meaning of it.

From its adoption in 1954 the Nigerian federal structure was fairly stable until 1964. After several constitutional conferences, Nigeria went into independence in 1960 with a unique arrangement.[15] There were three levels of government: the federal government, the regional governments, and the native administrations. There were three regional governments: Northern, Eastern, and Western. The federal government had a bi-cameral legislature, the House of Representatives and the Senate; the regional governments also had a bicameral legislature, Houses of Assembly and Houses of Chiefs. Each of the regional governments was powerful indeed. The areas of jurisdiction of the three levels of government were clearly demarcated in the constitution. Two legislative "lists" were compiled, the *exclusive* (federal) and the *concurrent* (federal/regional) lists. Of the items removed from the exclusive to the concurrent list shortly before independence, the most significant were the police and the maintenance of law and order. This gave the regional governments the opportunity to establish and maintain their own police forces for the maintenance of law and order.

At independence, the three regional governments together were more powerful than the federal government. They had significant control over their social and economic development programs and collected taxes on income and resources produced in the region. Although customs duties and mineral rents and royalties were collected by the federal government, the proceeds were returned to the regions of origin in accordance with the principle of derivation enshrined in the revenue allocation formula. Regional bureaucracies were strong, as very few qualified candidates sought positions in the federal government. Regional development and marketing boards were affluent and powerful. They took charge of regional economic development programs and gave subsidies to the fledging regional industries. Of course, regional premiers and those close to them had unlimited access to these revenues and often took questionable investment decisions. However, the issue here is the autonomy under which they operated.

The regional governments were so powerful that at independence the highest ranking political candidate in the country, the Sardauna of Sokoto, remained as premier of the Northern Region rather than take up the position of prime minister of Nigeria, a position to which he sent his deputy, Sir Abubakar Tafawa Balewa. Although southern political leaders such as Chief Obafemi Awolowo and Dr. Nnamdi Azikiwe pursued their careers at the federal level, they continued to take an interest in the politics of their respective regions. To further demonstrate their autonomy, the regional governments sent consuls to Europe and the Middle East to further their respective interests. Indeed, the federal system was alive. Doctoral dissertations were completed in the 1950s and 1960s which enthusiastically named Nigeria as one of the "new federations" and compared it with the Australian, Canadian, and Indian federal systems, among former British dependencies.

Another significant constitutional provision before independence was the bill of rights. The federal constitution affirmed certain "absolute" rights: to life, to protection against inhuman treatment, slavery, or servitude, to liberty, and to a fair trial. There was also a category of rights called "qualified" rights: to private life, freedom of conscience, expression, assembly, movement, and so on. The Nigerian bill of rights was not extensive, but a formal beginning was made. The tragedy is that subsequent political leaders and regimes governed as if the bill never existed.

To summarize, Nigerian federalism in 1954-1964 conformed to the six universal attributes of federalism compiled by Michael Reagan. There was a constitutional division of governmental functions such that each level was autonomous in at least one sphere of action; each government was final and supreme in its constitutionally assigned area; and both levels of government acted directly on the citizens. Both levels derived their powers from the constitution rather than from one another; neither could change the relationship unilaterally; and the regional governments existed as of their own right.

THE SLOW DEATH OF FEDERALISM

Nigerian federalism began a slow and painful decline in the early 1960s. This decline was the result of many factors but, as with many issues in Nigeria, scholars disagree on the significance of each of the factors. This chapter reviews seven factors. It takes the position that ethnic, religious, and other diversities and their politicization by members of the power elite have had negative effects on the operation of the federal principle. Nevertheless, it does not see these diversities as the cause of the failure of federalism. In a truly federal system, such plurality and diversity are managed effectively. Thus, ethnic and religious politics and conflicts are both symptoms (manifestations) and effects of the ailment; the root causes lie elsewhere. It is the intention of this chapter to find root causes, not symptoms.

In evaluating the slow death of the Nigerian federal system of government, perhaps the first place to start is the political crises of the early 1960s which reached their peak in the Western Regional crisis of 1964-1966.[16] In addition to factors that earlier studies have identified (such as constitutional crises, ethnicity, and personality conflicts), a major reason for the political crises was simply lack of experience. Of the three tiers of government, the one in which Nigerian political elites had no extensive experience prior to independence turned out to be the most important: the federal government. The key members of the federal executive were the president, the prime minister, and the ministers. The president was a ceremonial head of government. Originally the representative of the British crown, the president was also the commander-in-chief of the armed forces. The prime minister, on the other hand, was the person who held actual power. The problems for the Nigerian federal system arose in part from the fact that the federal government was a coalition government. The senior partner, the NPC, provided the prime minister; the junior partner, the NCNC, produced the president. The two failed to truly cooperate, except when it became necessary to silence the opposition.

Another dimension of the crises was institutional. According to Toyin Falola, the country had not developed the requisite institutions to operate both the parliamentary constitution and the federal arrangement. In his words,

> The country borrowed a parliamentary model but left out the conventions and practices that make it function appropriately. . . . The Northern House of Assembly, for instance, never had a record of sitting for as many as thirty days in a year. The membership of the legislature was mostly part-time, with the result that the executive had its way most of the time . . . The three branches of government often acted as one, and sometimes conspired for selfish reasons. In a few cases when one of the branches or any of its representatives tried to assert itself, the other two could gang up to frustrate it. For instance in 1963, when the Public Accounts Committee of the House of Representatives queried items of overspending in the audited accounts of the federal government, the executive quickly dissolved the committee, and it never met again.[17]

Another aspect of the crisis that had direct implications for federalism was the intervention of the federal government in regional affairs. Much has been written about the way the NPC-NCNC coalition federal government sought to muzzle the Action Group opposition in the House of Representatives by fueling the crisis in the Western Region.[18] The result was the creation of the Mid-Western Region in 1962. Federal government intervention continued well into the regional elections of 1964, occasioning a prolonged period of political violence, brigandage, and thuggery of immense proportions. It can be said that the Western Region provided the test case for the growing power of the federal government vis-à-vis the regional governments.

The second factor leading to the slow death of federalism was the military coup of January 1966[19] and, subsequently, the abolition of the federal system of government by Nigeria's first military administration, headed by General Aguiyi Ironsi. The impact of the Ironsi regime on Nigerian politics has not yet been fully assessed.[20] It was an embattled administration from beginning to end. We will never know what would have become of Nigeria had the regime lasted longer than it did. The killings, the erratic policies, the dismissal of Northern officers and promotion of Igbo officers, and especially the suspension of the republican constitution—these are the legacies usually associated with this embattled, ill-fated administration. Of particular relevance to this chapter is the abolition of federalism and reversal to unitarism. In just six months, the regime tore federalism apart, and began to undo the structure carefully and painstakingly crafted in the 1950s.

Ironsi did this in three overlapping stages. First, he militarized the federal structure. By a series of decrees, Ironsi suspended the republican constitution, abolished the offices of president and prime minister, dismissed the legislature, and placed the regional military governors directly under the control of the Federal Military Government (FMG). In essence, he transferred from military to civilian political life the centralized command structure of the armed forces. Thenceforth, all military governments in the country had legislative and executive powers. Next, Ironsi issued Decree no. 33, which abolished all forms of opposition to the military government and banned all political parties and ethnic/cultural organizations. Finally, he issued Decree no. 34, which dismantled the federal system and instituted unitary administration. All this contributed to the slow death of federalism.

By these decrees, Ironsi sought to remove most of the ills that had plagued the country since independence and had recently plunged it into violence: ethnicity, regionalism, and sectionalism. Furthermore, the decrees intended to promote national unity. To members of the northern political elite, however, the decrees only helped to confirm that Ironsi's goal was to impose Igbo domination on the country. Thus, rather than promote unity the decrees only managed to further divide the country; they fanned the flame of violence against the

Igbo, and quickly resulted in the counter-coup that brought Yakubu Gowon to power in July 1966.

Ironsi's administration was the first to openly pronounce federalism dead. Although the Gowon administration reinstated federalism, it was in name only. The central command structure instituted by Ironsi continued, as did the strengthening of the federal government at the expense of the states. The Ironsi regime in the mid-1960s plunged the country's federal system of government into a coma and it has never truly recovered.

The creation of states was the third major source of the slow death of federalism in Nigeria. In the thirty years between 1967 and 1997, the number of states has tripled from twelve to thirty-six. The more states the country has, the smaller their sizes, and consequently the less powerful they become. States have continued to resemble the provinces and divisions of the colonial administration, some in their size, others in their ethnic composition and territorial clustering. Their small sizes have made it impossible for them to compete with the federal government, challenge unfavorable policies emanating from the center, serve as initiators and sources of development at the state level, and perform their role in the administration of the country. In a federation where the praxis meets the theory, the people would be more inclined to think of the local and state governments as initiators of policies that affect their lives most; in Nigeria the people often see the federal government as the source of policies whose effects are immediately felt.

It is necessary to comment briefly on the background to state creation in the Nigerian federation. The federal principle necessitates state creation, which could be through fusion or fission. To qualify as a federation, a country must have coordinate and autonomous units, each responsible for legislative, executive, and judicial matters within its boundaries. Such units have been created in the United States, Malaysia, Canada, Germany, and Switzerland by fusion or aggregation, that is, where preexisting independent communities have agreed to shed part of their autonomy for the good of the union. In Nigeria, as in South Africa, Australia, India, Pakistan, and many other former British colonies and dependencies, the units have come about through a process called disaggregation or fission. This has meant that the country, formerly administered as a unitary state, is broken up into units each vested with legislative, judicial, and executive powers.

While the creation of "more" states has been extremely difficult in many federations, in Nigeria it has been fairly easily accomplished partly because of the incessant ethnic demands, the political calculations of the ruling elite, the desire to increase access to federally distributed revenues, and other considerations. In the older federations, such as the USA, Canada, and Australia, new states were created where some mainland territory existed unclaimed or was given up by any of the existing states. Nigeria has no such unclaimed land. Prior to 1900, the entire land area later organized as Nigeria had been occupied by various ethnic and linguistic groups. By 1914, when the Northern and Southern Protectorates were amalgamated, there were no new and "unclaimed" areas of Nigeria that could be organized as states. In fact, the Native Administrations, which were the only administrative divisions of note, were created out of political expediency and administrative convenience: they were not born out of British foresight with the idea of making Nigeria into a federation of numerous states. So, in 1953-1954 when Nigeria's political future was being considered in the London and Lagos constitutional conferences, the creation of states was not on the agenda. Although there were moves to effect a revision of boundaries, such proposals were not entertained; and the subsequent federal constitution recognized three regional administrations—the Northern, Western, and Eastern Regions—created in 1946 by the Richards Constitution.

How did the agitation for more states start? Who were the people responsible? The campaign for the creation of more states began immediately after the adoption of the federal system in 1954. There were two forces at work. First, in the south there was what has come to be dubbed the "fear of the North." The Northern Region was twice the geographical size of the south and it was also superior in population. Since voting patterns often followed ethnic and regional political party affiliations, it became apparent that elections would always be won by the North. To ensure fairness, the political elite in the south would prefer the splitting up of the Northern Region especially along ethnic lines.

The second reason for the emergence of state creation agitation in the late 1950s was the presence in all the regions of the "fear of ethnic minorities." The fear of minorities appeared so real in the 1957 constitutional conference that a commission was set up to study the issue and make recommendations to the colonial administration. It was expected that the findings and recommendations would be in favor of the creation of more states. The Minorities Commission reported in 1958. They did not support the creation of more states, partly because they reasoned that there was not enough time to accomplish such a change, and partly because they found that the fears of minorities were not real but imagined. Instead, they recommended the insertion in the independence constitution of a bill of rights and specific provisions to guide the creation of more states after independence. These provisions were used by the federal coalition government in 1962, under questionable political circumstances, to create the Mid-Western Region.

Beyond 1962, however, the agitation for state creation has thrived on two interrelated issues considered crucial by the Nigerian power elite: the desire to ensure the balance of political and economic power among the component units of the federation, and the desire to create centers of power, or "empires," which the elite would dominate. Here, again, we see the "fear of the North" coming into the political calculation. Northern elites continued to resist, but in 1967 they accepted the creation of six states out of their territory. In measure designed to prevent the imminent civil war, the military government under Yakubu Gowon gave the following explanation for breaking up the North: that no one state should be in a position to dominate or control the central government. This explanation goes to the heart of the argument of this chapter, that the creation of states has been one of the main factors undermining the federal system of government.

The 1967 state creation exercise was incomplete. The anomalies were to be addressed in a further exercise in 1976. In giving the country a nineteen-state structure, the Ayo Irikefe panel explained that they broke the Western State into three, the East Central State into two, and the North Eastern State into three because these states were upsetting the balance of the federal structure either in population or in geographical size. Strong supporters of the "balance of power" argument have continued to see areas of imbalance, and this has continued to propel the argument for the splitting of certain states and the merging of others. Thus, new states continued to be added, perhaps characteristically by military administrations, so that Nigeria currently has thirty-six.

The agitation for more states has also been fueled by the desire by members of the power elite to create empires for themselves. In a type of activity that probably started before colonial rule, ambitious leaders or failed regional politicians who craved a share of the "national cake" have called for the creation of particular states where they would have a better chance of becoming governors, judges, legislators, contractors, or members of the board of parastatals, and of gaining access to large sums of money for private personal enrichment. In many cases, these individuals have paraded themselves as ethnic leaders and organized state creation movements. Not surprisingly, their fears became amplified as the "fear of the minorities" and their aspirations were presented as those of their entire group.

Nigeria has not fully recovered from the civil war, and this constitutes the fourth cause of the slow death of federalism. This point is recognized by Toyin Falola, who has submitted that the war "promoted the development of a greater centralization of power which, in subsequent years, led to authoritarianism and the undermining of the federal system."[21] The secession of the Eastern Region shook the very foundation on which the country was built. On the other hand, it can be argued that the secession was a practical demonstration, albeit extreme, of the concept of state and ethnic rights. The Igbo as a people collectively had cause to feel that their very existence was threatened. Their secession was probably inevitable, given the political and security circumstances of 1966-1967. By the same token, the civil war that followed was an effort by the federal government to preserve the unity and national integrity of the country. Among other things, therefore, it would seem that two ideological positions were in contest: states' rights and stronger national government. The civil war enabled the federal government to strengthen itself vis-à-vis the states. The result was the triumph of the center. Coming in the wake of the war, the FMG consolidated its power in the 1970s and actually enjoyed the sympathy and active support of the political elites in the process. As successive military regimes became progressively more authoritarian, the FMG became progressively stronger, and the states it created became smaller, weaker, and economically more dependent on the federal government.

Since the military in power operated a hierarchical system, and since the state governors were usually appointed from the rank of junior officers, the strengthening of the federal government probably went on unnoticed, certainly unchallenged, until the brief interlude of civilian administration and multiparty democracy of the Second Republic, 1979-1983. By then, it was too late to reverse the process. Several states attempted to pursue certain policies—such as provision of free education and health care in states controlled by the Unity Party of Nigeria (UPN)—but soon realized their financial dependence on the federal government which was controlled by the NPN-NPP accord. By the 1990s, under the dictatorships of General Ibrahim Babangida and General Sani Abacha, the balance had shifted considerably in favor of the FMG.

Opposition to the Abacha regime took many shapes. It is especially remarkable that the leading pro-democracy group in the mid-1990s, NADECO, revived this notion of the rights of states and ethnic groups to secede. Thus, for some time before the death of Abacha, and as a last resort if the political transition under General Abdusalami Abubakar was not favorable to them, sections of the Yoruba leadership elite advocated secession from the union. Abroad in the United States, the Egbe Omo Oduduwa, an ethnic association, drafted the constitution of the envisaged Yoruba state. These activities were reminiscent of the 1960s when the Igbos challenged the powers of the FMG.

At the federal level, dictators developed a strong network of security operatives to silence all voices of reason or opposition. The argument always has been that the country needs national unity, but this has been the code name for fear of secession. Arising from this paranoia, the federal government looked at every type of criticism with suspicion. State security forces hounded the people, killed many, slammed others in jail, threatened religious leaders, deposed kings and chiefs, and generally suppressed any effort toward reasoned and reasonable discourse. Under the Babangida and Abacha regimes, hired assassins silenced opposition voices with guns, machetes, and bombs. For example, nine leaders of the Ogoni people, including Ken Saro-Wiwa, were executed on spurious charges; everyone knows that they were killed for fervently demanding fair and just treatment of the oil-producing communities and for leading the struggle for environmental justice and responsibility. One of the attributes of federalism in its purest sense is the guaranteeing of the rights of individuals; in Nigerian federalism after the civil war, these rights have been sacrificed for what has been touted as the need for unity, peace, and security.

The fifth cause of the slow death of federalism in Nigeria is military dictatorship. Military rule vested both the executive and the legislative powers in military leaders, thereby violating the principle of the separation of powers and threatening the independence of the judiciary. At the same time, the autonomy of state and local governments was eroded. It has long been recognized that dictatorship and federalism are incompatible. A federal government that operates under a military regime, or a totalitarian state with one political party, is simply a unitary system.

A discussion of human rights is relevant here. Appreciation and respect for states' rights (vis-à-vis the federal government) and local governments' rights (vis-à-vis the states) are possible only when the rights of the individual are recognized and respected. In the home, at the workplace, and in every walk of life there have been minor and major dictators. These are people who bend and break the rules at will, people who would like to exercise absolute powers. It is not an accident that since the Gowon era each successive military government has been progressively worse than the one before it. Each dictator has been more absolute than the one before him. By the same token, each federal military government has been less conversant with the principle of federalism than the one before it. Suspension of the constitution by the FMG has directly or indirectly prepared the government to violate the rights of states and individuals.

It is possible to argue that one of the reasons for this progressive erosion of the federal principle is that there are too many dictators waiting in the wings, too many corrupt politicians waiting to ascend to power. Children have the right to the love and care of their parents; employees have the right to decent treatment by their employer; women have the right to freedom, property, and the pursuit of happiness; and the citizen has the right to fair trial by an independent judiciary.[22] These changes in attitude and awareness must be achieved at the same time as states and local governments claim their independence and autonomy.

Without doubt, the sixth cause of the slow death of federalism in Nigeria has been economic: the reliance on petroleum as the source of national wealth.[23] Since the advent of petroleum in the country's economy, the only viable government in Nigeria has been the federal government, partly because of its control over this important revenue source. Oil revenue is considered to be a "national cake," but the expenditure of this revenue is skewed against the state and local governments of the areas where the crude oil is extracted.

A contributory cause of this is the system of revenue allocation. The formula adopted since 1979 has vested a larger proportion of all federally collected revenue (principally from petroleum) in the federal government than in the state and local governments combined. This conclusion has been reached from my extensive study of revenue allocation.[24] The four chapters on revenue allocation in a recent publication edited by Kunle Amuwo and others make the same point.[25] For most of the 1990s, the revenue allocation formula gave 53 percent of federally collected revenue to the federal government, 35 percent to *all* the thirty-six state governments, and 10 percent to *all* the local governments. This has been possible partly because the bulk of public revenue collected by the federal government since the 1970s has come from one source—petroleum—through sales of crude oil, and the collection of oil rents and royalties. The federal government's financial power has also been made possible by the fact that in the sharing of revenue among the states the principle of derivation has long been de-emphasized in favor of the principle of equality of states (40 percent) and the principle of inaccurate population size (30 percent).

Finally, it is the position of this chapter that the slow death of federalism was caused by the fact that capable politicians shun the state and local levels because of their understanding that real power and political influence (as well as the most money) reside in the federal government. From the Gowon era onward, only junior/young politicians could be found in the lower echelons of power, and they in turn consider this as a stepping stone to greater political heights in the not too distant future. Thus, rather than being viewed as a major branch of government, state and local governments are regarded as playgrounds for political novices. Major politicians probably began avoiding state and local governments as a result of the enlargement and consolidation of the federal government in the 1970s. This was a reversal of the situation in the heyday of the federal system—the 1950s through 1966—when the most capable candidates preferred the regional administration. The result is a cycle of poverty and powerlessness at the state-local levels because the "best" candidates have moved to the federal level.

CONCLUSION

As federalism began to collapse in the country, many of its attributes, identified earlier, began to erode. Although in theory there was a constitutional division of governmental functions, in practice the state-local governments are no longer autonomous in their spheres of action. Although in theory the federal, state, and local governments act directly on the citizens, in practice the effectiveness of the state-local governments has been limited by the power of the federal government to manipulate the revenue allocation system. State and local governments in Nigeria have been created at the whim of the federal government, often with disastrous consequences. They, therefore, derive their existence and powers from the federal government rather than the constitution; and under a military regime, the FMG is capable of changing the composition and structure of each state unilaterally. Thus, state and local governments no longer exist in their own right.

Federalism holds several advantages for Nigeria. It promises to provide a great measure of unity to the country's disparate component parts. It also holds the promise of advancing the pace of development through a competitive process in which no state will be held down to enable another to catch up. Federalism holds the promise of fulfilling the desire to tighten or loosen preexisting bonds and, when it operates as it should, federalism could prevent the rise of a despotic central government which might be a menace to private liberties.

It is perhaps with these advantages in mind that the country has begun to see resurgence in support for the federal, even confederal, principle since the beginning of the Third Republic. Contrary to what might be expected, some of this resurgence has been coming from the religious fundamentalists. Within two years of the beginning of the Obasanjo civilian administration, several states in northern Nigeria have declared the Shari'a as the official source and guide of the law. Many people in the south, even avid supporters of the federal principle among the Igbo and Yoruba, have been alarmed by the move. They have expressed their opposition, accused these states of Islamic fundamentalism, and have mobilized the press and public opinion against these states. Such a reaction is inconsistent with the principle of states' rights entailed in federalism and hitherto held by the same politicians. It is the position of this chapter that the adoption of Shari'a by some states is a good thing for federalism. As long as the fundamental rights of non-Muslims in the states are guaranteed, and as long as every individual's right to fair trial is assured, it may also be a good thing for Nigeria in the long run. The revival of federalism may, indeed, take an unexpected, religious route.

No idea, concept, or political system develops by chance. The federal arrangement in Nigeria was carefully crafted in constitutional conferences held in the country and in the United Kingdom between 1950 and 1960. The federal system was officially adopted in 1954 and continued to operate in a fairly orderly manner until 1964. In that decade of Nigerian federalism, the country structurally moved from a unitary system to a federal system. Federalism was actively cultivated, and maintenance work was carried out through constitutional talks. Since federalism did not develop by chance, its survival must not be left to chance. It must be redesigned and reinvented. At this stage, obviously, the country needs to reinvest in federal principles in order to revive the federal system of government. Until this is achieved, it must be understood that, as of the year 2000, Nigerian federalism is dead.

NOTES

1. Kenneth Clinton Wheare, *Federal Government* (London: Oxford University Press, 4th edition, 1963), 1.
2. See William S. Livingstone, "A Note on the Nature of Canadian Federalism," in Peter J. Meekison (ed.), *Canadian Federalism: Myth or Reality* (Toronto: Methuen & Co., 1968); William Riker, *Federalism: Origin, Operation, Significance* (Boston: Little, Brown, 1964), 106.

3. Amitai Etzioni, "A Paradigm for the Study of Political Unification," *World Politics*, 15 (1), 1962, 44-74.
4. Obafemi Awolowo, *Path to Nigerian Freedom* (London: Faber and Faber, 1947).
5. See Obafemi Awolowo, *Thoughts on the Nigerian Constitution* (Ibadan: Oxford University Press, 1966). Also see a review of Awolowo's views on federalism in Eghosa E. Osaghae, "Awolowo and Nigerian Federalism," in Olasope Oyelaran et al. (eds.), *Obafemi Awolowo: The End of an Era?* (Ile-Ife: University of Ife Press, 1988), 526-562.
6. *The Constitution of the United States of America*, Article VI.
7. Michael D. Reagan, *The New Federalism*, (London: Oxford University Press, 1972).
8. Ibid., 1.
9. Ibid., 7-9.
10. Wheare, *Federal Government*, 47.
11. L. Adele Jinadu, "A Note on the Theory of Federalism," in A. Bolaji Akinyemi et al. (eds.), *Readings on Federalism* (Lagos: NIIA, 1979).
12. *Encyclopedia Encarta*, 1996.
13. A. G. Adebayo, "Explaining the Choice of Federal System of Government in Nigeria: A Review and New Notes," *ODU: A Journal of West African Studies*, 33, 1988, 44-66.
14. See Eme O. Awa, *Federal Government in Nigeria* (Los Angeles: University of California Press, 1964); G. O. Odenigwe, "The Constitutional Development of Nigeria: The Origin of Federalism, 1862-1954," Ph.D. dissertation, Clark University, 1957; B. O. Nwabueze, *A Constitutional History of Nigeria* (London: Longman, 1982).
15. For a short review of the constitutional history of Nigeria, see S. G. Ehindero, *The Constitutional Development of Nigeria, 1849-1989* (Jos: Ehindero, 1991).
16. The most authoritative writings on this subject are those by Billy Dudley. See his *Parties and Politics in Northern Nigeria* (London: Frank Cass, 1968); *Instability and Political Order: Politics and Crisis in Nigeria* (Ibadan: Ibadan University Press, 1973); *Nigeria 1965: Crisis and Criticism* (Ibadan: Ibadan University Press, 1966); and *An Introduction to Nigerian Government and Politics* (Ibadan: MacMillan, 1982). Also see Remi Anifowose, *Violence and Politics in Nigeria: The Tiv and Yoruba Experience, 1960-66* (New York: Nok, 1980).

17. Toyin Falola, *The History of Nigeria* (Westport, Conn.: Greenwood Press, 1999), 99.
18. See Dudley, *Nigeria 1965*.
19. The 1966 coup and the subsequent civil war have been the subject of numerous writings. Works by participants in the coup and the war include the following: A. Ademoyega, *Why We Struck* (Ibadan: Evans, 1981); A. A. Madiebo, *The Nigerian Revolution and the Biafran War, 1967-1970* (London: Sidgwick, 1972); and Olusegun Obasanjo, *My Command* (Ibadan: Heinemann, 1980).
20. A very useful work on the era, with documents, is A.H.M. Kirk-Greene (ed.), *Crisis and Conflict in Nigeria: A Documentary Source Book, 1966-1969* (Oxford: Oxford University Press, 1971), 2 vols.
21. Falola, *The History of Nigeria*, 129.
22. The first reference to the need to guarantee these basic human and social rights was made by Chief Obafemi Awolowo over three decades ago. See Obafemi Awolowo, *Thoughts on the Nigerian Constitution*, 119-122. On the human rights imperative in Africa, see Akanmu Adebayo and Alma Riggs, "Human Rights in Africa: The Records, the Charter and the Priorities," *Journal of the Georgia Association of Historians*, 20, 1999, 53-92.
23. On petroleum and the Nigerian economy, see S. K. Panter-Brick (ed.), *Soldiers and Oil: The Political Transformation of Nigeria* (London: Frank Cass, 1978); and A. A. Ikein, *The Impact of Oil on a Developing Country* (New York: Praeger, 1990).
24. A. G. Adebayo, *Embattled Federalism: History of Revenue Allocation in Nigeria, 1946-1979* (New York: Peter Lang, 1993).
25. Kunle Amuwo et al. (eds.), *Federalism and Political Restructuring in Nigeria* (Ibadan: Spectrum Books, 1998), 211-275.

5

RELUCTANT DEMOCRACY: THE STATE, THE OPPOSITION, AND THE CRISIS OF POLITICAL TRANSITION, 1985-1993

Adebayo Oyebade

INTRODUCTION

Nigeria obtained political independence from Britain in October 1960 with the hope of building a stable and viable democratic state. However, the democratic experiment had lasted only six years when the First Republic ended violently via a bloody military coup on January 15, 1966. This coup brought about the first military government in Nigeria and marked the beginning of the institutionalization of the military elite in the political process. For the next thirty-three years, barring a short interlude lasting from 1979 to 1983 (the Second Republic), the country was governed by military dictatorships. The political instability inherent in these years could be seen in the occurrence of five successful coups and two abortive ones.[1] During the years of military rule, successive regimes never failed to reaffirm a commitment to returning power to a democratically elected government at a stipulated date. But military rule remained entrenched in national politics till the end of the century. It was not until May 1999 that Nigeria began another democratic experiment when the ruling military regime of General Abdusalami Abubakar handed over the reins of power to the elected government of President Olusegun Obasanjo.

The road to a democratic Nigeria was, however, fraught with uncertainties. Before the Abubakar transition program that eventually led to the transfer of power to a civilian government on May 29, 1999, two previous transition programs had played themselves out, both ending in dismal failure. The first transition program, instituted by General Ibrahim Babangida, commenced in 1986 and collapsed with the general's annulment of the result of the June 1993 presidential election. The aborted election not only failed to usher in a new democratic republic, it led to a state of national political crisis from which the country would not recover for a long time.

General Sani Abacha, who assumed power after eliminating the Interim National Government (ING) installed by Babangida shortly before his forced resignation in August 1993, embarked upon a new transition program in October 1995. From the outset, Abacha's program was a discredited one given its relentless drive to turn the military leader into a civilian president. The program was so grossly manipulated and teleguided by Abacha that it lacked any credibility either at home or abroad. This transition too, eventually ended ignominiously, with Abacha's death in 1998. Thus, within the space of thirteen years Nigeria had instituted two transition programs, neither of which led the country to democracy.

In this chapter the crisis of political transition in Nigeria is examined with particular reference to the Babangida program. The program is of particular significance in that it was the longest ever, the most elaborate, and consequently the most expensive in the political history of Nigeria. It began with laudable intentions but soon became fraught with so many contradictions that even if it had succeeded it is doubtful if it would have produced a viable and stable democratic state. The environment in which it was carried out was hardly conducive to a successful enthronement of democracy. During this transition, Nigeria's economy rapidly went downhill, creating severe hardship for millions of Nigerians especially the poor. Ethnic and religious tensions mounted, further poisoning the transition climate. Meanwhile, the state increasingly manipulated the transition program in such a way as to derail the genuine democratic aspirations of the people. Delaying tactics were employed which gave credence to the charge of a "hidden agenda" pursued by the military to entrench itself in power. The transition process inevitably drew opposition from the civil society. Organized pro-democracy and human rights groups emerged and combined with the society at large to oppose the growing authoritarianism of the state. This chapter will take a critical look at the Babangida transition program, the prevailing repressive atmosphere under which it was conducted, and the emergence and crystallization of civil opposition.

STRUCTURAL ADJUSTMENT REFORMS

In August 1985, Babangida came to power after overthrowing the military government of General Muhammadu Buhari, which itself had usurped power in December 1983 after terminating the Second Republic headed by President Shehu Shagari. Upon coming to power, Babangida declared the intention of his government to return the country to democracy as soon as possible.[2] Toward this end, an ambitious transition program was set in motion in January 1986 with the establishment of a seventeen-member Political Bureau entrusted with the task of conducting and monitoring a national debate on the political future of the country. The body also had the responsibility of drawing up a time schedule for the transfer of power to an elected government.[3] An electoral body, the National Electoral Commission (NEC), was established late in 1987 to handle the mechanism of the transition including registration of voters, clearance of candidates for election, and conduct of the elections. A constitution drafting committee was also inaugurated in 1987 to prepare a new constitution for the Third Republic.

The transition program was based on structural adjustment reforms. The reforms were aimed at improving political participation, eliminating endemic political corruption, and stimulating economic growth. The underlying assumption was that structural reform of the polity was necessary to ensure a viable Third Republic. The program of reforms was pursued in the political and economic spheres. These reforms will be examined, together with the extent to which they were successfully implemented, and their impact on the transition process.

Political Reform

Babangida seemed determined to remove the deep-seated political corruption that had characterized the Second Republic and partly brought about its downfall.[4] His reform innovation was to prevent the old discredited and corrupt political class from taking part in the new democratic experiment. He hoped to create a new breed of politicians untainted by the corruption of the past, patriotic in thinking, and selfless in service. He thus promulgated Decree no. 25 of 1987, which imposed a blanket ban on political participation by certain classes of people. These included all the politicians and bureaucrats who had served in the First and Second Republics, the "old brigades" and "moneybags" as they were often called, and people who had held public offices but had been dismissed or otherwise found guilty of corruption or other official offenses. The ban also affected police and military personnel who had held specific positions.[5] Also banned from the political process were people vaguely defined as "extremists." Babangida himself identified the so-called extremists as

> uncompromising, fanatical or immoderate in their views, who go beyond the limits of reason, necessity or propriety to advance their cause, or who exceed the ordinary, usually expected limits of de-

cency. . . . Extremists do not bother to delineate where their own rights end and those of others begin. They are not believers in the politics of equality; they are not democratic.[6]

"Extremists" invariably meant critics and opponents of the military regime. The restriction on political participation was perceived by the military as a sure way of cleaning the political stable and thus insulating the Third Republic from repeating the previous failed civilian eras.

The Babangida junta also wished to address the perennial problem of ethnic and religious cleavages, which were deeply entrenched in the Nigerian political culture. The answer to this divisive type of politics, in the government's view, was a two-party system in which the parties would be required to organize on a national and ideological basis that would make them transcend narrow ethnic and religious loyalty. The government then created two parties, the Social Democratic Party (SDP) and the National Republican Convention (NRC). The expectation was that the two-party system would develop a culture of political unity and stability that had eluded the previous republics.[7]

The regime's design to establish a new political order included the creation of a number of agencies and institutions designed to help establish a new order. The best known of these were the Directorate of Social Mobilization for Social Justice, Self-Reliance, and Economic Recovery (MAMSER), the Directorate of Food, Roads and Rural Infrastructure (DFRRI), the National Directorate of Employment (NDE), and the Better Life Program for Rural Women (BLP). MAMSER, established in September 1987, was charged with the responsibility of promoting political education and mobilizing the electorate for the transition to civil rule. Babangida hoped to use the program "to evolve a social order through the re-awakening and reorientation of Nigerians to face with determination, the challenges of nation building."[8] DFRRI was created in June 1986 to provide infrastructural improvements and facilities to the rural areas, enhancing rural development and productivity, and mobilizing the rural population. BLP was also expected to be involved with the rural population, with a particular focus on the well-being of women. NDE was created to foster self-employment in the private sector and to promote the development of small-scale business.

Reforms were also instituted in the administrative sector, including the creation of new local government areas and states. By 1991, the number of local government areas had increased from 301 to 589. New states were also progressively created, first in 1987, and then in 1991, making the country a thirty-state federation. The regime's purpose for this administrative reform was to effect grassroots access to government, and to enhance development, especially of rural areas.

Economic Reform

Measures were also undertaken toward restructuring the wobbling economy. Nigeria had entered a path of economic decline in the mid-1980s after a period of buoyant economy due to the oil boom of the previous decade. During the Shagari civilian government, corruption and mismanagement of resources rose to a height hitherto unknown in Nigeria. Despite the dwindling oil revenue, the politicians of the Second Republic indulged in a free-for-all looting of the treasury. By 1985 when Babangida took over power, the economy was in a distressed state. The huge oil revenues of the 1970s were no longer forthcoming, and successive Nigerian governments had failed to diversify the economy and shift emphasis from the oil sector. Oil boom had suddenly become oil doom. The Nigerian economy, which had steadily declined over the years, was now characterized by a huge budget deficit and debt burden. The dismal economic climate could hardly encourage external investment in the country.

As Nigeria faced a worsening economic crisis, like many other African nations, it turned to structural adjustment as the way of bringing the economy back on track. Although a national debate initiated by the Federal Government in 1985 rejected an International Monetary Fund (IMF) loan, Babangida went ahead to implement the fund's prescribed policies for economic revival.[9] This was done through the Structural Adjustment Program (SAP) introduced in July 1986. The basic objectives of the program are as follows:

1. Restructuring and diversifying the productive base of the economy with a view to reducing dependence on the oil sector and on imports.
2. Achieving fiscal balance of payments viability, that is, reducing and, possibly, totally eliminating budget deficits.
3. Lessening the dominance of unproductive investments in the public sector and improving the sector's efficiency, as well as intensifying the growth potential of the private sector.
4. Laying the grounds for sustainable non-inflationary or minimally inflationary growth.
5. Reducing the strangulating regime of administrative controls in the economic sector.[10]

These goals were to be realized through a number of measures including deregulation of the economy, devaluation of the naira, desubsidization of essential products such as petroleum, and privatization and commercialization policies.[11]

THE FAILURE OF REFORMS

The military regime's inability to successfully handle the reform programs it had embarked upon quickly became apparent. Most visible was the government's failure to improve the economy and raise the standard of living of the masses of the people. Although World Bank analysis attributed modest success to SAP, scholarly discourse on the program generally regards this as far from being the case.[12] Indeed, from the perspective of the common Nigerian who bore the brunt of its hardship, the program was a disaster. Rather than injecting vitality into the crumbling economy, SAP aggravated the suffering of most Nigerians, especially the poor and the working class. The high cost of living resulting from the devaluation of the naira, the removal of subsidies particularly on petroleum products, and the consequent increased inflation made life unbearable for many. The once powerful naira depreciated rapidly as a result of massive devaluation. Within a year of the commencement of SAP, the naira had been devalued by 75 percent in relation to the U.S. dollar, and by 90 percent by 1990.[13] The naira, which was at par with the U.S. dollar in value when Babangida took over power in 1985 had sunk well below it by 1993 when he left office.[14] The progressive depreciation of the naira began in late 1986 when the Second-Tier Foreign Exchange Market (SFEM) was introduced by the government. The burden of debt servicing was also taking a toll on the economy. During the structural adjustment regime, Nigeria's external debt increased considerably from a pre-SAP figure of $18.9 billion to about $40 billion in 1994.[15] Enormous resources that could have serviced social services like health care, education, and housing were diverted to debt repayment. Skyrocketing prices of goods and services, from food items to transport fares and housing rent, severely affected working people whose real incomes had diminished significantly given the growing inflation rate. Declining job availability and high-rate retrenchment of workers as a result of collapsing businesses or corporate downsizing led to an increase in social vices such as fraud, prostitution, and drug trafficking. Violent crimes, particularly armed robbery, were also on the increase.

The hardship of SAP for majority of Nigerians was, indeed, beyond anything yet known in the nation's history. But while the generality of the people especially the poor and the working class sank deep into the abyss of economic degradation under SAP, foreign interests and a tiny sector of the population emerged as the beneficiaries of the program. This tiny sector comprised, in the words of Julius Ihonvbere and Timothy Shaw, "drug pushers, currency traffickers, importers and exporters, contractors, used car dealers and landlords."[16]

Why did the economic reform program of the Babangida regime fail to rescue the economy? The execution of capital-demanding projects, wasteful spending, political patronage, and bureaucratic corruption all combined to thwart any potential gains from the program. Despite the obvious need for a tight budget in an economic emergency, the regime took on a number of projects that called for huge expenditures. These included the creation of more states and local government areas, the completion of a new federal capital at Abuja, and the championing of peacekeeping operations in the West African subregion. At a time when the vast majority of Nigerians were suffering from the effects of SAP, the government chose to pump enormous resources into these projects. The new states that were created, a total of eleven, required extensive financial support, at least initially in order to take off.[17] Although the perennial agitation for state creation in Nigeria could be justified on the ground of the need to bring the government nearer to the people and thus enhance grassroots development, yet, as some scholars have argued, not all the new states were created for this reason. As Eghosa Osaghae has pointed out, some were created more to compensate or reward allies.[18] As for the new capital at Abuja, it became the official seat of the federal government in 1990 at a great financial cost. Regional peacekeeping in West Africa, at that time principally in Liberia, was heavily reliant on Nigeria. In fact, Nigeria shouldered much of the financial burden of the peacekeeping operation.

Besides such expensive ventures, there was also the question of the effectiveness of the institutions and agencies created by Babangida to foster a new order. Though some of these institutions and agencies could be useful tools for this purpose, they mainly led to corrupt practices and patronage building. Indeed, during the Babangida regime, corruption soared high among the military class and its political collaborators. Gross mismanagement of the economy and reckless squandering of resources continued unabated despite the declining economy. Those who had access to the national treasury directly, or indirectly through patronage, simply helped themselves to it in order to alleviate the economic crunch. Such people lived in glaring, opulent splendor in the midst of poverty and economic depression. Some of them even insensitively flaunted their wealth by parading an array of expensive cars and imposing homes in wealthy areas of the cities.

In the political arena, the contradictions inherent in the Babangida's reform program were bound to make it a failure. First, the unprecedented creation of a two-party system by the government did not allow a political system to evolve naturally from the political culture and experience. When the ban on politics was lifted in May 1989, many political associations, as many as eighty-eight within the first month, emerged to compete for registration as one or the other party in the two-party system. Only thirteen of these associations eventually met the very stringent registration requirements of NEC, out of which six were short-listed to compete for the final two to be selected by the Armed Forces Ruling Council (AFRC). However, in October 1989, Babangida dissolved these political associations on the ground that they were under the influence of politicians already banned from the political process. Consequently, the government created the two parties on an ideological basis. The SDP was defined as "a little to the left," and the NRC as "a little to the right."

Justifiably, many political observers denounced as detrimental to democratic tradition the artificial creation of parties. According to a presidential aspirant of one of the unregistered parties, Dr. Tunji Otegbeye, "it is a misnomer and an assault on the intellect to style what we have at the moment as political parties."[19] The arbitrary imposition of the parties on the polity meant that politicians had no other choice but to join one of the two parties. Also, the removal of the old political class from the arena of Nigerian politics and the banning of others from the political process amounted to limiting political participation contrary to basic democratic tenets.

Besides the issue of negating democratic values, the government-manufactured political parties faced the problem of autonomy. The parties were not only state created, they were state funded as well for the greater part of their existence. The state drew up their manifestos and constitutions, designed their symbols, and provided them with vehicles and secretariats in all the state capitals and local government headquarters.

Their activities including conventions and primaries were also state funded. Many political observers thus termed them "parastatals," that is, state owned, publicly funded enterprises. A one time military head of state, General Olusegun Obasanjo (who would become the president of the Third Republic in 1999), went even further:

> Those who call the two government-created parties parastatals are even being generous. Parastatals at least have effective and accountable chief executives, who can enforce order and discipline. The same cannot be said about the government-created parties. And yet they are the vehicles through which it is hoped that a stable democracy will be built and nurtured. We delude ourselves.[20]

Given the parties' almost total financial dependence on the state, it could hardly be expected that they would be functionally independent especially in policy formulation. In fact, the government exercised a large measure of control over the parties and interfered at will in their affairs. For instance, in late 1992 after canceling the presidential primaries of the two parties, the government proceeded to dissolve their executive committees and replace them with caretaker committees. NEC also had the responsibility of supervising the parties.

Babangida's attempt at creating a new incorruptible political class for the Third Republic was also a huge failure. As soon as the junta announced the banning of the discredited politicians of the terminated First and Second Republics, this political class began to mobilize to undermine reforms opposed to their own political future and economic interest. Many discredited political heavyweights of the old era manipulated their way into the top hierarchy of government as ministers, chairmen of parastatals, and heads of one government agency or another. These elements, which the political reforms were designed to keep out of power, now occupied important positions where they could manipulate such reforms. The rehabilitation of this discredited political elite through patronage in the government was a dilemma for Babangida. He could not afford to alienate some of the political bigwigs who were still very powerful and influential, and their cohorts in the military. His own political survival depended on their goodwill toward him and so he could not oppose their desire for power. Thus, the supposedly banned politicians found their way into the transition process and actively participated by throwing their financial weight behind the parties. In this way, they could influence the process and steer it in the direction that served their political interest.[21] In the final analysis, Babangida was forced to throw open the political race. In December 1991 he lifted the ban on the old politicians.

Also, the agencies and institutions established by Babangida to foster political mobilization for the Third Republic failed to make any serious impact despite the government's huge expenditure on them. Whatever the good intentions of these agencies and institutions, they did not live up to expectations. Although the level of political awareness and participation increased considerably within civil society, it was not due to MAMSER. Rather, Nigerians were galvanized into political participation because they were tired of years of unproductive military dictatorship. Particularly, they were anxious to get rid of a recalcitrant, irritating military regime that appeared to be using delaying tactics to remain in power. As far as DFRRI was concerned, the body had little to show by way of success in rural development. The same can be said of Better Life, which seemed to focus attention more on wives of military governors and other high-class women than on rural women. It provided an opportunity, as Toyin Falola puts it, "for fashion parades rather than gender empowerment."[22] These institutions, as pointed out earlier, mainly served as yet another avenue for corrupt practices.

TRANSITION IN A CRISIS-RIDDEN ENVIRONMENT

Right from its inception as a political entity Nigeria had been troubled by ethnic and religious problems. The dominant groups in the north, the Hausa/Fulani, are Muslims, while the major southern groups, the Yoruba and the Igbo, are predominantly Christians. This ethno-religious difference between the north and the south has traditionally been a major cause of conflict. The three major ethnic groups identified above have lived in constant mutual suspicion of one another. One of the manifestations of the inherent ethnic antagonism is the Nigerian Civil War of 1967-1970.[23]

During the Babangida regime, ethnic and religious tension escalated significantly. The state's manipulation of ethnicity and religion was largely responsible for this tension. It was in this prevailing atmosphere of constant ethnic and religious crises that the transition program was implemented. Needless to say, this atmosphere was not conducive to a successful transition. It is important to look a little more closely at the nature of the ethnic and religious crises.

Ethnic Crisis

The Babangida administration played a politics of ethnic favoritism to serve northern interests to the detriment of the south. This led to great resentment among southerners, especially among the Yoruba and the Igbo who rightly felt marginalized in national politics. It was true that the north had a greater share of public offices within the federal government. For example, northerners held more cabinet positions than southerners in the administration, including the key ministries of foreign affairs, petroleum resources, internal affairs, and defense (held by Babangida himself). The president also appointed more northerners to the highest military ruling body, the Armed Forces Ruling Council (AFRC). Southerners accused the north of political dominance of the federation, and unwillingness to concede power to the south. This accusation would eventually be justified by Babangida's annulment of the result of the June 12, 1993, presidential election, which would have seen a southerner emerge as the president of Nigeria.

Apart from tension among the major ethnic groups, opposition to the state from the so-called minority groups also became commonplace during the Babangida era. An expression of minority opposition to the state was Major Gedion Okar's coup of April 22, 1990. This was a coup executed, according to Okar, on "behalf of the patriotic and well meaning peoples of the Middle Belt and the Southern parts" of Nigeria in order to liberate the regions from northern domination.[24] A cardinal objective of the Okar-led coup, if it had succeeded, was to expel the north from the federation. In his broadcast, Okar had, indeed, excised five northern states from the federation, namely, Sokoto, Borno, Katsina, Kano, and Bauchi. The coup expressed the extent of minority animosity toward the northern domination of the federation.

Another instance of ethnic minority opposition to the state came from the Ogoni people of the Niger delta region of Nigeria. Living in an oil-producing area, the Ogoni never really benefited from the enormous wealth obtained from their region. Instead, they had been victims not only of government neglect in terms of provision of basic amenities, but also of disastrous environmental degradation due to massive oil exploitation by multinational companies, particularly the Shell Petroleum Company. Environmental pollution from oil-spills posed serious health hazard to the people. Also, their land was routinely confiscated without benefit of compensation. Karl Maier describes the plight of Ogoniland and its people:

> Over the years, 634 million barrels of oil worth approximately $30 billion had been pumped from Ogoniland alone through a network of ninety-six wells hooked up to five flow stations. The Shell Petroleum Development Corporation (SPDC) ran the system with its joint venture partners the Nigerian National Petroleum Corporation (NNPC) . . . . In return, the Ogonis received much of the harm but few of the benefits the oil industry had to offer. Poverty is endemic in Ogoniland and the Niger Delta as a whole. Education and health facilities are primitive at best, and few Ogoni homes enjoy the

most basic services, such as electricity and running water.[25]

In 1990 the Ogoni people decided to protest the devastation to their land caused by the environmental problems created by Shell's extensive extraction of oil. A protest group, the Movement for the Survival of the Ogoni People (MOSOP), was founded by environmental activist and writer, Ken Saro-Wiwa, one of the most respected leaders of the people. The primary objective of MOSOP was to pressurize the government to halt Shell's abuse of Ogoniland and its people. As a beneficiary of huge revenues from Shell's operation in Ogoniland, the federal government responded to the Ogoni protests with a series of military assaults on the people, which literally turned the area into a war zone. For the Ogoni, intimidation, death, and destruction were the results of the campaign of terror unleashed on them by the Nigerian military. The death count in Ogoniland and surrounding communities at the hands of security forces has been staggering. For instance, a 1990 demonstration against Shell resulted in the killing of some eighty Ogonis by security forces.[26]

Religious Crisis

It could be said that the Babangida government compounded the persistent religious problem of Nigeria by infusing religion into the body politic of the nation. In February 1986, Babangida secretly took Nigeria into membership of the Organization of Islamic Conference (OIC), contrary to the secular nature of the country. Secret negotiation of Nigeria's membership was said to have been done even without its discussion in the highest decision-making body of the government, the Armed Forces Ruling Council.[27] As William Reno has rightly argued, Babangida was motivated in this action by the desire "to curry favor with Muslim elites who held key roles in state bureaucracies and military command . . . and to attract patronage from OIC member states."[28]

The membership of Nigeria in OIC, an exclusive club of Islamic states, alarmed Christian elements and organizations like the Christian Association of Nigeria (CAN). The tension generated by this action sparked off new rounds of religious unrest in the country. Muslim/Christian clashes occurred in several parts of the country, especially in the north. A religious demonstration at Ahmadu Bello University in Zaria, in May 1986, reportedly resulted in the death of many people, mostly students, following police intervention. In March 1987, there was another serious religious crisis when Muslim and Christian youths clashed at Kafanchan, in southern Kaduna State, with an equally high death toll. Violent confrontations between Muslims and Christians continued in the following years. In 1991 alone there were sporadic riots in Katsina in January and April, in Kaduna in February, in Bauchi in April, and in Kano in October. These confrontations almost always ended with heavy casualties on both sides of the religious divide.[29] Apart from destruction of lives, properties worth thousands of naira were also often casualties of these religious confrontations. Churches were frequently the targets of Muslim rioters.

STATE REPRESSION AND THE RISE OF ORGANIZED OPPOSITION

Opposition to authoritarian rule was nothing new in Nigeria. Previous military governments had experienced their share of civil society's opposition to draconian policies even during the days of economic boom. Traditionally, opposition had always come from radical groups such as student movements, trade and labor organizations, and the radical segment of academia and the press. But in the Babangida days, opposition to the state not only gathered unprecedented momentum, it also assumed a mass and organized dimension.

Opposition to SAP

Growing opposition to the state was in large part caused by the biting effects of the government's economic policies, to which Nigerians did not see an end in sight. Deprivation of the most basic needs of the majority of Nigerians forced on them by SAP produced widespread disaffection within civil society toward the Babangida regime. Obasanjo expressed the mind of many of his fellow countrymen when he severely criticized the government for insensitivity to people's sufferings. He accused the government of neglecting critical issues of employment, food, shelter, education and health, and, thereby, forcing on the people an economic program without a "human face, human heart, and milk of human kindness."[30]

Disaffection was rife particularly among the suffering masses of the people whom unequal distribution of the pains of SAP had turned into paupers. The harsh realities of the SAP regime had virtually wiped out the middle class. The living standard of many was ridiculously low, and access to all the good things of life including good education and health care was beyond their reach. By 1989, SAP-induced hardship for the majority of the people of Nigeria had begun to translate into civil opposition to the state. This opposition was expressed through civil unrest.

The rejection of SAP was manifested in May 1989 when Nigerians took to the streets in riots and demonstrations. Workers embarked on strikes and students of tertiary institutions demonstrated against the worsening economic condition of the people. In the following years, through demonstrations led by labor and students' movements, Nigerians expressed their anger against the unbearably high cost of living and the increase in transport fares brought about by persistent fuel shortages.

A Bungled Transition

But Nigerians were also reacting to the transition process itself, which was bedeviled by numerous problems. First, frequent and arbitrary changes in the process affected the credibility of the whole exercise and led people to question the sincerity of the military in handling over power to civilians. In January 1986 the government had indicated that military rule would terminate on October 1, 1992, when power would be relinquished to a democratically elected government. However, after the report of the Political Bureau was received in July 1987, the original date of power transfer was changed to December 1992. The transition program would again be altered to end in January 1993, and subsequently in August. The arbitrary shifting of dates meant that elections could not be held on schedule. For instance, the local government elections scheduled for late 1989 were not held until May the following year. State legislative and gubernatorial elections originally scheduled for the first half of 1990 were also delayed. Babangida blamed the delays in the transition schedule on either administrative lapses or wrangling within the political class. He used this excuse to justify the repeated government tampering with the transition process.[31]

Meanwhile, elections were often marred by irregularities when they were eventually held. NEC was compelled to annul some of the results of the December 1987 local government elections conducted on non-party basis, and to postpone further elections till March 1988. Although the violence and the electoral fraud that attended the elections have been blamed on NEC's inadequate preparations,[32] electoral malpractice could often, rightly be laid at the feet of the emerging corrupt and indisciplined political class. Many of the politicians were recklessly corrupt, indulging in bribery, vote buying, and rigging of elections. The gubernatorial elections of 1992 were, for instance, massively rigged by the parties, and were also fraught with other forms of electoral fraud. It was the irregularities in the conduct of the 1992 presidential primaries that prompted the government to cancel the entire exercise and to subsequently disqualify all the aspiring candidates.

The gross irresponsibility of the political elite is not entirely surprising, given the caliber of the politicians and the obvious reason for their quest for power. The politicians to whom the Third Republic was to be entrusted seemed interested only in personal gain and self-gratification, not in service to the people. Claude Ake has this to say about the politicians and their motivation:

> They ... demonstrated no genuine interest in identifying the needs of the masses .... The needs of the majority for basic sustenance such as food, proper health care, and education appeared to be no concern of theirs. None of them attempted to address the lack of basic infrastructure, such as reliable electricity, good roads, sewage disposal, potable water in rural communities, health care, and sanitation. Nigerian politicians spent enormous sums of money in their bid to gain power simply by buying votes or manipulating the machinery.[33]

Oppressive Measures

When the Babangida administration came to power in 1985 after dethroning the Buhari dictatorship that had no regard for human rights, the new junta gave the impression that it would operate an open government based on respect for the rights of Nigerians. One of the first acts of the government was to attempt to reverse the battered human rights image of the previous regime. After a review of cases of human rights abuse, the government released many prisoners including jailed Second Republic politicians, journalists, and others detained without trial. Those who were not released outright had their sentences drastically reduced. The government also scrapped the Buhari administration's principal instrument of human rights violation, the National Security Organization (NSO), noted for gross atrocities. Further, the administration reinstated professional and student organizations that had been banned by Buhari as a result of their critical attitude to his regime. These included the Nigerian Medical Association (NMA) and the National Association of Nigerian Students (NANS).

Perhaps the most popular step taken by the government to give an impression of a new regime ready to respect human rights was the abrogation of the hated Public Officers (Protection Against False Accusation) Decree no. 4, of 1984. This obnoxious decree was promulgated by the Buhari regime to stifle press freedom. It made punishable the publication by journalists of information which government considered embarrassing to state officials. Two journalists, Tunde Thompson and Uduka Irabor, charged with violating this decree were convicted and jailed. These two journalists were among the prisoners released by Babangida.

However, the image of a populist, human rights-sensitive regime did not stand the test of time. The pursuit of such an image was a deliberate and calculated attempt by Babangida to curry civil support and legitimize his regime. With the escalation of protests against the rapidly declining living standard brought about by SAP, the Babangida regime began to resort to increasing authoritarianism. The State Security Service (SSS) became the new apparatus for harassing radical scholars, students, journalists, lawyers, labor leaders, market women, indeed, all that dared to oppose the state.[34] Draconian laws were employed by the state to facilitate suppression of opposition. Babangida chose to retain the State Security (Detention of Persons) Decree no. 2 of 1984, promulgated by Buhari, ostensibly to enhance state security. This decree permitted the arrest without warrant of any person considered a security risk, and the detention of such a person without trial for up to six months (invariably, this meant indefinitely because it could be renewed). Although the total period of detention was eventually limited to six weeks, Babangida used the decree to frequently and arbitrarily arrest and detain without trial human rights activists, pro-democracy elements, striking workers, labor leaders, journalists, and others critical of the regime.[35]

One of the most vocal sectors of opposition particularly marked for liquidation by the government was student unionism. Stringent measures were decreed to intimidate that sector, including banning or regulating student union activities. In 1986 the radical student body, NANS, was proscribed in the aftermath of demonstrations. Heavily armed anti-riot policemen were often dispatched to campuses to break up demonstrations. The storming of campuses by security forces invariably resulted in the killing of students. Perennial closure of universities by the regime was also a measure to curtail student opposition. Between 1987 and 1993, higher institutions across the nation were regularly closed, often because of antigovernment protest.

Radical lecturers and professors were also often targets of state harassment. The list of detained or sacked academics during the Babangida regime is quite long. Particularly targeted were leftist academics, branded by the state as "extremists." This group of university teachers had always constituted the core of opposition to military dictatorship in academia. The government made no secret of its intention to curtail academic freedom and reduce university autonomy. One of the ways by which the regime tried to achieve this was to proscribe the national body for Nigerian academics, the Academic Staff Union of Universities (ASUU).

In the war against opposition, the radical arm of the press also experienced the wrath of the police and other security agents of the state. A landmark in the intimidation of journalists was the murder of Dele Giwa, the editor of *Newswatch*, a news magazine. A parcel bomb purportedly sent from the president was the cause of Giwa's death on October 19, 1986. The versatile journalist was believed to be preparing an article for publication that could implicate the president's wife in drug trafficking. Predictably, the government was unable to charge anyone for the violent crime, which lent credence to the suspicion of many Nigerians that it was the work of the state.[36] The clear message of this incident, intended for journalists, was that the junta would not tolerate any opposition. In effect, throughout the Babangida dictatorship, the offices of independent newspapers critical of the government were raided at will and their editors harassed from pillar to post. While some journalists avoided government repression by escaping into exile, others were not so lucky and found themselves in political prisons. Media houses that expressed opposition to the government were often closed down. In April 1987, *Newswatch* was proscribed for six months and its premises sealed up after it incurred the wrath of the government for publishing the report of the Political Bureau. Censorship, closure of newspapers, detention, jailing, and other forms of harassment of journalists continued to be the lot of media organizations. The witch-hunting of the press became particularly vicious after Major Okar's failed coup of 1990. The secret military tribunal that tried the alleged plotters also jailed a number of journalists. Newspapers, including *Punch*, *Newsbreed*, *Champion* and *Vanguard*, were also closed for publishing critical editorials and for carrying stories about the abortive coup. The months preceding the scheduled 1993 presidential election were also traumatic for the independent press. Suspicion that the government did not intend to honor its avowed declaration to hand over power to civilians in August had caused the press to become ever more critical of the regime. The junta's reply was to clamp down on the press. It seized magazines and newspapers containing offending articles, arrested and detained journalists, and invaded and sealed up media houses.[37] The effect of the constant harassment of journalists was to drive the critical press underground.

The labor movement, another opposition sector, was also marked for liquidation. Labor leaders were often arbitrarily arrested and detained. In March 1988, the leadership of the main labor union, the Nigeria Labor Congress (NLC), was dissolved and replaced by a sole administrator. Apart from using intimidation, Babangida also attempted to silence opposition by buying the support of opposition groups through monetary donations. The Nigerian Medical Association (NMA) and the NLC were in this way rendered ineffective. In

October 1992, Babangida donated N30 million to the Nigeria Media Foundation.[38]

THE END OF TRANSITION: THE JUNE 12 CRISIS AND THE RISE OF THE PRO-DEMOCRACY MOVEMENT

Opposition to the Babangida government initially rested primarily on the SAP-induced economic hardship. Most people opposed the regime because of the economic downturn, characterized by high inflation, rising unemployment, collapsing public institutions, crumbling medical services, and an escalating crime rate. The immediate demands of many groups, therefore, often had to do with better living standards.

However, the state's authoritarian tendency and the increasing doubts in the minds of Nigerians about the sincerity of the military promise to hand over power to civilians crystallized the opposition's demand for democracy. The unsteady transition program had not given people much encouragement that the end of military rule was in sight. The emergence of a number of pro-regime organizations and their campaigns for prolonged military rule heightened the suspicion of many Nigerians of a "hidden agenda" pursued by the military. It was generally believed that these groups, the most vocal of which was the Arthur Nzeribe-led Association for Better Nigeria (ABN), had the blessing of the government.

The seeming intention of the government to thwart the democratic aspirations of Nigerians, and the regime's increasing authoritarianism, found expression in the establishment of pro-democracy and human rights organizations. The Civil Liberties Organization (CLO), was founded in 1987 as a nongovernmental organization with the purpose of defending human rights and civil liberties. The Committee for the Defence of Human Rights (CDHR) was formed in 1989. In November 1991, the Campaign for Democracy (CD), essentially a coalition of pro-democracy and human rights groups, was established. These organizations campaigned against state repression, lack of respect for the rule of law, human rights violations, state corruption, and economic mismanagement. They criticized the inconsistencies in the implementation of the transition program, and demanded democracy. For their efforts, front-line activists such as Beko Ransome-Kuti, Gani Fawehinmi, Olisa Agbakoba, Femi Falana, and others became targets of regular government harassment.

The fear of the "hidden agenda" of the military was found to be justified when the government abrogated the electoral commission and annulled the result of the June 12, 1993 presidential election which was widely believed to be one of the fairest and freest in the nation's electoral history. Although the results of the election had not yet been officially released, returns from the states indicated that the SDP candidate, M.K.O. Abiola, had won the race, beating his NRC opponent, Bashir Othman Tofa.[39] However, Babangida abruptly annulled the election results on the pretext that the two candidates used money during the electioneering campaign to influence the electoral process. Many people especially from the south believed, however, that the north was unwilling to concede power to a southerner.[40]

What followed the annulment of the presidential election was a serious political crisis that pushed the nation to the brink of national disintegration. The annulment galvanized unprecedented civil protest, particularly among Abiola's Yoruba ethnic group. In major western cities, riots, demonstrations, road-barricades, and bonfires represented the populace's demand for an end to military rule. However, the pro-democracy coalitions and the NLC offered a more structured protest by masterminding nationwide strikes in July and August 1993. The massive civil protest eventually led to Babangida's resignation from office in August.

CONCLUSION

The transition program undertaken by President Babangida in 1986 was the most elaborate and the most extended in the nation's political history. It was promising at its inception with its lofty goal of creating a new political order to ensure the success of the Third Republic. Political and economic reforms were embarked upon to provide the bedrock of this new political dispensation. Yet, despite the enormous resources and time expended on the transition program, it ended in dismal failure. Its main economic element, structural adjustment, was a disaster. The transition program itself was manipulated at will by the military regime, and corruption, political repression, and ethnic and religious conflicts marred its implementation. In the end, the annulment of the presidential election in June 1993 brought about the ignominious end of the transition exercise.

The annulment not only aborted a new era of democracy, it ushered Nigeria into a period of political uncertainty and possible national disintegration. Nigeria, thereafter, was to see prolonged military rule, indeed, an era that can confidently be described as the most vicious dictatorship in the nation's history. The military government of General Abacha that succeeded the infamous ING took Nigeria to a new height in military authoritarianism.

The failure of the transition program underscores the contradictions inherent in a regime that claimed to be nurturing a new political culture that would ensure a viable democratic state, yet embarked on a virulently oppressive and autocratic path. The implementation of the program was marred by actions that negated the very principles of democracy. Political participation and expression were curtailed and a culture of repression pervaded the transition regime. Babangida's rhetoric of the sincerity of military disengagement from politics was, in the final analysis, a farce.

Further, the political class failed woefully to provide the effective leadership required for the success of the transition program. As the Babangida government tinkered with the program and introduced repressive measures to stifle civil opposition to the regime's undemocratic practices, the political elite largely kept its silence. Both parties, primarily because they were the government's creation, remained powerless and unable to challenge the regime's excesses. This became glaring during the June 12 crisis when the parties were unable to put up a united front against the annulment of the presidential election. The political class thus failed to lead the civil society and provide coherent direction to the burgeoning pro-democracy movement.

NOTES

1. The successful coups were those of Jan. 15, 1966; July 29, 1966; July 29, 1975; Dec. 31, 1983; and Aug. 27, 1985. The abortive ones were those of Feb. 13, 1976, and April 22, 1990. There were also rumors of a number of planned coups. In early 1986, a group of officers, including Major General Mamman Vatsa, minister of the Federal Capital Territory, Abuja, and a member of the Armed Forces Ruling Council (AFRC), were executed for plotting to overthrow the government of General Bababgida.
2. See his speech to that effect in Ibrahim B. Babangida, *Portrait of a New Nigeria: Selected Speeches of IBB* (Lagos: Precision Press, 1989), 33.
3. See *Report of the Political Bureau* (Lagos: Federal Government Printer, 1986).
4. For an analysis of the failure of the Second Republic, see the following: Toyin Falola and Julius Ihonvbere, *The Rise and Fall of the Second Republic, 1979-1983* (London: Zed Press, 1985); Ladipo Adamolekun, *The Fall of the Second Republic* (Ibadan: Spectrum Books, 1985); and Herbert Ekwe-Ekwe, "The Nigerian Plight: Shagari to Buhari," *Third World Quarterly*, 7, July 3, 1988, 610-625.
5. For details, see *Participation in Politics and Elections (Prohibition) Decree No. 25 of 1987* (Lagos: Federal Republic of Nigeria), Official Gazette, 74 (57), Oct. 9, 1987.
6. Cited in S. Ogoh Alubo, "Crisis, Repression and the Prospects for Democracy in Nigeria," *Scandinavian Journal of Development Alternatives*, 8 (4), 1989, 117.
7. The objectives of the so-called "grassroots party system" are well discussed in Tunde Adeniran, "The Two-Party System and the Federal Political Process," *Publius: The Journal of Federalism*, 21 (4), 1991.
8. Cited in *West Africa*, Aug. 3, 1987, 1506. See also Directorate for Social Mobilization (MAMSER), *Political Education Manual: Towards a Free and Democratic Society*, (Abuja: Integrated Press, 1989).

9. For a brief analysis of the IMF debate, see Herbert Ekwe-Ekwe, *Issues in Nigerian Politics since the Fall of the Second Republic 1984-1990* (Lewiston, N.Y.: Edwin Mellen Press, 1991), 38-44.
10. See Toyin Falola, *The History of Nigeria* (Westport, Conn.: Greenwood Press, 1999), 184. See also *Structural Adjustment Program for Nigeria: July 1986-June 1988* (Lagos: Government Printer, 1988).
11. The literature on SAP is quite extensive, including Richard Synge, *Nigeria: The Way Forward* (London: Euromoney Books, 1993), 44-45; Ishrat Husain and Rashid Faruqee, eds., *Adjustment in Africa: Lessons from Country Case Studies* (Washington, D.C.: World Bank, 1994); Adebayo Olukoshi, ed., *The Politics of Structural Adjustment in Nigeria* (London: James Currey, 1993); Eghosa. E. Osaghae, *Structural Adjustment and Ethnicity in Nigeria* (Uppsala: Nordiska Afrikainstitutet Research Report no. 98); and Julius Ihonvbere, "Structural Adjustment and Nigeria's Democratic Transition," *TransAfrica Forum*, Fall 1991, 61-81.
12. See, for instance, Claude Ake, *Democracy and Development in Africa* (Washington, D.C.: The Brookings Institution, 1996), 83-88; Eghosa E. Osaghae, *Crippled Giant: Nigeria since Independence* (Bloomington: Indiana University Press, 1998), 202-207. For a World Bank analysis, see Husain and Faruqee, *Adjustment in Africa*, 264.
13. Cited in Ekwe-Ekwe, *Issues in Nigerian Politics*, 52.
14. The exchange rate in 1993 was officially N22 to $1 while the so-called black market rate was N40-50 to $1. See Osaghae, *Crippled Giant*, 205.
15. Ake, *Democracy and Development in Africa*, 87.
16. Julius Ihonvbere and Timothy Shaw, *Illusions of Power: Nigeria in Transition* (Trenton, N.J.: Africa World Press, 1998), 116.
17. The two states that were created in 1897, Akwa Ibom and Katsina, were each given a take-off grant of about N33 million. See Osaghae, *Crippled Giant*, 228.
18. Ibid.
19. Cited in Ukechukwu Ihejirika, "Historical Perspective of the Nigerian Political Transition Arrangement," *African News Weekly*, Dec. 30, 1994, 6.
20. Olusegun Obasanjo, "Our Desperate Ways," *Nigerian Times*, March 1993, 14.
21. See William Reno, "Old Brigades, Money Bags, New Breeds, and the Ironies of Reform in Nigeria," *Canadian Journal of African Studies*, 27, 1993.

22. Falola, *The History of Nigeria*, 186.
23. The literature on the war abounds, including A.H.M. Kirk-Greene, *Crisis and Conflict in Nigeria: A Documentary Source Book 1966-70, 2 Vols.* (London: Oxford University Press, 1971); Z. Cervenka, *The History of the Nigerian War 1967-70* (Frankfurt: Bernard & Graefe, 1971); and John de St. Jorre, *The Nigerian Civil War* (London: Hodden and Stoughton, 1972).
24. For accounts of the coup, see *Newswatch*, May 7, 1990, and *The African Guardian*, May 14, 1990. A critical analysis of the coup is provided in Julius Ihonvbere, "A Critical Evaluation of the Failed 1990 Coup in Nigeria," *The Journal of Modern African Studies*, 29 (4), 1991, 601-626.
25. Karl Maier, *This House Has Fallen: Midnight in Nigeria*, (New York: Public Affairs, 2000), 80.
26. For more on repression in Ogoniland, see Ken Saro-Wiwa, *Genocide in Nigeria: The Ogoni Tragedy*, (Port Harcourt: Saros International Publishers, 1992); and Human Rights Watch/Africa, *Nigeria—The Ogoni Crisis: A Case Study of Military Repression in Southeastern Nigeria* (New York: Human Rights Watch, 1995).
27. See Ekwe-Ekwe, *Issues in Nigerian Politics*, 58.
28. William Reno, *Warlord Politics and African States* (Boulder, Colo.: Lynne Rienner, 1998), 187.
29. The Bauchi riots alone are said to have claimed the lives of an estimated 1,000 people. See Osaghae, *Crippled Giant*, 250. For a study of religious crises in Nigeria, see Toyin Falola, *Violence in Nigeria: The Crisis of Religious Politics and Secular Ideologies*, (Rochester, N.Y.: University of Rochester Press, 1998).
30. For the speech, see *National Concord*, Dec. 12, 1987.
31. It was claimed that the transition program was amended thirty-eight times. See *The News*, June 28, 1993, 23.
32. Ibid.
33. Ake, "Democratic Transition," 124.
34. The SSS and two other agencies, the Defence Intelligence Agency (DIA), and the National Intelligence Agency (NIA), replaced Buhari's NSO.
35. The decree was widely criticized. See, for instance, *Newswatch*, July 31, 1984.
36. This incident is discussed in Ekwe-Ekwe, *Issues in Nigerian Politics*, 61-65. Fourteen years after the unsolved murder of Giwa, some Nigerians still believe that the incident was state sponsored. In July 1999, at least two separate petitions were submitted to the Justice Chukwudifu Oputa Human Rights Violations Investigation

Commission, set up by President Olusegun Obasanjo to investigate human rights abuses before the return to democracy in 1999. The two petitions, from Newswatch Communication Limited, and from the radical human rights lawyer, Gani Fawehinmi, Giwa's lawyer, accused Babangida's government of masterminding the crime, and of a cover-up. See *Newswatch*, Dec. 18, 2000.
37. A special report on the government's clamp down on the press is provided in *Tell*, June 7, 1993, 31-36. See also Pita Agbese, "State, Media and the Imperatives of Repression: An Analysis of the Ban on Newswatch," *International Third World Studies Journal and Review*, 1 (2), 1989.
38. See *Tell*, June 7, 1993, 35.
39. The presidential election results were published in *The News*, June 28, 1994, 24.
40. For a critical examination of the annulment, see Osaghae, *Crippled Giant*, 251-261.

6

INTELLECTUAL PROPERTY LAW AND PROSPECTS FOR DEVELOPMENT

Adebambo Adewopo

INTRODUCTION

The development of intellectual property law in Nigeria stands tremulously on a historical threshold, primarily in the light of the inchoate domestic law reform process on the one hand and current global developments on the other hand. These two developments are both of enormous importance. The former, the intrinsic factor, relates to the prospective direction of the law, with specific reference to the proposed draft industrial property law. This proposed draft, if eventually passed into law, will usher the industrial property system into a new and dynamic era for the economic and technological development of the country. The latter, extrinsic, relates to the international dimension of intellectual property, particularly within the rubric of the multilateral trading initiative of which Nigeria is part. Current trends and developments in globalization as exemplified in the final completion of the Uruguay Round of the General Agreement on

Tariffs and Trade (GATT) in 1994 underscores the significance of intellectual property in the emerging global economy. It also signals the compelling need for countries to strengthen their intellectual property system for optimum comparative advantage in the global trade relations that are now intensely competitive.

Interestingly, Nigeria's intellectual property reform at its inception in the late eighties had the unique opportunity of coinciding with the period of the Uruguay Round of multilateral trade negotiations. It is significant to note that the Trade-Related Aspects of Intellectual Property Rights (TRIPs) Agreement was concluded in 1994 with the forming of the World Trade Organization (WTO), incorporating other multilateral and plurilateral agreements under a new GATT system. Nigeria is a founding member of the WTO and acceded to the TRIPs Agreement as a willing party to the new standard and instrument of trade in intellectual property. However, the Draft Industrial Property Law in Nigeria, though completed since 1991, has not been enacted into law. The Copyright Act was enacted in 1988 and has since been amended twice, in 1992 and 1999. More significantly, now that the transitional period of five years for developing country members has lapsed (by the year 2000), it has become crucial to revisit the Nigerian intellectual property regime. This is in view of the slow process of transition that has now characterized the landscape, spanning a decade, and which may well enter a second decade. This chapter, therefore, in giving an overview of intellectual property development in Nigeria, reviews the past, examines the present state of the law, and evaluates the prospects for future development of the law.

THE PAST

As would be expected, the historical evolution of intellectual property law in Nigeria followed the colonial pattern, although the pattern of introduction and administration of each of the three areas of the law differ. The first intellectual property law was in the area of trademarks, primarily because of the necessity to facilitate imperial trade in goods that had already filled the sprawling local market. The Trademarks Proclamation of 1900 was the first trademark law. By the proclamation, the United Kingdom Trademarks Act was made applicable to the then Southern Nigerian Protectorate. The proclamation became applicable by a 1914 ordinance to the whole of Nigeria with the amalgamation of the Southern and Northern Protectorates in 1914. This ordinance was, however, replaced with the Trademarks Ordinance no. 13 of 1926, which continued to be applied until after independence. The first postindependence intellectual property law was the Trademarks Act of 1965, which came into effect on June 1, 1967. It repealed the previous trademark legislation, which were consolidated in the 1958 revised laws.[1] The 1965 act is the substantive statute regulating trademarks in Nigeria after remaining on the statute books for about thirty-six years. The act was essentially fashioned after the English Trademark Act 1938, which itself was repealed by the Trademarks Act of 1994.

The first statute on copyright to be applied in Nigeria was the English Copyright Act 1911 applied by the Order-in-Council no. 912 of 1912. This law continued to apply until 1970 when the first post-independence copyright law was enacted in the Copyright Act of 1970. The Copyright Reciprocal Extension Order 1972 extended the application to the 1970 act of the Universal Copyright Convention, which Nigeria had acceded to in February 1962. The 1970 act was repealed and replaced with the Copyright Act of 1988. The Act was borne out of intense lobbying by the indigenous copyright industry which arose out of grave concern for the high level of piracy and lack of adequate copyright protection existing in the country.[2] The 1988 act preserved the 1972 order. With the 1992 and 1999 amendments to the copyright law, it could be said that copyright in Nigeria has witnessed more dynamic law reform initiative than the other areas of intellectual property.

The history of patent law in Nigeria has been a protracted one. It has spread over both independent and dependent eras.

The registration of U. K. Patent Ordinance of 1925 represented the dependent era, which provided for a re-registration of the United Kingdom patent system in Nigeria. Under it, patents were to be granted in the U. K., and enforced in Nigeria. Prior to this, there was the Patents Ordinance no. 30 of 1916, which in turn had repealed the earlier patent proclamation ordinances of 1900 and 1902, applicable to the Colony of Lagos/Southern Nigeria, and Northern Protectorate, respectively. In 1970, the Patents and Designs Act, the first postindependence patent statute, was promulgated. By this act, patents and designs rights could be granted in Nigeria without recourse to U. K. patent law.

THE PRESENT STATE OF THE LAW

Copyright

The background to the introduction of the 1988 Copyright Act with the two subsequent amendments has brought about remarkable law and policy reform with an accompanying mass of public interest in copyright issues. There is no doubt that the framework for protection as currently contained in the act has significantly extended the frontiers of copyright protection in Nigeria.[3] The framework of the act presents a comprehensive body of legislation that is remarkably responsive to conditions and to pressures for reform by the relevant copyright-based sectors. The act is in four parts and comprises five schedules. Within this thematic structure, the act establishes novel and far-reaching provisions in the development of a substantive and administrative regime of protection. Some of the salient features include a comprehensive threshold of rights under Part I, which comprises copyright provision dealing with substantive copyright protection. It includes, among other provisions, recognition and incorporation of the moral rights regime for the first time in the annals of copyright law in Nigeria. It defines the class of works eligible for copyright protection and the conditions for eligibility.[4] The protected works include literary works, artistic works, musical works, cinematograph film, sound recording, and broadcasts. It requires originality as the hallmark of eligibility for copyright protection as established in all copyright systems. "Originality" in copyright parlance relates to the expression of idea distinct from the ideas themselves.[5] In addition to originality, there is the condition of fixation, which requires that the work must have been fixed into a definite medium of expression from which it can be perceived, reproduced, or otherwise communicated either directly or with the aid of any machine or device. Also, the work must have been made by a qualified person who is a Nigerian citizen, or someone domiciled in Nigeria, or a corporate body under the laws of Nigeria.[6] Copyright in the protected classes of work vests "exclusive rights" of control in the copyright owner, who may not necessarily be the author. This brings to the fore the distinction between two important concepts, namely, authorship and ownership. While authorship describes a direct or inherent relationship between the work and its creator for which the moral right principle is applicable, ownership is much wider and more transactional in nature, encompassing different degrees of relationship of proprietary and juridical character with the work. Hence, "author" has been defined under the act in relation to the different classes of works.[7] A copyright owner would therefore include licensees and assignees of right in contractual transactions. The exclusive rights can be classified into three substantive types of rights under the act, namely, reproduction rights, performing rights, and publishing rights. They cumulatively describe the various acts over which the copyright owner can exercise exclusive right of control, in the nature of reproduction, publication, performance, distribution, communication, broadcast, translation, adaptation, or recording of the works as outlined in the act.[8] Ownership of copyright under the act is vested initially in the author, however, parties may vary the statutory position by contract or assignment.

For the first time in Nigerian copyright law, the regime of neighboring right protection for performers and expressions of folklore was introduced under Part II of the act. With this provision, live performances and traditional folklore, which are not copyrightable because of their inability to fit into the essential copyright paradigm, are now protected. This is perhaps, on the one hand, born out of response to international initiatives in the advancement of neighboring and indigenous rights fields, particularly the Rome Convention to which Nigeria is a signatory. On the other hand, it represents a progression in the dynamics of the copyright reform process in filling the lacuna created by the absence of performers and traditional folkloric renditions in the regime of protection. Very importantly, in Part III, the Act recorded another novel achievement in the establishment of the Nigerian Copyright Commission, a statutory body responsible for the administration and supervision of copyright matters. Since 1989, the commission has established the machinery for copyright administration in fulfillment of its statutory and regulatory functions. In doing so, the commission is complemented by other agencies such as the copyright inspectors, who are primarily responsible for public enforcement of copyright, and the copyright licensing panel, responsible for the granting of compulsory licenses. The commission is directly responsible for the approval of collecting societies.[9] Its regulatory activities under this provision in the last decade have far more than any other provisions of the act, affected the present state of copyright in Nigeria, particularly as it relates to the approval of collecting societies. It is important to note that it is in this area that the two amendments to the principal act were made. The 1992 amendment established the commission's framework for approval of collecting administration, and the 1999 amendment strengthened the commission's regulatory powers arising from the controversies generated, especially within the music industry, over the interpretation of the scope of its powers under the 1992 amendment. By the 1999 amendment, collective enforcement of copyright is heavily regulated by the commission.[10] Part IV generally provides for miscellaneous matters such as reciprocal extension of protection, presumptions, restriction of importation of printed copies, regulations, jurisdiction, and other matters.

Trademarks

The Trademarks Act defines "trademark" as:

> a mark used or proposed to be used in relation to goods for the purpose of indicating, or so as to indicate, a connection in the course of trade between the goods and some person having either as proprietor or as registered user to use the mark, whether with or without any indication of identity of that person.[11]

The definition appears unnecessarily complicated for a simple marketing device for indicating the origin and value of a product in the marketplace. This is especially so in view of the fact that the marks protected are restrictive in scope as the act only protects trademark or trade name, certification marks, and defensive registration of well-known marks. It does not, for example, protect service marks, collective marks, and distinctive shapes of goods or sensory marks which are part of the essential features of most trademark laws. The act provides for registration and registrability of marks under two registers, namely parts A and B. It outlines the essential particulars for registration under the registers. A mark is generally registrable for reason of distinctiveness. However, the distinctiveness may either be inherent or factual in nature.[12] The Act also provides for the procedure for registration.[13] It provides for transfer and assignment of marks. A mark can be assigned with or without the goodwill of the business. Although, registration under the act confers a right of action against infringement of a mark, it is also possible to bring a common law action for "passing off" in cases of unregistered marks,[14] thus, making the protection a dual one, for both registered and unregistered marks.

The high rate of counterfeiting and piracy has increasingly accentuated the importance of trademarks and the need to strengthen the protection of trademarks in the current national drive toward the attainment of economic and industrial development. Toward this end, the Trademark Act is complemented by two important pieces of legislation, namely, the Trade Malpractices Act of 1992 and the National Office of Technology Acquisition and Promotion (NOTAP) Act, originally of 1979 and amended in 1992. The former act appears to strengthen the enforcement of trademark rights by imposing criminal sanctions against counterfeiters for labeling, packaging, and selling. It also imposes sanctions on offering for sale, or advertising any product in a manner that is fake or misleading or is likely to create a wrong impression as to its quality, character, brand name, value, composition, merit, or safety. It introduces novel enforcement measures in the current war against piracy and counterfeiting through the establishment of special tribunals which provide a much-needed forum for an expeditious and effective prosecution of offenders. The latter act is significant from the standpoint of trademarks and patents, more generically described as industrial property as a vital instrument of transfer of technology with crucial relevance to the realization of rapid technological growth and to the foreign investment objectives contained in recent national economic policies. The NOTAP Act provides a framework for the transfer of technology involving trademark and patent rights. It provides a scheme for registration, licensing, and monitoring of transactions for the use or transfer of trademarks and patents. It essentially seeks to protect the Nigerian users or licensees of foreign marks or patented technology in any technical agreement or similar transaction for the overall purpose of promoting local technological development. In doing so, it gives NOTAP the power to refuse to register any contract containing clauses that are restrictive to technological development. This includes clauses limiting research and development by a transferee, tie-in-clauses, or onerous and unconscionable clauses.[15] The act provides for a voluntary registration scheme. Non-registration of a contract under the act does not render the contract invalid; it merely results in the loss of the privilege of remittance of foreign earnings. The act therefore has inadvertently made itself irrelevant in the matter of acquisition of technology for which it was initially introduced. The judicial endorsement of this position in the well-cited court of appeal decision in *Beecham Group Limited v. Essdee Food Products Limited* has consistently supported the common view that the provision undermines the underlying and laudable objective of the act in ensuring an effective transfer of industrial property rights and technology with the attendant flow of foreign investment.[16] Recent foreign investment legislation which ensures unrestricted transferability of funds in dividends, profits, or remittance of proceeds accruable to foreign investors as a way of promoting foreign investment has largely reduced the importance of NOTAP and, indeed, the contribution of industrial property to the economic and technological development of the country. What is required is a mandatory system of registration without unduly restricting the flow of transactional funds as a way of encouraging foreign investment.

Patents

The Patents and Designs Act 1965 contains provisions regulating the grant of patent and design rights in Nigeria. It provides for the protection of patents as a limited monopoly right for a one-term period of twenty years accorded to the statutory inventor on a first to file basis. It provides for patentability requirements, namely, that the invention must be new, result from inventive activity, and be capable of industrial application. The important requirement of disclosure in the act is consistent with the function of the patent system as an important information resource for inventors and industry. The scope of patents cover inventions in all fields of technology except those specifically exempted. The exempted inventions are, first, those in respect of plant or animal varieties or essentially biological processes for the production of plants or animals (other than micro-biological processes and products resulting from such processes) and, second, those whose use would be contrary to public order or morality. The act provides for enforcement of the patent rights in the event of infringement. The general thrust of patent rights under the act has been generally considered as entrenching a high standard of inventiveness which needs to be relaxed or moderated to fit into the country's level of technological development. It also involves incorporating utility models and reducing the range of disclosure from a universal to a national standard to allow indigenous inventive activity to take off.

FUTURE DEVELOPMENT

There are two important challenges to the future development of intellectual property in Nigeria. First, there is the current law reform effort represented in the Draft Industrial Property Law which presents a model for the future direction of the law. Public awareness of the of need for the protection of intellectual property has increased remarkably. The growth of entertainment and intellectual property-based industries and the marked sophistication of marketing strategies and recent sectored planning are important factors for consideration. The government's current drive toward establishing a sound industrial and technological base for sustainable development has more than ever before brought the economic importance of intellectual property to the fore. More particularly, the National Industrial Policy and the National Technology Policy have established the long-term goal of improving the technological skills and capabilities of the country. It is common knowledge that this cannot be effectively achieved through the present patent regime in the sense that a viable patents system must be used to stimulate innovation and the adaptation of existing technology to the country's peculiar needs, particularly as a developing country in search of economic and technological development. The copyright regime has traveled on a faster track, though not necessarily on a better lane. The copyright act has expanded the threshold of the substantive rights of authors, and with the introduction of moral, and neighboring, including artist's resale rights, has significantly enhanced the regime of protection. Although, it has not completely solved the problem of collective administration, largely because of the volatility of the subject and the politics of the copyright industry, there is no doubt the momentum for reform is already set.

It is important to note that the Draft Industrial Property Law, which was prepared by the Nigerian Law Reform Commission in 1991, has addressed some of the substantive and administrative law reform initiatives in the development of the law of patents, designs, and trademarks in Nigeria. It has also set the law on the path of future growth. The establishment of a central Industrial Property Office (IPO) with a greater degree of autonomy than the present Trademark and Patents Registry is instructive. Under the new IPO, the draft law proposes the following registries for an effective and efficient intellectual property regime in Nigeria:

a. Patents, Utility Certificates, and Designs Registry;
b. Trademarks Registry;
c. Technology Transfer Registry; and;
d. Industrial Property Documentation Center.[17]

Overall, nine registers are to be established to administer the wide spectrum of rights which the draft law proposes to protect. These include the registers of patents, utility certificates, industrial designs, trademarks, service marks, certification marks, collective marks, industrial property contracts, and industrial property agents. These far-reaching substantive and administrative reforms when legislated will certainly secure an enhanced intellectual property regime in line with the general requirement of TRIPs. One essential TRIPs concern about the Nigerian law relates to enforcement of intellectual property, which cannot be divorced from the wider problem of law enforcement and administration of justice. TRIPs' extensive civil and criminal procedures, including the provisional measures and the special border measures with regards to enforcement of intellectual property in member countries, have raised compatibility questions. TRIPs' general obligation enjoins member countries to ensure an effective and expeditious system of enforcement of its agreements.[18] The enforcement of intellectual property therefore faces TRIPs' critical test, particularly as an integral part of the general administration and enforcement of law in Nigeria, commonly regarded as inefficient and lack-luster. Within this context, the importance of the draft law is underscored by the establishment of the Industrial Property Tribunal (IPT), because of its crucial role in the enforcement of industrial property in line with TRIPs standards.

The development of intellectual property law in Nigeria has had a unique and checkered history. It has continued to engage contemporary debate in the tension between its role in the economic and technological development of the country and the current global demands for uniform global standards and increased protection by all countries. The resolution of the tension for a developing country like Nigeria involves due recognition of the national condition and how the law could best fulfill its developmental needs. Happily enough, the law reform initiative has captured the cardinal philosophy of protection within the context of relevant national policy measures but, sadly this reform effort has not yet been matched with the commensurate political will, the most decisive of all factors.

NOTES

1. The Revised Edition (Laws of the Federation and Lagos) Ordinance, 1958.
2. Bankole Shodipo, *Piracy and Counterfeiting: GATT, TRIPS and Developing Countries* (Boston: Kluwer Law International, 1997), 27.
3. Adebambo Adewopo, "Legal Framework for Copyright Protection in Nigeria," in Lanre Fagbohun and Bambo Adewopo (eds.), *Developments and Reforms: Nigeria's Commercial Laws* (Lagos: Lagos State University Law Center, 1998), 41 and 45.
4. Copyright Act, 1988 as amended, Section 1.
5. *University of London Press v. University Tutorial Press*, 1961, 2 Ch. 601, and *Sony Music Corp. of America v. Universal City Studios*, 1984, 464, U.S., 417.
6. Copyright Act, 1988 as amended, Section 2.

7. Ibid., Section 39.
8. Ibid., Section 5.
9. Ibid. Section 32B.
10. Ibid. Section 15A.
11. Trademark Act, 1965, Section 67.
12. Ibid., Sections 9 and 10.
13. Ibid., Sections 17-25.
14. Ibid., Section 3.
15. NOTAP Act, Section 6.
16. Draft Industrial Property Law, Section 11.
17. Draft Industrial Law, 1991, Section 13.
18. Ibid., Part III, particularly Article 41.

PART B

ECONOMY AND SOCIETY

7

POLITICIZATION OF MERCHANT CAPITAL DURING DECOLONIZATION: EUROPEAN BUSINESS IN NIGERIA, 1948-1951[1]

G. Ugo Nwokeji

INTRODUCTION

The legacy of merchant capital is strong in contemporary Nigeria.[2] The United Africa Company (UAC), Patterson Zochonis (PZ), Shell, Bata, Cadbury, and John Holt are significant players in the distribution-oriented economy. A thriving compradorial class fortifies the system.[3] These realities resulted from struggles over conflicting ideas about decolonization during its early phase, 1948-1951. The politicization[4] of merchant capital was central to these struggles. Politicization involved an attempt by European business to influence the other political actors, particularly the officials.[5] This process entailed a public relations offensive geared to the Nigerian mass media and civil society. It also involved demands for increased representation in the legislature and special consultation in public policy formulation. In other words, merchant capital attempted to be a direct player in the constitutional negotiations for independence and to secure institutionalized roles in post-independence state structures. For its part, officialdom favored a compromise solution that took into consideration the new realities of post-World War II politics. Officialdom sought to get European business to link its interests to those of the capitalist-oriented nationalist elite, rather than to constitute a parallel political movement. This chapter examines these struggles. It stresses that, and explains why, officialdom compelled merchant capital to act in a particular manner at that particular time. This approach derives from the belief that an accurate description of the events will provide a basis for future inquiries, such as an inquiry into the utility of the approach that merchant capital was compelled to adopt.

The politicization of merchant capital during decolonization in Africa has attracted the attention of only a few scholars.[6] The works of D. K. Fieldhouse, Josephine Milburn, and Sarah Stockwell stand out. Milburn concluded that merchant capital was lukewarm to the political changes in post-World War II Ghana.[7] For his part, Fieldhouse has stated that merchant capital "certainly . . . did not regard [decolonization] as the logical consequence of a process of restructuring colonial economies to the point at which political control was no longer necessary or desirable."[8] This comment is particularly insightful. It means, by extension, that merchant capital pursued a policy of political intervention. This view differs from Milburn's view of a politically lukewarm merchant capital. Yet, Fieldhouse declares that merchant capital never thought very clearly about the prospects of decolonization.[9] With privileged access to the records of UAC, Fieldhouse maintains that the company appraised post-World War II nationalist tide as politically inspired anti-UAC sentiments, but that there "seems to have been no sense that a new world was being born."[10] In effect, Fieldhouse maintains his earlier argument that politicization came later, in the 1950s. The first mention of politics and indigenous opinion that survives in the company's records is in 1953; and thereafter political considerations became a predominant theme in Unilever calculations.[11] To Fieldhouse, therefore, merchant capital's political involvement would fall outside the time frame of the present chapter.

Fieldhouse's views on merchant capital's politicization during decolonization demand detailed attention because of their significance. Although Fieldhouse's recent major work, *Merchant Capital*, confines its focus to UAC, it embodies data that are extremely valuable in illuminating the events, especially with respect to intra- and inter-firm relations. UAC was a central player in these relations. Fieldhouse recognizes that anti-UAC feelings were strong and that "company relations" appeared regularly on the agenda of UAC's board.[12] But, to him, this development represented merely a postwar intensification of the long-standing but previously spasmodic anti-UAC sentiments.[13] He therefore treats UAC's reactions during 1948-1951 elements of routine internal reorganization. In spite of the insights that Fieldhouse has brought to politicization, his non-use of the Colonial Office records reflects not only on his periodization but also on his conclusions regarding the aims, motivations, and methods of merchant capital. His inferences differ significantly from the impression that one can draw from the Colonial Office records. Fieldhouse's rich data are therefore most usefully complemented with these records. His data should be combined with the government records and with the Nigerian conjuncture for a fuller understanding of the events of the era.

More recently, Stockwell has shown in the Ghana case that merchant capital fought vigorously for the incorporation of its interests when decolonization came to the table.[14] Although the pace of political change was too fast to be anticipated by British businessmen (and officials, one may add), "talk of political change featured" among them as early as 1941.[15] Unlike Milburn and Fieldhouse, Stockwell incorporates evidence from the recently declassified Colonial Office records. Stockwell has called for similar work to be done on other colonies.[16] The present chapter addresses this problem as it pertains to Nigeria on which no such work has yet appeared. The fact that merchant capital had a larger presence in that country, certainly during decolonization, makes the Nigerian case particularly relevant. It is important, therefore, to examine precisely how merchant capital responded to decolonization in Nigeria. After all, businesses traditionally change with their environments.[17] The dearth of relevant work on Nigeria must be at least partly responsible for scholars' assumption that merchant capital and officialdom had unproblematic relations, and for the tendency to conflate the two social forces. Olukoju's recent work on the interwar period is a remarkable departure. That work indicates that merchant capital responded politically to the demands of the time.[18] This tradition of quick response continued and, for the obvious reason of decolonization, intensified during the 1948-1951 period. The politicization of merchant capital during this period also witnessed a broadening of methods, particularly the use of a strong London lobby. Although Stockwell stresses in her work on the Gold Coast that British businesses held conflicting visions regarding appropriate political responses, these conflicts apparently did not reflect on merchant capital's platform or achievements in Nigeria.

In examining merchant capital's approach to politicization in Nigeria, I will first characterize the internal developments that conditioned the official reactions. My analysis terminates in 1951 because the various interests involved had accepted the principle of decolonization by that year, when the Macpherson Constitution enshrined the principle of independence.[19] The provisions of this document have been analyzed and are well represented in the Nigerian constitutional historiography.[20] But because the works came out before the relevant Colonial Office records were declassified, it was not possible for their authors to describe the struggles that enabled merchant capital to achieve increased representation in the center and representation in the regions. The tendency to confine analyses to the relations that existed between officials and nationalists obscures the political role of merchant capital during the period. Merchant capital was an important political actor. To underline this point, merchant capital's political role should be situated, even if only briefly, in its theoretical and historical contexts.

CONTEXT

Political scientists have articulated the conditions for the politicization of business around several assumptions. The basic assumption is that politicization is rare because it is difficult to pursue. The competing demands of the share/stakeholders, the customers, and the local and international communities are among the commonly identified impediments to successful politicization. Other problems arise from the multiplicity of businesses, divergent political tendencies, sectional biases, and interfirm competition.[21] These standard theoretical assumptions originated in industrial democratic polities. By 1948, they either did not, or had ceased to, obtain in Nigeria. Although not homogeneous,[22] the European business community was a close-knit circle without such impediments as endemic ethnic and sectarian conflicts. Even if business tends to avoid political involvement in the absence of strong peer support,[23] this support was solid in Nigeria behind UAC's leadership. Further, it was not just profit or the life of a single firm that was at stake during decolonization, but the future of merchant capital itself. These conditions enabled the Association of West African Merchants (AWAM), regarded as "a semi-moribund organization," effectively to project the political interests of merchant capital.[24]

Following World War II, officialdom began to redefine its relationship with merchant capital in a way that accommodated the burgeoning nationalist elite. This trend arose from three interrelated historical developments involving the colonial state, the Nigerian nationalist elite, and European merchant capital itself. The politicization of merchant capital occurred in the context of the growth, expansion, and consolidation of the three social forces. These processes gave intensity to the struggle and great significance to its outcome. The processes merit close examination. It is appropriate to start with the developments that occurred within the business community.

These developments center on the march toward the consolidation of many small and competing European enterprises from the late nineteenth century onward. Consolidation gained momentum with the depression of the late 1920s and the 1930s. Its most important landmark was perhaps the formation of UAC in 1929. By 1945, all the substantial expatriate firms in West Africa, except PZ and John Holt, were subsidiaries of UAC.[25] UAC was henceforth largely representative of European business in Nigeria. Despite its strategic dissociation from local subsidiaries, UAC controlled its varied colony/country operations through a regional general manager. This officer and "his very large staff throughout the colony constituted virtually a parallel administration" to the government. The general manager "was almost always the leading figure in the local chamber of commerce" which consisted mostly of representatives of UAC's subsidiaries. He was often a member of the Legislative Council and "had close contacts" with the governor.[26] Then "the whole character of Unilever's stake in Africa began to change fundamentally" with the establishment of the Produce Marketing Boards in 1947. African agents came increasingly into produce-buying, hitherto the preserve of expatriate firms.[27] This trend is relevant to the politicization of merchant capital in the 1948-1951 period. It is by definition part of the Africanization program that merchant capital would oppose in that period.

The second element in the politicization of merchant capital relates to the circumstances of the colonial state. In postwar Nigeria, the state had grown strong enough to assert itself more forcefully. Through the Colonial Development and Welfare (CD&W) program, Whitehall mounted a development offensive, involving massive state intervention in the economy. This process has aptly been termed the "second colonial occupation."[28] The most important question that arose "was whether the British Empire could negate . . . the autonomy of the individual British capitalists and bear the burden of becoming a fully-fledged, centralized imperial state capable of carrying out this mission."[29] Simultaneously, the new version of interventionism exposed the state to all the economic grievances of the colonized peoples.[30] The nationalists and the workers mounted sustained pressure, explicitly demanding the withdrawal of the British from Nigeria.[31] The colonial state tried to address these pressures through a combination of political and economic reforms as well as security measures. I have elsewhere chronicled with recently available data the systematic manner by which the state combined coercive and reform tactics during the period.[32]

The third process relevant to the postwar politicization of merchant capital was the culmination of what Ken Post calls the "militant phase of the nationalist movement"[33] in the 1945-1951 period. This was the era when the Nnamdi Azikiwe-led National Council of Nigeria and the Cameroons (NCNC), an ideologically unstable party, was at the center of the Nigerian nationalist movement. Radical nationalism under the umbrella of the Zikist Movement (an NCNC affiliate) gained momentum after the "Accra riots" of March 1948.[34] Through Azikiwe's group of newspapers, which the Zikists seem to have dominated, the radicals stepped up their propaganda campaign. They emphasized that the colonial state existed to serve British interests, especially in merchant capital. The Accra incident, according to Zikists, had rendered self-government imminent in the Gold Coast and reinforced the relevance of violent action. A secret intelligence report of the time captures these developments and also gives insight into the economic conditions in the country:

> Interest in the ["Accra riots"] might have waned were it not for the fact that certain elements mostly connected with the NCNC began to use the prevalent economic ills to stir trouble. The main planks in the propaganda platform were the price paid to farmers for cocoa compared with the price obtained for it overseas; conditional sales and the black market, believed to be organized by Europeans, for their own profit; the high price of imported goods arbitrarily fixed by Government for the benefit of Europeans; the belief that the UAC and Government are hand in glove in exploiting Africans and, of course, the iniquities of the AWAM. Attempts were made to make the people believe that only [through] boycott and rioting could these evils be remedied.[35]

The nationalist movement had reached its peak. As the ideological differences between the moderate and radical nationalists crystallized, the colonial regime exploited the crisis. It began more actively to incorporate the moderates, whom it never really regarded as fundamental enemies.[36] The dangerous elements were the radicals, the members of the Zikist Movement and militant labor who tended to articulate an alternative political economy. These were the ones who were arrested, imprisoned, shot and exiled.[37] The strategy of actively incorporating the moderate nationalists informed officialdom's response to merchant capital's demands during the period 1948-1951.

It is clear from the foregoing that the nationalists, the colonial state, and merchant capital had all gained significant strength. The nationalists were now a formidable force. The colonial state was now strong enough to mediate, if not to stave off, crises. And merchant capital was now well-placed to make its case forcefully, striving to do so in an atmosphere of perceived government "hostility."[38] Thus, the trio—the state, merchant capital, and the nationalist elite—was set for a confrontation that must be decisive even if it did not produce clear victors.

POLITICAL DEVELOPMENT AND RESPONSE

Merchant capital's political response followed the agitations of UAC's African workers in 1948. These agitations germinated under the auspices of the Amalgamated Union of UAC African Workers' Union (UNAMAG), the largest union in colonial Nigeria. This union was formed and led by Nduka Eze, a young and radical Zikist with strong and well-known views on British colonialism, merchant capital, and the desirable direction of Nigerian nationalism. Eze succeeded in fusing labor and the Zikist Movement when he took over the acting presidency of the Zikist Movement. When the major union combine, the Trades Union Congress (TUC), disaffiliated from the NCNC in 1949, Eze formed the Nigerian National Federation of Labor (NNFL) and remained with the NCNC. This move attenuated the effect of the TUC's disaffiliation from the nationalist movement. More importantly, labor and the Zikist Movement were fused under the double influence of Eze, known in the secret intelligence community as "an avowed Communist."[39] By this move Eze, who was also a member of the NCNC cabinet, accomplished his dream of "linking the labor movement to the Zikist Movement for revolutionary action."[40] Contrary to the impression that Fieldhouse gives, UAC, whose workers Eze was organizing, did not take these developments merely as a politically inconsequential intensification of familiar anti-UAC feelings. As we will see below, UAC's political measures from 1948 seem to have been taken in either anticipation of, or response to, the Eze-led agitations.

The secretary of UAC's board, A.R.I. Mellor, recommended in April 1948 that European personnel officers might "constitute themselves [as] an unofficial intelligence service for discovering and reporting on outside trends or movements."[41] Mellor also recommended that a team of experts visit West Africa. This team was to include an anthropologist, a sociologist, a psychologist, and "particularly someone with organizational experience."[42] It is unclear if any such team went to West Africa. What is clear is that Mellor himself visited West Africa in mid-1948. Evidently, Mellor's activities during that visit were political. He held meetings with the European and African managers, and with senior government officials including the governors. He also sought audience with "local African rulers, African traders, and as representative a sample of public opinion . . . as could be mustered outside the Company."[43] That Mellor spent all eight weeks of his visit in Nigeria (except for five days spent in the Gold Coast) is an indication of the political importance of the Nigerian end of UAC's operations.

The report that Mellor wrote at the end of his visit was clearly political, a political response to a political situation. Mellor emphasized the need for rapport between the European and African staff of the company. He recommended the holding of regular meetings and the forging of closer interaction between the two groups. The report also enjoined senior European staff to participate actively in community affairs. This call specified the surreptitious encouragement of the politically ambitious African senior staff who wished to stand for election to the Legislative Council. Mellor addressed the need for public image-making and the immediate establishment of a newsletter to publicize the social schemes of the company. The image-making component of the political strategy called for extra-company "contacts" with the indigenous press and a move to overcome the hostility of government officials and the nationalistic and "anti-white" orientation of Nigerian youth. Therefore, school children needed regular lectures by the UAC staff whose aim would be to reorient the young people. Mellor's report recommended the establishment of technical training schools that would produce "a corps d'elite." To this end, there was a need to appoint a "lecturer" who must "be a spell-binder [and who] would talk about the Company's history and role, and to give the African a really unvarnished history of his own country."[44] In the meantime on 17 June 1948, UAC made "a gift of £1,000 per annum for two years [to] Lagos ex-servicemen.... UAC consider their support 'politically' desirable."[45] The political importance of ex-servicemen in post-World War II West African politics requires no emphasis. The company also appointed one Mr. Newman as "Information Officer" in mid-1948. The appointment was also made as a result of the agitations of UAC workers under the auspices of Eze's UNAMAG.[46] This appointment is important because of the political role that Newman would attempt to play in the following year. Mellor's recommendation for the appointment of a "lecturer" indicates that the appointment of an information officer was inadequate in the scheme of UAC strategists. This "Company's role" in the "unvarnished history" of Nigeria might imply driving home the point that the history of the country and the company were inseparable. UAC's precursor, the Royal Niger Company, ruled much of Nigeria by a royal charter before the British government took over direct control of the colonial venture in 1900. Given this background, a spellbinder could generate tomorrow's leaders' gratitude to the UAC for founding their country!

Mellor also recommended less overt political measures, but measures that had a clear strategic coloration. The measures included the award of scholarships to African staff and their children, and the rejuvenation of the existing scholarship schemes for junior staff. Nigeria received six of the nine scholarships available in 1948.[47] The scholarships for employees' children were valued at £20 to £50 annually over a five-year period.[48] At about the same time, UAC established non-restricted scholarships for students of the newly established University College, Ibadan, approvable by the Company's Panel of Experts.[49] Pedler commented that "nothing did more to improve UAC's reputation among West Africans."[50] Indeed, the authors of the political intelligence summaries in mid-December 1948 included these scholarships among the main politically significant events.[51] A late 1948 intelligence report projected, like UAC, that the scholarships would ensure for the affected children "the educational opportunities necessary to fit them to play a worthy part in their country's development."[52] In the context of decolonization, these are weighty words. UAC's public relations strategy appeared to place merchant capital in line with the path which the Colonial Office had favored since late 1947.[53] But the European firms had plans for direct intervention in Nigerian politics. They did not plan to be mere spectators in the decolonization process.

BATTLING FOR THE STAKES

By early 1950, the colonial secret intelligence community had known for some time that "certain firms *were* indeed willing to keep a larger European staff than *was* commercially justifiable in order to permit their members to participate in the work of the legislature."[54] This practice probably began as early as 1948 when UAC, for instance, could make "politically desirable" donations, set up an intelligence unit to report on other movements and organizations, and appoint an "information officer" and a "lecturer." That same year, UAC's managing director, Frank Samuel, visited Nigeria. The scanty available record[55] of Samuel's visit indicates that he made news voicing concerns about the problem of swollen shoot disease in cocoa, thus giving the impression that he was in West Africa because of the disease.[56]

Given the political atmosphere of the times and UAC's appreciation of the events, it is unlikely that the managing director/sole administrator of UAC was in Nigeria at that time merely to discuss swollen shoot disease, or that he would fail to score political points, using this opportunity. The fact that he kept the agenda of his visit hidden, apparently even from the lower-rank officers who wrote the intelligence reports, suggests that his visit was of a political nature. There is compelling evidence for this. First, the intelligence summaries of 14 January 1949, which referred to "Samuel's recent visit", managed to suggest a liaison between colonial officers and merchant capital in regard to "the political situation."[57] Second, Samuel titled his report to the UAC board on 28 January 1949, aptly, "the political aspects of the situation." We find in the sketchy available information that the "Nigerian press just lately has been the most violent and abusive that can be imagined against Government and against white English. Newspapers [are] read by all the youths just leaving school." The UAC chiefs noted the ethnic cleavages within the Nigerian nationalist movement and speculated on their impact on the future of the country. They also noted the people's disillusionment with colonial development. The attitude of the nationalist elite toward the company drew cynical comments. "In Nigeria [as opposed to the Gold Coast, the] situation is different and all they think of is what advantages they will gain by destroying UAC."[58]

The first known specific attempt to interfere directly with politics was in July 1949 when Chief Public Relations Officer Newman of UAC went to initiate contacts with the Colonial Office. He made the political nature of his visit crystal clear. He even asked to see the colonial secretary himself. But the Colonial Office officials could not recognize the political content of Newman's suggestions. Newman had gone to inquire about the extent to which "the British commercial interests in West Africa would be consulted in regard to the forthcoming constitutional changes."[59] His tactics for coping with the volatile political situation included fraternizing with Nigerian newspaper editors in order to "instill into them unobtrusively some of the ethics of journalism, e.g. the separation of news from views, in the effort to break down distrust." Newman intimated that he was working in close collaboration with the public relations department of the Nigerian government.[60] Yet, Blackbourne, the official who received him at the Colonial Office, thought that UAC's image maker had merely wished "to show himself as being a person of some consequence—and not that he wishes to raise any practical matter." Blackbourne dismissed Newman as a former unsuccessful junior applicant for employment in Blackbourne's department. Blackbourne opposed the idea of Newman meeting with the colonial secretary because it "might create an unfortunate impression in West Africa if the news got abroad that Unilever's P.R.O. deals directly with the Secretary of State." Other officials shared this appraisal.[61] The reasons for the Colonial Office action are fairly clear. These reasons are related to intensified nationalist activity and the new policy on Africanization. Africanization was perceived as a precondition for decolonization.

Officialdom had begun to articulate a program of Africanization of political and bureaucratic posts in early 1948 at the latest. This program involved giving in to some of the yearnings of the commercial section of the Nigerian elite.[62] Officialdom thought that the most effective means for merchant capital to secure its interests was to court the friendship of the modernizing elite. Any gestures to the contrary were discouraged. For example, in late 1948, newly appointed Governor Macpherson expected that the Nigerian Legislative Council members would oppose the UAC's push for £250,000 in annual royalties on mines and he advised that

> the Company might be induced to further badly needed goodwill by an offer to plough back any capital sum they might receive by constituting a trust fund which would be devoted, e.g. to University College endowments, development schemes for workers in industry, etc. It is expected that the Governor will explore this suggestion with Company representatives.[63]

Officialdom knew that merchant capital could not on its own actualize its version of the neocolonial agenda. Officialdom also knew that the British State would be called upon ultimately to deploy the coercive instruments necessary to deal with anticipated mass uprisings. The British State could not do this simultaneously in the Far East and in East, Central, and West Africa.[64] The Colonial Office instructed the Nigerian government in August 1949 that UAC and other firms "will not in any circumstances be consulted behind the scenes about constitutional changes."[65] But the UAC board in London decided in October 1949 that the proposals for representation in Nigeria did not adequately represent European interests, and to bring this "to the notice of Members of the two Houses [of Parliament]."[66]

Further developments in Nigerian politics seemed to place merchant capital's goals farther from realization. In November 1949, the colonial police shot and killed twenty-nine miners, and wounded many others, at the Enugu colliery. This incident triggered a flurry of events. It greatly embarrassed the state and presented it with a set of challenges. It also led to a national (if temporary) coalition of the different factions of the nationalist elite, labor and other indigenous groups. This coalition resulted in the formation of the National Emergency Committee (NEC).[67] The shooting provided Zikists with further reasons to organize violent mass protests in Aba, Onitisha, and Port Harcourt. In their national conference held in Kaduna in December 1949, the Zikists passed a vote of "no confidence in the British Government which has become destructive to the ends for which governments of people are instituted." They also resolved, among other things, to withhold tax payment from government and to pay tax instead to national organizations in order "to paralyse Britain's economy;" institute a military training program for young Nigerians; and "to carry out reprisals bordering on assassination of British officers viz., Commissioners, Residents, Governor, Chief Secretary and so on."[68] The ensuing crackdown on the movement prevented the consummation of their plans. But the lessons were clear. This kind of incident should not reoccur. Moreover, the moderate nationalist intelligentsia, who collaborated with the colonial establishment in destroying the Zikist Movement, could not continue to collaborate against radicalist insurgency if they were not stakeholders in the political economy. The *Economist* in July 1947 had already called for concessions to "intelligent Africans" as "counterweight to Zikism."[69]

In spite of the setback of the colliery shooting, AWAM continued to press its case for increased representation in the proposed central legislature. But it waited till June 1950 to renew its request for an audience with the colonial secretary and for European business to present its views on the political negotiations for independence, as it had done in the Gold Coast. Mellor observed correctly that political developments in Nigeria appeared "to be reaching a decisive stage."[70] The Colonial Office agreed to a meeting with AWAM's representatives.[71] In the meeting, AWAM submitted a memorandum that commented extensively on the political situation in Nigeria and West Africa as a whole and on the political interests of merchant capital. The document was couched in corporate-sector arrogance. AWAM claimed that the proposed constitutional reforms for Nigeria would compromise European business interests should merchant capital not partake in the negotiations. Such a situation, it warned, would undermine merchant capital's confidence in the government. The memo connected the interests of merchant capital to those of the British State. "The economic development of West Africa is important not only to the external economy of the United Kingdom, but also to the equilibrium of world trade in general." The thrust of the document was a demand for merchant capital's direct participation in constitutional negotiations. Business felt that Governor Macpherson of Nigeria had pandered to the nationalists when he proposed that only three members of the proposed central legislature would "represent interests . . . not otherwise adequately represented." In their view, this number "would be entirely inadequate to achieve the desired purpose." AWAM also made a case for its purported indispensability in the political process. It claimed that its position in the country bestowed special experience and knowledge of the country that its members would bring to the legislature. It would provide legislative experience and knowledge which are not available from its African members but are vital to a successful solution of economic development with which the country will be faced as it advances on the road of self-government . . . . The experience and knowledge which we think should be available to the legislature are obtainable in [the merchant capitalist] communities and nowhere else; not even in Government Departments which deal with Commerce, Industry and kindred subjects. The need for such special members is even stronger in Nigeria than in the Gold Coast [where such membership had been granted], because Nigeria is so much larger, more diversified and less developed than the Gold Coast.[72]

AWAM made specific proposals on the future structure of the Nigerian State. It argued that the "specialist advice" that its members were already offering to the government would be most suitably realized in the lower chamber of a bicameral legislature. In this connection, the quota of "special members" of the lower chamber of 122 members should be set at a ratio of 1:10. This would bring the Nigerian situation up to par with that of the Gold Coast where 6 to 8 "special members" were being proposed in a legislature of 70 members. The important issue was not that the ratio be accurate; rather, it was that the minimum merchant capitalist representation in Nigeria be 10 members so as to enable AWAM experts more effectively to impart their special knowledge. One clause demanded "special interest" representation in the regional legislatures and made a case for even higher ratios there than in the Gold Coast. The rationale for this calculation was that each of the Nigerian regions was as large as or larger than the whole of the Gold Coast, and had a far higher population. Moreover, the memo continued, the Nigerian federal structure provided "a much more advanced measure of decentralization." This high degree of autonomy made it critical that merchant capitalist interests be well represented in the proposed regional Houses of Assembly. AWAM also demanded for a special clause in the proposed constitution against racial and religious discrimination. The ostensible basis for this demand was that the possibility of discrimination would "discourage the inflow of capital and technical skill."[73] This was aimed to counter Africanization and was probably intended as protection against possible nationalization and indigenization of businesses by nationalist politicians.

Finally, AWAM argued that in Nigeria the chambers of commerce, through which the government customarily consulted merchant capital, were no longer "suitable for the purpose" of representing merchant capital's interests. (Africans had been represented in the chambers of commerce since 1929).[74] AWAM proposed the establishment of an Economic Advisory Council (EAC) in place of the chambers of commerce. By presenting this proposal, AWAM aimed at undercutting the indigenous rivals of merchant capital. AWAM urged that the proposed EAC not be enshrined in the proposed constitution, in order for the council to outlive constitutions and governments.[75] This way, AWAM hoped to perpetuate and institutionalize the dominance of merchant capital and to secure it from nationalist power. AWAM was bidding for guarantees. It called for "anti-discrimination legislation", while insisting that control of the police "remain in the hands of an ex-officio member of the legislature."[76] This measure would guarantee that the coercive instruments of the state remained in European hands. Given the elaborate security measures that the British State was putting in place for the colonies,[77] the colonial state was not in a hurry to relinquish police control in the first place.

Thirteen representatives of the various European enterprises and syndicates operating in Nigeria met with the colonial secretary on 27 June 1950 to discuss AWAM's proposals. In attendance were representatives of UAC, John Holt and Co. (Liverpool) Ltd., Cadbury Brothers Ltd., Shell Company of West Africa Ltd., British Bata Shoe Co., Nigerian Hardwoods Ltd., Taylor Woodrow Ltd., the Nigerian Chamber of Mines, and the Joint West Africa Committee.[78] These representatives made their interests clear enough, even if they couched their motives in ambiguous terms. They reaffirmed commitment to their shareholders, who were members of the British public, and solicited the "advice" of the colonial secretary on how best to serve their primary constituency. Business representatives claimed to be aware of the presence of "a core of sensible Africans who appreciated the value of European interests in the territory." AWAM indicated that it would like to continue to encourage these individuals. Having made this important concession, AWAM went on to press its case. It recognized that the safeguard that it was proposing "might cause some friction in Nigeria but [that it was] better to have some friction now rather than forego safeguards whose absence would be most dangerous in the future."[79]

The Colonial Office team rejected AWAM's demand for increased representation in the proposed central legislature. The officials advised once again that "the most effective protection for the firms was clearly that they should link themselves with the aspirations of the Nigerian peoples and with the desire of those peoples to raise their standard of living."[80] The Colonial Office repose to merchant capital does not signify a lack of sympathy. In addition, it does not signify that merchant capital should become depoliticized. Instead, officialdom wanted merchant capital to continue to be involved in politics, but to do so covertly through indigenous surrogates or simply under the aegis of the nationalist intelligentsia. It was a tactical difference in how to best achieve the interests of merchant capital. It was because of officialdom's sympathy that the colonial secretary kept the channel of communication open. He appointed Cohen, colonial office official, to liaise between the Colonial Office and merchant capital. The secretary of state would consult with the Nigerian governor and then meet again with AWAM.[81] The secretary of state acceded to AWAM's demand for the establishment of the EAC, but Cohen wrote the Nigerian government on 30 June 1950 asking for limitations in the jurisdiction of the proposed committee. His reason was that a powerful EAC would unduly favor merchant capital since the EAC would provide it with advance knowledge of policy. Merchant capital could exploit this advantage to stifle any plans for local industrialization.[82] But, as will be seen below, the Nigerian government had no plans for the EAC.

Merchant capital's reaction to this move carried the most ominous and authoritative tone that the London business establishment could muster in the face of a perceived insult. AWAM furiously denounced what it deemed the Nigerian government's interference in Colonial Office matters. It insinuated the irresponsibility of the Colonial Office, accused new Colonial Secretary James Griffiths of disregarding its views, and implied adverse consequences of such a course.[83] In return, the Nigerian government denounced merchant capital's disregard of government counsel, claiming that business representatives had been consulted at all stages. Merchant capital's approach might lead to the loss of political ground if pursued. According to the deputy governor, "My advice to the firms would be that they should be satisfied with what they have got with willing consent of Unofficial Members [i.e., nationalist representatives] and that they should not prejudice willing consent by asking for more."[84] That officialdom pressed on with this line of action indicates that it did not take seriously AWAM's repeated claim to represent the interests of Nigerians (instead of those of its member companies) or, for that matter, business's claim to be the repository of all human knowledge. As a matter of fact, the Nigerian government observed that there were "few members of the European unofficial community with sufficient calibre" to provide the requisite expertise.[85]

Merchant capital's other argument rested on a frequent reference to satisfactory representation in the Gold Coast. In July 1950, the Colonial Office dismissed this attempt to capitalize on Gold Coast gains: the situation there differed from that of Nigeria. In the Gold Coast, the government invited merchant capital as soon as the Coussey Commission report was published. But in Nigeria, "the local proposals had all been published well in advance of any statement of H.M.G.'S general views." Cohen expressed surprise that business was accusing the colonial secretary of being unwilling to help. If the colonial secretary stressed the African point of view, it was because "in Nigeria as in the Gold

Coast it is the African members of the Legislative Council whom we have to carry with us in whatever is proposed about representation." Cohen reiterated that "the most effective protection for the firms was for them to be able to convince Nigerian opinion that they were linking themselves with the aspirations of the Nigerian people."[86] The Nigerian government concurred once more, insisting that the number of special members of the proposed legislature must be limited. Even the provision of a limited number was, in their opinion, only to be allowed because the special members would "probably alone deal with financial questions." Otherwise, special members appropriately belonged to the ceremonial upper house. This was because the indiscriminate allocation of votes to special members "would be untidy, invidious and might lead to recrimination." As a result, the number of special members with votes in the lower house must be restricted to three.[87]

In the meantime, AWAM continued to exert pressures at both the Nigerian and London ends. Its strategy now included trying to carry Nigerians along with it, but on its own terms. AWAM designated one Mr. Rogers, probably an unofficial Legislative Council member, to lobby certain indigenous delegates to the Ibadan Constitutional Conference in support of merchant capital's demand for higher representation. But the Nigerians made it clear that their support for any representation at all for merchant capital was contingent upon confining its demand to three representatives. The Nigerian government was aware of this lobbying and did not support it.[88]

But the Colonial Office soon yielded to the pressures of merchant capital's London lobby.[89] The Colonial Office's policy on merchant capital's representation suddenly changed. In a dispatch on 5 August 1950, Cohen, on behalf of the colonial secretary, urged the Nigerian government to "devise something comparable" with the Gold Coast situation. The ostensible reason was that it was difficult to insist on only three special member representatives for Nigeria because the Gold Coast had a smaller house and yet had as many as six such representatives. These representatives would be elected by the European constituency, as in the Gold Coast.[90] By mid-September 1950, the new constitutional proposals had accommodated six voting members in the 148-member central legislature. This was the same number as in the Gold Coast, but works out as a much smaller proportion of the size of the legislature. From this time onward, the Colonial Office lent its full weight to merchant capital's quest for representation, although the cause of this volte-face is still unclear.[91]

The presence in London of the Nigerian governor, Macpherson, who was spending what must have been a well-timed working leave there at this decisive moment, is interesting. Unless being in London had been more important than being in Nigeria at the time of the colony's most far-reaching constitutional negotiations, the governor would have stayed on to monitor the conference that he had inaugurated. But the governor's actions in Nigeria before the Colonial Office turn-around do not suggest that he was in the United Kingdom to support merchant capital's demands. Neither did Macpherson return from leave radically compromised. The opposition to AWAM's demand that emanated from the deputy governor's office during the time of AWAM's intense lobbying seems to have had Macpherson's blessing. It is possible that he had gone to London to thwart the efforts of AWAM, lest it succeed in persuading the colonial secretary to pursue a line of policy that the governor considered to be dangerous. If the governor ever met with the colonial secretary, as seems likely, the proceedings of such a meeting or meetings have not yet been made public.

The fact that the Colonial Office succeeded in getting enough nationalists to support merchant capital's quest for representation in the proposed legislature underlines the influence of the British state over the colonies at the time. Also, the Colonial Office's volte-face shows that its bureaucrats did not pursue consistent ideologies but followed the line of the secretary of state. Most importantly, the acceptance of the volte-face testifies to the willingness of the Nigerian nationalists to collaborate with merchant capital. AWAM's leader in London, Mellor, later noted that unidentified nationalists had helped in the achievement of representation for merchant capital.[92] That the nationalists did not protest vehemently against the proposals[93] indicates that Rogers had made a lot of headway in his lobbying venture, this time with the colonial secretary's blessings. The nationalists conceded more than the colonial state functionaries had learned to expect from them. Indeed, merchant capital had carried the nationalists in its aspiration for increased representation.

Securing representation for merchant capital in the regional assemblies was harder. The main obstacle was the absence of collaborating insiders such as had existed in the struggle for representation at the center.[94] The Colonial Office was determined to help merchant capital overcome this obstacle. On the one hand, it instructed the Nigerian government not to leave any stone unturned in ensuring that European special interests were not disadvantaged in securing representation in the regions on account of lack of collaborators. On the other hand, the Colonial Office offered merchant capital a game plan. This strategy involved an attempt to influence events, but to do so informally through (a) unofficial business representatives in the Legislative Council; (b) the Nigerian members of the Legislative Council and their non-council nationalist colleagues; and (c) liaison with the acting governor.[95] This strategy meant that lobbying the nationalists would complement the efforts of the colonial state, which had to be subtle. The plan worked, and this reflects on the legislative representation that the Macpherson Constitution of 1951 provided. European Business achieved its goal of six members to represent special interests in the 148-member House of Representatives. Out of the six, three represented commerce, one each was for mining and shipping, and one was Nigerian. But these six were to be appointed by the governor rather than be "elected by the constituencies concerned" as AWAM had desired. Merchant capital also won representation in the three regional assemblies: not more than ten in the North, and not more than three each in the East and West.

After the resolution of the representation matter, the next battle between the colonial state and merchant capital concerned AWAM's demand for anti-discrimination legislation. Merchant capital had gone on the defensive. By insisting on the promulgation of an anti-discrimination law, it now opposed the practice that had placed it in a privileged position. The government rejected this request in September 1950. To do otherwise would have thwarted the Africanization program that had become part of decolonization since 1948. This program incorporated a "native lands law and [a] policy of encouraging Nigerian commercial enterprise." Consequently, the government insisted that anti-discrimination provision must be limited to religious matters.[96] Merchant capital continued to push for the promulgation of an all-embracing anti-discrimination law. As the government had feared, all attempts to get the Nigerian nationalists, particularly the Northern elements, to accede to this law had failed up the end of 1950. The Colonial Office had begun to search for a formula "which would remain short, simple and general but nevertheless both leave existing discriminatory legislation untouched and enable us to amend and replace it whenever necessary in future."[97] The Colonial Office also decided on the establishment of committees to look into this question and other unresolved issues that AWAM had raised. The EAC was one of these unresolved matters. It is in this matter that the differences between the Nigerian government and the Colonial Office became clear.

The colony's administration was more cautious in acceding to merchant capital's demands than the Colonial Office. Instead of Economic Advisory Council, the Nigerian government established the Lagos Trade and Industrial Advisory Committee (LTIAC) in October 1950. Whereas the EAC's function would have been the protection of merchant capital's interests, LTIAC's terms of reference centered on advising "on means whereby Nigerians may be encouraged and assisted to play a larger and more efficient part in trade and industrial enterprise." The membership of the committee included three persons each of the following organizations: the Nigerian Association of African Importers and Exporters, the Association of African Importers and Industrialists, the Industrial Planning Committee, and the Lagos Chamber of Commerce. The committee also included the "1st nominated member" of the Legislative Council, a representative of the director of education, and a director of the African Development

Corporation. One European, R. C. Irving, and one Nigerian, Mobolaji Bank Anthony, were appointed in their personal capacities. A member of the Department of Commerce would serve as secretary of the committee while a director of the same department would serve as chair.[98]

Following the formation of LTIAC, the Nigerian deputy governor, Hugh Foot, informed Cohen that the formation of an EAC was not possible at the time. According to Foot, there were obstacles to plans to form committees with balanced European and African representation. The obstacles derived from the difficulty in getting enough qualified Nigerians. Any new committees must have a sufficient number of Nigerians to protect indigenous interests. The problem that arose from this dilemma was twofold and reflected the struggles of the time. In the first place, the disposition and sensitivities of merchant capital's representatives disqualified them from taking "a special position in relation to the formation of a Nigerian policy." Expatriate business were ill-suited for this role because "some of [them] find it difficult to adjust themselves . . . and it seems that some of them have a lot to learn regarding the usefulness of Committees on which there is Nigerian representation."[99] Second, predominantly European committees would elicit criticisms in Nigeria. These obstacles contributed to the indefinite postponement of committee formation.[100] Although the deputy governor told Cohen that LTIAC's "functions would overlap" with those of an EAC,[101] the supposed dearth of manpower did not prevent the government from establishing LTIAC. With the sudden formation of a committee for the purpose of encouraging indigenization, LTIAC, rather than an EAC, AWAM intensified its push for an EAC, and demanded to be consulted before the inauguration of a new policy or any change in existing policies.

Probably to break the deadlock, Governor Macpherson in London asked at the end of October 1950 to meet with the representatives of merchant capital at the Colonial Office.[102] A meeting took place swiftly, on the same day, 31 October 1950, that the Colonial Office communicated Macpherson's wish to meet with AWAM. The struggle for both the EAC and an antidiscrimination law continued in this meeting: "the commercial interests while anxious to be fully cooperative over the new Constitution, wished to be sure that any representations which they might have to make were put forward at the appropriate stage and before final decisions were taken." The representatives of merchant capital also reiterated the necessity of an anti-race clause, demanding to see it beforehand. Governor Macpherson and Colonial Office officials discounted the possibility of such a clause ever coming into effect. The officials actually reneged on their earlier agreement to establish an EAC, albeit a more limited body than merchant capital desired. They placed on merchant capital the onus of providing more convincing reasons why an Economic Advisory Council was necessary.[103] Apparently, the convincing reasons did not emerge. Neither did an EAC.

Soon after this meeting with Governor Macpherson, a meeting that was unfavorable from AWAM's point of view, the colonial secretary's point man, Cohen, advised merchant capital's representatives to liaise with the acting governor in Lagos.[104] AWAM addressed a petition to the Nigerian government early in December 1950, again arguing the case for prior consultation. Such a procedure would give the governed the opportunity to provide input on policy. In fact, AWAM's case for prior consultation contains everything—cushioning state functionaries from nationalist attacks and being advantageous to the Nigerian people—except the point that such a procedure would benefit merchant capital itself. The significant new element in AWAM's position is that merchant capital was now ready to accommodate Nigerians in the EAC that it proposed. The EAC

> would further provide a means of protecting the Government and Ministers from organized agitation on any particular problem and from that of insidious personal and family pressure which are common in Africa and the East. Also (since membership of the Committee would not be confined to Europeans) it would afford an excellent training ground and education of Africans with little experience on economic matters in

the wise conduct of the affairs of their country. It might even be that [with] the intimate exchanges possible at a Committee meeting privately held, and with the assistance of experienced Europeans, Africans possessing extreme views might be persuaded that such affairs should be examined objectively.[105]

The names of Gbadamosi, Dr. Maya, L. P. Ojukwu and Oba Adele II of Lagos were put forward in this connection.[106] This idea of incorporating indigenous elements tallied with the advice, unheeded before now, that officialdom had been giving to merchant capital.

The seeming contradiction in the Nigerian government's explanation—for establishing the LTIAC rather than an EAC—is noteworthy. The government simply did not want to form any committee whose main function would be to cater for merchant capital's interests. The government was less sympathetic to AWAM's demand than Cohen and the colonial secretary had become. Being closer to nationalist pressure, the Nigerian State functionaries were less enthusiastic than the new colonial secretary about merchant capitalist interests playing a major role in the decolonization process. The officers in the colony apparently formed and publicized the LTIAC hurriedly, before the colonial secretary (and Cohen) had a chance to stop it. The fact that the colonial state refused to act at the behest of capital is not difficult to understand. The determination of the Nigerian nationalists ensured that only through force could the state intervene to grant all of merchant capital's demands. Such a strategy would certainly alienate the nationalists further. Unlike the Colonial Office officers who were far removed from the scene, the administrative officers thought that such a development was uncalled for, given that the mainstream nationalist intelligentsia did not after all articulate an alternative political economy—a development that wide-scale insurgency could generate.

Officialdom could not grant all the demands of merchant capital, but met it halfway with support for increased representation in the central legislature and representation in the regional assemblies. For its part, business stepped up its social schemes. The companies established educational development programs, publicizing their names through the schemes. The focal point was Nigeria's first university. In March 1951, the UAC donated £61,000 toward the erection of an assembly hall proposed.[107] The magnificent Trenchard Hall resulted solely from the UAC's contribution. The edifice was opened with fanfare on the Foundation Day of the University College (17 November) in 1954, and named after Viscount Trenchard, UAC's chairman (1936-1953).[108] For its part, John Holt established the John Holt Scholarship in October 1952.[109] UAC would donate an "Independence Gift" of £25,000 to the University College in 1960.[110] By getting business to toe the line of collaboration, the colonial officials co-opted merchant capital to their version of decolonization. UAC instituted scholarships which tallied with the government program already in train.[111]

CONCLUSIONS

Politicization was an attempt to structure the Nigerian State according to merchant capital's interests. It aimed to secure exclusive European electoral constituencies, entrench merchant capital as a permanent organ of state through the agency of an extra-constitutional Economic Advisory Council, and retain British control of the security forces. AWAM began to press this case by mid-1948. The idea of decolonization only began to crystallize in the last days of 1947.[112] Therefore, merchant capital was not late in the pursuit of politicization. It does not seem to me that merchant capital recognized the political trend significantly later than officials themselves did. Merchant capital argued throughout the struggle for representation in Nigeria on the basis of its prior input on the Gold Coast resolutions. Because merchant capital had already been involved in such negotiations in the Gold Coast, the idea that it was late in realizing the political trends can hardly apply to Nigeria. And the fact that merchant capital did succeed in getting the Colonial Office to reverse its policy on European representation in Nigeria means that Merchant capital's efforts in Nigeria were, thus, not as ineffectual as Fieldhouse has suggested. UAC's appointment for the first time, in mid-1948, of a public relations officer was a politically motivated move made in response to the changing political environment. In 1948, UAC pursued a policy of sponsoring politically ambitious Nigerian staff for election. AWAM's leader Mellor's visit to West Africa led to his far-reaching recommendations in late 1948. Managing Director Samuel's visit soon afterward also had a political objective. UAC's public relations officer, Newman, visited the Colonial Office to seek support for his political projects as early as July 1949. The officials did not take him seriously. This happened in spite of the fact that no less an officer than the Nigerian governor had mentioned Newman to Colonial Office officials "in complimentary terms" before Newman appeared at the Colonial Office.[113]

Officialdom merely compelled merchant capital to broaden its strategy. The evidence suggests that officialdom told AWAM that European business was late on the scene as a way of keeping merchant capital out of direct participation in the political process so that an Africanization program could be carried through. Colonial officials feared that merchant capital's direct participation would draw the hostility of the nationalists at a time when the imperial state was trying to contain an empire-wide cycle of unrest. Frederick Cooper has eloquently summarized the pervasiveness and intensity of the postwar labor crisis and shown that this led to policy reappraisal, not only in the British African colonies but also in the entire colonial world.[114] The Nigerian share of the unrest has been given some attention in this chapter. The "restoration of confidence" in the colonies preoccupied the British colonial establishment at the time. Despite the different approach that new Colonial Secretary Griffiths adopted, the strategy for decolonization current at the time was reiterated in mid-1950. In view of the "transfer of power [and the British inability to set a definite timetable], the solution to the difficulties faced by many officials lay in their being as friendly and as helpful as possible so that the people of the territory would wish them to stay when self-government was achieved."[115] Indeed, the state acted against certain segments of the dominant class "to renovate the structures and ideology of domination and accumulation."[116] Although the state considered the interests of capital, the interests of the indigenous social forces also mattered. This fact is crucial in understanding the politicization of merchant capital in Nigeria, at a time when sections of the fractious nationalist elite were prepared to collaborate with desperate merchant capital.

The Nigerian case shows that merchant capital maintained its historical dominance of the economy. The intensification of nationalist activity in the post-World War II period had threatened this dominance by opening merchant capital to double-pronged pressure. First, officialdom compelled it to compromise with the moderate nationalist intelligentsia. Second, the anticapitalist ideas and activities of nationalist radicals occasioned officialdom's admonitions. Upon finding decolonization inevitable, merchant capital sought to ensure that it continued "to exercise political influence at the highest levels, and in particular that [it] should have an entrenched role in the new legislatures."[117] It achieved some success. In 1953, one of the UAC members of the House of Representatives, J.W.W. Johnson, reported that the company's image had improved radically among the Nigerian members.[118] At this point, UAC, which had sponsored Nigerian political contestants in its employment, began to suspend the politically involved staff.[119] Officialdom initially did not want business to participate in decolonization at all. It was merchant capital's struggles that ensured representation. The state was not hostile to capital beyond the hostility forced on it by nationalists' efforts. There was considerable sympathy for business in the secret intelligence reports of the period.[120]

To complete this picture of the politicization of merchant capital during decolonization, two areas call for research. The first is the latent disagreement between the functionaries in the colony and the new colonial secretary over the role of merchant capital. Both the Colonial Office and the Nigerian government were committed to decolonization and Africanization. But the colony-based officers in particular pursued a version of the Africanization program that had less scope for merchant capital's designs. The "sandwich element" concept that Kirk-Greene uses to depict the district officer's role at the local level[121] could apply to the role of colony officers in liaising among the Nigerian nationalists, merchant capital, and the Colonial Office. The second line of enquiry with prospects for illuminating the politicization of merchant capital is the possible role of the British shareholders of the expatriate firms. It could be that, rather than act as a check on politicization, as the theory goes, the shareholders' anxiety about the political future of the colonies actually fueled politicization during the decolonization period.

NOTES

1. The Graduate School of Memorial University of Newfoundland, Canada, supported the research for this chapter with a grant in the Summer-Fall of 1992. For all his help, Chris Youé deserves acknowledgment in all my work that originated in Memorial University. I presented an earlier draft of the chapter at the Canadian Association of African Studies 23rd Annual Conference held at Trent University, Peterborough, Ontario, Canada, in May 1995. Andrew Okolie made useful comments on it.
2. The term "merchant capital" has been used to characterize the pre-capitalist precursor of modern finance capital. See D. K. Fieldhouse, *Merchant Capital and Economic Decolonization: The United Africa Company 1929-1987* (Oxford: Oxford University Press, 1994), vii. Merchant capital's historic manifestation in Britain was "the complex of services and consumer industries which sustained wealth in the south-east of England [and provided] the means of perpetuating gentle-manly values, status and power." This phenomenon has been referred to as "gentlemanly capitalism." See P. J. Cain and A. G. Hopkins, *British Imperialism: Crisis and Deconstruction 1914-1990* (London: Longman, 1993), 5.
3. I am not suggesting that expatriate firms have had unproblematic relations with the independent Nigerian State. The most trying time in these relations was the early 1970s when the military government effected a sweeping program of indigenization. With the notable exception of Shell, these firms have also stepped up divestment since the 1980s. In spite of this, the European firms maintain their promi-

nence in the commercial arm of the organized private sector.
4. By "politicization," I mean the process by which European business enterprises acted as a cohesive group and interfered in matters that were beyond the traditional concerns of businesses. The concept of politicization goes beyond mere resistance to state intervention in market relations. It involves, among other activities, exerting influence on public policy. See Kris W. Kobach, *Political Capital: The Motives, Tactics, and Goals of Politicized Businesses in South Africa* (Lanham, Md.: University Press of America, 1990).
5. I use the term "officialdom" to describe both the Nigerian government and the Colonial Office where the distinction of the two bodies is inessential. At a point in this paper, it becomes necessary to differentiate between the two bodies. "The differences between metropolitan and colony officers cut deep." These differences were a function of the practical difficulties that faced administrative officers whose daily work involved ruling unwilling peoples. See G. Ugo Nwokeji, "Slave Emancipation Problematic: Igbo Society and the Colonial Equation," *Comparative Studies in Society and History*, 40 (2), 1998, 318-355.
6. Much of the work that followed Hopkins' call for the study of business history, like the call itself, focused on entrepreneurship and the other traditional concerns of business. See A. G. Hopkins, "Imperial Business in Africa Part I: Sources," *Journal of African History*, 17, (1) 1976, 29-48; "Imperial Business in Africa Part II: Interpretations," *Journal of African History*, 17 (2), 1976, 267-290; "Big Business in African Studies," *Journal of African History*, 28 (1), 1987, 119-140.
7. See J. F. Milburn, *British Business and Ghanaian Independence* (London: C. Hurst, 1977).
8. D. K. Fieldhouse, *Black Africa: Economic Decolonization and Arrested Development* (London: Allen and Unwin, 1986), 9.
9. Ibid.
10. See Fieldhouse, *Merchant Capital*, 338.
11. D. K. Fieldhouse, Unilever Overseas: *The Anatomy of a Multinational 1895-1965* (London: Croom Helm, 1978), 361-32.
12. To be sure, the hostility of the indigenous Nigerian press was regularly mentioned in the secret intelligence summaries that began to appear in 1946. For a detailed analysis of these summaries as they pertain to Nigeria, see G. Ugo Nwokeji, "Britain's Response to Post-Second World War Colonial Crises, 1947-50: Findings and Reflections from the Nigeria Research," *Frankfurter Afrikanistitsche Blät-*

ter, 6, 1994, 78-79.
13. Fieldhouse, *Merchant Capital*, 337-378.
14. See S. E. Stockwell, "Political Strategies of British Business during Decolonization: The Case of the Gold Coast/Ghana, 1945-57," *Journal of Imperial and Commonwealth History*, 23 (2), 1995, 277-300. The present chapter, like Stockwell's article, utilizes the more recently declassified Colonial Office records.
15. Ibid., 279, 280.
16. Ibid., 293.
17. Kobach, *Political Capital*, 3.
18. During the interwar years, merchant capital was able to achieve "all practical concessions" by utilizing various forums and strategies. Among the methods that merchant capital adopted was highlighting the purported benefits that would accrue to Nigerians if capital's policy preferences were adopted. The platforms for the pursuit of interest included the Legislative Council, banquets, AGMs, deputations, committees, the press, and the chambers of commerce. See A. Olukoju, "Anatomy of Business-Government Relations: Fiscal Policy and Mercantile Pressure Group Activity in Nigeria, 1916-1933," *African Studies Review*, 38 (1), 1995, 23-50.
19. G. Ugo Nwokeji, "Colonialism in Transition: Shifting Foundations of Rule and Collaboration in Nigeria, 1900-51," M.A. thesis, Memorial University of Newfoundland, 1993, 3.
20. J. S. Coleman, *Nigeria: Background to Nationalism* (Berkeley: University of California Press, 1971); Kalu Ezera, *Constitutional Developments in Nigeria* (Cambridge: Cambridge University Press, 1960); S. O. Okafor, *Indirect Rule: The Development of Central Legislature in Nigeria* (Lagos: Nelson Africa, 1981); G. O. Olusanya, *The Second World War and Nigeria 1939-1953*, (Lagos: University of Lagos Press, 1973); R. Sklar, *Nigerian Political Parties: Power in an Emergent African Nation* (Princeton, N.J.: Princeton University Press, 1963); J. White, *Central Administration in Nigeria, 1914-1948* (Dublin: Irish Academic Press, 1981).
21. It is untenable for many businesses to collaborate with their rivals and potential rivals. The innate risk-phobia of businesses constrains their willingness to challenge the incumbent government. For details on these impediments, see Kobach, *Political Capital*, 8-9.
22. Stockwell, "Political Strategies," 278. The heterogeneity that Stockwell reveals in Ghana is similar to the Nigerian case. But the disagreements that she reports regarding inter-firm ideas on political strategies (see 280, 282) are not found to be a significant factor in

the Nigerian case.
23. See Kobach, *Political Capital*, 9-10.
24. AWAM came in to being during World War I as an umbrella organization for the British and French companies. Its original role was to coordinate policies among member-companies and to influence the governments in gaining advantages over African and Levantine rivals. Fieldhouse, *Merchant Capital*, 127, 236; A. G. Hopkins, *An Economic History of West Africa* (London: Longman, 1973), 259; Milburn, *British Business*, 5.
25. Its parent, Unilever, merged with the Dutch Margarine Union in 1929. This move augmented the UAC share of the African market. UAC began that same year to buy up A&E and completed the process in 1939. It also acquired G. B. Olivant (GBO) in 1933, SAT in 1936 and Gottschalcks in 1940. These were the most important acquisitions. See Fieldhouse, Merchant Capital, 9-18, 25.
26. Fieldhouse, Merchant Capital, 27.
27. C. Wilson, *Unilever 1945-1965: Challenge and Resistance in the Post-War Industrial Revolution* (London: Cassel, 1968), 214-215.
28. D. A. Low and J. M. Lonsdale, "Introduction: Towards the New Order 1945-1963," in D. A. Low and A. Smith (eds.), *History of East Africa, Volume 3* (Oxford, Oxford University Press, 1976).
29. M. Cowen and R. Shenton, "The Origin and Course of Fabian Colonialism in Africa." *Journal of Historical Sociology*, 4 (2) 1991, 166.
30. Coleman, *Nigeria: Background to Nationalism*, 252.
31. Nwokeji, "Britain's Response," 75, 80-81; E.E.G. Iweriebor, "Radical Nationalism in Nigeria: The Zikist Movement and the Struggle for Liberation, 1945-1950," Ph.D. thesis, Columbia University, 1990; J. F. A. Ajayi and A. E. Ekoko, "Transfer of Power in Nigeria: Its Origins and Consequences," in P. G. Clifford and Wm. Roger Louis (eds.), *Decolonization and African Independence: The Transfer of Power, 1960-1980* (New Haven, Conn: Yale University Press, 1988); T. Abdul-Raheem and A. Olukoshi, 'The Left in Nigerian Politics and the Struggle for Socialism," *Review of African Political Economy*, 37, 1986, 64-67.
32. For details, see Nwokeji, "Britain's Response."
33. Ken Post, "Nationalism and Politics in Nigeria: A Marxist Approach," *Nigerian Journal of Economic and Social Studies*, 6 (2) 1964.
34. Members of the radical Zikist Movement admired the action of the Gold Coasters. In their view, the leadership of the Gold Coast nationalism believed in action, unlike its Nigerian counterpart which

just talked too much. Public Record Office (PRO) CO 537/3649/47272/2/A: Political Intelligence Reports, West Africa, Nigeria, No. 24, Secret, March-April 1948, p. 9. My reliance on the intelligence reports on nationalist activities does not mean that this evidence is irreproachable. Their significance as evidence derives mainly from the fact that their authors believed in what they wrote and/or wanted administrative officers and the Colonial Office to believe what they wrote.

35. The labor movement became more politicized during this period. Even domestic servants in the employ of UAC were mobilized to demand improvements in their working conditions and remuneration with some success. CO 537/3649/47272/2/A: Possum No. 24, 1948.
36. The nationalist elite defined their interest in capitalist terms. The economic motive, the control of productive resources, dominated the calculations of the mainstream nationalist elite during this era. Post, 172. For a more detailed account of this, see Nwokeji, "Colonialism," chapter 6: "Contradictions of Nigerian Nationalism."
37. Post, "nationalism," 172. See also Chinweizu, *The West and the Rest of Us* (New York: Random House, 1975), 1-2; E. Ekekwe, "The State and Economic Development in Nigeria," in C. Ake (ed.), *The Political Economy of Nigeria* (Ibadan: Longman, 1985), 157.
38. Fieldhouse, *Merchant Capital*, 338, 339.
39. CO 537/364947272/2/A: Possum No. 27, 1948.
40. For details see Sklar, *Nigerian Political Parties*, 76.
41. Fieldhouse, *Merchant Capital*, 338. Emphasis is added.
42. Ibid., 338-339.
43. Ibid., 339.
44. Ibid., 339-340.
45. "BWAC: AWAM and MFA Meetings, Liverpool, 17th June 1948," Research note of Anshan Li. I am grateful to Li for this material.
46. See CO 537/4645/33539/231 1949: Blackbourne to Gorsuch, 14 July 1949; CO 537/2679/14355/6 pt. 31949: West African Intelligence Summary, No. 3, 14 Jan. 1949. Fieldhouse refers to this appointment only in passing– "a press officer was to be appointed." See Merchant Capital, 340.
47. Fieldhouse, Merchant Capital, 339.
48. See CO 537/2678/4355/6: Political Intelligence Summary, No. 2, 14 Dec. 1948.
49. J. T. Saunders, *University College, Ibadan* (Cambridge: Cambridge University Press, 1960), 217-218.
50. Cited by Fieldhouse, in *Merchant Capital*, 339.

51. See CO 537/2678/4355/6: General Colonial Political Intelligence Summary, No. 2, 14 Dec. 1948.
52. CO 537/2678/4355/6: General Colonial Political Intelligence Summary, No. 2, 14 Dec. 1948.
53. See Sir Charles Jefferies, "The Political Significance of African Students in Great Britain," December 1947. See CO 537/2573: "Proceedings of the Informal Committee on the Political Significance of Colonial Students in Great Britain," 1947. The significance of Sir Charles's memo has been analyzed. See Nwokeji, "Britain's Response," 76-78.
54. CO 537/5789/30453/11 1950: See memo of a meeting with AWAM representatives. Emphases are added to signify that this trend was not new in 1950.
55. Even Fieldhouse, to whom the company gave its records, notes that the reports of Samuel's visit are hazy. See *Merchant Capital*, 342.
56. See CO 537/2679/14355/6 pt. 3 1949: General Colonial Political Intelligence Summary, No. 3.
57. CO 537/2679/14355/6 pt. 3 1949: General Colonial Political Intelligence Summary, No. 3.
58. The information on Samuel's visit is from Fieldhouse, Merchant Capital, 342.
59. CO 537/4645/33539/231/1949: Gorsuch to the Nigerian Governor, 6 Aug. 1949.
60. CO 537/4645/33539/231/1949: Minutes prepared for Cohen.
61. CO 537/4645/33539/231/1949: Gorsurch to Walson, 18 July 1949. See also Walson to Gorsuch, 18 July 1949.
62. For instance, the Nigerian Cocoa Marketing Board guaranteed the Bank of British West Africa loans for its agents, the Ibadan Traders' Association Ltd., up to the sum of £7,000, and the Ijesha Trading and Transport Co. Ltd., up to £5,000. See Nigerian National Archives (NAI) MN/X28 vol. 1: Nigeria Cocoa Marketing Board. Minutes of 7th to 12th Meetings 15 Nov. 1948 to 28 Sept. 1949. Appendix 49A "Bank Guarantees."
63. CO 537/2678/4355/6: General Colonial Intelligence Summary, No. 2, West African Political Intelligence Summary, No. 2, 14 Dec. 1948.
64. Nwokeji, "Britain's Response," 79-80. This is by no means the only explanation for the decision to decolonize. Many scholars have discussed this matter. The more nuanced discussions include D. Austin, "The Transfer of Power: Why and How?," in W. H. Morris-Jones and G. Fisher (eds.), *Decolonization and After* (London: Frank Cass,

1980); John Darwin, *Britain and Decolonization: The Retreat from Empire in the Post-War Period* (New York: St. Martin's Press, 1988); R. D. Pearce, *The Turning Point in Africa: British Colonial Policy 1938-48* (London: Frank Cass, 1982); A. N. Porter & A. J. Stockwell, *British Imperial Policy and Decolonization, 1938-64* (New York: Macmillan, 1987).

65. CO 537/4645/33539/231/1949: Miscellaneous, Visit of P.R.O., United Africa Co., to Colonial Office: Gorsuch to the Nigerian Governor, 6 Aug. 1949.
66. Fieldhouse, *Merchant Capital*, 344.
67. The Zikists had persuaded the miners to allow certain cases of mining explosives to be removed from the stores, for if they were removed the colliery management would feel free to renege on the arrears of payment due to the miners, and even sack them. The Zikists intimated that they would seize on this punishment to embarrass the government. In reality, however, the Zikists also needed those explosives for a showdown. The fact that thirty cases of the explosives had been stolen already probably unnerved the security forces. Coleman, *Nigeria: Background to Nationalism*, 299.
68. The plan also included the destruction of all "storage centres, Government Houses, Government departments and so on." Settlement with Britain was predicated on conditions which not only included immediate expatriate withdrawal but also payment of compensation for past misdeeds. See Iweriebor, "Radical Nationalism," 386-387, 388.
69. Cited by G. O. Olusanya, "The Nationalist Movement in Nigeria," in O. Ikime (ed.), *Groundwork of Nigerian History* (Ibadan: Heinemann Educational Books, 1980), 564.
70. CO 537/4645/33539/231/1949: Mellor to Secretary of State, 9 June 1950.
71. CO 537/4645/33539/231/1949: E. Hallet (UAC) to Kirkness (C.O.), 16 June 1950.
72. CO 537/4645/33539/231/1949: Memo by European business interests addressed to the Secretary of State, 21 June 1950.
73. CO 537/4645/33539/231/1949: Memo by European businesses addressed to the Secretary of State, 21 June 1950.
74. See Olukoju, "Anatomy of Business-Government Relations," 24.
75. CO 537/4645/33539/231/1949: Memo by European businesses addressed to the Secretary of State, 21 June 1950.
76. CO 537/4645/33539/231/1949: Memo by European firms addressed to the Secretary of State, 21 June 1950.

77. See Nwokeji, "Britain's Response," 78-80.
78. See CO 537/5789/30453/11/1950: Mellor to Gorsuch, 14 July 1950. See also Minutes of meeting with AWAM's representatives.
79. See CO 537/5789/30453/11/1950: Minutes of meeting with AWAM's representatives.
80. Ibid.
81. Ibid.
82. See CO 537/5789/30453/11/1950: Cohen to Nigerian Governor, 30 June 1950.
83. See CO 537/5789/30453/11/1950: Mellor to Secretary of State, 13 July 1950.
84. See CO 537/5789/30453/11/1950: Nigerian Governor's Deputy to the Secretary of State, 24 July 1950.
85. CO 537/5789/30453/11/1950: Nigerian Governor's Deputy to the Secretary of State, 24 July 1950.
86. CO 537/5789/30453/11/1950: Cohen to Mellor, 21 July 1950.
87. CO 537/5789/30453/11/1950: Deputy to the Nigerian Governor to the Secretary of State, 24 July 1950.
88. CO 537/5789/30453/11/1950: Deputy to the Nigerian Governor to the Secretary of State, 24 July 1950.
89. Fieldhouse has suggested that Creech Jones' successor as colonial secretary, James Grifiths, was harder for merchant capital to deal with than his predecessor, who had lost his parliamentary seat in a general election, in July 1950. See Fieldhouse, *Merchant Capital*, 344. This does not appear to be so, as will be seen below.
90. CO 537/5789/30453/11/1950: Cohen to the Nigerian Governor, 5 Aug. 1950.
91. Cohen's expression of surprise that the colonial secretary, Griffiths, who replaced Creech Jones after the 1950 British election, was being perceived as anti-business, which suggests that the new pro-business policy may have originated from the new colonial secretary himself. Co 537/5789/30453/11: Cohen to Mellor, 21 July 1950.
92. CO 537/5789/30453/11/1950: Mellor to Cohen, 15 Nov. 1950.
93. NCNC leader Azikiwe did criticize the provision, but only after the constitution had been published. See G. O. Olusanya, "Constitutional Developments in Nigeria 1861-1960," in O. Ikime (ed.), *Groundwork*, 533.
94. CO 537/5789/30453/11/1950: Mellor to Cohen, 15 Nov. 1950. It appeared that that the proposals to have appointed members to represent special interests were accepted only in the North. See CO 537/5789/30453/11/1950: Foot to Cohen, 22 Sept. 1950.

95. CO 537/5789/30453/11/1950: Gorsuch to Foot, 20 Nov. 1950.
96. CO 537/5789/30453/11/1950: Foot to Cohen, 22 Sept. 1950.
97. CO 537/5789/30453/11/1950: Foot to Cohen, 11 Dec. 1950.
98. CO 537/5789/30453/11/1950: "Press Release," n.d.
99. CO 537/5789/30453/11 1950: Foot to Cohen, 16 Oct. 1950.
100. Ibid.
101. Ibid.
102. CO 537/5789/30453/11/1950: Gorsuch to Mellor, 31 Oct. 1950.
103. CO 537/5789/30453/11/1950: "Note on a Meeting at the Colonial Office on 31st October to Discuss Representations Made about the Nigeria Constitutional Review by the Representatives of European Interests in Nigeria."
104. CO 537/5789/30453/11/1950: Cohen to Mellor, 21 Nov. 1950.
105. CO 537/5789/30453/11/1950: Mellor to Acting Governor of Nigeria, 7 Dec. 1950.
106. CO 537/5789/30453/11/1950: Mellor to Acting Governor of Nigeria, 7 Dec. 1950.
107. UAC did not buy the government's idea that the company establish an endowment fund. It feared that inflation would reduce the real value of the investment. The company offered instead to invest in a capital project. K. Mallamby, *The Birth of Nigeria's University* (London: Methuen, 1958), 100-101, 109.
108. See Saunders, *The University College*, 56-59; T.N. Tamuno, "The Formative Years, 1947-56," in J.F.A. Ajayi (ed.), *The University of Ibadan*, 1948-73 (Ibadan: Ibadan University Press, 1973), 26, 46.
109. Saunders, *The University College*, 217.
110. J. O. O. Abiri, "The Making of the University of Ibadan, 1957-62," in Ajayi (ed.), *The University*, 61.
111. The blueprint was Sir Charles Jefferies' memo of December 1947. CO 537/2573: "The Political Significance of African Students in Great Britain."
112. CO 537/2573: See "The Political Significance."
113. CO 537/4645/33539/231/1949: Blackbourne to Gorsuch, 14 July 1949.
114. Frederick Cooper, *On the African Waterfront: Urban Disorder and the Transformation of Work in Colonial Mombasa* (New Haven: Yale University Press, 1987): 2, 4, 249-263.
115. CO 537/5789/30453/11/1950: memo.
116. J. Lonsdale and B. Berman, "Coping with Contradictions: The Colonial State in Kenya, 1895-1914," *Journal of African History*, 20 (4) 1979, 490.

117. Fieldhouse, *Merchant Capital*, 343-344.
118. Ibid., 344-345.
119. Ibid., 345.
120. For instance, when the West African Court of Appeal in December 1948 reduced the fine imposed on UAC for food over-charge (from £90,000 to £4,000), the anonymous authors of one report expressed delight. They found it necessary to remark that the "fine was imposed by Mr. Justice Scipio Pollard (a West Indian) who delivered himself a particularly severe judgment on the defendants." CO 537/2678/4355/6: General Political Intelligence Summary, No. 2, 14 Dec. 1948.
121. A.H.M. Kirk-Greene, "Preface," in A.H.M. Kirk-Greene (ed.), *Africa in the Colonial Period II—The Transfer of Power: The Colonial Administrator in the Age of Decolonization* (Oxford: University of Oxford, 1979).

8

AGRICULTURAL TRANSFORMATION, STATE POLICY, AND AGRICULTURAL DECLINE IN EASTERN NIGERIA, 1960-1970

Chima J. Korieh

INTRODUCTION

Rural development has continued to be a major concern of government policy and public discussion as a result of agricultural decline. This chapter contributes to the discussion by outlining some of the important ways in which state agricultural policies contributed to this decline. I intend to highlight the ambivalent nature of state agricultural policies and their role in the decline of agricultural production in Nigeria. Engaging some of the policies and programs of the Eastern Region government in the first decade of independence can set Nigeria's agricultural development in historical perspective.

The analysis begins with the changes taking place in Nigerian agriculture during the colonial period in order to show that the agricultural decline in Nigeria is rooted in colonial policy. It examines how colonial policies and the emphasis on primary production made their impact in the colonial period. It then examines the attempts by the regional government to deal with the issue of agricultural development and the reason for its inability to do so successfully. It will be argued that the postindependence regional government in Eastern Nigeria also emphasized cash crop agriculture. As a result of the neglect of subsistence production, the emphasis on cash crops, and the marketing and plantation policies of the regional government, what emerged in the first decade of independence was a development pattern that contributed to agricultural decline in the region's agricultural economy.

OVERVIEW OF AGRICULTURAL CHANGE IN THE COLONIAL PERIOD

During most of the first half of the twentieth century, the colonial government took steps to encourage the production of primary products. The steps were few, often hesitant, and largely misdirected, but their effects were long lasting. Agricultural policy remained ambivalent, sometimes encouraging export crop production and African commerce, and at other times limiting it as administrators struggled to balance competing African and European interests. As in other West African societies where there were no European settlers, local peasants in Nigeria embarked on rapid expansion of production for export.[1] One remarkable result of the expansion of the export economy was the stimulation and enlargement of the local producer's socioeconomic base in the exchange economy. Therefore, the production of primary commodities for export was unquestionably the most dynamic feature of Nigeria's economic life in the first five decades of the colonial era and was apparently responsible for most of the growth in per capita income during the colonial period.[2]

The centrality of agricultural products to the colonial economy is reflected in the emphasis placed on its expansion at different times. It is therefore possible to identify four phases in the history of colonial participation in agricultural development in Nigeria. The first phase, 1887-1900, can be characterized as the "botanical garden era" when agricultural policy was limited to the importation of plants, the study of their behavior, and their adaptation to local conditions. Kay argues, in the case of Ghana from 1889 to 1905, that the role of the colonial state in this period was limited to horticulture rather than crop production.[3] This was certainly the case in early colonial Nigeria. The second phase, 1900-1921 of colonial participation in agriculture resulted from the directive of the Colonial Office that the Forestry Department assume responsibility for the Botanical and Agricultural Department in the "interest of the economy."[4] During this phase the structure of the department changed, leading to the establishment of agricultural departments in the Northern and Southern Provinces, an experimental plantation at Lagos, and the Moor Plantation at Ibadan.

In the Southern Provinces, the period was marked by a strong campaign, calling on farmers to expand the area under oil palm in the region. Although the palm products exported in 1912 were valued at approximately £4.5 million, the colonial campaign did not receive an enthusiastic response from peasant producers.[5] Local peasants viewed with suspicion the call to expand oil palm cultivation. The lack of enthusiasm for developing commercial oil palm plantations was strongest in the Owerri and Calabar Provinces in eastern Nigeria. The peasants' attitude in this period was related to the fear of losing their land and oil palms as a result of the government's involvement in agricultural production.[6] According to the director of agriculture,

> So strong has this sentiment proved, that repeatedly individuals or families have decided to try planting palms, but have later given in to the strong adverse public opinion of their neighbours.[7]

The initial rejection of large-scale oil palm planting was also related to the nature of the local agricultural economy in eastern Nigeria, especially the limited land available for agricultural production in many parts of the region.

In most of eastern Nigeria, especially the Igbo areas, a high population density had already decreased the carrying capacity of the land. By the first quarter of the twentieth century, much of the land in Igboland was already in an advanced stage of degeneration. Reporting on the food situation in eastern Nigeria in 1912, the director of agriculture noted:

> In some districts and even divisions we have not yet been able to get even one tiny plot of palms planted by any farmer. And it is in these areas, with their heavy populations of trees and palms that the matter is of most urgency. This is not merely because this is the "palm belt" par excellence, nor even merely because neither the people nor ourselves know of any other export crop which will succeed on these poor acid soils. A more important reason for the urgency of this work in these areas lies in the poor food crops that the poor soil yields and their inadequacy to feed such a heavy population. If the yield of the areas that are occupied by palms could be doubled, as they easily could by the substitution of plantations for wild trees and groves, then more land would be available for food crops or much more money would be obtained wherewith the people could purchase food imported from other parts of Nigeria or from abroad.[8]

While the total export of palm oil and kernels was 52,771 tons valued at £1,655,914 and 153,354 tons valued at £2,831,688, colonial officials paid no attention to subsistence production.[9] Although primary production was on the increase, food production was becoming precarious because the expansion of cash crop production posed a major treat to subsistence production.

In the third phase, 1921-1953, the Agriculture Departments of the Northern and Southern Provinces were merged to form a single Department of Agriculture. During this period, palm produce remained the single most important product not only for eastern Nigeria but also for Nigeria as a whole.[10] The government was determined to maintain the momentum and expand production of other cash crops despite the threats the expansion of the oil palm sectors posed to agricultural sustainability. In 1927, for example, the Chief Secretary's Office acknowledged that decreased production of native foods had resulted in a rise in prices in the producing areas. But the colonial government's agricultural development strategy was seen as the quickest way to introduce the benefits of Western experience.[11] This development ideology was not suited to the local conditions in eastern Nigeria because the expansion of cash crop production created problems in sustaining an adequate food supply. Nevertheless, great strides were achieved in the commercial sector in terms of level of production. The government's persistence resulted in the export figures for palm oil and palm kernels increasing to 246,638 tons and 127,111 tons respectively in 1928.[12]

By 1929, the value of exports had increased more than sevenfold and export volume fivefold, implying "compounded annual growth rates of 7 and 5.5 percent respectively."[13] Overall, export production amounted to 5 to 7 percent of the GDP. Revenue from palm kernels exported in 1921 amounted to £3,189,000 and by 1930, this stood at £4,429,000 and contributed 62 percent of Nigeria's export earnings. For palm oil, the 1921 government revenue was £2,520,000, and in 1930 it was £3,375,000.[14] Between 1928 and 1932, about 200 new native-owned palm plots were started, and 54 plots were extended by previous owners in the Southern Provinces.[15]

In 1951, the Department of Agriculture was split into three departments based on the three regions in Nigeria, each under a regional director. The regionalization of the agricultural authority did not affect the basic principles of agricultural policy. But the peasants increasingly switched the focus of agricultural production to the expansion of export production. Their success in increasing the acreage of oil palms led to extensive and intensive use of land and to the intensification of the agricultural crisis in the region.[16] The fourth phase, 1954-1960 began as a result of the granting of regional autonomy in 1954. Regional autonomy led to the devolution of the technical departments to the regions, with the Central Agricultural Department reformed in 1954 as an Agricultural Research Department. Regional directors of agriculture were now responsible for agricultural development in the different regions.

Suffice it to say, however, that agricultural policy throughout most of the colonial period was consistent in the emphasis placed on export crops, the neglect of local social and economic conditions, and the neglect of the food sector. Colonial agricultural policies were synonymous with efforts to increase the export of primary agricultural products, mainly to Britain. But the contradiction between European economic interests and the best interests of the local farmer was evident from the neglect of subsistence agriculture through the pursuit of a cash crop economy.

AGRICULTURE IN THE POSTINDEPENDENCE PERIOD

The history of indigenous agricultural policy began before political independence in 1960. The Nigerian Constitution of 1954 allocated responsibility for all agricultural matters other than research to the regional governments.[17] In contrast to the previous five decades, economic and social development initiatives were transferred to the regions, and thus began the indigenization of agricultural policies in Nigeria. Agriculture was strategically important to the economy of the regional authorities and Nigeria as a whole. Agriculture was to provide the revenue necessary for the postindependence authorities to implement their development programs.

Kolawale Balogun, the federal minister for research and information, emphasized the strategic importance of agriculture to the economic and industrial development of the country:

> The rapid increase in population now taking place together with the plans underway for industrializa-

tion will of necessity entail more intensive use of land, but this will not be possible without a high level of technical efficiency in the production of both food crops and export crops.[18]

This policy statement appears people-oriented, but it also reveals an acceptance of the need for an appropriate agricultural policy. However, the agricultural policy pursued by the regional and later state governments was government oriented and had a strong developmentalist flavor.[19] As I show later, the policies were structurally defective, hurriedly developed, and implemented without consideration of their long-term implications.[20] The extent of state intervention in agriculture was much greater than in the colonial era, and the approach was not gradualist, due in part to the "rivalry" between the different regions, which were trying to out-do each other. This approach stemmed from the lack of centralized planning in Nigerian agriculture in this period.[21] Although Stolper viewed the relative independence of regional policies as a strength in terms of their response to "grassroots" needs, the government's attempt to expand agricultural production was driven by economic rationalism, with no consideration for the social cost, an approach that accelerated the rate of agricultural decline.[22]

From 1960 onward, the government stressed the need to maintain the prominence given by the colonial administration to the export sector and viewed the expansion of commodity production as fundamental to national economic development. Minister for Economic Development Jaja A. Wachuku reemphasized the importance of the agricultural sectors for the development of the country. It was abundantly clear, he argued,

> that in spite of the great efforts necessary in the industrial field, that the impetus of an agricultural productivity must be maintained and increased if our ambitious plans are to be fulfilled.[23]

Although the government continued to emphasize increased cash crop production, the need to increase food production was raised as part of the official agricultural policy. But the paternalistic attitude of the state toward peasant production continued. Agricultural planning continued to be productionist in orientation while questions of rural equity or gender were largely ignored as planners followed a technocratic approach to agricultural development.[24] The continued neglect of women farmers and emphasis on cash crops in the postindependence period is understandable because the indigenous bureaucrats were the products of the colonial system.

Successive postindependence governments adopted a combination of the improvement approach—inherited from the colonial era—and the radical transformation approach to agricultural and rural development. The interventionist policies of the regional and later state governments, the emphasis on cash crops, and the continued neglect of women farmers, all rooted in colonial ideology, worked against agricultural development. During much of the first decade of independence, however, the performance of the agricultural sectors was still impressive, contributing about 80.3 percent of the total value of Nigeria's exports. However, in 1967, the average share of agriculture in the total export earnings of Nigeria fell to about 58.8 percent.[25] At this time, there was evidence of a crisis in the agricultural sector as food items were increasingly imported.[26] The decline in the value of agriculture is manifested in the dwindling contribution of the sector to the national GDP. The contribution of agriculture to the GDP by 1970 had declined to 48.23 percent.[27] By the same year, Nigeria's export of palm oil and kernels, the major cash crops from eastern Nigeria, had declined from 165,000 tons and 411,000 tons to 8,000 and 182,000 tons respectively.[28]

Several factors influenced the nature of state control in the postindependence era. State capitalism was the dominant model in the agricultural sector and the preferred means of dealing with the issue of development. The dominance of the state raises important questions: first, regarding the persistence of state capitalism in Nigeria; and second, regarding the fate of the Nigerian peasants who constitute the majority of the Nigerian population and who must be the focus of development. But since the rhetoric of the Eastern Region government was local economic development, the regional authority saw its mission as a noble one. Not surprisingly, then, the regional government increased its hold on the peasants through market intervention and direct participation in agricultural production using peasant labor and land. The large number of state-owned agricultural projects in the early postindependence period highlights the increased involvement of the regional government in the agricultural sector.

Unlike the colonial administrators, however, the regional government interfered directly in the organization and marketing of agricultural products. Its control of the peasants, as was the case in the colonial period, was arbitrary, lacked cohesion, and threatened the stability of rural life and agricultural production. The continued state intervention in agriculture exerted pressures on the agricultural sector. The case of the Eastern Region will now be assessed.

OVERVIEW OF AGRICULTURAL DEVELOPMENT, 1960-1970

The regional government saw control of agricultural production and indeed greater state participation as the ideal economic development strategy. Although there was no clear break from the past, state control of the agrarian economy became stronger and more effective. The government invested directly in cash crop agriculture and created conditions favorable to the expansion of export crops. Table 1 below gives some idea of the importance of the cash crop sector to the regional government.

The Eastern Region was keen on rapid local infrastructural, social, and economic development. The government expanded existing programs and launched new ones intended to revolutionize agriculture in the region. The determination to achieve the goals of development through agriculture is seen in the estimated capital expenditure devoted to the sector

Table 1: Government Investment Priorities in Agriculture

Sector	Estimated Amount of investment (£1,000)	%
Tree crops for export	22.784	61.9
Other crops (food)	2.795	7.6
Animal health & husbandry	2.831	7.1
Extension/research/training	5.711	15.3
Fisheries/Forestry	.403	1.1
Land use & conservation	.997	2.7
Supporting services	1.500	4.1
Total	36.821	100.0

Source: *Eastern Nigeria Development Plan 1962-1968, Official Document No. 8.* Enugu: Government Printer, 1962.

in the Eastern Nigeria Development Plan. With 40 percent of a total expenditure of £75,192,000 set aside for agricultural development, revised in 1964 to 37 percent, agriculture towered over all other sectors in the government's development plans.[29] This policy was continued not only because government revenue depended on the export trade, but also because bureaucrats had a fixed view of what constituted development and the best way to achieve it.

The agricultural development programs in the region consisted mainly of the establishment of farm settlements and plantation schemes, which were staffed and populated by peasant farmers. In addition, the marketing arrangements for agricultural produce were restructured to ensure effective control of peasant production and enable the government to maximize revenue generation from agriculture. A review of the marketing strategy and of various agricultural schemes will throw more light on the region's mechanisms of exploiting peasants and the ways the region's agricultural policy exacerbated agricultural decline.

Marketing Boards

The Eastern Nigeria Marketing Boards (ENMB) were established in 1954 and held the monopoly in selling agricultural produce overseas.[30] The marketing boards were charged with the responsibility for palm oil, palm kernels, cocoa, bennised, soya beans, groundnuts, copra, and any of their derivatives.[31] The boards were, among other things, to stabilize producers' prices by fixing legal minimum buying prices for a whole season and minimizing price alterations between one season and the next. In addition, the boards were required to help maintain legally prescribed grades and standards of quality and to improve the quality of export produce. The boards were also charged with the allocation of funds to appropriate authorities by through grants, loans, investments, and endowments for the purposes of economic development and research.[32]

However, the marketing boards did not improve agriculture. The boards' pricing policies used a quarter to a third of the potential gross income of farmers to finance development in infrastructure, state plantations, and farm settlements, and research in agriculture.[33] The activities of the marketing boards and their pricing policies reduced potential producer income by keeping prices in the region of 50-70 percent of actual market value.[34] While the middlemen and the boards made huge profits, farmers in the Eastern Region suffered as a result of low producer prices.[35] This translated into massive accumulation of funds by the boards. In 1958, for example, the total revenue the government realized from the F.O.B. price per ton in the case of cocoa was 43.7 percent, which represents the proportion by which the farmer was underpaid. A decade later, in 1968, the proportion under the postindependence government was 49.1 percent and it continued to rise until 1977.[36]

The repressive nature of the state control structures implemented though the marketing boards exacerbated agricultural decline because farmers were unwilling to re-invest in agriculture. The dilemma faced by the peasant producers led to a dramatic decline in the officially marketed output of crops for export in Nigeria although the world market price for these products was rising.[37] Moreover, the income generated was not ploughed back into agriculture or used to improve producer income but was used for development in other sectors. The production of major exports continued to decline because the high prices agricultural produce fetched in the world market did not reach the peasant producers. The rate of outmigration increased as the income of rural producers declined.

REGIONAL PLANTATION SCHEMES

With the movement toward political independence, the indigenous elite began to reverse British plantation policy by 1952.[38] The development of a Unilever oil palm plantation in Calabar and the Dunlop Rubber Estate of over 21,000 acres in 1956 marked the beginning of the "plantation decade."[39] The regional government through the Eastern Region Produce Development Boards (later the Eastern Nigeria Development Corporation, or ENDC) initiated the development of oil palm, rubber, cocoa, cashew, and coconut plantations. The activities of the regional agricultural development program were organized around ENDC plantations or estates, community plantations and farm settlements. The first significant steps in this direction were the region's tree crop programs implemented through the Ministry of Agriculture (MOA).

Tree Crop Programs

In the Ministry of Agriculture's major tree crop programs, oil palm rehabilitation, rubber planting, and cocoa planting, were intensified to boost export production. The Ministry supplied seedlings, fertilizer, and instructions without charge for a period of five years. Over a five-year period—the normal period for oil palms to reach maturity—the farmer was paid up to $28.00 per acre in cash.[40] There was enthusiasm on the part of farmers especially toward the oil palm rehabilitation program. Purvis's survey indicates that a variety of means was used to acquire land for the project including outright purchase.[41] By the end of 1966 the area planted with oil palm totaled about 50,000 acres, and over 4,000 farmers had participated in the scheme in the five years of its operation.[42]

However, the impact of the tree crop programs was minimal as peasants continued to produce under the traditional system because of land scarcity in many parts of the region. Very few farmers could provide five acres of land as required by the Agricultural Department. The Agricultural Sample Survey for 1963-1964, for example, indicates that over 85 percent of the region's farmers cultivated less than 2.5 acres annually.[43] In fact, by the 1960s and 1970s, the fallow period had been shorted or even disappeared in many areas due to land scarcity. In the Mbaise, Owerri, Mbano, and Obowo areas of the Eastern Region, continuous cropping had become routine as a result of scarcity of land. Thus, the regional government's tree crop programs were implemented under conditions of acute land scarcity, which limited their success, but at the same time put pressure on the local agricultural economy. The state's intervention under conditions of land scarcity and its emphasis on permanent tree crops failed to consider the conditions under which the Eastern Nigerian peasant operated. But the regional government continued this approach to agricultural development with the establishment of plantation schemes.[44]

Community Plantations

The community plantations were at the heart of the region's rural development agenda. As a major component of the six-year development plan, the regional government aimed at changing rural land tenure patterns to guarantee larger land holdings to genuine farmers.[45] As Floyd observed, the scheme aimed at "changing and modernizing village life in *toto*."[46] In formulating the community plantation policy, the government capitalized on existing social structures, which emphasized cooperative efforts in achieving common goals. The community development programs therefore aimed to use local resources especially "abundant labor as a substitute for scarce capital."[47] Thus, the self-help method became a key component of the rural development program.

In each location, the government acquired land which it then handed over to individual members of a farmers' cooperative. The land, which was leased for sixty to ninety-nine years, was to be planted with cash crops in addition to food crops from which the farmer maintained himself and his family.[48] With assistance in the forms of free seedlings and fertilizer under the "Tree Crop Subsidy Program," the farmer maintained the crops till maturity. Although the proceeds from cash crops went directly to the farmer, the marketing arrangements and the supervision of the scheme by a rural development officer placed the farmer effectively under government control.

As Table 2 below indicates, the community plantation projects involved large-scale land alienation. By 1965, there were twelve community plantations with 970 participants, occupying a total land area of 11,750 acres. The establishment of the scheme in some heavily populated parts of the region reduced the land available for subsistence production and led to agricultural intensification. The continued emphasis on cash crops further relegated food security and subsistence production to the backburners of the government's agrarian development policy. The gender bias in official policy remained, as women were left out of the agricultural development schemes. The implicit assumption that the farmer was male denied women access to new agricultural technology and participation in improvement schemes.

Table 2: Rural Development Community Plantations, Eastern Nigeria, 1965

Location	Division & Province	Size (Gross Acres)	Approx. No. of Participants	Period of Lease (Years)	Crops	Pop. Density Zone
Oban	Calabar (Calabar)	Approx. 5760	50		Rubber	Low
Abia Ohafia	Bende (Umuahia)	1500	170	99	Oil palm	Low-Medium
Ugwuaka	Okigwe (Owerri)	1500	30		Oil palm	Medium
Ikwa and Ikot Ita	Opobo (Uyo)	700	145		Oil palm	Medium
Akwete	Aba (Umuahia)	530	95	99	Oil palm	Medium
Inyong Oron and Iwoma	Opobo (Uyo)	420	100	99	Oil palm	Low
Ajbaja Umukabia	Okigwe (Owerri)	400	100		Oil lm	Medium-High
Akoliufu Alayi	Bende (Umuahia)	400	100	99	Oil palm	Low-Medium
Lekwesi	Okigwe (Owerri)	400	70		Oil palm	Medium
Itigidi and Adadana	Afikpo (Abakaliki)	185	34		Oil palm Rice	Low
Umuogbo Nkwerre	Orlu (Owerri)	90	25	60	Oil palm	High-Very High
Affa	Udi (Enugu)	25	50		Vegetables (tomatoes, onions, peppers)	Medium

Source: Floyd: *Eastern Nigeria: A Geographical Review* (New York: Frederick C. Prager Inc., 1969), 216-217.

In actuality, the schemes constituted obstacles to peasant production and subsistence because the evidence suggests that when resources are directed to women, agricultural productivity and efficiency increase.[49] The state, nevertheless, continued with the gender-biased ideology of the male farmer and the neglect of food production.

ENDC Plantations/Estates

Beside community-level schemes, the regional government began to mount a vigorous program of agricultural development along commercial plantation lines under the Eastern Nigeria Development Corporation.[50] A total of 148,930 acres was acquired for plantation development in twenty-two locations in the first five years after independence.[51] By the end of 1965, 67,000 acres (45 percent of the area acquired) had been planted with cash crops and 85 percent coverage was projected by the end of the Six-Year Development Plan period in 1968.[52] Provided with modern facilities including maternity homes and schools, and equipped with modern farming implements, these plantations represented the most ambitious of the agrarian development programs. This was the regional government's attempt to create a "modern," self-supporting settlement for farming households, where men would be responsible for plantation operations while women provided domestic services and raised children. But structural, administrative and social factors created obstacles to the realization of the stated goals. The lack of sensitivity to local structures and conditions resulted in implementation problems.

Although most of the plantations were located in areas of relatively "low" population density in the Calabar and Uyo Provinces, the rubber plantations at Ameke in Umuahia Division, and Emeabiam and Obiti in Owerri Division were located in areas of high population density. In most of Igboland, even areas of "low" population density were relatively high in density by national standards.[53] The policy of large-scale land alienation and emphasis on permanent tree crop development reduced the land available for food production in these highly populated areas.

The system of operation and supervision provided effective government control of the estates. But the plantations were inefficient as commercial enterprises because they were staffed by laborers and supervised by government employees. Moreover, the mechanized nature of their operation did not generate the desired employment for thousands of school leavers. The Six-Year Plan estimated that the plantations would employ 80,000 elementary school leavers, 15,000 school certificate holders, and 2,000 university graduates.[54] Judging from the employment figures in 1966, the region did not meet the optimistic targets of labor absorption estimated in the Six-Year Plan.[55]

The plantation projects failed to achieve their employment targets, not only because of the mechanized nature of the plantations but also because agriculture was becoming an increasingly unattractive option for young school leavers.[56] The inability of the projects to achieve an agricultural revolution or increase the desire of the youth to take up agriculture is borne out by the continued rural-urban migration that occurred in the region. The mechanization of operations in the plantations also effectively eliminated women from the scheme.[57] The gender division of labor led to women being overloaded with tasks in subsistence production, and to a reduction in agricultural productivity.[58]

The projects faced other problems besides improper projections. The field surveys necessary for the production of topographic, pedologic, and cadastral maps were not carried out. Incorrect soil analysis and planting of crops on unsuitable soils led to crop failures.[59] The dilemma is exemplified by the failure of the Ubani section of the Umuahia cocoa estate and much of the Arochukwu and Oburba cocoa estates to produce healthy trees despite the heavy cost involved in the initial establishment of the plantations.[60] This prompted the replanting of Ubani plantation with coffee and Arochukwu with oil palm. There is no doubt that improper feasibility studies were a major obstacle to the realization of the government's objectives. The government's policy of establishing plantations on large tracts of land created problems in a society where land was communally owned. The structure of the land ownership and the traditional land tenure system made a plantation system difficult to set up. The intricacy of the ownership structure meant that establishment of ownership was not easy. Disputes between village groups over the ownership of particular tracts of land occurred frequently.[61] Furthermore, there were severe problems for peasants who lost their land and began to depend largely on the market for subsistence.

Farm Settlements

The region's agricultural strategy continued with the establishment of farm settlements though which the state further intervened in agricultural production. The farm settlements scheme dates back to the post-World War II period. With money from the Colonial Development and Welfare Fund, the Nigerian administration put more effort into producing cotton and groundnuts with the first schemes established in Talabakwa, Mokwa, and Baiduara in Northern Nigeria. The schemes involved settling farmers in villages with government financial and technical support. The rapid shift in policy toward collectivization was often imposed on an unwilling peasantry and implemented under unfavorable social conditions.[62] The farm settlement projects, unlike similar projects in China and Vietnam, were adopted under a capitalist system without the kind of moral/political authority commanded by socialist states.

The farm settlements reversed traditional land tenure systems and deprived peasant farmers of their autonomy. Baldwin argues that:

> The failure of the scheme was not due to any lack of factors of production—land, labor and capital—but to the inability of the farmers to combine them effectively into an economic unit.[63]

But the inability of peasants to combine the different factor elements is not a plausible reason for the failure of the scheme. Peasants have been producing for the market on their own terms and using the same resources in an economic and rational manner for many years.

The regional government ignored the social, economic, and cultural context in which the scheme was to operate. The settlement projects, which amounted to forced villagization and relocation of peasants, failed because they disrupted local social and production patterns. They operated under a labor arrangement which limited settlers' ability to call upon traditional forms of labor procurement. Under the traditional forms of labor arrangements, a household relied on the labor of the immediate family, the lineage and various work groups to carry out its farming tasks. This labor was often provided free. But the settlement schemes often took settlers away from their immediate locality, which tended to sever kinship-based labor networks.

In addition, many settlers saw themselves as civil servants working for the government and did not regard settlement farms as their own private profit-oriented enterprises.[64] Government officials also misjudged peasant response to the settlement scheme. Officials did not adequately consider the numerous variables that informed settlers' decisions whether to stay in the program or the effect of new agricultural techniques on peasants. By 1954, the early settlements had ceased operation because peasants did not believe in their viability. Moreover, the settlers found some of the modern agricultural techniques, which required a certain level of education, very frustrating.[65]

The failure of the earlier schemes did not deter the Eastern Region government from establishing farm settlements. The regional government chose the option of agricultural advancement through the introduction of radical, novel ideas based on cooperative farming. In the Western Region, the government established a farm settlement scheme in 1959 to demonstrate that by careful planning, farms can be operated by young people to provide a comfortable standard of living comparable with or even higher than that gained by persons of the same status in other forms of employment. The settlement scheme was also expected to provide an alternative to the traditional efforts of extension services in disseminating new techniques to farmers throughout the region as well as to promote the social integration of different ethnic groups and communities.[66] The Eastern Region decided to pursue this line of agricultural development and its settlement scheme became its most ambitious agricultural development scheme.

In 1961, the premier of the Eastern Region, Dr. M. I. Okpara, undertook a tour of Israel to access the viability of farm settlements in his region. His return with a team of Israeli experts marked the beginning of the farm settlement project in the region. The premier announced in a speech in 1961 that a number of farm settlements would be established, each at the cost of £500,000, to include 400 young men and families with individual farms.[67] A farm settlement scheme based on the Israeli model was initiated.

The Israeli model, based on the "smallholders village" (moshavin),[68] was adopted in the form of "regional settlements" allegedly suitable to African societies.[69] This adaptation to African conditions must be qualified. The scheme's success in Israel is not unrelated to the peculiar historical circumstances in which the members of the Jewish Diaspora found themselves. With little agricultural experience, the scheme offered them the chance of acquiring agricultural knowledge in a new environment. The Eastern Nigerian peasants already had centuries of agricultural skills and many years of commercial agriculture experience behind them. The new system, however, was to operate under radically different socioeconomic and political conditions.[70]

By 1966, the Eastern Region had set up multipurpose settlement schemes at Ohaji, Igbariam, Erei, Boki, Ulonna South, Ulonna North, and Uzouwani (See Table 3 below). Like its predecessors, the regional scheme aimed at the development of cash crops and targeted male settlers as the principal beneficiaries. Although the farm settlements cultivated food crops such as yams, cocoyams and maize in their compound land, all the farm settlements except Uzouwani grew oil palm. Some settlements grew other crops in addition, while Uzouwani grew rice.[71]

Table 3: Farm Settlements in Eastern Nigeria, 1962-1966

Settlement	Total area planned		Area planted December 1966		Type of crop	No. of settlers by Dec. 1966	Date started
	Acres	Hect.	Acres	Hect.			
Boki	11541	4616.4	528.65	211.5	Oil palm, citrus	240	16 Nov., 1962
Uzouwani	10562	4224.8	619.00	247.6	Rice	190	24 Mar., 1965
Igbariam	6560	2624.0	1775.00	710.0	Oil palm, citrus	350	1 Nov., 1962
Erei	10385	4154.0	1338.00	535.2	Oil palm	360	23 Oct., 1964
Ulonna South	2018	807.2	892.00	356.8	Oil palm, rubber	240	9 April, 1964
Ulonna North	5780	2312.0	623.00	249.2	Oil palm, rubber	120	23 Jan., 1965
Ohaji	14929	5971.6	2053.40	821.4	Oil palm, rubber	360	15 Nov., 1962
Total	61,775	24,710.0	7,829.05	3,131.7		1,860	

Source: H. I. Ajaegbu, Urban and Rural Development in Nigeria (London: Heinemann, 1976), 65.

The objectives of the scheme were set out in various policy statements. According to Minister of Agriculture, P. N.

Okeke, the farm settlement scheme was to serve as a model for the masses of the peasant farmers to emulate. This was the most important long-term aim of the scheme as outlined by the government.[72] The government believed that the trickle-down effects of the scheme would ultimately improve peasant production methods and increase agricultural production in the region. The scheme was also to help resettle school leavers and stem the rural-urban drift that had been a major feature of the region since the 1940s. The government believed that modernization of agricultural methods would rouse the interest of young people in farming.

As in the days of the colonial administration, research was to be an important component of the new agricultural scheme, partly because the settlers, already familiar with the traditional methods of cultivating these crops, would be particularly useful participants in the research. In addition, government would not have to spend any extra money establishing special research stations.[73] The scheme was also supposed to enable commercial farmers to overcome some of the constraints on large-scale farming in Eastern Nigeria, including the indigenous land tenure system.[74] The government's view was that fragmentation of farm holdings acted as a disincentive to large-scale farming in the region. Indeed, the regional government saw its role as the implementation of its political ideology of "Pragmatic African Socialism."[75]

Whether critics of the settlement scheme were right to state that the scheme and choice of sites were politically motivated is not the issue here. We are, rather, concerned with the implications of the scheme for agricultural development in the region.[76] To what extent did the scheme facilitate or inhibit agricultural development? The system seemed ideal in theory, but it did not work in practice for obvious practical and ideological reasons.

The scheme did not revolutionize agriculture in the region. Given the mechanized form of operation, the whole idea of creating employment was doomed to failure. The farm settlements were capital intensive and not labor intensive and therefore employed very little labor. Mechanized agricultural production prevented the realization of the government's stated objectives. The number of settlers (1,860) in 1966 was very limited compared with the number of unemployed people in the region. Intakes of settlers continued to remain low and by 1970, the settlements had only 3,350 families, which represents what Floyd called "a drop in the bucket" compared with the employment needs of the region.[77] Similarly, the system did not do much to relieve congestion in high-density areas as had been envisaged. The Igbariam scheme in particular led to the movement of tenant-squatter farmers away from the area. Since they were forced to forfeit their livelihood from the Igbarian area, they added to the rural overpopulation and underemployment in other parts of Onitsha Province.[78] The growth of dependency on imported food items was an indication of the failure of the settlement and other agricultural schemes.

The poor level of local adaptation created other problems. The whole idea of a farm settlement was "strange," stated a social anthropologist attached to the settlement at the Uzouwani scheme.[79] Dormitory life, communal feeding, and separation from local environments were like "taking a plunge into the unknown."[80] This leads to a state described as "settler shock," and Floyd and Adinde argued that sociologists or human geographers who have studied the farm settlements could detect this phenomenon without difficulty.[81] The change of environment imposed a lot of psychological strain on the settlers.[82] The obsessiveness with which the regional government pursued its agricultural development scheme led to disaster because the government did not count the social and environmental costs or the long-term implications for agriculture in general. Furthermore, the management style that was introduced was not in line with indigenous ideas. The activities of government supervisors, the overcentralization of decision-making, and the bureaucratic approach of the civil service made work frustrating.[83]

But the government was eager to make the project succeed by facilitating its efficient operation. To achieve this goal, the government forced settlers to enter into a contract that made them tenants-at-will to the government of the region for a period of thirty-five years, which was considered the length of the active working life of the first settler.[84] Settlers could not sublet or fragment their holdings. Settlers undertook to work hard each day in accordance with a regimented timetable. Absence from work except in cases of certified illness attracted a fine of £1.[85] A tenancy could change hands under three conditions. First, by a man's son inheriting the holding on the death of his father; second, on eviction, if conditions of entry into the settlement were violated on which case the new settler inherited the capital liabilities involved in establishing the holding; and third, by a voluntary decision to leave the settlement, after which the holding was granted to a new settler on the same conditions as above.[86] Since the settlers had to repay a subsistence loan of three shillings per day provided for the first two years, it is doubtful if many easily broke away from the contract.

Besides being forbidden to form trade unions, the settlers were forced to belong to a farm settlement cooperative society and to sell their produce to the cooperative society for wholesale marketing.[87] But the organizational structure, the insecurity, the fear of eviction, and the regimented settlement life could not have made for optimum production.

There were other problems associated with the settlement scheme. The alienation of large tracts of land created problems for local communities and the environment. Since settlers were to enjoy the right of ownership, tension arose between locals and "foreign" elements in the settlement communities. Some villagers opposed the recruitment of non-indigenes, in particular, non-Igbos into the settlements located in the Igbo areas. As one village group argued;

> Since each settler enjoys rights of ownership of his plantation land in perpetuity, a time will eventually come when a large proportion of our productive land will pass into the ownership of non-indigenes. It is a dangerous threat to our interests and those of our posterity.[88]

By 1966, a total of 7,828.05 acres of land had been alienated from rural communities for the settlement schemes.[89] With population densities far above the national average in a land hungry society, land alienation was a potential source of frustration and conflict.[90] The government-sponsored farm settlements, in addition to the activities of migrant farmers, the piecemeal expansion of land-hungry communities, and the various plantation schemes, took a "heavy toll on the natural vegetation of the region."[91]

We must not lose sight of the gendered nature of the settlement program. The regional government concentrated its efforts on male farmers. Although full statistics are not available, indirect evidence shows that men were the targets of the scheme. The mechanization of agriculture under the different schemes initiated by the regional government led to the domination of new agricultural knowledge by men.[92] With a masculinist view of agriculture, extension services, new technology, and inputs went directly to men, leaving women in subordinate positions. While women continued to produce most of the food crops, their reduced return from agriculture forced many to diversify into nonagricultural sectors. On their part, many men were not ready to accept agriculture as an occupation as opportunities in other sectors offered better incentives. The government, however, continued to bring its message of an agricultural revolution to the peasants through community-centered projects. The settlement scheme did little to incorporate traditional social structures or integrate methods based on local farming patterns and local technology. Thus, agricultural production levels did not improve in any significant degree.

In the settlement schemes in particular, the social organization of production was modified to take advantage of scale economies and crop specialization and to maximize marketed output. This led to a loss of women's usufruct rights to land, to a loss of female income in male-headed households, and to a less varied cropping pattern.[93] There continued to be priori assumption that men were the farmers. This revealed a failure to perceive women as producers and as an important part of any innovations in agriculture. Extension agents continued to be mostly males and often tended to work with males. This was a major flaw in government's approach to agricultural development.

The settlement schemes did not produce the desired revolutionary result. Described as "a colossal waste of public funds," the farm settlements had achieved little when the civil war broke out in 1967.[94] Commenting on the Uzouwani Farm Settlement in particular, Umoh, a member of the Eastern Nigeria House of Assembly, noted:

> Having studied the Uzouwani farm settlement, I have come to the conclusion that we erred when we authorized the expenditure of thousands of dollars on such [a] white elephant. Unemployment persists; rural-to-urban migration of youths continues.[95]

In a case study of the Igbariam Farm Settlement, Floyd argues that "positive" gains were made in the physical landscape, as exemplified in the neatly kept farms and villages and the regimented lines of modern cement-block and tin-roofed houses as opposed to "primitive" dwelling structures.[96] Floyd's opinion reflects the planners' notion that the key to agricultural development lay in the transformation of peasant modes of production.[97] This certainly came at a cost in the form of social disruption and waste of human and material resources.[98] The entire program was far too costly and any achievement came at a high environmental and ecological cost. As was the case in Western Nigeria, the farm settlement scheme failed because it did not yield a compensatory output to justify the resource input committed to it. The desired objective of social integration and improved economic status for the settlers was not attained, and the scheme failed to arrest rural-urban drift, thus failing to achieve the employment-creating objective.[99]

By 1966, five years after the establishment of the Uzouwani scheme, 75 percent of the settlers still needed regular allowances from the government for subsistence.[100] The bureaucratic nature of the farm projects and the form of organization established in the settlements that removed settlers from their roots did not make for the realization of the goals of the project. The project did not lead to the production of more food or improve agriculture in the region. The project functioned as a state enterprise in an area where peasants have been the backbone of export production. The failure of the state to recognize that peasants have other interests and motivations and are part of a cultural milieu that recognizes the primacy of locality meant that the settlers saw themselves as strangers in the settlements. Very often, local farmers know better than "experts" do, but the bureaucrats had no place for indigenous knowledge, making the settlers mere laborers instead of owner-operators.

The struggle of the regional government to control peasant production, access to land, and the crops to be produced created tension and contradictions because the state acted as the "owner" in establishing agricultural projects and the intervention that followed disrupted rural life and removed any incentive to remain in farming. State intervention became a means of extracting peasant surplus and disrupting agricultural productivity.[101] At the same time, government programs ignored the cooperative nature of production in the traditional economy. The schemes made the relationship between men and women highly individualized, leading to the erosion of community resource management systems.

In the Eastern Region, the government's approach to agricultural development is important in understanding some of the dynamics of the agrarian crisis in the region. This is because the attempt to transform agriculture was taking place in a region that was already involved in intensive agriculture and heavily burdened by high population pressure. Government activities in this era gave rise to a relationship in which state capitalism and control of peasant agriculture became more aggressive. The relationship between the state and the peasants and the increased attempts by the state to intervene in peasant production frustrated agricultural development. The effects of state agricultural policies reverberated in the rural economy, seriously undermining subsistence production and the ability of peasants to control production. But there were other factors during the period that affected the course of agricultural development in the region, including the Biafran-Nigerian Civil War.

NIGERIAN-BIAFRAN CIVIL WAR AND AGRICULTURAL DECLINE, 1967-1970

By 1966, the Nigerian federation was in a political crisis that led to a civil war between the predominantly Igbo-speaking people of Eastern Nigeria and the rest of the federation.[102] The political crisis created an economic crisis for the Igbo as many migrants returned to Igboland. In a region partly dependent on other regions to meet its food needs, the civil war exacerbated the agricultural and food crisis in Igboland. The civil war disrupted the production and supply mechanisms on which the food security of the whole of Igboland depended. The crisis resulted in higher food prices in 1966 and 1967.[103] This prompted a major food promotion campaign early in 1967 because the reduction in supplies, especially from the North, resulted in shortages of meat and onions.[104]

Compounding the food crisis was the number of returnees to the Eastern Region. Estimates of their number have varied from a few hundred thousands to millions.[105] Whatever the accurate figures, the large influx of returnees and displaced persons in the region created social and economic problems never previously experienced there. Insecurity made it difficult to farm. Tremendous increases in population created other problems. Refugees harvested crops that were not ready, and uprooted freshly planted seed yams as food. Even after the war, it was difficult to rebuild the decimated villages and rural economy. Public agricultural projects remain abandoned.

Looking back on those years, a number of those who lived through the civil war on the Biafran side remembered the resourcefulness of the Igbo people more than they cared to recall the heartbreaks. Those who survived the horror reminisced about women's and old men's trading activities, and the ability of many households to survive on whatever they scratched from the bush. The forced repatriation of Igbos into the Biafran enclave put increasing pressure on the already fragile environment. As one informant recalled,

> Refugees scouted farms and pulled out seed yams from the ground. Stealing of farm produce increased astronomically. This would have been an abomination in the past. But the war created a situation where people had to survive at all cost.[106]

While some households were able to farm, the majority could not. "How could you plant with all the insecurity when you were not sure of harvesting your crops?"[107] one informant asked. This was the beginning of serious de-agrarianization for many peasant farmers. Many never recovered from their losses. For many of the peasant farmers in the Biafran enclave, who lost their crops, especially yams, this marked the end of farming as a primary occupation.[108]

The food crisis in Igboland was exacerbated by the economic embargo imposed by the Federal government on the Biafran Republic. The fact that after thirty months of war, the Igbo could not sustain themselves is indication enough of the precarious nature of the agrarian economy, especially in crop production. The loss of labor created further crises for the agrarian sector. An informant sums up the implication of this episode for agriculture in most of Eastern Nigeria:

> The war and the disruption it brought created the kind of poverty and hopelessness never experienced in this region in the past.[109]

The effects of the war continued after its end in 1970. Many who survived the war did not remain in the rural areas to farm, but were attracted to the urban centers as they sought to rebuild their lives.

The plantations in the region as well as the farm settlements could not function under war conditions. In Eastern Nigeria, the major cash crop, palm produce, witnessed decreased exports from 1967 and disappeared from the world market, although palm kernels continued to be exported into the 1980s. Although there was increased local use of palm oil, prices fluctuated sharply from the 1970s onwards, making household income unstable. Despite increased local use of palm oil, there was an overall decrease in the contribution of agriculture to GDP with the exit of palm produce. For the Igbo people of Eastern Nigeria, this represented a major decline in income derived from sales of agricultural produce. Although peasants continued to produce and earn income from palm produce, the inflationary trends in the country reduced real peasant income considerably. At the same time, the high cost of imported food items, the large-scale rate of de-agrarianization and increased movement into the urban areas, the expansion of infrastructural development, and an urban-biased development policy all took their toll on agriculture. All these circumstances disrupted and altered the pattern of subsistence production.

The Biafran government responded to the crisis of the late 1960s by changing the priority, which had hitherto been placed on export production, in favor of food production.[110] But success was limited and the peasants bore the burden of the crisis in the agricultural sector within Biafra. The resourcefulness of the Igbo was what prevented many households and the Biafran army from starving to death. Women organized food production campaigns and supported the Land Army Scheme, which aimed at producing more food within Biafran territories that were not directly affected by the war.[111] After the civil war, farming no longer dominated the regional or national economy. By this time, farming had ceased to be the major source local subsistence or export revenue due to withdrawal from the sector and the expansion of the petroleum industry.[112]

CONCLUSION

Since independence, Nigeria has made efforts to reverse the trend of agricultural decline. The object of this chapter has been to try to identify the pattern of change in the Eastern Region. The chapter has argued that state intervention was characterized by a variety of systems of control, all of which imposed more constraints on the agricultural potential of the region and the ability of many peasants to continue operating in the agrarian sector. It has argued that the role of the state in agricultural transformation has indeed led to agricultural decline as a result of the emphasis on a cash crop economy which is often affected by world market fluctuations, the neglect of subsistence production, and the state's imposition of its will on the peasants.

The contradiction inherent in the attempts to improve agricultural production led to their failure. State sponsored agricultural projects could not produce the desired effect, but in fact limited the ability of peasants to achieve the objective. By imposing new systems of agricultural production, the regional government constructed new economic systems, which entailed a radical redefinition of production relations within the household. Yet the government did not usually understand the social changes entailed in such a transformation, much less the importance of gender relations in the socioeconomic system. In many cases, women gained no benefit from official agricultural programs.

The policies adopted had a negative impact on agriculture as a result of the emphasis on commodity production. Agricultural planning in the postindependence era implied a consistent effort by the government to replace peasant farming with capitalist farming. The government acted out of near contempt for the peasant farmer who is generally regarded as incapable of spearheading higher productivity.

Overall, government agricultural development projects provide some insight into the problems associated with the interventionist approach to rural development in Eastern Nigeria. The evidence shows that the deteriorating condition of agriculture in the region can be traced to state interventionist measures and the fallout created by these measures since the colonial period.

NOTES

1. Colonial agricultural policies in Africa were expressed differently in each colony depending on imperial interests. For an analysis of British agricultural policy, see for example, G. B. Kay (ed.), *The Political Economy of Colonialism in Ghana: A Collection of Documents and Statistics, 1900-1960* (Cambridge: Cambridge University Press, 1972), 330.
2. See Sara Berry, *No Condition is Permanent: The Social Dynamics of Agrarian Change in Sub-Saharan Africa* (Madison: University of Wisconsin Press, 1993).
3. Kay, *The Political Economy of Colonialism*, 199.
4. Public Record Office, London, CO/879/65/635/208, "Colonial Office to Governor MacGregor," 29 December 1900.
5. Nigeria: *Annual Report on Agriculture, 1912* (Lagos: Government Printer, 1912).
6. Interview with Chief Eneremadu, aged 96, Mbutu Mbaise, December 1999.
7. Nigeria: *Annual Report on Agriculture 1912,* (Lagos: Government Printer, 1912), 23.
8. Ibid.
9. Nigeria: *The Nigeria Handbook,* 1927 (Lagos: Government Printer, 1927), 255-256.
10. Helleiner, *Peasant Agriculture Government and Economic Growth in Nigeria* (Homewood, Ill.: R. D. Irwin, 1966), 5.
11. This was the strategy adopted by Hugh Clifford, governor-general of colonial Nigeria from 1919 to 1925.
12. Nigeria: *The Nigeria Handbook, 1929*, (Lagos: Government Printer, 1929), 246.
13. Helleiner, *Peasant Agriculture,* 5.
14. I.E.S. Amdii, "Revenue generating capacity of the Nigerian Customs and Excise, 1875-1960," in I.E.S. Amdii (ed.), *100 Years of the Nigerian Customs and Excise: 1891-1991* (Zaria: ABU, 1991) 12-47.
15. Nigeria: *Annual Report on the Agricultural Department, 1932* (Lagos: Government Printer, 1932), *22*.
16. For a recent analysis of the crisis in "Third World" agriculture, especially its colonial origins, see Mafoud Bennoune, "The

Causes and Consequences of Famine in the Third World," in Christine Ward Gailey (ed.), *Dialectical Anthropology: Essays in honor of Stanley Diamond* (Gainesville: University of Florida Press, 1999), 227-267.
17. Nigeria: *Annual Report on the Department of Agriculture, 1953/1954* (Lagos: Government Printer, 1954), 1.
18. Nigeria: *Annual Report on the Agricultural Department, 1958/1959* (Lagos: Government Printer, 1954), 3.
19. For an examination of agrarian policy and its relation to economic development in this period, see Jerome C. Wells, *Agricultural Policy and Growth in Nigeria, 1962-1968.* (Ibadan: Oxford University Press, 1974).
20. For a critique of the uncoordinated nature of economic planning in the era of regionalism, see Peter B. Clark "Economic Planning for a Country in Transition: Nigeria", in Everett E. Hagen (ed.), *Planning Economic Development* (Homewood, Ill.: Richard D. Irwin, Inc., 1963), 261.
21. See Wells, *Agricultural Policy,* 83.
22. For a similar analysis, see Stolper Wolfgang "Economic Growth and Political Stability in Nigeria: On Growing Together Again", in Carl K. Eicher and Carl Liedholm (eds.), *Growth and Development of the Nigerian Economy* (E. Lansing: Michigan State University Press, 1970), 328-351. Cited in Wells, *Agricultural Policy,* 83.
23. Nigeria: *Annual Report on the Agricultural Department, 1959-1960,* (Lagos: Government Printer, 1960), 1.
24. For a critique of state approach to agricultural development, see, for example, A. Labo, "Social Research, Agricultural Policy and Rural Social Change in Nigeria" paper presented at the Ninth General Assembly of the Social Science Council of Nigeria, University of Lagos, 25-27 March 1966.
25. A. Kolawole "Agricultural Stagnation, Food Crisis and Rural Poverty in Nigeria," Center for Social and Economic Research: Ahmadu Bello University Seminar Series, 1984.
26. For food import figures and values see, for example, D. A. Iyegha, *Agricultural Crisis in Africa: The Nigerian Experience* (London: University Press of America, 1988), 37; O. Awoyemi, "Character of Nigerian Agriculture" *Bullion,* 6, (4) 1983, reproduced in T.S.B. Aribisala, "Nigeria's Green Revolution: Achievements, Problem and Prospects," NISER Distinguished Lecture Series, 8. See also Federal Office of Statistics, *Annual*

Abstract of Statistic sand Nigeria Trade Summary (Lagos: Federal Office of Statistics), for various years.
27. Iyegha, *Agricultural Crisis*, 32.
28. For statistical data on exports see, Federal Office of Statistics, *Review of External Trade* (Lagos: Government Printer, 1979-1983).
29. Nigeria: *National Development Plan. Progress Report 1964* (Lagos: Federal Ministry of Economic Development, 1964), 63.
30. The origin of the marketing boards dates back to the post-World War II reconstruction era. The problem of postwar reconstruction gave rise to a reorganization of the colonies and the setting up of marketing boards. In the postcolonial era, the marketing boards were further reorganized as instruments of "heavy taxation and unremitting exploitation of the peasantry." For further analysis, see Iyegha, *Agricultural Crisis*, 90.
31. Nigeria, *Handbook of Commerce and Industry in Nigeria* (Lagos: Government Printer, no date), 122.
32. Ibid., 123.
33. See Wells, *Agricultural Policy*, 40.
34. Ibid., 40.
35. Interview with Elija Agu of Mbaise, aged about 90, December 1998. See also Iyegha, *Agricultural Crisis*, 89-90.
36. Ibid., 92.
37. Ibid., 90
38. The colonial government discouraged the development of a plantation culture for obvious political and economic reasons. The colonial authority was aware that a radical change in the land tenure system and large-scale alienation of peasant land would result in social and economic problems. Moreover, the peasants in the region as elsewhere in the country met European needs for the most important agricultural produce including palm oil and kernels. This policy continued with little or no modification till the end of 1951.
39. Barry Floyd, *Eastern Nigeria: A Geographical Review* (London: Macmillan, 1966), 213. For a historical analysis of the development of plantations in the region, see R.K. Udo, "Sixty Years of Plantation Agriculture in Southern Nigeria, 1902-1962," *Economic Geography* 12, (1965), 356-368.
40. As an important part of the six-year development plan in the Eastern Region, farmers who wanted to join the scheme were required to provide a minimum of five acres. The farmers also signed a

formal agreement with the Ministry of Agriculture, obliging them to clear, space, mulch, and maintain their land according to government specifications. Gerald D. Hursh et al, *Innovation in Eastern Nigeria: Success and Failure of Agricultural Programs in 71 Villages of Eastern Nigeria* (East Lansing, Michigan: Michigan State University, 1968), 22.
41. Malcolm J. Purvis, *Report on the Survey of the Oil palm Rehabilitation Scheme in Eastern Nigeria*, cited in Wells, *Agricultural Policy*, 258.
42. Wells, *Agricultural Policy*, 257-258.
43. In Hursh et al, *Innovation in Eastern Nigeria*, 19.
44. For the organization of the Eastern Region's agricultural schemes, see Floyd, *Eastern Nigeria*, 213.
45. The use of the term genuine farmer here denotes practicing farmers. Floyd, *Eastern Nigeria*, 215.
46. Ibid., 216.
47. Ibid.
48. Ibid.
49. See especially Janice Jiggins, "Gender-Related Impacts and the Work of the International Agricultural Research Center," *CGIAR Study Paper No. 17* (Washington, D.C.: World Bank, 1986).
50. The Eastern Nigeria Development Corporation (ENDC) was government owned and ran many commercial enterprises, such as cold stores, a soft drink factory, the Obudu cattle ranch, the Progress Hotels. Through its connection with the Ministry of Agriculture, it managed many large cocoa, rubber and oil palm estates, and also ran the "Pioneer Oil Mills". See Hursh et al., *Innovation in Eastern Nigeria*, 196.
51. Floyd, *Eastern Nigeria*, 219.
52. Ibid.
53. For the location of different plantations, their sizes and laborers, see ibid., 219-220.
54. See M. K. Mba, *The First Three Years. A Report of the Eastern Nigeria Six-Year Development Plan* (Enugu: Government Printer 1965), 9, cited in Floyd, *Eastern Nigeria*, 223.
55. Floyd, *Eastern Nigeria*, 219.
56. Nigerian National Archives Enugu, RIVPROF 8/5/661, Registrar of Cooperatives Societies to Chief Secretary.
57. D. Elson (ed.), *Male Bias in the Development Process* (Manchester and New York: Manchester University Press, 1995), 9.
58. Ibid., 10.

59. Floyd, *Eastern Nigeria*, 221-222.
60. Ibid.
61. Ibid.
62. Not in the Chinese or Vietnamese sense of collectivism as part of a socialist ideology.
63. K.D.S. Baldwin, *The Niger Agricultural Project* (London: Blackwell Co. Ltd.).
64. Okoro C. Odiri, "The Uzouwani Farm Settlement and Socio-Economic Development in the Anambra Basin, 1961-1971", M.A. thesis, Department of History, University of Nigeria, (May 1986), 4.
65. Ibid.
66. O. F. Ayadi and C. O. Falusi, "The Social and financial implications of farm settlements in Nigeria," *Journal of Asian and African Studies*, Vol. 31, no. 3-4, (1994),191-206. For a review of the Western Nigeria experiment see O, Okediji, "Some Socio-Cultural Problems in the Western Nigeria land Settlement Scheme: A Case Study," *Nigerian Journal of Economic and Social Studies*, November, 1966, pp. 301-310; and W. Roider, *Farm Settlements for Socio-Economic Development: The Western Nigeria Case*. (Munchen: Weltforum Verlag, 1971).
67. Government Press Conference, *ENIS Bulletin* No. E2,200. (Enugu, January 18, 1961). Cited in Barry Floyd and Monica Adinde, "Farm Settlements in Eastern Nigeria: A Geographical Appraisal" *Economic Geography*, Vol. 43, no. 3 (1967), 189-230.
68. *Moshavin* is a plantation system of commercial agriculture in which the settlers have secure title on their holdings through which they can draw income and are part of a larger cooperative that runs the scheme.
69. M. E. Krenin *Journal of Farm economics* 45 (3), (1963), 35, cited in Okoro, "The Uzouwani Farm Settlement," 5.
70. See, for example, T. C. Yusev, *The Economics of Farm Settlements in Israel* (New York: Express Printers Inc., 1963); and F. C. Gorman, *Social Relations in Israeli Farm Settlements* (Tel-Aviv: Zester and Rox Ltd., 1957).
71. Okoro, "The Uzouwani Farm Settlement", 11.
72. Ministry of Agriculture, *Agricultural Extension Newsletter*. (Enugu, Government Printer, 1963).
73. Mary Jones, *Farm Settlements and Social Transformation in Eastern Nigeria* (New York: Tyndale Inc., 1963), 9.
74. Okoro, "The Uzouwani Farm Settlement", 18.

75. See, *Nigerian Spokesman*, 10 April 1964.
76. Major critics of the scheme included the opposition party in the Eastern House of Assembly, the Action Group (AG). See, *Daily Express*, 10 November 1962.
77. Floyd, *Eastern Nigeria*, 233. See also H. P. Elliot, *Farm Settlements in Eastern Nigeria: Background and Objectives as a Means of Farm Training*, p. 51.
78. Floyd, *Eastern Nigeria*, 233.
79. J.C.U. Eme, "Sociological Problems Connected with Farm Settlement Schemes", *Technical Bulletin*, No. 4. (1963), 61. See also Njaka Imelda, "Socio-Psychological Problems in the Farm Settlements" A Paper presented at the Conference of Agricultural Officers, (Abakiliki, 8 September 1964), 6-9.
80. Okoro, "The Uzouwani Farm Settlement" 44.
81. Floyd and Adinde, "Farm Settlements", 223.
82. Eme, "Sociological Problems", 61. See Floyd and Adinde, "Farm Settlements", 223.
83. Okoro, "The Uzouwani Farm Settlements" 45.
84. Floyd and Adinde, "Farm Settlements", 193.
85. Okoro, "The Uzouwani Farm Settlement" p. 29.
86. Eastern Nigeria, "Eastern Nigeria Farm Settlement Scheme" *Agricultural Bulletin* No. 2, (n.d.), 10.
87. Eastern Nigeria, "Eastern Nigeria Farm Settlement Scheme", 3.
88. Okoro, "The Uzouwani Farm Settlement" 43.
89. H. I. Ajaegbu, *Urban and Rural Development in Nigeria* (London: Heinemann, 1976), 65.
90. For estimates of percentages of population and area experiencing pressure on land (rural), see ibid., 15.
91. Floyd, *Eastern Nigeria*, 163.
92. See for example, M. A. Klein (ed.), *Peasants in Africa: Historical and Contemporary Perspectives* (London: Sage Publications, 1980), 33.
93. See Jiggins, *Gender Related Impacts*, 48.
94. West Wariboko, *Tribune*, 15 April 1966, 10
95. See debate in Eastern Nigeria House of Assembly, *Hansard*, 17 May 1966.
96. Floyd, *Eastern Nigeria*, 232.
97. For discussion on mode of production in the African context, see, for example, Bowlig Simon, *Peasant production and market relations: A Case Study of Western Ghana*, (Copenhagen: Third World Observer Publishers, 1993), 7.

98. Floyd, *Eastern Nigeria*, 232.
99. Ayadi and Falusi, "The Social and Financial Implications", 194.
100. Cox N. George, Mimeographed lecture, cited in Okoro, "The Uzouwani Farm Settlement", 49.
101. For an analysis of state interventions in African economy, see D. Siddle and K. Swindell, *Rural Change in Tropical Africa: From Colonies to Nation-States* (Oxford: Basil Blackwell, 1990), 152ff.
102. For historical studies of the Biafran-Nigerian Civil War, see Mok Chiu Yu and Lynn Arnold (eds.), *Nigeria-Biafra: A Reading into the Problems and Peculiarities of the Conflict* (Adelaide: Adelaide University Quaker Society, 1968); Forsyth Frederick, *The Making of an African Legend: The Biafra Story* (Harmondsworth, England: Penguin Books, 1977); and Herbert Gold, *Biafra Goodbye* (San Francisco: Twowindows Press 1970).
103. Hursh et al., *Innovation in Eastern Nigeria*, 213.
104. The yam and rice producing areas of Abakiliki and Ogoja were particularly important in meeting the food needs of other parts of the region. The insecurity that followed the invasion of the Biafran State affected these frontier regions in such a manner that they could not meet the food needs of other parts of Igboland. The same applied to the riverine regions such as Etche and Ikewere in the south, which were important sources of processed cassava (*akpu*) and fish respectively. The Igbo also depended on the north for beef. The war disrupted supplies thereby worsening the food crisis in the Igbo heartland.
105. See for example, Axel Harneit-Sievers et al, *A Social History of the Nigerian Civil War: Perspectives from Below* (Enugu: Jemezie Associates, 1997), 89-90.
106. Interview with S. Mbagwu, aged 74, Mbaise, December 1998.
107. Interview with Susan Iwuagwu, aged 55, Mbaise, December 1999.
108. Many of the farmers I spoke to relate this experience of losing their barns as a result of the war. Many never recovered from their losses.
109. Interview with Alpelda Korie, aged about 65, Mbaise, 28 December 1998.
110. See Eastern Nigeria: *Economic Development Plan*, 8.
111. Harneit-Sievers, et al., *Social History*. See especially chapters 3 and 4.
112. Anthony Kirk-Greene and Douglas Rimmer. *Nigeria since 1970: A Political and Economic Outline* (London: Hodder & Stoughton, 1981), 70.

9

DEVALUATION AND ECONOMIC CRISIS: A POLITICAL ECONOMY ANALYSIS

J. I. Dibua

INTRODUCTION

The 1980s saw Nigeria's economy witnessing a very severe crisis. The crisis has worsened since then. Among other things, the crisis is manifested in balance of payment deficits, huge external and internal debts, heavy budget deficits, a high rate of inflation, smuggling, a low level of capacity utilization in the manufacturing industries, the intolerably worsening material condition of the majority of the populace, and political instability. Although the severity of the crisis became apparent in 1982 with the collapse of the world oil market and the subsequent drastic reduction in government revenue, its beginnings can be traced to the late 1970s, when Nigeria embarked on heavy external borrowing. This resulted in a phenomenal growth of the country's external debt. For instance, Nigeria's external debt jumped from $1.2 billion in 1978 to $12.8 billion in 1983 and to $30 billion dollars in 1989. Since then, the external debt has stabilized at between $30 and $32 billion dollars. The huge amount needed to service this loan has siphoned a great deal of money out of the country. The Nigerian debt situation is a reflection of the situation in Africa generally.

In accounting for this crisis, successive Nigerian governments from the late 1970s, the international financial institutions (IFIs)—in particular the World Bank and the International Monetary Fund (IMF)—and various neoliberal scholars have emphasized issues like the overvaluation of the naira, the overregulation of the economy, the overdependence on oil as the main source of foreign exchange and government revenue, and the high level of corruption, among others.[1] It is argued that by introducing many distortions into Nigeria's economy, these factors made massive external borrowing and therefore the debt crisis (which is central to the economic crisis) inevitable.

Based on the above explanations of the causes of the economic crisis, a number of policies aimed at resolving it were implemented between 1978 and June 1986. The policies include the introduction of various forms of austerity measures; a ban on the importation of certain items in order to conserve scarce foreign exchange; an increase in import duties on a wide range of finished and intermediate goods; the encouragement and protection of local industries; and the restriction of government expenditure to essential projects. In spite of these measures, the country's economic crisis continued to worsen. By 1986, it was becoming increasingly difficult to service Nigeria's huge foreign debts while external creditors were reluctant to extend more credit facilities to the country. This was the context within which the Ibrahim Babangida administration introduced the Structural Adjustment Program (SAP) in July 1986.

Although the Nigerian government claimed that SAP was a "home-grown" program, it is clear that its introduction was dictated by the IFIs. Indeed, the IFIs had consistently made the introduction of the World Bank-designed SAP a condition for debt restructuring and further financial assistance to Nigeria. Previous requests for an IMF loan by the Shehu Shagari and Muhammadu Buhari administrations failed due to disagreements on the IFIs' insistence on the implementation of a SAP which among other things required the massive devaluation of the Nigerian currency, the privatization of public enterprises, and the removal of government subsidies from social services. Babangida promised in his inaugural address to break the impasse with the IMF over the request for a loan. He subjected the issue of the IMF loan to a nationwide public debate. The outcome of this debate was an overwhelming popular rejection of the loan. This fact notwithstanding, the administration with the covert assistance of the IFIs went ahead to introduce SAP.[2] The centerpiece of SAP is the deregulation of the Nigerian economy through the ascendancy of market forces. A cardinal aspect of this deregulation is the massive devaluation of the naira through the agency of market forces. In fact the overvaluation of the naira was seen as one of the fundamental factors responsible for the economic crisis.

This chapter situates devaluation within the context of the neoliberal explanation of the causes of Nigeria's economic crisis and the solution the neoliberals proffered. It examines the extent to which overvaluation of the Nigerian currency and overregulation of the economy contributed to the economic crisis. It is noted that while these factors contributed to the crisis, they were at most symptoms of more fundamental factors that center around the dependent and neocolonial political economy that has existed in the country since the attainment of political independence. To be able to understand and overcome the crisis it is important to understand the dependent capitalist system that existed in the country. The chapter also examines the effects of devaluation and deregulation on Nigeria's economy. To what extent have these factors, which are the centerpiece of SAP, contributed to the resolution of the economic crisis? The next section will examine the various ways in which the overvaluation of the naira was said to have contributed to the economic crisis.

OVERVALUATION AND NIGERIA'S ECONOMIC CRISIS

Proponents of the overvaluation theory based their arguments on the nature of foreign exchange management in Nigeria in the period between 1960 and 1986. It is pointed out that at the time Nigeria obtained political independence in October 1960, its currency, the Nigerian pound, was tied to the British pound sterling. When Nigeria joined the IMF in March 1961, its pound was pegged at par with the British pound sterling. In addition, the exchange rate between the American dollar and the British pound sterling was used to determine the exchange rate between the Nigerian pound and the dollar. This situation continued until August 1971 when the dollar-gold convertibility was suspended. Since the dollar now became the principal reserve currency, many countries responded by floating their exchange rates. Nigeria then adopted a policy of mainly using the floating rates of the pound sterling and the dollar to determine the value of the Nigerian pound vis-à-vis the various currencies. But in April 1974 Nigeria stopped using the exchange rates of foreign currencies to determine the value of its own currency. This was partly an outcome of the change of the currency's name from the pound to the naira in January 1973. Other means of independently determining the value of the naira were introduced.[3]

It has been pointed out that apart from a 10 percent devaluation of the naira on February 14, 1973, to tally with the devaluation of the dollar two days earlier, no substantial devaluation took place between 1973 and 1986.[4] This is in spite of the fact that other major currencies experienced some considerable devaluation during the same period. Even then, for a variety of reasons, one of which was the government's expansionary policy, the 1973 devaluation was ineffective since the effective rate of devaluation was substantially lower than the nominal rate. Moreover, the increased revenue from oil as from 1973 made the Nigerian authorities embark on a very high degree of public expenditure. In addition, the government adopted a policy of progressively appreciating the naira, which was partly reflected in the adoption of an inflexible nominal exchange rate policy. Thus while the economy experienced a high degree of domestic monetary expansion and therefore a very high rate of inflation, the currency continued to appreciate against other major currencies instead of depreciating. All these factors contributed to the very high overvaluation of the naira that in turn had adverse effects on the economy.[5]

It is claimed that the very high degree of overvaluation of the naira introduced great structural defects into the economy. It made imports cheaper while locally produced goods were overpriced and therefore more expensive. This created a great demand for imported goods, thereby encouraging profligate consumption of foreign goods, there was a disincentive for local industries to produce export-oriented goods. For instance, between 1974 and 1978, imports increased nearly fivefold, rising from N1,737.3 million to N8,368.7 million. This exceeded the growth rate of exports, which rose from N5,794.8 million to N6,542.7 million in the same period, representing a growth rate of 12.9 percent in four years or an average of 3.2 percent per year.[6] At the same time, it was not profitable to produce primary commodities for export purposes. Agriculture therefore stagnated. As a result, the country became dependent on crude oil for over 90 percent of its foreign exchange earnings.

This import dependency resulted in a very high demand for foreign exchange, far in excess of what was available. This in turn gave rise to an elaborate system of foreign exchange controls like import licensing, quotas, and tariffs. Apart from the fact that the implementation of the system was expensive, it resulted in bureaucratic bottlenecks that in turn encouraged a great deal of corruption. There was therefore a booming business in foreign exchange speculation and racketeering, and many people resorted to the thriving black market. There was a great deal of inefficiency in the allocation of foreign exchange since factors other than the merits of individual applications were taken into account. Furthermore, there was a disincentive for autonomous capital inflow while, on the other hand, there was flight of capital out of Nigeria.[7]

In short, the distortions that resulted from the overvaluation of the naira were, among other things, corruption, lack of diversification of the economy, and a non-export orientation of the economy. It was argued that given these defects, the way out was to seek the real value of the currency through substantial devaluation. This could appropriately be done through the agency of market forces. Yet in spite of the economic expediency of this position, political considerations, rather than economic logic, made successive Nigerian administrations up to 1986 not to subject the determination of the real value of the naira to the interplay of supply and demand for foreign currencies.[8]

There is no denying the fact that the overvaluation of the naira contributed to the emergence of the economic crisis. But it is debatable whether it should be accorded the central position in the emergence as well as the solution to the crisis. It is my position that overvaluation has been given undue emphasis, to the neglect of more fundamental factors responsible for the crisis. Overvaluation and overregulation of the economy were at best by-products of more fundamental factors that center on the existence of a dependent, neocolonial political economy in Nigeria. Placing a premium on devaluation to the neglect of these fundamental factors is not acceptable. The next section will briefly summarize the factors I consider fundamental to the emergence of the economic crisis.

DEPENDENT CAPITALISM AND THE EMERGENCE OF NIGERIA'S ECONOMIC CRISIS

The fundamental factors responsible for Nigeria's economic crisis are traceable to the political economy of surplus accumulation under the dependent, neocolonial capitalist system in the country. These factors have been adequately documented in a number of studies.[9] I will briefly summarize them here. However, to understand the factors, it is necessary to appreciate the nature and character of the Nigerian State and the Nigerian bourgeoisie. Both of them owe their origin to the colonial period during which they served the exploitative desires of the British imperialists. On the attainment of political independence, their character did not undergo any meaningful transformation. It therefore follows that the post colonial state continued to serve the interests of the erstwhile colonial masters and continued to promote the subjugation of the country's economy to the interests of international monopoly capital.

The immense administrative, economic, and coercive apparatus at the disposal of the Nigerian State turned it into the primary instrument of surplus accumulation and capitalist development in the country. The state therefore serves as an organ of capital accumulation both for the domestic bourgeoisie and for the foreign bourgeoisie.[10] This function of the Nigerian state was enhanced by the oil boom of the 1970s which the Nigerian bourgeoisie saw as an opportunity to strengthen their weak material base through large-scale capital accumulation. The state capitalist model of accumulation was installed.[11] Nevertheless, the predominance of the comprador faction of the Nigerian bourgeoisie in the country's political economy ensured that surplus accumulation hardly went beyond the primitive stage.[12] Worse still, while the wealth of the country was being dissipated, its dependence on international monopoly capital was accentuated.

The ascendancy of the comprador faction of the Nigerian bourgeoisie in the country's political economy resulted in a situation that can be described as a sort of buccaneer capitalism.[13] The comprador elements include middlemen, contractors, consultants, and importers/exporters. Ake noted that these people thrived mainly on commerce, contracts, and political access and were most strongly disposed toward unproductive capitalism. For them, capital came "less from productive activity than the manipulation of social status and political power."[14] As a result these people are greatly prone to corruption. Indeed the monumental acts of corruption in which they have been involved have been ably documented in the reports of various commissions of inquiry. We have already noted the fraud associated with imports. It will suffice to cite a few more examples here. A ministerial committee on factors responsible for the excessive cost of government contracts, headed by Professor S. Essang, reported in July 1980 that the cost of government projects given to contractors was 200 percent higher in Nigeria than in Kenya, and 130 percent higher than in Algeria.[15] Also, in February 1985, the Odama Committee reported that most contracts in Nigeria were deliberately inflated with the result that their costs were three times higher than those in East and North Africa, and four times higher than those in Asia.[16]

Given the dependent nature of the Nigerian bourgeoisie, it could not take any bold steps that would significantly advance its interest and that of the country's economy vis-à-vis international capital. Hence the indigenization decree of 1972 (revised in 1977), which was supposedly a bold and progressive step aimed at greatly reducing the influence of foreign capitalists in Nigeria's economy, merely ended up strengthening the position of international monopoly capital. Although the decree led to the takeover by the Nigerian bourgeoisie of merchandizing and small-scale industrial enterprises that had been mainly owned by Asians, it ended up promoting the ownership and control by the foreign bourgeoisie of highly state protected and subsidized high technology enterprises. This supposedly progressive policy merely resulted in the further consolidation of international monopoly capital in Nigeria and therefore the further subordination of the Nigerian economy to the interests of foreign capital.

Moreover, the dependent nature of the Nigerian bourgeoisie made it impossible for the bourgeoisie to replace the inherited industrial strategy that emphasized import substitution with a strategy that emphasized productive, self-reliant, and self-sustaining industrialization. By promoting the establishment of high import dependent consumer goods industries to the neglect of intermediate and capital goods industries, the import substitution strategy not only led to the massive expatriation of capital from Nigeria, but also prevented the creation of linkages between various sectors of the economy. This in turn discouraged the diversification of the economy, which became almost entirely dependent on crude oil.

What is apparent from the brief discussion in this section is that with the installation of a neocolonial system in Nigeria in the 1960s, the economic crisis was latent. Due to the oil boom, it did not become apparent until the early 1980s. Yet given the increasingly monumental nature of capital expatriation from Nigeria as from the 1970s, it was clear that the crisis was bound to manifest itself with or without the oil glut. The drastic reduction in the revenue from oil in the early 1980s merely triggered off the crisis. Central to the crisis are the pattern of surplus accumulation and the dependent structure of the economy. It thus follows that the factors responsible for the crisis are certainly more fundamental than the alleged overvaluation of the naira and the over regulation of the economy. At best these were by-products of the dependent capitalist system in the country. Making devaluation of the naira, through the agency of market forces, the core element of the SAP, therefore, amounts to tackling only the peripheral issues responsible for the crisis. This will in all probability aggravate the crisis rather than help to resolve it.

DEVALUATION AND THE ECONOMIC CRISIS

The IMF and the World Bank's conception of the causes of Nigeria's economic crisis center around the perceived overvaluation of the naira, excessive credit expansion and excessive government intervention in the economy. As a result, at the center of the SAP are demand-management policies through a credit squeeze and economic liberalization that will grant ascendancy to market forces.[17] In a nationwide address introducing the SAP, Babangida stated that the program "puts emphasis on price mechanism as a means of strengthening the existing demand management policies; it encourages . . . a more realistic rate of the naira; promotes replacement of direct administrative controls with greater reliance on market forces and the rationalisation of public enterprises."[18] The main objectives of the SAP are to dismantle exchange controls and adopt a market-determined exchange rate policy; to restructure and diversify the productive base of the economy in order to reduce dependence on the oil sector and on imports; to achieve fiscal and balance of payment viability; to liberalize the trade regime, rationalize customs tariffs and excise duties, and abolish price controls; to privatize and commercialize public enterprises and abolish marketing boards; to lay the basis for a sustainable non-inflationary or minimally inflationary growth; and to lessen the dominance of unproductive investments in the public sector, improve the sector's efficiency, and intensify the growth potential of the private sector.[19]

Given the claim that the grossly overvalued naira introduced severe distortions into Nigeria's economy, a substantial devaluation of the currency constitutes a core element of SAP. It has been noted that the overvaluation of the naira made the exchange rate of the currency highly inflated in relation to other major currencies. The outcome was the high import dependency ratio of the economy, many imports being irrelevant consumer and luxury goods, while production for export was discouraged. The adjustment of the exchange rate was therefore seen as crucial for the economic recovery program. However, this exchange rate adjustment was to be achieved through the agency of the "free" market system.

This fact accounts for the central position which the Second-Tier Foreign Exchange Market (SFEM)—later replaced by the Foreign Exchange Market (FEM)—occupy in the adjustment program. In fact it was specifically stated in the SAP document that the SFEM was set up to correct the serious overvaluation of the naira through the interplay of "free" market forces.[20] It was believed that massive devaluation of the naira would improve Nigeria's balance of payments position while at the same time diversifying the economy and improving the efficiency of resource allocation. This was to be achieved through the perceived positive effects of devaluation. The supposed positive effects included the discouragement of imports, which would become very expensive; the stimulation of non-oil exports, which would become more profitable; the achievement of a realistic exchange rate of the naira through the forces of supply and demand; a more efficient allocation of foreign exchange; eventual elimination of the black market involving the currency; an increase in industrial capacity utilization, an expansion of domestic production, and, therefore, a reduction in unemployment; and the restoration of creditors' confidence in the economy, thereby encouraging an inflow of capital and foreign investment.

In spite of the innovations that were introduced into the exchange rate market—the change from SFEM to FEM, the change from weekly bidding to fortnightly bidding, and subsequently the introduction of daily inter-bank bidding—the underlying philosophy remained the same. That is, reliance on the "free" market system of demand and supply to determine the appropriate value of the naira. But it should be pointed out that reliance on the so-called free market forces of demand and supply to determine the realistic value of the naira is patently defective. For one thing, a "free" market system does not exist anywhere in the world. Even in the advanced capitalist economies, which are usually touted as "free" market economies, this is in practice not really the case. In fact since the post-World War II period, the governments of these countries have actively intervened in their economies in order to achieve their economic objectives. Callaghy described what exists in these societies as "embedded liberalism." According to him,

> Contrary to popular assumption and official rhetoric, orthodox liberalism, especially its free-market core, has not been the dominant form of political economy in the industrial West since World War II. Instead, the dominant political economy has been a form of compromise called "embedded liberalism," which involves the use of quite extensive state power simultaneously in the interests of domestic political and social stability and well-being on the one hand and international economic adjustment on the other.[21]

Moreover, in developing countries, the conditions required for the effective functioning of what comes close to a "free" market system are completely lacking. For instance, in Nigeria, the efficient functioning of the FEM presupposes adequate funding, which in practice is not available. Furthermore, the Central Bank of Nigeria (CBN) is virtually the monopoly supplier of foreign exchange to the FEM in a system in which an oligopolistic group of banks bid for foreign exchange. From time to time, the CBN has been compelled to intervene in the market to change the "market"-determined exchange rate of the naira.[22] Thus, in such a grossly imperfect market situation it is unrealistic to rely on market forces to determine the actual value of the naira.

It should be recalled that one of the reasons why the (S)FEM was introduced was the bureaucratic corruption and bottlenecks associated with the import license system. Though the foreign exchange market succeeded in eliminating these problems, the locus of corruption shifted to the banks. This is partly responsible for the unacceptable level of devaluation of the naira since the introduction of the SAP. Until January 1989, the FEM and the autonomous market existed side by side. Although the rate at which foreign currencies could be sold at the FEM was regulated, the same was not the case with the autonomous market. The cost of foreign currencies in the autonomous market was therefore very high (for instance, in December 1988, the exchange rate of the naira to the dollar was N10 to $1). Thus, in order to make huge profits, banks diverted most of the foreign exchange they earned from the bidding sessions into the autonomous market. This situation resulted in the proliferation of banks while at the same time they diverted their attention from those regular banking functions that are vital to the overall economic development of the country.

In an attempt to curb the corrupt practices of banks and shore up the value of the naira, the federal government in the 1989 budget merged the autonomous market with the FEM while introducing daily inter-bank foreign exchange bidding. But this did not yield any positive results. The cancellation of the autonomous market did not go down well with the bankers and even with some exporters, who started clamoring for the reintroduction of the autonomous market. Even though the government introduced Bureaux de Change where individuals could sell and buy foreign currencies using licensed private dealers, the ceiling on the volume of transactions did not make the Bureaux sufficiently attractive to exporters, many of whom preferred leaving their money in foreign banks. Consequently, the inflow of foreign exchange into the Bureaux was very low and this did not positively affect the fortunes of the naira.[23] In another attempt to deal with the situation, the Central Bank of Nigeria (CBN), in May 1989, ordered all government agencies and parastatals to withdraw their accounts from commercial and merchant banks and lodge them with the CBN. It was felt that the resultant liquidity squeeze would help to raise the value of the naira. But this did not yield any positive result. On the contrary, between 1989 and 2000, the exchange rate of the naira against the dollar declined from N10 to $1 to over N100 to $1.

Thus, from a position of purported overvaluation of the naira, the currency became so extremely undervalued that the outcome was spiraling inflation. This high level of inflation in turn had adverse effects on the economy. For instance, official figures showed that the rate of inflation more than doubled between 1987 and 1988, rising from 10 percent to 25 percent[24] and then to 80 percent in 1995.[25] Given the dependent nature of the country's production structure, this situation deepened the economic crisis. The adverse effects on the manufacturing sector have been clearly demonstrated by various annual reports of the Manufacturers Association of Nigeria (MAN). For example, the MAN report on the performance of Nigeria's industries showed that average capacity utilization in manufacturing industries declined from 40 percent in 1988 to 32 percent in 1989 and further declined to 27 percent in 1995. The reasons given for the low level of capacity utilization include the massive devaluation of the naira, the high interest rates, and the inadequate credit supply to enterprises, all of which led to the escalation of the cost of production and the prices of finished goods.[26] Also, local sourcing of raw materials declined from an average of 51 percent in 1988 to 46 percent in the first six months of 1989, and further declined to an average of 40 percent in 1999. The reasons adduced for this decline include the increases in both the cost of local raw materials, due to pressure from exports, and the cost of imported machines and spare parts due to the massive devaluation of the naira. Furthermore, between 1988 and 1989, the cost of both imported and local raw materials rose by an average of 111 percent and 98 percent respectively. This contributed to the rising cost of production and ex-factory prices of goods, and therefore a considerable decline in the demand for locally manufactured goods.[27]

Furthermore, it should be noted that in the face of the astronomically high prices of goods, the income of workers remained virtually static while as a result of inflation, the real income of the working people declined considerably. The very high level of unemployment did not help the situation. It is therefore not surprising that various surveys by the MAN recorded a very marked decline in demand. The outcome was the closure of many medium and small-scale industries. Yet it is a well-known fact that small-scale industries in particular play a very crucial role in the economic development of developing countries. A related issue is the impact of liberalization of the trade regime on the industrial sector. The deregulation policy of the SAP fails to take into account the immense advantages that foreign and well-established industries have over Nigerian industries. Exposing Nigerian industries to the chilly winds of international competition under the pretext that the magic of the marketplace will force them to be more efficient is misguided, if not dishonest. In addition, the fact that the adjustment program ignored supportive policies specific to the industrial sector and also the recessions caused by the harsh economic policies has led to "contraction without restructuring" in manufacturing. In the face of this stifling environment, Nigerian industries were not able to compete with cheap imported goods. The unfavorable policies resulted in a deindustrialization process in Nigeria. Ojo adequately captured the adverse impact of devaluation and trade liberalization on the industrial sector in Africa generally when he wrote:

> In Africa, the massive devaluation of most national currencies and the liberalization of trade regime inherent in current (SAP) policies are not geared toward an alteration of the existing comparative advantage. Indeed, they are favoring the indiscriminate importation of cheap foreign goods, while at the same time national industries are operating below capacity because of the devaluation-induced high domestic currency costs of imported raw materials and other restrictive policies. As a consequence, local industries cannot compete with these imports, and the stage is being set . . . for a gradual process of "Deindustrialization" in most African countries.[28]

Moreover, the liberalization of imports adversely affected Nigeria's industries while on the whole entrenching the import dependency of the economy. Making foreign exchange considerations the centerpiece of the SAP is antithetical to the program's avowed intention of ending import dependency through the diversification of the economy. In fact, many local manufacturers abandoned their industries in favor of the importation and distribution of finished consumer goods. The demand for imported consumer goods did not contribute to the elimination of the parallel "black" market; on the contrary, it greatly helped to further promote smuggling. At the same time, the industrial policy and the Debt Equity Swaps promoted by the SAP had the effect of significantly reversing some of the few gains of the indigenization program. These, together with the unrestricted desire for the inflow of foreign investments, tended to promote the re-colonization of Nigeria's industries by foreign capitalists.[29]

While the inflationary situation occasioned by the SAP created very difficult times for local manufacturing industries, the banking sector experienced an unprecedented boom, as demonstrated by the proliferation of banks, especially merchant banks. One factor that influenced this proliferation of banks was the monetarist as opposed to productionist policies promoted by the SAP. Perhaps more important is the huge amount of profit that the banks made, primarily from foreign exchange speculation. The fact that these banks concentrated on foreign exchange speculation to the neglect of the normal banking functions of helping to promote the development of the economy demonstrates the detrimental impact on the country's economy of the proliferation of banks. It is probable that it is the lucrativeness of the banking business that made the MAN the umbrella organization of all manufacturers in the country, apply for a license to establish a merchant bank in September 1989.[30]

The huge profit margin of the banks, among other things, introduced great distortions into the country's labor market. For instance, by offering emoluments that were far beyond what the manufacturing industries could pay, the banks attracted some strategically highly skilled personnel to the banking industry instead of the manufacturing industry. Yet as Phillips has argued, since Nigeria's economic crisis was caused mainly by the country's production structure, meaningful attempts at overcoming the crisis should comprise primarily structuralist rather than monetarist strategies.[31]

One of the main reasons which the proponents of devaluation used to justify it was that it would help to end the reliance on crude oil as the principal source of foreign exchange through the diversification of the export base of the country. It was argued that making imports more expensive while at the same time significantly increasing the value of exports would encourage Nigerian farmers to produce more cash crops for export. As a result, the ratio of non-oil exports would increase considerably. Furthermore, in line with the discredited policy of comparative advantage, it was argued that it was in Nigeria's interest to concentrate on agricultural production, in which the country has the advantage, as opposed to industrial production. It was equally stated that this would help to stimulate the rural economy and therefore improve the economic well-being of rural dwellers who had been neglected by successive Nigerian administrations.

At the initial stage it appeared as if devaluation had helped to boost non-oil exports. This was as a result of the phenomenal increase in the prices of cash crops. For instance, a ton of cocoa which sold for N1,500 in September 1986 sold for N27,000 in January 1989. But by May 1989 (within a period of five months), the price of a ton of cocoa crashed to N7,000 per ton, representing an enormous 286 percent decrease. The initial great increase in the price of cocoa had made a number of farmers mobilize their resources and borrow a lot of money in order to increase the amount of cocoa they could cultivate. As would be expected, the sudden crash created a great deal of misery for cocoa farmers and even resulted in the dislocation of some families. A significant question is how do we account for this serious crash in prices? The conventional explanation usually given for this kind of occurrence includes the inelastic nature of the demand for primary commodities in the world market and the availability of synthetic substitutes. But Fadahunsi has pointed out that the phenomenal increases in the price of cocoa and other agricultural commodities were in the first place artificial. As he puts it:

> Between 1987 and 1989, bogus cocoa merchants invaded the cocoa trade once government yielded to IMF/World Bank pressure to disband the cocoa and other commodity marketing boards. The newbreed cocoa merchants turned out to be mostly foreigners and their Nigerian fronts who were desperately trying to repatriate some of their genuine and ill-gotten profits that had accumulated in Nigeria during the regime of controlled exchange rates. Because these foreign entrepreneurs no longer had confidence in the viability of the Nigerian monetary system and the economy, they were seeking for means to take their money out of Nigeria at all cost.

He further decried the fact that

> What makes the cocoa experience particularly unfortunate, and with it the blind ideological pursuit of the policy of deregulation by the political authorities, is the damage that has been done to the country's leading potential non-oil export and to the welfare of the cocoa farmer. There was no moment during the period when the "newbreed" cocoa farmers were offering over N20,000 per tonne to farmers that the export value of the commodity was more than . . . N15,000 . . . A more caring government should have become suspicious of the intentions of the merchants and therefore interfered in the interest of the nation and the farmers. The hands of the Nigerian state are apparently still tied by its avowed commitment to "deregulation" and the interplay of market forces in the commodity and foreign exchange markets.[32]

One significant effect of the collapse in the prices of primary commodities was the drastic decline in the volume of the exports of these commodities. Hence, cocoa exports declined from 19,526 metric tons in January 1989 to just 905 tons in August of the same year, representing a 95 percent drop. Consequently, the contribution of non-oil exports to the country's foreign exchange earnings was very low. Of the expected revenue of $1.14 billion from non-oil exports between January and August 1989, only $405 million was realized.[33] In addition, the crash in prices of primary commodities negatively affected the income of the rural peasant producers. The very high degree of inflation considerably reduced their real incomes. The situation was not helped by the escalating increase in the prices of foodstuffs, which put them virtually out of the reach of the overwhelming majority of farmers. Indeed, in noting the worsening standard of living of the rural dwellers, the 1989 MAN mid-year report stated that "cases of hunger and malnutrition, the worst in the last decade were recorded in the rural areas of the country."[34] By the mid-1990s, the situation had become desperate and cases of kwashiorkor, a disease caused by malnutrition in children, had become common place in the country. These monumental economic hardships forced many farmers and youths to resort to what Hirschmann has described as the exit option by abandoning farming and migrating to the urban centers, thereby worsening the already acute employment situation in these areas.[35] It is therefore ironic that devaluation, which was supposedly aimed at increasing the income of farmers, ended up further impoverishing them. Given the empirical evidence that has been presented, the argument that devaluation would greatly stimulate the production and export of non-oil products, thereby enhancing the standard of living of the rural dwellers, has been proved to be incorrect.

By promoting an astronomical increase in the cost of social services like health and education, devaluation put these crucial services out of the reach of the majority of the populace. This has been worsened by the removal of government subsidies from these services as recommended by the SAP.

Thus while on the one hand devaluation made these services unaffordable for the vast majority of the populace, the high costs of equipment occasioned by devaluation and the huge decline in government allocations have led to a virtual collapse of the health and educational sectors in Nigeria. This collapse is manifested in the poor conditions of service for staff and the consequent extremely low morale, the lack of facilities, libraries that are devoid of current books and journals, and hospitals that have become consulting clinics and virtual mortuaries. It is from this perspective that the incessant strikes and other crises that have characterized the health sector can be explained, as can the massive brain drain that these sectors experienced from the mid-1980s onward. Yet adequate performance of the health and educational sectors is crucial for the development of any country.

With regard to the effect of devaluation and adjustment programs on the social sector in Africa generally, Sahn has argued that the above scenario is not an adequate characterization of their impact on social services. He pointed out that there were many instances where funding of education and health experienced considerable increases. To him, the major issue is not "whether adjustment affected the level of spending; but whether adjustment affected the way available resources were being allocated within the social sector." In a rehash of some of the familiar arguments of the proponents of devaluation and adjustment policies, he stated that too much money was being spent on secondary and university education as opposed to primary education, on subsidizing the urban elite as opposed to the rural dwellers, and on curative, hospital-based services for the urban population as opposed to preventive services, most of which would have benefited the rural dwellers.[36] Of course this is not a correct assertion. The massive brain drain from both the health and education sectors, the frequent strikes by academics and health workers, and the numerous student demonstrations in Nigeria are clear manifestations of the adverse effects of devaluation on these services.[37]

In addition, the debilitating effects of devaluation have discouraged virtually all forms of productive activities, and promoted capital flight, disinvestment, and worst of all, the flooding of Nigerian markets with used goods from various Western capitalist countries, a situation which Abutudu has appropriately described as the *"tokunboh"* culture.[38] Apart from the fact that devaluation discouraged production, it not only reinforced and sustained the existing emphasis on distribution, but in fact did this in the worst possible way. While previous distribution efforts concentrated primarily on the importation of new goods, the emphasis under the devaluation regime has been on the importation of used goods. Moreover the primary concern with foreign exchange speculation by Nigerian banks helped to promote the worst form of "buccaneer" or, at best, compradorial capitalism in Nigeria.

In fact, other African countries which have substantially devalued their currencies on the basis of SAPs share similar experiences with Nigeria: their economic problems have been aggravated. This has led to riots and strikes in most of these countries and in some instances repudiation of the policy. A good example is Zambia, which in June 1984 became one of the first African countries to adopt a floating exchange rate through foreign exchange auctioning. For this it was widely praised by the IMF, the World Bank, and various liberal scholars as a model for reforms in developing countries. But in May 1987, the worsening economic crisis forced the Zambian government to abandon the foreign exchange auctioning program and return to the fixed exchange rate regime while imposing a ceiling on debt servicing. This action was seriously criticized by the Bretton Woods institutions, the Western capitalist countries, their media, and liberal scholars. But as Sano pointed out, these critics missed the point because they were not well informed about the realities and dynamics of the Zambian and, indeed, the African situation.[39] Another illustration of the debilitating effects of devaluation is Zimbabwe, whose economy was still on a relatively sound footing when it made the "fatal" mistake of swallowing the bitter pill of SAP in the early 1990s. The outcome has been a virtual collapse of the economy, which is largely responsible for the serious unrest and upheaval that the country has recently experienced. Indeed, in Nigeria and other African countries that have implemented adjustment policies and substantially devalued their currencies, the ravages of these policies have worsened rather than helped to resolve the economic crisis.[40] It is obvious that devaluation cannot contribute to the resolution of the economic crisis; on the contrary, it leads to a dead end in Africa's development.[41]

CONCLUSION

It is apparent from the preceding discussion that the role of overvaluation in bringing about Nigeria's economic crisis has been exaggerated. The fundamental causes of the crisis can be located in the political economy of the dependent, neocolonial capitalist system existing in the country. Central to this crisis is the accumulation process. In other words, the fundamental causes of the crisis go very much beyond the so-called inadequacies of the monetary policies pursued in Nigeria prior to 1986. It thus follows that solutions that emphasize devaluation and deregulation will not have much success; on the contrary, they are bound to aggravate the crisis.

Extreme devaluation of the naira set in motion a serious inflationary situation that resulted in the worsening of the distortions in the country's economy. Many manufacturing industries ceased to exist while the extreme decline in the real income of working people and the extremely high level of unemployment (a situation which MAN described as unacceptable) combined to pauperize the overwhelming majority of Nigerians.[42] Some of the results of this situation are the increased level of crime, other social vices, violence, and instability in the country. Phillips adequately captured the debilitating effects of devaluation and deregulation on Nigeria when he noted that the policies have made the cost of development so high that development might elude the country for a long time.[43] Similarly, in a statement released by the Nigerian Economic Society (NES) after its millennium conference on Economic Development held at Abuja in September 2000, it was noted that devaluation might make "good politics on the short run [but] dangerous economics in short to long run." The statement added that the effects of devaluation scare away foreign investment while promoting macroeconomic instability, unemployment, poverty, and low investment in the real productive sectors.[44] At the same time, extreme devaluation and deregulation have helped to further entrench the subordination of Nigeria's economy to the interests and dictates of international monopoly capital. This is hardly surprising, for the IFIs that insisted on the implementation of these policies are agents of international monopoly capital.

A related issue is the fact that the implementation of the deregulation and devaluation policies marked a significant loss of autonomy on the part of the Nigerian government over the implementation of economic policies. Right from the Shagari period there has been widespread opposition in Nigeria to the devaluation of the naira. The public debate that the Babangida regime conducted over the IMF loan equally reflected widespread opposition to the taking of the loan, implementation of the SAP, and devaluation of the naira. But acting contrary to popular opinion, the 1986 Babangida budget incorporated most of the main elements of the SAP. Among other things, the budget contained a package of export incentives incorporating trade liberalization, reduced the petroleum subsidy by 80 percent, and made a commitment to privatization. But although the budget mentioned an exchange rate adjustment, the naira was not devalued. The absence of devaluation from the budget made the Western creditors and the IFIs reject the reform package in the budget. In the face of this opposition, the Nigerian government decided to go against the popular will by introducing an adjustment program "whose central feature was a two-tier system to devalue the naira," in August 1986.[45] It is thus clear that the SAP and devaluation were implemented under the *diktat* of the agents of international monopoly capital.

It should be noted that the practice of leaving the determination of the value of national currencies completely to market forces does not, strictly speaking, exist anywhere in the world, even in the advanced capitalist countries. Various steps are taken by different advanced capitalist countries to ensure that their currencies are valued at levels that are conducive to the growth of their economies. The case of the recently introduced Euro currency is a good illustration of this point. Worried by the continuous decline in its value, European member countries and even the United States, which is not a member of the European union, directly intervened to shore up its value. The argument was that an uncontrolled decline in the value of the euro would promote economic recession in the advanced capitalist countries. The same argument holds true for Nigeria and other African countries. Indeed, various Nigerian experts and manufacturers are of the opinion that the naira is so unacceptably undervalued that if steps are not taken to considerably increase its value, the economic crisis will continue to worsen.[46]

Given the ravaging effects of devaluation it is clear that any solution aimed at overcoming Nigeria's worsening economic crisis should not only halt the ill-advised extreme devaluation of the naira but should also terminate the IFI-inspired SAP. Examples from all over Africa demonstrate that these adjustment policies are highly detrimental to the development of African countries. In fact, in view of the contributions of neocolonial dependency to Nigeria's economic crisis, merely adjusting the neocolonial structures as prescribed by the SAP is not a credible solution. What the country needs is structural transformation programs that will help to terminate the prevailing neocolonial dependency.

NOTES

1. See, for instance, D. Rimmer, "The Overvalued Currency and Over-Administered Economy of Nigeria," *African Affairs*, 84, 336 (1985), 435-446; N. B. Tallroth, "Structural Adjustment in Nigeria," *Finance and Development*, September 1987; and R. Faruqee, "Nigeria: Ownership Abandoned," in I. Husain and R. Faruqee, eds., *Adjustment in Africa: Lessons from Country Case Studies* (Washington, D.C.: World Bank, 1994), 238-285.
2. Callaghy has pointed out that after the public debate in which the IMF loan was massively rejected, experts from the IFIs covertly worked with Nigerian officials in an inter-ministerial committee set up by the Babangida regime to formulate a SAP program. See T. M. Callaghy, "Lost between State and Market: The Politics of Economic Adjustment in Ghana, Zambia, and Nigeria," in J. M. Nelson, ed., *Economic Crisis and Policy Choice: The Politics of Adjustment in the Third World* (Princeton: Princeton University Press, 1994), 306-309.
3. C. O. Obute, "Floating Exchange Rates and Structural Adjustment in Nigeria," in *Structural Adjustment in Nigeria: Proceedings of the Nigerian Economic Society Annual Conference, Ile-Ife, May 3-7, 1988* (Ibadan: Nigerian Economic Society, 1988).
4. A national debate on the alleged overvaluation of the naira started in 1981. But it was not until 1984 that the government adopted a policy of gradually devaluing the currency. Thus, from a rate of N1 to $1.3359 in January 1984, the naira was devalued to N1 to $1.2046 in January 1985, and then to N1 to $1.0004 in December 1985. In short, between January 1984 and June 1986, the naira exchange value depreciated by 57.54 percent against the pound

sterling and 50.27 percent against the dollar. See I. Aluko-Olokun, "An Appraisal of the Second-Tier Foreign Exchange Market (SFEM)," in A. O. Phillips and E. C. Ndekwu, eds., *Structural Adjustment in a Developing Economy: The Case of Nigeria* (Ibadan: NISER, 1987), 56-57.

5. Obute, "Floating Exchange Rates and Structural Adjustment in Nigeria"; and Tallroth, "Structural Adjustment in Nigeria."
6. Federal Republic of Nigeria, *Guidelines for the Fourth National Development Plan: 1981-85* (Lagos: Federal Ministry of National Planning, 1981), 10.
7. I. Ajayi, "The Exchange Rate Issue," *First Bank Monthly Business and Economic Report*, July 1986, 3-24; and Aluko-Olokun, "An Appraisal of the Second-Tier Foreign Exchange Market (SFEM)," 55-56.
8. Rimmer, "The Overvalued Currency and Over-Administered Economy of Nigeria," 441.
9. See, for example, A. Abba et. al., *The Nigerian Economic Crisis: Causes and Solutions*, (Zaria: Academic Staff Union of Universities, 1985); B. Onimode, *Imperialism and Under-development in Nigeria* (London: Macmillan, 1983); B. U. Ekuerhare, "Recent Pattern of Accumulation in the Nigerian Economy," *Africa Development*, 9, 1 (1984), 63-64; and J. I. Dibua, "The Post-Colonial State and Development Planning in Nigeria, 1962-1985," *Journal of Eastern African Research and Development*, 24 (1994), 212-228.
10. B. Beckman, "Neo-Colonialism, Capitalism and the State in Nigeria," in H. Bernstein and E. Campbell eds., *The Contradictions of Capitalist Accumulation in Africa* (Beverly Hills: Sage Publications 1985).
11. B. U. Ekuerhare, "Crisis of State Capitalist Model of Accumulation and the Collapse of the Second Republic in Nigeria," paper presented at the 12th Annual National Conference of the Nigerian Political Science Association, held at the University of Ilorin, Ilorin, Nigeria, May 7-11, 1985.
12. J. I. Dibua, "Conflict among the Nigerian Bourgeoisie and the Demise of the Second Republic," *Africa Development*, 13, 4 (1988), 84-85.
13. See A. O. Adeoye, "Of Economic Masquerades and Vulgar Economy: A Critique of the Structural Adjustment Programme in Nigeria," *Africa Development*, 16, 1 (1991), 23-44.
14. C. Ake, "The State of the Nation: Intimations of Disaster," Presidential Address to the Nigerian Political Science Association,

1982; and C. Ake, "Introduction," *Africa Development: Special Issue on Nigeria*, 9, 3 (1984).
15. Federal Republic of Nigeria, *Report of the Ministerial Committee on the Causes of the Excessively High Cost of Government Contracts in Nigeria (Essang Committee)* (Lagos: Federal Government Printer, 1981).
16. Cited by Y. B. Usman, "Middlemen, Consultants, Contractors and the Solutions to the Current Economic Crisis," *Studies in Politics and Society*, 2 (1984), 23-24.
17. Federal Republic of Nigeria, *Structural Adjustment for Nigeria, July 1986-June 1988*, (Lagos: Federal Government Printer, 1986).
18. Cited by A. Fadahunsi, "Devaluation: Implications for Employment, Inflation, Growth and Development," in A. O. Olukoshi, ed., *The Politics of Structural Adjustment in Nigeria* (London, Ibadan and Portsmouth, N.H.: James Currey and Heinemann, 1993), 38.
19. A. O. Phillips, "A General Overview of SAP," in Phillips and Ndekwu eds., *Structural Adjustment in a Developing Economy*, 2; and Faruqee, "Nigeria: Ownership Abandoned," 247.
20. Federal Republic of Nigeria, *Structural Adjustment for Nigeria*, 9.
21. T. M. Callaghy, "Political Passions and Economic Interests: Economic Reform and Political Structure in Africa," in T. M. Callaghy and J. Ravenhill, eds., *Hemmed In: Responses to Africa's Economic Decline* (New York: Columbia University Press, 1993), 507.
22. M. I. Obadan, "The Theory and Practice of the Second-Tier Foreign Exchange Market in Nigeria: Nine Months After," in Phillips and Ndekwu, eds., *Structural Adjustment Programme in a Developing Economy*, 36-39.
23. The adverse effects of the limit placed on the amount of foreign exchange transactions the Bureaux de Change could carry out, made their umbrella body, the Association of Bureaux de Change Operators of Nigeria (ABCON)), petition the CBN in September 2000, requesting a revision of the maximum amount allowed per transaction. Even though the maximum amount allowed per transaction had earlier in the year been raised from $2,500 to $5,000, they argued that this amount was not enough. They further argued that the limit placed on the amount of transactions they could carry out was a contributory factor to the continuous depreciation of the value of the naira. See *Guardian* (Lagos, Nigeria), September 4, 2000.
24. *Guardian*, January 4, 1989.

25. United Bank of Africa (UBA), *Monthly Business and Economic Digest*, September/October 1995, 5.
26. UBA, *Monthly Business and Economic Digest*, August 1989, 1-2; and September/October 1995, 5.
27. See UBA, *Monthly Business and Economic Digest*, August 1989, 1-2; and *Guardian*, May 29, 2000.
28. O. Ojo, "Beyond Structural Adjustment: Policies for Sustainable Growth and Development in Africa," in G. A. Cornia and G. K. Helleiner, eds., *From Adjustment to Development in Africa: Conflict, Controversy, Convergence, Consensus* (New York: St. Martins Press, 1994), 131.
29. J. F. E. Ohiorhenuan, "Re-Colonising Nigerian Industry: The First Year of the Structural Adjustment Programme," in Phillips and Ndekwu, eds., *Structural Adjustment Programme in a Developing Country*.
30. *Guardian*, September 28, 1989.
31. Phillips, "A General Overview of SAP," 7.
32. A. Fadahunsi, "Devaluation: Implications for Employment, Inflation, Growth and Development," in Olukoshi, ed., *The Politics of Structural Adjustment in Nigeria*, 48-49. Also see E. A. Walker, " 'Happy Days are Here Again': Cocoa Farmers, Middlemen Traders and the Structural Adjustment Program in Southwestern Nigeria, 1986-1990s," *Africa Today*, 47, 2 (2000), 151-169.
33. UBA, *Monthly Business and Economic Digest*, August 1989, 2 and 7.
34. Ibid.
35. A. O. Hirschmann, *Exit, Voice and Loyalty* (Cambridge, Mass.: Harvard University Press, 1970).
36. D. E. Sahn, "Economic Crisis and Policy Reform in Africa: Lessons Learned and Implications for Policy," in D. E. Sahn, ed., *Adjusting to Policy Failure in African Economies* (Ithaca, N. Y.: Cornell University Press, 1994), 382.
37. See, for instance, B. Beckman and A. Jega, "Scholars and Democratic Politics in Nigeria," *Review of African Political Economy* (*ROAPE*), 64 (1995), 167-181; and K. A. Shettima, "Structural Adjustment and the Student Movement in Nigeria," *ROAPE*, 56 (1993), 83-91.
38. *Tokunboh*, which is derived from the Yoruba language and usually given as a name to someone born overseas, was popularized in the SAP era in Nigeria by a company named Tokunboh which specialized in the importation of used motor vehicles. Generally the term is used to describe the massive importation of used con-

sumer goods like motor vehicles, electrical and electronic equipment, clothing and shoes, and other items from Europe. See M. I. M. Abutudu, "Globalization and 'Tokunboh': Tentative Notes on Structural Adjustment, Culture and Politics in Nigeria," paper presented at the 22nd Annual Conference of the New York African Studies Association, held at Binghamton University, Binghamton, April 24-25, 1998.
39. H. Sano, "The IMF and Zambia: the Contradictions of Exchange Rate Auctioning and Desubsidisation of Agriculture," *African Affairs*, 87, 349 (1988).
40. B. Founou-Tchuigoua, "Africa Confronted with the Ravages of Neo-Liberalism," *Africa Development*, 21, 2-3 (1996), 5-24.
41. J. I. Dibua, "Journey to Nowhere: Neo-Liberalism and Africa's Development Crisis," *Comparative Studies of South Asia, Africa and the Middle East*, 18, 2 (1998), 119-130.
42. In its half yearly report for the period July to December, 1999, MAN stated that "a situation where over 130 member-companies of the Manufacturers Association of Nigeria shut down operations during the year under review . . . left much to be desired." It equally observed that "unemployment in Nigeria, which at present, is at an unacceptable level, poses a great threat to the political, economic and social stability of the nation as crime, destitution, social exclusion and similar vices become prevalent." Cited in *Guardian*, May 30, 2000.
43. Phillips, "A General Overview of SAP," 7.
44. Cited in *Guardian*, September 20, 2000.
45. See Faruqee, "Nigeria: Ownership Abandoned," 244-245. Indeed, the case of Ghana, the so-called star pupil of the IFIs' adjustment programs in Africa, clearly illustrates the implications of the implementation of these programs for the autonomy of African countries. For details, see Callaghy, "Political Passions and Economic Interests: Economic Reform and Political Structure in Africa," 486-487.
46. Fadahunsi stated that most experts, producers, and genuine traders he interviewed agree that the appropriate exchange rate of the naira to the dollar should be between 2.50 and 3.00 to one dollar. They argued that anything more than that would be damaging to the economy. See Fadahunsi, "Devaluation: Implications for Employment, Inflation, Growth and Development," 42. The prominent Nigerian economist, Professor Sam Aluko, shares a similar opinion. See his interview in *Guardian*, August 27, 1989.

10

STATE-CORPORATION RELATIONSHIP: IMPACT ON MANAGEMENT PRACTICE

Nimi Wariboko

INTRODUCTION

The nature of the postcolonial state in Africa, especially in Nigeria, is highly problematic to many political scientists. It is even more so when organization theorists try to figure out the possible ways in which the state in Nigeria affects corporate management practice.[1] Thus, we must proceed gingerly as we unravel the interesting ways in which the very nature of the postcolonial state "creates," impacts, and nudges specific corporate management practices in Nigeria. The practices of Nigerian corporations are very diverse (from large multinationals to locally owned small-scale operations) and are still evolving—a moving target indeed. Inevitably, one has to rely on generalizations for simplicity's sake, with the understanding that the broad truths discussed here are not timeless.

This chapter dwells on the character of the relationship between the state and corporations as a factor influencing the nature and direction of organizational management practices in Nigeria. The concern of this chapter with the state-corporation relationship does not extend to the debate on the "developmental state." This is not the place to enter into the debate on the question: does political authoritarianism have some "redeeming features," and if a state is controlled by a disciplined political class with the goal of economic development, can the government actively orchestrate industrial promotion and export expansion? There is a burgeoning literature on the issue for the interested reader to consult.[2] Most of these works adequately present the pros and cons and the nuances of the "developmental state" thesis and discuss how governments of such states deliberately steer their companies to particular entrepreneurial activities. However, they fail to discuss the impact of the state-company relationship on corporate management practice.

Here I go beyond the developmental state thesis in three senses. First, I try to move beyond the very common argument on the relationship between state power and capital accumulation. I argue that a fuller understanding of the inability of the Nigerian state to insulate itself from particularistic interests and the limited development of productive forces demands an analysis of Nigerian corporate management practices, which are influenced by the ongoing political and social processes. Second, it is my thesis that forms of management practice are generated by the experience of the wider social group in which the firm is situated. The Nigerian firm and its attendant management practices are the product of definable social experience, which need have nothing to do with competition or technology. This position challenges the generally held belief that management practices are basically responses to market or technology.[3] My argument is that the selection of optimal management practices/policies depends largely on the lack of bureaucratic *cohesion* and absence of *depoliticization* of the state in Nigeria (put simply, the absence of state autonomy).

Third, the penetration of the state into the society (at any rate, if not by its *infrastructural power*, by its *despotic power*) have countered the modern worldwide trend of the development of the corporation as an independent and competing center of power in Nigerian society.

The history of the modern corporation is a history of movement away from the state, avoiding being subjugated by one central authority. The legal history of the corporation goes back to the time of the Romans when corporate bodies were organized to run cities, guilds, and even monasteries. In the fourteenth century the Crown in England started to give charters to trades and universities. By the seventeenth century the charters were being granted to joint-stock companies (such as the East India Company and the Hudson's Bay Company) which were not only profit-making organizations but also instruments of the state. As agents of the state in its colonial adventures, they were granted monopoly rights and quasi-government authority over their territories. As Thomas K. McCraw contended, "by the early [eighteenth] century the principle of private corporate activity undertaken for a public purpose and possessed of monopoly rights was lodged firmly within the body of the English legal system."[4] The granting of charters by government remained generally in effect until 1844 when it became possible to incorporate without a special grant; and by 1855 firms were granted the right of limited liability.[5] This was a major innovation, which marked the beginning of the real reduction of the traditional powers of government over corporations. Peter Drucker did not mince words:

> this new "corporation," this new "Societe Anonyme," this new "Aktiengesellschaft," could not be explained away as a *reform*, which is how the new army, the new university, the new hospital presented themselves. It clearly was a genuine innovation.... It was the first new autonomous institution in hundreds of years, the first to create a power cen-

ter that was within society yet independent of the central government of the national state.[6]

The next major innovation that occurred in the corporate institution—the managerial revolution—took root in the United States. The severe management difficulties that the railroads encountered in the 1850s as they grew to substantial sizes spurred the development of complex organizational hierarchies. There was a basic difference between the response of Americans and that of Europeans to the complex management, operational, and capital challenges of the railroads. In Europe the solution was sought via government ownership and control. But managerial hierarchies invented in America provided a smooth way for firms to exploit economies of scale and scope, to control operations and ensure safety, to operate the firm as an internal capital market, and to separate ownership from control. The essential message is that Americans because of anti-statist feelings rejected the public operations of large industrial complexes. The new corporate form that evolved in the "Second Industrial Revolution" was under private initiative and ownership. According to McCraw,

> Corporations gradually drifted away from their historic public-purpose status and became separated from government. The focus of managers shifted from the relationship of corporations to government to internal operations. Each company began to conceive of itself as a freestanding entity, just as individual Americans characteristically insisted on independent citizenship for themselves. Corporate managers saw their organizations as autonomous bodies beyond the interference of government or any powerful institutional force. The corporate form was hardening into a mold that was efficient for the conduct of business that would prove almost impossible for public authority to crack.[7]

We are now in what business historians have termed the "Third Industrial Revolution," "postindustrial society," "postcapitalist society," or the "knowledge society." The corporation's relentless search for autonomy is now symbolized by the diversified multinational organization located in various economies and increasingly operating independently of any specific national regulations. Increasingly, the interests of corporations are dissociated from those of their home or host countries. This new postcapitalist society imposes new imperatives on corporate managers. The dynamics of modern knowledge society demand three systematic practices. According to Peter Drucker, it requires a continuing improvement in everything a company does; the company must learn to exploit its knowledge, that is, to develop the next generation of applications from its successes; it must learn to innovate; and innovation has to be organized as a systematic process.[8] This compelling demand creates the need for the organization to seek greater autonomy from its surrounding society. For it must seek to "constantly upset, disorganize, and destabilize the community" (the organization needs to be an innovator), be free to close factories on which local communities depend for employment, and "live *in* a community but not be *of* it." Drucker puts it succinctly when he declares that "the organization cannot submerge itself in the community nor subordinate itself to the community's ends. Its 'culture' has to transcend community. It is the nature of the task, not the community in which the task is being performed, that determines the culture of an organization."[9] The modern corporation arguably more "soulful" than its ancestors is no longer the handmaiden of the state and has emerged as an autonomous and competing center of power in society. As a corporate citizen, a legal person with rights and duties, it has, like the individual, emerged as an essential unit of political action in the modern nation-state. It has transformed the modern nation-state into the pluralistic society of competing and autonomous, specialized, and single-task tools called organizations. This far-reaching transformation has created new tensions such as the corporate need for autonomy versus the care of the common good. It is in the light of above the historico-theoretical sketch that I would investigate the state-corporation relationship and its attendant management practices in Nigeria.

There are seven doorways through which I will closely examine the state-corporation relationship and its impact on corporate management practice in Nigeria. First, I investigate the connection between the character of the postcolonial state and politics on one hand and the weak material base of the ruling elites and wealth accumulation on the other. Next my investigation focuses on the nature of capital accumulation and corporate attitude toward risk. I try to find out if the Nigerian capitalist economy truly forces or encourages managers to behave capitalistically. Closely related to the attitude toward risk is the issue of how environmental uncertainty, created and largely sustained by the state, fundamentally affects the choice of corporate forms. Third, I look at why firms have become "states" in Nigeria. They provide their own security and infrastructure ranging from electricity and water to garbage disposal. Every firm is forced to be a government because of public infrastructure deficiencies and the inability of the Nigerian state to adequately protect life and property. Fourth, I examine how the postcolonial ideology and paradigm of development affects the ideology and paradigm of management in the postindependence era. Fifth, I investigate the corruption in the public and private sectors as it relates to the development of productive forces, the limited commodification of the economy and the appropriation of surplus that is not mediated by commodity exchange but by political power. Sixth, I examine the authoritarian management style of Nigerian managers as it harks back to the days of the resident and district officers of the colonial state. Finally, I look at the state-society relationship and analyze its effects on management practices in Nigeria.

These seven areas are by no means exhaustive, but it is my hope that they will make my point clearer and help us to better understand management in Nigeria. They encompass the historical, theoretical, and practical fields of interaction of the state and the corporation. More fundamentally, they bring to the fore the objective conditions and the dynamics of social forces that define and drive such interactions. The presentation will entail "thick" description of the interaction between the state and the corporation, and inferences should be taken with the understanding that every interaction between any human organizations is imbued with multiple, frequently contending, values, meanings and interpretations.

THE COLONIAL STATE IN NIGERIA

We must begin with the colonial state and its economic and political legacy. The postcolonial state is after all a successor or a child of the colonial state. What was the nature of the colonial state, especially the aspects of it that throw light on the issue at hand? The colonial state started as a commercial concern, the Royal Niger Company. Its charter, granted by the British government in 1886, empowered it to "maintain law and order, levy and collect duties, to maintain free trade, to administer justice and to secure the abolition of slavery." It was also given charge of the overall economic development of Nigeria. The company not only acted as a state in this regard, it also helped to extend British imperialism with coercion. Thus the state in Nigeria started as a crude tool of capital. The primary function of the colonial state was to create and maintain the political and economic conditions under which the accumulation of capital could proceed through the extraction and exploitation of Nigeria's resources by the metropolitan bourgeoisie. This task was to be carried out at minimal cost to the colonizers. This economic consideration resulted in the imposition on the country of a minimalist Weberian bureaucracy, a highly centralized public administration system that emphasized control and centralized power.[10] In performing its role as promoter of the interests of the foreign bourgeoisie, the state established bureaucratic network, built roads, railroads and ports to facilitate the export of raw materials and the import of manufactures, attended to the supply of labor, sometimes using forced labor, created legislation that introduced or rationalized taxes, broke up traditional institutions and social relations of production, and accelerated the atomization of society. The state built schools and hospitals and went into the buying and selling of commodities. All this was done to create a capitalist-oriented economy dependent on Britain and on foreign capital. According to Claude Ake, "the colonial state was statist, its statism consisted in ubiquitous and heavy handed control of economy and polity."[11]

The colonial state needed to carry out its mission and to survive in the face of the hostility of the colonized. Its power was not only absolute but also arbitrary. It accelerated the destruction or restructuring of any local institution that did not serve its purpose, rejected any restrictions on its power, and extended its rights to powers. The absoluteness and arbitrariness of the colonizers' powers were to structure politics in Nigeria and flavor it long after the departure of the British in 1960. According to Ake,

> Since the colonial state was for its subjects, at any rate, an arbitrary power, it could not engender any legitimacy even though it made rules and laws profusely and propagated values. Accordingly, in struggling to advance its interests, the colonial subjects did not worry about conformity to legality or legitimacy norms. Colonial politics was reduced to the crude mechanics of opposing forces driven by the calculus of power. For every one in this arena, security lay only in the accumulation of power.[12]

There is another area that we need to touch upon in our characterization of the specificity of the colonial state. Ake contends that the state as a specific modality of class domination has two important features: class domination is mediated by commodity exchange and the system of mechanisms of class domination is autonomized.[13] The combination of these features ensures that the system of institutional mechanisms of domination is differentiated and disassociated from the ruling class, appearing as an independent, objective force (independent of social classes, even the hegemonic class) standing alongside the society, mediating the struggle for the appropriation of the society's surplus value. This conceptualization of the state sees it as an expression of relations between classes in society. For the effective performance of its role of creating favorable conditions for the general and fundamental interests of the capitalist class, it has to mask its role as an instrument of domination and the subjection of the non-capitalist class. Now how can this be done or how can class domination assume this form? According to Ake, "Essentially it does so by virtue of its mediation by the thoroughgoing generalization of commodity exchange."[14] The state mediates and creates the conditions for the preservation of pervasive commodification and market relations and the subsequent atomization of society, which compel everyone to be first and foremost a commodity bearer (even if it is only labor power), producing for exchange value and falling into a web of mutual dependence. A common and mutually beneficial dependence is established and maintained by the market, the laws of supply and demand. By virtue of this mutual, society-wide dependence and exchange domination are autonomized and conceived by many as market forces that dominate and subordinate all players. In a typical market economy, no one can escape this tyranny. Behind these impartial, impersonal market forces are real human beings, but the domination of one social group by another is masked, "seems autonomized, seems to operate independently of the social group which dominates."[15]

The mediation of commodity exchange also produces autonomization and attendant masking of domination in the political sphere. The operative norms of market capitalism are competition, individualism, freedom, property rights, exchange, and formal equality, allowing every one to act in self-interest and inexorably promoting exchange in an increasingly atomized society. This community of formally free and equal agents requires an independent agency to maintain law and order and maintain conditions for the free exchange of values in conformity with the rule of law. This independent agency enacts laws and regulations for the creation of conditions necessary for the sustenance and development of market relations and the realization of exchange value. This agency guarantees the worker's right to sell his labor power, the capitalist's right to extract profits and keep them, rigorous adherence to the rule of law, and equal treatment of the unequal before the law, which are the conditions underlying capital relations and domination of labor by capital. The appearance of autonomization is also sustained by the periodic election of managers of the state by a free and competitive process, harking back to the "neutrality and objectivity" of the market. According to Ake, autonomization is the very essence of the state as a modality of domination and the state is essentially (not exclusively) a capitalist phenomenon.[16]

But the problem in Africa, especially in colonial Nigeria, was that the state enjoyed only limited autonomy, limited independence from the hegemonic class, and thus was immersed in the class struggle. Why was this so? It was due to the rudimentary development of commodity production and exchange, the relatively elementary nature of the productive forces. Exchange relations, which undergird and propel autonomization of class domination, were limited because the capitalist sector was still small in Nigeria, market relations had not fully penetrated many portions of the economy, especially the rural areas, and the society was not highly atomized. The operative norms of capitalism were very rudimentary. Capitalism remained enclave capitalism. In short, precapitalist relations of production and exchange defined transactions in many parts of the economy and politics. In the absence of pervasive commodification and related autonomization of the state and institutionalization of formal equality and open competition for offices, the colonial government lacked even the appearance of legitimacy and objectivity. For Nigerians, colonial power was arbitrary. In the absence of autonomizing mechanisms, the colonial state had to frequently resort to brute coercion to create conditions for the expansion of capital. Thus the accumulation and monopolization of power was the top priority of everyone and security laid in the control of power. State power was used for the accumulation of wealth; simply put the colonial state was not an autonomous force to impartially deal with the issues of capitalist reproduction. Ake states that

> Without coercion the equilibrium of the colonial system would have been destroyed. In the colonial economy, force became the key instrument of the profit motive. Force was used to allocate roles, force was used to ensure the supply of labour, and force was used to extract and allocate the economic surplus.[17]

The colonial systems, as would be expected, denied Nigerians political freedom and choice of state managers. Colonization in Nigeria did not provide liberal democracy as the political correlate of capitalism and instead imposed a state that was not a product of society.[18] It was these contradictions arising from the conditions of production in Nigeria that led Ake to say that politics in colonial Nigeria was driven by the calculus of power. The problem of the limited autonomy of the state and its control by hegemonic interest, in this case Britain, meant that there was little confidence in resolving contradictions between Nigerians and British interests. Differences between groups were presented as absolute, and politics was thus essentially the "determination of two exclusive claims of rulership."[19]

I have gone to this length to explain the colonial state and indeed the notion of state in general, for at least four very important reasons. First, the non-autonomization of class domination has serious implications for politics and the accumulation of capital in Nigeria in the postcolonial era. The ruling class is obliged, because of the underdevelopment of commodity relations, to follow a negative form of accumulation and reject liberal democracy in favor of authoritarianism. Second, the rudimentary development of productive forces and exchange mediation carry implications for the way corporate managers see their roles in the economy. The pattern and means of accumulation of wealth in the economy are not particularly conducive to the growth of capitalism and have largely disassociated wealth from entrepreneurial activities. Needless to say, corporate managers are ultimately responsible for creating shareholders' value or wealth for their owners. Third, the appropriation of surplus by mechanisms other than mediation of commodity exchange makes wealth accumulation appear as theft or corruption. Fourth, the underdevelopment of commodity relations has often meant the intervention of force in the labor process and the unrestrained exploitation of workers, which threaten workers' ability to reproduce themselves for benefit of the corporations.

THE POSTCOLONIAL STATE IN NIGERIA

Like the colonial society, postcolonial Nigeria is still characterized by limited commodification. The society is largely non-atomized and hence difficult to characterize as a market society. Sixty-four percent of people depend largely on subsistence farming and less than 10 percent are involved in wage labor. Social relations are still characterized by mechanical solidarity, based on ethnic solidarity and primary loyalties. The state is still immersed in a class struggle, unable to arbitrate economic and political competitions impartially.

According to Ake, the character of the postcolonial state can be summarized as follows. The state is totalistic in scope, it tries to do everything, and unlike the colonial state it has extended statism into entrepreneurial roles.[20] State capitalism is justified by government officials as a sure way to mobilize capital for development and as the logical outcome of the state's control of large portions of the society's surplus.[21] State capitalism is also a means by which the national ruling elites try to create a surplus in order to appropriate an ever-bigger share of wealth. This change from mere statism to entrepreneurism has to be understood in another context. Unlike the colonial state, which could afford to carry on exploitation without development, the postcolonial state managed by Nigerians could not afford to ignore development and was understandably in a hurry to effect some development. The second feature of the postcolonial state is that the power of the state is still absolute and arbitrary. It rejects any restriction on its power. It is an apparatus of violence and relies for compliance on coercion rather than authority. Fourth, the Nigerian state enjoys a narrow base of support, as it is essentially hostile to the bulk of its populace. The state is often an instrument of class struggle. The state is co-opted for the service of the dominant faction of the elite. There is an undue emphasis on capturing political power and an intense fear of losing to rival parties. For this reason, political competition assumes the character of warfare and has become a zero-sum game, "an anarchy of dedicated self-seeking."[22] The leaders are often engrossed in a struggle for survival.

Most importantly, the tendency is to use state power for the accumulation of capital/wealth. Politicians and bureaucrats use state power to create or strengthen their material base.[23] In this highly statist economy and warring polity, economic success and personal security and welfare depend on access to state power. To quote Ake:

> To become wealthy without the patronage of the state was likely to invite the unpleasant attention of those in control of state power. For any one outside the hegemonic faction of the political elite, it was generally futile to harbor any illusions of becoming wealthy by entrepreneurial activity or even take personal safety for granted. For anyone who was part of the ruling faction, entrepreneurial activity

was unnecessary, for one could appropriate surplus with less risk and less trouble by means of state power.[24]

This is not conducive to economic development.

The above is only a thumbnail sketch of the nature of the state in Nigeria. The rest of this chapter will investigate the state-corporation relationship in the context of how it aids an understanding of management practice in a developing society.

WEAK MATERIAL BASE OF THE RULING ELITE

Often we hear people complain about management or its quality in Nigeria. This presupposes that "management" is going on in Nigerian ventures. Even in this chapter I have assumed that there is management going on in the Nigerian corporation. This point is really contestable, because in a very fundamental sense, management is not on the agenda in most Nigerian companies. By all indications, entrepreneurial activity is unnecessary in accumulating a surplus. One can make all the desired profits and accumulate wealth with less risk and trouble if one has access to state powers. One does not need to articulate any management philosophy, set up proper management structures to coordinate and monitor the flow of activities, or plan for efficient allocation (spatial and temporal) of resources. The entrepreneur does not need to make investments in production, marketing, and management to create and maintain competitive capability. This is a serious, if not deadly, dilemma for the manager in Nigeria. Caught in the struggle for survival in a capitalist economy that does not promote capitalistic behavior, the entrepreneur can afford, therefore, not to focus attention on building managerial hierarchies and addressing management philosophy, yet he cannot abandon the idea of management. The entrepreneur or manager cannot abandon it because at the minimum it is seen as the means by which he hopes to reproduce his wealth someday outside the corridors of power. For in the postcolonial society, business and politics are woven together. Wealth is necessary to build political structures and power bases. Political power is necessary to acquire more wealth. More importantly, corporate management helps to bring some kind of coherence to the various fragmented contracts a manager is executing for the state. In this circumstance, the real response of the entrepreneur is to make token gestures toward the idea of management by employing a team of professional managers. For a firm's fortune is not essentially defined by its ability to solve problems and run its internal administration, but its capacity to direct both personal and corporate resources toward opportunities for profits. According to Berry, the expansion of the firm in Nigeria

> is often directly related to the amount of time and energy the proprietor spends away from the shop, cultivating good relations and potential customers, creditors, and bureaucrats who control access to key resources. Thus the entrepreneur faces a contradiction between developing his enterprise and keeping it running. Expansion of a firm often undermines its performance.[25]

Why has management in Nigeria taken this kind of turn? To understand why this is so, one has to examine the ruling elite's lack of a strong material base, especially immediately after independence. During colonialism, Nigerians were, by and large, denied access to wealth. In order to strengthen its material base, the elite that took power from the departing colonialists had to quickly find ways to appropriate more of the wealth of the society. This precluded the usual method of private capitalist investments, risk taking and exploitation of profits, given the urgency of the situation and the relatively small size of the capitalist enclave. What was most efficient in the short run was the use of state power to engage in coercive expropriation of economic surplus or the means of production. The objective character of the ruling elite did not allow it to behave capitalistically in the classical sense of the word but forced it to specialize in the maintenance of the political conditions necessary for accumulation and surplus appropriation by political power rather than commodity exchange.

ATTITUDE TOWARD RISK AND ENVIRONMENTAL UNCERTAINTY AND CHOICE OF CORPORATE FORM

The inclination of the Nigerian ruling class to use state power for capital accumulation has a profound influence on attitudes toward risk and organizational design. It is true to say that there are many genuine capitalists in Nigeria who have made their money outside the corridors of the state, but most of the capitalists in Nigeria have found a method additional to the usual method of private capitalist exploitation. Such people do not want to act capitalistically—to invest and take risks and reap profits or losses—and do not want to depend on the inexorable working of the laws of demand and supply. They have to depend on occasions when the power to make political decisions or enforce laws provides effective and significant opportunities to give or take surplus from individuals or taxpayers. Given that it is easier to make money through the award of contracts, the enforcement of laws, the siting of public projects and the appointment of officers to economically rewarding posts, not many people are interested in taking the risks that usually and inevitably develop productive forces in a capitalist economy.[26]

Often because of political interests and struggle for state power, policies are changed too frequently. In fact, one nagging characteristic of the business environment in Nigeria is the uncertainty and risk associated with the turns and twists in policy regimes. As we would expect, we have seen the prevalence of short-term orientation to investments, crippling inflation, high discount rates, and a strong preference for current consumption and trading. The future is indeed abstract and far away for many actors in the economy. This type of business environment not only affects attitudes toward risk, but also influences organizational design.

Organization theories would suggest that these conditions of uncertainty, which increase the likelihood of parties cheating and acting opportunistically, should produce vertical or horizontal integration, hierarchies, and boundary expansion of firms.[27] But in Nigeria we have not seen a discernible trend toward increase in organizational size, building of managerial hierarchies, or investment in managerial or administrative coordination. If anything, we have seen movement in the opposite direction, away from increased managerial hierarchies and toward a strategy of spreading risks. The typical Nigerian entrepreneur is involved in many ventures (no intensification of capital; he or she invests by diversifying), rather than expanding and focusing on one. As macroeconomic policies change, he or she quickly changes to capture new opportunities and move on to the next ones. Often, this strategy of spreading risks is a defense against deliberate attempts by hostile governments to impoverish their political enemies and economic competitors, and a protection against the direct use of coercion to appropriate economic surplus or the means of production. According to Ake,

> Sometimes this [direct appropriation] is done under the cover of political conflict; some people are denounced for some political crime and then murdered or imprisoned and their property seized. Sometimes, it is done gangster style. Sometimes it is done under the cover of religious or ethnic conflict; a religious or ethnic group is denounced for being unpatriotic and subversive, or for economic exploitation of other groups, and popular hatred is built up against them. Then, under cover of this popular antipathy, the unfortunate group is abused,

sometimes to a point amounting to genocide, and their property taken from them.[28]

Before ending this section, let me state that the above analysis is not meant to suggest that state policies are the sole causes of organizational design, but to show that they influence the organizational business structure.

THE FIRM AS A STATE

Any analysis of management development in Nigeria must pay close attention to the context in which the public is privatized and the private "publicized." From the beginning of European contact in Nigeria, monopolistic tendencies were present. Because of the large amounts of capital needed for ventures into Africa, the poor state of communications, or the extensive fortifications of ports, only large-scale enterprises or state-supported companies could undertake the risks of enterprise in Nigeria. These monopolistic tendencies, rather than decreasing at the close of the nineteenth century were intensified because of the rivalry between European companies of which the scramble for and partition of Africa was just one ugly aspect of it. The need for a more secure market base drove the British government to increase statism and the monopolization of the Nigerian economy. The British government brought an increasing range of geographical territories, economic activities, and powers of government under the control of the Royal Niger Company, notably by granting of charter powers and by anti-competitive enactments, to facilitate accumulation by means of state powers. The Royal Niger Company was given charge of the overall economic development of its territories. Nigerians whose territories were carved up were unhappy. The Brass and Akassa raids in the 1890s were some of the manifestations of discontent among the "natives." The Royal Niger Company dealt with the tide of popular discontent among Nigerians by enforcing conformity through coercion. The big trading company, which had its own security forces, used coercion to restrain political and economic rivalry and competition. Political power became a means to economic power. Economic competition now assumed the character of warfare and paved the way for the ascendancy of the rapacious, violent, colonial state with absolute and arbitrary power. It is very important for us to understand this phase of the development of corporate organization in Nigeria: the monopolization of economic powers, the political and military character of accumulation, with companies functioning as the state, and the close link between state and commercial enterprise. Herein lies a great key to the understanding of management and entrepreneurship in postcolonial Nigeria.

Thus, today we should not be surprised when we hear that the Nigerian police force is the often-preferred means of settling industrial disputes in the country. Sola Fajana studied the resolution of industrial conflicts in Nigeria from colonial times to 1986. His study reveals that the police have been highly effective in bringing strikes to an end. Nigerian managers prefer to call in the police to settle industrial disputes rather than to negotiating with workers. According to Fajana,

> Nearly all the cases of disputes were terminated by police intervention, the figure reaching as high as 84 per cent. On the other hand, only 3.08 percent were handled by management without the intercession of the police. Only 4 per cent were resolved by recourse to the joint determination provision in the statutory settlement procedure. (Viz. collective negotiations, mediation, conciliation, arbitration and industrial court.)[29]

This tendency of Nigerian managers, whether in the public or private sector, to use the armed forces and the coercive apparatus of the state in their management of industrial dispute, dates back, as we have seen, not only to the formative years of the Nigerian state, but also to colonial days. The state has never been a neutral arbiter between labor and capital. Not only did the colonial state use forced and convict labor in private enterprises, it also enacted repressive laws to subjugate workers in the interest of capital. The colonial police saw every worker's protest as protest against the colonial administration. The colonial government even admitted that "the Chief Commissioners (Police) have given it as their opinion that there can be no comfortable line of demarcation between labour affairs and politics...and that in consequence, labour policy becomes mainly the concern of Provincial administration itself."[30]

Today, many petroleum exploration companies have their own private, armed police force (such as the "Shell Super-numerary Police") or a detachment of the Nigerian police stationed at their facilities. These forces have not only harassed employees, but also intimidated oil communities for protesting against environmental degradation and pollution. On November 1, 1990 while the people of Umuechem in Rivers State were asleep after two days of protest against Shell, the largest oil producer in the country, the Nigerian Police, invited in by the powerful oil company, killed eighty people.[31] Reports of other collaborations with the coercive apparatus of the state were rampant during the Ogoni crisis of 1993-1995, which culminated in the hanging of Ken Saro-Wiwa and eight other Movement for the Survival of Ogoni People (MOSOP) members by the rapacious military government of General Sani Abacha. Less than a year after the hanging, newspapers reported that Shell was negotiating the importation of arms for the Nigerian Police. It was even mentioned that the oil giant had in the past imported arms for the Nigeria Police, ostensibly to be used by the company's supernumerary police who are, technically, accountable to the Nigerian Police Force. In May 1998, 120 young men climbed onto Chevron's Parabe platform, off the coast of Ondo State, shutting down production and taking some company staff hostage for several days. In response to this act, Chevron called for the intervention of security forces, and provided three helicopters to fly in the navy and a paramilitary force, Mobile Police Unit, who killed two of the unarmed protesters. About seven months later, state security forces (about a hundred heavily armed soldiers) were invited again by Chevron into the two small Ijo communities (of roughly 500 people each) of Opia and Ikenya in Delta State, and the soldiers fired indiscriminately as they approached the villages. This resulted in the killing of dozens of people and the wounding of many others. The soldiers also burnt villages and destroyed properties. What was the offense? According to Chevron, it was believed that "youths from the two communities had demanded money from soldiers guarding a nearby [Chevron] rig."[32] So much for the neutrality of the police and the state!

Shell and Chevron not only exemplify the over reliance of Nigerian firms on security cooperation in dealing with labor disputes and community protests, but they also show the character of Nigerian firms as states. Shell and Chevron have their own hospitals, mini-water works, and power generating systems, and other types of "public goods." In a recent survey of 179 manufacturing establishments in five states, including Lagos and Kano, conducted by the World Bank, the extent of private provision of infrastructure was revealed. About 92 percent of Nigerian firms surveyed had their own generators to supplement (by as much as 37 percent) the inadequate supply of electricity by the state agent, the National Electric Power Authority (NEPA). In terms of boreholes or artesian wells, 44.1 percent of the firms surveyed did not rely on public supply. Firms also had their own radio equipment for communications and vehicles and motorcycles for the shipment of goods. The percentage of firms having vehicles for workers' transport was 26 percent. Many firms also provided their own garbage disposal systems, with 13 per cent having vehicles for garbage disposal.[33] According to Lee and Anas, whose article relied on the World Bank survey, the total share of capital investment in private infrastructure (including generators, boreholes, radio equipment, motorcycles and other vehicles) was 14 percent of total capital.[34] The costs manufacturers bear go beyond the capital expenditure of installing their services; they pay a heavy price compared with the price of services provided by the state agents. The average cost per kwh of self-generated power is 69 U.S. cents in Nigeria, which is 10 times higher than the international unit cost of efficient utilities. When the survey was conducted in 1987, NEPA was charging 1.74 U.S. cents at the then exchange rate of four naira to the dollar, meaning that the average cost of privately generated electricity was 40 times higher than NEPA's price.

The massive public infrastructure deficiencies not only force companies to act like states, they affect companies in more ways than the inconvenience of providing services. For instance, firms seldom relocate because of the switching and high setup costs related to capital investment in utilities even when there may be better market opportunities elsewhere. Of the 179 firms surveyed only two percent indicated that they had moved from another location. According to Lee and Anas,

> This absence of mobility is striking considering that the average annual moving rate observed in large cities in other developing countries such as Seoul and Bogota is about 5 per cent. The relative immobility of Nigerian firms is consistent with the fact that the capacity, regularity and quality of infrastructure vary from bad to worse within and across cities. This tends to limit the gains in infrastructure quality that can be achieved by moving to new locations.[35]

THE IDEOLOGY OF NATIONAL DEVELOPMENT AND THE IDEOLOGY OF MANAGEMENT

Economic development is without question the most urgent task facing Nigeria. Development was seen as the overriding task of the nation's leaders after independence in 1960 as it was imperative that the black man quickly eradicate the humiliation of the white man's colonization of Africa. In this regard, in the last forty years, the state has been variously perceived, depending on the development perspective in vogue, to be the key player and given a particularly important role in the development process or as the obstacle to the liberation of the energies of its people. In the 1960s and early 1970s, when the "trickle down" and "basic needs" approaches to development were the predominant perspectives, the state was characterized as the key actor to command the heights of the economy in initiating development. Later, in the 1980s and 1990s when "small is beautiful," and "enabling environment" developmental perspectives became the darling of policy makers and economists, there was the belief that many institutions needed to be consciously incorporated into development efforts and the state's role reduced.[36] Looking at this change, one may conclude that the ideology of development has changed. In actuality, however, it has not changed. My argument here is that there is a pervasive ideology of development that has reigned supreme since independence in national development.[37] By examining it, we will discover a salient aspect of the state-corporation relationship in Nigeria. The ideology of development has a corollary in corporate management, which I call the ideology of management. Our understanding of the relationship between state and corporation will be severely limited unless we examine this.

The development orientation of the Nigerian State (or the hegemonic faction that controlled the state) accepted Western development precepts. There was a naive assumption that every thing traditional was bad and development could be brought about by modernization and Westernization. At the core of this ideology was the perception that the way to overcome underdevelopment is to remove a set of specific technical obstacles. These are lack of entrepreneurial skills, inadequate manpower and technology, low levels of savings and investments, low productivity, low inflow of foreign investment or technical assistance, and low achievement motivation. Given this type of analysis of the problem, the process of development involved stimulating investments, encouraging savings, mobilizing capital, and modernizing attitudes, and in a word "catching up with the West" which has apparently overcome these obstacles. What needed to be done to further development also involved changes in the vertical relation between Nigeria and wealthy Western nations: better access to Western markets, more aid on lenient terms, debt forgiveness, transfer of technology, more foreign investment, and so on. When development was conceptualized this way, the preferred characteristics of the economically developed Western society became the goal of social evolution. This approach to development marginalized those who should have been its means and ends, ignored the transformation of society, and viewed development as independent of politics and culture. What was more important was the correction of technical obstacles. Conceiving development in this manner (development being independent of culture and institutional framework) gave the ruling elites unrestricted liberty to pick and choose what aspects of Nigerian institutions and culture would allow them to "maintain and exploit power" and to discard what was not useful for them. Thus, they would use traditional non-oppositional politics to argue, without acknowledging the African concept of participative development and consensus building, that dissent was not to be allowed in the development effort.

The real core of this exogenous development strategy was that it was a strategy of power employed by the leaders of the nation—and it is in this regard that we can draw out the connection to corporate management practice. After independence when the nation's leaders were pressured for redistribution, they argued that the people needed to work harder to produce the surplus which then could be shared. They conveniently shifted the emphasis from the radical nationalist demands for redistribution, equality, and structural transformation of the colonial economy to hard work.

Today, the Nigerian corporate ideology of management also views improvement in administration as becoming more like the West and is driven by a calculus of power.[38] Once again the ideal characteristics of the Western corporation are seen as the goal of corporate culture, of managerial evolution, and anything traditional is construed negatively or treated with hostility. The highly educated, acculturated managers in the big corporations, in the formal sector have swallowed hook, line, and sinker the ideology's image of the inferiority of traditional African management practice and the superiority of Western styles. Being more like a Western corporation means increasing resource flows (management principles, models, and fads) from America or Britain and denying the validity and integrity of African management principles. One obvious illustration of this is managers' preference for hiring foreign consultants to solve local management problems or to run corporations. Managers long to come to Western educational institutions for so-called management training and believe that foreign experts always know better than Nigerians.

CORRUPTION AND THE ECONOMY

Corruption is a management practice in Nigeria. Observers are in substantial agreement about this, and should thus not detain us here. What is contestable is the cause of corruption. Many commentators explain the willingness of corporate managers to bribe state officials or to accept gratification as due to individuals' weakness. It is also suggested that managers engage in corruption because the practice is so endemic that without it no one can really do business in the country. These explanations see the problem as psychological or sociological rather than economic, meaning that corruption is primarily a function of the development of the productive forces and commodity exchange, and of the objective character of Nigerian capitalists. Corruption is particularly linked to the limited commodification of the economy, which makes the appropriation of surplus by non-formally equal exchange possible, and to the limited autonomy of the state. When exchange and appropriation of surplus in a capitalist society is not done by the market, through the mediation of commodity exchange, surplus has to be appropriated by political power, at the point of making political decisions to collect for the state or transfer resources to it. We have learnt that the state and the market hide domination and the common subordination of man by man and give them the appearance of autonomous force. But where the state and market are not *there* or are not functioning properly to coordinate individually produced exchange values, commodity exchange appears in its "true character as theft." Nonetheless, according to Ake, it is "an exchange of sorts, but one which, to the misfortune of the bourgeoisie that is obliged to appropriate surplus in this way, has the connotation of corruption."[39] During the time of feudalism or the very early days of capitalism in Europe, when the market was not well developed and the state was not developed enough to be outside the class struggle or protect the individual and institutionalize equal treatment of the unequal, the exploitation of the one who mainly sold his labor power or was landless was conspicuously corrupt, oppressive, and often brutal. It was also often done by direct use of force, by what has been described as "primitive accumulation."

The point I am making is that corruption in the corporate and public sectors is primarily a function of the limited autonomization of the state and the partial atomization of the society in Nigeria. These in turn reflect the rudimentary level of the development of productive forces, commodity production, and exchange. So the nature of the Nigerian state is very important in understanding this nagging area of corporate management. When the state promotes nonproductive primitive accumulation it makes the business environment nonconducive for entrepreneurs and managers to develop the productive forces which will liberate the state itself from privatization by special interests.

NIGERIAN MANAGERS AS THE DESCENDANTS OF THE COLONIAL DISTRICT OFFICERS

We cannot really understand the management practices of Nigerian firms until we look at the influence on them of the management style of the top colonial civil servants. Dia has argued that the foundation of the administrative style of African managers lies in the colonial era. According to Dia, "the pattern of centralized authority [created by the colonial masters] has carried over to today with managers mainly intent on controlling and micro-managing the individual and organizations below them."[40] The prototype of today's Nigerian manager is the colonial district officer. The district officer in colonial times was not exactly the European bureaucrat of the Weberian formulation but rather an admixture of the European civil servant and the traditional African chief as he was perceived and wanted to be understood in Africa. Dudley wrote:

> The District Officer saw himself not just as a system-functionary; in fact he took on the role of a "father-figure" not unlike the image of the traditional elders and chiefs, and one in which the local population were encouraged to see him. In the role of the "father-figure" he was the embodiment of law. He did what he thought was good for "his" people, not what the people wanted. People sought his good will through "gift" of kind. To maintain his image, he should not appear easily accessible and therefore had to be guarded by a series of intermediaries and agents. He lived on the "hill," far removed from those he "governed" and whose affairs he administered and from where, in the words of Jomo Kenyatta, he presumably "communed with the ancestral spirits." From his exalted position, the District Officer gave instructions and orders which had to be followed and obeyed, never to be questioned. In

complying with the orders of the District Officer, one was not only complying with a bureaucratically sanctioned order, compliance was performance of one's moral obligations.[41]

Beyond the district officer (D.O.) in the colonial system was the resident, a higher order of man, a conqueror and god. From time to time he would descend from his Olympian heights to "'survey" his "domain," master of all he saw.'" More pompous and dictatorial than the district officer, the resident was not answerable to anyone in his domain. The African if wronged could sometimes "appeal" from the District Officer to the Resident but with the latter there was no recourse. His rulings were 'settled in heaven' and were questioned only at dire personal risk and 'wrath of hell fire.'[42] We need no further analysis to show that this was hardly the administrative model required to inculcate in the colonial subjects the participatory management style of modern corporations.

The few Nigerians who became "colonial praetors" were even more interesting than the white officers because of the complexity and contradictions of their lives. By examining this category of officers we can glean various characteristics which combined to form the complex tapestry we call Nigerian corporate management practice. The Nigerian district officer was also authoritarian with his own people because of the logic of the law-and-order administration of colonialism. Similarly, he was inaccessible as there were many intermediaries and agents around him—such people were often not regarded by him as causing obstruction but as a measure of his status and wealth-in-people. But his inaccessibility created a cultural problem, which the white D.O. did not confront. Though the chiefs in precolonial and colonial Nigeria were highly dignified, they were approachable. Thus, the Nigerian D.O. must balance approachability against over-familiarity. He was often unwilling to informally chat with a junior official in the corridors of his office but agonized over the fact that "starched collar" management eroded any sense of belonging in the organization by workers. As a successful man in the white man's organization he was in the position of a chief in his village. Like his village counterpart he was expected to cater for his people and be a source of inspiration, encouragement, and help to his people, including those in his organization and members of his extended family. He was also expected to use his position and status to draw resources from the establishment and polity to meet the needs of his corporate village group. He was the representative of his village, clan, or ethnic group in the white man's world.[43] As a warrior for his people in the violent and rapacious world of the colonizers he must conquer and bring home the spoils of office. The colonial era was indeed the beginning of what Goran Hyden has called the "economy of affection" at the state level.[44]

Decision-making was also another area of contradiction for him. In the traditional Nigerian culture (to which the Nigerian D.O. retired after work each day and during weekends, holidays, and vacations) decision-making was consultative in the sense that decisions seemed to emerge. Elders did not take unilateral decisions without informally consulting with other members of the society, namely, the youths. In this context, disagreements about authority were not so much about where the authority was located as about the desire to be consulted. But in the new hierarchical structure and bureaucratic style of management of the colonial oppressors, the Nigerian D.O. was expected to make unilateral decisions, being at the top meant being the smartest and expected to exercise authority and decision-making. Besides, the labor unions, spurred on by the nationalist leaders, questioned his authority and openly expressed doubt about the legitimacy of the whole colonial enterprise.

STATE AND SOCIETY RELATIONSHIP: POINTER TO MANAGEMENT PRACTICES

The definition of the rights and duties of the individual, the way the state defines an individual, and the character of the relationship between state and society provides a crucial point of departure for investigating how the state influences the management practices of the firm. The evolution of civil society, the relationship between the state and society in the West, has yielded some guidelines for understanding management practices in Europe and America. In the West, the state essentially started with the fusing of competing and autonomous centers of power. There were feudal lords, autonomous craft guilds, "free" cities, tax exempt bishoprics and autonomous monasteries, private armies, and so on. The development of the state meant the subjugation of these competing and autonomous centers of power under a central authority. This process not only led to the development of central authority, but also fused society and state together. But as society developed and became more complex, becoming more differentiated and requiring specialized agencies to satisfy its needs, the state was gradually separated from its encompassing society.[45] As a product of its encompassing society right from its beginning, the state was principally expected to execute the mandate of society. Given this largely harmonious relationship between the state and society, the citizens of the West see the state as a public good with which they can identify. The next trend in this development of the state-society relationship was the progressive empowerment of the individual after the end of the medieval era. The individual, from being a subject of the state (king or prince) and enclosed in the kinship and community frameworks of fixed hierarchies, "has more or less replaced such corporate entities as kinship groups and village communities as the significant political units of the medieval world and has emerged as the elemental unit of political action in the modern nation-state."[46] This development of the recognition of the worth of the individual—

the growth of individualism—is intrinsically linked with the development of the corporation. According to Scott, both individualism and organizations evolved as part of a dual process. The same social forces that brought about individualism—"the freeing of individuals from all-absorbing social structures"—promoted the growth of organizations: "the freeing of resources, including individuals, which can be mobilized in the service of specialized purposes."[47]

In Nigeria the state and society have drifted apart (starting in the era of the slave trade, intensified by colonialism, and exacerbated by postindependence politics) and the individual has steadily been attacked by the forces of the state, which has refused to recognize his worth or citizenship. The terms of exchange between the state and the individual are ill defined. The individual is alienated from the state and his or her attention is focused more on the *primordial public* such as kin and ethnic groups, which are independent of the postcolonial state.[48] All this, as Ake has cautioned, is "not to suggest that the Nigerian masses are not a political force or that they do not participate politically in any way." He contends that

> They remain a powerful political force, but largely potentially and as an externality (that is, to the state). They break into the state intermittently through anomic interest articulation and at those periods in which the ruling class makes a show of formally consulting them in order to buttress their legitimacy as governors. It is important to note that on these occasions of formal consultation they are mobilized by charismatic politics and appeal to primary loyalties.[49]

The Western corporate world has not only witnessed the growth of individualism, but has also seen an increasing appreciation of the worth of the worker. This has changed greatly from the time in the Middle Ages when corporate bodies such as guilds, manors, and villages "wholly contained their members and possessed full authority and responsibilities over them and workers' rights were acquired via memberships in these bodies."[50] In contrast to the nineteenth century, when employers believed that workers needed employers more than employers needed workers, we are today (in the postcapitalist, knowledge society) seeing corporations marketing for membership as much as they market products and services, and corporations contain only the resources vested in them by their members or owners and the services of their agents.[51] So business leaders talk about people as "the greatest assets" of the corporation and of "human resources" instead of "labor." From the days of command and control management style, we have come to the time when essentially the manager, though still having considerable authority, like the state, does not command but inspires and has equals working as a team, not subordinates. As Drucker puts it, "because the modern organization consists of knowledge specialists, it has to be an organization of equals, of colleagues and associates. No knowledge ranks higher than another; each is judged by its contribution to the common task rather than by any inherent superiority or inferiority."[52] The acceptance of the individual as an asset, as an equal, as the knowledge worker who owns his "means of production," allows the conception of the corporation as a public stake in which the worker has a major share, both as a contributor to it and as a beneficiary of its resources. The corporation is thus not seen by management as a place where the costs of workers and raw materials are processed into profits but as a repository to which all stakeholders contribute and from which they expect to receive benefits. In the Nigerian corporate world the picture is different. The workers are an externality to management, a powerful and useful force which management has to work with but essentially a factor in the corporate environment, where managers' right is coextensive with might. In this intemperate environment, the police and other coercive apparatuses of the state are quickly brought in to suppress workers' genuine demands. Earlier, we learnt how the oil companies routinely use soldiers and police to suppress demands of villages and we know of industrial disputes that are "settled" by brutal police actions. These modes of corporate behavior reflect the reality of the state of the development of individualism, especially the relationship between the state and the individual or the civil society, and the failure of the state to carry out the mandate of its encompassing society.

CONCLUSION

This chapter has investigated the nature of the state-corporation relationship in Nigeria and highlighted its effects on management practice. Before I summarize our findings, it is necessary to review the "nature" of the state and the corporation's in the country. The state has not risen above society; it is immersed in class struggle and often privatized by the hegemonic faction of the ruling elites. The corporations (capitalists) still largely dependent on access to state power as a means of wealth accumulation, have not yet developed a collective consciousness sufficient to make the state provide appropriate conditions for capitalist development or for a common rationality which allows common rules of competition to be accepted. These two "natures" define the character of the relationship between state and corporation as a factor influencing the development of management practice.

There are seven characteristic features that help to explore the state-corporation intercourse and its impact on management practice. First, the weak material base of the ruling elite impels it to accumulate wealth by the use of state power, not permitting it to behave capitalistically. Second, the pervasive conditions of uncertainty, often created or sustained by the intense struggle among the factions of the hegemonic elite to gain the political power necessary for accumulation, have forced many business owners to abandon or downplay the importance of managerial hierarchies and to move toward a strategy of spreading risks. There is a preference for diversification rather than intensification of capital in Nigerian ventures. Third, the failure of the state to meet its infra-structural duties has inevitably turned firms into states. Today, we have companies which are essentially states, with the necessary coercive apparatus. Fourth, the ideology of management, which fundamentally drives thinking about the place of management in Nigeria's development, the capability of indigenous managers and consultants, and the potential for the adaptation of African traditional management techniques, is borrowed from the bankrupt ideology of development cherished by the Nigerian state. Fifth, corruption is a management practice in Nigeria. I have argued that corruption in the corporate and public sectors is primarily a function of the limited autonomization of the state and the partial atomization of the society in Nigeria. These in turn reflect the rudimentary level of the development of productive forces and commodity production and exchange. Sixth, the root of the administrative style of Nigerian managers lies in the colonial era. The colonial district officer who is the prototype of today's Nigerian manager was authoritarian and pompous, behaved as a conqueror and god, and was questioned by Nigerians only at dire personal risk. Finally, the poor and hostile relationship between the state and civil society in Nigeria helps to define the character of workers' relationship with their managers. In Nigeria the state and society have drifted apart, and the individual is attacked by the forces of a state which has refused to recognize his worth or citizenship. The worker is essentially an externality to management, a mere factor in the corporate environment where managers' right is coextensive with might. In this intemperate milieu, the police and the coercive apparatus of the state are easily brought in by firms to suppress the genuine, legitimate demands of workers.

Taken by itself, each of these seven fields of interaction of the state and corporation may amount to little. But taken together, they highlight three major characteristics of the Nigerian business environment. First, the modern corporation is not an autonomous and competing center of power. The corporation has not dissociated itself from the public (state) and has failed to evolve an inward-looking, private organization focused on internal operations. It has not shifted from its relationship with government; it is still wary of conceiving itself as a freestanding entity and hence is unable to develop its managerial hierarchies and style under private initiatives and ownership. Second, the corporation has not emerged as a citizen (with rights and duties) in the society, as a member of the political community, as a central political actor with whom the state has to deal. This is quite opposite to what is happening in the West; granted, the firm is treated as a legal person in Nigeria but it has not dissociated itself from the government as happened in the 1850s in the United States. This is not surprising; the individual has not even really emerged as a full-fledged citizen of the nation-state of Nigeria. The individual in Nigeria is still the object of persecution, either by the state or through its agency. Third, managerial practices in Nigeria are a product of definable social experience, and need have nothing to do with competition or technology. The selection of optimal management practice is driven largely by the non-autonomization of the Nigerian State.

NOTES

1. We are not necessarily concerned with state and economic development, or with the state and the private sector, or with how the state facilitates a policy framework within which investment and production can thrive. I am focused narrowly on state and corporate management practice.
2. Steve Chan, Cal Clark, and Danny Law, *Beyond the Development State* (New York: St. Martin's Press, 1998); World Bank, *The East Asian Miracles* (New York: Oxford University Press, 1998); Harvey Brooks, Lance Liebman, and Corinne S. Schelling (eds.) *Public-Private Partnership: New Opportunities for Meeting Social Needs* (Cambridge: Ballinger Publishing Company, 1984); and Amartya Sen, "Democracy as a Universal Value." *American Educator*, 24, (2), 2000, 16-22, 50.

3. Alfred D. Chandler, *Strategy and Structure* (Cambridge: Harvard University Press, 1966); Alfred D. Chandler, *The Visible Hand: The Managerial Revolution in American Business* (Cambridge: The Belknap Press of Harvard University Press, 1977); Oliver Williamson, *Markets and Hierarchies: Analysis and Antitrust Implications* (New York: Free Press, 1975), and Oliver Williamson, *The Economic Institutions of Capitalism* (New York: Free Press, 1985).
4. Thomas K. McGraw, "The Evolution of the Corporation in the United States," in John R. Meyer and James M. Gustafson (eds.), *The U.S. Business Corporation: An Institution in Transition* (Cambridge: Ballinger Publishing Company, 1988), 3.
5. French business people enjoyed limited liability as early as 1807 when they formed *societes anonymes* as corporations were and are still called. But it was not until 1867, thirteen years after the English that French citizens could incorporate without specific authorization. Germany only gave its citizens the right to incorporate without special grants in 1870.
6. Peter F. Drucker, "The New Society of Organizations," *Harvard Business Review*, Sept.-Oct. 1992, 170.
7. McGraw, "The Evolution of the Corporation in the United States," 7.
8. Drucker, "The New Society of Organizations," 97.
9. Ibid., 98.
10. Mamadou Dia, "Indigenous Management Practices: Lessons for Africa's Management in the 90s," in Ismail Serageldin and June Taboroff (eds.), *Culture and Development in Africa*: Proceedings *of an International Conference held at the World Bank* (Washington D.C.: World Bank, 1994), 169-170, and Philip Curtin et al., *African History* (London: Longman, 1978).
11. Claude Ake, *Revolutionary Pressures in Africa* (London: Zed Press, 1978), 74.
12. Claude Ake, *Democracy and Development in Africa* (Washington, D.C.: The Brookings Institution, 1996), 3.
13. Claude Ake, "The State in Contemporary Africa" in Claude Ake (ed.), *Political Economy of Nigeria* (Lagos: Longman, 1985), 1-3.
14. Ibid., 1.
15. Ibid., 2
16. Claude Ake, "The State in Contemporary,"1-5, and "The Nigerian State: antimonies of a periphery formation," in Claude Ake (ed.),

Political Economy of Nigeria (London: Longman Group Ltd.1985), 9-10.
17. Ake, *Revolutionary Pressures*, 83.
18. Ake, *Democracy and Development*, 1-3; and Peter Ekeh, "Social Anthropology and the Two Contrasting Uses of Tribalism in Africa," *Comparative Studies in Society and History*, 32, (4), 1990, 683-686.
19. Ake, *Democracy and Development*, 3.
20. Ibid., 3-6.
21. The current attempts at privatization are changing this viewpoint.
22. Ake, *Democracy and Development*, 129
23. Segun Osoba, "Corruption in Nigeria: Historical Perspectives," *Review of African Political Economy*, 23 (69), 1996, 371-386.
24. Ake, *Democracy and Development in Africa*, 7.
25. Sara Berry, *Fathers Work for Their Sons: Accumulation, Mobility, and Class Formation in as Extended Yoruba Community* (Berkeley: University of California Press, 1985), 10.
26. Ake, "Indigenization: problems of transformation in a neocolonial economy," in Claude Ake (ed.), *Political Economy of Nigeria* (London: Longman Group Ltd.1985), 198.
27. Williamson, *The Economic Institutions of Capitalism*; and William G. Ouchi, "Markets, Bureaucracies, and Clans," *Administrative Science Quarterly*, 25, 1980, 120-142.
28. Ake, *Revolutionary Pressures*, 71
29. Sola Fajana, "The Police and Conflict Regulation in Industry," in Dafe Otobo ed., *Further Readings in Nigerian Industrial Relations* (Lagos: Malthouse Press Limited, 1992), 187-188.
30. Cited in Fajana, "The Police and Conflict Regulation," 184.
31. Rivers State of Nigeria, "Judicial Commission of Inquiry into Umuechem Disturbances under the Chairmanship of Justice Opubo Inko-Tariah" (Port Harcourt: Rivers State of Nigeria, 1991), 12, 14, 22, and Appendix G.
32. Bronwen Manby, "The Role and Responsibility of Oil Multinationals in Nigeria," *Journal of International Affairs*, 53 (1), 1999, 291.
33. World Bank, *Nigeria Infrastructure Project Establishment Survey*, 1988
34. Kyu Sik Lee and Alex Anas, "Costs of Infrastructure Deficiencies for Manufacturing in Nigerian," *Urban Studies*, 36 (12), 1999, 2135.
35. Ibid., 2140.

36. Goran Hyden, "Changing Ideological and Theoretical Perspectives on Development" in Ulf Himmelstrand, Kabiru Kinyanjui and Edward Mburugu (eds.), *African Perspectives on Development* (London: James Currey Ltd., 1994), 308-319.
37. For details, see Ake, *Democracy and Development*, 8-17.
38. To monopolize decision-making, sustain authoritarianism and retain a top-down, nonparticipatory management style, all necessary for the exclusive hold on power at the expense of labor, and for the maintenance of huge inequalities in compensation.
39. Ake, "Indigenization," 198.
40. Dia, "Indigenous Management Practices," 169-170.
41. B. J. Dudley, *Instability and Political Order*, (Ibadan: Ibadan University Press, 1973), 37.
42. Ibid., 38.
43. See F. C. Ikoli, "The Dilemma of Premature Bureaucratization in the new states of Africa: The case of Nigeria," *African Studies Review* 23, (2), 1980, 12; and Samuel M. Muriithi, *African Crisis: Is There hope?* (Lanham, MD: University Press of America, 1996), 88-89; and Chan, Clark and Law, *Beyond the Development State.* (New York: St. Martin's Press, 1998).
44. Goran Hyden, *No Shortcuts to Progress: African Development Management in Perspective* (Berkeley: University of California Press, 1983).
45. See Peter Ekeh, "Colonialism and the Two Publics in Africa: A Theoretical Statement," *Comparative Studies in Society and History*, 17 (1), 1975, 91-112; Peter Ekeh, "Social Anthropology and the Two Contrasting Uses of Tribalism in Africa," *Comparative Studies in Society and History*, 32 (4), 1990, 660-700; Peter Ekeh, "The Public Realm and Public Finance in Africa," in Ulf Himmelstrand, Kabiru Kinyanjui and Edward Mburugu (eds.), *African Perspectives on Development* (London: James Currey Ltd., 1994), 234-236; and Drucker, "The New Society of Organizations," 103.
46. Ekeh, "The Public Realm and Public Finance in Africa," 235.
47. W. Richard Scott, *Organizations: Rational, Natural and Open Systems*. (Englewood Cliffs, NJ: Prentice Hall, 1981), 136-137, 162.
48. Ekeh, "Colonialism and the Two Publics in Africa," and Ekeh, "Social Anthropology."
49. Ake, "The Nigerian State," 15
50. James S. Coleman, *Power and the Structure of Society*, (New York: W. W. Norton & Co. 1974), 29.

51. Drucker, "The New Society of Organizations," 100.
52. Ibid., 101.

11

ECONOMIC BASES FOR POLITICAL DEVELOPMENT

Michael O. Anda

INTRODUCTION

In the years following independence, Nigeria focused primarily on issues of political development and only secondarily on devoting scarce resources to economic development. By the 1990s, it was clearly evident that the nation had not even achieved a stable political system. Coups and counter-coups, leading to frequent changes in government, amply demonstrate this. This chapter examines political development in Nigeria and views political instability as partly a function of economic underdevelopment. Despite enormous human and material resources, the nation has remained politically and economically underdeveloped. This chapter argues that dynamic growth can be achieved with pragmatic government policies and a disciplined, hard-working population that responds to the right incentives.

LITERATURE REVIEW: INSIGHT FROM EXISTING RESEARCH

The existing research has focused on such questions as the impact of regime types and other institutional arrangements on economic reform and the political and economic origins of various economic policies in developing countries. Often such analysis makes a general comparison between East Asia's economic success and the recent stagnation or decline of many African, Middle Eastern, and Latin American economies. Though East Asia's governed market approach to successful policy reform is touted for its refutation of more simplistic neoliberal analysis, it is not necessarily useful for regions still grappling with severe administrative problems or strong interest group pressures.[1]

East Asia, which structured its import substitution industrialization, provided postcolonial rulers with a coalition of state bureaucracies and statecentered industries while effectively marginalizing the rest of society. Economic decline and neoliberal reform in Africa have caused statist coalitions to disintegrate and have undermined the region's long-standing authoritarian regimes.[2] Democratization, particularly the highly managed type that is occurring in Africa, represents an attempt by politicians to cope with these shifting coalitions and gain the support of winners.[3] The governed market approach has spurred much useful debate about the role of government intervention in developing economies.

The relationship between democratic stability and economic development is a theme that scholars like Lipset and Bollen have pursued.[4] Their studies stress the need for institutional continuity and harmony as a prerequisite for economic development. Thus, development and order are critical, and disorder makes development difficult, if not impossible. The Nigerian experience is an example of a country alternating between civilian and military regimes. Military regimes are certainly no guarantee against frequent changes in leadership due to coups and counter-coups. Civilian governments have been weak and ineffectual. One can argue that Nigeria's recurring ethnic and regional conflicts, its institutional weaknesses, and the general failure of its leadership have done great harm to the nation's economic programs. Another dimension here is that the poor economic situation has found expression in antisocial behavior, some of which could be serious enough to threaten national security. Victor Okafor and Sheriffden Tella noted that

> The current nose-diving trend of Nigeria's economy has greatly multiplied the number of marauding armed bandits whose operations have defied any solution from the authorities. In the face of a practically helpless police force, life and property of law-abiding citizens remain unsafe. The nation is practically held hostage perpetually.[5]

The explanation given for Africa's failure to reform is the weak political capacity of states in relation to long-entrenched ethnic and interest groups. To bolster the investor confidence that is crucial for long-term economic growth, according to some scholars, political capacity must include a disciplined, competent bureaucracy and the establishment of the rule of law rather than rule by arbitrary decrees.[6]

This view represents a significant step away from the previous conventional wisdom, namely, that developing nations' economic troubles were often derived from too much government.[7] The World Bank and the International Monetary Fund (IMF), for example, were major proponents of government retrenchment during the 1980s and the implementation of their recommendations produced adverse consequences for the living conditions of the people. Implementing IMF programs led to belt-tightening and removal of subsidies on certain products and services. The resulting deterioration of the standard of living has been a cause of civil strife capable of threatening national stability and security. For instance, the removal of oil subsidies in Nigeria in 1992 greatly affected the people and caused tensions that found resounding expression in civil disorder during the abortive 1993 political transition program. A similar attempt by the Obasanjo government to remove oil subsidies in June 2000 almost produced widespread civil strife.

More recent analyses have come to focus on the type (civilian or military) rather than the scope (degree) of state intervention. Lawrence Summers and Vinod Thomas contend that governments have done too much of the things they cannot do well, that is, regulating markets and producing ordinary goods, and too little of the things they must do well, that is, maintaining macroeconomic stability and making necessary public investments.[8] Jeffrey Herbst, Julius Ihonvbere, and Wayne Nafziger stress the lack of a legal and political system that could establish an environment promoting business confidence as a key factor in economic decline in Africa.[9]

DEVELOPMENTS IN NIGERIA

In 1960, when Nigeria attained political independence from Britain, there was no clear policy for economic development. Nigeria's industrialization program at that time was modest. The concern of the British colonial administration had been mostly commercial and was aimed at promoting the transfer of agricultural commodities to Europe.[10] Colonial policy did not permit indigenous technological development, and after the transfer of power, the new country continued its dependence on imported European commodities and technology.

Decisions concerning appropriate technology are critical responsibilities of governments in developing areas, and the absence of an agreed upon national and industrial development policy has done considerable damage to the Nigerian economy. Acknowledging this problem, in the 1980s, the military junta emphasized both industrialization and the development of an indigenous, "home grown" technology. One could not be successfully pursued without the other. A key issue concerned the construction of the nation's technological base. The first need, therefore, was to end Nigeria's almost total dependence on the importation of foreign technologies. The fact that so much technology was imported did not mean that Nigeria did not possess a local technological base. But that base and its more appropriate character suffered as a consequence of the demand for imported technologies that were not as useful to the developing economy. Moreover, the preference for imported technology had resulted in Nigeria's technological dependence on the more developed nations, and an outflow of capital that could be better invested at home.

Soon after independence, the federal government introduced legislation aimed at safeguarding foreign investments in the country. This legislation led to an upsurge of investments in the country which amounted to U.S.$45 million during the period of the country's First National Development Plan, 1962 to 1968.[11] The government launched this development plan, in large part, to stimulate the establishment and growth of national industries. In order to ensure the success of this plan, in 1964, the government created the Nigerian Industrial Development Bank (NIDB) to assist private enterprises. Although the full implementation of this program was affected by the Nigerian Civil War of 1967-1970, it nevertheless recorded some successes. For example, private sector investments rose from $1,237.6 million in 1962/63 to $1452.1 million in 1968 and 1969.[12]

At the end of the civil war, the government launched the Second National Development Plan (1970-1975). This plan had several stated aims including (1) a united, strong, and self-reliant nation; (2) a dynamic economy; (3) a just and egalitarian society; (4) an increase in opportunities for all Nigerians; (5) and the building of a free, just, and democratic society. Unfortunately, these aims were not realized in spite of the huge revenues derived from the sale of oil during the oil boom of the 1970s. In fact, the lucrative sale of petroleum seriously distorted the implementation strategy of the development plan and resulted in the total neglect of meaningful national industrial development.

Nigeria is one of the world's major oil exporting countries.[13] The drilling, refining, and marketing of high-quality, low-sulfur petroleum should be a boon to the country's economy, but Nigeria's political instability and uncertainties, caused in part by military rulers, have prevented the nation from realizing its economic potential. Oil is very central to the development of Nigeria and constitutes the backbone of the economy. In the 1990s, petroleum production accounted for 25 percent of its GDP, and oil exports accounted for over 95 percent of its total export earnings and about 75 percent of total government revenue. Petroleum operations in fact provide the only immediate hope for the development of the rest of the economy. The real story of oil in Nigeria is one of opportunities missed by the military, administrative disorganization, and resource mismanagement.[14] From 1966 to 1999, except for the years of the Shehu Shagari and Olusegun Obasanjo civilian governments, the army directed all facets of Nigerian political life. A majority of the governors of the Nigerian states were military officers, and senior military officers managed the country's corporations or served on the boards of directors. Military officers were made ambassadors to different countries or led Nigerian delegations at international conferences. The military establishment has always justified its intrusion in the country's political life by asserting the need for political stability. But while Nigeria has enjoyed little political stability, its higher military officers have reaped substantial personal rewards. Having noted these circumstances it would be useful to explore both the military and the civilian roles in the country's economic development.

THE MILITARY'S ROLE
IN ECONOMIC DEVELOPMENT

The Nigerian economy suffered as a result of the civil war. According to Oyediran, investment dropped by 3 percent a year in 1966 and 1967.[15] Agricultural exports were affected and the money supply increased at the rate of 7 percent a year.[16] At the conclusion of the war, the head of state, General Gowon, promulgated the Second National Development Plan (1970-1975), which projected a strategy of economic development and diversification.[17] The plan recognized the need to diversify the economy rather than rely solely on the oil boom.

The Third Development Plan (1975-1980) was the largest and most ambitious ever launched by an African country.[18] It was the first major effort at maximizing the oil resources for the development of the whole country.[19]

In 1973, world oil prices skyrocketed and Nigeria received a fourfold increase in revenue from its petroleum exports. The quadrupling of oil prices enriched Nigeria but created several problems. There was port congestion, biting inflation, and fuel shortage in an oil-rich country. The 1970s also witnessed the retardation of agricultural growth and the stagnation of the industrial sector. During the peak years of the oil boom, the regime of General Gowon and the successor regimes of Generals Murtala Mohammed and Olusegun Obasanjo followed a strategy of state capitalism. The core of this strategy, according to William Graf, involved pumping oil revenue directly into the economy, but mostly on terms likely to benefit the military establishment.[20] Thus, the complaint was courageously made that "The lion's share of the oil revenue still goes to maintaining the 250,000 strong armed forces with no enemies but the Nigerian people who, after many rough encounters with the swaggering troops, no longer regard them as saviours."[21] In effect, the junta reserved most public revenue for itself and distributed what remained to state and local governments. For example, vast sums were set aside for defense and a large amount of this was to be spent on capital equipment such as new barracks.[22]

Nigeria in the mid-1970s was in a state of transition. It had emerged from the postcolonial era of reliance upon the old metropolitan power though it still had some colonial problems. It had passed through a devastating civil war, and had begun to reap the benefits of vast oil resources. It was embarking upon a new era in its history.[23] By the mid-1980s, Nigeria's economic problems could be characterized in at least six categories summarized as follows:

1. A slow rate of agricultural growth which failed to keep up with population increase.
2. An export trade totally dependent on crude oil.

3. A dependence on the importation of consumer goods, raw materials, and technology.
4. A widening gap between the very rich and the very poor.
5. Inattention to the creation of a sophisticated indigenous technological capability and conflicting views on the proper role of government in industrial development.
6. The inflated role of the public sector in promoting and managing economic activities.

These problems raised serious questions about the future of Nigeria's economic development. In order to address them, the military expanded central planning and imposed a strict regulatory authority. It encouraged public investment and called for diversification in the industrial sector. Public enterprises were developed in petroleum, capital goods production, transportation, large-scale manufacturing, and light industry. All were made possible by the oil boom.

The military government built bridges and roads, expanded port facilities, and constructed new airports. Many of the activities were carried out with military needs in mind. Military installations were improved and new facilities were constructed. The government modernized officers' messes, expanded offices and stores, and built sport fields, new living quarters, and shooting ranges. Only rarely did the military undertake the construction of similar civilian projects. Olatunde Odetola argues that the earnings from oil during the Gowon administration were enjoyed by a small elite composed of senior military officers who were sometimes also federal ministers, members of the governing council, the Supreme Military Council, and state military governors. This elite group extended its largesse to business friends and civil servants, and to a lesser extent, lower-level army personnel.[24] The Gowon regime's method of awarding inflated contracts to Nigerian agents of foreign corporations became a major avenue for personal capital accumulation. Inequalities were ignored, and rising food prices and higher rent levels made life virtually impossible for the lower salaried classes. The military did not restructure the Nigerian economy, or move it from its dependence on the Western industrialized nations. An indigenization decree, which purported to give Nigerians some say in the running of their economy and reduce foreign control and indebtedness, only served to regularize the relationship between the Nigerian high command and foreign financial interests. Indigenization of the economy basically meant the selling of shares to Nigerians capable of buying into the foreign companies operating in the country. But the military did not address the pervasive forms of foreign economic domination, particularly in the area of appropriate technology.

The regimes of Generals Mohammed and Obasanjo witnessed a deteriorating economic situation with a decline in petroleum sales and a massive rise in agricultural imports. In April 1978, the military imposed an extremely stringent budget by introducing a development plan that was expected to right the wrongs of the Gowon government. Unfortunately, however, the envisaged projects were rarely integrated with one another, nor did they fit the socioeconomic environment of the country. Partly because it was unable to address the country's needs, in 1979 the military handed over power to the civilian government of President Shehu Shagari whose Second Republic epitomized the height to which corruption could climb in an African country. (See section on civilian role in economic development.) The Shagari government was very short-lived, however, and the usual problems associated with urban overcrowding, unemployment, and extreme poverty continued to multiply.

The military regime of General Muhammadu Buhari, which followed Shagari's civilian government, imposed stringent austerity measures. It reduced capital expenditure as well as the government budgetary deficit, but it did not curtail federal and state spending in the military sector. As a consequence, the nation's manufactures fell during Buhari's regime by 18 percent, and the construction industry was in a state of collapse. Inflation rose to over 40 percent, unemployment soared, food prices increased, and consumer products disappeared from the marketplace. Buhari was forced to take drastic action as he tightened the clamp on imports, introduced counter-trade strategies involving other countries, and even imposed financial discipline on military spending. The latter policy proved unacceptable to some in the army. Buhari was overthrown and replaced by General Ibrahim Babangida, who tried another approach, but also failed to control corruption and to stabilize the economy.[25] The further collapse in world oil prices at the beginning of 1986 plunged the Nigerian economy into deeper crisis. Seeing a need for concerted action, Babangida introduced the structural adjustment policy, believing it might be one answer to the country's problems. But the impact of this policy, coupled with political instability, resulted in less than 40 percent utilization of the nation's manufacturing capacity. Babangida's policies caused banks to close and inflation to rise. Amid corruption and ineptitude, his successor, General Sani Abacha (1993-1998), was unable to reverse the downward spiral as he ran government "primarily for the private benefit of himself and his favored associates."[26]

THE CIVILIAN ROLE IN ECONOMIC DEVELOPMENT

The first six years of independence were deeply troubled ones for Nigeria. In the Western Region the deep rift in the Action Group between Obafemi Awolowo and S. L. Akintola threatened to split the region disastrously by 1962. An attempt at a census in 1962 was canceled because of distorted figures. There was a successful general strike in 1964 in which more than 800,000 workers took part and the government was forced to accept higher wage levels than it had previously been willing to concede. The First Republic government of Tafawa Balewa (1960-1965) was unable to cope with chronic political and economic problems including corruption. The Second Republic was bedeviled by corruption. According to Okafor and Tella:

In 1979, when the military left the political stage, Nigeria's external reserve was $5.1 billion. The country, in addition, earned some $51.6 billion from petroleum and non-oil exports between 1979 and 1983. By the time the civilian administration was terminated by a military coup in December 1993, the country was indebted externally and internally to the tune of $26 billion. This means that in four years, the government of the Second Republic had access to over $82 billion out of which $17.1 billion could not be accounted for.[27]

In sum, economic underdevelopment and corruption especially among the rulers, both civil and military, had become endemic. The political campaigns leading up to primaries and main elections were characterized by high levels of electoral rigging, bribery, violence, and fraud. Upon assuming office, politicians looted the treasury in an attempt to recoup their money.[28]

The only regime that dealt squarely with corruption was the Murtala Mohammed administration. Mohammed attacked corruption and abuse of office and produced a major retrenchment exercise in the months following the coup. There were a number of sackings and retirements of governors and top military personnel. Thereafter, the government turned its attention in great detail to the whole civil service, both federal and state.

Basil Davidson has described Babangida's disgust with civilians of the Second Republic. He argued correctly (to a point) that

> dissidents and patriots emerged, and sometimes survived. They too tried, whenever possible, to take hold of this caricature of nation-statehood and make it function as its prophets had believed it could. Some of the soldiers were among them, and among these—exceptionally, in this case, during the 1980s—was a military ruler of the Federation of

Nigeria, General and then President Ibrahim Babangida. He was one of those not-so-few Nigerian soldiers who stood historically in the position of other patriots such as Murtala Mohammed and Olusegun Obasanjo. These were men who had worked to keep the federation together. They were pledged to the conviction that military rule had no developmental value.[29]

The present Obasanjo civilian government has had to deal with ethnic and interest groups' demands, which would have been muted or mitigated if the country's resources had been managed competently and conscientiously. However, Nigeria's governments, both civil and military, have looted or failed to prevent the looting of the country's treasury, consequently reducing the pool of funds for distribution and for real, substantial development. Whether this attitude has now changed remains to be seen. However, since Abacha's death in 1998, the government has uncovered billions of dollars of looted funds that Abacha and his aides had stashed away in foreign banks. As Ibelema notes, ultimately, "the specter of another military coup and even civil war should work in favor of amicable solutions and [elite] accommodation."[30] But there is a general failure in Third World countries, including Nigeria, to make a positive impact on their citizens despite moving from military dictatorship to democracy.[31]

MANUFACTURING AND AGRICULTURE

Nigeria's manufacturing sector provides employment for only a fraction of the country's workforce. Its light industries are limited to the production of consumer products for the limited internal market.[32] Despite the military's desire for rapid industrialization, Nigeria's unreliable electricity supply, restrictive policies (for example, requiring foreign companies to accept Nigerian partnership terms), foreign exchange controls, fixing of arbitrary prices for finished products, and shortage of skilled workers have been problematical.

Agriculture is another sector in which successive military and civilian governments have declared their interest, but in actuality done very little.[33] Capital expenditure in the agricultural sector accounted for only 7 percent of the total during the years 1975-1980. It is estimated that between 1970 and 1982, yearly production of the main Nigerian cash crops, cocoa, rubber, cotton, and peanuts, fell by 43, 29, 65, and 64 percent respectively.[34] Agriculture was by far the most important sector of the economy in the years immediately following independence. It provided almost all of Nigeria's jobs and export earnings. It was also the major source of government revenue. David A. Iyegha noted that

> Since Independence, even though increasing attention has been devoted to government sponsored land settlements and government-owned plantations, to the neglect of small farms, the small farmers have been performing much better than the government sponsored schemes.[35]

But agricultural output which increased between 8 and ten 10 percent in the 1960s, saw only a 3 percent increase in the 1980s and 1990s[36] with the appearance of oil and the military.[37] For some years—the whole of the 1970s in fact—agriculture was making a declining contribution to the GDP even though it was increasing in absolute terms. There was poor agricultural performance during the years of the Second Plan. Both military and civilian governments promised ambitious major project initiatives to boost agricultural production, for example, Operation Feed the Nation (1976-1979), the Green Revolution (1979-1983), and Shagari's Food Production Plan (1980). The Third National Development Plan allocated N2.2 billion to agricultural projects and aimed especially to make it possible for farmers to obtain fertilizers, pesticides, and other agricultural inputs at heavily subsidized prices.

But inefficiency and poor funding ruined the chances for successful programs. The failure of Nigeria's agricultural sector is the most significant cause of the country's economic decline. There is also the lack of adequate food processing and packaging facilities, for example, to produce canned and frozen food crops for marketing and consumption. The responsibility rests mainly on the military governors, who have given lip service to the problem, but whose policies have only accelerated the downward spiral.[38] Henry Bienen has noted that the military lacks the wisdom, the skills, the training, and the mindset for genuine economic development.[39]

ECONOMIC POLICIES: MANUFACTURING INDUSTRIES AND TECHNOLOGY

The Federal Ministry of Science and Technology has passed through various phases in the evolution of what might be termed a national technology policy.[40] The first phase dates from the colonial and postcolonial years to the introduction of the indigenization decrees. During this phase, the small amount of technology in use in local industries was foreign owned. The second phase started with the inauguration of the indigenization decrees in the 1970s and lasted until the early 1980s. (The indigenization decrees were policies introduced by the military government to nationalize all foreign-owned businesses in Nigeria.) It encouraged industrial incentive programs that gave modest attention to developing Nigeria's technology. The largest allocations were for the development of the industrial sector so as to make Nigeria self-sufficient in petroleum products, petrochemicals, pulp and paper, sugar, and strategic minerals. Until the period of the Third Plan, manufacturing in Nigeria had been principally concerned with light consumer goods such as beer, soft drinks, cigarettes, shoes, and textiles. The plan aimed at ensuring an industrial revolution so that Nigeria could start producing its own trucks and cars (as opposed to merely assembling them) and also engage in iron and steel development and petrochemical production.

The more developed third phase focused on raising the proportion of indigenous ownership of industrial investment for the purpose of maximizing local retention of profit, while at the same time promoting foreign investment. This new industrial policy, which was introduced in the 1980s, was intended to attract foreign investment and technology, but also to produce a high degree of indigenous ownership. It fostered a review of the indigenization laws which were perceived as creating an undesirable hostile foreign investment climate. Import substitution had produced a manufacturing sector with low employment capacity and low productivity. Nigeria had experienced little internalization of technical knowledge and its industrial output had been confined to consumer goods. It was not unexpected, therefore, that these production areas were among the first to be reorganized with national needs in primary view.

Enwere Dike asserts that the transition to local production of iron and steel, which began in 1982, marks the turning point in Nigerian industrialization.[41] The country's three rolling mills at Oshogbo, Jos, and Katsina, were established in the early 1980s to provide broadbased linkages with the iron and steel plants at Ajaokuta and Warri. Prior to the establishment of these modern plants, Nigeria depended on imports and the rather limited output from small-sized cast-iron works (for instance, the Niger Steel Works at Emene near Enugu) to supplement imports. It is estimated that, despite setbacks to the iron and steel project during the course of the development plans, the project will go ahead since it is expected that demand will reach several million tons of steel a year. Specifically, Nigerian consumption of steel products had grown from 123,000 metric tons in 1950 to 226,000 metric tons in 1962, and expanded thereafter to 3.5 million metric tons in 1987.[42] In the mid 1980s, iron and steel was a successful and growing industry, expected to reach 7 million metric tons of production by the year 2000.

Oil production is a major industrial area for the country and a major source of foreign exchange earnings. Nigeria is a leading member of the Organization of Petroleum Exporting Countries (OPEC). Oil production after the civil war and the subsequent rise in oil prices led to massive increase in government revenue. Nigeria built four oil-refineries with a capacity of over 450 million barrels per day, the largest in Africa. It also expanded the petro-chemical industry which now processes crude oil into various petroleum products. There have been efforts at diversification, and chemical fertilizers, and oil-based synthetic materials such as heavy alkydresin, polypropylene and benzene are now being produced. Oil has been the most successful revenue producing industry in Nigeria, but it was asked to cover too many of the national costs and it could not satisfy expectations when world oil glut caused prices to fall in the 1980s. And despite being a major oil producing country, Nigeria cannot sometimes meet the domestic demand for refined oil (and kerosine). This was a major problem in June 2000 when there was a strike by workers because of a hike in oil prices. Some suggested that saboteurs of the Obasanjo government destroyed some refineries in order to gain contracts as Nigeria imported oil from abroad for domestic consumption. Consequently, corruption and some degree of maladministration are still very much a part of the national life-style even with the departure of the military.

Analyses of the manufacturing sector from the Nigerian *Central Bank Reports* (1990-1995) reveal that the share of industry in Gross Domestic Product (GDP) rose almost three-fold between 1960 and 1982, specifically 12 percent per year between 1960-1966 and 32 percent per year between 1980-1982. The share of manufacturing in the industrial GDP, however, was 41% for 1960-1966 and 27% for 1980-1982; and the share of manufacturing in an economically active population was 10% in 1960, 17% in 1980 (the peak of the oil boom), and 8% in 1983.[43] The net result is that resources and technology required for the operation of the Nigerian manufacturing sector and the engineering sector were by 1986, still largely imported from abroad. Nigeria needs engineering products to complement consumer products, and technological self-sufficiency is also indispensable for industrialization. The country, however, reveals a continuing inability to exploit imported technological systems from which it can develop the new technologies appropriate to its needs in the 21st century.

Fifteen years after independence, in 1975, manufacturing still represented only 8 percent of the GDP which compared unfavorably with many of the developing countries whose manufacturing sectors stood at between 15 and 20 percent. Nigeria has virtually no engineering industry and a few of the subsectors that go with such an industry. The industry is dominated by assembly activities which import content is high. There is the real and apparently continuing dependence of Nigeria upon expatriate industrial investment and know how. As discussed already, the largest economic sector is mining. In 1962, mining provided 1.1 percent of the GDP; by 1972, this figure had reached 15.9 percent; and mining had replaced agriculture as the highest contributor to the GDP. The government obtained a controlling interest in oil. Coal production is expected to grow and exports of coal to increase, the biggest problem remaining the transportation of coal from the mines to the ports. Substantial resources need to be allocated to mining and quarrying. The country's superstructure needs to be enlarged and the economy diversified, particularly in the fields of mining and manufacturing, so that Nigeria would become—or start to become—a modern, diversified economy.

ECONOMIC CRISES OF THE 1980's - 1990's

In the early 1980s, a severe foreign exchange earning crisis contributed to the political and economic upheavals engulfing Nigeria. Exports, of which oil accounted for 96 percent, fell by almost 50 percent from their peak in 1980. It fell from $25.7 billion to $13.1 billion in 1985, and they were then halved again in 1986 to $5.0 billion.[44] The build-up of sizable trade deficits, especially between 1981 and 1983, as well as the need to repay medium and long-term debts magnified Nigeria's economic difficulties. When the price of world oil suddenly collapsed in the world market towards the end of 1981-1982, a crisis of immense proportions, much more severe than the relatively mild one suffered in 1977-78, impacted the Nigerian economy. The price of Nigerian oil fell from the 1980 level of $44.4 barrel to about $28 per barrel in 1985, and to less than $10 per barrel in early 1986. The country's revenue from oil fell dramatically from its peak $10 billion in 1979 to about $5.161 billion in 1982. Nigeria's oil output declined from 2.05 million barrels a day in 1980 to 1.294 million barrels a day in 1982 and to 0.8 million barrels a day by 1983-84.[45] As a result of the crisis, Nigeria's GDP fell about 1 percent in 1982 and by a further 8 percent in 1983 to record an annual growth rate of minus 4.5 percent. The current account recorded a deficit of 4.9 billion in 1982 and N2.9 billion in 1983.

The budget deficit for 1983 alone was N6.231 billion, representing more than 50 percent of total government expenditures.[46] This crisis also intensified Nigeria's debt problem. External reserves fell sharply and foreign debt increased in the face of rising imports.

As the crisis escalated, basic social services collapsed, the agricultural sector continued its steep decline, the construction boom in the economy ended, and infra structural facilities like highways and the refineries deteriorated very rapidly. The government's deficit widened and efforts at containing the more adverse developments created other serious problems, such as economic depression, rising prices and unemployment. The situation was made even worse by the gross mismanagement of available resources. By 1985, the economic downturn had deteriorated in spite of a number of austerity policies adapted by the government to assist in stemming the tide. The supply of raw materials and spare parts to the import dependent manufacturing sector was drastically reduced leading to extensive plant closures, a substantial drop in capacity utilization, and the layoff of workers. By the end of 1985, real per capita GDP and consumption were well below the level recorded in the early 1970s. The outstanding external debt rose to over $18 billion out of which about $5 billion represented trade arrears, and the external debt service obligation increased to 32 percent of the GDP.[47]

While servicing on medium and long-term debts was not interrupted until 1986, rescheduling had by then become imperative if a unilateral default was to be avoided. The World Bank and the IMF became increasingly more prominent in shaping economic policy. The government, hit by worsening terms of trade for oil, and pressed for credit facilities, entered into negotiations with the IMF for a stand-by loan facility. In 1983, the civilian government of President Shagari could not agree to the full IMF conditionality because elections were near and he was concerned with his political survival. It was against this background that in 1984 the military again took over the government. The new regime headed by General Buhari, however, was reluctant to accept the whole IMF package, especially, the devaluation of the Naira (the Nigerian currency),[48] the removal of the petroleum subsidy, the liberalization of trade, and an across the board privatization of public enterprises.[49] As a result, no agreement with the IMF could be concluded. Matters were further complicated by Nigeria's reluctance to accept an IMF loan package, the normal prerequisite for rescheduling its outstanding debts by the Paris[50] and London[51] Club of Creditors.

As available data are not consistent with known facts, the exact magnitude of Nigeria's outstanding debt is not exactly known. While Nigeria quoted a figure which indicated a debt burden of $26 billion, World Bank and IMF statistics projected a figure closer to $30.5 billion.[52] The more conservative Nigerian figure of $26 billion was still enormously larger when compared with Nigeria's total 1986 GNP, said to be N82.46 billion, or less than $13 billion. Moreover, the amount needed annually to service the Nigerian debt was about N9.9 billion in 1988.[53] Due to the absence of a rigid command structure, debt may be exaggerated in civilian rule rather than in military regimes because in the former the government has little control over state expenditures.[54]

In August 1985, General Buhari was ousted from office in a bloodless coup by General Ibrahim Babangida who created an Armed Forces Ruling Council (AFRC) made up of most of the members of the Supreme Military Council (SMC). Babangida's new regime opened negotiations with the World Bank and IMF. It was against this background of crisis, austerity measures, economic need and dependency that his Administration introduced the Structural Adjustment Program (SAP) in June 1986. Thus, the severity of the economic crisis of the mid-1980s and the urgent need for change led to the introduction of SAP—the austerity program aimed to move towards a liberalized and market-determined exchange rate. It devalued the national currency, removed domestic fuel subsidies and liberalized trade by terminating import licenses.[55]

The goal of SAP is technological development, economic reconstruction and self-reliance. Indigenization should be approached with an aura of cautious optimism. As is elsewhere on the Africa continent, there is, in Nigeria, great emphasis upon indigenization of the economy. Yet the extent to which this is done, or possible in Nigeria, varies enormously from one area of development to another. But Nigeria cannot achieve these goals without a domestic technological base. The major drain on the country's foreign exchange and the main cause of its foreign debt was the importation of equipment and spare parts. That situation has not altered, as Nigeria is still dependent on imported technology. What the nation needs is Nigerian technologies that utilize locally available raw materials and resources to produce consumer products that will satisfy its needs. Appropriate technology for Nigeria should entail a shift in emphasis from imported machinery materials and spare parts to the production of equipment that can be made and used domestically. There is also the need at some point to improve on information technology.

The key to much of Nigeria's future development lies with current efforts at industrialization. At first Nigeria should want to supply its own industrial needs. In the long run, however, it must aim at becoming a major industrial exporting country. An appropriate technology would involve the use of mineral resources such as iron, tin, gold, columbine, limestone and petroleum that are abundantly available in Nigeria, as well as the nation's skilled and unskilled labor force. Nigeria should focus on homegrown as opposed to imported talents. What is yet to develop are home stimulants to self-generating growth. Indigenization should avoid products that require scarce resources and capital.

The development of engineering and new technologies requires experience in the production of machine tools, and other capital goods. It requires design and creative skill as well as applied research. An appropriate technology for Nigeria must also be cost effective for Nigeria is a poor country with a per capita income of $250 per year.[56] An adequate technology for Nigeria must use local resources, save foreign exchange, be labor intensive, involve capital saving and produce low cost products. Technological development and poverty alleviation are two challenges before President Olusegun Obasanjo's government, which is why they assume prominence in virtually all the government-sponsored fora. What seems important is the act of using Nigerian grown technology to fight the Nigeria poverty quagmire. "Recently, the Federal Ministry of Science and Technology, in conjunction with the National Office for Technology Acquisition and Promotion NOTAP) organized an exhibition in Lagos during which 60 innovators and inventors, among research institutions, showcased their products."[57]

CONCLUSION

Five unfavorable scenarios can be deduced in the analyses in this chapter. These are:

1. Periodic chronic political instability in Nigeria
2. Chronic economic instability (economic underdevelopment and high rate of inflation).
3. Continued dependence on external technology.
4. Sporadic, serious banking problems.
5. Increasing burden of an expanding foreign debt.

Nigeria has suffered from political, economic and social distress for many years and continues to do so. It cannot build a self-reliant economy or a resilient, integrated society in the absence of a stable, civil society and government. Hopefully, the current civilian administration of President Obasanjo will prove up to the task. As a democracy, Nigeria may finally have a real chance at experimenting with people-centered "populist" measures such as the recent government decision to reverse its decision to reduce the subsidies on petroleum. It is not always helpful to blame the British and the colonial legacy for the contemporary predicament. In sum, the military, civilian and bureaucratic elites bear responsibility for the dislocation of the national economy. Nigeria should encourage appropriate exchange rate and non-discriminatory export incentives for its agricultural products. The government should promote export infrastructure, such as better telecommunications, electricity, warehousing, storage and refrigeration. "Improvement in the industrial sector is also important for economic growth .... Nigeria must invest more in the manufacturing industry. Leonard Gonchanov has suggested that without national industries, any attempt to attain a self supporting growth of the economy and bridge the gap with major capitalist countries in the development levels is impracticable."[58] The government should focus its spending on promoting competitiveness in the private sector. Nigerians, in turn, must change their orientation from import dependence to export orientation which will require the establishment of new structures, diversification, and additional investment which will include investment in American and European technology. Nevertheless, there is still the enduring Nigerian problem of the geographical concentration of oil and the greater preparedness of Southerners to compete efficiently in a global economy that may revive legitimate Northern fears of being left out of Nigeria's economic development.[59]

NOTES

1. Robert Wade, *Governing the Market: Economic Theory and the Role of Government in East Asian Industrialization*, (Princeton: Princeton University Press, 1990).

2. Robert Dibie, "Cross-National Economic Development in Indonesia and Nigeria," *Scandinavian Journal of Development Alternatives and Area Studies*, 17 (1), March 1998.
3. Henry Bienen, *The Military and Modernization*, (Princeton: Princeton University Press, 1971).
4. Seymour Martin Lipset, "Some Social Requisites of Democracy: Economic Development and Political Legitimacy," *American Political Science Review*, 53, 1959, 69-105, and K. Bollen, "Political Democracy and the Timing of Development," *American Sociological Review*, 44, 1979, 572-587.
5. Victor Okafor and Sheriffden Tella, "Economic Development and the Prospect for Economic Security in Africa," in Adebayo Oyebade and Abiodun Alao, (eds.), *Africa after the Cold War: The Changing Perspectives on Security*, (Trenton: Africa World Press, 1998), 26.
6. Richard Sandbrook, "Taming the African Leviathan," *World Policy Journal*, Fall 1990, 673-701; Efiong Essien, *Nigeria Under Structural Adjustment*, (Ibadan: Foundation Publishers, 1990); and Julius O. Ihonvbere, *Nigeria: The Politics of Adjustment and Democracy*, (New Brunswick: Transaction Publisher, 1994).
7. Deepak Lal, "The Political Economy of Economic Liberalization," *The World Bank Economic Review*, 1 (2), 1986, 273-299.
8. Lawrence Summers and Vinod Thomas, "Recent Lessons of Development," *The World Bank Research Observer*, July 1993, 249.
9. Jeffrey Herbst, *The Politics of Reform in Ghana 1982-1991*, (Los Angeles: University of California Press, 1993), 160; Ihonvbere, *The Politics of Adjustment and Democracy*; and Wayne Nafziger, *The Economics of Developing Countries*, (Upper Saddle River: Princeton Hall, 1997).
10. See K. Onwuka Dike, *Trade and Politics in the Niger Delta* and Walter Ofonagoro, *Trade and Politics in Southern Nigeria*.
11. Dave O. Imoko, "The Development of Nigerian Manufacturing Sector," *The Nigerian Interpreter*, October 1990.
12. Ibid.
13. Nigeria is the largest producer of oil in Africa and the largest producer of sweet (almost sulfur free) crude petroleum among OPEC member states. See Sarah Ahmed Khan, *Nigeria: The Political Economy of Oil*, (New York: Oxford University Press, 1994).
14. Ibid., 2.
15. Oyeleye Oyediran, *Nigerian Government and Politics under Military Rule 1966-79*, (New York: St. Martins Press, 1979).
16. Ibid., 53.

17. The first republic politicians drew the First National Development Plan of 1962 to 1968 (later extended to 1970), and it was mainly financed by the agricultural sector. See David A. Iyegha, *Agricultural Crisis in Africa: The Nigerian Experience*, (New York: University Press of America, 1988), 117.
18. Ibid., 65.
19. The Fourth National Development Plan (1981-1985) was launched to improve upon the former plans, especially the Third Plan. See Iyegha, *Agricultural Crisis in Africa*, 131.
20. William Graf, *The Nigerian State, Political Economy, State Class and Political System in Post-Colonial Era*. (Portsmouth: Heinemann Press, 1988).
21. *Nigeria Tribune*, 10 July 1975, quoted in Guy Arnold, *Modern Nigeria*, (London: Longman Group, 1977), 15.
22. Arnold, *Modern Nigeria*, 76.
23. Ibid., 35.
24. See Olatunde Odetola, *Military Regimes and Development: A Comparative Analysis of Africa*, (London: George Allen Press, 1982); and Dibie, "Cross-National Economic Development," 71-72. The inquiry into the administration of Gowon only absolved two of his twelve governors of corruption and mismanagement.
25. The Babangida regime developed the simple formula of allowing the leadership and those who cooperated with them to make as much money as possible in a short time and then step aside for others. A dimension of this problem later became known as the "settlement" syndrome.
26. William Reno, *African Studies Review*, 1999, 106.
27. Okafor and Tella, "Economic Development," 21-22. See also, Alaba Ogunsanwo, *The Transformation of Nigeria: Scenarios and Metaphors*, (Lagos: University of Lagos Press, 1991), 19.
28. Bolanle Awe, "Conflict and Dialogue: Government and Society in Nigeria," *African Studies Review*, 42 (3), Dec. 1999, 12.
29. See Basil Davidson, *The Black Man's Burden: Africa and the Curse of the Nation-State*, (New York: Random House, Inc. 1992), 229.
30. Minabere Ibelema, "Nigeria: The Politics of Marginalization," *Current History: A Journal of Contemporary World Affairs*, May 2000, 214.
31. United Nations Development Program (UNDP), *2000 Human Development Report* (HDR). The report noted that arbitrary use of power has marred many new democracies (including Nigeria's), and it accused many emergent democracies of making policies

behind closed doors. See *Guardian* (Nigeria) Friday June 30, 2000.
32. Adedotun Phillips and Eddy Ndekwu, *Structural Adjustment Programs in a Developing Economy: The Case of Nigeria*, (Ibadan: NISER Publication, 1992).
33. Where in both relative and actual terms Nigeria's economy is weakest—and should be the strongest—is in agriculture despite the fact that "the country's land is among the best on the continent south of the Sahara, in terms of climate." Iyegha, *Agricultural Crisis in Africa*, 6. Agriculture and rural development is and must remain the most important single activity of the economy, for it provides the livelihood for the great majority of the population.
34. Cited in Sarah Ahmad Khan, *Nigeria: The Political Economy of Oil*, 187.
35. Iyegha, *Agricultural Crisis in Africa*, 4-5.
36. Enwere Dike, *Economic Transformation in Nigeria*, (Zaria: Ahmadu Bello University Press), 295.
37. Under military rule, the oil boom increased the prices of "labour-intensive export crops of the southern states" due to increased demand, thereby causing a consumption switch to cheaper imports. Whatever the timing and influence of the oil boom on the agricultural sector, it is clear that the loss of agricultural productivity, particularly after the oil boom and during military rule was severe. See T. Forrest, *Politics and Economic Development in Nigeria*, Oxford: Westview Press, 1993, 184-186. Forrest also disputes the claim that the switch in consumption in favor of wheat and rice exports was due to a production crisis. In his view, the decline in agricultural output for export had started before the surge in revenues and was only exacerbated by the latter as well as by the drought of 1973-74. See also Khan, *Nigeria: The Political Economy of Oil*, 187-188.
38. Khan puts it thus: "While lip service continued to be paid to the importance of agriculture, the country could no longer feed itself and was dependent on food imports," ibid., 189.
39. Bienen, *The Military and Modernization*, 1971.
40. Akin Adubifa, *Technology in Nigeria*, (Ibadan: NISER Press, 1990), 27.
41. Dike, *Economic Transformation in Nigeria*, 1994.
42. Ibid.
43. *Central Bank: Annual Report and Statement of Accounts*, (Central Bank of Nigeria, 1994).

44. Adebayo Olukoshi, Omotayo Olaniran and Femi Aribisala, *Structural Adjustment in West Africa*, (Lagos: Pumark Nigerian Limited, 1994).
45. Aham Anyanwu, *Nigerian Structural Adjustment Program: A Multi-Sectoral Analysis*. (Enugu, Nigeria: ABIC Books and Equipment Limited, 1992).
46. *Central Bank: Annual Report and Statement of Accounts*, (Central Bank of Nigeria, 1986).
47. B. A. Oke, "Structural Adjustment and the Role of the Central Bank of Nigeria: The Nigerian Experience and Future Direction," *Central Bank of Nigeria: Economic and Financial Review*, 28 (1), 1990, 36.
48. From a position of parity in the Naira/US $ exchange rate up to 1985, the currency had devalued to about N9.9 per US $ in 1991, N17.3 per US $ in 1992, and finally fixed at N22.0 per US $ at the end of 1993 by the military government of Abacha. See Khan, *Nigeria: The Political Economy of Oil*, 190.
49. Anyanwu, *Nigerian Structural Adjustment Program*.
50. The club is composed of largely Organization of Economic Cooperation and Development (OECD) members. As a point of fact, over 65 percent of Nigeria's external debts is owed to the Paris club.
51. Members of the London club are in the main International Commercial Banks in Western Europe and North America. The group is also referred to as the Commercial Bank Advisory Committee. It grants loans not only to governments but also to government agencies and private enterprises. Such led to the created avenue for indiscriminate borrowing purportedly to finance projects. Between 1979 and 1983 the resort to arbitrary borrowing resulted into a multiple increase in the level of debt outstanding. See John Nwokocha, "Solving Nigeria's Huge Debt," *Sunday Vanguard*, 9 July 2000, 19.
52. Olukoshi et al., *Structural Adjustment in West Africa*, 83. With the clamor for reduced debt repayment, some estimate the national debt at $30 billion or greater. As one report states, "Burdened by a debt-portfolio of $33 billion, Nigeria is asking creditors to reduce repayment rate to give the country's economy a fresh breadth. The country wants the current repayment of $3.5 billion reduced to $1.5 billion for subsequent years." See "Clinton Coming to Nigeria with 1,500-Man Entourage," *The Guardian*, 16 July 2000, 1-2. See also Khan, *Nigeria: The Political Economy of Oil*, 194. Some argue that what is at stake is debt forgiveness. "With a

staggering $32.8 billion external debt portfolio the government is embattled..." Nwokocha, "Solving Nigeria's Huge Debt," 19. He continues: "World Bank statistics revealed that accumulated interest payment as at 1985 stood at $5.8 billion and rose to about $21 billion in 1998. It further revealed that the loans were secured at between six and seven percent interest but was later linked to 12 percent which accounts for the rise in debt stock."
53. *World Bank Report*, 1990.
54. The nature of the federal government and state relationship in which states enjoyed political autonomy from the federal government but yet relied on federal funding, has led to increased fiscal irresponsibility as regards public expenditure at the state level. See T. Forrest, *Politics and Economic Development in Nigeria*, (Oxford: Westview Press, 1993), 51.
55. How favorable the impact of SAP has been on the national economy is a matter of much debate.
56. Some place the GNP per capita at $240. See Khan, *Nigeria: The Political Economy of Oil*, 191-192.
57. See *Sunday Vanguard*, 9 July 2000, 18.
58. Leonard Gonchanov, "The Critical State of the African Economy: Its Causes, Characters, and Ways to Overcome It," in Olusegun Obasanjo and Hans d'Orville, eds., *The Leadership Challenge of Economic Reforms in Africa*, (New York: Crane Russac, 1991), 27-36, cited in Okafor and Tella, "Economic development," 35.
59. Reno, *African Studies Review*, April 1999, 120.

PART C

GENDER AND ETHNICITY

12

BREAKING ETHNIC BARRIERS AND URBAN INTERETHNIC CONFLICTS: THE GENDER IMPERATIVE

Gloria I. Chuku

INTRODUCTION

Several works[1] on ethnic conflicts in Africa in general and Nigeria in particular have suggested that the solution to the deep-rooted conflicts and antagonisms existing between various groups in most African countries lies in the democratization of these polities. According to such works and even to some African leaders, the panacea for the crisis is political, that is, transferring power to the masses so that they can directly or indirectly manage their governments. For example, *Africa Recovery* has reported Boutros Boutros-Ghali, the then UN secretary general, as saying "I see democracy as the missing link between peace and development, because democracy safeguards peace, and because sound development is unimaginable without democracy, self democratization is the key to the future."[2] Ghali's belief in the power of democracy to bring about peace ignores the paradox of democracy.

Democracy, in striving to maintain social cohesion through the encouragement of dialogue, also breeds competition and conflicts through the affirmation of individual autonomy and freedom, especially where the machineries for social consensus and reconciliation of divergent interests are lacking. An important question before us is: To what extent has democracy tended to encourage peace or conflict in Nigeria (or Africa)?

The Nigerian experience has shown that one of the major causes of interethnic conflicts in the country is politics or the process of democratization, the quest to control political and, subsequently, economic power through electoral processes. The open competition and freedom that democracy engender have escalated into group conflicts and deepening of the crisis. As K. A. Owolabi puts it, "group differences are either employed and further amplified by the incumbents to gain undeserved victory or promoted by them to ferment crisis when unfavored [sic] groups are about to claim electoral victory."[3] Politicians have usually increased ethnic hostility when they have used ethnic issues to enhance their electoral support. As Chinua Achebe observes, the use of ethnic sentiments to score political goals was first manifested in Nigeria in the 1951 Western House of Assembly election when the leadership of Western Nigeria was "stolen" by Chief Obafemi Awolowo (a Westerner) from Dr. Nnamdi Azikiwe (an Easterner).[4] Since then, according to Achebe, things have never been the same again; it has remained "to your tents oh Israel" when it comes to politics and elections in the country. Such observations have led some people to argue that democratic processes in Nigeria are ill motivated and not products of a genuine and sincere desire to install popular governance.

Similarly, E. Osaghae in the introduction to one of his works admits that democratization processes, by their very nature of mobilizing greater participation and placing the question of control (and sharing or distributing) of state power and resources at the top of the political agenda, exacerbate ethnic conflicts and tensions and therefore make their management a critical matter.[5] As Osaghae argues further, constitutions (recommended by some scholars as a way out) are not sufficient conditions for the regulation of ethnic conflicts. He therefore suggests that they have to be complemented and underpinned by a mass of other formal and informal devices and institutions that focus directly on the conflicts. Such devices according to him are federalism; the creation of more states and more local government areas; the federal character principle; and the quota system. The debate on whether these devices have achieved any degree of success is the subject of research and discussion outside the scope of this chapter. However, some of the weaknesses of these devices are mentioned to demonstrate the relevance of the gender imperative to the resolution of the crisis.

The Federal Government of Nigeria has made some attempts to tackle interethnic conflicts in the country. Some of these include the creation of federal colleges (popularly known as "Unity Schools") since the 1960s to cater for students from all parts of the federation; the National Youth Service Corps (NYSC) program, inaugurated in June 1973 to provide quasi-military training to Nigerian youths, and to inculcate in them the spirit of self-reliance, the sense of common belonging and patriotism; and the provisions in the 1979 and 1989 constitutions on the need to encourage interethnic marriages and mutual cooperation. Others include national festivals and arts and culture festivals. These efforts have been intended to encourage and promote interethnic linkages, understanding, and cooperation, but the extent to which they have succeeded in checking urban interethnic conflicts is another matter.

Urban interethnic (as well as religious) conflicts are still plaguing Nigeria as a nation-state in spite of the attempts made by the government to encourage interethnic cooperation. The danger in such conflicts makes this issue important. This is because, if not checked and solved, the conflicts, which threaten the fundamental basis of Nigeria as a nation-state, might lead to its disintegration. In this chapter, some cases of urban interethnic conflicts, which date back to the colonial era in the country, will be mentioned. Using available relevant literature and evidence from field surveys, an attempt will also be made to show how some devices employed especially by government, to resolve urban interethnic conflicts have failed to achieve any significant success. This demonstrates the need for an alternative approach to resolving them, an approach, which is offered in this chapter. The thesis of this chapter is that it will be almost impossible for any solution to the problem of urban interethnic conflicts to work in Nigeria unless the female gender (the women question) is taken into consideration. An attempt is made to justify the need to explore the intrinsic attributes and power of the female gender in resolving such problems in Nigeria. This is because, for so long the male gender has been dominating the scene (either causing the conflicts or formulating and implementing policies to resolve them) without listening to females. But Nigerian women since the precolonial period have demonstrated both intrinsic attributes and actions in controlling conflicts and fostering intergroup relations. Historical evidence has shown how Nigerian women have used their qualities to foster intergroup relations and understanding, within their communities and at the regional and national levels. This is why I suggest strongly in this chapter the need to involve women and exploit their talents in resolving urban interethnic conflicts in the country. Having said this, it is important at this juncture to examine concisely, the history of the Nigerian nation-state, which has been plagued with urban interethnic and religious conflicts in spite of the measures employed to contain them.

THE NIGERIAN NATION-STATE
AND URBAN INTERETHNIC CONFLICTS

Nigeria as a nation-state is not a product of historical evolution; rather, it is a British colonial creation. The British colonizers lumped together divergent sociocultural and linguistic groups without considering their traditional differences, inasmuch as the situation was favorable to their administrative convenience and economic interests. From 1951 to the present, politics in Nigeria has been characterized by ethnicity and the struggle for national power has been regarded as a struggle for dominance among the various ethnic groups especially the major ones: the Hausa-Fulani, Yoruba, and Igbo.

Nigeria's constitutional development, which started during the colonial period, has resulted in the regionalization of politics and the politicization of ethnicity.[6] The parties that emerged in the 1950s elections toed ethnic lines: the Action Group (Yoruba party), the Northern Peoples Congress (Hausa-Fulani party), and the National Council of Nigerian Citizens (Igbo party). Even close to two decades later, this scenario had not changed. The political parties that emerged in the 1970s were all recreations of the 1950s parties. The Nigerian Peoples Party (NPP: Igbo), the National Party of Nigeria (NPN: Hausa-Fulani), and the Unity Party of Nigeria (UPN: Yoruba). Ethnic hostility and schism helped to delay Nigeria's independence from 1956 to 1960, caused the ethnic massacres of 1966-1967, and the bloody civil war of 1967-1970. Some scholars[7] and even past Nigerian leaders have attributed the collapse of the First and Second Republics to ethnic conflicts. For example, General Olusegun Obasanjo,[8] (the Nigerian military head of state between 1976 and 1979, but currently the executive president of Nigeria) has attributed the failure of the civilian governments to regionalism, sectionalism, and ethnicity. Similarly, Alhaji Shehu Shagari, the first executive president of Nigeria, stigmatized ethnicity as the curse of the First Republic.

Ethnic schism has also led to the 1990 abortive *coup d'etat* whose organizers planned to dismember the country; the political domination of Nigeria by the north (predominantly, the Hausa-Fulani); and the almost endless transition to civil rule program, which culminated in the annulment of the June 12 presidential elections of 1993. B. O. Nwabueze has opined that the grave danger which ethnicity poses to the stability and corporate existence of Nigeria was never more frighteningly demonstrated than in the crisis that followed the annulment of the June 12 presidential elections.[9] On a similar note, O. Nnoli has observed that the annulment of the June 12 presidential election in 1993 led to ethnically based disputes as the southerners protested the annulment, which they saw as a design by the north to prevent a southerner from becoming president of the country.[10] According to Nnoli, "the virulence of the southern protest generated insecurity in the north which some northern politicians exploited to fan the embers of ethnicity and regionalism for their selfish ends. From then on, the ethnic factor returned with a vengeance to the political arena as the country tottered at the brink of disintegration." Traces of ethnic politics were also evident in the 1998-1999 presidential elections. But the prolonged transition to civil rule came to a conclusion with the election and swearing-in of General Olusegun Obasanjo as the executive president of Nigeria in May 1999.

Regionalization of national wealth, which is also traceable to the colonial period, has brought about uneven development and imbalance between the regions. During the colonial period, three unequal regions were created. This pattern of development policies and programs pursued in the colonial period unfortunately continued after independence. Coupled with this regionalization of national wealth is the unresolved minorities problem.[11] All these have resulted in fears of oppression, nepotistic distribution of scarce public jobs and other national resources, prejudice, and discrimination as well as the denial of liberty and equality; all these attend ethnic group exclusiveness in Nigeria. Ethnic conflict in Nigeria has usually arisen from the insecurity of members of groups engaged in intense sociopolitical and economic competition, especially for access to political power.

Patterns of intergroup migration and settlement in Nigeria have tended to breed ethnicity. The migration patterns between the north and the south are such that most northern cities have a larger concentration of southerners who live in "strangers' quarters" (Sabon Gari) in comparison to northerners in the south. The establishment of Sabon Gari in some northern cities which started during the colonial period (1911 in Kano) has made it difficult for the settlers to assimilate into their host communities and also for the hosts to understand the sociocultural orientation of the settlers. Such settlement patterns make intergroup integration and peaceful coexistence difficult to achieve.

Nigerian urban centers are made up of people from different ethnic, sociocultural, religious, economic, and political traditions. As Nnoli aptly observes, it is not the contact between groups in these urban centers in itself that breeds intergroup conflicts but the extent of socioeconomic competition between them. The intensity of competition for wealth and power could be said to be the prime determinant of the degree of ethnic hostility in Nigeria.[12] That is, the nature of the relationship between urban settlers and their host population often depends on the extent of the competing claims between the two groups. Similarly, A. Shack and E. P. Skinner observe that "more than other activities, the economic aggressiveness of strangers is often responsible for hostility to them by members of their host communities."[13] I. Albert has stated that where the sociocultural characteristics of two groups are diametrically opposed to one another, the host-stranger relationship is often characterized by animosity, and this has resulted in urban interethnic and religious conflicts in Nigeria.[14] The attitudes of the settlers have not helped matters either. This is because, according to M. Kuka "the *average Nigerian* first belongs to a family, a clan, a village-community, a tribe, and an association (occupation and religious group). In the city, he finds out where his people are mainly concentrated and registers his presence."[15] These attitudes of the settlers, together with the reactions and at times the aloofness of the host population, have resulted in ethnic violence in Nigeria. Thus, we have recorded in Nigeria numerous cases of violent clashes between hosts and settlers, such as the Kano riots of May 1953; March 29, 1966; October 1966; and October 1991. Others include the Kafanchan riots of March 1987; the Tafawa/Bauchi riots of 1991; the Bauchi riots of 1991; the Zangon-Kataf/Hausa conflict of February and May 1992; the Yoruba/Hausa riots of 1999 in Lagos; the Kaduna riots of

1999; the Hausa/Igbo riots of 1999 in Aba; and the Ilorin riots of 1999, to mention but a few.

The Nigerian nation-state has remained both a target of ethnic competition, as all ethnic groups struggle to gain access to it, and also an instrument of interethnic conflict resolution. The Nigerian government embarked on the creation of states totaling twelve in 1967, nineteen in 1979, twenty-one in 1987, thirty in 1991, and thirty-six in 1997. More local government areas were also created, all with the purpose of creating multiple centers of power and development. This is in line with the theory of decentralization as a strategy for ethnic management. Unfortunately, these creations have been ineffective in checking interethnic conflicts because of the lack of infrastructural development and the near complete lack of autonomy of these states and communities. Osaghae, thus, opines that the greatest impediment to managing ethnic conflicts in Nigeria remains the continued uneven levels of development among the groups, where states and local authorities discriminate against non-indigenes no matter the length of their domicile, in order to keep the available scarce resources for indigenes.[16] The government also introduced the principle of federal character (a distributive principle aimed at preventing the domination of government and its resources by people from only one group or a few groups) and the quota system or ethnic arithmetic formulas, which were intended to guarantee every group access to power and national resources. In practice, however, these principles have their weaknesses and, therefore, have not achieved much in terms of managing and checking ethnic conflicts. As Osaghae's work confirms, these principles in practice have recorded modest successes, especially in the area of furthering peaceful coexistence.[17] They have been inadequate to solve the Hausa-Fulani domination of federal power, especially the office of the head of state, as the work of Okechukwu Okeke demonstrates.[18] They have not helped to solve the problem of the marginalization of minorities. Recent protest demonstrations in the Delta region attest to the lingering of the minorities' problem in the country.

The federal government has tried to reduce the ethnic conflicts arising from competition for state power and resources through economic deregulation. Privatization and commercialization of some federal government holdings were embarked upon to reduce its control as repository of all resources and controller of the economy. But these measures have not achieved any recognizable success because of the haphazard manner in which they have been implemented. We still experience in Nigeria the dependence of all groups on the state and, therefore, intensive struggles over its control.

We have seen the nature of urban interethnic conflicts in Nigeria, the various measures employed to check them, and the persistence of the problem. The problem still plagues the existence of Nigeria as a nation-state in spite of the measures employed to resolve it. Kuka has noted that "The ethnic, cultural and political composition of Nigeria is such that its problems have defied any neat solution."[19] Thus, there is still competition for scarce resources, unevenness in resource endowment, structural inequalities among groups in terms of size, education, and access to state power and resources, features that are especially prominent in Nigerian urban centers. In addition to the above factors, Osaghae has concluded that the existence of about 300 ethnic groups in Nigeria together with a highly developed and fractionalized indigenous bourgeoisie, has made Nigeria's ethnic situation perhaps the most complicated and the most difficult to deal with in Africa.[20] Ethnic and regional forces in Nigeria have encouraged wasteful and anarchic allocation of resources, as well as employment in the public sector at times precludes merit and efficiency criteria. These features retard development rather than promote it; and here lies the major problem of urban interethnic conflicts in Nigeria. It is partly because of the fact that Nigeria's urban interethnic conflicts have defied the existing devices used to contain them, and partly because such conflicts have remained the bane of national integration and development in Nigeria, that the gender option is considered in this chapter.

Although ethnic units are primordial groups, which differentiate themselves in the struggle for power and resources, it is at the level of the individual that the deliberateness of the ethnic strategy is most clearly seen because at any point in time, the individual has several identities from which to choose in furtherance of his or her interests.[21] But such identities as class, gender, political party, and so on are not as likely as ethnicity to threaten the fundamental basis of the state. In the words of Osaghae, "ethnic cleavages do not die, ethnicity is real, and to the extent that it cannot be wished away, it requires careful handling because it is capable of destroying the state, and has proven to be more intractable than other conflicts, including class conflicts."[22] Ethnic conflicts are fluid and dynamic, and therefore require dynamic, careful and, conscientious consideration and the contribution of the totality of the population to bring about civil peace and the coexistence of people of different groups in Nigeria.

THE GENDER IMPERATIVE IN URBAN INTERETHNIC CONFLICT RESOLUTION

The problem of ethnic conflicts still plagues Nigeria as a nation-state because the talents of the female gender have not been properly utilized in resolving the problem. Attempts will be made below to justify the above statement by examining the various ways in which Nigerian women have demonstrated their potential, especially in the area of intergroup relations and coexistence, cooperation, understanding and national integration.

Political Role

The political role of Nigerian women is examined here through the activities of famous women who have individually and collectively distinguished themselves in the political history of Nigeria by using politics to foster group development and intergroup and interethnic integration since precolonial times. Long before the advent of colonialism, such women as Amina of Zazzau, Moremi of Ile-Ife, Inkpi of Igala, Daurama of Daura, and Kambassa of Bonny were women of repute, who sacrificed themselves in the service of their various communities. While Daura offered herself as an object of settlement between a warrior stranger who killed a dangerous snake menacing Daura and the Daura people, Moremi used her femininity to seduce men who were menacing her people, and learnt their secrets, which she revealed to her people to enable them to defeat the strangers. Moremi proved to her society that women could achieve success where men had failed. Amina's intervention in her community was a demonstration of military prowess. Kambassa pioneered the militarization of the Bonny state.[23] Awe has called these women "the saviours of their societies," who played the part of preventing disaster and hardship, and who by virtue of this role "attracted the supernatural, acting as the *deus ex machina* when all else seemed impossible."[24]

The colonial period could be said to have witnessed the greatest mobilization of female political power in Nigeria.[25] Through their resistance movements, Nigerian women demonstrated their ability to mobilize for political action. The retention of their economic independence and the reopening of avenues of influencing decisions of government became the primary objective of their mass movements in colonial Nigeria. Most of these resistance movements took place between the 1920s and 1950s. The movements accorded women the position of being one of the most powerful groups who participated in the anticolonial resistance in Nigeria. One of the most notable of these movements was the 1929 Aba Women's War, which J. S. Coleman has described as "traditional nationalism."[26] Some women I interviewed in 1993 confirmed that a major reason behind their wars in colonial Nigeria was nationalism. A quote from one of them will clearly illustrate the women's philosophy: "We fought to build an independent Nigeria from the colonialists and therefore, will be foolish to destroy what took us several years to build in the name of demonstrations and ethnic politics. We are nation-builders and not destroyers."[27]

Colonial Nigeria witnessed such women's mass movements as the 1925 demonstrations, the 1928-1930 women's war in Igboland; the Egba women's movement of the 1930s and 1950s; and the 1950s women's movements in Eastern Nigeria protesting against the introduction of school fees. The introduction of school fees in 1956-1957, for example, sparked off organized women's demonstrations in the area, which involved women in Yenegoa, Port Harcourt (in the then Rivers State); Awka and Onitsha (in the former Anambra State); and Owerri and Orlu (in Imo State). The women's actions resulted in the reduction of the fees.[28] In the colonial period and, to a lesser degree, in the postcolonial era, there have been historical examples of women warring against men who sell out the interests of their communities to enrich themselves and become allies of the dominators (either alien or indigenous). Women embarked on anti-tax demonstrations, market closures, road-blocks, produce holdups, unseating traditional rulers and warrant chiefs as well as kidnapping officials of government to register their grievances. For example, Mrs. Ransome-Kuti and the Abeokuta Women's Union (AWU) were able to force the Alake of Egbaland, Chief Ademola, out of office because he defended the brutality of tax collectors toward women in the 1940s.[29]

Various Nigerian women played active roles in Nigerian politics through their own participation and the mobilization of the mass of women in politics. Such women include Mrs. Ransome-Kuti, Mrs. Mary Nzimiro, Mrs. Margaret Ekpo, Hajia Gambo Sawaba, Mrs. Janet Mokelu, and others. While Mrs. Kuti was mobilizing women in the west, Mrs. Ekpo was doing the same job in the east, and Hajia Sawaba in the north. Some of these women contested and won elections in their various regions. The outstanding role of Mrs. Ransome-Kuti and Mrs. Ekpo in the National Council of Nigerian Citizens (NCNC), their political party, resulted in their selection by the party to represent Nigerian women in the various constitutional conferences held in London in the 1940s and 1950s.

Some of these women formed political parties of their own during the 1950s and 1960s. Mrs. Kuti, for example, formed the Commoners Peoples Party (CPP) to support her candidacy when she was expelled from the NCNC following her refusal to step down for Mr. J. Akande in the 1959 elections into the House of Representatives.[30] Adunni Oluwole formed the Nigeria Commoners Liberal Party (NCLP) in 1954. She demonstrated remarkable and enviable leadership qualities in running her party, a party in which men formed the great majority. Her leadership qualities resulted in the party winning a seat in Osun North (Ikirun) in the Western Region, defeating the NCNC and Action Group candidates in the elections of 1954 into the regional House of Representatives. This was a great feat because it was achieved barely five months after the formation of the party. Another quality of Mrs. Adunni Oluwole was her strong belief in the unity of Nigeria. She was strongly opposed to regionalism because of her conviction that the only way by which the country could achieve rapid progress and play an active role in international affairs was to remain strong and united. She was also a great champion of women's rights who constantly demanded representation of women at all the constitutional conferences that were held. She promised that her party would oppose any constitutions that seemed likely to create wrangling among political leaders, exploitation of the masses, and disunity in Nigeria. Unfortunately, the party did not last long enough to achieve these objectives due to lack of adequate financial resources among other constraints.[31]

Through the activities of these women and their associations, such as the Abeokuta Women's Union (1946), the Nigerian Women's Union (1949), and the Federation of Nigerian Women's Societies (1957), the interests and aspirations of the silent majority of the Nigerian population were articulated and presented to the government. Continuous pressure was put on the colonial administration and later the Nigerian government to enable women to participate actively in government. Among other things, women demanded the nomination of women into membership of local councils, the extension of the franchise to northern women, the extension of educational opportunities to women, and the improvement of women's social status. These actions have led to the appointment and election of women into political offices in the country.

In the postindependence era, especially in the 1970s, there were women commissioners such as Flora Nwapa (East Central State, 1970); Folake Solanke and Ronke Doherty in Oyo State; and Kofoworola Pratt in Lagos State. Chief Janet Akinrinade was elected and four other women appointed to membership of the 1975-1977 Constituent Assembly. Between 1979 and 1983, the Shehu Shagari administration appointed three women as ministers: Mrs. Ebun Oyagbola for National Planning, Mrs. Ivase for Education, and Chief Akinrinade for International Affairs. The military government of General Buhari excluded women from federal levels of government. But under General I. B. Babangida, two women were elected as local government council chairpersons; two were appointed to the Political Bureau; two were appointed as university vice chancellors (University of Benin and Lagos State University); two as deputy state governors (Mrs. Celia Ekpenyong for Cross River and Alhaja Sinatu Ojikutu for Lagos State). There were also five women directors-general at the federal level; one woman senator out of ninety-one; thirteen women members in the National House of Assembly; and twenty-seven women members in the states' houses of assembly.[32] The current administration of Olusegun Obasanjo has also included women in government.

In spite of the achievements of Nigerian women in governance and political participation, efforts are still needed to include more women in government. Nigerian women should not be contented with their modest achievement, which some have called "political tokenism" or even "political exclusion." However, there is an interesting aspect of the "political tokenism" of Nigerian women. The few women who have been given the opportunity to participate actively in politics and governance have demonstrated, more than their male counterparts, a degree of success in terms of dedication to duty, hard work, integrity, and responsibility. For this reason, they should be given more opportunities to serve their motherland, Nigeria.

Social Role

Nigerian women have used their social power of production and reproduction to achieve successes in the maintenance of social order, peaceful intergroup relations, and tranquil coexistence amongst Nigerian peoples. They have been able to achieve these through interethnic marriages, and by their role in family socialization processes and watchdogs of the society. They employ their age-old weapons of social control, that is, "sitting on the men," with uprisings, and "wars" as a last resort. As some scholars have shown, Nigerian women throughout the twentieth century have exercised social power to solve societal problems and issues directly affecting them.[33] As Turner and Oshare rightly observe, "among women's strengths is that their struggles and resistance start with a politics of mothering and by extension, a politics of fertility and creativity which includes, in many societies, the employment of collective nudity as a compelling tactic."[34] Scholars have defined the social power of women in various ways. While it was "traditional nationalism" to James Coleman,[35] it was "sitting on a man," to Van-Allen;[36] and while it was the "anatomy of female power" to Chiweizu,[37] it was "indigenous feminism" to Turner and Oshare.[38] It has been suggested that only through uprisings and the successful consolidation of the social power marshaled through them could women be empowered. But Nigerian women have used uprisings as a last resort, when all avenues for dialogue have proved unsuccessful in calling the opposing party to order, because they are naturally peacemakers.

Nigerian women have through their social functions helped to facilitate the growth of cultural diffusion and assimilation as well as intergroup understanding, thereby breaking ethnic barriers and preventing urban interethnic conflicts in the process. Women more than men have played a role in the use of interethnic marriages to foster group understanding, cooperation, and integration in Nigeria. The numbers in which Nigerian women shake off their previous family ties and culture, and integrate into and assimilate the culture of their husbands is worthy of emulation. Their role in the socialization of their children has more than men placed them in a position to blend the various cultures of Nigerian peoples to produce what could be regarded as a Nigerian culture, which is a means to national integration and the peaceful coexistence of the various groups in Nigeria. An examination of the activities of such women as Mrs. Margaret Ekpo will further illustrate this point.

Margaret Ekpo, an Efik (from the present Cross River State) married Dr. John Udo Ekpo, an Ibibio (from Akwa Ibom State) in 1940. Their parents opposed the marriage because of their ethnic differences. But Margaret, being a broad-minded woman, saw nothing wrong in marrying a man from a different ethnic group. In spite of protests from friends and relatives, she readily married Dr. Ekpo. By this act, she taught Nigerians one of the best ways to maintain the unity of the country and ensure its survival. The national integration process and intergroup relations could only progress beyond what is written in the Nigerian constitutions through interethnic marriages and other forms of cultural association. The action of Margaret Ekpo has earned her recognition as "one of the earliest detribalized Nigerians."[39] Through her family life, in her choice of place of residence after marriage, and in her political career, Margaret has demonstrated in practical manner the concept of *One Nigeria*. After her marriage to Dr. Ekpo, Margaret made Aba (an Igbo town) her second home. She became the president of the Aba Women's Association. At Aba, also, she became a top woman leader in the NCNC; there she was appointed a chief in the Eastern House of Chiefs; and there she was elected twice, in 1961 and 1964-1965, to represent Aba Urban North Constituency in the Eastern House of Assembly, defeating several prominent and wealthy Igbo men.

Her victory in these elections was very significant, not only because she was a woman, but also because she won outside her original home, Calabar. She was not an indigene of Aba either by birth or by marriage. But her victory at Aba signified her full acceptability in the area on account of her sincere services, loyalty, and dedication to the cause and aspirations of the people of Aba. Stella Effa-Attoe and S. O. Jaja conclude that "Until then, never in the history of Nigerian politics had any Nigerian woman gained so much influence and risen meteorically to political prominence outside her home base and without the support of her ethnic group and her kith and kin."[40] Margaret Ekpo became synonymous with the word "Aba," and in connection with politics and women's mobilization, reference began to be made to her as "Margaret Ekpo of Aba" throughout Nigeria. Her efforts became a shining example of how to answer in practice the Nigerian national question of citizenship and nationality. She provided a direct answer to the burning question about the role of residential qualifications in the determination of rights and privileges which has remained a major factor in fanning the flames of urban interethnic and religious conflicts in Nigeria. Margaret Ekpo offered a practical example of how to break ethnic barriers and minimize urban interethnic conflicts. The activities of the Igbo, especially the Igbo women in Aba who encouraged Margaret through their support, should also be commended and emulated. They put ethnic sentiments aside, and supported an Efik/Ibibio woman because they believed she had the ability to pursue their cause and achieve their goals. Margaret Ekpo lived up to their expectations. She never disappointed them.

Economic Role

Nigerian women through their membership of such groups as market women's associations and the Nigerian Association of Women Entrepreneurs have used their market power to empower themselves and foster interethnic relations in the country. For example, it was reported that in 1946, the market women of Abeokuta felt alienated from the Alake (king) and his administration because they were not consulted over the issue of tax, which affected them, and because the tax collectors were brutal to them. As a result, these women, under the able leadership of Mrs. Ransome-Kuti, forced one of the most powerful traditional rulers in Nigeria, King Ademola, out of office in 1948. By 1950, the Abeokuta Women's Union had changed its name to the Nigerian Women's Union and was documented as having about 80,000 members. It began to open branches in other parts of Nigeria, and in Abeokuta, it operated a weaving corporation, ran a maternity and child welfare clinic, and conducted classes for adult women.[41]

At Aba, at the height of the Enugu Colliery crisis in 1945, women demonstrated the use of their market power in handling national issues. Under the dynamic leadership of Mrs. Margaret Ekpo, the Aba (Ekeoha) Market Women Association boycotted the market, which remained closed for several days. Women throughout Eastern Nigeria as a sign of solidarity took similar actions. Women throughout Eastern Nigeria declared a Day of National Mourning for the victims of the Enugu Colliery massacre and attracted sympathy throughout Nigeria and abroad for the unfortunate widows of the deceased miners, those wounded, and those otherwise affected.[42] The anti-school fees uprising in Eastern Nigeria in the 1950s is another example of women's use of their market power to address national issues. Also in the 1950s, women from Eastern Nigeria, through their market associations, shook Enugu city. This came about because of the murder of one Mrs. Onyia, a wardress, by an irate warder when she resisted his attempt to seduce her. The women who trooped to Enugu insisted that justice must prevail. The warder was tried, found guilty, condemned to death, and subsequently hanged. The list of similar cases in which market women acted in solidarity over national or regional problems before Nigeria's independence is numerous. But as I have shown in one of my studies,[43] there has been a decline since independence in the use of the market power of women to address national questions. The market power of women, however, is still strong and effective at the communal level. Examples include the Ogharefe women's uprising in 1984; the Ughelli women's tax protests of 1985-1986; the Ekpan women's uprising of 1986; and the Abiriba women's protest of 1992.

The market power of Nigerian women could be revived through networking by market women's associations in the country to address national questions. Such networking could help to break ethnic barriers and foster interethnic relations leading to national integration and development. Interethnic cooperation and interaction is already fostered by the composition of the membership of these women's associations, especially in the urban centers. Members come from various ethnic, political, and religious backgrounds but are united by common economic interests.

CONCLUSION

Some of the people I interviewed during my fieldwork in 1993 suggested that urban interethnic conflict could be resolved and interethnic understanding and national integration fostered through women's organizations. They recommended the formation of an umbrella women's organization, which will act as a parent body to other associations. This parent body will be responsible for coordinating the activities of other organizations for the primary purpose of cleaning up Nigerian society—fighting corruption, checking public officers, and fighting against the oppression and exploitation of the masses. My informants believed the National Commission for Women could have played this role if it had not been an organ of the state. Therefore, they recommended the use of a nongovernmental women's organization, if it could remain nonpartisan, secular and free from control by the state.

Another group of my informants argued that members of such an umbrella organization could act as vigilante groups for the purpose of suppressing ethnicity and its conflicts. This might sound difficult to achieve but with hard work, determination, and the high sense of commitment which Nigerian women have been known for; it could be achieved in Nigeria. This is because women's associations, especially the nongovernmental ones, have served as representatives of civil virtues and as a vast reservoir of untapped energy, eager to participate in national and local development, and prepared to engage in selfless actions to promote the common good and to assist the less fortunate members of society. As they did in the colonial period but even more effectively, the women's organizations could serve as bulwarks against state power if given the opportunity to function independently, and could serve as mechanisms for those seeking to make the state more accountable and responsive to the people.

Women's organizations have demonstrated their capability to serve as intermediary brokers or links between the state and societal interest groups. What the Mothers in Nigeria (MIN) did in the federal government/Academic Staff Union of Universities (ASUU) impasse in 1996 is an example of such a mediating role. Through MIN's intervention, the Federal Military Government agreed to meet some of ASUU's demands, and the latter called off its several months old strike action. Through the mediating role of Nigerian women, the macro-policy objectives of the state and the particularistic interests of society's groups could be adjusted to each other by a process of dialogue and bargaining. Nigerian women have demonstrated that they can more than men, and through their associations, better link the state and society together and, therefore, enhance the state's legitimacy.

Through the active participation of a reasonable number of women in politics and in the affairs of the state, the negative aspects of democracy prevalent in the Nigerian system could be eliminated for the good of all. But this can work only when the politics of exclusion and tokenism in the country are buried forever, and only when the principles of equity and equality are applied to both genders in terms of access to and control of political and economic power. It is only when this is done that ethnic loyalties and values can be transformed and used as an engine of national cohesion, integration, and development.

Nigerian women through their various organizations and their individual efforts have helped to create a cosmopolitan spirit among Nigerians in the cities. They have proved worthy stabilizers of their society and builders of their nation. Women by nature are not violent but peace loving. They not only have the interests of their children and their families to protect, but also those of their society. Nigerian women have historically demonstrated that they are better equipped than men to break down ethnic barriers and resolve urban interethnic conflicts in Nigeria; therefore, they should as a matter of urgency be given the opportunity to serve and save Nigeria from disintegration and collapse. There are, however, some Nigerian men who through their actions have proved to be true Nigerians, who know no ethnic boundaries. Professor Toyin Falola, to whom this book is dedicated, is among such Nigerian men. His actions, especially in the United States of America, in assisting Nigerian students and young scholars have known no ethnic barriers. He is one of the most detribalized Nigerians I have ever known. I hope others will emulate his exemplary life.

NOTES

1. Eghosa Osaghae, *Crippled Giant: Nigeria since Independence* (Indianapolis: Indiana University Press, 1998); E. Osaghae, *Ethnicity and Its Management in Africa: The Democratization Link*, Center for Advanced Social Science Occasional Monograph, No. 2 (Lagos: Malthouse Press Ltd., 1994); D. Olowu et al. (eds.), *Governance and Democratization in Nigeria* (Ibadan: Spectrum Books Limited, 1994); *Africa Recovery*, United Nations, 7, 2 (Oct. 1993); O. Otite, *Ethnic Pluralism and Ethnicity in Nigeria*, (Ibadan: Shaneson C.I., 1990); *Ethnicity, Citizenship, Stability and Socio-Economic Development in Africa*, Proceedings of the Regional Conference held in Tripoli, Libya, August 1989.
2. "Boutros-Ghali: No Democracy, No Peace," *Africa Recovery*, United Nations, 7, 3 (1993): 6.
3. K. A. Owolabi, "Group Interests versus Social Cohesion: Democracy and the Deepening Crisis of Social Order in Africa," paper presented at the CODESRIA 8th General Assembly, Dakar, Senegal, 26 June-2 July 1995, 9.
4. Chinua Achebe, *The Trouble with Nigeria* (Enugu: Fourth Dimension Publishers, 1983), 5.

5. Osaghae, *Ethnicity and Its Management*, 1.
6. O. Nnoli, *Ethnic Politics in Nigeria* (Enugu: Fourth Dimension Publishing Co. Ltd., 1978); and Okechukwu Okeke, *Hausa-Fulani Hegemony: The Dominance of the Muslim North in Contemporary Nigerian Politics* (Enugu: ACENA Publishers, 1992).
7. O. Otite, *Ethnic Pluralism and Ethnicity*; P. P. Ekeh and E. E. Osaghae (eds.), *Federal Character and Federalism in Nigeria* (Ibadan: Heinemann, 1989); R. A. Joseph, *Democracy and Prebendal Politics in Nigeria: The Rise and Fall of the Second Republic* (Cambridge: Cambridge University Press, 1987); Nnoli, *Ethnic Politics in Nigeria*; U. Okpu, *Ethnic Minority Problems in Nigerian Politics* (Uppsala: Acts Universitalis Uppsaliensis, 1977); B. J. Dudley, *Instability and Political Order: Politics and Crisis in Nigeria*, (Ibadan: Ibadan University Press, 1973); and P. C. Lloyd, "The Ethnic Background to the Nigerian Crisis," in S. K. Panter-Brick (ed.), *Nigerian Politics and Military Rule: Prelude to the Civil War* (London: The Athlone Press, 1970), 1-13.
8. Olusegun Obasanjo, *My Command: An Account of the Nigerian Civil War, 1967-70* (Ibadan: Heinemann Educational Books, Nigeria, Ltd. 1980).
9. B. O. Nwabueze, *Nigeria '93: The Political Crisis and Solutions* (Ibadan: Spectrum Books Limited, 1994), 133.
10. O. Nnoli, "Ethnic Conflicts and Democratization in Africa," paper presented at the CODESRIA 8th General Assembly, Dakar, Senegal, 26 June-2 July 1995, 20.
11. The Willink Minorities Commission of 1957 could not help to resolve this problem. See Ken Saro-Wiwa, *Genocide in Nigeria: The Ogoni Tragedy* (Port Harcourt: Saros International, 1992); Okpu, *Ethnic Minority Problems*; and Lloyd, "The Ethnic Background," 6.
12. Nnoli, *Ethnic Politics in Nigeria*, 69-70.
13. A. Shack and E. P. Skinner (eds.), *Strangers in African Societies* (Los Angeles, CA: University of California Press, 1979), 6.
14. I. O. Albert, *Inter-Ethnic Relations in a Nigerian City: A Historical Perspective of the Hausa-Igbo Conflicts in Kano, 1953-1991* (Ibadan: French Institute for Research in Africa [IFRA], Occasional Publications, 2, 1993), 1.
15. M. H. Kuka, *Religion, Politics and Power in Northern Nigeria* (Ibadan: Spectrum Books Limited, 1993), 245.
16. E. Osaghae, *Trends in Migrant Political Organizations in Nigeria: The Igbo in Kano* (Ibadan: IFRA, 1994), 40.
17. Osaghae, *Ethnicity and Its Management*, 34.

18. Okeke, *Hausa-Fulani Hegemony.*
19. Kuka, *Religion, Politics and Power*, 245.
20. Osaghae, *Trends in Migrant Political Organizations*, 29.
21. Ibid., 5.
22. Ibid., 5-6.
23. Bolanle Awe, "The Iyalode in the Traditional Yoruba Political System," in A. Schlegel (ed.), *Sexual Stratification: A Cross Cultural View* (New York: Columbia University Press, 1977), 140-160; B. Awe (ed.), *Nigerian Women in Historical Perspective* (Lagos and Ibadan: Sankore Publishers Limited and Bookcraft Ltd., 1992); Michael G. Smith, *The Affairs of Daura: History and Change in a Hausa State, 1800-1958* (Berkeley: University of California Press, 1978); Nina Mba, *Nigerian Women Mobilized: Women's Political Activity in Southern Nigeria, 1900-1965* (Berkeley: California Institute of International Studies, 1982); C. J. Johnson, "Grassroots Organizing: Women in Anti-Colonial Activity in Nigeria," *African Studies Review*, 16, 2/3 (1982): 137-158; Oladipo Yemitan, *Madame Tinubu: Merchant and King-Maker* (Ibadan: Ibadan University Press, 1987); B. J. Callaway, *Muslim Hausa Women in Nigeria: Tradition and Change* (New York: Syracuse University Press, 1987); and LaRay Denzer, "Yoruba Women: A Historiographical Study," *The International Journal of African Historical Studies*, 27, 1 (1994): 1-39.
24. B. Awe, "Saviours of their Societies," in Awe, *Nigerian Women*, 9.
25. Gloria Chuku, "The Militancy of Nigerian Women since the Colonial Period: Evolution and Transformation," in *UFAHAMU*, 26 (1), 1998, 55-76; G. Chuku, "The Changing Role of Women in Igbo Economy, 1929-1985," Ph.D. dissertation, Department of History, University of Nigeria, Nsukka, 1995; Cheryl Johnson-Odim and Nina Emma Mba, *For Women and the Nation: Funmilayo Ransome-Kuti of Nigeria*, (Urbana: University of Illinois Press, 1997); M. N. Noah, "The Role, Status and Influence of Women in Traditional Times: The Example of the Ibibio of Southeastern Nigeria," *Nigeria Magazine,* 54, 4 (1984), 24-31; Mba, *Nigerian Women Mobilized*; Johnson, "Grassroots Organizing"; Caroline Ifeka-Moller, "Female Militancy and Colonial Revolt: The Women's War of 1929, Eastern Nigeria," in Shirley Ardener (ed.), *Perceiving Women* (New York: Wiley, 1975), 127-157; and Judith Van Allen, "Sitting on a Man," Colonialism and the lost Political Institutions of Igbo Women," *Canadian Journal of African Studies*, 6, 2 (1972): 165-182.

26. J. S. Coleman, *Nigeria: Background to Nationalism* (Berkeley: University of California Press, 1958), 172.
27. Interview with Lolo Margaret Nwogu, c. 60 years, women's leader and trader, Umuokwaraikuku, Umuna, 30 July 1993.
28. Chuku, "The Militancy of Nigerian Women; Mba, *Nigerian Women Mobilized*; and E. Amucheazi, "A Decade of Church Revolt in Eastern Nigeria, 1956-1966," *Odu,* 10 (1974): 45-65.
29. Johnson-Odim and Mba, *For Women and the Nation.*
30. Nina Mba, "Olufunmilayo Ransome-Kuti," in Awe, *Nigerian Women,* 147.
31. G. O. Olusanya, "Olaniwun Adunni Oluwole," in Awe, *Nigerian Women,* 123-131.
32. A. Mama, "Feminism or Femocracy? State, Feminism and Democratization in Nigeria," *Africa Development,* 20, 1 (1995): 42-55; and my field notes.
33. Chuku, "The Militancy of Nigerian Women: T. E. Turner and M.O. Oshare, "Women's Uprising against the Nigerian Oil Industry in the 1980s," *Canadian Journal of Development Studies,* 14, 3 (1993): 329-357; Awe, *Nigerian Women*; Ifi Amadiume, *Male Daughters, Female Husbands: Gender and Sex in an African Society* (London: Zed Books Ltd., 1987); Mba, *Nigerian Women Mobilized*; and Van Allen, "Sitting on a Man."
34. Turner and Oshare, "Women's Uprising," 342.
35. Coleman, *Nigeria: Background to Nationalism,* 172.
36. Van-Allen, "Sitting on a Man."
37. Chiweizu, *Anatomy of Female Power: A Masculinist Dissection of Matriarchy* (Lagos: PERO Press, 1990).
38. Turner and Oshare, "Women's Uprising," 330.
39. Stella A. Effah-Attoe and S. O. Jaja, *Margaret Ekpo: Lioness in Nigerian Politics* (Abeokuta: ALF Publications, 1993), 15 and 148.
40. Effa-Attoe and Jaja, *Margaret Ekpo,* 149-150.
41. Johnson-Odim and Mba, *For Women and the Nation.*
42. Chuku, "The Changing Role of Women; and Effa-Attoe and Jaja, *Margaret Ekpo.*
43. Chuku, "The Militancy of Nigerian Women."

13

MORE THAN FARMERS' WIVES: YORUBA WOMEN AND CASH CROP PRODUCTION, c. 1920-1957[1]

Olatunji Ojo

INTRODUCTION

The participation of Yoruba women in agriculture in the period before 1970 remains a matter of debate among historians. In analyzing their economic roles, scholars have described them severally as "traders," "wives," "homemakers," "farm assistants," but never as farmers. The colonial authorities seemed to have shared this view; hence cash crop production and virtually all agricultural policies were targeted at male farmers. This is strange because farming/agriculture remains the biggest and most strategic sector of the economy.[2] This chapter, based largely on primary sources, provides another perspective by looking at the different tasks of farming. It focuses on who carried out what task and how; on time allocation; and on the effects of farming tasks on other activities. My research is based on Ekiti renowned for its farming, rurality, scarce labor, and semi-forest vegetation. It shows that Yoruba women were heavily involved in farming, not just as helpers but in their own right, and therefore qualified to be called farmers. More importantly, their involvement, during the period 1920-1957 transformed preexisting duties, disrupted old vocations and at the same time created new opportunities.

Until 1920, Ekiti remained a food-producing district with special emphasis on yams, maize, guineacorn, and vegetables. It nevertheless produced some cotton and tobacco. However, a different wind was blowing. Between about 1850 and 1920, commercial activities in non-food products, popularly called cash crops, began and expanded. By the latter date, the colonial state was more or less dependent on cocoa, palm produce, timber, and peanut production for its foreign trade and the local payment of taxes. Given the low prices of food crops, farmers gradually drifted into cash crop production or into more remunerative vocations. In Ekiti, although the land was not very good for cocoa, it still attracted many farmers, some of whom soon built new houses, acquired more wives, and titles.

It is impossible to date accurately when cocoa was introduced into Ekiti but it is not unlikely that it arrived about 1895 when freed slaves and Christians arrived with their notion of Western civilization and the concept of "the bible and the plough." These returnees came primarily from the Lagos Colony and other cocoa growing Christian regions such as Ibadan, Ondo, and Ilesa and retained their contacts with these regions. Nevertheless, cocoa farming was not widely accepted in Ekiti until the 1920s. The change of attitude was partly a response to the introduction of British currency and colonial taxation in 1919 and 1920 respectively and partly a response to the profits that were anticipated. Aware of the potential income, a significant number of Ekiti youth traveled to Ijesa, Ibadan, and Ondo where they worked as laborers on cocoa farms.[3] While the wages were welcome, many of them used the opportunity to learn the art of cocoa cultivation. These young men began returning in the 1930s, signaling the beginning of an agricultural revolution in Ekiti. Many received plots from their families on which they made cocoa farms. Less fortunate individuals, who had no family access to land, opted to borrow or lease land. Lease agreements involved an annual fee paid to the owner of the land, who could be either an individual or a lineage. The amount varied from place to place. Critical factors in determining the fee were the kinship relationship between the contracting parties and local custom. In some areas, the fee was paid in palm wine and kolanuts; in others, the landlord took a stipulated percentage of the annual harvest.[4]

Because of their knowledge of the procedures involved in cocoa production, the first cocoa planters were men. Women quickly learnt that the change from subsistence farming to cash crop farming entailed modifications in their work schedules and expectations. Traditionally, women were required to help their fathers and husbands in planting, weeding, and harvesting crops, and later in processing the harvest into products for household use or sale in the markets. At various times in its growth cycle, the new crop demanded intensive attention, which exceeded the nurturing required by subsistence crops. Moreover, as male farmers expanded the amount of land devoted to cocoa, they began making demands for labor and transport that far exceeded those associated with traditional agriculture. Women found that they no longer had time for their personal farming, weaving, work in other crafts, and trading, all of which had yielded income they controlled. If their husbands were well-off, migrant laborers would be hired to perform tasks associated with cocoa, leaving women in the household free to engage in their own endeavors as before. But less well-off husbands were compelled to ask their wives to increase the amount of time spent on cocoa-related duties.

Another way women supplied labor was through betrothal of daughters to prospective husbands who were thought to be hardworking. Such acts involved regular labor obligations on the part of intending husbands on their in-laws' farms. Since girls were often betrothed while still very young, the fiancé was obliged to labor for many years. He would invite an *owe* (bridal labor group) of his relations and friends, the size depending on the extent and type of work to be done and the fiancé's ability to mobilize people. The advantage of *owe* was that it provided labor whose quantity, timeliness, effectiveness, relative cheapness would otherwise have been unobtainable. Women realized that the switch to cash crops eroded their traditional rights, and sought compensation from their husbands for the increase in their workload on the farms. This could take the form of cash, cloth, gifts, or taking responsibility for the children's school fees and material welfare.

FEMALE FARMERS ON CASH CROP FARMS

Work in cocoa cultivation had a gender dimension. Men took responsibility for bush clearing, tree felling, bush burning, and heaping. Time spent on these tasks depended on the thickness of the bush, the number of trees on the plot, and the nature of the soil. Initially, cocoa farms were made on virgin forest land, an arduous task necessitating many hours of effort, especially since Ekiti farmers did not use the axe. Wives and children were mobilized to help burn down the trees.

The entire family might take part in planting the cocoa seedlings, but it was not uncommon for men to leave the actual planting to their wives and children. Pa Samuel Adebayo[5] told me that he cleared his farm in 1935, and his family planted cocoa in April and May 1936. To his surprise, he later discovered that the seedlings planted by himself had failed to germinate while those planted by his wife thrived. When he replanted his seedlings, they again failed to grow. But when his wife helped him plant this portion of the farm yet again, the seedlings grew very well. Investigating the situation, he found that his wife dug deeper holes and made sure that the soil around the seedlings was firmly pressed down, making it difficult for rodents to dig the seedlings up. His own planting method had been less thorough.

Young cocoa trees were interplanted with food crops like cocoyams, plantains, bananas and maize. Such crops met the family's immediate food needs and served a cover for the young cocoa plants.[6] Cocoa was planted in the months of June and July, after which Ekiti farmers attended to weeding their yam farms and preparing new plots for the following season. Women tended to be left to plant the cover crops to safeguard the cocoa seedlings.

The expansion of cocoa cultivation in Ekiti coincided with the economic depression of the early 1930s. Again, women were called upon to work longer on cocoa farms, because their husbands could not afford to hire migrant laborers. Yet families now depended more on women's incomes from their trade and food processing. Taxation added to the farmers' burdens, resulting in resentment against the colonial administration. In 1931, the administration cut taxes (then one-fortieth) on income, which ranged between six shillings and fifteen shillings. Despite the cut, tax riots broke out in Ido Ekiti and Akure. In Ido, angry rioters could not agree on the extent of the cuts they wanted. Some demanded the total abolition of taxes while others only wanted a 50 percent reduction. Meanwhile, some women rebelled against their husbands' assertion of the traditional prerogatives of labor obligations, obedience and deference.

Some women were in a better position to assert their autonomy vis-à-vis their husbands, particularly if they were old or had junior co-wives in the household over whom they (the senior wives) exercised the right to assign labor duties. Some of these older women began to export to Osogbo the cotton they grew on their personal farms, rather than weave it at home.[7] Others sought new opportunities in palm kernel cracking and retail trading. Both occupations followed patterns established earlier. Though cracking palm kernels was not necessarily highly remunerative, during the depression, it provided sorely needed income. Table I shows how palm kernel prices fluctuated in the period 1931-1937.

Table 1: Palm Kernel Prices, 1931-1937 (per ton)[8]

Year	£	s	d
1931 (Average)	6	10	5
1932 (February)	8	7	6
1932 (June)	5	2	6
1933 (Average)	6	6	3
1936 (Average)	14	12	6
1937 (Average)	6	0	0

Cocoa prices fared much better than those for palm kernels. Cocoa opened at £17.5s. in 1931,[9] averaged £19.3.s throughout 1936,[10] and plummeted to £14.10s. in 1937.[11] The difference between the prices of cocoa and palm kernels accentuated the social cleavages that had become apparent as cocoa expanded. Cocoa farmers were perceived as socially more important than non-cocoa producers. Since few women engaged in cocoa farming in their own right, this exacerbated gender disparities.

WORLD WAR II AND ITS AFTERMATH

Colonial policy reinforced the dominance of male-oriented social structures in Ekiti by encouraging men to transfer to cash crop agriculture. This adversely affected the patterns of the gender division of labor.[12] Men's preference for cocoa farming and other forms of cash crop production led to a growing neglect of food production. By 1933, cocoa production was not only expanding but had ushered in a period of prosperity in Ekiti. In the Annual Report for Ondo Province, the District Officer for Ekiti, F. B. Carr commented on "the emergence of new and improved houses."[13] This trend continued through World War II and afterward.

Since women found it less easy to enter into cocoa farming, they focused on the production of palm products. During the war, the colonial authority launched a huge production drive for palm oil as part of the Win-the-War Campaign.[14] The administration's effort to expand palm production was only partially successful. Official reports constantly complained about the perceived apathy shown by the Ekiti to gathering palm fruit.[15] But it was at least clear that the administration had reached a better understanding of women's role in the production process. It was accepted that the Ondo palm kernel trade was controlled by women.[16] Long before, however, a John Holt agent in Ekiti had observed "a large export of palm kernel and palm oil from Ikole area in northern Ekiti to Lokoja."[17] Several years later, the British resident officer reported on the large amount of palm oil supplied to Owena village from as far away as Ado Ekiti, sixty-three miles away.[18]

Low market prices, however, discouraged palm products producers. In 1933, the price for palm kernel stood at £3.10s. To crack palm kernels worth a halfpenny, one woman required three pence worth of food to supply the necessary energy. A woman's head load of palm kernels fetched only 4d. During the war, some administrators urged that the price of palm kernels should be raised to between £7 and £7.10s. per ton.[19] This measure was not adopted in the end, but the provincial authorities tried to strike a balance between mandating production of palm products and allowing the people to continue their activities in more profitable ventures. Women objected to the forced production of palm products because transport was scarce, and if available, its cost was so high they could not realize a profit.[20] Although the administration toyed with the idea of raising import quotas to raise consumption, it was easier to earn the money needed to purchase goods through weaving, trading, and gari production. These were enterprises that had expanded during the war. In 1943, an agricultural officer was appointed to "look after" price adjustments, motor transport, and control of movement and prices of local foodstuffs.[21] The increase in the palm kernel price to £6 in July 1943 encouraged production, but this alone may not explain the rise in output.[22]

Production figures for Ekiti between 1939 and 1950 showed a sharp rise between 1943 and 1946, followed by a gradual decline. The increase was due to an increase in the price of palm kernels in 1943 and 1944 concurrent with a fall in the demand for cocoa which reduced its cultivation; hence more women, who were released from duties connected to cocoa cultivation, engaged in palm kernel production. The end of World War II, however, reversed this trend. The demand for cocoa rose in the world market, causing a substantial rise in prices. This prompted many families to return to their abandoned cocoa farms.

Table 2: Production of Palm Kernels in Ekiti, 1939-1957[23]

Year	Production	Year	Production
1939	226	1946	1,699
1939/40	609	1947	773
1941/42	499	1948	1,226
1942/43	980	1949	1,829
1943	1,423	1950	2,560
1944	2,222	1955/56	2,171
1945	2,002	1956/57	1,054

These figures were not exclusive as they did not include unrecorded products that were smuggled and sold outside Ekiti or those processed locally into a lotion called *adin*. Although we do not have figures for these, we can reasonably assume that a substantial amount was involved. This we may adduce from the fact that a large number of Ekitis used *adin* as a body cream. Palm kernels also constituted one of the major trading products in the inter-district commerce between Ekiti, Ilesha, Osogbo, Ilorin, Lokoja, and Akure. In 1943, the police reported that "empty vehicles were going to Ekiti for produce."[24]

From the palm kernel figures, we may infer that the production of palm oil must have been quite substantial since the ratio of oil weight to palm kernel was 10:7.[25] To assess the role of women in the production of palm oil, we must examine the gender division of labor. Men did the initial harvesting, for it was considered taboo for women to climb palm trees in most places. Thus, professional male climbers specialized in cutting down the ripe fruit. Until the 1950s, the majority of these men were migrant laborers: Urhobo (called Isobo), Igbo, and Igbomina. Both male and female farmers hired such laborers. Usually, the children and wives of the farmers followed the harvesters to gather the cut bunches of palm fruit and take them to a nearby collection place. Although stripping the fruit from the bunches was usually done by men, women sometimes carried out this task when there were only few bunches to be stripped. After that, women took over the rest of the processing tasks. They sorted out the fruit, transported it, pounded it, mashed it, pressed the fruit into oil, and processed the oil for use in the household or for sale in the market. When women farmers had a large harvest, they would hire female processors who were either paid in cash or given a stipulated percentage of the oil. In the 1950s, the going rate for this work was between a half *kongo* (a unit of measurement) and a full *kongo* or 1-2d per day.

Apart from cocoa and oil palm, other important cash crops were tobacco and kolanuts. In the early days, farmers' wives sold kolanuts to traders who resold the produce in the markets or their homes. After the introduction in the 1920s of a new variety of kolanut, *gbanja* (*kola acuminata*) the kola trade expanded, for the new type of kolanut did not have the same ritual value as the Ekiti *abata* (*kola nitida*). *Gbanja* was cultivated purposely for its commercial value at home and abroad. This trade was dominated by women, who bought the kolanuts directly from the farmers and hired porters (usually women) to transport the crop from Itaji, Iyin, Igede, and

Aramoko to Egosi (now Ilupeju), the leading bulking center in Ekiti.

The processing of kolanuts was a laborious task which male producers refused to carry out. Hence, they sold the kolanuts to women at relatively low prices. Initially, Ekiti farmers did not know the technology involved in preparing *gbanja* for marketing. They merely removed the testa, often scarring the nuts in the process, washed the nuts, and took them to market for sale. A large amount of spoilage occurred. Such poor processing resulted in a fall in kolanut prices in the 1930s. But women traders soon learned the necessary techniques required for fermenting the kolanut then removing the testa, decorticating the nuts, and preparing them for dry storage. To facilitate the marketing of Ekiti kolanuts, associations of kolanut traders were organized in Ekiti and Lagos. A particularly noteworthy one was founded in Ado-Ekiti by Madam Emily Patience Fayemi, a daughter of the nineteenth-century warrior, Chief Sajowa.[26] Through these associational networks, Ekiti kolanuts were traded to Lagos, where they were sold, often by Ekiti women migrants. An obituary published in 1948 recorded the death of Madam Ayisatu Fajobi Labinjo, the mother of the editor of the *Daily Service* "an active kolanut trader," who was the head of the Labinjo family of Lagos and Aramoko.[27]

Cash crop production adversely affected gender relations which had previously centered on the traditional values of complementarity and division of labor. The European colonialists pursued their goal of expropriating wealth from the colonies and in doing so were guided by Victorian values, which presumed men performed the bulk of agricultural tasks. According to Esther Boserup, "the unfamiliarity of Europeans to women farmers led to the belief that men in the region of female farming were lazy."[28] Thus, colonial policy makers failed to notice the spheres of women's dominance in African agriculture and made no provision for them in constructing development policy. Clashes occasionally developed, as was the case in the 1920s and 1940s when the administration attempted to introduce palm oil presses and crackers. Traditionally, women did the work these machines were designed to do. They saw the new machines as a threat to their economic rights, and refused to have anything to do with them. Cash crop producers, however, realized the importance of women in the cultivation process, for often women worked such long hours on their husbands' farms that they could not pursue their own income-generating activities. Women were forced to limit the time they spent on their weaving (or other craftwork) or working on their own farms. Sara Berry observes that in order to compensate their wives for this loss of income, "men helped by wives on their cocoa farms gave them capital to enable them to participate in trading activities."[29] This, however, was subject to the availability of wage labor and to an individual farmer's ability to hire workers. Wealthier farmers in the older cocoa areas like Ado, Ilawe, Igede, Ise, Emure, and Ikere had incomes substantial enough to give their wives money to engage in trade. Moreover, in the 1940s and 1950s there was plenty of migrant labor from Igbira and Yorubaland (especially from Iresi).[30] Smaller farmers or farmers in the new cocoa areas could not afford to release their wives from their farms, except perhaps during the dry season when duties connected to cocoa were lessened. But even then, the period October to February, when the harvest period for cocoa was at its height, required significant help from women to gather the pods, remove the beans, and transport them first to the fermentation sites, then to the drying sites and then again to the produce buyers. A wise husband compensated his wife or wives in the form of cash and/or new cloths. He was also expected to buy new furniture, to build new houses if possible, and to provide the school fees for his children as well as buy them cloth and books. Moreover, wives expected financial assistance for social functions that took place in their natal homes, especially marriages or burials.[31] In tobacco growing areas, women experienced much the same situation. In Igboho, Oyo State, Babalola and Dennis observed that:

the extent to which such an arrangement [giving capital to women for trading purposes] was implemented depended on the availability of hired migrant labour at an acceptable rate with which to replace the wife's labour contribution. A man with less access to migrant labour was less apt to compensate his wife (wives) in capital to initiate trading.[32]

In my research, I found this same pattern among the wives of tobacco farmers at Aisegba, Ijan, and Iluomoba, and it is more than likely that the same situation exists in other parts of Ekiti. Madam Oyewumi Obarinde told me that tobacco production needed a reliable, permanent source of family labor, meaning that:

Women were unable to work for money except on market days when we begged our husbands to allow us to sell our goods at the community market. Some women, who had only livestock to sell, would some-times give them to *alagbata* or *onisowo* [professional traders] to sell for them on the agreement that the *alagbata* would take her commission for the assistance rendered.[33]

Nevertheless, it must be noted that cash crop production did improve the status of women in certain respects. Not only did they receive from their husbands cash remuneration and gifts for services rendered, but the commercialization of land enabled significant numbers of women to gain access or to buy or inherit land which they could use in their own right.

CASH CROP PRODUCTION, WOMEN, AND LAND REFORM

Unlike the precolonial period when it was held that women had no right to inherit land, the production of cash crops (palm oil, cocoa, tobacco, and others) set in motion a process of land reform which benefited Ekiti women.

The earliest Ekiti women to engage in cash crop farming were widows, who after the death of their husbands took over their farms and managed them together with their children. Earlier, the tradition was that a deceased man's properties, including his wife (wives) and children, were inherited by his relations, especially when the children were young. After the introduction of colonialism, divorce became legal, and this allowed women the opportunity to leave men if they wanted. In selecting new husbands, women were guided by their personal aspirations and their economic and social needs. Closely related to the growing popularity of divorce among women was the growing tendency to reject traditional ideas concerning widow inheritance, particularly among those who converted to Christianity. Previously, the young wives (and even older wives) of a deceased man were expected to be inherited by his brothers and children, subject to the condition that a woman's son could not inherit his mother. From 1940 onward, widows who had children in school could no longer tolerate a situation whereby they would be inherited by a brother-in-law who was unwilling to sponsor their children's education. Such widows would persuade their children to disallow the inheritance of their father's farm by any of his brothers. Instead, the widows and their children would manage the farm themselves. In such instances, the bereaved family usually became cash crop farmers, with the woman as the household or family head. In many cases, women who engaged in both trade and farming preferred to concentrate on their trading activities while hiring a farm manager (*alagbase, alagbaro, or onise odun*) to oversee their farm(s). They compensated the manager in one of two ways. Either they shared the profits or harvest on a 50-50 basis, or the owner received two-thirds of the profits or harvest and the hired manager one-third.[34] Other male laborers would be hired on a contract basis to carry out specific work such as weeding, spraying, and harvesting. Children would also assist in these tasks on

Saturdays and during school holidays. During the harvest season, the farm took precedence over trade, and everyone pitched in, especially if the farm was small or only a small number of pods were to be harvested.[35]

Apart from widows, older married women and divorcees [*omo osu*] preferred to remain close to their fathers in order to secure land to plant their own cocoa or to inherit a part, or the whole, of the father's farm should he have no son. In 1944, one Victoria Bola of Ikere Ekiti sued her husband, Samuel Ojo, for divorce.[36] She told the court that she had inherited a cocoa farm from her late brother, Komolafe. From the money she realized from the sale of the cocoa harvest, she kept £33.10s., which she gave to her husband for safekeeping. Without her knowledge or permission, Ojo then spent £6 of this amount on a new wife. Infuriated, Bola broke into Ojo's room and removed £14, and sued her husband in court to get the remaining balance of £8.10s. She won her case. Another case involved a Mrs. Kolade, who was sued by her brother, Gabriel Ojo, who objected to her inheriting her father's farm at Ogotun. He accused Mrs. Kolade and her husband, along with the Ologotun-in-Council of wrongfully sharing the property of his father, who had died in 1945. He claimed that a woman should not inherit land. The Ologotun-in-Council, who had presided over the original sharing, however, justified their action on the grounds that only Mrs. Kolade had financed the burial and the clearing of her father's debts, amounting to £22.11s.[37] Although the case file did not contain the view of the district officer who tried the case, the fact that the Ologotun-in-council accepted Mrs. Kolade's right to inherit her father's farm showed a distinct change in Ekiti society. In other cases, women's rights over land were clear. For example, one Oluseju of Arigidi (now Ayegbaju) gave his daughter a portion of the lineage land to farm. Through this woman, the land passed on to her son who planted both cash and food crops. Sometime later, a land dispute arose between Arigidi and Ifaki in which one James Dada, a grandson of Oluseju from a male line, lost his portion of family land to

Ifaki. He then decided to claim land farmed by J. K. Daramola, a grandson of Oluseju's daughter, on the basis that the land belonged to his lineage and not to Daramola whose rights derived from a woman. The Native Court at Oye Ekiti, however, ruled against Dada, stating that the plot belonged to Daramola, who might, if he so wished, permit James the use of part of it. Not content with this decision, James appealed to the Divisional Court, which upheld the decision of the lower court, maintaining that long usage had changed the ownership of the land. Planters of cash crops could not be separated from their land.[38]

Women's increased assertion of rights over land enhanced their role in agriculture. They assumed more responsibilities in their natal and marital homes. Besides performing the usual duties expected by their husbands, friends, and children, they now managed their personal farms, marketed crops, provided credit, subsidized the family food supply, and generated income from other sources. Such changes began to affect the formulation of government policy. In 1952, when the administration made its preparations for conducting the census, R. Bromage, the district officer of Ekiti Division, wrote to enumerators that "a woman who markets her own or her husband's produce should be regarded as engaged in agriculture."[39] This showed a better understanding of the structural organization of the agricultural sector than the definition used ten years later by the Federal Office of Statistics, whose 1962 development plan statistics maintained that whoever worked on another man's farm or pledged his labour to another farm was not a farmer. With the new conception of who was a farmer, the 1952 census for Ekiti showed a preponderance of women agriculturalists, who numbered 55,617 as against 35,301 women engaged in trading or clerical work (See Table 3).

In Ekiti, the lack of adequate credit facilities posed a serious problem for farmers. Many had such low incomes that it became impossible for them to hire wage laborers or buy new farming implements, seedlings, herbicides, or insecticides. Nor

Table 3: Occupations in Ekiti by Gender, December 1952[40]

Occupation	Male	Female
Agriculture and Fishing	62,317	55,617
Trading and Clerical	41,890	35,301
Crafts	6,729	*NA
Administration and Other	1,951	*NA
Other Occupations	3,477	*NA

Not available

Source: Western Region of Nigeria, *Population Census of the Western Region of Nigeria 1952* (Ibadan: Government Printer, 1953), 16.

were they able to meet other social obligations. For farmers who had little or no surplus, the situation was even worse. The outbreak of blackpod disease in the early 1940s exacerbated the problems. The price of cocoa fell sharply from £28 in 1937 to £14 the next year.[41] There was no significant improvement in prices until the end of World War II. After the war, farmers in the affected areas cut down infested trees, planted new seedlings, and sprayed their crop with *Gamallin 20* or *Bordeaux*. Since many farmers did not have enough money to buy new seedlings or insecticides they resorted to traditional credit schemes arranged with produce merchants and traders, some of them women. These arrangements varied. Some traders provided credit facilities on condition that the debtor would pay back his or her loan during the following harvest period. Other farmers pawned their farms and children as collateral for the amount of credit advanced.

Sometimes female betrothal was in a real sense child pawning, disguised as a formal marriage transaction. Parents pawned their daughters to creditors and the credit was converted into dowries. Through this, farmers were able to raise cash or buy seeds for their farms. When farms were pledged, the creditors had a lien on the cocoa harvest until the full amount of the debt was paid. The profit thus realized was considered as interest paid on the original amount of credit. An example of such an agreement is the one made in 1957 between one J. A. and E. O. [possibly Elizabeth Oguntubi] of Ado-Ekiti. The agreement read:

> Know all ye men that I, J. A. of Igbehin Street, Ado do hereby receive the sum of £50 (fifty pounds) on loan from Madam E. O. of [I] joka Street, Ado and I do hereby pledge my cocoa farm which is situated at Oke Epa farm and which is lying between Y. F.'s cocoa farm on the right and S. O.'s cocoa farm on the left as a security against the above sum for a period of three years. That she, Madam E. would hold the cocoa farm for a period of three years as from 1/3/57 to 28/2/60. She will be reaping the cocoa crops of the said farm and make sales of it for her own purpose, and if I fail to refund the said £50 at the expiration of the time, she would call for a fresh document to be made.[42]

As indicated in the above document, the creditor possessed the right to harvest the cocoa crop on the pledged farm but did not gain the right to harvest other cash crops, such as kolanuts, palm products, cocoyams and oranges, grown on the farm. However, a badly pressed debtor might pawn these crops as well. Should the debtor fail to pay at the stipulated time, his or her farm might pass into the possession of the creditor, but local practices often counteracted such alienation of land. The friends and relations of the debtor might intervene to settle the matter by "begging" the creditor to release the farm to the debtor if he or she agreed to pay back the original loan. This happened in Emure-Ekiti in 1956. Abraham Akosile and Madam Theresa Faluyi were the offspring by different mothers of the late Pa Akinola, once a leading cocoa farmer in Emure-Ekiti. When the time came for Akosile to pay his children's school fees in 1956, he pledged his cocoa farm to his half-sister, Theresa Faluyi, for two years in return for £28. At the end of the stipulated term, Akosile defaulted. In 1962, when he was finally able to repay the loan, his sister refused to take it, claiming that the agreement had lapsed and the farm was now hers. Only after friends and relations intervened in 1963 was the conflict settled and the farm returned to Theresa's half-brother.[43]

Women's ability to offer credit facilities depended on their capacity to accumulate capital, the bulk of which derived from their trading enterprises. Through trading, women were able to muster enough capital to enable them to become moneylenders or creditors. Thus, they advanced credit to friends and prospective customers for both trade and farming. Successful traders like Madam Comfort Oguntubi and Madam Tinubu Egbeyemi,[44] both still flourishing today, are prominent figures in Ado-Ekiti. Aged about ninety, Madam Oguntubi is the Iyaloja (titled market leader) of Ado-Ekiti and the town's most popular woman. As a young girl, she learned weaving and trading from her parents. In the 1920s, she started out as an itinerant trader traveling between Ado-Ekiti and Ile-Ife. By the mid-1930s, she had accumulated enough capital to specialize in imported textiles. Between 1960 and the late 1980s, she owned the biggest textile shop in the town. A progressive woman, she co-founded the Egbe Ifelodun, an elite women's organization dedicated to fashion and modernization. She played a leading role in the town's political crisis of 1940-1942. Since then, she has often been consulted on community issues. Equally committed to modern development is Madam Egbeyemi, who also played an important part in the Egbe Ifelodun. Early in her life, she engaged in weaving and selling *akara* (a type of bean cake), but by the 1930s, she was one of the leaders in the palm oil trade. These two women controlled the textile and palm oil trades from 1945 to 1980, keeping in close touch with farmers engaged in cocoa and oil palm cultivation.

Unlike many male produce buyers or scale owners, women produce merchants and farmers went directly to the source of their supplies where they purchased harvested crops and arranged for porters (often women) to transport them to the markets from which they operated. Thus, they were able to assess the size of the harvest and the quality of the produce, using this knowledge to set market prices. They could also monitor the movement of labor on the farms. In addition, they sometimes advised farmers on market trends and suitable crops. Some of my male informants told me that they were often guided by such advice when deciding what crops to plant. Possibly, a factor in making their decision was their need to obtain credit facilities from these women. Such loans were used to educate their children, hire farm laborers, and purchase insecticides and fertilizers.

CONCLUSION

The discussion in this chapter has demonstrated the adaptability of women to changing economic circumstances. This facilitated women's participation in the development of cash crop production and marketing in Ekiti. They provided labor on the farms, organized marketing, and processed the harvests into marketable products. Since the Yoruba inheritance system was flexible, women were able to extend the boundaries of acceptable custom, making it possible for them to gain greater access to and control over land. While some women were more successful in these endeavors than others, the bulk of women farmers operated at small scale levels. Nevertheless, they laid the groundwork for more forceful demands for women-oriented policy in development.

NOTES

1. I owe special debts to Dr. Laray Denzer and Prof. Paul Lovejoy, in whose classes I learned women and economic history. Their comments made me think more clearly.
2. For a full review and critique of the literature on the economic roles of Yoruba women, see Olatunji Ojo, "Ekiti Women in Agricultural Production,1890-1960," M.A. thesis, University of Ibadan, 1996.
3. J.D.Y. Peel, *Ijeshas and Nigerians: The Incorporation of a Yoruba Kingdom, 1890s-1970s* (Cambridge: Cambridge University Press, 1983), 122; Sara Berry, *Cocoa, Custom and Socio-Economic Change in Rural Western Nigeria* (Oxford: Clarendon Press, 1975), chapter 5; R. Galletti, K. D. S. Baldwin, and I. O. Dina, *Nigerian Cocoa Farmers* (London: Oxford University Press, 1956), 206; Nigerian National Archives Ibadan (NAI), CSO 26/06027, Annual Report, Oyo Province, 1921.
4. See Peter C. Lloyd, *Yoruba Land Law* (London: Oxford University Press, 1962), 88-94, 207-222; Berry, *Cocoa, Custom*, chapter 5; Galletti et al., *Nigerian Cocoa Farmers*, 116-118.
5. Interview with Pa Samuel Adebayo, 80+ years, 37 Ereguru Street, Ado-Ekiti, 9 October 1995.
6. Galletti et al., *Nigerian Cocoa Farmers*, 183; interviews with Madam Alice Adedoyin Ojo, farmer, 67 years, at 10, Matthew Street, Ado-Ekiti, 22 May 1995 and 10 October 1995.
7. NAI, CSO, 26/1/11874, vol. 9: Annual Report, Ondo Province, 1931 (by H. C. Aveling), 664.
8. NAI, CSO, 26/1/11874, vols. 9-14: Annual Reports, Ondo Province, 1931-1937.
9. NAI, CSO, 26/1/11874, vol. 9: Annual Report, Ondo Province, 1931, 663.
10. NAI, CSO, 26/1/11874, vol. 14: Annual Report, Ondo Province, 1936, 778.
11. NAI, CSO, 26/1/11874, vol. 14: Annual Report, Ondo Province, 1936, 838.
12. Z. Tadesse, "An overview of the Tripartite African Regional Seminar on Rural Development and Women in Africa," Dakar, Senegal, 1981.
13. NAI, CSO, 26/1/11874, vol.11: Annual Report, Ondo Province, 1933 (by F. B. Carr), para. 26.

14. NAI, Ib. Min. Agric. 1/373: Palm Produce: Compulsory Measures, 1943-45, 25-26, Acting Chief Commissioner, Western Provinces, note on Palm kernel situation, 15 May 1944.
15. NAI, Ib. Min. Agric.1/285, 2-11: E.V.S. Thomas, Senior District Officer, to Secretary Southern Provinces, Enugu, 6 July 1938.
16. Ibid.
17. NAI, Ekiti Div. 1/2/236, 7-8: Superintendent of Agriculture, Akure, to District Officer, Ekiti, 21 April 1934.
18. NAI, Ib. Min. Agric. 1/285, 6: Report on Palm Oil Survey, 1938-1940.
19. NAI, Ib. Min. Agric. 1/208: Resident, Ondo Prov. to Secretary, Western Provinces, 19 January 1934.
20. NAI, Ondo Prof. 1/4/O.C. 29, 3-5: Production and Trading of Palm Kernel, 1943-1946.
21. NAI, Ib. Min. Agric. 1/4447, 40-42: Hugh Marshall, Acting Secretary, Western Provinces, to Chief Secretary, 9 October 1943.
22. NAI, Ib. Min. Agric. 1/358,vol. 2: Production of Palm Kernel, Western Provinces, 317.
23. Official records gave monthly production for some years. This table is a summary of entries in NAI, Ib. Min. Agric. 1/324, 3; NAI, Ib. Min.Agric.1/358 vol.2, 280; NAI, Ekiti Div.1/655A, vol.1; NAI, Ekiti Div. 1/102 vol. 11, 30; NAI, Ekiti Div. 1/102, vol. 12, 22. The production figures are in tons.
24. NAI, Ekiti Div. 1/655A, vol. 1, 17: Police Post Erinmo to Assistant Transport Control Officer, Ado-Ekiti, 18 July 1943.
25. NAI, Ondo Prof. 2/1/D28, 109: Palm oil industry in Nigeria, Development, 1946-1953.
26. *Daily Service*, 27 June 1949, 3.
27. "Editor Daily Service Loses Mother," *Daily Service*, 22 January 1948, 1.
28. Esther Boserup, *Women's Role in Economic Development* (London: Allen and Unwin, 1970), 54.
29. Berry, *Cocoa, Custom*,163-165.
30. Interviews with Chief Ojo Ajanaku, about 70 years, of Odo-Adin Street, Ilawe-Ekiti; Adeyemi Falayi, 62 years, 23A, Okebedo Street, Ilawe, 13 October 1995; and Joseph Ojo, Iwoye Street, Omu-Ekiti, 10 May 1995.
31. Galletti, Baldwin and Dina, *Nigerian Cocoa Farmers*, 460-493. A popular practice in Ekiti was to arrange major ceremonies to coincide with the cocoa season.

32. S. O. Babalola and Carolyne Dennis, "Returns to Women's Labour in Cash Crop Production: Tobacco in Igboho, Oyo state," in Jean Davison (ed.), *Agriculture, Women and Land: The African Experience* (Boulder, Colo.: Westview Press Inc., 1988), 80-81.
33. Interview with Madam Oyewumi Obarinde, about 75 years, king's palace, Ijan Ekiti, 29 May 1995.
34. Galletti et al., *Nigerian Cocoa Farmers*, 211-214.
35. Interviews with Madams Ola, Ogundare, and Comfort Olaoba, all of Omu Ekiti, 10-12 May 1995.
36. NAI, Ekiti Div. 1/1/153/1: Ikere native court suit number 14/1944, Victoria Bola (F) vs. Sam Ojo (M), court sitting of 20 January 1944.
37. NAI, Ekiti Div. 1/1/77, vol. 2: Ogotun district, Matters arising, 83, 84, 93, 97.
38. Ekiti Divisional Court, 134/1949, and Oye Native Court 2/1949; cf. Lloyd, *Yoruba Land Law*, 212-213.
39. NAI, Ekiti Div. 1/1/918F: Census, towns, villages and quarters etc. Hints for enumerators, 1952.
40. Women engaged in crafts (weaving, spinning, and so on) were counted as traders. The table shows the occupations of adults, but the majority of children would have also been engaged in farming.
41. Berry, *Cocoa, Custom,* 22.
42. Lloyd, *Yoruba Land Law*, 311.
43. Interviews with Madam Theresa Faluyi, 83 years, 21 and 23 May and 11 and 12 October 1995. See also R. O. Adegboye, "Procuring Loan through Pledging of Cocoa Trees," *The Nigerian Geographical Journal*, 12 (1&2), December 1969, 63-76.
44. Interviews with Chief Elizabeth Oguntubi, about 85 years, at Erekesan market, Ado-Ekiti, 17 January 1993 and 22 May 1995, and Madam Egbeyemi, about 80 years, at Ogbon Oba Street, Ado-Ekiti, 16 January 1993.

14

NATIONALISM, ETHNICITY, AND NATIONAL INTEGRATION: AN ANAYLSIS OF POLITICAL HISTORY

Julius O. Adekunle

INTRODUCTION

Like so many aspects of social and political history, nationalism and ethnicity are attracting attention from historians, political scientists, and sociologists. Judging from the past and present social and political experiences of Nigeria, national integration has been elusive. Frequent conflicts among the major ethnic groups and the claim to margnalization by the minorities consistently weakens the process of national integration. The purpose of this chapter is to analyze the intersections of nationalism, ethnicity, and the process of national integration in Nigeria. The chapter discusses the main political developments in Nigeria as they relate to the issues of nationalism, ethnicity, and national integration. Before and since independence, the historiography of Nigeria has centered on these three issues, although how nationalism and ethnicity can be used in the process of national integration has hitherto not been critically examined.

Nationalism and ethnicity are two fundamental issues in the process of nation building. Depending upon how they are used, both can be instruments to build or to destroy national unity. Ethnic diversity should be a centripetal factor where every group brings its cultural values to facilitate nation building, but conflicts and violence make national integration very slippery. Similarly, nationalism has been used as a means of national integration, especially in Europe, but in modern history, it has been employed as a negative force to cause violence.[1] During the era of colonialism, the European powers adopted the policy of "divide and rule," which hindered national integration. Although Nigeria has never been a homogenous society, the policy of "divide and rule" made national unity more difficult to achieve. After independence, it became imperative for Nigerians to adopt the principle of "unity in diversity" in order to build a strong nation. Building a nation is a slow process that involves a combination of factors. The development of a national consciousness in spite of ethnic divisions is important in national integration considering the Nigerian political structure and the vicissitudes the country experienced before and after independence. Since independence, there have been political shifts, which have led Nigeria to oscillate between democracy and military dictatorship. During this period, the concepts of nationalism and ethnicity have been used to determine government policies, and now that Nigeria has returned to democracy after a long period of military rule, it is possible to reexamine the roles of nationalism and ethnicity in national integration.

THE ENIGMA OF NATIONALISM AND ETHNICITY

Nationalism and ethnicity are thorny issues, not only in Nigeria but also in modern world politics and from time to time, every country grapples with them. Conflicts have arisen in many countries as a result of religious differences or an overly ostentatious sense of ethnic nationalism. Particularly in

Africa, ethnic rivalry or ethnic chauvinism has caused major political and social problems, both in the past and in the present. In Nigeria, the problem of ethnic antagonism began during the period of decolonization when nationalist leaders formed political parties on ethnic lines. As a result of the imbalance in Western education, religious orientation, and political consciousness, there was a dichotomy between the northern and southern regions.

The political structure that evolved after independence exposed Nigeria to world criticism in several ways for acts of corruption, nepotism, favoritism, and discrimination that resulted from ethnic rivalry. Ethnonationalism became a growing factor acting against efforts geared toward national integration. The sociopolitical, interethnic, and intraethnic problems can be associated with the European imperialism that led to the formation of a country including peoples of divergent backgrounds without their consent to living together. This accounted for the weak foundation of the country and was a potential cause of conflict.

On behalf of the Royal Niger Company (RNC), Captain Frederick Lugard signed treaties of protection with traditional rulers in every part of what now constitutes Nigeria. He signed treaties with the Yoruba, with Nupe, Benin, Borgu, and the rulers of northern Nigeria. Out of desperation, to make indirect rule operate among the Igbo, the British appointed and imposed "warrant chiefs" on the people. This situation ignored the traditional political structure and caused intraethnic antagonism. Without traditional support, and considered as traitors and collaborators, the warrant chiefs became unpopular and corrupt.[2]

Lugard constituted the West African Frontier Force (WAFF), consisting largely of Nigerians, with whom he fought the rulers who refused to sign treaties. The RNC therefore became the instrument through which the imperial aims of the British in Nigeria were accomplished. Lugard became the governor of Nigeria in 1912 and in 1914, he amalgamated the Northern and Southern Protectorates and took the personal title of governor-general.[3] It was clear right from the outset that the British ideology of "divide and rule" encouraged conflicts and left an enduring legacy of ethnic or regional rivalry between northerners and the southerners. The British favored the northerners, to the displeasure of the southerners who were denied opportunities they deserved because of their more advanced political and economic development.

The British ruled Nigeria through constitutional and political processes. In the Richards Constitution of 1946, which introduced the concept of regional division, Nigeria was divided into three disproportional regions.[4] The Northern Region was larger in size and population than the two southern regions combined. This constitutional development left in its wake conflicts and unsavory relationships between northerners and southerners. Thus, colonial policies heralded the idea of separatism. Most political conflicts and upheavals have been interwoven with the spirit of nationalism and ethnicity. Complex and bloody issues have erupted and rather than declining, ethnic animosity and religious violence continue to ravage the fabric of Nigerian society even after the return to democratic rule in May 1999.

A pertinent question to ask is what comes first: ethnic loyalty or national interest? For a thorough analysis, several interconnected factors have to be taken into consideration. Fred W. Riggs was of the opinion that "the most powerful motivators for contemporary ethnonational movements were generated by nationalism. State elites and intellectuals initially promoted nationalism as a motor for assimilation and nation-building."[5] A majority of Nigerian societies did not understand the philosophy of nationalism because it was foreign to them. Nigerian societies owed allegiance to their different ethnic groups as a result of their primordial and cultural setting. That is ethnonationalism. The centralized kingdoms, such as Oyo, Benin, Nupe, Jukun, and the Hausa states, and the Igbo societies were not constituted as nation-states; therefore the concept of national consciousness or integration was non-existent. As a consequence, it has been difficult to bring the societies together under a national political organization, which would mean placing national interest above ethnic loyalty.

NATIONALISM

Nationalism is an inescapable aspect of human history, which operates within a nation-state structure. Being a nation-centered ideology, it has become an important factor in the process of development and nation building. As an instrument of nation building, nationalism remains part of human thought through which national aspirations, values, and ideas are expressed. It is a means of inculcating national interest in the minds of citizens; a means of suppressing ethnocentricism and of generating loyalty to the nation. Nationalism fosters national integration and promotes political, economic, and social growth. While theoretically nationalism may be abstract and its definition unsuitable to some conditions, its practical application may produce unity among the citizens of a nation.

The emergence of nationalism in political history can be traced to Europe, especially England, in the nineteenth century. According to Boyd Shafer, "any use of the word nationalism . . . before the eighteenth century is probably anachronistic."[6] The Age of Enlightenment contributed to the growing patriotic or national interest that led to the birth of the Italian and German nations in the second half of the nineteenth century, and the growth of intellectualism also encouraged the spread of nationalism. Max Skidmore traced the rise of nationalism to the French Revolution that began in 1789. He argued that France became a nation-state when power shifted from the king to the nation.[7] Since its rise, nationalism has consistently played a prominent role in influencing French political ideologies.

In Africa, the concept did not appear until the late nineteenth or early twentieth century and it was used to cover a wide range of ideas and expressions. It was used to express patriotism, loyalty, or national consciousness. It was also used as an instrument to liberate people from foreign rule or a means of promoting national identification. In some cases, nationalism emphasizes sentimental attachment to territory, which may result in border disputes, a problem that Nigeria has been dealing with for a long time.

Ali Mazrui distinguished "national consciousness" from "nationalism." While national consciousness is a "sense of a shared national identity," nationalism is "a more assertive or more defensive degree of that consciousness."[8] This is important because nationalism not only implies a common origin but also the sharing of common identity. Shafer contended that "nationalism" might be used to denote "that sentiment unifying a group of people who have a real or imagined common historical experience and a common aspiration to live together as a separate group in the future."[9] Shafer's idea corresponds with Hapsburg rule in parts of Europe.[10] Three elements apply to the Nigerian situation. First, the "sentiment of unifying a group of people"; second, "a real historical experience" of colonialism; and third, "a common aspiration to live together." Robert Jordan stated that a nationalism that unites diverse groupings of peoples "springs from their desire to live together within a common political system. But a nationalism which divides peoples into majority and minority groupings is born out of mutual fear of what will happen if they remain together."[11] In the Nigerian situation, the concept of a "common aspiration to live together" was not mutually agreed by the numerous communities but imposed by the British colonial power. The British drew the present political map of Nigeria, which led to the birth of nationhood and the genesis of a national identity. In Nigeria, the fear of monopoly of power by the major ethnic groups and the marginalization of the minority has proven Jordan right.

Max Skidmore further pointed out that "nationalism was compatible with virtually any culture or any political system."[12] This is relevant in Nigeria where different political structures existed before the incursion of the Europeans. Reference can be made to Hausa nationalism, Igbo nationalism, or Yoruba nationalism. Clearly, nationalistic sentiments cannot be completely free from ethnocentrism but at the same time, nationalism does not necessarily encourage unhealthy rivalry. Nationalism attempts to purge the nation of potential weaknesses and elements of disunity and therefore works toward empowering the people and the smooth running of a democratic government.

Unlike Britain, where James Coleman argued that the modern nation-state was attained through technology or industrialization,[13] the process of achieving nationhood in France, Italy, Germany, and Eastern Europe was, conducted by violent means. In contrast, the Nigerian nationalist struggles during the colonial period were not bloody. The mechanisms through which nationalism was expressed and propagated included powerful speeches, pungent articles in papers, pamphlets, and magazines, and strong delegations to Britain. Aided by printing technology, Nigerians founded newspapers such as the *Lagos Weekly Record*, the *Nigerian Chronicle*, the *Nigerian Pioneer*, the *Nigerian Times,* and the *West African Pilot* to express their nationalistic opinions to their colonial masters.[14] They countered the Europeans' erroneous assumption that Africans were not capable of self-government.

The concept of nationalism began to receive much attention in Nigeria during the interwar years (1920-1939) as a reaction to the economic and political realities of the period. It did not appear that the nationalists accomplished much. Their struggle was not based on self-rule because, considering the strong colonial control and the lack of social unity among the various societies, it was inconceivable that a homogenous nation could evolve. For example, in 1922, Bishop Alfred Jones declared that it would be many generations before Africans could be ready for any form of autonomy and that cooperation between the white and the black races was the true road to independence.[15] Nationalist activities were restricted to urban centers and to a small group of people. From the colonial point of view, as represented by Sir Hugh Clifford (governor of Nigeria, 1919-1925), the early nationalists were "a handful of gentlemen drawn from a half-dozen coast towns."[16] Another colonial official described them as "unreliable, ill-educated, undisciplined, lacking in integrity, self-control and respect for authority of any kind, 'unfitted to hold posts of trust and responsibility where integrity and loyalty are essential'"[17] because they demanded more participation in government.

The formation of the Pan-African Movement led by Edward Blyden (1832-1912), who advocated "Africa for the Africans," Marcus Garvey (1885-1940), and W.E.B. Du Bois (1868-1963) provided a stimulus for African nationalists.[18] In the Pan-African Congress of 1919 held in Paris, fifty-seven people attended, with emphasis being placed on Africans participating in government and on the idea that Africa should be ruled by the consent of its people. Subsequent meetings in 1921, 1923, 1927, and 1945 similarly focused on democracy and self-rule for Africans. Chief Samuel Akintola was one of the Nigerians who attended the 1945 meeting.[19]

In the vanguard of the political struggles were nationalists such as Herbert Macaulay, H. O. Davies, Ernest Ikoli, Ladipo Solanke, Dr. J. C. Vaughn, Dr. Nnamdi Azikiwe, and Chief Obafemi Awolowo, who were the precursors of modern Nigerian nationalism. Although E. A. Ayandele described the educated elite as collaborators with the British and co-exploiters of the unlettered masses, their contributions to the emergence of Nigeria as an independent nation cannot be completely ignored.[20] The actions of the nationalists included mass mobilization and the creation of political awareness among the people through the formation of economic, professional, and ethnic associations. Through the organizations and associations, nationalism flourished within and outside Nigeria. At this point, according to John Mackintosh, the nationalists had become a powerful group that put pressure on the British government to grant self-rule to Nigeria.[21] Ladipo Solanke, the founder of the West African Students Union, emerged as "an outstanding figure in the nationalist awakening in Nigeria."[22] To gain national support, Solanke solicited the cooperation of traditional rulers such as the Alake of Abeokuta and the Emir of Kano.

Although the nationalists provided leadership, the formation of political parties remained grounded on ethnic affiliation. In the north, the leader of the Northern Peoples' Congress (NPC), Sir Ahmadu Bello, the Sardauna of Sokoto, claimed that the southern parties were merely the followers of prominent individuals.[23] This situation weakened the hope for a united and vibrant Nigeria that would be devoid of ethnic loyalty. Thus polarized in political ideologies and agenda, independent Nigeria entered into an era of continuing segmentation.

ETHNICITY AND THE EMERGENCE OF A NATION-STATE

The word "tribes," which the Europeans used to describe African peoples, is derogatory, inappropriate, and unacceptable.[24] Although numerous and coming from varying historical and cultural backgrounds, African peoples are better referred to as "ethnic groups." Paul Mercier described an ethnic group as "a closed group, descended from a common ancestor, or, more generally, having the same origin, sharing a homogeneous culture, and speaking a common language."[25] While members of an ethnic group share many common traits, political ideology may not be one of them. For example, the Yoruba have the three elements (common ancestor, homogeneous culture, and common language) but they evolved autonomous political structures such as the Oyo, Ijebu, Ekiti, and Egba kingdoms. As ethnicity constitutes a form of identity, the *ebi* (family) system of the Yoruba served as a symbol of unity. It should be added, however, that kinship relations also failed to prevent warfare as revealed by the Yoruba Civil Wars of the nineteenth century and the rivalry among the Hausa states. In modern times, intraethnic conflicts as demonstrated in the Ife-Modakeke episodes have proven that kinship affiliation may not necessarily foster unity.

Made up of about 250 ethnic groups with numerous languages, Nigeria fits into the paradigm of ethnic, cultural, and religious diversity. Each of the groups whether large or small distinctly displays a rich historical and cultural background. Some, such as the Bini, Yoruba, and Hausa, evolved powerful centralized political structures; others, such as the Igbo, adopted a gerontocratic form of government. The formation of Nigeria as a country encompassing many ethnic and political groups was carried out to satisfy the administrative needs of the British. Since then, Nigeria has been besieged by ethnic conflicts,[26] characterized by the Nigerian Civil War (1967-1970), which threatened the political and economic development as well as the national unity of the country. Ethnic affiliation has been used not only to compete for the allocation of the nation's wealth, but also to mobilize political interests. The deterioration of ethnic relations increased conflicts and violence.[27]

Another divisive element was and still is religion. The displacement of traditional religions by Islam and Christianity brought about religious differentiation and conflicts that have continuously hindered the processes of unity. In his discussion of the causes of internal conflict, Michael E. Brown pointed out that "the driving forces behind these conflicts [include] the 'ancient hatreds' that many ethnic and religious groups have for each other."[28] It is believed that the war in Serbia between Serbs, Croats, and Muslims was incited by "age-long animosities."[29] The Nigerian experience since colonialism fits into this model of long-standing ethnic and religious conflict, between the Muslim north and the Christian south.

The British respected and preserved the Sokoto Caliphate structure because it suited their administrative system. They even created two artificial emirates in Borgu, which was not a Muslim region. Furthermore, they prevented the Christian missionaries from the south from spreading their religion to the north. Thus according to Ayandele, "the British conquest of Northern Nigeria was a cultural and religious compromise. The compromise was that Islam would be left intact whilst the infidel British exploited the economic resources of the country."[30] This indicated that the British played a politics of convenience, creating an atmosphere that became inimical to the national unity of Nigeria.

After the amalgamation of the Southern and Northern Protectorates in 1914, Lugard proceeded to create the Nigerian Council of three members as an advisory body in 1916.

The membership reflected the favor that Lugard gave to the north because of the three members, two came from the north—the Sultan of Sokoto and the Emir of Kano—while only the Alaafin of Oyo was chosen from the south. That council was short-lived. Unarguably, the British favored the Islamic north against the Christian south. Ethnic segregation was introduced into the army when Lugard recruited more soldiers from the north than the south.[31] Subsequent governors followed Lugard's style of segregational administration. Nigerians realized the danger of the administrative games that the British were playing but the more they struggled, the more they became entangled in ethnic consciousness, and the more they drifted apart. In 1943, H. O. Davies, a nationalist, advocated togetherness in a poem in which he stated that

> We've had our dose of squabbles, lies and hate,
> And cursed each other worse than pagans do,
> We've all been spiteful and revengeful too!
> Let's learn to appreciate each other's worth,
> And give to everyone his rightful due.
> Together pull for country of our birth.
> Nigeria will be prosperous, free and now.[32]

Taking advantage of the disunity among Nigerians, Sir Arthur Richards came up with the idea of decentralizing the administration of Nigeria. This led to the division of Nigeria into three regions in the constitution of 1946. According to Arthur Richards,

> I do not think that Nigeria is yet a sufficient coherent whole, whether in the political, social or economic sphere to be capable of immediate and full self-government. The new Constitution is designed to encourage the sense of unified interest beyond the realm of tribal [ethnic] jealousies, and to provide the training for ever swifter advance towards self-government.[33]

The objectives of the constitution were to "promote the unity of Nigeria; to provide adequately within that unity for the diverse elements which make up the country; and to secure greater participation by Africans in the discussion of their own affairs."[34] However, nationalists indicated that because the Northern Region was larger in size and population than the two southern regions combined, the constitution could not achieve the intended goals. The regions were more powerful than the federal administration and therefore the foundation for national integration became weak. Although the establishment of a central administration was possible, the integration of the disparate ethnic groups and societies was not successful. Thus the Richards Constitution neither provided self-rule nor promoted ethnic unity.

There was uneven development in the three regions as indicated by Sir Abubakar Tafawa Balewa, who declared that "Nigeria is one country in name, but the Regions have reached different stages in development."[35] In his *Path to Nigerian Freedom*, Chief Obafemi Awolowo addressed the issue of multiethnic composition by stating that "Nigeria is not a nation. It is a mere geographical expression."[36] Awolowo was correct in that before European imperialism and colonization, Nigeria did not exist as a political entity, but, as Funso Afolayan has indicated, the ethnic and cultural "differences and distinctions should not be exaggerated" because the "societies and groups were not self-contained and exclusive units."[37] However, Nigeria as a nation-state emerged with colonialism. If Nigerians had allowed national integration to take place, the gulf of ethnic or religious differences would not have been so glaring because national interest would have taken precedence over sectional issues.

The British artificially created Nigeria as a nation-state but it was impossible for them to enforce the spirit of nationalism or to forge unity among the diverse ethnic groups. Toyin Falola indicated in *Violence in Nigeria* that

> Colonial Nigeria was nothing more than an artificially constructed agglomeration of diverse ethnici-

ties and other loosely united groups. Built by conquest and subjugation, the state never acquired any enduring legitimacy or trust from the various indigenous groups and nationalities. Older loyalties to kings, gods, and religions continued until the end of colonial rule in 1960.[38]

The divisions among Nigerians worked in favor of the British government. The Action Group (AG) was led by Obafemi Awolowo with its stronghold among the Yoruba; the National Council of Nigeria and the Cameroons (NCNC), founded and led by Dr. Nnamdi Azikiwe, was Igbo controlled; and the Northern People's Congress under Sir Ahmadu Bello held sway in the north.[39] Each ethnic group gave its support to "the son of the soil" and the pattern continues to feature in the formation of political parties today. Religiously, southern-based parties were regarded as Christian while the NPC was Muslim.

POSTINDEPENDENCE POLITICAL EXPERIENCES

The preparations for independence began in earnest in 1958 and were followed by the elections of 1959. The results of the elections clearly reflected the tripartite political division of Nigeria.

Table 1: 1959 Election Results

Party	North	East	West	Lagos	Total
NPC	142	--	--	--	142
NCNC/NEPU	8 (NEPU)	58	21	2	89
AG	24	14	34	1	73
Independent	--	--	8	--	8
Total	174	72	63	3	312

None of the three main parties was able to gain an overall majority, as a result of which a coalition agreement was reached between the NPC and NCNC, leaving the AG as the opposition party. While Abubakar Tafawa Balewa became the prime minister, Dr. Nnamdi Azikwe became the governor-general in 1960. Thus at independence in 1960, Nigeria inherited political, economic, and social problems and divisions that have continued to dominate the country's political history. In spite of the existence of a coalition, there was still evidence of lack of unity. The euphoria of independence was short-lived because the ethnic cleavages that had been created by the colonial administration were not easy to resolve. In addition to the lack of a strong nationalist spirit, incessant ethnic conflicts helped to dash the hopes of integration and national development in the post-independence era. Understandably, nation building is a slow process that requires the cooperation of all the ethnic groups. To alter the colonial ideology of "divide and rule," a new attitude and a new political orientation have to be developed. Nigerians have to imbibe the culture of unity in diversity.

The domination of the south by the north at the federal level created some problems and tensions. First, crises erupted in 1962 over the census. It was alleged that the population of the north was overestimated. Second, the coalition of the NPC and NCNC at the federal level did not work out well because of conspicuous and conflicting characteristics and programs that were difficult to harmonize. For instance, while the NPC was "regionalist, Muslim, and aristocratic, the [NCNC] was nationalist, Christian, and populist."[40] Third, the southern politicians had received Western education while most of the northern leaders had received Islamic education. These differences made it difficult for the NPC and NCNC to work together effectively and efficiently. This served as a warning of the national disaster that was soon to follow. Fourth, chaos erupted in the Western House of Assembly in 1962 and the prime minister, Sir Abubakar Tafawa Balewa, was alleged to have collaborated with some members of the House to destroy, disrupt, and discredit the laudable programs of the Action Group (the ruling party in the West).[41] The most badly disrupted program was free primary education, which had enabled the Yoruba to advance in Western education. After allegations of corruption were made, the federal government supported Chief Samuel Akintola as the Governor of the Western Region against Chief Awolowo. As a result, there were internal political disturbances in the region and increasing hostility between southerners and northerners.[42] Ultimately, in January 1966, the military struck in a bloody coup, which ushered in Major-General Aguiyi Ironsi, a southerner and an Igbo, whose period of rule lasted only six months. In the counter-coup that occurred in July 1966, Ironsi was assassinated and a Christian from the Middle Belt, Lieutenant-Colonel (later General) Yakubu Gowon, was installed as the head of state. Southerners were unhappy that leadership went back to the north. Nigeria shifted from democracy to military dictatorship. Within a short time the military ushered in new political experiences characterized by decrees and stringent socioeconomic measures. Political thinkers and observers agree that under successive military regimes, the concept of nationalism was suppressed while that of ethnicity gained firmer roots. The situation was exacerbated by the unbalanced composition of the military. Claiming to have usurped power in the national interest, the military has not conscientiously pursued policies and programs that would allow intermingling of ethnic groups within the country. That would have been a positive and impelling force toward national growth but instead, Nigeria was plunged further into national chaos.

The Nigerian Civil War (1967-1970) was heavily infused with ethnic connotations. The conflict between the Hausa and Igbo clearly demonstrated the cleavage that existed in Nigerian society. The war was not fought for the Igbo or Hausa alone; it was fought for the whole country. The whole story is too complex and lengthy for a thorough analysis here; suffice it to say that in all respects the civil war revealed the delicate balance on which the Nigerian political system rested. The civil war was only an incident in the much larger picture of ethnic separatism, rivalry, and conflicts over power. Lieutenant-Colonel Odumegwu Ojukwu believed that, as the most senior officer, he was supposed to be made the head of state. Refusing this position was tantamount to marginalizing the Igbo people.[43]

That episode accelerated the severance of interethnic relationships in the early years of independence. The heavy loss of life, the huge destruction of property, and the untold damage done to the political system has required years of reconciliation, rehabilitation, and reconstruction. To demonstrate the height of ethnic impairment that arose from the civil war, N. U. Akpan quoted an elderly Igbo woman as saying, "as far as what the Hausa have done to our people is concerned, we shall neither love, nor forgive, nor forget. If that is what will send us to hell, then we are prepared."[44] This single voice represented the general sentiment and feeling of the time. A broken heart does not think of forgiveness or unity and even if forgiveness is possible, it is difficult to forget. Nevertheless, measures have to be carried out to allow effective progress and national unity. That was why the federal government embarked on programs that promoted reconciliation, rehabilitation, and reconstruction.

General Gowon was ousted in 1975 when General Murtala Mohammed came to power, only to be assassinated in 1976, General Olusegun Obasanjo became the head of state. In October 1979 when General Olusegun Obasanjo (a southerner, Yoruba, and Christian) handed over political power to Alhaji Shehu Shagari (a northerner and Muslim), there ensued a dispute that almost propelled the nation into another round of ethnic confrontation. Chief Obafemi Awolowo challenged the declaration of Alhaji Shehu Shagari as the winner of the presidential election. The judicial scuffle over what constituted a two-thirds majority dragged on for a long time but ultimately ended in favor of Shehu Shagari.

THE 1990S AS A DECADE OF TURMOIL

Nigeria has not enjoyed a long period of democratic rule because there have been frequent military coups.[45] Since independence in 1960, Nigeria has elected only two heads of state—Shehu Shagari in 1979 and Olusegun Obasanjo in 1999. Rather than being a period of consolidation and movement toward national unity, the 1990s turned out to be a decade of political turmoil, ethnic conflicts, and religious violence. It was a period Toyin Falola has described as "the Age of Warfare."[46]

When General Ibrahim Babangida ousted General Muhammadu Buhari in 1985, he promised to return Nigeria to democratic rule in 1987, but the date was later changed to 1993. Not long after assuming office, Babangida entrenched his dictatorship and his northern factor came into greater play. Perhaps the most explosive example of ethnic problems in Babangida's era was the presidential election of June 1993. The election was peacefully and successfully conducted but in spite of this success, as acknowledged by international observers, Gen. Babangida annulled the results under the pretext of accusations of corruption but more accurately because of the ethnic factor. Chief Moshood Abiola, a Yoruba and a Muslim convincingly won the elections against Alhaji Bahir Tofa, a Hausa and a Muslim. With the annulment of the election results, the unity of Nigeria was at stake.

The Yoruba interpreted Babangida's action as marginalization and many of them called for "the balkanisation of the country."[47] This incident provided an opportunity for southerners to describe the Lugard's amalgamation of 1914 as "an accident of history," or an "unholy alliance," which had to be dissolved.[48] Dare Babarinsa of *Tell* magazine described Nigeria as "a nation in distress," and Asikpo Essien-Ibok from Akwa Ibom State reiterated that there must be social, economic, and political justice for Nigeria to remain as a country.[49] In order to placate the Yoruba, Babangida chose Chief Ernest Shonekan as the chairman of the interim government. After three months, Gen. Sani Abacha seized power and Nigeria was thrown into another round of political, economic, and social turmoil.

The highhandedness of the military regime in the 1990s remains indelible in the political history of Nigeria. Abacha's regime was characterized by indiscriminate arrests of journalists and government critics. As part of his repressive measures, on November 10, 1995, Abacha had Ken Saro-Wiwa and eight other Ogoni activists hanged for protesting against the Shell Oil Company for destroying their land and livelihood.[50] As in the annulment of the election results, the Ogoni people saw the execution of their leaders as marginalization and social injustice perpetrated by the Abacha government. After this episode, international observers became more critical of Abacha's lack of respect for life and of his flagrant violation of fundamental human rights. The incident almost shattered all expectations of a strong united Nigeria and it tarnished the international image of the country.

Tensions were high and Nigeria was in political, economic, and social disarray when, in spite of all the hardship he subjected the people to, Abacha prepared to turn himself into a civilian president. The editor of Vanguard Newspapers aptly described the political and ethnic warfare of the 1990s in the following words:

> The guns are still in Warri and the Niger Delta region. Ijaws versus Itsekiris; Ijaws versus Ogonis killed themselves and were in turn killed by the state. They soak the creeks in blood, they torch their assets with fire of hatred! Move upland to the cradle of [the] Yoruba race, Ile-Ife. The bloodletting between the Ifes and the Modakekes has left hundreds dead, thousands maimed [51] and billion-naira assets wasted. The war is far from being over. Hoodlums have been replaying the Niger Delta creek war in the jungles of Ifeland, since August 1997. What of the Jukuns against the Kutebs? These reflect hundreds of our new "civil wars," North, East, West, South, etc. waiting to be exploited for partisan politics. How do we save the fatherland and remove the best attraction for military adventurers to return to power if and when they quit power in May 1999? How do we stop the carnage?[52]

The sudden death of General Abacha on June 8, 1998, was a turning point in the recent political history of Nigeria. His death marked the demise of dictatorship and the chance to usher in democracy. General Abdulsalami Abubakar succeeded Abacha on June 9, 1998, and he moved toward national integration by releasing some political prisoners, including Olusegun Obasanjo and Olu Falae (both of whom ran for the presidency in 1999). Abubakar pursued other wide-ranging political, economic, and social reforms with the objective of returning the country to democracy. He was determined to redeem the image of the military as well as that of the country. On the international scene, he won the support of some powerful democratic countries such as Britain and America. Internally, he reduced political tension with an approach like that of Nelson Mandela. Abubakar's style of governance was politics without bitterness, which helped to reinforce the principle of nationalism and reduce ethnic antagonism.

Expectations were high that Abubakar would release Chief Moshood Abiola and June 12 would become a reality. However, the sudden death of Abiola in July 1998 triggered off violent reactions, especially among the Yoruba, who had claimed that the results of the elections of June 12, 1993, were authentic and therefore should be accepted and Abiola should become the president of Nigeria. The violent demonstrations that followed the announcement of Abiola's death clearly illustrated the Yorubas' continuing mistrust of the military and of the northerners. With the death of Abiola, the realization of June 12 became impossible.

Gen. Obasanjo, who had been released from prison, became a presidential candidate in the process of returning Nigeria to democratic rule. He won the election and was installed on May 29, 1999. In August 1999, shortly after Obasanjo was inaugurated as the president of Nigeria, various ethnic and religious conflicts erupted that threatened the nascent democracy. For instance, in the ethnic clashes between the Ijaw and Ilaje, hundreds of people were killed. There has been a mixture of ethnic and religious clashes as illustrated by the Kafanchan episode of May 1999. In opposition to the dominance of Islam, revolts broke out among the indigenous people, mostly Christians or traditional worshipers, against the Muslims. Like other occurrences, the Kafanchan outbreak was a struggle for identity, and self-determination. In a week of violence that began in Sagamu, Ogun State, about one hundred people (mostly Hausa) were killed. In retaliation, the Hausa in Kano launched an onslaught on the Yoruba in which about one hundred people were also killed. The killings revealed the insecurity of life and brought about ethnic demographic movements. The ethnic and religious violence at the beginning of the year 2000 claimed thousands of lives. Before the idea of introducing the Sharia'a was dropped in Zamfara and Kaduna, hundreds of people had been killed. Bloody riots erupted between Christians and Muslims in February and May 2000. Clearly, some people hide under the cloak of religion to perpetrate violence. In the Sharia'a states, such as Sokoto, Niger, Zamfara, Kano, Katsina, Jigawa, Yobe, and Borno, peaceful ethnic relations were destabilized. In another outbreak of interethnic violence between the Yoruba and Hausa in October 2000, over one hundred people were killed and about 20,000 were forced to evacuate their homes. All these ethnoreligious conflicts encourage a rethinking of the unity of Nigeria. They also threaten to destroy the present democratic system. Tixo Tokuta declared that Nigeria was "in a state of war."[53] No nation has ever thrived or triumphed in ethnic and religious warfare. International organizations such as the Commonwealth and United Nations and the world community expressed grave concerns over the ethnic animosity and religious intolerance that have pervaded Nigerian politics and social interactions.

NATIONAL INTEGRATION AS A CHALLENGE

It is clear that Nigeria has not been able to find a lasting solution to the problem of ethnic and religious conflicts or the problem of national integration.[54] Unity is an instrument of social engineering as well as a means of fostering the political stability and economic growth of Nigeria. It is an important driving force that can intensify the growth and development of democracy, which Nigerians want to enjoy after a long period of military rule. In spite of many obstacles to unity, Nigerians want to build a great nation that will regain international respect, regain leadership in African politics, and live up to the slogan "Giant of Africa." Taking advantage of unity in adversity will increase the chances of improvement and collective responsibility.

Cooperative effort among ethnic groups is a powerful means to remove excessive control by a domineering group. For example, the Eritreans united first against Italy and later against Ethiopia. The people of Kenya, although led by the Kikuyu, formed the Land and Freedom Army (which the British called Mau Mau) to resist the continued acquisition of their land. At independence, Jomo Kenyatta (1963-1978) was able to integrate the people of Kenya by structuring the educational system through the integration of all ethnic groups. He called on his people to underplay ethnic divisions and uphold national unity.[55] When Nelson Mandela came to power in South Africa, he declared to South Africans that "we are starting an era of hope, of reconciliation, of nation building."[56] Under a democratic government, Nigerians can rededicate themselves to reconstruction, rehabilitation, re-conciliation, and nation building.

Looking at the political history of Nigeria, it is apparent that national integration has become a challenge and a task that involves the participation of all Nigerians. While it is impossible to get rid of ethnic diversity, and cultural fusion is totally impracticable, the advantages of diversity can be utilized to the benefit of the country. The problems that governments have been facing in terms of domestic and foreign policies can be solved partly by putting national interests ahead of ethnic divisions.

Openness, respect for other ethnic groups, and cooperation in the name of national interests are some of the key ingredients for a united, vibrant, and progressive country. Frontline nationalists should utilize their foresight and experience to boost a national spirit and ethnic integration. For Nigeria to remain a country to reckon with in world politics, a new framework has to be evolved to increase ethnic cohesion and harmony and to repair the damaged internal and external relations and image of Nigeria. Building a greater Nigeria is the task of every Nigerian. Ethnic criticism or antagonism is not a means to unity and no ethnic group can exonerate itself from the troubles that Nigeria has experienced since 1960.

In his inauguration speech, President Obasanjo described May 29, 1999, as the "beginning of a genuine renaissance" in the political history of Nigeria. If Nigeria is to achieve this bridging the ethnic and social gap is the task that has to be seriously addressed. One positive measure taken to encourage integration is demilitarization, to guard against the political ambition of the soldiers. Nigeria has suffered severely and too long at the hands of dictatorial and rapacious military juntas. It is time to enjoy an enduring democracy. According to Seymour Lipset, if demilitarization is "the struggle of various groups . . . against one another and against the group that controls the state, then demilitarization levels the playing field by increasing the participatory power of countervailing groups in society."[57] One ethnic group should not dominate either the military or Nigerian politics, and that has been a major problem contributing to disunity and instability.

CONCLUSION

Nigeria realizes the problem of nationalism and ethnic rivalry. Several steps have been taken to achieve national integration. For instance, the quota system was evolved partly to recognize and cater to the needs of all the ethnic groups through equal representation, and partly to reduce the domination by any region or ethnic group of the allocation of offices or economic resources. Using education as a tool for achieving national integration, successive federal governments have established, funded, and controlled "unity schools" or federal government high schools or colleges. This approach has not been fully successful, but it is a positive approach in a multiethnic society. Some Nigerian languages are also widely taught in schools with the purpose of creating a sense of national awareness and unity in school children.

It is time to pay greater attention to the inculcation of a strong nationalist spirit in younger people. Nationalism is a useful device for forging social and political unity and for building a powerful and cohesive nation. Inclusive nationalism (where every ethnic group is represented) brings progress and integration but exclusive nationalism (which marginalizes) destroys integration and creates ethnic, political, and social tension. Inclusive nationalism strives for equity by recognizing minority groups. At the same time, Nigeria cannot ignore the ethnically diverse basis on which its early political structures were founded. But strength lies in unity. Rather than concentrating on the dysfunctional aspects of ethnic diversity, its advantages should be articulated to promote amicable and lasting interethnic relations. Ethnicity can be employed to accomplish national growth and integration.[58] As a result, Nigeria will be in a good position to pursue sound policies that will bring about much-needed development.

Nigerians realize that conflicts and violence are normal phenomena in the process of nation building. While violence divides, resolution unites. Conflict resolution is a constructive civil mechanism for preventing the country from being torn into pieces. Ali Mazrui rightly says that "conflict resolution may not be a sufficient condition for national integration, but it is certainly a necessary one."[59] Conflict resolution is therefore an essential ingredient of national development and national integration. By constant dialoguing, with a deliberate effort to understand each other, all the ethnic or conflicting groups can develop a capacity not only to discover their areas of compatibility but also to work together in the national interest and in unity. Such dialogues will also promote a bold determination to rid the mind of ethnic prejudice. They will lead to respect for other people's ideas, values, and aspirations.

Peaceful coexistence remains essential for political stability and economic prosperity. For Nigeria to regain its former image and international integrity, it has to grow in positive dimensions. The continuing ethnic friction is a kiss of death for the nation. The federal government should rise to the task of repairing, rebuilding, and renewing Nigeria in order to make it a better place to live in. To ensure a radical departure from the past structure of ethnic politics and propaganda, and to achieve enduring integration, Nigerians should incorporate nationalism and ethnic cooperation into their political culture.

One hopes that leaders and politicians will permit national interest to override ethnic consciousness. In his "Myth of Northern Domination," Felix Edjeren pointed out that "peace among ethnic nationalities would only be possible when we become willing to drop some of our inward-looking tribal [ethnic] wisdom in favour of a broad nationalist outlook."[60] In other words, the minds of Nigerians have to be decolonized from ethnic nationalism. Okwudiba Nnoli also suggested that steps should be taken toward "deconcentration and decentralization of state power to check ethnic conflicts and limit their negative effects on development."[61] Equity in the sharing of federal jobs, national resources, and social amenities will promote national integration. According to Alex I. Ekwueme,

> National integration can be fostered by deliberately attempting to evolve a policy of accommodation, compromise, give and take, and resolution with a view to giving every part of the country a sense of belonging and a sense of nationality no matter how democratic it may appear to do otherwise.[62]

Nigeria has all the resources (human, natural, and mineral) to build a virile and sustainable country. It is, however, necessary to harness these resources, as it is crucial to forge unity to achieve national integration. Nigeria also needs a change from a culture of violence and corruption to one of national consciousness and peaceful interethnic relations. In order to invest in the future unity of the country, each ethnic or religious group should be recognized and respected. Cooperation and not competition will help to build a vibrant nation.

The issue at stake now is how long shall Nigeria wait to put its house in order? Fragmentation into three regions has created both geopolitical and ethnic problems, which leaves Nigeria to find an alternative political framework that will generate enduring national integration. The solution may be found in a renewed form of nationalism, a renewed form of north-south cooperation and collaboration, and a renewed form of political understanding. Ethnic cleavages cannot create a united and strong nation. Equity and political power distribution will help to prevent one ethnic group from dominating others as well as prevent ethnic marginalization. Nigeria also needs to strengthen political education at the grass roots. These measures perhaps constituted the objectives of the 1979 constitution that "sought to guard against the domination of the country's affairs by one or more ethnic groups by incorporating provisions which would promote national unity and reflect 'the federal character' of the new Nigeria."[63] But with the demise of the Second Republic in 1983, the constitution was discarded. While the potential of ethnic rivalry to destroy a nation should not be under-estimated, neither should the power of ethnic collaboration for national integration.

NOTES

1. For integrative and disintegrative nationalism in Europe and West Africa, see Robert S. Jordan, *Government and Power in West Africa* (Benin City, Nigeria: Ethiope Publishing Corporation, 1978), 10-14. While Jordan used Britain as an example of integrative nationalism, he referred to the tensions in Nigeria that culminated in the 1967-1970 civil war as an example of how nationalist movements including various ethnic groupings can cause fragmentation. On the issue of violence in modern history, see William Pfaff, *The Wrath of Nations: Civilization and the Furies of Nationalism* (New York: Simon and Schuster, 1993), 13.
2. Michael Crowder, *The Story of Nigeria* (London: Faber and Faber, 1966), 259.

3. J. A. Atanda, "Indirect Rule in Yorubaland," *Tarikh,* 3 (3), 1979, 16-28.
4. During the colonial period, several constitutions were adopted upon which the colony operated. There was the Clifford Constitution in 1922, the Bourdillon Constitution of 1939, the Richards Constitution of 1946, the Macpherson Constitution of 1951, and the Lyttlelton Constitution of 1954. Each of the constitutions was intended to move Nigeria toward self-government.
5. Fred W. Riggs, "The Para-Modern Context of Ethnic Nationalism," http://www2.hawaii.edu/~fredr/7-cip1a.htm.
6. Byod C. Shafer, *Nationalism: Myth and Reality* (New York: Harcourt, Brace & World Inc., 1955), 5.
7. Max J. Skidmore, *Ideologies: Politics in Action*, second edition (New York: Harcourt Brace Jovanovich College Publishers, 1993), 258.
8. Ali A. Mazrui, "Pluralism and National Integration," in Leo Kuper and M. G. Smith, eds., *Pluralism in Africa* (Berkeley: University of California Press, 1969), 336.
9. Shafer, *Nationalism*, 10.
10. Benedict Anderson, *Imagined Communities: Reflections on the Origin and Spread of Nationalism* (London: Verso, 1991).
11. Jordan, *Government and Power*, 13.
12. Skidmore, *Ideologies*, 153.
13. James Coleman, "Nationalism in Tropical Africa," in P. J. McEwan and R. B. Sutcliffe, eds., *The Study of Africa* (London: Methuen, 1965), 160.
14. A. Adu Boahen, *African Perspectives on Colonialism* (Baltimore, MD: Johns Hopkins University Press, 1987), 68.
15. *Leisure Hours*, April 1922, 52, cited in E. A. Ayandele, *The Educated Elite in the Nigerian Society* (Ibadan: Ibadan University Press, 1974), 67.
16. Crowder, *The Story of Nigeria*, 255.
17. Nigerian National Archives Ibadan (NNAI) CSO/26/2, vol. 1, "Memorandum by Director of Education Northern Provinces," 1927, cited in Ayandele, *The Educated Elite*, 65.
18. Boahen, *African Perspectives*, 21-22.
19. J. D. Anderson, *West Africa and East Africa in the Nineteenth and Twentieth Centuries* (London: Heinemann Educational Books, 1972), 160-163.
20. Ayandele, *The Educated Elite*.
21. John Mackintosh, *Nigerian Government and Politics* (Evanston, IL: Northwestern University Press, 1966), 21.

22. James S. Coleman, *Nigeria: Background to Nationalism* (Berkeley: University of California Press, 1965), 207.
23. Sir Ahmadu Bello, *My Life* (Cambridge, Cambridge University Press, 1962), 111.
24. William Tordoff, *Government and Politics in Africa* (Bloomington: Indiana University Press, second edition, 1993), 72-73.
25. Paul Mercier, "On the Meaning of 'Tribalism' in Black Africa," in Pierre L. Van Den Berghe, ed., *Africa: Social Problems of Change and Conflict* (San Francisco: Chandler Publishing Company, 1965), 484.
26. Ugbana Okpu, *Ethnic Minority Problems in Nigerian Politics: 1960-1965* (Stockholm: LiberTryck AB, 1977), 3.
27. Okwudiba Nnoli, *Ethnicity and Development in Nigeria* (Warwick, England: UNRISD, The Centre for Research in Ethnic Relations, 1996).
28. Michael E. Brown, "The Causes of Internal Conflict: An Overview," in Michael E. Brown et al., eds., *Nationalism and Ethnic Conflict* (Cambridge, MA: MIT Press, 1997), 3-25.
29. Brown, "The Causes of Conflict," 3.
30. Ayandele, *The Educated Elite*, 64.
31. J. Gus Liebenow, *African Politics: Crisis and Challenges* (Bloomington: Indiana University Press, 1986), 246.
32. H. O. Davies, "Let's pull Together," *West African Pilot*, November 4, 1943.
33. Legislative Council Debates, March 20, 1947, 6-8, as cited in G. O. Olusanya, *The Second World War and Politics in Nigeria 1939-1953* (Lagos: University of Lagos, Evans Brothers Limited, 1973), 83.
34. "Progress towards Independence in Nigeria: A Review," in P.J.M. McEwan, ed., *Twentieth-Century Africa* (London: Oxford University Press, 1968), 53.
35. "Extract from a Speech by Sir Abubakar Tafawa Balewa on the Review of the Constitution," in G. O. Olusanya, ed., "Documents and Speeches on the Nationalist Movement in Nigeria," unpublished manuscript, 131-133.
36. Obafemi Awolowo, *Path to Nigerian Freedom* (London: Faber and Faber, 1947), 194.
37. Funso Afolayan, "Nigeria" A Political Entity and a Society," in Paul A. Beckett and Crawford Young, *Dilemmas of Democracy in Nigeria* (Rochester, N.Y.: University of Rochester Press, 1997), 45-62.

38. Toyin Falola, *Violence in Nigeria: The Crisis of Religious Politics and Secular Ideologies* (Rochester, N.Y.: University of Rochester Press, 1998), 52.
39. A good discussion of the Nigerian political parties during the decolonization period is found in Richard L. Sklar, *Nigerian Political Parties: Power in an Emergent African Nation* (Princeton, N.J.: Princeton University Press, 1963).
40. Helen Chapin, ed., *Nigeria: A Country Study* (Washington, D. C.: Library of Congress, 1992), 48.
41. Robin Hallet, *Africa since 1875: A Modern History* (London: Heinemann, first published 1974, reprinted 1980), 383-384.
42. Anderson, *West Africa and East Africa*, 184-186.
43. In most recent times, the Igbo have claimed to be marginalized, especially when Dr. Alex Ekwueme lost the presidential primary election to Gen. Olusegun Obasanjo (rtd). The Igbo also allege that Obasanjo has not appointed enough Igbo people in his cabinet.
44. Ntieyong U. Akpan, T*he Struggle for Secession 1966-1970* (London: Frank Cass, 1971), xi-xii.
45. Aside from several attempted coups, there have been eight successful ones. Of the thirteen past and present leaders, eight came from the military, including the current president who was formerly an army general.
46. Falola, *Violence in Nigeria*. 193.
47. Philip Oluwole Ukanah and Idowu Samuel, "Echoes of Break-Up," *Sunday Tribune*, August 9, 1998, 9.
48. Ukanah and Samuel, "Echoes of Break-Up."
49. Dare Babarinsa, "Journey to the Unknown," *Tell*, no. 39, October 4, 1993, 10-13.
50. The following people were hanged along with Ken Saro-Wiwa: John Kpuinen, Baribor Bera, Saturday Dobee, Felix Nwate, Nordu Eawo, Paul, Levura, Daniel Gbokoo, and Dr. Barinen Nubari Kiobel.
51. Editorial, *Guardian*, June 4, 1999.
52. This appeared on the home page of the *Vanguard Newspapers*, http://www.vanguardngr.com/vag.htm.
53. Tixo Tokuta, "Deception of a Federation," *Vanguard Newspapers*, http://www.afbis.com/vanguard/pn2-120199.html.
54. Pade Badru, *Imperialism and Ethnic Politics in Nigeria* (Trenton, N.J.: Africa World Press, Inc., 1998), 151-154.

55. R. M. Maxon, "Social and Cultural Changes, " in B. A. Ogot and W. R. Ochieng, *Decolonization and Independence in Kenya* (London: James Currey, 1995), 143.
56. Nancy Gibbs, "Cover Story: Why? The Killing Fields of Rwanda," *Time*, May 16, 1994, 1-4.
57. Gilbert M. Khadiagala, "The Military in Africa's Democratic Transitions: Regional Dimensions," *Africa Today*, January 1, 1995, 1-12.
58. Immanuel Wallerstein, "Ethnicity and National Integration in West Africa" in Van Den Berghe, *Africa: Social Problems of Change*, 472-482.
59. Mazrui, "Pluralism and National Integration," 33-335.
60. Felix Edjeren, "Myth of Northern Domination," ViewPoints, *Vanguard Newspapers*, http://www.afbis.com/vanguard/vp3-180199.html.
61. Nnoli, *Ethnicity and Development*.
62. Alex I. Ekwueme, "Power Shift and National Integration," text of a lecture delivered at Bayero University, Kano, January 15, 1999.
63. Tordoff, *Government and Politics*, 73.

15

POLITICAL ETHNICITY IN WESTERN NIGERIA: CHIEFTAINCY, COMMUNAL IDENTITIES, AND PARTY POLITICS

Olufemi Vaughan

INTRODUCTION

Scholars of African politics generally agree that communalism poses a major obstacle to the political stability of the postcolonial African state. Firmly rooted in a colonial encounter with complex societies, this persistent problem is expressed in the neo-traditional and patrimonial character of the African state and society. Analyses of this recurring problem, expressed through evolving communal identities, must assess the interaction between the formation of modern political institutions and the construction of legitimacy doctrines.

Through a detailed case study of the Yoruba of southwestern Nigeria (one of Africa's most dominant ethnic groups), the present chapter analyzes the interaction between the processes of Nigerian state formation and the conflicting manifestations of communal identities since decolonization in the 1950s. Specifically, the chapter contends that the collective political action engendered by the imposition of liberal democracy intensified the rapid pace of communal identity among the Yoruba people during the democratic transitions of 1951-1966 and 1978-1983. I address three interrelated questions. First, with a view to conceptualizing the dynamic nature of communal identities in Yoruba towns, I show how an imposed federal structure led to paradoxical expressions of pan-ethnic and intra-ethnic collective political action after decolonization. Second, mindful of the absence of viable modern political institutions, I show how in their preoccupation with mobilizing political followings, a political class of career politicians, military administrators, and traditional rulers propagated communal doctrines in local communities. Finally, drawing on a detailed case study of Oyo State (Yorubaland's most prominent area), especially its major city, Ibadan, in the Second Republic,[1] I argue that communal identities were further shaped by the prevailing political alignment that had emerged during the historical moment of decolonization. In short, Yoruba political action was shaped by an array of historical and contemporary sociopolitical forces in the colonial and postcolonial periods. Yoruba communal identities are analyzed in the context of the entrenched ethnoregionalism that emerged out of the struggle for state power in the 1950s. These persistent problems have serious implications not only for the political viability of contemporary Yoruba communities but also for Nigeria's post-independence political stability.

EXPLAINING COMMUNAL IDENTITY AND POLITICS IN YORUBA COMMUNITIES

Studies in communal identity and politics in postcolonial Africa have generally emphasized the intense struggles among the political classes of ethnic groups for the distributive resources of the state. Given the severe centrifugal pressure of political ethnicity, analysts agree that these conflicts have undermined the corporate structure of the postcolonial state. The Nigerian Civil War of 1967-1970, the ethnic conflicts in Burundi and Rwanda in the 1980s, the Sudanese Civil War, South Africa's ethnic conflicts at the end of apartheid, and the Rwanda genocide are only some notable examples of the carnage that can result from extreme ethnic conflicts when the legitimacy of the postcolonial state is in doubt. Responding to these persistent crises, African states (Nigeria in 1979 and 1991, Ghana in 1969, 1979, and 1992, Burkina Faso in 1978, Mali in 1979, and Uganda in 1980, to mention only a few important examples) embraced "the science of ethnic engineering and the amenability of ethnicity to constitutional constraints."[2] However, the pre-occupation with these ethnic confrontations has obscured the fluid intra-ethnic interactions in local communities. In Nigeria, with its contentious politics of federalism, Yoruba collective political action has consistently been reflected through ethnic cohesiveness and communal fissures within the dominant ethno-linguistic group.

Historians of modern African studies generally agree that these manifestations of communal identities in contemporary politics have their roots in the nature of colonial encounters with complex societies. In the case of colonial southern Africa, Terence Ranger concludes that an enduring legacy of the British system of indirect rule lies in a systematic reconstruction of communal identities, customary law, and traditional practices.[3] Reinforced by British objectives, these "invented" identities of "tribe, gender and generation," he contends, not only distorted pre-existing sociopolitical arrangements but also redefined power relations among chiefs, elders, and local communities. Similarly, Leroy Vail linked the political, economic, and ecological developments in colonial southern Africa to the rapid pace in the reconstruction of communal consciousness.[4] Thus, political development since the colonial period witnessed a process in which, despite remarkable continuity with the past, communal identity was radically disrupted.[5] These expressions of communalism assume greater political significance in postcolonial African states and societies.

Despite the intense competition for influence among leaders (obas, chiefs, and educated elites) of Yoruba hometowns within colonial administrative dispensations, a Yoruba intelligentsia constructed a pan-ethnic doctrine with relative ease during decolonization.[6] This pan-Yoruba collective action resulted from the exigencies of the regionalization of power that the British (with the tacit approval of the dominant ethno-regional political classes) had imposed on its most complex African colony. Both the pre-colonial and the colonial past (especially the nineteenth-century internecine wars and the communal agitations of the colonial period), coupled with the political interest of a modernizing regional elite, challenged the effectiveness of a pan-Yoruba political consciousness in the postcolonial era.

Illuminating studies by J.D.Y. Peel and David Laitin provide a conceptual framework for the study of the conflicting expressions of communalism in the Yoruba region since the colonial period. Peel shows in the case of the Ijesha (a major Yoruba subgroup) that electoral politics after the decolonization process defined a paradoxical type of collective political action along the lines of an ethnic (Yoruba) and a sub-ethnic (Ijesha) consciousness.[7] Party political allegiance among the Ijesha was shaped by Nigeria's volatile politics of federalism and the prevailing political conditions in the region. In a critical application of Gramsci's theory of hegemony, Laitin contends that Yoruba "political calculations have been consistently based on the exploitation of ancestral city fissures."[8] Political action in these communities were not shaped by the dominant world religions—Christianity and Islam—which had radically transformed Yoruba communities since the mid-nineteenth century, but by a sub-ethnic consciousness based on strong loyalty to major Yoruba hometowns. By stressing the Yoruba's firm political allegiance to the hometown, Laitin de-emphasizes the situational character of Yoruba politics. While "ancestral city fissures" are critical expressions of

Yoruba politics, Yoruba communities have equally demonstrated considerable pan-ethnic political cohesiveness within Nigeria's contentious federal politics. Frank Salomone is therefore right when he notes that "flexibility has been the hallmark of a successful Yoruba leader. The political system rewarded the person who could juggle various interests and roles while forming alliances among competing factions."[9]

The role of the political class is central to the development of these communal blocs. In the context of an arduous nation state project, with its rapidly shifting political forces during decolonization, the political class appropriated communal doctrines, myths, and symbols as a strategy for political mobilization and support.[10] Rather than undermine primordial values, the modernizing elites in fact unleashed the politicization of ethno-regionalism and promoted a strong sense of sub-ethnic identities. Thus, the exigencies of Nigerian politics since decolonization prompted the Yoruba political class to construct a cohesive pan-ethnic ideology among its historically diverse subgroups. As this pan-ethnic project confronted prevailing communal (hometown) identities, the "partisans" of ancestral hometowns emerged as defenders of the natives' interest and values against an intruding regional political class.[11] Peel's study of an Ijesha hometown collective political action within the context of the politics of colonialism, decolonization, and federalism, and Laitin's skillful application of Gramsci's theory of hegemony to Yoruba politics underscore the critical role of a local elite as the defender of a perceived local interest against external adversaries. The political development in Ibadan during the Second Republic discussed later in this chapter underscores the reconstruction of a nativist doctrine by a local elite to protect against the perceived adverse policies of the dominant pan-Yoruba political party.

Despite these manifestations of communalism at the grassroots, a straightforward instrumentalist perspective which solely links ethno-regional consciousness only to the struggle for state controlled resources still dominates the discussion of this subject in contemporary Nigerian politics. Howard Wolpe's influential study of Port Harcourt is an exception, looking at the interaction between communalism and the formation of the postcolonial Nigerian state.[12] Emphasizing the absence of unifying state structures capable of sustaining cross-cutting sociopolitical alliances, subtle analyses of the impact of politics on communal identity in Nigeria must emphasize the interaction between class formation, the regionalization of state power, and neocolonialism.[13] In turn, the prevailing political arrangement has entrenched an "ethno-clientelist" system in which ethno-regional elites define collective political action for the purpose of disbursing unlimited patronage.[14]

This conceptual framework will not only show the dynamic interplay between shifting communal boundaries and the competition for limited resources, but will also underscore the interaction between communal groups and the construction of legitimacy doctrines.[15] Thus, it will be argued that in addition to the dominant instrumentalist perspective that underscores the significance of political ethnicity, party politics at the grassroots has reflected the politicization of communal symbols, sentiments, histories, and myths as expressions of legitimacy doctrine.

HISTORICAL CONTEXT OF YORUBA POLITICAL ALIGNMENT AND COMMUNAL IDENTITIES

In his pioneering work on party politics in Nigeria, political scientist Richard Sklar argues that politics during the decolonization process was sustained by the political interests of the dominant ethno-regional political classes in the Eastern, Northern, Western, and Mid-Western Regions.[16] In these four regions of the federation, three dominant regional parties became the vehicle for the advancement of the fortunes of the political class. Parliamentary democracy thrived because it provided a framework for party leaders to dominate state institutions. Thus, the major constitutional[17] and political initiatives adopted during decolonization intensified the regionalization of power and the preexisting process of the development of communal identities. In Yoruba towns, conflicting communal expressions were shaped by the interests of powerful groups and individuals who projected their objectives as the real aspirations of local people. Political mobilization was based on prevailing social and economic issues, especially matters pertaining to regional government policies on decisions having direct relevance to power. The politics of decolonization in the Western region led to the construction of a pan-ethnic movement under the leadership of a Yoruba bureaucratic and commercial class. The political and economic objectives of this modernizing elite were consequently built on the organizational structure of an ethnically based political party, the Action Group (AG). The party's preeminence was ensured by the propagation of ethnic myths (especially the reinvention of a Yoruba myth of origin), the mobilization of hometown social organizations, and the alliance between politicians, obas, chiefs, and elders who had served as the cornerstone of the colonial Native Authority system.

While this trend toward elite consensus prevailed in most parts of the region, it was met with stiff resistance in some Yoruba towns. This schism between the pan-Yoruba project of the dominant intelligentsia and the nativist aspirations of hometown leaders was expressed in Ibadan where a major local party, Mabolaje, under the leadership of the charismatic politician, Adegoke Adelabu, mobilized chiefs and local groups against the Yoruba party, the AG.[18] Mabolaje's short-lived control of Ibadan politics from 1951 to 1958 can be attributed to Adelabu's skillful resistance to AG government reforms. Communal political action was determined by the interests of powerful actors at the local and regional levels. Mabolaje politicians and chiefs as local powerbrokers portrayed the reform policies of the Yoruba political class as a deliberate attempt to advance the interests of the non-Ibadan Yoruba in local politics and commerce. Thus, at least in the short term, Mabolaje politicians successfully projected their political objectives as those of the general community by appealing to nativist sentiments. As the politics of federalism entrenched the AG's control over regional resources and patronage, Ibadan leaders who were initially disposed to support the local party, Mabolaje, realized that the cost of their support was political marginalization within the regional power structure.[19] Confronted with the AG's domination of the regional government, these leaders adopted a more favorable position toward the regional authorities.

AG domination of regional politics was suddenly interrupted by the historic Western Region Crisis of 1962-1966. Two consequences of this crisis are significant here. First, the split in the AG leadership not only led to the formation of a new political party, the Nigerian National Democratic Party (NNDP), but also transformed Yoruba political alignment in the following decades. The AG's disintegration resulted from the radical opposition of party leader Awolowo and his supporters to the regionalization of power by the AG's adversaries in the coalition federal government—the Northern Peoples Congress (NPC) and the National Council of Nigerian Citizens (NCNC)—following the AG's defeat in the 1959 federal election. Since the NNDP lacked popular support in Yoruba communities, it relied exclusively on patronage and intimidation of opponents.[20] The spirited resistance of politicians and obas (AG loyalists) not only undermined the credibility of the NNDP, but also resulted in recurrent political crises and ultimately the intervention of the military in politics.[21] Opposition to the NNDP-NPC alliance was ensured by AG loyalists' projection of the new arrangement as a deliberate ploy to marginalize the Yorubas in Nigeria's federal structure. Second, the crisis further enhanced the popularity of Awolowo who was convicted of treasonable felony in 1962.[22] The persecution of the most prominent Yoruba politician by the Northern and Eastern Region alliance that controlled the federal government enhanced the status of the AG leader among the Yorubas. For example, after his release from prison by General Gowon in August 1966, Awolowo, who had emerged as the symbol of Yoruba unity, enjoyed the support of most obas, elders, and the intelligentsia.[23] Indeed, the imposing leadership of Awolowo in regional and national politics shaped Yoruba political alignment in the years of military rule.[24]

This political development was sustained by the policies of successive military regimes. Under military rule, ex-politicians and new aspirants were not deterred by military promulgations prohibiting all forms of partisan politics. Seeing the military's failure to enforce its edicts, regional politicians of the previous democratic period simply assumed a more clandestine approach in preparation for the eventual lifting of the ban on party politics. Instead of discouraging the temptation to engage in competitive politics, the style of military administration in fact encouraged continuity with the preceding era of civilian government. Thus, despite the cohesiveness that characterizes military structures[25] and the claims of these regimes to be able to solve the country's sociopolitical problems, Nigeria's military officers still harbor strong regional sentiments. Moreover, the lack of effective organizational structures further encouraged successive military regimes to co-opt the support of the ethnic powerbrokers who generally mediate the interaction between holders of state power and local communities.[26] And with no real ties to local communities, Gowon appointed prominent ex-politicians as commissioners in the federal executive committee and as leaders of federal corporations.[27]

Similarly, in the old Western Region, the Fajuyi (January 1966-July 1966), Adebayo (1966-1972), Rotimi (1972-1975), and Jemibewon (1975-1979) administrations adopted policies that entrenched the existing political alignment. For example, intent on reversing the policy of the NNDP civilian government, Fajuyi's regional government adopted policies that advanced the position of the beleaguered AG during Fajuyi's short spell as military governor.[28] Similarly, with a state executive council dominated by former regional politicians, the Adebayo administration depended on the assistance of politicians for the resolution of major crises in the region, cians for the resolution of major crises in the region, notably the Agbekoya Rebellion of September 1968-July 1969.[29] Thus, despite their goal of rationalizing the country's economic and political systems, successive military administrations perpetuated the conflicting interests of the entrenched ethno-regional power structures and other sub-national political alliances which had emerged in the preceding democratic era. The case study of a major Yoruba state—Oyo—will demonstrate that the interaction between personalities and communal identities was also crucial in collective political action during the Second Republic from 1978 to 1983.

PARTY POLITICS AND COMMUNAL IDENTITIES IN OYO STATE

As in other regions of the federation, the origins of political parties in the Yoruba states[30] were firmly based on Nigeria's entrenched ethno-regional structure and a strong communal ideology. In these states, the pan-ethnic foundation of the preeminent political party was reinforced by historical and contemporary factors. A key political association, the Committee of Friends, which existed as an informal organization of former AG partisans during the years of military rule, provided the framework through which the dominant faction of the Yoruba political class was able to mobilize support. Under the leadership of Awolowo, the group was subsequently transformed into the Unity Party of Nigeria (UPN). The strategy adopted by the UPN in its formative months of 1978 and 1979 differed significantly from that of its precursor, the AG, in the early 1950s. Unlike the latter, which had relied on the patronage of Yoruba obas and influential local personalities, through a sociocultural organization, the Egbe Omo Oduduwa, the UPN by 1978 had consolidated its position as the most dominant political bloc in the region. A pan-ethnic ideology welded Yoruba constituencies to this pan-ethnic party. The need for pan-Yoruba sentiments had progressed from the concept of egbe (organization) to the more assertive notion encapsulated in capsulated in one of the 1979 election slogan, *Ti wa ni ti wa*, a popular Yoruba saying: what is ours is definitely ours.

Beyond mere political slogans, the party, along with a social democratic manifesto,[31] staked its claim to legitimacy in Yoruba communities on the leadership of Awolowo and the Yoruba myth of origin. Ethnic cohesiveness was ensured by Nigeria's entrenched regionalization of power, Awolowo's dominant personality, and a formidable alliance with obas. In a manner reminiscent of the formative years of the AG, party leaders projected the institution of obaship as the ultimate expression of a pan-ethnic (Yoruba) group.[32] In a specific reference to the significance of this institution, Awolowo, despite the changes in the country, noted during this period that "a good politician, as the representative of the people, should support any institution which is respected by the people."[33] In short, the party's electoral success is connected to Yoruba ethnic cohesiveness and to continuity with the previous, unsuccessful parliamentary years. Thus, political scientist Billy Dudley notes that "the Unity Party of Nigeria (UPN), which, with some justification, could be taken as a recreation of the AG, polled in 1979 over 80% of the votes in the states which in 1959 formed the Western Region."[34]

The ethno-regional identity that led to this electoral victory became a major feature of UPN government strategy after the elections. Adopting electoral tactics is one thing; formulating and implementing policies in states with contentious communal and elite interests is another. Oyo State politics provides an instructive example during the Second Republic. Like UPN political leaders in other Yoruba states, Bola Ige, the dynamic governor of Oyo State, at various periods attempted to consolidate the gains of his party within an ethnic framework. Like AG policies during decolonization, UPN strategy reinforced the preeminence of Awolowo's vision and the ideology of an ethnic myth of origin that was traced to the legendary cradle of Yoruba civilization, Ile-Ife. Like their predecessors in the AG three decades earlier, the leadership of the UPN in Oyo State (and other Yoruba states) projected a unifying pan-ethnic ideology similar to what Stephanie Lawson in the case of ethnic Fijians referred to as "the myth of cultural homogeneity."[35] Given the major political changes which had taken place in Nigeria, the complex nature of Yoruba communal identities, and the turbulent history of Yorubaland, the mythological construction of an ethnic identity invariably promoted the interest of specific personalities and groups at the expense of others. In Oyo State, this strategy led to old as well as new forms of alliance and conflict.

The most significant expression of this was the protracted controversy over the state council of chiefs. Less than a year after his gubernatorial victory, Governor Ige advanced the status of his ally the Ooni of Ife, Oba Sijuade Olubuse II, by appointing him the permanent chairman of the Oyo State Council of Chiefs in September 1980.[36] This political strategy adversely affected the Alaafin of Oyo, Oba Lamidi Adeyemi III, who had given tacit support to the opposition party, the National Party of Nigeria (NPN) in the 1979 elections.[37] By embarking on a policy that projected the supremacy of the Ooni, the UPN government attempted to use an ancient mythology to legitimate its power in a modern political environment. The enhanced status of the Ooni was, however, short-lived, as Dr. Omololu Olunloyo's NPN government reversed this policy immediately after the controversial 1983 election.[38] Finally, this policy with its political implications for obas and local politicians echoes the observation of Eric Hobsbawm in the case of "invented" traditions in Europe:

> It is clear that plenty of political institutions, ideological movements and groups—not least in nationalism—were so unprecedented that even historic continuity had to be invented, for example by creating an ancient past beyond effective historical continuity.[39]

Communal tension was also apparent in the UPN's local government reform program. One of the main features of politics in the First Republic was the consistent attempt by the political parties in control of the regional government to dominate local politics through electoral and extra-electoral methods. In the North for example, the Northern People's Congress (NPC) utilized the Native Authority (NA) structures to crush opposition and consolidate its position in local communities, while the NNDP government in the West dissolved local government councils and replaced them with management committees that mirrored its objectives.[40] In spite of constitutional provisions designed to prevent such abuses, the state governments elected to power in October 1979 were no less relentless in their desire to dominate local politics. This trend was exacerbated by the confrontations that ensued between the NPN federal government and the twelve states controlled by non-NPN parties. The general trend between 1979 and 1983 was for these state governments to dissolve duly elected local authorities and replace them with management committees. Since the committees were staffed by party supporters, they reflected the wishes of the state governments rather than local aspirations. In addition, the state governments created new local authority jurisdictions at will. So serious was the proliferation of local councils that their number increased from 301 in October 1979 to 701 by December 1981, only two years after the civilians assumed power.[41] This control of local government structures was thus "a means not only of distributing patronage, but was also an exercise in gerrymandering."[42] Local authority size and boundary delimitation, were "a logistical, party political or federal constitutional issue and not a means of linking the corporate structures of government with local forms of governance."[43]

It would however be disingenuous to suggest that the local government reform initiated by the Oyo State government was established with the sole purpose of advancing UPN political objectives. Undoubtedly, the state authorities had some good intentions in constituting a commission of inquiry to recommend a more effective method of local government administration and to redefine the boundaries of local government councils. To UPN state officials, the local authority jurisdictions established by the military government, through the 1976 Local Government Guidelines, had failed to address the perennial problems of local administration in the state: maladministration, social divisions, poor communication, and inadequate resources remained endemic throughout the state.

Despite this profound crisis of governance, it was soon realized that any meaningful local government policy undertaken within a party political framework would intensify communal struggles. In the Oranmiyan Central Local Government Area of the state, for instance, local government reform meant the reemergence of historical tensions between the Ife and Modakeke people between 1979 and 1983. The bitter political violence that brought the conflict to a head in 1980 was shaped by the partisanship that emerged from the politics of decolonization.[44] In Ibadan, the state capital, the Olubadan (the city's oba), his senior chiefs, local leaders, and politicians in the two major parties in the city, the UPN and the NPN, mobilized the support of various interest groups against the state government's plans to reorganize the Ibadan Municipal Government (IMG). To these Ibadan leaders, Governor Ige's argument in favor of local government efficiency was not convincing. They contended that the proposed policy was an insidious attempt by a non-Ibadan governor (although a resident of Ibadan since his youth, Bola Ige is a native of the Ijesha town of Esa Oke), to achieve an earlier AG goal that was perceived to be detrimental to the interests of the "indigenous" population. Thus, as a strategy to mobilize Ibadan natives, chiefs and local politicians argued that this was similar to the old AG ploy that was initially introduced in the 1950s to advance the interest of non-Ibadan Yoruba, especially the Ijebus, in local politics.

In the view of the UPN state government, however, a comprehensive local government reform policy was long overdue in Ibadan. State authorities argued that it was problematic for a central municipal authority to effectively administer the affairs of the second largest city in sub-Saharan Africa from the town hall in Mapo. To curb corruption (considered by some to be the bane of city administration in the recent past), the state government proposed the division of Ibadan into smaller administrative units, advocating what Governor Ige described as a greater council for central Ibadan, in which a number of county councils for adjacent areas would be included.[45] These councils would be expected to manage most of their affairs semi-autonomously from the greater Ibadan council. In his desire to overhaul the anachronistic structure in Ibadan and elsewhere, the governor, only two months after his election, appointed a commission of inquiry under the chairmanship of Mr. Justice Yekini Adio to propose methods of reforming local government administration in the state.[46] The following case study of Ibadan politics between 1979 and 1983 shows the impact of the Oyo State local government policy on communal identity in this critical Yoruba city.

COMMUNAL POLITICS AND LOCAL GOVERNMENT REFORMS IN IBADAN

The line of action taken by the Ibadan political class on the proposal for local government reform was crucial to the nature of political alignment in Ibadan from 1979 to 1983. It was political leaders—politicians and chiefs—who constructed a town based ideology, contending that the state government reform would further advance the interests of non-native Ibadans at the expense of the core of the city where the "indigenous" population resided.[47] The strategy adopted by Ibadan leaders was similar to those employed by their predecessors in the 1950s. The Olubadan and the senior chiefs were quick to mobilize popular support by calling on artisans' guilds, women traders, farmers' groups, and other associational interests to oppose the government's policy. The chiefs also sought the support of influential personalities—sons and daughters of the soil—in the city and in other parts of the country. Memoranda from many influential personalities were sent to the Adio Commission, opposing the proposed reforms. Various groups also made their impact felt, sending petitions to the commission in support of the Olubadan. They printed pamphlets attacking the UPN government and the small group of Ibadan politicians who supported the reorganization, whom they accused of having "sold out" for self-serving political reasons.[48]

The best organized of these groups was the Ibadan Committee of Concern (ICC), an amalgamation of diverse voluntary groups cutting across party lines, formed with the specific purpose of frustrating the government's objectives. The ICC consisted of an alliance of chiefs, politicians, senior civil servants, businessmen, and wealthy traders. The group, which claimed as its sole objective "the orderly growth and development of that geographical entity in Yorubaland formerly known as Ibadan Province" identified three political goals: first, it committed itself to the promotion of the status of the Olubadan and his chiefs, whom it regarded as the custodians of the city's cherished values and culture; second, it called for the economic and social advancement of the city; and third, it pledged to uphold peace and harmony among local people.[49]

The ICC's major activities were, however, centered on its attacks on the UPN government and the small group of Ibadan politicians who had actively campaigned for the proposed reorganization of the city's administration. The strategy adopted by the anti-reformist movement is similar to the communal agitation of the late colonial period. In an attempt to mobilize community support, local elites at home and abroad embraced traditional symbols and reconstructed myths for political purposes. Specifically, their political objectives were legitimated by an appeal to the cherished heritage of their city and the promotion of what was left of its chieftaincy structure. Moreover, the controversy surrounding reorganization was not unconnected to the historical experiences of the diverse communal groups within the city. The layouts in Oke Ado, Oke Bola, Ijebu By-Pass, and Ago Taylor (referred to in the 1940s and 1950s in colonial and 1950s in colonial parlance as "Native Settler Areas", in which the Ijebus were prominent) had assumed a distinct character when compared to the core of the city. These areas, whose residents are by heritage predominantly non-Ibadan Yorubas, especially Ijebus, Egbas, and Ijeshas, have done better economically than the central section of the city, in which the majority of Ibadan natives still live and which has suffered from benign neglect at the hands of successive state authorities. Hence, coalition leaders projected the government's reform policy as the final death knell for the social and economic aspirations of the "indigenous" population, as reorganization would mean the removal of the administrative control of the IMG from Ibadan natives.

It was therefore apparent by mid 1980 that this grassroots coalition was poised to undermine the credibility of the government in the city. The inclusion in this organization of powerful groups and native sons of diverse political persuasions under the "spiritual" leadership of the Olubadan was what turned this fringe coalition into a formidable opposition. Indeed, this appeal to atavism in a modern political situation can be clearly seen in one of the organization's most pointed attacks on pro-reform politicians:

> One would like to ask these agents of instability and avowed apostles of disunity, precisely who and what they set out to reform? Our age-old culture and traditions that have seen us through many years of wars and have earned Ibadan the unique prominent place among the Yorubas and Nigerians? Are we so unreformed a people that we need to be reformed by a gang of institutional destroyers . . .?[50]

In the end, although the Adio Commission recommended a significant increase in the number of the state's local government councils, it suggested that the IMG should be retained in its existing form, contrary to the state authorities' objectives. The IMG was also allowed to maintain control over all sections of the city under its jurisdiction.[51] Fully aware of its opponents' popularity, the government abandoned its vision of local administration in the city and accepted the recommendations of the commission. As a consequence, Ibadan, the second largest local authority in the country, prevented the implementation of the government's reform, despite its severe administrative problems. Thus, more than any other political issue in the Second Republic, the reorganization controversy had a profound effect on political alignment in the city. Indeed, it can be argued that it partially transformed the preexisting political alignment in Ibadan. This perspective is based on the assumption that the confrontation would have worked to the disadvantage of the party in power, the UPN, which was considered the villain by those who opposed the reform. More importantly, by leading to events that undermined the UPN government's popularity in Ibadan from 1980 to the 1983 elections, the conflict transformed the political allegiance of important personalities in the city. Opponents of the UPN administration presented the government's proposal as an indication of what they considered the administration's general anti-Ibadan disposition. In fact, these leaders went as far as to attack the government for a perceived imbalance in the allocation of state resources.

It was however, the opposition party in the state, the NPN that benefited the most from the reorganization controversy. To prominent leaders of the Ibadan branch of the NPN who had suffered a shocking setback in the 1979 gubernatorial and legislative elections, the local government reform policy was the perfect political instrument through which they could undermine the pan-ethnic base of the UPN in Ibadan. As in other areas of the state, where communal tensions had persisted since the UPN victory in 1979,[52] NPN leaders in Ibadan used the controversy as an instrument for reviving the historical divisions between Ibadan natives and the descendants of Ijebu immigrants. In fact, Laitin claimed that this strategy was pervasive not only in Oyo State, but also in other parts of the region:

NPN strategists [in the 1979 and 1983 elections] . . . worked through the ancestral city divide, hoping to recruit Oyos and Egbas in a common stand against the Ijebu, Awolowo.[53]

The NPN projected itself as the party sympathetic to Ibadan and by extension, to the advancement of chiefly influence.[54] Thus, the chiefs embraced the propaganda of the NPN, which portrayed the reform proposal as an attack on the interests of the indigenous population.

The Ibadan branch of the UPN was also disenchanted with the government's reform proposal. It was generally felt by this group that Ibadan was not receiving its rightful share in the decision making process and in the distribution of state resources. Thus, by late 1981 a major division had emerged within the coalition that had united to support the UPN in Ibadan only two years earlier. So apparent was the animosity between the UPN government (principally the governor) and prominent leaders of the Ibadan UPN the antigovernment group disavowed the leadership of the governor. In fact its leaders issued a press release in April 1982 withdrawing its support for Governor Ige in the 1983 election:

> It is our candid opinion that this present administration has not adequately compensated for Ibadan's support in 1979 and after, except in verbiage. We shall not support the extension of this administration beyond 1983. Enough is enough.[55]

Beyond its denunciation of the governor, the group stated that a pro-Ibadan position would guide their decision to support a gubernatorial candidate. The group called for an Ibadan native as the party's candidate in the 1983 gubernatorial elections.[56] A gallant political warrior and a man of supreme confidence, the governor was not intimidated by a group of politicians he dismissed as "traitors and detractors." Their failure to prevent the re-nomination of Governor Ige as the party's gubernatorial candidate in 1983 was the last straw. Thus, they called on Ibadan natives to vote the UPN administration out of power and support a native son as the NPN gubernatorial candidate. Ibadan-centered slogans such as *Omo wa ni e je o se* "We want a native son for governor", and *Ibadan o se ru mo, gomina la o se* "Ibadan will no longer be slaves, we now want to be governor" became popular during the election campaign.

The 1983 election in Ibadan was presented by the opponents of the UPN government as a family affair in which all members should support a native son, Dr. Omololu Olunloyo, the NPN gubernatorial nominee in the state. The campaign slogan in Ibadan encapsulates this sense of brotherhood and camaraderie: *Ohun ti agbe kale o ju ija lo, ara Ibadan o ba ti ija wa—Ohun ti a gbe kale yi ju ja lo* "This issue is more than a mere tussle [election]; it is actually about survival". A new consciousness reminiscent of the populism of the Ibadan political boss in the 1950s, Adegoke Adelabu, emerged; indeed the spirit of the legendary Adelabu was conveniently injected into the NPN campaign. The NPN campaign in Ibadan was "packaged" as *oro a la jo bi* "a kith and kin affair." The NPN emphasized a communal identity that mirrors Laitin's conceptualization of an ancestral hometown ideology in Ibadan as well as in other cities in the state. For example, the NPN campaign was injected with the eulogy of prominent native sons, such as Adelabu in Ibadan and Akintola in Ogbomosho,[57] who at various periods and for different reasons had mounted an effective local opposition against the pan-Yoruba ideology of a regional political class.

Although the NPN candidate won the 1983 gubernatorial election, the evidence suggests that the victory was far from fair, as electoral fraud was rife in the state. Significantly, however, instead of experiencing the violence that often accompanies the defeat of a Yoruba political party in a rigged election,[58] Ibadan was relatively peaceful after the 1983 election. This unusual occurrence may be attributed to a three-year nativist campaign against the UPN in Ibadan. The victorious leaders of the NPN embraced major conflicts such as those in Ibadan and Ife as justifications for the election outcome.

CONCLUSION

Since the period of decolonization, electoral politics have consistently given impetus to a complex manifestation of communalism in Yoruba communities. In reaction to Nigeria's entrenched ethno-regionalism, which had emerged with the regionalization of state power during decolonization, the Yoruba political class, like their counterparts in other parts of the federation, consistently constructed a communal ideology along broadly defined ethnic lines. Under the leadership of a modernizing political class, this pan-ethnic project paradoxically led to severe tension among Yoruba subgroups such as the Ibadan, Oyo, Ijebu, Ijesha, Ekiti, Egba, and others during the democratic transitions of the First and Second Republics.

As the case studies from Oyo State and Ibadan city demonstrate, Yoruba communities, responding to shifting sociopolitical and economic conditions, embraced pan-ethnic and hometown doctrines that drew heavily from reconstructed notions of traditional myths and local historical interpretations. And despite the claims of military regimes to rationalize Nigeria's political system, this process persisted during the years of military rule. Thus, in the context of an intense struggle for state power, party politics in Yoruba communities since the period of decolonization has encouraged the development of a shifting types of communal political action, usually along ethnic and sub-ethnic lines.

NOTES

1. This is a term popularly used by Nigerian political analysts to describe the country's second experiment with democratic rule.

2. A.H.M. Kirk-Greene, "Ethnic Engineering and the 'Federal Character' of Nigeria: Boon of Contentment or Bone of Contention?" *Ethnic and Racial Studies*, 6, 1993, 459.
3. Terence Ranger, "The Invention of Tradition in Africa," in Eric Hobsbawm and Terence Ranger (eds.), *The Invention of Tradition* (Cambridge: Cambridge University Press, 1988). See also Terence Ranger, "The Invention of Tradition Revisited: The Case of Colonial Africa," in Terence Ranger and Olufemi Vaughan (eds.), *Legitimacy and the State in Twentieth Century Africa*: Essays in Honour of A.H.M. Kirk-Greene (London: Macmillan, St. Anthony's College, Oxford series, 1993).
4. Leroy Vail (ed.), *The Creation of Tribalism in Southern Africa*, (London: James Currey, 1989), 10.
5. Martin Chanock, *Law, Custom and Social Order: The Colonial Experience in Malawi and Zambia* (Cambridge: Cambridge University Press, 1985), 3.
6. Richard Sklar, *Nigerian Political Parties: Power in an Emergent African Nation* (Princeton, NJ: Princeton University Press, 1963).
7. J.D.Y. Peel, *Ijesha and Nigerians: The Incorporation of a Yoruba Kingdom 1890s-1970s* (Cambridge: Cambridge University Press, 1983).
8. David D. Laitin, *Hegemony and Culture: Politics and Religious Change among the Yoruba* (Chicago: University of Chicago Press, 1986), 132.
9. Frank A. Salamone, "Playing at Nationalism: Nigeria, a Nation of 'Ringers,'" *Geneve-Afrique*, 30, 1, 1992, 69.
10. In his study of Arab nationalism, Bryan S. Turner argues that, despite their training in Western science and rationality, Arab nationalists have generally mobilized their various communities on the basis of strong Islamic and traditional values. *Marx and the End of Orientalism*, (London: Allen & Unwin 1978).
11. Myron Weiner, *Sons of the Soil: Migration and Ethnic Conflict in India* (Princeton, NJ: Princeton University Press, 1978), 350.
12. Howard Wolpe, *Urban Politics in Nigeria: A Study of Port Harcourt* (Berkeley: University of California Press, 1974) 233.
13. Toyin Falola and Julius Ihonvbere, *The Rise and Fall of Nigeria's Second Republic* (London: Zed Books, 1985).
14. Richard Joseph, "Class, State, and Prebendal Politics in Nigeria," in Nelson Kasfir (ed.), *State and Class in Africa* (London: Frank Cass, 1984), 30-31. See also Richard Joseph, *Democracy and*

Prebendal Politics in Nigeria (Cambridge: Cambridge University Press, 1987).
15. William Arens and Ivan Karp (eds.), *Creativity of Power* (Washington D.C.: Smithsonian Institution Press, 1989), xiii-xiv.
16. Sklar, *Nigerian Political Parties*. See also his "Contradictions in the Nigerian Political System," *Journal of Modern African Studies*, 3, 1965, and "Nigerian Politics in Perspective," *Government and Opposition*, 2, 1967.
17. These political and constitutional reforms can be seen in major landmark documents such as the 1947 *Dispatch of the Secretary of State for the Colonies to African Governors* (London: H.M.S.O., 25 February 1947); The 1947 (Richards) Constitution; The 1951 (Macpherson) Constitution; The 1960 (Independence) Constitution; and the Western Region 1952 Local Government Law.
18. The communal significance of this local party can be seen in the meaning of Mabolaje. In this particular context Mabolaje simply means, "do not destroy the honor of the nobility," who were generally seen as the ultimate symbol of communal values. For a detailed discussion of the performance of this party in Ibadan politics, see Kenneth Post and George Jenkins, *Price of Liberty: Personality and Politics in Colonial Nigeria* (Cambridge: Cambridge University Press, 1973).
19. As in the two other regions of the federation (Eastern and Northern), a trend toward single party domination was apparent by 1960. In fact, the AG in the August 1961 local elections, after almost a decade's struggle with Mabolaje in Ibadan, succeeded in removing this local menace by gaining control of the Ibadan City Council. See John P. Mackintosh, "Electoral Trends and the Tendency to a One Party System in Nigeria," *Journal of Commonwealth Political Studies*, 1, 3, 1962.
20. This was particularly the case in those towns where its most prominent politicians remained loyal to the Yoruba-based party, the AG. While some major politicians who defected to the NNDP were at varying levels able to attract the allegiance of significant sections of their towns to the new party, their inability to achieve a critical mass in many Yoruba towns demonstrated that the new party lacked legitimacy in its home region. Its desire to maintain power through authoritarian measures, despite its rejection by obas, politicians, community leaders, and the masses of local people, soon led to social strife.

21. For a detailed analysis of the pre-military crisis, see Kenneth Post and Michael Vickers, *Structure and Conflict in Nigeria, 1960-1966* (London: Heinemann, 1973).
22. Richard Sklar, "Nigerian Politics: The Ordeal of Chief Awolowo, 1960-1965", in Gwendolen M. Carter (ed.), *Politics in Africa: Seven Cases* (New York: Harcourt, Brace and World, 1966).
23. In fact, Awolowo's release from prison can be regarded as one of the best tactical moves made by General Gowon, who immediately gained Yoruba support as the pre-civil war crisis intensified.
24. For example, Awolowo was appointed federal commissioner for finance and vice-chairman of the National Executive Council by General Gowon. It is common knowledge that he played an active role in sensitive regional issues such as the Agbekoya Crisis of 1967-1968 and the appointment of the Alaafin of Oyo in 1970. Moreover, he was chosen by prominent Yoruba personalities to lead the Western delegation to the influential "Leaders of Thought" conference, set up by the Gowon administration to recommend a solution to the country's pre-civil war crisis. Much to the dismay of his political adversaries, especially ex-NNDP politicians, Awolowo was given the chieftaincy title of Asiwaju (leader) of the Yorubas by the obas of the western provinces. See Sklar, "Nigerian Politics in Perspective," 533.
25. See Robert Price, *Society and Bureaucracy in Contemporary Ghana* (Berkeley: University of California Press, 1975), 213.
26. See for example, Bala J. Takaya, "Politics of Hegemony and Survival?" paper presented at the National Conference on the Role of Traditional Rulers in the Governance of Nigeria, Institute of African Studies, University of Ibadan, 11-14 September 1984.
27. Billy Dudley, *Instability and Political Order, Politics and Crisis in Nigeria* (Ibadan: University of Ibadan Press, 1973).
28. In addition to dissolving NNDP management committees and relieving NNDP appointees of their positions in public corporations, Fajuyi adopted policies which advanced the status of ex-AG politicians. For example, he reversed the previous government's appointment of the Alaafin of Oyo as chairman of the regional council of obas, and reappointed the pro-AG Ooni of Ife in his place. Fajuyi's policy also led to the deposition of the NNDP loyalist, the Olowo of Owo, Sir Olateru Olagbegi. See *Western Nigerian Gazette* (Ibadan: Government Printer, 1966).
29. See C.E.F. Beer, *The Politics of Peasant Groups in Western Nigeria* (Ibadan: University of Ibadan Press, 1976); and C.E.F. Beer

and Gavin Williams, "The Politics of Ibadan Peasantry," in Gavin Williams (ed.), *Nigerian Economy and Society* (London: Rex Collings, 1978).

30. After the division of the four regions (the creation of the Mid-West in 1963 made Nigeria a four-region federation) into twelve states by the Gowon administration in 1967, the country was further divided into nineteen states in 1976. The Western (Yoruba) State was carved into three, namely Oyo, Ogun, and Ondo. The city of Lagos as the federal capital and its neighboring towns and villages became a state in 1967. See the *Report of the Panel Investigating the Issue of the Creation of more States and Boundary Adjustments in Nigeria* (Lagos: Government Printer, 1976).

31. For a detailed discussion of the ideology of the UPN, see Richard Joseph, "Political Parties and Ideology in Nigeria" *Review of African Political Economy*, 13, 1978.

32. Olufemi Vaughan, " Chieftaincy Politics and Social Relations in Nigeria," *Journal of Commonwealth and Comparative Politics*, 29, 3, 1991.

33. Reproduced by the *Nigerian Guardian*, 7 June 1987, after the death of the UPN leader in May of the same year.

34. Billy Dudley, "The Nigerian Election of 1979: The Voting Decision," *Journal of Commonwealth and Comparative Politics*, 19, 1981, 277.

35. Stephanie Lawson, "The Myth of Cultural Homogeneity and Its Implications for Chiefly Power and Politics in Fiji," *Comparative Studies in Society and History*, 32, 4, 1990.

36. In an attempt of promote this policy, Deputy-Governor Afolabi, while announcing the government's approval of Prince Sijuade as the Ooni elect, declared that the chairmanship of the state council of chiefs would automatically accompany the Ooni's appointment by the state government. The deputy-governor further claimed that the selection of the Ooni as chairman was based on his "traditional" seniority among obas in Yorubaland. *Daily Sketch*, 18 September 1980.

37. This policy revived the traditional rivalry between these two preeminent Yoruba obas and prominent sons of their historic towns. In the pro-UPN newspaper, the *Daily Sketch*, local Ife historians projecting the mythological supremacy of the Ooniship among Yoruba obas defended the policy adopted by the government. Conversely, a group called the Oyo Traditional Defence Committee consistently refuted the historical claim of the Ife elites and the

policy of the government in the pro-NPN newspaper, the *National Concord* See *Daily Sketch*, 18 September 1980; 12 December 1980; 16 December 1980; *Sunday Concord,* 16 December 1980.

38. For a detailed discussion of Governor Olunloyo's policy, see *Oba's Council Chairmanship Tussle Resolved—Olunloyo Speaks: Text of the Broadcast in Ibadan by the Governor of Oyo State on 2nd December 1983* (Ibadan: Ministry of Home Affairs, Information and Culture, Government Printer, 1983).
39. Eric Hobsbawm, "Introduction: Inventing Tradition," in Hobsbawm and Ranger (eds.), *The Invention of Tradition,* 7.
40. For a good analysis of the case of the Western Region see Alex Gboyega, "Local Government and Political Integration in Western Nigeria," unpublished Ph.D. thesis, University of Ibadan, 1975; and Olu Fadahunsi, "The Politics of Local Administration in Western Nigeria, 1958-1968," *Quarterly Journal of Administration*, January 1977.
41. So severe was this abuse of power by the state governments that a notable publication observed that virtually all local authorities had failed to comply with the clause of the 1979 constitution that required each state to ensure the existence of a system of democratically elected local government councils. See *West Africa*, 10 January 1983.
42. Daniel Bach, "Managing a Plural Society: The Boomerang Effects of Nigerian Federalism," *Journal of Commonwealth and Comparative Politics*, 27, 2, 1989, 228-229.
43. Jane I. Guyer, "Representation without Taxation: An Essay on Democracy in Rural Nigeria, 1952-1990," Boston University, African Studies Center Working Papers.
44. For a discussion of the post-World War II historical background of this conflict, see Oyeleye Oyediran, "Modakeke in Ife: Historical Background to an Aspect of Contemporary Ife Politics," in Oyeleye Oyediran, *Essays in Local Government Administration* (Lagos: Project Publication, 1988).
45. Interview with Governor Bola Ige (Ibadan, February 1987).
46. The commission, which was chaired by Mr. Justice Y. O. Adio, an Ibadan High Court judge, consisted of a University of Ibadan historian, Dr. Wale Oyemakinde, and a retired senior civil servant, P. P. Ladipo. For a detailed discussion of the terms of reference of the commission, see *The Report of the Commission of Inquiry into Local Government Reform in Oyo State* (Ibadan: Government Printer, 1981).

47. For the historical origins of the tension between Ibadan indigenes and native settlers, see Toyin Falola, "From Hospitality to Hostility: Ibadan and Strangers, 1830-1904," *Journal of African History*, 26, 1985. For political developments in the late colonial period see Post and Jenkins, *Price of Liberty*.
48. Interview with Dr. Wale Oyemakinde, member of the Commission of Inquiry, and Dr. Busari Adebisi, chairman, Department of Political Science, University of Ibadan (Ibadan, February 1987).
49. *Press Release of Ibadan Committee of Concern (ICC) on the Situation Created by Misguided Efforts to Balkanise Ibadan Municipality*, Ibadan, 1982, 3.
50. Ibid.
51. Oyo State Local Government Law, Ibadan: Government Printer, April 1981.
52. This was particularly the case in the Oranmiyan Central Local Government Area, where the support of the UPN state government for the Ife people led to a major political realignment in the town. In the midst of all the tension and the tragic riots, NPN leaders with remarkable success sought to split the UPN Yoruba bloc vote of the previous election by using the myth of Oyo origin as a rallying cry for Modakeke discontent. For a detailed discussion, see *The Report of the Judicial Commission of Inquiry into the Communal Disturbances in Oranmiyan Local Government Area of Oyo State* (Ibadan: Government Printer, 1981).
53. Laitin, *Hegemony and Culture*, 157.
54. This objective was not difficult to achieve, as Ibadan native sons, notably A.M.A. Akinloye, national chairman of the NPN, and R.O.A. Akinjide, attorney general and minister of justice in Shagari's NPN federal government, were prominent leaders of the party.
55. *Press Release of the Unity Party of Nigeria (UPN) Ibadan Branch, Nomination for Oyo State UPN Gubernatorial Candidate in 1983: Our Stand Today*, 4 April 1982, 6.
56. Ibid.
57. Interview with Dr. Olunloyo, NPN governor of Oyo State, October 1983-December 1983 (Ibadan, March 1987).
58. The crisis that accompanied the rigged 1964 federal elections, the 1965 Western Region elections, and the 1983 Ondo State elections all bear witness to the specter of political violence in Yoruba towns. See Post and Vickers, *Structure and Conflict in Nigeria;* and Andrew Apter, "Things Fell Apart? Yoruba Responses to the

1983 Elections in Ondo State, Nigeria." *Journal of Modern African Studies*, 25, 3, 1987.

16

THE EVOLUTION OF AN ETHNIC IDENTITY: THE OWAN OF MID-WESTERN NIGERIA

Onaiwu W. Ogbomo

INTRODUCTION

Ethnic competition has been a major factor in the history of Nigeria since its establishment by the colonial British in 1914. The negative aspects of the competition led to a 30-month civil war lasting from 1967 to 1970. Through various pathways, Nigerian ethnic groups have defined and expressed their identities. For most ethnic groups,

> Ethnic identity is a matter of shared self-perception, the communication of that perception to others and, perhaps most crucially, the response it elicits from others in the form of social interaction.[1]

The Owan are a sub-group of the Edo-speaking peoples of southwestern Nigeria. Occupying two local government areas (Owan West and East Local Government Areas) of Edo State, Nigeria, the Owan people inhabit eleven major communities:

Emai, Evbo-Mion, Igue, Ihievbe, Ikao, Iuleha, Ivbi-Ada-Obi, Ora, Otuo, Ozalla, and Uokha. These were the divisions recognized by the British colonial officials. While nine of these communities conform to precolonial realities, Evbo-Mion includes six pre-colonial communities and Ivbi-Ada-Obi includes three. Thus, there were eighteen independent communities prior to colonialism. In linguistic terms the Owan people speak north-central dialects of the Edo language which constitutes a branch of the Kwa linguistic group. A classification by G.B.L Oyakhire[2] states that the Owan dialects can be grouped into five related categories. The categories are as follows: (a) Emai, Ihievbe, Iuleha, Ake, Ora, and Uokha; (b) Errah and Ozalla; (c) Ivbiaro and Warrake (Ivbi-Ada-Obi community); (d) Arokho, Ikhin, and Iruoke (Evbo-Mion community); and (e) Igue, Ikao, and Otuo. Oyakhire also states that the dialects in groups A, B, and C are closer to each other in terms of mutual intelligibility than D and E, but these two also share commonalties. In the same vein Rudy I. Ohikhokhai reports that "[t]he dialects of Ighue, Ikao, Ikhin Otuo at the extreme north are more closely linked and are at the same time relatively different from the dialect of the rest of Owan. The dialect is made up of largely Bini [Edo] words with some sprinkling of Yoruba and other corrupted words."[3]

With the exception of some assumed ties and linkages which they trace to their founder heroes, all Owan communities were independent of each other in the precolonial era. Hence, they referred to themselves separately as Ora, Ozalla, Uokha, Ihievbe, Otuo, Emai, Iuleha, Ivbiaro, Warrake, Ohami, Ake, Ikhin, and so on. However, over time these disparate names and separate identities merged into one. This chapter seeks to explore the evolution of ethnic consciousness among the Owan people. This exploration will involve an explanation of the reasons and processes behind the identity formation of the Owan people from earliest times to the present. In examining the central issue of identity formation, I will examine the role of historical narratives, rituals, and religion, and colonial and postcolonial politics. I will also focus on the emblems and symbols of Owan ethnic identity.

ORAL NARRATIVES AND OWAN IDENTITY

Major components of any ethnic group's history are the legends and myths, which trace the origin or origins of the particular group. As George De Vos has noted "[a]n ethnic group is a self-perceived group of people who hold in common a set of traditions not shared by the others with whom they are in contact. Such traditions typically include 'folk' religious beliefs and practices, language, a sense of historical continuity, and common ancestry or place of origin."[4] In Owan, the narrative traditions can be classified into three categories. These include the aboriginal traditions, the traditions of Yoruba origin, and the Benin traditions.

The narrative tradition focusing on an aboriginal population in Owan before Benin and Yoruba migrants arrived can be found among the Ivi-Ada-Obi group of communities. In Ivbiaro, the people claim they have no tradition of migration from anywhere. Rather, they are descendants of a god-like being whom they called Ada-Obi. Ada-Obi was said to have married a woman called Aro. They had four sons who established the villages of Iyokuoto, Abogwan, Ebese, and Isogben. Another community in which narrative traditions point to an aboriginal group is Otuo. While Otuo tradition claims that migrants came to the region from Benin and Ife, it is accepted that the migrants met an aboriginal population about whom historians know very little today. In a larger study, I have argued that in the development of Owan communities, the aborigines had reverence for snake and plant totems.[5] I concluded that "two of the Otuo community totems are the boa and groundnut, which indicates the existence of an aboriginal population before the coming of either Yoruba or Benin settlers."[6] In other communities such as Uokha and Igue there are hints of aboriginal populations based on an analysis of totemic observances. The narrative traditions alone are not very helpful in locating where the aboriginal population came from. Hence, one has to rely on logical analysis of both narrative and totemic evidence. Taking all this together, what is incontrovertible is that in the development of Owan communities, an aboriginal group played a significant role. However, narrative tradition today says very little about them. As Ohikhokhai concluded,

> Not much is now known about the aboriginal people [in Owan]. Many of the migration accounts involved peaceful absorption of the aboriginal inhabitants who themselves may have been relatively small in number. Though Otuo traditions conceded the fact that the Ife migrants met a group of aboriginal people, [they are] however, silent on their origin.[7]

The peaceful absorption Ohikhokhai is talking about refers to the assimilation of the aboriginal group by the Yoruba and Benin migrants as they moved into the Owan area. What was the nature of the Yoruba and Benin traditions? Among the eleven Owan communities, four claim Ife-Yoruba origins. The communities are as follows: Otuo, Uokha, Ikao, and Iuleha. Uokha and Otuo also claim Benin origins. At this juncture I will try to examine the traditions of Ife-Yoruba origins.

In Otuo, the tradition states that Otuo was founded by Gbadejo, the son of an Oni of Ife. He was said to have been a temperamental and impulsive young man. Hence, he was nicknamed Otuaka ("He scatters").[8] Gbadejo left Ife on a hunting expedition which took him to Idogun through Ilesha, Akure, and Owo. He married wives and finally settled in Okotheko or Igbobi brook in Otuo area. This narrative tradition stated that while the Ife migrants met an aboriginal group in Otuo, the Benin migrants came later. As Lawani noted, "It appears from the Otuoka story that Otuo was an admixture of two separate stocks, one from Benin and the other from Yorubaland."[9] So Otuo traditions have clearly established three major groups in the development of that community: the aboriginal group, the Yoruba migrants and the Benin migrants.

In Uokha, the Yoruba tradition of origin claims that two brothers, Akpewewuma (Akhuema) and Uvbie (Ovie), who lived at Use in Ondo region were famous traditional doctors. Uvbie was said to have moved to Benin, but because of his peculiar behavior he was driven out of Benin. Hence, he decided to join one Odion at Uokha. Later Akpewewuma joined Odion and Uvbie. Today the descendants of Uvbie are in Evbuvie in Uokha. On the other hand, H. F. Marshall, a British colonial official, recorded another version, which claims that Akpewewuma was a deranged priest who migrated from Ife to Benin, but was driven from Benin as a result of rude behavior.[10] He then decided to move to what is today Uokha. The claim is that he was the founder of Uokha, and Uvbie was his son. Whatever version is adopted, we can gather from the narratives that in the development of Uokha community Yoruba elements featured in the process. Related to the Yoruba traditions in Uokha is the tradition in Iuleha community group. According to Iuleha tradition, Irimo, the founder of the community, was a follower of Akpewewuma. Irimo was said to have migrated from Ife like Akpewewuma. From Ife he moved to Benin, from which he was expelled. He decided to settle in Uokha. The tradition went on to state that it was from Uokha that he founded Iuleha community.

Of the four communities which claim Yoruba origins, only Ikao people claim full Ife descent in their traditions of origin. Ikao, the founder, whose name the community bears today, was said to have left Ile-Ife with his family and settled in Idoani in Owo region. As a result of a quarrel, he and his family moved to what is today known as Ikao. There he had three sons whose names the three component villages bear today. Marshall expressed doubt about Ikao's Yoruba origins. According to him, "the hereditary system of the clan headship by primogeniture indicates more of Benin origin than Yoruba."[11] Even though the people claim a Yoruba origin, Marshall tries to infer a Benin origin. This is undoubtedly the result of the fact that Benin influence has been very pervasive in Owan since the precolonial period. For the majority of Owan communities, Benin is their ancestral home. And in terms of linguistic analysis, most Owan dialects are closer to the Edo language than to Yoruba.

The orthodox explanation for the exodus of migrants from Benin has been that they were renegades who were escaping justice or injustice.[12] In addition, informants claim many migrants from Benin left because they were opposed to the ruthless and hierarchical rule of the obas of Benin. Nine of the eleven Owan communities claim Benin origins. These include Emai, Ora, Ozalla, Otuo, Ihievbe, Igue, Ivbi-Ada-Obi, Evbo-Mion, and Uokha. The classic traditions of Benin origin can be found in Uokha, Ora, and Ozalla. For reasons of lack of space I will focus on Uokha and Ora traditions.

Throughout Owan, Uokha is recognized as the earliest settlement in the region. Uokha is said to have been founded by Odion, the son of Oba Eweka I (c.1320-1347). J. U. Egharevba, the Benin historian, explains that "Omorodion's (Odion's) claim to the crown after the death of their father was passed over. He, in consequence, left Benin City in anger, with his family and followers, and became the founder of Uwokha [Uokha] in Ivbiosakon [Owan]."[13] Uokha narrative tradition has it that Odion was the elder of two brothers. The younger was named Omo. Odion was said to be a very hard working farmer who spent most of his time in the farm. At the death of their father, Eweka, Omo succeeded to the throne. When Odion came back he was infuriated by this development. He left Benin for Uokha after seizing Omo's *ada*, his state sword.[14] Odion lived and died in Uokha.

Ora tradition on the other hand claims that the founder of that community was Prince Uguan, the son of Oba Ozolua. He was banished from Benin for indiscipline. Uguan decided to leave Benin with his followers and stopped at various locations before finally reaching Oderere, close to the present site of Uokha. Uguan was said to have married Akpewewuma's daughter. Not long afterward, his wife became pregnant. She had a difficult delivery and so they consulted a diviner who advised that Uguan should return to the location (Oderere) where he had previously killed a leopard. His wife finally delivered a son who was named Erhae-Ekpen (Ora-Ekpen), the "fiery leopard."[15] The "fiery leopard" had numerous sons who according to the community charter founded the six villages which together made up the Ora community. In commemoration of the birth of Erhae-Ekpen, Ora people adopted the leopard as their community totem. Incidentally, the leopard is also the royal totem of the Benin Kingdom. Without doubt, totemic evidence supports the narrative traditions which claim that the founder of Ora community came from the royal family in Benin.

An analysis of Owan narrative traditions reveals that many Owan communities, while trying to maintain their independence, also place emphasis on the claim that their founders were either related to or were members of a migrant group who moved out of Benin or Yorubaland. Thus, in interpreting the ethnic origins and identity of the Owan people, the narrative traditions take cognizance of the relationship which existed between the different groups from the beginning. It is important to consider some of these traditions here.

In Otuo, the traditions of Benin origin claim that the founders of Otuo descended from the twelve age grades (Otu ni 'egbeva) which accompanied Prince Uguan from Benin to Ora.[16] Clearly, what this tradition tries to establish is that while Otuo is independent of Ora in the post-migration period, nevertheless, there exists a bond if not a kinship relationship between Ora and Otuo people. In Ihievbe community the traditions of origin claim that its founder, Obo (c.1504-1536) was a contemporary of Prince Uguan and a relative of Uzuanbi of Emai.[17] In the same vein, we have noted above that Iuleha traditions claim that Irimo, Iuleha's founder, was a follower of the priest Akpewewuma[18] who sought refuge with Odion the founder of Uokha. Again, what we have here is a narrative tradition which explicitly points to a strong connection between two Owan communities even though they prefer to identify themselves as different communities. If anything there is a shared history between them. Ora and Ozalla traditions assert that their founders were the sons of Oba Ozolua. Whereas Ora's founder was said to be Uguan, Ozalla people point to Iyelolo as their progenitor.

Thus using the narrative traditions, I have established that in searching for the ethnic origins of the Owan people, one has to look to three groups: the aborigines, the Yoruba migrants and the Benin émigrés. Today, the traditions of the Benin migrants are dominant, with remnants of aboriginal myths and very limited reference to Yoruba origins. As I have argued elsewhere,

> On the whole, what can be said about the ethnic composition as far as current evidence will allow is that three major groups made up the Owan communities. First, were the aboriginal people who are seldom recognised. Clearly, they lived in all Owan communities as against Marshall and Ohikhokhai's assertion that they existed only in Ivbiaro. Second, Yoruba migrants from Ife and Ondo area have been identified as comprising sections of Uokha, Iuleha, and Otuo communities. Last were the Benin migrants who have dominated all narrative traditions which points to the fact that they might have formed the most important and prestigious of all the groups which moved into Owan.[19]

SYMBOLS, RITUALS, RELIGION, AND IDENTITY

Symbols, rituals, and religion illuminate the ethnic identity of the Owan people. Totemic observance was one way Owan people defined their ethnic and kinship identity. Totemism could be characterized as a set of processes which defined individual and group identity. Totems place individuals "into groups under the emblem of a common totemic species (animal or plant usually, but sometimes also objects, and natural phenomena) and set them apart from groups claiming common substance or origin under other species."[20] So for an average Owan person, totems define both their ethnic identity and their kinship relations. Because they have reverence for particular animals and plants, Owan people see the killing or eating of their totems as self-destruction. Thus, when totems die or are accidentally killed, Owan people give them formal burials as is done for deceased humans. Totems started out as practices based on religious and ritual beliefs. With time they became kinship emblems, social and cultural symbols which defined the people's identity. In every Owan community in which totemic observances exist, oral narratives explain the adoption of the totems by the people. Through oral tradition, societal norms are transmitted from generation to generation. Hence, it is possible to retrieve the narratives from informants through interviews. In the next few pages I will try to examine the narrative traditions which illumine the basis of Owan totemic practices.

The story of the "fiery leopard" in the Ora tradition of origin is a classic case of totems explaining community or ethnic identity. Following his migration to Ora, Uguan created the leopard as the "national" totem and created a shrine to the leopard for all the citizens of Oraland. He had been a prince of Benin and the leopard had been the royal emblem of the kingdom. The traditions declare that when Uguan was expelled from Benin he turned against the leopard. Nevertheless, when his wife had difficulty in birth, a diviner insisted that he return to his totemic emblem, the leopard. He did. His son was named Erhae-Ekpen (Ora-Ekpen) after the leopard. From then on the leopard became a community totem in Ora. Thus, the ethnic and kinship symbol of the Ora people emerged. The leopard provided Ora people with the framework for a shared cultural identity.

Throughout Owan there exists a level of totemic unity among the aboriginal groups. As a consequence of my analysis of totemic observances I came to the conclusion that the aboriginal population in Owan revered plant totems. Also associated with the early period was the reverence of snakes as totems, the most noticeable being boa-python reverence. This totemic practice possibly arose from an earlier python cult. In Owan communities such as Igue, Uokha, Otuo, Ihievbe, and Evbo-Mion, aboriginal groups combine boa-python totems with those of plants. Looking back at pre-colonial totemic practices, one can infer a common identity for these aboriginal groups in

Owan. As I have noted elsewhere, "the snake groups have been associated with authority in the early matriarchal societies. The snake totems are the most widespread and are found in fifty-one wards in nine communities, the python alone existing in thirty-seven, also in nine communities.... The boa-python is the community symbol in three communities and a village totem in four others."[21]

In Owan, religious beliefs and ritual practices have also formed part of the peoples' identity since earliest times. According to Schwartz, "Religion is ... one among the features of an identified or self-identifying group that could be taken by members of that set of ethnic groups as ethnonomonic."[22] The Owan people, while utilizing religious beliefs as identity symbols, have also employed them in their day to day life since the precolonial period. While they pray to their gods and goddesses for good health, bumper harvests, rains and protection from evil, religious practices also regulate their behavior both in private and public life. In the process, the Owan over the centuries have created a pantheon of gods and goddesses which now define them as a people. Among the Edo people of Nigeria, the mere mention of Ada-Obi shrine takes a person's mind to Owan. For them it is a known fact that the Owan are associated with Ada-Obi, even though it is really a shrine dedicated to the ancestors of only the Ada-Obi community. A number of other deities exist in the region.

For instance, Afuze in Emai community is home to the Oviagbede shrine, a shrine dedicated to the memory of a female figure who was the daughter of a blacksmith. Being an only child, she was barred by her father from marrying, because he wanted her to remain in her paternal home to bear a male child, so the child could inherit his property. Unfortunately she never had a child. At death she was deified. Contemporary oral tradition remembers her as "a woman who fought for the welfare of other women. She was very wealthy and prosperous. She did not marry. She was energetic and powerful. She challenged the powers of men."[23] Today Oviagbede represents different things to the two genders. For women, she is a fertility goddess. To men, she is a protector during wars. "Afuze indigenes believe that she is always concerned for their welfare. The feeling is prevalent that Ovia-gbede protects her people even without being asked. It is for this reason they annually offer sacrifices for the good she has brought them during the past year."[24]

The classic narrative tradition of deification in Owan relates to the story of Omouwa (Owan). She was said to have been from Uhonmora in Ora community. She married an Otuo man. For years she lived with her husband in Otuo. At her death her husband's relatives chose to bury her in Otuo rather than return her corpse to her paternal home in Uhonmora.[25] In most Owan traditions, it is customary at death for a woman's corpse to be returned to her place of birth, failing which her husband may be charged with treating his deceased wife as a slave. Oral tradition reports that following her burial, in the course of tracing her way back to Uhonmora, Omouwa turned into a river—the Owan. The name "Owan" was said to have been a corrupted version of "Omouwa." For centuries this deification was restricted to Uhonmora alone. Following the deification, the people of Uhonmora adopted all the species of fish in River Owan as their totem. It is from the name of the river that the Owan people later took their name. While for the most part deification in Owan communities was specific to villages and communities, Omouwa became an Owan-wide phenomenon.

On the eve of British colonialism in the area, the Owan people saw themselves as independent groups with narrative traditions pointing to social, political, and economic connections. These separate identities changed in the colonial and postcolonial periods. The next section will examine the environment in which Owan identity germinated.

COLONIALISM AND OWAN IDENTITY

The notion of ethnic identity is formed through the interaction of both internal and external forces. I have tried up to this point to examine the internal dynamics in the formation of

Owan identities. In this section of the paper I will try to explore the external influence, that is, British colonial impact on the formation of Owan identity. The first collective name to describe the Owan people was adopted by the British. The name "Ivbiosakon" came into use after the British established its rule in the region. A colonial assistant district officer, Mr. H.F. Marshall, later used the name in his intelligence report of 1937.[26] Before this time the term Ivbiosakon (meaning "children of one who files his or her teeth") referred specifically to the Ora people. The Ora people inherited the name by virtue of being descendants of Uguan, the son of Oba Ozolua. Oba Ozolua's nickname was "Obanosakon" ("the king who filed his teeth"). Without thorough investigation, the British applied the name to all the Owan people. However, the practice of filing the incisor teeth was previously common among the Northern Edo people in general (Ivbiosakon, Etsako, and Akoko-Edo people).

Following the defeat of the Benin Kingdom by the British in 1897, a colonial administrative system was established in the region. The British replaced the Benin monarchy in Owan. Owan communities came under the control of the district commissioner, who resided in Benin. Because only minimal control could be exercised from Benin, a district commissioner was stationed in Ifon District (which was considered to be closer than Benin) and he took control of the Ivbiosakon communities.[27] In 1905 the first "native" court was established at Afuze (Emai community) and this marked the beginning of the reference to the people as Ivbiosakon. From 1905 to 1937 the Owan people were administered as the Ivbiosakon districts of the Ishan and Kukuruku divisions.

In 1937 Marshall was instructed to carry out investigations and write an intelligence report to enable the colonial government to implement administrative reorganization. In his "proposals for the future" Marshall noted that,

> It is important to stress the fact that, while the Clans [Ivbiosakon communities] are closely connected by ties of custom, and tradition, each Clan has been in-

> dependent and has paid direct allegiance to the Oba of Benin. There never has been any form of central Iviosakon (sic) Council. At the present time, while all the Clans are anxious to recognize the ties which exist between them, and are perhaps even more anxious that the existence of the Iviosakon (sic) Clans should have the recognition of Government, they are not at present willing to forego any of their independence. I cannot, therefore, recommend any Central Native Administration with a Central Native Authority.[28]

Whereas Marshall was reluctant to recommend a central "native" authority for the whole of Ivbiosakon (Owan), the British colonial officials inadvertently created a conducive atmosphere for the growth of a new Ivbiosakon (Owan) identity. In fostering confederation for the Owan groups, the colonial officials were very careful not to antagonize the local people. The colonialists were praying fervently that the colonized should accept the new colonial dispensation and designs. This they did. As Marshall revealed, a clan (community) representative once noted, to the delight of the British, that "We want to have control over our own affairs, particularly over our money, but we do want a central Treasury for all Iviosakon (sic) for, how else are we going to get Iviosakon (sic) to combine?"[29] While the goal of the British was to create a confederal administrative system in the area, the colonial officials were willing to wait for the Owan people to demand it, rather than be seen to be imposing it on the Africans. For Marshall the amalgamation of the Owan communities into a confederation was only a matter of time. According to him,

> [t]here is little doubt in my mind, that, in the course of time, the Clans will agree to combine for all purposes, but the danger of complete confederation at the present time would be that, to the mind of the general public, the governing body would be too large and too remote to be anything but an innova-

tion of the "White Man," and the people would learn no more of the meaning of Native Administration than they know at present, which is practically nothing . . . Confederation should be the ultimate objective, but it must come from the people.[30]

The people had asked for a separate Ivbiosakon Division independent of Benin, Ishan, and Kukuruku divisions. However, because of insufficient personnel to administer a new division, Marshall leaned toward the incorporation of all Ivbiosakon communities into Ishan Division. The implementation of this recommendation was delayed by the outbreak of World War II in 1939. It was only in April 1945 that the Ivbiosakon communities were brought under the control of Kukuruku Division. In addition, an Ivbiosakon Federal Native Authority was established with executive authority for all Ivbiosakon communities. Its headquarters was located at Afuze. This arrangement lasted until 1952 when the people were consulted about the best local government system for the area. In 1954 a new Ivbiosakon District Council came into being. This became the administrative framework for the area up to 1960 when Nigeria gained its independence from the British. Clearly the attempt by the colonial government to institute a workable local administrative system helped to solidify a new identity for the Owan people. Thus, the Owan and the colonial government accepted the new identity, which was "Ivbiosakon people." This identity was not to remain unchanged for too long. The postcolonial period saw new demands and challenges for both the independent government and the Owan people. Nigeria's civilian government lasted for only six years before it was toppled by a military junta. Within a few months the country was plunged into a thirty-month civil war. One of the causes of that war was negative ethnic competition over the control of social, political, and economic power in the new nation-state.

POSTCOLONIAL OWAN IDENTITY

At independence the Owan people remained a minority ethnic group in the Nigerian polity. Even under a military regime, the creation of local governments was seen as a viable means of bringing government closer to the people. In order to achieve this goal, in February 1967 the military governor of what was then Mid-western Nigeria appointed a commission to look into the creation of a separate division for the Ivbiosakon.[31] The commission, which was headed by Mr. D. B. Patridge, had the following terms of reference:

a. to enquire into and ascertain the wishes of the people of Ivbiosakon as to: (i) the siting of the headquarters of the new Administrative Division created for their area; (ii) a suitable and acceptable name of the new division.
b. having regard to all related administrative, social and historical factors, to submit recommendations in respect of the matters specified above.[32]

There was no debate as to the necessity of the creation of a new division for the Ivbiosakon people. However, it was not easy to arrive at a new name for the division. The people suggested six different names. They were Owan, Edion, Ivbiosakon, Odion, Okugbe, and Ozolua. While five communities supported the adoption of "Owan," one each chose other names as listed. Some reservations were expressed about the name Owan. One was that the Owan River runs through only six of the eleven Owan communities. Nevertheless, in recommending Owan, the report took into consideration the fact that the name "should be as widely acceptable as possible and . . . should have some relevance to historical fact, or to prominent geographical features."[33] In picking Owan, Partridge argued that "I consider OWAN must be chosen since in spite of its shortcomings it can nevertheless be reasonably held to enjoy majority support."[34] Even though alternative names were suggested, the name "Owan" won the day. The military government went ahead to approve the recommendation of the commission. From 1967 Owan became both a name and an emblem of Owan people's identity. Today the people proudly call themselves by the name, and two local governments, Owan East and West Local Government Areas, remain as a testimony of the faith the people have in the name. It defines who they are, what they stand for, and their aspirations for the future.

CONCLUSION

I have in this short essay tried to explore the origins and evolution of Owan ethnic identity. Through an analysis of Owan narrative traditions and totemic observances, I have tried to establish that Owan ethnic origins are traceable to three groups: the aboriginal population in the area, the Benin migrants and the Yoruba migrants. The chapter also argues that religious practices, rituals, totemic symbols, and belief system define who the people are. Furthermore, it is clear from the analysis that Owan's ethnic identity has been dynamic; hence, that identity has changed according to the social and political exigencies of the time. It is certain that precolonial, colonial, and postcolonial developments have influenced the tone and content of Owan's ethnic identity. More importantly, the Owan people have remained aware of who they are in Nigeria's multiethnic society.

NOTES

1. Quoted in Gerald Bereman, "Bazar Behavior: Social Identity and Social Interaction in Urban India," in George De Vos and Lola Romanucci-Ross (eds.), *Ethnic Identity: Cultural Continuities and Change*, (Palo Alto, Calif.: Mayfield Publishing Company, 1975), 71.
2. G.B.L. Oyakhire, "The Institution of Traditional Chieftaincy in the Owan Culture Area of Bendel State in Nigeria, " unpublished manuscript in possession of the author, Benin City, Nigeria, 1981, 21.

3. Rudy I. Ohikhokhai, "Owan and the Benin Kingdom: An Analysis of a Relationship up to the Twentieth Century," M.A. thesis, University of Benin, Benin City, Nigeria, 1986, 2.
4. See George De Vos, "Ethnic Pluralism: Conflict and Accommodation," in De Vos and Romanucci-Ross (eds.), *Ethnic Identity,* 9.
5. Totems are plants and animals for which people have reverence. Totemism is based on the belief that the souls of their ancestors and ancestresses live in the plants and animals. Hence, they will not kill or eat the plants or animals.
6. Onaiwu W. Ogbomo, *When Men and Women Mattered: A History of Gender Relations among the Owan of Nigeria* (Rochester, N.Y.: University of Rochester Press, 1997), 49.
7. Ohikhokhai, "Owan and the Benin Kingdom," 28.
8. S. I. Lawani, *A History of Otuo* (Ibadan, Advent Press, 1947), 14.
9. Lawani, *A History of Otuo*, 14-15.
10. H. F. Marshall, *Intelligence Report on the Ivbiosakon Clans in Ishan and Kukuruku Division*, (Benin City: Ministry of Local Government and Chieftaincy Affairs, 1937), part 5, 4.
11. Quoted from Military Governor's Office, Mid-Western State of Nigeria, Benin City, *Investigation into the Role of Chiefs in the Mid-Western State, Divisional Report in Respect of the Owan Division* (Benin City: Military Governors Office November 1971) 59.
12. Jacob U. Egharevba, *A Short History of Benin* (Ibadan: Ibadan University Press, 1968).
13. Egharevba, *A Short History of Benin*, 85.
14. Owan Historical Text (hereafter referred to as O.H.T.) #92, interview with Mr. J. Ohiochoioya Afeinkhena, (66) Uokha, November 6, 1990; O.H.T. #94, interview with Pa. Akharumen Amaize (85), Uokha, November 8, 1990; O.H.T. #96 interview with Chief Edegbai Esezobo, (80), Uokha, November 9, 1990; O.H.T. #98 interview with Chief Ikhianvbode J. Ogboro (90), and Mr. Ikpekhai Evbotokhai, (80), Uokha, November 15, 1990. See also Ohikhokhai, "Owan and the Benin Kingdom."
15. See Ogbomo, *When Men and Women Mattered*, 29-30.
16. See Marshall, *Intelligence Report on the Ivbiosakon Clans*, Part 8, 3; Ogbomo, *When Men and Women Mattered*, 48; Ohikhokhai, "Owan and the Benin Kingdom," 21.
17. O.H.T #211 interview with Mr. Romanus O. Gbadamosi (58), and Mr. Andrew O. Isunuoya, (55), Ihievbe, September 13, 1990; O.H.T. #212 interview with Mr. Mosaidu Sedenu, (62), Ihievbe,

September 13, 1990; and O.H.T. #214 interview with Chief Aliu Ikpekhia (82), Ihievbe, September 14, 1990. See also Marshall, *Intelligence Report on the Ivbiosakon Clans,* Part 9, p.4.
18. O.H.T. #154 interview with Mr. Abraham Alukpe (54), and Mr. Christopher Alukpe, (32), Okpuje, March 17, 1991; O.H.T. #155 interview with Chief Eduke Ogedengbe (80), Avbiosi, March 18, 1991.
19. See Ogbomo, *When Men and Women Mattered*, 53.
20. Theodore Schwartz, "Cultural Totemism: Ethnic Identity Primitive and Modern," in De Vos and Romanucci-Ross (eds.), *Ethnic Identity*, 106.
21. See Ogbomo, *When Men and Women Mattered*, 53.
22. Schwartz, "Cultural Totemism," 108.
23. O.H.T. #76 interview with Madam Ilekesun Againe (85), priestess of Oviagbede shrine, Afuze, September 10, 1990.
24. Ogbomo, *When Men and Women Mattered*, 75.
25. O.H.T. #12 interview with Mr. Theo A. Esele, (58), Eme-Ora, September 7, 1990; O.H.T. #16, interview with Chief Okpaise Idornijie (88), Uhonmora, September 2, 1990.
26. Marshall, *Intelligence Report on the Ivbiosakon Clans.*
27. See Marshall, *Intelligence Report on the Ivbiosakon Clans*, Part 1, 12.
28. Marshall, *Intelligence Report on the Ivbiosakon Clans*, Part 1, 20.
29. Ibid.
30. Ibid., 20-21.
31. The commission came out with a report: D. B. Patridge, *A Report of an Inquiry into Certain Matters Connected with the Creation of a Separate Division for the Ivbiosakon Area*, (Mid-Western State of Nigeria, 1967).
32. See Patridge, *A Report of an Inquiry,* 1.
33. Ibid., 19.
34. Ibid., 20.

PART D

LANGUAGE, CULTURE, AND ART

17

THE MATA KHARIBU MODEL AND ITS OPPOSITIONS: CONFLICTS AND TRANSFORMATIONS IN CULTURAL VALUATION

Oyekan Owomoyela

INTRODUCTION

On Thursday September 7, 2000, Ato Quayson, the Ghanaian director of the African Studies Centre at Cambridge University, gave a lecture on "The Culture Hero in African Literature and Politics" at the Institute of African Studies of the University of Ghana, Legon. He led off with an endorsement of what Western thinkers like Charles Taylor (the Canadian philosopher), James Ferguson, Raymond Williams, and others have variously characterized as multiple modernities, fractured modernities, different social imaginaries, and so forth. However designated, the concept is very much like the old multiculturalism, an ideology that discourages, in whatever guise, the homogenization of experience and consciousness into a uniform modernity, which always tends to bear Western imprints.

Quayson's opinion, in which he appeared to be advocating an inclusive modernity that would have a place for African contributions, fits snugly into a long-standing debate among African writers and intellectuals on the relevance of the African experience in our time, a debate that goes back to colonial times, and that forms a record of the transformations African self-perception has undergone over the years. I propose in this essay to outline some of the highlights of the debate, and to discuss its implications for the African condition at the beginning of the new millennium. Wole Soyinka's vision, first expressed on the occasion of Nigeria's independence and continually elaborated since, provides the anchor for the ensuing discussion, with other African writers and scholars (mainly Nigerian and Ghanaian) providing support.

DUELING TENDENCIES

Derogation

Since the intrusion of Europeans into the African world with its devastating effects, Africans have been plagued by ambivalence about themselves, their past, their heritage, and their place in the world. Some commentators have expressed the conviction that the vicissitudes that the continent and its people have experienced are the consequences of pervasive and long ignored moral corruption, without which it would have been impossible for so few foreigners to effect the subjugation and colonization of so vast a continent.[1] Opposed to such thinkers have been cultural patriots who see the pre-European African world as no worse than that of its European conquerors, visionaries who believe that the European conquest in fact condemns the victors more than the vanquished.[2]

The dawning of the era of independence in Africa, with Ghana's attainment of self-rule in 1957, also witnessed the beginning of a campaign by African writers to deflate the euphoria that swept the continent. Their message was that the recovery of African history and heritage from colonial usurpation was no cause for celebration. The African legacy, they sneered, was rife with debasement and debauchery, and they held out little hope or expectation that the future would be any different. The prime example was Wole Soyinka, who shocked a nation exhilarated by the reality of release from colonial bondage, aglow with pride in the past accomplishments of its constituent peoples, and buoyant about its billing as the awakening giant of Africa, with his iconoclastic play *A Dance of the Forests*.[3] The planners of Nigeria's official independence celebrations had commissioned their most illustrious dramatist to produce a drama fit for the occasion, but what they got was far different from what they expected. It was duly performed as part of the festivities, but to a less than enthusiastic reception, for which its studied obscurity and ponderousness was only partly to blame.

According to *Forests*, Africa's inglorious past was peopled with murderous, megalomaniacal, self-indulgent rulers like Mata Kharibu, acquiescent, sycophantic hangers-on like his Court Historian, and degenerate courtesans like Madame Tortoise. What is more, the play suggests, the continent's history has been a recycling of these blights on humanity, and its future will be plagued by the repercussions of their offences. As a voice of vision from the past sums up the prognosis, "Unborn generations will be cannibals .... Unborn generations will, as we have done, eat up one another."[4]

A short while later a writer from so-called Francophone Africa took up Soyinka's refrain. In *Le Devoir de Violence* (1968; *Bound to Violence*),[5] Malian author Yambo Ouologuem traces the history of the Nakem Empire of the Saif dynasty from 1202 until the present. What he unearths is quite similar to Soyinka's findings about the African past—profligacy, lecherousness, incest, cannibalism, and worse, if that were possible. But the two works differ in a significant respect. In Soyinka's play the activities of foreign agencies on the continent are irrelevant; African perversion is native, home grown, and essential. By contrast, by the time Ouologuem's history opens, Islam is already entrenched in the Nakem Empire, and the account testifies to the effective presence of Christianity (and its European agents). As Soyinka has observed in his discussion of Ouologuem's narrative, "Nakem's history of pederasty, sodomy, sexual sadism, etc.," as Ouologuem recounts it, is in essence "a sanguinary account of the principal rival to the Christian mission in Africa [in which] Ouologuem pronounces the Moslem incursion into black Africa to be corrupt, vicious, decadent, elitist and insensitive."[6]

For all that, however, Ouologuem's primary target was not Islam or its Arab agents but the African past. Like Soyinka, he too was intent on dousing the jubilation attendant on the attainment of self-government, and the concomitant tendency on the part of euphoric Africans to regard their precolonial past as a golden age, the danger of which, Robert Fraser says, Soyinka had warned against in *Forests*. Fraser contrasts the two authors, though, by observing that whereas Soyinka incorporated into his play "a mechanism for the redemption of the past," Ouologuem allowed himself to fall "prey to self-mockery, and . . . 'inoculated' himself with a heavy dose of cynicism so as to attain resistance to the prevailing bug."[7]

Soyinka points out that Ouologuem's thoroughgoing debunking of African history begins at a point at which he does not have to describe pristine Africanity. Its main intention is to expose the thoroughly evil aspects of Islam in Africa, and, says Soyinka, his thoroughness in the enterprise, his "total and uncompromising rejection," leads inevitably to one question: "what was the authentic genius of the African world before the destructive alien intrusion?"[8] Put differently, what is Ouologuem's version of the picture Soyinka had himself offered in *Forests*? Soyinka goes on to suggest that Ayi Kwei Armah in *Two Thousand Seasons*[9] took it upon himself to fill in that lacuna in Ouologuem's account.[10] In other words he sees Armah's work as an elaboration of the project he had inaugurated in his celebrated play.

Armah's epic novel depicts a traditional African world organized around what he describes repeatedly as "our way, the way," an ethos characterized by systemic, egalitarian reciprocity, the embrace of life, and an expansiveness that welcomed strangers with open-armed hospitality. This last quality, in his telling, proved a disastrous vulnerability, because foreigners took advantage of it to insinuate themselves into the Africans' midst, and thereafter proceeded to destroy the existing order, short-circuit the life of "the way," impose servitude on the people, and finally sell multitudes of them into slavery. The foreigners reportedly came in two waves: first on the scene were the perversely licentious Arabs from out of the desert, predators who like the desert knew only how to take but not how to give; they were followed (after their gruesome overthrow) by Europeans who emerged like maggots out of the sea, and were bent on carting their African hosts into slavery across the oceans.

Like Ouologuem, Armah lumps Arabs and Europeans together as bloody invaders of the African world and renders them indistinguishable in their single-minded rapaciousness. He stresses their shared whiteness, and follows the negritude writers in reversing the color symbology of colonialism. Accordingly he assigns to black, usually associated with African peoples, all the positive values (of "our way, the way") while attaching their opposite to white. In his discussion of *Seasons*, Soyinka nevertheless absolves the novel of all racist intent, arguing rather that it "functions as a wide swab in the deck-clearing operation for the commencement of racial retrieval."[11] The novel, he adds, represents a "quest for . . . the black cultural psyche," whose loss "began as a result of the deliberate propagation of untruths by others, both for racist motives and to disguise their incapacity to penetrate the complex verities of black existence."[12] In the recovery effort, Armah's work serves, in this view, as a necessary (ritual) destruction of Europeans and Arabs as a preliminary to unearthing the positive African world that they had destroyed—the world of "our way," which is the way of reciprocity, of connectedness, and of life.[13]

Fraser is in substantial agreement with Soyinka in exonerating *Seasons* from any racism. Armah's version of "antiracist racism" is in Fraser's opinion excusable because the work is not art but rather myth, legend, and racial memory, something intended to "provide a strong, healing mythology." He adds, "In the context of the massive communal inferiority complex [prevalent in

Africa] . . . there is only one antidote, a heightening of self-respect, and we need fear no over-dosage. Armah's concern is to provide an overwhelming counteraction to the colonialist distortion of history."[14]

Soyinka's reading of Armah's work and Fraser's are valid, but only up to a point. Armah might be transported by adoration for "the way, our way," but it takes people to actualize a way, however one defines it, to *live* it, and in Armah's telling only a handful of the people, an almost negligible minority, actually did. By contrast, first the patriarchs (and men in general) betrayed the spirit of reciprocity and, emulating the mores of the predators from the desert, reduced the women to "things—things for pleasure, things for use, things in the hands of men,"[15] until the women revolted and ended the rule of men. Later, in the era of the destroyers from the sea, rulers who should have led the people in fighting off the plague instead colluded with its purveyors, thus facilitating the enslavement of their own people in return for trinkets and rum. As for the common men, they found a niche for themselves in the new economy, serving the foreigners as *askaris* and *zombis*, hired guns with no scruples about killing their own people in order to protect the foreign abusers. The collaborators harassed and persecuted the handful who hewed to "the way, our way," and sold them to the slavers, because their stubborn adherence to the path of virtue was an unbearable irritant to the rulers. Armah's disgust with the people (with the exception of the women and the faithful handful, his *fundis*) is so profound that he devises ingeniously horrid deaths for them and their foreign mentors, so horrid and gruesome that even Soyinka finds them objectionable: "the humane sensibility tends to recoil a little," he remarks.[16]

Affirmation

While the Soyinkas, the Ouologuems, and the Armahs looked at the African past and saw perdition, other Africans looked and saw a heritage that inspired pride, and cultures that were, in human and spiritual terms, if not in material terms, far superior to the Western impositions. As Fraser has pointed out, the gloomy portraits of the past were in fact an overcompensation for what Soyinka and his followers considered as unwarranted, or excessive glorification of the past, a tendency that they believed threatened to induce complacency in the face of an urgent need to confront moral and structural deficiencies. The tendency was exemplified par excellence in Chinua Achebe's seminal novel *Things Fall Apart*,[17] and in the poetry of negritude.

Achebe's partisan defense of traditional Africa would be included (along with negritude poetry) in what Fraser described as unwarranted or excessive glorification of the African past. Like the poets, Achebe was provoked to take up a pen because of his dissatisfaction with the colonialist misrepresentations of Africa that he had read. As a student of English at the colonial University College at Ibadan, he had had to read works like Joyce Cary's *Mister Johnson*, Joseph Conrad's *Heart of Darkness*, and Graham Greene's *The Heart of the Matter*. At a certain point he realized that what he had before him were supposedly true depictions of Africans and the African world, but he could not recognize himself or the world he knew in the portraits. He therefore decided to challenge the colonial distortions with his own version of the African world and his experience of it.

Things Fall Apart, as the title suggests, represents the intervention of Europeans in African affairs as a disruptive rather than salutary event. The Igbo world, particularized in Umuofia, stands for the entire continent. Achebe painstakingly documents its ordered and harmonious life, giving the lie to colonialist claims that before the arrival of the Europeans a figurative darkness enveloped the land and its people. Though by no means perfect or perfectly egalitarian, Achebe shows, the society had devised effective remedies for whatever eventuality its past experience had taught it to anticipate: unfriendly acts by neighboring villages like Mbaino; incidences of wife beating by stubborn men like Uzowulu; even the accidental but still abominable shedding of kindred blood, the event that resulted in Okonkwo's banishment to his mother's lineage village of Mbanta and the destruction of his compound in Umuofia. In sum, Achebe's thesis is that the world Africans inhabited before the European intrusion, imperfect though it was, "was not one long night of savagery from which the first Europeans acting on God's behalf delivered them."[18]

Armah, as we have seen, faults the people of "the way" for their unquestioning hospitality and unstinting receptiveness toward strangers, an unfortunate virtue that afforded the predators and destroyers an opening to insinuate themselves into the heart of the community and thereafter destroy it from inside. Similarly, Achebe testifies to Umuofia's learning, after the destruction of Abame, the expediency of tolerance of foreigners, and the wisdom of avoiding precipitate action in the face of events and phenomena the likes of which they had never known or heard about. Thus when strange white beings arrived in their midst, they avoided the Abame response of destroying the stranger (and strangeness) that they perceived as a portentous abomination. Umuofia's hospitality and perspicaciousness did spare it immediate destruction, but not eventual disorientation and disintegration. The white intruders soon usurped traditional authority and imposed their own version of disorder on the people. In place of the court over which the nine *egwugwu* presided, for example, the tribunal whose Solomonic wisdom was manifest in the matter of Uzowulu the wife beater, the white men "built a court where the District Commissioner judged cases in ignorance."[19] Most importantly, in Obierika's summation, they put a knife to what held Umuofia together and caused the community to fall apart.

The negritude poets' approach to championing the cause of African cultures at the expense of Western cultures took both negative and positive forms. The negative strand consisted in exposing the insufficiency of Western habits that their apologists represented as the apogee of human accomplishment, while the positive demonstrated the splendor of the African ways that the colonialists maligned. An example of the former approach is David Diop's encapsulation in "Hammer Blows" of the process and practice of colonization, which for the poet bespoke the inhuman, murderous propensities of Westernity:

> The White man killed my father
> My father was proud
> The White man raped my mother
> My mother was beautiful
> The White man bent my brother under the sun of the roads
> My brother was strong,
> The White man turned towards me
> His hands red with black blood
> And said in his Master's voice
> "Boy! A drink, a towel, some water!"[20]

Léopold Sédar Senghor's poem, "Snow Upon Paris," addresses the Lord in a less strident but no less telling accusation against the brute might of the West that lays both humans and Nature to waste, brute might embodied in

> White hands that fired the shots which brought the empires crumbling
> Hands that flogged the slaves, that flogged You
> Chalk-white hands that buffeted You, provided painted hands that buffeted me
> Confident hands that delivered me to solitude to hatred
> . . . .
> They cut down the dark forest for railway sleepers
> They cut down the forests of Africa to save Civilization,
> for there was a shortage of human raw-material.[21]

In another poem, "New York," Senghor explicitly compares Africa and the West, juxtaposing African and Western values and unequivocally favoring the former. Aggregating to coalesce into the phenomenon that is the city of New York are such elements as blue metallic eyes, skyscrapers with muscles of steel and skins of weathered stone, birds falling dead on bald sidewalks, and legs stuffed into nylon stockings. Absent from the picture are pastures, children's laughter, and tender words from mouths that are lipless anyway. Moreover, the city offers neither peace nor love, only "Insomniac nights . . . tormented by fatuous fires, while the klaxons cry through the empty hours // And dark waters bear away hygienic loves, like the bodies of children on a river in flood."[22]

In contrast to what some Western critics of Africa (taking their cue from Soyinka and company) would conclude, Senghor recommends an ameliorating and humanizing infusion of the spirit of Africa into the heart of the West, a spirit that is ready to hand right there in the midst of the West, in the heart of New York City, if the city (or the West) would only open its eyes and mind:

> New York! I say to New York, let the black blood flow into your blood
> Cleaning the rust from your steel articulations, like an oil of life
> Giving your bridges the curve of the hills, the liana's suppleness.[23]

Apostasy

The postindependence disasters that vindicated Soyinka's pessimistic predictions of what the future held also lent credence to his unflattering construction of the past. He has dutifully documented the unfolding morass in later works like *Madmen and Specialists* (1971), *The Man Died* (1972), *Season of Anomy* (1973), *A Play of Giants* (1984), and *The Open Sore of a Continent* (1996). As in *Forests*, Nigeria provides the particular contexts of his portraiture, but the entire continent is in fact implicated. The works constitute a record of betrayal and usurpation—betrayal of the people's hopes and aspirations by corrupt leaders, and usurpation of power by military rulers who took advantage of the civilians' own enabling corruption. The pervasive disillusionment has, not surprisingly, cured staunch defenders of the African experience of their sanguine outlook and plunged them into despair. For instance, Achebe's personal involvement on the Biafran side of the Nigerian Civil War inspired the essay, *The Trouble with Nigeria*,[24] in which, although the author concentrates on the Nigerian condition, his message can be generalized across the whole continent. It opens with a categorical statement:

> The trouble with Nigeria is simply and squarely a failure of leadership. There is nothing wrong with the Nigerian character. There is nothing wrong with the Nigerian land or landscape or water or air or anything else. The Nigerian problem is the unwillingness or inability of its leaders to rise to the responsibility, to the challenge of personal example which are the hallmarks of true leadership. [25]

But in a later revision of his diagnosis he included the general populace in his indictment. He makes Ikem tell the student body at Kangan University in *Anthills of the Savannah* (1987) that there was also a failure of followership—on the part of workers who go on strike because they are denied perquisites the departed colonizers had devised for themselves, and on the part of students who criticize the leadership for corruption while themselves engaging in buying votes during their elections, and destroying public property because they are not as pampered as they would wish.[26] And although Achebe asserts in his essay that there is nothing wrong with the people's character, his fiction, in which Kangan represents Nigeria specifically and all of Africa by extension and implication, seems to suggest the opposite, for example, when the people behave as though a gruesome public execution of armed robbers is a funfair.[27]

Achebe's *Anthills* signals a significant volte-face from his stance in *Things Fall Apart*, no doubt partly in response to the counterattack Western apologists for the colonial, civilizing, and missionizing enterprises, whose influence on African writers is quite considerable (for obvious reasons), have mounted against African complaints against the rape of the continent. The refrain from the apologists has been that Africans should stop blaming

Europeans for the continent's problems and accept their own responsibility for them. But an apposite Yoruba proverb goes, *Wón ní, Amúkùún erù é mà wóò. Ó ní ìsàlè ló ti wó wá* ("They say, 'Deformed one, your head load is crooked!' He responds, 'The crookedness starts all the way from the ground'"). Its import is consistent with Edward Said's insistence that when we consider the sorry state of affairs in postcolonial situations we "take the disorder back to the colonial intervention in the first place—which is what Chinua Achebe did . . . in his great novel *Things Fall Apart*."[28] In *Anthills,* Ikem contributes a pertinent comment in his Kangan University speech in the form of another proverb: "If you want to get at the root of murder . . . you have to look at the blacksmith who made the matchet." He adds, however, that "it was only intended to enlarge the scope of our thinking not to guide policemen investigating an actual crime."[29] In other words, it does not suggest that one should arrest the blacksmith who manufactured the matchet, but that one should acknowledge, at least, his part in making the crime possible. An appropriate analogy is the discussion in the United States regarding handguns. Opponents of handguns insist more and more that gun manufacturers be held culpable for crimes in which their product is used, almost to the same degree as the criminals who actually committed the crimes, even though the manufacturers are not guilty of actively inciting or inducing the criminals. No such extenuation is available to European colonizers and neocolonizers, whose primary responsibility for the African condition is as direct as their manipulation of events on the continent is continuous, so much so that only historical myopia and deliberate self-delusion can explain the minimization of their agency.

The Walk and Its Reception

Bí a ti nrìn la se nkoni. So goes another Yoruba proverb, meaning, "The way you walk determines the reception you get." In other words, self-presentation largely dictates the regard others accord the self. If some influential Africans are disposed to accept the imputation of native African perversion, the reaction from outside to the anomie that has perennially threatened to become the permanent state in Africa is typified by the writings of the brash Afrophobe, V. S. Naipaul. His essays and novels set in Africa unsurprisingly speak eloquently of his antipathy toward the continent and its people. He is offensive enough in essays like "A New King for the Congo: Mobutu and the Nihilism of Africa"[30] and "The Crocodiles of Yamoussoukro"[31] and his novel, *A Bend in the River*.[32] The depth of his disdain becomes even more evident when the sentiment forces itself into a work that has nothing to do with Africa. *Among the Believers: An Islamic Journey*,[33] a record of his travels in Islamic Asia, provides him with ample opportunities to indulge his characteristic superciliousness toward any culture that deviates from his beloved Western one, and to lampoon any people not descended from European stock. The Asian setting of his travelogue does not, however, prevent him from venting his hatred of Africa, as in the following passage where he is describing the everyday street scenes that assail his vision in an Asian city and fill him with terror: "Africans, camel carts, dwarfs in green turbans: they were not memories that could be trusted. They were more like ideas suggested by nerves, my nerves at being in the subcontinent for the first time."[34] A while later he records a conversation with his Pakistani (Sind) host whom he describes as a newcomer to Islamic fastidiousness. The issue is the relative merits of different religions, and Ahmed is arguing the superiority of Islam over earlier religions, specifically Judaism and Christianity:

> Moses, he said, was all law; that was too harsh. Jesus was all compassion. Ahmed said, "In a world where there are people like Africans and Negroes, that doesn't make sense. If you turn the other cheek to a primitive fellow, it annoys him."[35]

Perhaps the reference to Africans and Negroes in that context seared itself into Naipaul's memory because of its sheer gratuitousness, but it probably found fertile soil in his consciousness because of its congruence with opinions he has himself often propagated in his writings about "nihilistic" Africa.

Africa as Disabling Tag, and Sign of Disability

To reiterate, writers like Soyinka and Ouologuem presumably wrote their gloomy tales of the African past (and in Soyinka's case prognostications for the future) expressly because they felt a necessity to deflate the unwarranted soaring pride of people finally coming into their own after centuries of abuse and decades of subjugation. In this view, they saw a need to bring down to earth such starry-eyed cultural patriots who dared to confidently assert the superiority of their world, and to proclaim, like the Martiniquan Aimé Césaire, a "strange pride" in African ancestry generally:

> those who invented neither gunpowder nor compass
> those who tamed neither stream nor electricity
> those who explored neither sea nor sky
> but without whom the earth would not be the earth.[36]

The pride is "strange" precisely because it is a pride in the obverse of the qualities and "successes" that enabled the West to impose its sway over other peoples in every corner of the earth, and that thus (supposedly) confirmed its superiority over the rest.

Whether as testimony to the constancy of the African reality or as evidence of the circularity of time and history, sentiments such as Soyinka's and Ouologuem's are increasingly resurgent among disillusioned Africans, who ridicule ideas like Césaire's as wrong headed or degenerate. Philosophers steeped in European thought are embarrassed by the kind of traditionalism evident in his "strange pride," advocating instead an embrace of "the spirit of Europe."[37] Doing so, of course, entails a corresponding distancing from the spirit of Africa, inasmuch as the discourse of colonialism and its successors have cast Europe and Africa in manichean opposition. One form the distancing has taken is the *de*legitimizing (or erasure) of Africanness as a viable identity option.

Of the projects Kwame Anthony Appiah pursues in his book, *In My Father's House* (1992), the most dogged is the assault on the notion of race and other bases for racial identification and identity.[38] It forms part of an undoubtedly serious intellectual debate on a subject that many scholars consider important, but I am interested more than anything in the rationale for it. Without benefit of statistics from a scientific survey, I would aver that the popularity of the intellectual movement against race and race-based identity has been more marked among non-Europeans, or non-Westerners, Africans especially, than among people who can claim, say, English, French, German, Spanish, or Russian descent. It also has, as far as I can tell, only a very small following among the Chinese or the Japanese, despite the latter's well known adoration of Western cultural productions.

In the chapter entitled "African Identities," Appiah not only questions the validity of the conventionally accepted concept, "African," but he also challenges "invented" subordinate identities, like Asante, Igbo, Shona, or Yoruba.[39] That does not mean, though, that he believes the continent is empty of all identity, for he acknowledges that as a result of European activities on the continent—explorations, missionizing, and the establishment of Western schools—"there is no doubt that now . . . an African identity is coming into being."[40] This new identity is not contestable, he suggests, because it is free of the falsehoods according to which the others have been theorized: "race, a common historical experience, a shared metaphysics . . . falsehoods too serious for us to ignore."[41]

But Appiah's assigning so powerful an identity-creating agency to European actions leads one to question an earlier argument of his. At the beginning of his discussion he invokes nostalgic recollections of African childhoods by Soyinka (in *Aké*) and Camara Laye (in *L'Enfant Noir*) and fictional accounts of pre-European Africa by Achebe as proof that even children weaned early from their parents' and grandparents' traditional cultures nevertheless remained immersed in those cultures. "To insist in these circumstances on the alienation of (Western-) educated colonials, on their incapacity to appreciate and value their own traditions," Appiah contends, "is to risk mistaking both the power of this primary experience and the vigor of many forms of cultural resistance to colonialism."[42] Yet, according to him, the primary experience is not vigorous enough to resist the supplanting, by colonially imposed alternatives, of the identities it sanctioned.

A quotation from Chinua Achebe, which Appiah uses as the epigraph for his final chapter, offers a clue as to the impulse that underlies his contentions. In it Achebe refers to "tags" like "African" by which he might be identified in a Cambridge shop. A few pages into the chapter Appiah returns to it, writing, "The passage from Achebe . . . continues in the words: 'All these tags, unfortunately for the black man, are tags of disability.' But it seems to me that they are not so much labels of disability as disabling labels."[43] Conceived as a label of disability or a disabling label, Africanity would in either case be unattractive to people, especially to upwardly and outwardly mobile cosmopolitans and celebrities, to whom more attractive options are available, and who are free to choose. In Appiah's words,

> If an African identity is to empower us . . . what is required is not so much that we throw out falsehood but that we acknowledge first of all that race and history and metaphysics do not enforce an identity: that we can choose, within broad limits set by ecological, political, and economic realities what it will mean to be African in the coming years.[44]

Nothing here about culture, habits of the mind, or "the way, our way," but everything about ecological, political, and economic determinants, perhaps (in other, frank, plain parlance) "the spirit of Europe."

Africa in the World: Pariah or Partner

I return now to Quayson and his talk of multiple modernities, and to the prospects of making something of Africa a component of it. Two years before Quayson delivered his lecture at Legon, on August 24, 1998, to be precise, his compatriot Kofi Annan, the secretary general of the United Nations, paid a triumphal visit to his native country to receive an honorary degree from the University of Science and Technology at Kumasi in recognition of his achievements. In his address to the audience assembled for the occasion, he observed that Africans had demonstrated their capabilities to other peoples around the world, and urged them to continue living up to expectation. According to a *Daily Graphics* reporter, "He stressed that this is an age where peoples all over the world must learn from each other [rather] than the era in which people from the so-called Third World had to learn from the First World."[45]

While Quayson seemed initially to be saying something very much like what Annan had earlier advocated, divergences became apparent as Quayson went farther into his speech. What had sounded like a space-clearing gambit gradually took on a different tenor as he proceeded to enumerate certain African practices of which he disapproved, and which would have no place in his modernity, implicitly because they were at variance with Western modalities that have proved effective and efficacious. For example, he declared, in accord with what has become standard (but highly suspect) knowledge about African gender relations, that traditional African practices were characteristically "counter-women." Perhaps because the talk was not specifically on gender relations, to which he alluded only in passing in the course of discussing some novels, he did not substantiate the declaration, treating it rather as a given, a settled proposition, and the audience accepted it as such.

He was also critical of what he described as the African tendency to personalize transactions, giving as his example a hypothetical youth seeking menial employment at the University of Ghana at Legon. Such a youth, said Quayson, would be directed by his father to seek out a certain Mr. So-and-So, husband to a cousin on the father's mother's side, who held a job at the university, and who, therefore, would arrange for a suitable job for the youth. The point, of course, was that Africans in such situations placed knowing people, and the people they knew, above possessing skills, and the appropriateness of the skills for the employment in question, and trusting in a "blind," therefore impartial and transparent, selection process.

Obviously a conflict exists between Quayson's valuation of African approaches, or the African "way," and Annan's. Whereas Annan suggests that the African difference might have something to teach the world, Quayson's belief, for which his characterization of African gender proclivities and his citation of the personalization of transactions are illustrations, seems to be that Africans would do well to abandon their "way" and embrace the spirit of Europe. Since he did not dwell on the gender question, I too will skip over it. And since I have sought elsewhere to make the case for the African preference for the personal (or human) approach to transactions,[46] I will not rehash the argument here. I will point out, though, that the impersonal, automatized Western habit Quayson favors is no more than a contingency of the liberal necessity to govern at a distance. This governmental strategy requires that everything, people included, be reduced to statistics, be quantified, and be made amenable to generalized formulaic manipulation.[47]

Towards an African Modernity: Sotrek and Stall 72

Quayson's dig at African personalization of transactions brought to my mind two conflicting Accra experiences, both involving approaches to marketing. Sotrek Groceries is a modern store in the Osu area of the city, patronized mainly by the Westernized elite and the expatriate community. It offers the same complement of processed and packaged goods (most of them imported) that one will find in modest supermarkets in European and American cities. Outside the store, a permanent African market composed of stalls maintained by a few women has established itself. The wares on sale in this open-air mall include such items as yams, plantains, potatoes, vegetables, peppers, and the like, commodities that by some understanding are not on sale in the grocery store. Sotrek patrons therefore customarily make supplementary stops at the outdoor stalls after completing their shopping inside the establishment.

While Sotrek's prices are fixed, the women's are subject to negotiation: seller and buyer match negotiating skills and conclude a sale if they reach an agreement, or forego one if no terms can be agreed. Done in the right spirit, the negotiating is an exhilarating exercise, which for many African traders, buyers and sellers alike, is the most pleasant aspect of trading. It establishes a human bond between merchant and customer, and at the conclusion of the process, whether it results in a sale or not, both feel a warm glow of human contact and look forward to the next encounter.

In the traditional Yoruba world, the largest market in any sizable town is usually the *ojà oba*, literally "the king's market," because it is customarily situated in front of the king's palace. It is typically a sprawling open-air complex that is the focus of life in the community when it is in session. Characteristically a chaos of clamorous transactions, it generates high decibels of noise audible from miles away, and the noise level is an index of the vitality of the market, which in turn reflects that of the community; in other words, the noisier the market the wealthier, healthier, and more prosperous the community is. But what explains the noise? The haggling and bargaining, of course; but a Yoruba proverb places an instructive construction on it. It says, *Gba wèrè, ng ò gba wèrè, lojà fi nhó* ("Accept the imputation of imbecility;" "I will not accept the imputation of imbecility": that is the reason why the market is noisy). The idea is that for a prospective buyer to agree to the amount the seller asks initially is to accept the seller's imputation that the buyer must be an imbecile; and for the seller to accept the amount the prospective buyer offers initially would be to accept the buyer's imputation that the seller must be an imbecile. The exchange, which is conducted with considerable wit and humor, is in fact a performance that incorporates much that is aesthetic and that is often as important as the conclusion of a sale, if not more so. It is as much a display of mental acuity as a celebration of vitality, and a ritual of community and fellowship.

The phenomenon of bargaining is not peculiar to the Yoruba world but pervades Africa, including Ghana. Unfortunately, the traders outside Sotrek have become so familiar with the supermarket pricing culture, and have become so used to Western and westernized African clients, that they have developed some impatience for the odd customers who want to engage in protracted haggling instead of paying the asking prices which, though high by local market standards, are still quite modest in comparison with Sotrek's. I happen to delight in bargaining and in the good-natured banter that normally accompanies it (at least in the right contexts); I was therefore chagrined to be met with irritation and insulting asides when I gave reign to my haggling proclivities at the stalls, which I had mistaken for an African environment.

The other, more pleasant anecdote concerns my experience at African Things, also known as Stall No. 72, at the beachfront Arts Centre also in Accra. On sale here are assorted items of merchandise like leather jewelry boxes, leather chess sets and desk pads, Asante stools, wood and soapstone figurines, brass bracelets, *kente* strips, and other assorted goods. African Things is unique in this section of the centre in being managed by a woman, as the women's domain seems to be the more permanent structure to the front, dedicated mainly to textiles. The main attraction of African Things is the quality of the goods, which is far higher than that of the stock in the neighboring men-owned stalls. More important for me, though, was my discovery that the proprietress delighted in bantering and bargaining with her customers. My visits to the shop became such a welcome experience for both of us that always on seeing me she invited me to sit with her in the raised recess from where she supervised her wares. There, behind a low platform of leather items, we discussed prices, politics, and other topics of mutual interest.

We were thus occupied one afternoon when a gentleman dressed in the sort of dark gray pinstriped suit that African diplomats favor came shopping. From his accent I surmised that he was from a Francophone African country. With him was another man who seemed to be an aide. The diplomat was interested in a small Asante stool, a battery-powered wall clock shaped like the map of Africa, and a wood carving stained to simulate ebony—the usual touristy stuff. He asked the proprietress how much they were, and she gave him her usual inflated starting prices. The diplomat consulted perfunctorily with his companion and then asked if the woman would wrap the items while he looked at other stores for more articles of interest to him. On his return he asked his companion to take the articles to the car, and counted out the amount the woman had asked in payment. After his departure I commented jokingly that my hostess must love customers like him, since they gave her what she asked and spared her the trouble of haggling. No, she said; the greatest pleasure she derived from her occupation was the opportunity it gave her to talk to people and get to know them. You could not really know buyers who simply gave you what you asked and walked away with their purchases, whereas you could know those who lingered to chat with you, disagreed with you over prices, tried to bend your will to theirs, and dared you to bend theirs to yours.

I mentioned this latter experience to Quayson during the question period following his talk and asked his view. To his credit he agreed that the human contact that characterizes African transactions is indeed something worth preserving, even propagating.

The Reality of Africa, and the Uses of the Past

Appiah's discourse on African *identity* to which I referred earlier is in the main an argument for pluralizing the noun; it also establishes a hierarchy of identities based on legitimacy, the one resulting from European influence apparently sitting somewhere near the top, and those erroneously theorized (in his view) on the basis of "race, a common historical experience, a shared metaphysics" and the like lying somewhere in the nether regions. The same argument, one assumes, would apply to African culture(s), and to Armah's "our way, the way."

I have also cited Quayson's endorsement of multiple modernities—of a variety of social (and cultural) imaginaries, of what earlier thinkers have characterized as cultural diversity—in our contemporary human community, the implication being that some space must be cleared on the world stage for African inclusion and active participation. I have also referred to Annan's earlier expression of his belief and hope that Africa would make meaningful contributions to the world's pool of assets, that Africa would be a source, a donor, and not always a recipient. The question we need to answer, then, is: What did Annan and Quayson have in mind as African contributions? One assumes that they were not referring to technological or material commodities—South African diamonds or Nigerian petroleum, for example. One assumes further that they did not mean the regurgitated concepts and practices that modernized, Westernized, Europeanized Africans internalized in the first place in the course of their fashioning in Western institutions. Such warmed-over westernisms, with all their African veneer, cannot logically meet Annan's wishes, and are not consistent with the imperative of agglomerating truly multiple modernities that Quayson reminds us is necessary. One suspects, therefore, that they meant such things as would be subsumed under "our way," things specifically, and uniquely, African.

What the foregoing indicates is *African* alternatives, habits of the mind that characterized the cultures that inhabited the African space before the arrival of Europeans and their influences. For my purposes it matters not at all that these cultures cannot be totalized (that is, cannot be presumed to be invariable and homogenous in all particulars) as scholars like Appiah suggest is intended by the application of a collective designation to them. The caveat that there is no such uniformity as the collective modifier "African" implies is in the nature of a red herring, a copout, since one can say the same of the classifier "European" or "German." It matters only that, in their diversity, Africans, traditional Africans (and I use the designation deliberately and advisedly, fully mindful of a host of possible challenges to its conceptual validity), evolved specific and characteristic ways of thinking, and living, and being, that served them well for centuries before the white men arrived. Nor can we allow ourselves to be sidetracked by the contentions that hankering for treasures from the African past amounts to uncritical traditionalism, or suggests a fixation on fossilized anachronisms. These too are derogations attributable to embarrassment by the African connection. There are, certainly, updated and usable traditional approaches to life and the universe that bear the stamp of uniquely African ways of being and adapting.

Moreover, one assumes that Annan, certainly, and Quayson, probably, meant African beliefs and practices that they adjudge as superior (or at least as good alternatives) to those available in all other cultures elsewhere in the world; the very opposite, that is, of the sort of things the "First World" cites as grounds for, as it were, keeping Africa quarantined lest it infect the rest with its pathologies. That being the case, one would assume that ascertaining marketable African "ways" would be the primary preoccupation of African and Africanist scholars, that conscientious Africanists would be busily assembling a catalogue of such contributable Africanisms in the interest both of rehabilitating the African image and of enriching the world therewith. Experience has, unfortunately, proved the contrary as this essay has sought to demonstrate. For a variety of reasons, self-demonizing self-criticism has proved powerfully attractive to numerous self-professed African champions of the African cause, and Africanists have been no less vociferous than others in the campaign.

Amply apparent from this discussion is the readiness, even eagerness, with which African writers and scholars have embraced the project of self-criticism. Taking Soyinka's *A Dance of the Forests* as a starting point and moving through works like Ouologuem's *Bound to Violence*, Armah's *Two Thousand Seasons*, Soyinka's *Season of Anomy*, Achebe's *Anthills of the Savannah*, and, finally Soyinka's *The Open Sore of a Continent*, one must concede that such earlier impulses to celebrate as were evident in Achebe's *Things Fall Apart* have gone into conspicuous abeyance, rendering passé the reason Fraser cited for the iconoclastic spirit of the years immediately following independence, and making such calls as Soyinka recently made for Africans to stop blaming others for their problems and accept responsibility somewhat superfluous. Moreover, the Africa that the "corrective" self-criticism has presented to the world has unfortunately been one of near-general malignant patriarchy; near-general compulsive urges to sell kith and kin into slavery; near-general spontaneous orgies of fratricidal murders (such as the world recently witnessed among the Tutsi and the Hutu in Burundi); and near-general cravings to mutilate women and children (as Foday Sankoh and his "force" exhibited in Sierra Leone). The rationalization for such imaging, namely, that we must face the truth about ourselves if we are ever to deal effectively with our shortcomings, must be seen for the self-serving subterfuge that it often is. It suggests either that *as a whole* Africans are a worse lot than the rest of the world *as a whole*, or that unless (and until) Africans become uniformly more perfect than the rest of the world they must be proclaimed pariahs. Indeed, it seems as though we have willed ourselves into forgetting the inescapable truth that European adventurers inaugurated the disordered springs that ushered in the continent's subsequent seasons of anomie.

My conclusion is that Africans and Africanists err if they believe that they serve Africa's best interest by devoting their geniuses to reducing the continent to a mere invention without substance, and the identities stemming from it to chimerical outcomes of erroneous theorization, when they exercise their mandarin freedom to choose other (supposedly uninvented), non-African identities, or when they envelop the continent and its people in a seemingly essential pathology that the rest of the world must be protected from. Africa's best interest will be served by affirmation of its rightful place in the world, by recuperation of the best of the continent's cultural heritage, and by taking the present difficulties confronting the land and its people to their sources, to those, that is, who ordered the disordered spring(s) in the first place, while also striving, of course, for positive change.

NOTES

1. Kwasi Wiredu, *Philosophy and an African Culture* (Cambridge: Cambridge University Press, 1980), 61.
2. Edward Said's discussion of the European conquest of most of the world, in *Culture and Imperialism* (New York: Knopf, 1983), is most instructive on this issue.
3. Wole Soyinka, *Five Plays: A Dance of the Forests, The Lion and the Jewel, The Swamp Dwellers, The Trials of Brother Jero, The Strong Breed* (London: Oxford University Press, 1964).
4. Ibid., 55.
5. Yambo Ouologuem, *Le Devoir de Violence* (Paris: Editions du Seuil, 1968); *Bound to Violence*, translated by Ralph Manheim (New York: Harcourt Brace Jovanovich), 1971.
6. Wole Soyinka, *Myth, Literature and the African World* (Cambridge: Cambridge University Press, 1976), 105.
7. Robert Fraser, *The Novels of Ayi Kwei Armah* (London: Heinemann, 1980), 67–68.
8. Soyinka, *Myth, Literature and the African World*, 105.
9. Ayi Kwei Armah, *Two Thousand Seasons* (London: Heinemann, 1979).
10. Soyinka, *Myth, Literature and the African World*, 106.
11. Wole Soyinka, *Season of Anomy* (New York: Third Press, 1974), 105.
12. Ibid., 107.
13. Armah, *Two Thousand Seasons*, 111–112.
14. Fraser, *The Novels of Ayi Kwei Armah*, 73.
15. Armah, *Two Thousand Seasons*, 59.
16. Soyinka, *Myth, Literature and the African World*, 111.
17. Chinua Achebe, *Things Fall Apart* (London: Heinemann, 1958).
18. Chinua Achebe, *Morning Yet on Creation Day* (Garden City, N.Y.: Anchor, 1976), 59.
19. Achebe, *Things Fall Apart*, 156.
20. David Mandessi Diop, "The Time of the Martyrs," in *Hammer Blows and Other Writings*, translated and edited by Simon Mpondo and Frank Jones (Bloomington: Indiana University Press, 1973), 40–41.

21. Léopold Sédar Senghor, "Snow upon Paris," in *Selected Poems*, translated and introduced by John Red and Clive Wake (New York: Atheneum, 1969), 7.
22. Léopold Sédar Senghor, "New York," in *Selected Poems*, 70.
23. Senghor, "New York," 79.
24. Chinua Achebe, *The Trouble with Nigeria* (London: Heinemann, 1983).
25. Ibid., 1.
26. Chinua Achebe, *Anthills of the Savannah* (New York: Anchor Books, 1989), 144–148.
27. Ibid., 36–39.
28. Said, *Culture and Imperialism*, 234.
29. Achebe, *Anthills*, 146.
30. V. S. Naipaul, "A New King for the Congo: Mobutu and the Nihilism of Africa," in *The Return of Eva Peron, with The Killings in Trinidad* (New York: Alfred Knopf, 1980).
31. V. S. Naipaul, "The Crocodiles of Yamoussoukro," in *Finding the Center: Two Narratives* (London: André Deutsch, 1984).
32. V. S. Naipaul, *A Bend in the River* (New York: Alfred Knopf, 1979).
33. V. S. Naipaul, *Among the Believers: An Islamic Journey* (New York: Knopf, 1981).
34. Ibid., 94.
35. Ibid., 111.
36. Aimé Césaire, *Return to My Native Land*, translated by John Berger and Anna Bostok (Baltimore, Md.: Penguin, 1969), 74.
37. Paulin Hountondji, *African Philosophy: Myth and Reality* (Bloomington: Indiana University Press, 1983), 172.
38. Kwame Anthony Appiah, *In My Father's House: Africa in the Philosophy of Culture* (New York: Oxford University Press, 1992).
39. Ibid., 177–180.
40. Ibid., 174.
41. Ibid.
42. Ibid., 7.
43. Ibid., 176.
44. Ibid.
45. *Daily Graphic*, "UST Honours Kofi Annan," 25 August 1998, 3.
46. Oyekan Owomoyela, "African Philosophy: The Conditions of Its Possibility," in *The African Difference: Discourses on Africanity and the Relativity of Cultures* (Johannesburg: Witswatersrand University Press, 1969), 59.

47. See Nikolas Rose, "Governing 'Advanced' Liberal Democracies," in Andrew Barry et al., eds., *Foucault and Political Reason: Liberalism, Neo-Liberalism and Rationalities of Government* (Chicago: University of Chicago Press, 1996), 37–64.

18

UNDERSTANDING THE NIGERIAN STATE: POPULAR CULTURE AND THE STRUGGLE FOR MEANING

O. B. Lawuyi

The Nigerian nation, even to the least critical intellectual, is in a sorry state. The state utilities are inefficient, indeed, in many cases, dysfunctional. The economic infrastructure has crumbled. The citizens are despondent and have resorted to crime, a brain drain, rapid urbanization, and unconstitutional goals. It is indeed intriguing that the military, which engages in interethnic marriages, encourages professional mobility across the state, promotes the acquisition of knowledge at any relevant institution, and relies on multilingualism as an effective means of communication, could rule the country for so many years and fail to promote these ideals and the unity of the country. Equally difficult to explain is the failure of a thriving popular culture, emerging around "Babariga" as a dress code, pepper-soup consumption as a form of relaxation, "broken-English" as a means of communication, and slogans written on motor vehicles as a means of articulating public consciousness, to create a distinctively Nigerian identity and promote effective communication among Nigerians. What is more, the winning mentality taken to the stadium when the Green Eagles, the national soccer team, play and the enthusiasm for chieftaincy titles (which have become numerous and commonplace) cannot, for the elite, create a consciousness of healthy competition, a preference for the ideal, an approval of merit, and an interest in a creative individualistic ethos. Even if, undoubtedly, the state is a geographic reality—a point which is debatable according to some—the issue is that within the state's popular cultures, there is a struggle for meaning.

There is a struggle for the definition of the real Nigerian and for what he/she is worth. There is a struggle for the process of change to be directed to a meaningful end. The intellectual interest in this struggle for meaning leads to private and public debates, and promotes an array of local and international seminars, symposia, and conferences. Nigerians and foreign authors struggle to analyze and to understand the various aspects of a sordid state. Even Toyin Falola, the renowned Nigerian historian, is caught in the web. He has written extensively on the Nigerian State from historical, cultural, and politico-economic perspectives.[1] In most, but certainly not in all of his works, he has raised the issue of culture as central to the development process.[2] Although the complex links between culture and development are not always analytically clear or theoretically interrogated—Falola, of course, is one who shies away from theoretical expositions, and prefers expository, descriptive, yet analytical tales that illuminate a process—what is obvious is his concern with corruption.[3] His arguments can be reduced to the idea, also widely shared by international scholars, of corruption as a factor responsible for the crippling of state power, for the disempowerment of the citizens, and for the befuddlement of collective vision. The dominant form of state culture is corruption, even if some other cultural expressions can, and often do, exist. But why?

The concept of "culture," in Falola's view, is the result of an act: rarely dramatic, rarely guided by a text, and rarely educative, yet unarguably very effective in its impact on economy and governance. As an act, culture stems from a historical consciousness, and is a particular adaptation to an environment. In this sense, the act is rational. But it could also, as a contextually influenced variable, be impulsive. The selective impulses by which Nigerians choose their options are, therefore, not likely to be just physiological. They are cultural as well.

The rationally organized corruptive act is meaningful at three analytical levels: the individual thoughts, the public/ private exchanges, and the community ethos. The first level is most likely, as a minded activity, to be socio-psychological; while the second level deals with options, strategies, partnerships, values, and historical consciousness. At the third level, the concerns are with issues of policy making and ethics. The historian Falola prefers to operate at the second level and not the first or the third level of the discourse. And much as we may want to shift the discourse away, into the analysis of other important aspects, we should also stay at the second level for a single purpose: to theorize and systematize behaviors, symbols, and thoughts. The discourse is only just appropriate since corruption has replaced ethnicity as a National Question since the 1980s, and it is creating more and more problems for economic exchange and the welfare of Nigerians.

The effects are devastating on the national psyche as well as on structures. The disappointment of intellectuals engaged in the search for meaning of the state is obvious. Eghosa Osaghae, a Nigerian political scientist, says the state is a "crippled giant."[4] Wole Soyinka writes that it is "the open sore of a continent."[5] Falola and Ihonvbere once observed the "fall" of the republic.[6] But it is Wole Soyinka's position that is the most provocative and his attack on institutions and personalities that is the most vicious. As far as he is concerned, the sore is a self-inflicted wound; primarily because the military men who have ruled Nigeria for most of its four decades of independence, lack a sense of history, of purpose, and of intellectual interrogation. They transferred the theatrics of war into the theatrics of politics, removing dialogue from the public dictionary and creating, instead, a deadly power game of surprise, attack, ambush, destruction, and captivity. The character of military politics, whether in the Buhari-Idiagbon regime (1983-1985) or Babangida's rule (1985-1993), or Abacha's authoritarianism and Kleptocracy (1994-1998), is self-centered, conceptually inept, corrupt, undemocratic, and schizophrenic. Soyinka sees all of these people as opposed to the state they ruled, in that they fired their "artillery" at will, in order to disarm, to cripple, or to demolish the ruled. The civil society was thrown into chaos.

A long lasting chaos has prevailed as one regime has collapsed due to the assault of another. The military minds, as Soyinka argues, are simply incapable of handling the complexity of the architectural structural relations (built by the British colonial masters on weak foundations and with engineering defects). The concept, architecture, is not merely descriptive of networks and exchanges, but also analytical—in particular of political pragmatism and cultural aesthetics. The inherited political architecture[7] may be illogical, nonfunctional, and tension prone. But the military ensured that the remaining bit of humanism in it, and which it represents, was removed. The stark reality is a nation that heads for a predicament: "[the] national capsule is . . . cracked internally, and the watchers [begin] . . . a drastic interrogation of history, of the beginnings and affective meaning of . . . national identity."[8]

For much of their period in power, the incompetent military militarized the space with symbols and icons of violence, with memorials of wars, and with literature of heroes and heroines of doubtful intentions. They militarized the space with commands, generating incessant chaos (strikes, riots, closures, and so on) and promoting expedient decisions, a murder instinct, a tactical withdrawal consciousness, and the shelling and ambush of selected, targeted civilians. Uncertainty rules. They have simply depersonalized the civil person into a state of confusion, identity crisis, begging, and opportunism. A lasting legacy, no doubt, is a character that has become identifiable with Nigerians: exhibiting resistance, aggressiveness, eloquency, dare-devil risks, opportunism, and intolerance.

But, still, there is another legacy: the act of corruption. The act might not have started with the military.[9] It probably dates far back into the colonial era. But the military ensured its place as a public issue. Because their military regimes were prone to chaos, the discourse of corruption was prominent at times of identity crisis, credibility challenge, chaotic climate, religious bigotry, and undiplomatic international relations. The state moved away from its respectable place within the comity of nations to join the rogue states and finally ended up as a pariah. Nigerians at home and abroad were, and are still, discreditably treated with contempt and suspicion at international borders. Moreover, they are paralyzed by fear of the known and the unknown. The social engineering of corruption has led to an unproductive climate, to capital flight, to industrial decay, and to images of an aimless, senseless, drift.

A concern with restoring dignity to the nation motivates Falola—having moved away from the indeterminacies and unpredictability of a "primitive" state to settle in a modern, orderly atmosphere—to return in various ways to an archaeological dig, revealing an architecture and culture of chaos.

THE CHAOTIC OVERVIEW

The archaeological images of the Nigerian state are faulty in one sense: the culture of corruption is not just a refraction of structural imbalance, it reflects, itself, a culture of chaos. This reflection is ignored in analyses because of the major preoccupation with political structure which, certainly, is an important issue, important because it creates an awareness and an interest that enrich the social consciousness of the average Nigerian and his/her inclinations toward divisions. Yet, it is interesting to note that the Fulani herdsman turns to and interprets the news from Radio Kaduna while he is operating in the southwest of the country. Also, the exiled Nigerian craves for news from "home." Many exiles know the frequencies of the BBC's "Voice of Africa"[10] and tune in at the appropriate times, eager for news. The situations in other countries might interest them but that of Nigeria matters most to a sense of nationalism trying to struggle to the fore. These examples are merely indicative of a certain interest in and commitment to a "community."

For, undoubtedly, there is a sense of community; even though the attitudes of involvement, the ethics of practice, and the sense of purpose may be questioned in terms of how elevating they are. It is arguable that Nigerians really think that their community recognizes the value of their membership, or that there is a market opportunity for their potential. By tuning to the BBC or Radio Kaduna they are probably trying to reconcile some contradictions: the mixture of love and hate, primordialism and modernism, individualism and collectivism, corruption and wealth. We suspect that the impulse to hear from home shifts within these loyalties in order to create self-integrity.

The impression to be developed here is not that there is no structural imbalance, but that the imbalance yields a culture of chaos. The structural imbalance makes Nigeria a place where contradictions provoke a simultaneous feeling of pity and arrogance; a choice of materialism or of spirituality. The state itself emerges from a contractual relation negotiated by individuals for or on behalf of their communities. The contractual relation is supposed to be voluntaristic. But because needs differ, resources are limited, the market is unstable, and greed exists, some coercive interventions are necessary and applied. The use of force, military or police, however, is useless because it does not generate surplus production and because it restores advantage only to a favored client. In essence, the contractual structure may be a necessary condition for the state. But it is not a sufficient one. And the evidence is in the dominant chaotic culture.

A Nigerian intellectual narrates how, at Ibadan,[11] he waited at a traffic light for it to turn green. For a long time nothing happened. While he waited, a public transport vehicle maneuvered its way to the front of a queue (there were many vehicles waiting by then) and finally broke away as the "conductor" reminded those still waiting that they were fools. "The light does not work." Soon after the public transport vehicle went through, others attempted to follow. There was chaos. However, when the intellectual had, himself broken away, and looked back through the mirror, he discovered that the traffic light was now green! The impulsive acts, the suspicion and lack of trust in symbols, combine to generate an excitement revealed in chaos. The atmosphere is characterized by a rush, abuse, failure of technology, unchanneled competition, and a large acquisitive impulse. While you wait, the "best" has been shared!

Buhari and Idiagbon thought they had an understanding of the state problem. They introduced the War Against Indiscipline (WAI). But they failed when they were themselves caught in the web of chaotic contradictions. Mohammed and Obasanjo, heroes of the civil war of 1967-1970, wanted to instill order. They retired the "lazy" (?), "redundant" (?) workers. But this amounted to a limited change, primarily because it lacked an understanding of chaos. Chaos has its own logic. It can be likened to a sandstorm in a desert. First, there is no reason why the sand is where it is. Consequently, the social impulse is to seek a mythical, religious, human, or accidental explanation, but rarely a scientific rationale. Second, the movement depends on the strength and the direction of an external force, the wind. The materials travel in waves, creating varied and various patterns of distribution. The architecture, which emerges, is not due to any logic, any reason, any historical consciousness, or any value system. It is an impulsive act concerned only with distribution. Change has to be externally motivated, to be meaningful, and it has to be applied forcefully. The results are unpredictable owing their direction to the strength of the wind. But one thing is sure: the pattern of things changes when the "weak" wind takes over (metaphorically, development slows down and consolidation of power begins).

The third element of chaos theory is that particles, which move land on a space, have their own constitution. They are, therefore, an imposition over a nonresistant (or weak) force.

As the strong leader imposes its will, a structure emerges. Of course, the sight of this structure may be aesthetically appealing to tourists. However, of what use is its potential to itself (and lest we forget, there are human beings on the site that may be permanently blinded; and many have to run for their life or cover up their faces!)?

The demonstration of chaos is everywhere in Nigeria. Those who travel need only take an aerial view of Lagos or Kano. The intellectual would ask, what is the logic of the housing construction? How are the road networks planned? How suitable are the industrial settings? Why is there no light? The streets meander like a river; there is a mix up of industrial and residential quarters; and recreation and leisure life is paralyzed by a failed lighting system. Horrifying images. The sum total of the view is that ideas and aesthetics inhabit different universes of thought. Chaos is obvious.

Even on the ground, chaos is obvious. Oshodi, in Lagos, is a classic example. There is a mass of people moving in and out of the web of streets known as its market. Everybody appears to be in a rush. They sweat themselves out, laboring in high temperatures or heavy rainfall. There is a jostling for space, and a struggle for movement (whether forward or backward) from a center that appears confused and confusing to somewhere that may be equally chaotic. The passengers struggle with "epileptic" vehicle (run by Big Men behind the scenes), moving slowly towards its destination, and having to be ignited now and then, or otherwise be pushed. Meanwhile, passengers jump in or out of the moving vehicle, invariably hurting themselves or others in the process. Those hurt hurl abusive language at the perpetrators. Tension is high. On board, there is a struggle to find a seat; and one may be found after some polite or hot exchanges of words. The passengers are uncomfortably seated, looking here or there, rising occasionally to see the traffic ahead, and eager not to miss their destinations. At Oshodi, the Big Men are nowhere to be found. But for the poor there is an intense competition for space, for comfort, and for mutual understanding. They survive under an imposed order, direct or indirect. Their freedom is a luxury, as life itself is a hard negotiation for a pittance.

As a mirror of the bigger Nigerian space, Oshodi is an arena for the tough, for the migratory (who can never settle permanently for one reason or another), for the risktakers, and for the vagabonds. The decent try to stay away. But not many people enjoy the luxury of having options. They are condemned to a life of struggle, to a danger intrinsic to their motivating urges; the vehicle itself is in constant danger of being transformed into a sporting arena or zone. The personal integrity of workers is compromised: a critical comment here; an acerbic joke later. There could be a blow for the resistant, or a push for the reluctant. The atmosphere is dominated by the smell of rotten materials in stacks. Everywhere, there is unease. Some materials have been stolen. Other passengers are busy looking for their wares. The preoccupation is with survival.

The mixture of the expected and the unexpected, of realism and illusion, of order and chaos, of neatness and dirtiness, give the Oshodi market its special character. Tourists and even natives cannot rely on any script to give them an idea of success in this situation—except to count on the memories and experiences of themselves or close friends and relatives. The situation is constantly improvised in nature of language, in style of dress, and in personality. Invariably sentimental and escapist, the struggle (as well as the tension) generates a façade of genteel personality. The gentility can be misinterpreted as coolness or stupidity. But the façade disappears as quickly as a provocative incident arises; particularly one which drives a wedge between aspiration and expectation, ego and identity.

In Nigeria, popular obsession with survival has reached psychotic proportions characterized by lack of guilt, identity confusion, and speedy fortune. The market culture promotes crime, corruption, wrongdoing by public officials, drug abuse, family breakdown, brain drain, coup d'états, forgery, and assassination. The struggle between morality and development is a recurring act. As the moral framework shifts so does the struggle. Either the end justifies the means, or the means justifies the end. In a chaotic community everything is adrift and there is a struggle, a contestation for meaning (of language, action, and predictions).

The drift drives the moral appraisals by altering what is needed; how it is got; where it is got; how it is to be used; and whether it can be lived with. At one level, this promotes rapid urbanization of those who want things fast. At another, it encourages policy around the issue of numbers (you have, we don't have, and so there is imbalance). The number of universities has therefore grown. But they still cannot admit all the qualified candidates. Ironically, the number of graduates has grown, but there is a high rate of unemployment. Public buildings are in a state of dilapidation. Equipment is inadequate in the hospitals, the teaching institutions, and the media houses. The only place of relative success appears to be the religious setting. A new church or mosque opens daily. In a street there may be up to twenty churches.[12] Many services are conducted in the open. Many of the centers lack adequate seats or ventilation. Half-literate clergy who can hardly read or interpret the religious texts leads the members. But their message resonates well with the drift in a chaotic society: "anyone can achieve saving grace through . . . struggle against sin."[13] In a similar vein, you can be wealthy through struggle against barriers. However sin is defined, the motivation is to achieve and be somebody. However struggle is defined, the best conceivable end is opportunity.

THE STATE AND THE CHAOTIC COMPLEX

But the resources that once prompted pride, the pride of the "elephant," of the "giant" of Africa unified in the 1970s temporarily by the spirit of success, have diminished. Instead a marked sense of hierarchy, favoritism, and opportunism is established. Competition has intensified. But the morals of the market are increasingly questionable. Characterizing the human drift is a movement from the "Oshodi" mentality to the church/mosque mentality; or vice-versa, from the church/

mosque culture to the Oshodi culture. This is what we have termed the chaotic complex. Oshodi market sets the pattern for the mode, duration, and scale of competition; it indicates the complex interaction between space and time; it reveals the process by which values are generated; underscores rural tendencies; and promotes the performance from which Big Men emerge. It demonstrates the superiority of distribution over production, it is sensitive to the science of networking, and it educates on the techniques of mass action as a public voice. In contrast, a critical appraisal of the church/mosque culture will show how the ethics of competition and rivalry are developed, and what the ethos of success is. Space may not permit an extensive elaboration on each characteristic as indicated here. But of major importance, especially in the religious context, is the use of codes. The codes are not taken from texts, the Koran or the Bible. They embody religious interpretations of sociopolitical events that constitute historical consciousness. The interpretive rules are, to a large extent, individualistic. The interpretations can gain a wide currency when verbalized by the Big Men of the religious setting: the Sheiks, Imams, Prophets, Bishops, Evangelists, and others. And as soon as the Big Men of the Oshodi subculture hear (these are the politicians, the entrepreneurs, and the military), they mobilize their constituencies for action. Because the Big Men of the Oshodi subculture understand the codes quickly, they are able to exploit the drives, initiatives, and metaphors of success. They return later to the church/ mosque for thanksgiving; donating heavy sums of money and celebrating with a party. This gesture makes the Big Men of the church/mosque rich and relevant to the political process.

In reality, the church/mosque will accept the membership of the poor and the rich. But it is the rich, the successful in the Oshodi subculture, that are valued, praised, rewarded (with titles), and set up as models of achievers. Meanwhile, the reciprocity between the two domains of national culture allows the Prophets, the Imams, the Evangelists, and the Sheiks to cultivate a significant voice in the dramatic productions of power politics.

So, how is the state? The answer depends on whom you talk to. The Big Men's complaint is that they are not allowed greater roles in shaping the organization, course, and destiny of the nation. But the poor not only count themselves out of the power equation, they engage in a dream of self-potentiality. Theirs is a hope for a better future, one that is better than the present. While the Big Men seek a wider space from which to perform, the poor have to struggle against the loss of space, and of their properties, which can be taken by the exploitative Big Men.

As the drama of this chaotic complex unfolds, on the national stage, the irony is that failure produces and reproduces failure. The failed leader is replaced by a failed leader. A failed policy is reintroduced, and there appears to be no solution in sight. Big Men continue to rule in spite of the irrelevance, ambiguity, and disingenuity of their performances. As their colleagues rotate the chair of head of state, they serve as ministers, head of parastatals, envoys, and chairpersons of corporations. They are rotated amongst ministries; even though in the earlier one they headed, no reasonable accounts of expenditure and incomes were kept. Under their leadership, files were hidden away by officials seeking bribes. Moreover, state materials, including drugs, vehicles, copiers, or phones, systematically disappeared. The point is that within the chaotic complex, leadership is not to be judged by its performance. There are some assumptions of natural right, due to origin of birth and club membership. The failed leader can be circulated and recirculated because of rules of exclusivity intrinsic to networking: the ability to interpret the coded messages of the Big Men and to make "returns" (largely financial) to the mentors. For this reason, certain problems have remained unresolved. Such problems as fuel shortages, the introduction of the Shari'a, and crime, have to be addressed by virtually all regimes.

REFORMING THE MARKET

In line with a thesis of chaos, it is difficult to organize a good government on a weak economic base; particularly on an economy in which there is no organized forum of exchange; in which policies are externally imposed; and in which rational decisions are supplanted by mythical and religious explanations. An orderly and progressive economy does not grow from a flair for distribution of resources, retail trading, monopoly, hoarding, and a lack of skills. It is not an economy that survives with the undervaluing of skills, the overcentralization of resources and capital, and the wastage of surplus through the extravagant ceremonials (as in a peasant economy). As at now, what is available is, (a) the feeling that anything is possible through luck, charms, prayer, or violence. Such reasoning promotes the importance of "emergency contractors" who just happen to be on site at the right time to take a job for whose completion they are lacking in skills, capital, and experience. After all, (b), service is the major form of exchange and it is regulated by physical and biological forces (beauty, strength, mobility, and so on). There is only one issue of importance in this agenda: a discussion of what to pay for having rubbed your back. Which then leads to point (c), that usually there is no planning or adequate feasibility studies of market sites because choices are the result of personal luck, friendly advice, reciprocity, and proximity to "secured" identity. Indeed (d), the market does not operate on principles of political liberty or civil rights; rather the opposite. The absence of the rule of law gives motivation for ransacking the market, exterminating the entrepreneur, and burning down industries in the attempt to impose the values of the Oshodi-religious complex. Thus (e), any change in the market is noticeable for its disorganization, for its consumption, and for the presence or absence of security of life and properties.

The chaotic complex has ensured that the industrial base of production is weak. Because the security of the market cannot be guaranteed, capital is on the run. The consequence is that many people are unemployed, and they live in penury.[14] And based on their concerns with survival, they reject or distance themselves from state symbols. There is no motivation to display the national flag or sing the national anthem. There is no reason to share a national hero/heroine; hence, all streets in a community are named after local heroes. "Made in Nigeria" goods are inferior and are hardly patronized. Nigerian embassies in foreign countries are rarely visited. Abuja and Lagos are tribal centers for those of different ethnicity. To change this culture of alienation, democratic values are vital:

> Democracy, which is valuable in its own right, may not be especially effective economically all the time, but it comes into its own when a crisis threatens and the economically dispossessed need the voice that democracy gives them. Among the lessons of the Asian economic crisis is the importance of social safety nets, democratic rights and political voice. Political deprivation can reinforce economic destitution.[15]

The destitution caused by the military interventions for and on behalf of the chaotic complex leadership makes democracy all the more important; and, of course, turns it into a valuable ideal to be jealously guarded.

However, as Nobel Prize winning Amartya Sen warns in the passage quoted above, democracy is not enough. A focused economy must be organized now. The options available are very limited; and they are within the ideas of Western capitalism, which has attracted the bulk of highly trained Nigerian skills. The West has cultivated three types of economy, which run parallel and are compatible: the industrial, the informational, and the bio-technological economies. There are indications that Nigeria participated briefly in the industrial economy during the 1970s when there was an oil boom.[16] But whatever infrastructure was raised crumbled under the chaotic complex. The emphasis in the economy was on consumption, and so on an import-dependent economy. There were no concrete structures to activate competitive performance and create value for labor. Consequently, as oil prices began to fall in the 1980s, the state's response was to artificially maintain a high exchange rate, and increase its purchasing needs. The consequence, as Alos noted, is that the import demand could not be sustained.[17]

The raw materials for industrial expansion were not available locally. Although a few industries, especially in the beer consumption sector, attempted to diversify production and make it dependent on local materials, they were faced with uncontrollable inflation. Capacity utilization began to decrease. And a Structural Adjustment Program (SAP) had to be introduced in 1986. But it was too late. And it may have been irrelevant at this stage. Nothing better has emerged. On the contrary, "there is a relatively passive private sector which tended to embrace short termism as the best way of sustaining operations. These cost inefficiencies have resulted in higher product prices which in turn lead to lower demands and lower capacity utilization, and finally to lack of re-investment."[18]

The industrial economy has stagnated. As yet there is no plan for either informational or bio-technological economies. By the 1980s, Nigeria had lost a chance of becoming an economic power. It did have some skilled persons, some of whom would hardly commit themselves and their resources to rebuilding the industrial economy (undervalued labor makes it imperative for them to seek greener pastures). But it failed significantly to develop appropriate values. Yet now, it must contend with skills and languages totally different from those of the industrial economy and of which many of its citizens are unaware. This widespread illiteracy can constitute a clog in the wheel of progress. Nor are the concerns of ill-informed shari'aists, wanting to impose religious values, relevant.

The state needs to reshape its educational curricula and begin to address the needs of scientists, science administrators, laboratory technicians, and artists. The state needs to re-order its priorities and bring to the forefront of the national agenda the development of information technology. This process cannot wait on outside aid, not just because there is a need to take control of the process but also because there is a need to domesticate it. Moreover, it complements the educational agenda so well that it increases the rapid liberation of potential. Once outsiders take control of it, they automatically also take control of the development process. Because there must be investments in skills that are appropriate to a process of globalization—a web from which Nigeria cannot extricate itself—there is a lesson or two to learn from India. Though, as the Indian case also demonstrates, there must equally be a move to attempt a process of poverty alleviation through the cultivation of a market sensitive to social deprivation and equitable distribution.

A national asset, physical or human, is for all communities, and not just for the area where it is produced. The Nigerian situation is lopsided in many ways: some areas have the skills, some have the physical resources, and some have the weather suitable for agricultural production. The federal structure dictates that it would be improper to develop a market where capital concentrates in only one spot, or to reduce the states to a beggar's stance. It would be uneconomical for a government to raise earning power without sensitivity to production level or engage in production of goods where it is most uneconomical. Of course salaries must be paid promptly, and adjusted appropriately in line with the inflation rate. Where capital is restricted, skills are restricted. Tension then rules labor-management relations and the atmosphere is thrown into the chaotic complex.

Economies have come in various shapes. They are likely also to take on various patterns as the human intellect grows and visions become more revolutionary. The dynamics of economies, as Stan Davis and Christopher Meyer hint, rest upon the fact that "economies end not because they peter out but because a challenger supplants them."[19] In the West, the motivation is to raise the stakes of challenges, to resist a tendency toward complacency, rigidity, and equilibrium. As any politician in America knows, the dynamics of the economy determine the tenure of the political officeholder. The image and reputation of the government is shaped by economic growth. An African state that intends to participate in competition with America must either hold the same values or develop better ones.

Nigerian politics must be played as if in the arena of a market economy, which means that ascriptive criteria must be put aside. Production must become a measure of worth. The market must be open, free, and fair. The good politician is one who makes good choices, makes meaningful exchanges, critically assesses inputs and outputs, accepts order, and is not suspicious of change. There are other challenges:

> The industrial era was accompanied by pollution and environmental degradation. The major problem of the information age is privacy. In the bio-economy, the issue is ethics. Cloning, bioengineered foods, eugenics, genetic patenting and certainty about inherited diseases are just a few of the many developments that are already creating a storm.[20]

These are also issues that many Nigerians would expect a good leadership to be sensitive to. A proper sensitivity calls not only for adequate compensation where necessary, but also for respect for the environment and human dignity. Moreover, insofar as science and scientific productions are key to the dynamics of the capitalists' economy, it is imperative that the leadership understand and appreciate the thematic evolution of science, progressing from the complex to the simple, from the slow to the fast, from the narrow to the broad, from the private to the public, from the possibility of death to the possibility of life.

The chaotic complex that now rules Nigeria endangers its political structure. The chaos may last much longer as Big Men recycle ideas and paradigms derived from the coded messages of Oshodi-religious cultures. Chaos may last longer if there is no willingness to shift emphasis: from the collective to the individual; from individuality to partnership; from mysticism and chance to experimentation; from authoritarianism to democracy; from centralization to decentralization; from corruption to accountability; and from chaos to the rule of law. In this contrast, and in their choices, in organizing relationships lies the future and meaning of the Nigerian State.

CONCLUSION

This chapter does not dispute Wole Soyinka's idea that the political architecture of the Nigerian State is faulty and needs to be corrected. It does not argue with Toyin Falola's contention that corruption increases the instability of the state and reduces the worth of the citizens, as well as their contributions. The context of this chapter's contribution is the chaotic culture which has emerged from and continues to reflect the architectural defects of the state and the dynamics of corruption. Arguing from evidence which is socio-psychological and cultural, rather than only political and historical, chaos is conceptualized as a structure emerging from a process; a process with a locus in the scenarios of popular cultures.

The point here is that even if the political structure of Nigeria was imposed, and the one imposed is defective, a proper relation to the market economy would have ensured that factors which disable, or distort, state power and confuse its meaning and functions in the minds of the citizens (and observers) are not allowed to operate. However, since such factors, termed the chaotic complex, flourish, it is necessary to redefine and reconceptualize the economy and let the state structure emerge from new contractual relations and established rules.

NOTES

1. Toyin Falola, *Development Planning and Decolonization in Nigeria* (Gainseville: University of Florida Press, 1996; Toyin Falola, *The History of Nigeria* (Westport, Conn.: Greenwood Press, 1999); Toyin Falola (ed.), *Nigeria and Britain: Exploitation or Development* (London; Zed, 1987); Toyin Falola and Julius Ihonvbere, *The Rise and Fall of Nigeria's Second Republic, 1979-84* (London: 2ed, 1985); and Toyin Falola, *Violence in Nigeria: The*

Crisis of Religious Politics and Secular Ideologies (Rochester, N.Y.: University of Rochester Press, 1998).
2. See Toyin Falola and Akanmu Adebayo, *Culture, Politics and Money among the Yoruba* (New Brunswick, N.J.: Transaction Publishers, 2000); Toyin Falola, (ed.), *Oil and Nigerian Economy and Society* (Lagos: Longman, forthcoming); Falola, *Violence in Nigeria*, 247; Falola, *The History of Nigeria*, 108.
3. Falola, *The History of Nigeria*, 108; Falola and Adebayo, *Culture, Politics and Money*, 253.
4. Eghosa, E. Osaghae, *Crippled Giant: Nigeria since Independence* (London: Hurst and Company, 1998), 3.
5. Wole Soyinka, *The Open Sore of a Continent* (New York: Oxford University Press, 1996), 3.
6. Falola and Ihonvbere, *The Rise and Fall of Nigeria's Second Republic*, 10. What is interesting is to compare the pessimism of the later years with the optimism of some earlier authors. For instance, see O. Arikpo, *The Development of Modern Nigeria* (Harmondsworth, England: Penguin, 1967); S. Afonja and T. O. Pearce (eds.), *Social Change in Nigeria* (Harlow, England: Longman, 1984) and P. Kilby, *Industrialization in an Open Economy: Nigeria 1945-1966* (Cambridge: Cambridge University Press, 1969).
7. Soyinka, *The Open Sore,* 17-60.
8. Ibid., 128.
9. See Falola and Adebayo, *Culture, Politics and Money*, 253-274.
10. The BBC is the British Broadcasting Corporation. In my own part of the world, South Africa, I have not met any Nigerian that does not tune to the BBC and is not eager to debate the essence or thrust of what is heard.
11. Gbade Alabi, describing a situation at Adamasingba, Ibadan, Dec. 8, 1998.
12. Conversation with Matthew Ojo, an eminent Nigerian authority on new religious movements, 1999.
13. Robert J Samuelson, "The Limits of Materialism," *Newsweek*, May 15, 2000, 4.
14. Albert J Alos, "Creating Value under Uncertainty: The Nigerian Experience," *Journal of African Business* 1 (2000), 9-24.
15. Amartya Sen, "Will There Be Any Hope for the Poor?" *Time*, 155 (2000), 62.
16. Adedotun Phillip and Olu Ajakaiye, *Nigerian Economy and Society: Economic Policy and Development* (Ibadan, NISER, 1993); T. Biersteker, *Multinationals, the State, and Control of the Nige-*

rian Economy (Princeton, N.J.: Princeton University Press, 1987); S. P. Schatz, "Obstacles to Nigerian Private Investment," *Nigerian Journal of Economics and Social Statistics*, 4 (1962), 66-73.
17. Alos, "Creating Value under Uncertainty," 10.
18. Ibid., 12.
19. Stan Davis and Christopher Meyer, "What Will Replace the Tech Economy," *Time* 155 (2000), 56.
20. Ibid., 57.

19

THE POET AS HISTORIAN: FORM AND DISCOURSE IN CONTEMPORARY NIGERIAN POETRY

Yinka Agbetuyi

INTRODUCTION

I begin this chapter by justifying the parameters of delimitation in time and space. The poems to be discussed in the following pages are those written after political independence, because it was from that period that Nigerians formally normalized what has variously been defined as a "mere geographical expression" by an act of collective self-assertion as a nation.[1] The materials to be examined do not include performed oral poetry.[2] This is for the simple reason that I intend to argue that the written forms of poetry that we have had from Nigeria since political independence have been striving to complement, on paper, the function which oral poetry performed in "pre-literate" societies. It is for this reason that contemporary Nigerian poetry may be defined as the writings on the collectively shared experience of Nigeria, presented in a highly wrought language.

The question which consequently immediately engages our attention is how does the poetic apprehension of history differ from the craft of the traditional historian? The answer to this question has been partly answered in the definition proffered above. Perhaps we need to explore in depth what this linguistic difference is, and add that the form itself is the other marked aspect of distinction between the two areas. While emphasis is laid on denotative language in the narration of traditional historiography, with only a sprinkling of connotative language, poetry, as the parent of all the other verbal arts, thrives more on the connotative use of language. This is combined with the evocative use of imagery in a manner which, in traditional history, would be regarded as mere embellishment. Also the most unusual syntactic arrangements are the province of poetic license.

Whereas in conventional historiography, narration is linear, in poetry, narrative form is more contrived and could be concentric with a cyclic time frame.[3] The use of myth also differs in poetry and historiography. The latter concentrates on myths of origin and tries to see how these shed light on the chronology of the narrated events. The use of myth in poetry, however, is more diverse and there is an acknowledged mythmaking process immanent to the craft of the poet. Thus for the poet, the symbolic significance of events matters more than the concatenation of the bare facts of events: what do they mean for the people concerned and how can the poet intervene to affect this meaning-creating process?

Finally, even though both conventional historiography and poetry may narrate past poetic and oral forms, the poet attempts to demonstrate or "perform" these forms by a re-enactment, thereby securing a doubly coded history—narratively and histrionically. Thus, as was noted above, modern Nigerian poetry incorporates rather than describes elements of oral poetry. I now proceed to examine how some poems have tried to reflect Nigeria's history within their artistic forms.

CHRISTOPHER OKIGBO
AND MYTHIC ECLECTICISM

Nigerian poets have responded to history in two basic ways. The first is the articulation of mythic history which often features the deployment of appropriate historical art form and trope, like the praise poem, the elegy, or incantatory poetry. Poets have also responded to contemporary history by delineating, in poetic tropes, the import of recent social events for Nigerians. These often take the form of ruminations where the poet, often with heightened sensibilities, redraws the contours of such events, foregrounds their impact on the daily grind of the commonality. Among the celebrated Nigerian poets who were initially averse to the effect of this practice on the craft of the artist was Christopher Okigbo, in his strictly universalistic stage. Thus he was to say of direct engagement with national issues:

> I don't think that this sense of responsibility is fulfilled only by writing directly about . . . social change. I believe that any writer who attempts a type of inward exploration will in fact be exploring his society indirectly. Because the writer isn't living in isolation. He is interacting with different groups of people at different times.[4]

But at the peak of his career, as Dubem Okafor has argued, Okigbo came out fully on the side of the people, "the quadrangle," with whom he had always covertly identified.[5] We commence the examination of mythic history in Nigerian poetry with a look at Okigbo's work, *Labyrinths*, since Okigbo was one of the celebrated three at Nigeria's independence (the other two being Wole Soyinka and John Pepper Clark) who were the active poets of the Mbari Club.

Between Okigbo and Soyinka lay the onerous task of formulating the serious business of Nigerian postmodernism in the sixties—a movement that was later sanctified in the America of the seventies. In pursuance of this task, one of the most enduring hallmarks of what I have called elsewhere *"manifest* postmodern-eclecticism" was the most notable feature of Okigbo's poetry. Writing on the prolific eclecticism in Okigbo, Dan Izevbaye has made a distinction between two forms: literary echoes and literary borrowings.[6] Literary echoes he sees as the resonance of an original work. In his view, to get a full experience of the poem, the reader requires some knowledge of the original. He, however, situates much of Okigbo's eclecticism within literary borrowings.

This eclecticism is remarked both in form and in the syncretism of myths that pervades the whole of *Labyrinths*. Many scholars have noted this syncretism, which saw Okigbo conflating biblical creation myths with Mesopotamian lore as well as Igbo and Yoruba myths. The initial sequence, "Heavensgate" commences with a blend of the biblical creation myth with Okigbo's native myth of the goddess Idoto:

> BEFORE YOU mother Idoto,
> naked I stand
> before your watery presence . . .[7]

On the following page, Okigbo hints at the biblical myth in Genesis:

> DARK WATERS of the beginning . . .[8]

In "Limits V" he writes, conflating Egyptian and Mesopotamian myths:

> ON AN empty sarcophagus
> hewn out of alabaster,
> A branch of fennel on an
> empty sarcophagus . . .[9]

In the third stanza he continues:

> Smoke of ultramarine and amber
> Floats above the fields after

> Moonlit rains, from tree unto tree
> Distils the radiance of a king ...[10]

Here he merges two myths together and suggestively incorporates them into the quest for self-discovery of the poet-protagonist, who is on the triple mission of spiritual self-discovery, poetic amplification, and the refiguration of the collective consciousness of his people, which is seen as buried under neocolonial cultural domination.

In this mission, in which Okigbo sees the poet also as a prophet, the story of the apotheosis of Christ after the crucifixion is invoked (this in turn is suggestive of a recasting of Leonardo da Vinci's supposed portrayal of his own features in his portrait of Christ):

> HE STOOD in the midst of them all
> and appeared in true form,
> He found them drunken, he found none
> thirsty among them,
> who would add to your statue,
> or in your village accept you?[11]

That Okigbo the poet believes his calling to be intertwined with priesthood is shown by his avowed belief in reincarnation. He was reported to have admitted to being a "changeling" linked to the spirit world. As he puts it:

> My maternal grandfather was the head of a particular type of religion which is intimately connected with my village and since I am a reincarnation of my maternal grandfather, I carried this on.[12]

Okigbo here foregrounds the role of the poet as the preserver as well as the creator of myths by his manner of reinscribing the myth of reincarnation by personal identification and by the use of ritual throughout the sequences of *Labyrinths*.[13]

WOLE SOYINKA AND MANIFEST POSTMODERNISM

If Okigbo saw the craft of poetry as the vehicle for drawing attention to the universalism of mythmaking, largely by the juxtaposition of similar myths and an invitation to the reader to deduce the similarity, Wole Soyinka's task was slightly different in emphasis. Whereas Okigbo displayed learning overtly by recounting the major classical myths he had come across, Soyinka chose instead a synthesized translational strategy in mythopoesis.

Soyinka's use of Western myths was sparing, but he displayed a near total concentration on indigenous Yoruba myth as a vehicle for the explication of his internalized principles of the mythic archetypes of the world. In Soyinka the other classical myths, in particular Greek mythology, lay simmering below the surface, to surface occasionally in the landscape of his poetry, which was largely dominated by the reformulation of the Yoruba Ogun myth. Soyinka's "writing" of mythic history as an inauguration of his project of post-modernism was contained primarily in his epyllion, *Idanre*.[14]

For Soyinka, *Idanre* was the opportunity to debunk the Negritudinist claim that Africans were not technically minded enough to create metallurgical artifacts, their strong points being only in the oral arts and choreography. He was in this position at one with Okigbo, who so resented the message of black essentialism being promoted by the Negritudinists that he once rejected a prize won by his poem "Limits" at the Negro Festival of Arts in Dakar. According to Donatus Nwoga, he found "the whole idea of a Negro arts festival based on colour quite absurd."[15] It was perhaps for the same reason that Soyinka was reported as making his famous statement that "a tiger doesn't have to proclaim his tigritude."

Thus, Soyinka's project in *Idanre* was to establish the argument that the same fount underpins poetic creation as well as technological creation. The vehicle to achieve this goal lay in the mythic figure of Ogun, the Yoruba God of creativity and metallurgy. Soyinka thus sought to show through myth that Ogun being the God of creativity and metallurgy simultaneously underscores the non-exclusiveness of all areas of creativity. Like Okigbo's *Labyrinths*, Soyinka's *Idanre* began with a scene redolent of the biblical creation myth, but the similarity here, unlike *Labyrinths,* is inferred in the image evoked and not the actual words of Genesis. This is clearly a creation myth on the poet's own cultural terms with the thunderous and portentous heraldry of a visitant:

> The flaming corkscrew etches sharp affinities
> (No dream, no vision, no delirium of the dissolute)
> When roaring vats of an unstoppered heaven deluge
> Earth in fevered distillations, potent with
> The fire of the axe-handed one. [16]

The alliteration in the second line suggests in its thudding sound a tumultuous rude awakening, the prelude to the entrance of an awesome being. The tone from the outset, in comparison with the ruminative introverted tone of "Heavensgate," is extroverted as well as panegyric and celebratory in form. This is not a poem lamenting the loss of culture but a poem revalidating a dear possession. By the fifth stanza, the poet had begun the mythic identification with Ogun which was the bedrock of his rhetoric of an independent precolonial metallurgical technology:

> He catches Sango in his three-fingered hand
> And runs him down to earth. Safe shields my eaves
> This night, I have set the Iron One against
> All wayward bolts.[17]

Here, the Iron One is being used in several senses: Ogun is the tough, formidable god of war; he is also the patron god of the metallurgical arts and the mining of rare ores. Integral to this myth is the suggestion of an autochthonous Iron Age of the Yoruba people, and the evolution of metallurgical technology, which negated the Negritudinist self-denigration couched in the praise of the Africans "who had invented nothing." Again, setting the Iron One against all wayward bolts is reflexive of the first line of this stanza, where the metallic three-fingered projectile of the thunder catcher is seen as the handiwork of Ogun. This is used to trap the lightning associated with Sango, another Yoruba mythic figure and the God of thunder.

Soyinka's use of the Ogun myth suggests his alignment with what Isidore Okpewho has called the Euhemerist school of thought,[18] since his preface to *Idanre* describes his visit to "the rockhills of that name, a God-suffused grazing of primal giants and mastodons, petrified through some strange history, suckled by mists and clouds."[19] The poet, however, incorporates elements of oral performance within his mythic reenactment. This is what Okpewho has identified as the ability of the oral performer to weave elements of contemporary reality into the myth that is being retold.[20] Hence the poet weaves the myth into the coeval use of metallurgical products:

> His head was lost among the palm towers
> And power pylons. Through aeons of darkness rode
> the stone
> Of whirling incandescence, and cables danced
> In writhing ecstasies, point to point, wart to wart
> Of electric coils.[21]

Two stanzas later, Soyinka's project of postmodernism, which sought to show that the division of the various scientific disciplines and the arts into different compartments was merely a modernist invention, has begun:

> In the blasting of the seed, in the night-birds'
> Instant discernment, in the elemental fusion, seed
> To current, shone the godhead essence:
> One speeds his captive bolts on filaments
> Spun on another's forge.[22]

The poet further explores the idea of the multiform existence of nature, rather than individualized linear forms, through a related myth, the Atúnda myth. This myth, suggests

Soyinka, makes it imperative for Africans seeking a revolutionary model for social engineering to look inward[23] rather than replace one colonialism (Western) with another (Soviet):

> Rather, may we celebrate the stray electron
> Of patterns, celebrate the splitting of the gods
> Cannonisation of the strong hand of a slave who set
> The rock in revolution—and the Boulder cannot
> Up the hill in time's unwind . . .
> All hail Saint Atúnda, First revolutionary
> Grand iconoclast at genesis— and the rest is logic
> Zeus, Osiris, Jahweh, Christ in trifoliate
> Pact with creation, and the wisdom of Orunmila, Ifa
> Divining eyes, multiform . . .[24]

Niyi Osundare, member of a younger generation of Nigerian poets, has attempted an etymological archeology of the import of Soyinka's recourse to the Atunda myth. He differentiates the two morphological realizations and identifies a link in the principle of recreative and regenerative imperative immanent to African cosmogony, as has been shown in the creative use of reincarnation and the Ogbanje myth by Okigbo. Osundare's analysis show that Atunda means to recreate, to make or to fashion. Atooda, on the other hand, is analyzed to mean something created from hand or someone making something from hand. He then links the common element between them as the penchant to fashion.[25]

The variable linguistic manifestation itself reinforces the semantic articulation of continuous and multiple creativity envisioned in the myth, which was a calculated barb directed at the unitarist African Marxist school of criticism.

Soyinka's use of the Atúnda myth also nullifies Kwame Anthony Appiah's claim that Soyinka's engagements with myth in his work foreground a "presupposition that there is, even at quite a high level of abstraction, an African worldview."[26] Appiah's misconception lies in assuming a unified, immutable worldview, but as the project of African postmodernism encapsulated in the Atooda myth suggests, any of the splinters in the shards of African worldviews, because they bear an inflection of Africanness recognized by Africans, would suffice as just such an African worldview.

THE LYRICAL POETRY OF BEKEDEREMO-CLARK

Bekederemo-Clark is another Nigerian poet who used mythology to drive home his poetic vision. In "Abiku" Clark explores the myth of the constantly returning child, which demonstrates the belief in reincarnation shared by many African cultures.[27] In the first three lines, the poet chides the child asking him to make up his mind to stay with his companions in the spirit world or to stay permanently in the world of the living:

> Follow where you please your kindred spirits
> if indoors is not enough for you.[28]

In lines five to fourteen, the poet tries to ascertain what might be responsible for the Abiku's transience and evokes images of an uncomfortable homestead, sodden, cold, and at the mercy of the elements. He then attempts to persuade the wonder child to stay for good:

> True, it leaks through the thatch
> When floods brim the banks,
> And the bats and the owls
> Often tear in at night through the eaves,
> And at harmattan, the bamboo walls
> Are ready tinder for the fire
> That dries the fresh fish up on the rack.[29]

The poet next delves into the myth surrounding the recognition of an Abiku, the practice of marking children from families bedeviled with the constant death of their children; he then goes on to warn the wonder child that the game is up. The accusatory tone is deliberate, for it is believed that such children knowingly engage in this pastime to inflict punishment on the family into which they have been born:

> We know the knife scars
> Serrating down your back and front
> Like beak of the sword-fish,
> And both your ears, notched
> As a bondsman to this house,
> Are all relics of your first comings.[30]

The last two lines also suggest that the ploy of the Abiku in refusing to stay for good is directed at preventing sibling rivalry which could occur if he stays and other children come after him to share the mother's affection.

THE TROPES OF CONTEMPORARY HISTORIOGRAPHY

The second part of this chapter considers how Nigerian poets have "written" history in their poems by incorporating contemporary events within the framework of their poetic creativity. We again proceed by way of the demiurgics straddling both sections.

Ime Ikiddeh's study of "Path of Thunder"[31] has shown a definite shift from Okigbo's earlier position, in a move he traced back to the writing of "Silences" following the assassination of Patrice Lumumba and the incarceration of Obafemi Awolowo. The effort to make this ideological realignment, according to Ikiddeh, is what the poet has described symbolically as "How does one say NO in thunder" in the opening lines of the "Lament of the Silent Sisters." The gravity of the situation the poet tries to convey is inscribed in the word "Lament." But the poem allows the poet to tidy up the details of what many critics have identified as the obscurity of his earlier poetry. After the cleansing ritual in "Heavensgate," which was only introductory to another round of cleansing rites in "Limits," the poet has finally found the form that will contain his poetic message.

The charge of obscurity in Okigbo's earlier poetry would seem to have arisen because his protagonist's persona carried within his single structure several voices. Readers and critics perhaps for this reason often are at a loss as to which voice is speaking at each moment. Okigbo has tried to situate these voices within psych'e'analytic—that is, the African originary roots of Western psychoanalysis—by describing them as the 'selves' of the protagonist-poet.

In "Silences," however, the poet, having been "cleansed of foreign influences" hindering the form of his art, would now dip into the oral-histrionic resources of his traditional background for a form that would liberate him from "straining thin among the echoes." "(Limits II)"

In realizing his priestly-poetic calling, he would then construct a dramaturgic piece like "Lament of the Silent Sisters," which featured a crier and a chorus. By his remarkable build up of imagery, Okigbo again evokes a sense of foreboding, of an impending martyrdom, in "Lament of Silent Sisters II and III":

> They struck him in the ear they struck him in the eye;
> They picked his bones for scavenging...[32]

The feeling of impending doom is reinforced in "Lament III":

> Crier: This is our swan song
> This is our senses' stillness;
> Chorus: We carry in our worlds that flourish
> Our worlds that have failed...[33]

The internal structure of the African traditional epic poem has also been adopted here. This is demonstrated by an initial formula in the first line of a poem,[34] which is slightly altered in the second line for a development of the poem. An example of this is the "This is our" formula. Thus this poem and "The Lament of the Drums" justify the earlier assertion that many modern African poets try (within limits permissible by literate culture) to incorporate elements of oral narrative within their poetry. Indeed, Okigbo's lament poems confirm to a large extent Okpewho's insight that "a good oral performance depends on the maintenance of a healthy balance between the tale, the music, the histrionics and everything else to which the performer lends his genius."[35] Okigbo therefore seems to have set his eyes on the task confronting the modern African writer faced with cultural sections that are still largely oral, which in the view of Abiola Irele is "to write an oral culture."[36]

Okigbo's last sequence, "Path of Thunder,"[37] is also marked by the collective voice which bears the burden of contemporary sociopolitical comments, buried in the familiar Okigbo symbolism of "Thunder, Iron, Elephants, and Eagle." The poems constituting this sequence were written between the month preceding Nigeria's first military coup and the month preceding the counter-coup (six months).

Ikiddeh has sought to group the undated "Elegy of the Wind" with "Come Thunder," but the fact of its being undated and the seemingly different subject matter suggest that Okigbo intended it to belong to yet another sequence after "Path of Thunder."

Okigbo in his manner of couching events in mythic history would appear to have used the symbolism of the elephant again to depict the "biggest" casualty of the January 1966 military takeover, Ahmadu Bello, the Sardauna of Sokoto, the charismatic leader of the Northern Region. Thus Okigbo's use of the classical title "tetrarch" identifies Roman history with Nigeria in which there were then four regions. The poet celebrates the Sardauna's prominence:

> The elephant, tetrarch of the jungle:
> With a wave of the hand
> He could pull four trees to the ground;
> His four mortar legs pounded the earth:
> Wherever they treaded,
> The grass was forbidden to be there.[38]

In "Elegy for the Slit-Drum," the poet tries to put into perspective the fate that befell the Sardauna, especially as he was not involved among the corrupt officials identified by the coupists:

> the elephant has fallen
> the mortars have won the day
> the elephant has fallen
> does he deserve his fate . . .[39]

The panegyric tone of the sequences in "Path of Thunder" is another feature that has been widely acclaimed (whether a bloody coup deserves to be celebrated is another matter entirely; notwithstanding the fact that a wide section of the populace seemed tired of the inept politicians).

Omolara Ogundipe-Leslie has traced the roots of Okigbo's eclecticism to the elephant praise songs of the Ijala hunters. In one of Okigbo's minor poems, "The Lament of the Masks," she claims that some of the lines were a reworking of actual praises of the Timi (ruler) of Ede (a town in Yorubaland).[40] Whether the title "lament" should preface a panegyric would seem to be a matter for discussion.

Since the coup initially celebrated by Okigbo in time spawned the July 1966 counter putsch, perhaps this is an appropriate place to appraise the response of an equally formidable poet to these events of national prominence.

"For Fajuyi"[41] was Soyinka's testament to the effect of that counter-coup on the principal member of the Ironsi government in the Western Region. Col. Adekunle Fajuyi had the unenviable but tragic role of being General Ironsi's host when the coupists came calling. For that fortuitous reason, he had to make the ultimate sacrifice with his supreme commander.

The poet begins with the word "honour" and draws our attention to the fact that Fajuyi chose to be killed (in military fashion) with his supreme commander, in order to obviate suspicions that the Western Region was colluding with the North to exact revenge for the January coup. This notion of honor is encapsulated in the phrase "chivalric steel." The poet feels this sacrifice has redeemed those living from a vicious cycle of bloodletting that could otherwise have broken out nationwide. It is also for this spirit of sacrifice that the poet describes Fajuyi as "flare too rare.[42]"

The respite which the poet hoped would attend the sacrifice, however, did not materialize; the counter-coup eventually led to a series of events culminating in the civil war which claimed the life of fellow poet, Christopher Okigbo, who fought on the side of the secessionist Biafra.

The poet Soyinka found himself incarcerated while trying to shuttle between the warring sides to end the war. In "To the Madmen over the Wall," one of the poems he wrote in detention, Soyinka deplores the fact that the country is being torn apart by centrifugal forces. In the first stanza, he cries that he does not wish to be a party to the dismemberment of the country. He captures the lack of unity more vividly in the second stanza:

> Your wise withdrawal
> Who can blame? Crouched
> Upon your ledge of space, do you witness
> Ashes of reality drift strangely past?
> I fear
> Your minds have dared the infinite
> And journeyed back
> To speak in foreign tongues.[43]

One of the foremost Nigerian nationalist leaders, Nnamdi Azikiwe, also recorded his feelings about the war in a poem titled "War and Peace." In the first stanza, the poet states that there is no cause, however just, that is worthy of the sacrifice of human lives. In stanza after stanza of rhyming couplets, the poet drives home the miseries attendant upon the horrors of war:

> War brings out the worst in man,
> Stultifying divine plan,

> Man's base instincts it lays bare
> Bringing awful death and fear . . .[44]

The poet further stresses the advantages of peaceful coexistence and ends by referring to the madness inherent in the cultivation of hate.

OJAIDE: POETRY AS A CLARION CALL TO ARMS

As Nigeria settled down to the task of healing its wounds and giving democratic governance a try again, a new crop of younger poets began to make their voices heard alongside the remaining established poets.

Among this younger group, two names stand out for consistency of form as well as for narration of the concept of nation, within the new dispensation: Niyi Osundare and Tanure Ojaide. Although the democratic polity inaugurated in 1979 was not sustained beyond four years, the creative vision and spirit that it produced survived it, and was one of the planks of resistance to the long-term return of military dictatorship.

In "Epilogue: Spoken by a Chorus"[45] Tanure Ojaide returns to a theme broached by Okigbo in "Elegy for Alto," where Okigbo discerned the hidden hands of politicians influencing the military authorities of the day. Okigbo summed up this feeling thus:

> Politicians are back in giant hidden steps of howitzers, of detonators.[46]

Ojaide in "Epilogue: Spoken by a Chorus" adopts the traditional song form as did Okigbo in much of his poetry. The poet cannot see any essential difference between the performance of the military and the politicians. As he appears to suggest in the poem, politics and military dictatorship are but two sides of the same coin in the Nigerian experience:

> When a flash storm gathers tyrannical strength, it breaks the only tall palm of the land.

> Politics and the military are the breeding grounds
> for a summit of torturers.[47]

Ojaide wondered at the end of the poem whether there was not active collaboration between the two, particularly as military officers see their tour of duty as an opportunity to amass wealth to fight future political battles:

> We have cut the Cobra's tail
> but already the enemy throws its head loose
> and the land has no rest from raids.
> May it not re-appear with a more poisonous tail.[48]

Ojaide's preoccupation in "The Flight" is similar. The poem was probably composed in the era of the "brain drain" that accompanied the near-total wrecking of Nigeria that attended the return of the military to power in 1983. Then the common wisdom among the intellectual elite was that the situation was beyond redemption and that it was now everyman for himself. This meant flight to greener pastures overseas.

The poem opens with the fantastic tales brought back by the temporary returnees from the initial exodus. In the last two stanzas, the poet then expresses his desire for such intellectual leaders of the community to stay in their own country and make it as wondrous as those far flung places whose tales they bear:

> But whoever stood the stampede,
> whoever shunned the fashionable flight ...
> taller than a million fugitives ...
> to minister to the deserted soil
> gladdens my native heart ...[49]

In "The Music of Pain," the poet sets out his poetics and what he believes must be the task of a poet in a country such as Nigeria. In the third line, he tells us that for him, a poem occupies the functional position of songs in a traditional setting. As a corollary to this, he therefore thinks each poetic moment must be lived by the poet performing a function for the society in which he lives. For the moment, he identifies that function as resistance to the tyranny of power:

> I do not cry in vain.
> For my song I sought
> the chorus of resistant cries
> to excoriate the land's scurvy conscience . . .[50]

In the next four lines, the poet justifies the use of mythology, which he says is needed to search for archetypes in the past, to highlight people's deliverance from oppression and the denial of freedom of speech by tyrants. For the poet, the art of poetry is a noble one: an effective weapon for reflecting the yearnings of the majority of the people. For those who fault the efficacy of poetry as songs of deliverance, the poet retorts:

> And I say:
> They have the bite of desperate ones!
> They are fine-filed matchets
> in the hands of the threatened!
> They are a swarm of mystery bees
> haunting robbers of the proud heritage . . .[51]

NIYI OSUNDARE'S POETRY AND THE REFIGURATION OF ESU'S SIGN

Perhaps more noted for his identification of the relationship between poetry and songs is the poet Niyi Osundare. His collection, *Songs of the Marketplace*,[52] covers in detail that period in Nigeria's history pejoratively referred to as the "civilian interregnum" of 1979-1983. His poetics are delineated at the outset in "Poetry Is"[53] which tries to locate the art—imagery and idiom—within the purview of the poet and his immediate audience. Osundare does not subscribe to the view of the earlier Okigbo that poetry should be the insular preoccupation of the poet and his coterie of friends. Hence he declares in the first stanza,

> not the esoteric whisper
> of an excluding tongue
> not a claptrap
> for a wondering audience
> not a learned quiz
> entombed in Grecoroman lore . . .[54]

In the following five stanzas, the poet rolls out his vision of the function of poetry in the community. As he puts it in the third stanza,

> Poetry is
> the hawker's ditty
> the eloquence of the gong
> the lyric of the marketplace
> the luminous ray
> on the grass's morning dew . . .[55]

It would appear that it was just such an engagement with the definition and redefinition of the art by poets such as Wole Soyinka, Christopher Okigbo, Tanure Ojaide, and Niyi Osundare that has prompted theorists of the postmodern to define artistic postmodernism as the tendency by the demiurgics to be self-reflexive and to redefine their craft[56] as they go along. Henry Louis Gates, Jr., one of the theorists of the postmodern, has sought to construct an African-American semiotic theory of the Sign based on these praxes.[57] The model can however be said to have only a limited advance over the Saussurean model and is (contrary to Gates' assertion) not uniquely African-American, since it still possesses two axes that are linear in movement (even granting that the "rhetorical axis" is dual-directional). Esu's axis which is the truly hermeneutical axis of signification that "plots" meaning on both earlier axes, semantic and rhetorical, can only be represented by a broken line and like the compass operates in a swivel to generate meaning from the other two (see Figure 1). Only a model that adequately represents the postmodern Sign can cope with the infinite demands of "multiple coding" which theorists have identified in postmodernism. A ready example of this is the three-dimensionality of representations of the postmodern as in the televisual.

Figure 1

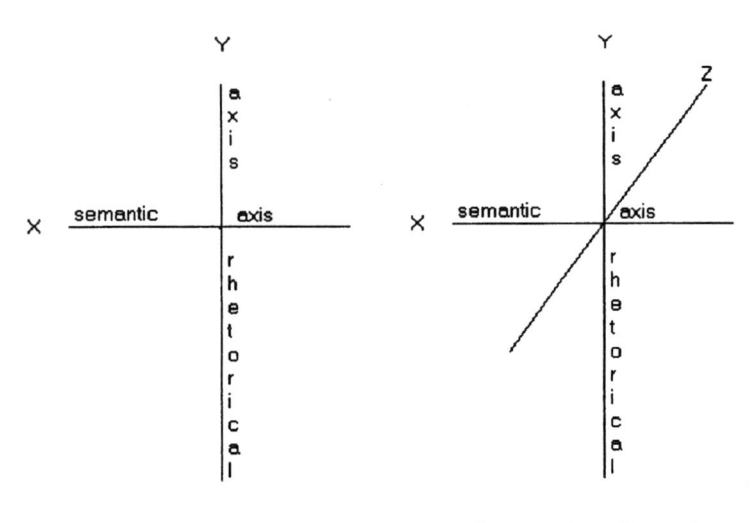

```
                Y                              Y
                |a                             |a        Z
                |x                             |x       /
                |i                             |i      /
                |s                             |s     /
    semantic    |    axis          semantic    |axis /
X ──────────────┼──────────    X ──────────────┼────────
                |r                             |r   /
                |h                             |h  /
                |e                             |e /
                |t                             |t/
                |o                             /o
                |r                            /|r
                |i                           / |i
                |c                          /  |c
                |a                             |a
                |l                             |l
```

    Neo-Saussurean   Postmodern Spatial
      Signification   Signification

We can see that under a postmodern model of the Sign, signification occurs as a result of the interaction among trinary rather than binary axes, anywhere within the force-field of the axes, facilitated by the hermeneutic, mobile Esu axis. Since the third axis is broken and operates synaptically (reflecting the alloyed essence of Esu) it is the repository of mythic meaning which is always involved in all significations including poetic visions. This assertion is relevant to the vision Osundare has projected (and Soyinka before him) that it is through myth that the sensibilities of most audiences are reached and the more immediate and accessible the myth, the more effective the poet. In addition, because the Esu axis is synaptic and syncretic, it can serve as the translatory storehouse of myths as well as the combinatory bedrock of lyricism and other art forms. Finally, it is the generator of electromagnetism with its import for the televisual.

In *Songs of the Marketplace*, Osundare's "Excursions" begins with a kaleidoscopic survey of the Nigerian countryside, with a haunting lyricism and images that speak of the untold neglect of the rural populace by their government. The graphic imagery of hunger and want etched on the faces of the people is forcefully delineated to evoke pathos and make readers identify with the poet's sense of outrage:

> We see village boys' kwashiorkor bellies
> hairless heads impaled on pin necks
> and ribs baring the benevolence
> of the body politic . . .[58]

The sense of deprivation is further deepened by the portrayal of pregnant women scavenging for both themselves and their children:

> in city fringes pregnant women
> rummage garbage heaps for
> the rotting remnants of city tables
> above, hawks and vultures hovering
> for their turn . . .[59]

In the fourth movement, the poet continues by telling us of the people's discovery of the cause of their woes and the increasing restlessness of the people. Here, Osundare's tone is unmistakable as that of an *ewi* exponent (a Yoruba traditional singer of poetic songs which observe and correct contemporary ills):

> In the streets
> people whisper their rage
> about a million million
> naira of our blood

multiplying foreign fortunes
and the damnable years
of our blind slavery.[60]

In *Waiting Laughters (A Long Song in Many Voices)*, Osundare is at his best in the appropriation of the stylistic resources of the traditional oral performer for the medium of print. The use of many voices is the first striking device used to sustain interest in a long narrative lyric.

The "song" opens with a lead singer who performs a form of verbal *feu de joie* to the Muse, to which the choral response is:

Tonalities. Redolent tonalities . . .[61]

The poet next enters into the use of the formula:[62]

Truth of the valley
Truth of the mountain

Truth of the boulder
Truth of the river . . .[63]

The body of the poem is then made up of over ninety pages of verse, woven round the ramifications of the motif of waiting, which constantly explores the possibilities of further subtexts.

Another stylistic device of the oral performer in this poem is the use of the ideophone[64] introduced in the panegyric to the rain:

The rain is oníbánbántibá
The rain is oníbànbàntibà
The rain which taunts the root's dusty
laughter . . .[65]

The dexterity of Osundare's word play is here triumphal and gleeful, with each word play opening up a pathway of further significations, yet the motif of waiting persists:

> Passports are pass ports
> The Atlantic is a wilderness of barbed walls
> brooking no windows, its door of deafening
> steel . . .[66]

By the time we reach the climax of the first movement, we discern that the poet is not engaged in word play just for the fun of it, and that the waiting is not envisaged to be in vain, but for the rulers' day of reckoning:

> Waiting
> like the Bastille for the screaming stones
> of turbulent streets
> their bread is stone
> their dessert garnished sand from the kitchen
> of heartless seasons
> And when the humble axe finally heeds its
> noble task
> the head descends, lumpen dust in its royal mouth.[67]

Also notable is the poet's bold experimentation in graphicacy, which is initiated in the second movement. Here, the phrase "diverse paces with diverse persons" is graphically represented on the page by scattered indentations.

The poet begins the third movement with a sense of the urgency of the waiting game, and the impatience that is beginning to shape itself into an iron resolve. He maintains this fevered pitch till the closing line of the para-epic, in which he calls for a change in strategy to achieve the lofty goals of the perennial waiting game:

> The season calls for the lyric of other laughters
> New chicks breaking the fragile tyranny
> Of hallowed shells.
>
> A million fists, up,
> In the glaring face of complacent skies
> A matchet waiting, waiting
> In the whetting shadows of stubborn shrubs.[68]

The phonic metathesis between "waiting" and "whetting" is the closing stylistic device employed by the poet to reinforce his underlying message.

CONCLUSION

I have tried to distinguish between the craft of the traditional historiographer and that of the poet weaving history through the tapestry of his art. In the former, narrativity is the overriding means and goal; the language is more denotative than connotative. The historiographer's craft involves researching, interpreting, and cataloguing of events. The poet on the other hand gives primacy to the connotative use of language, using images, symbols and extended symbolism; with these he attempts an amplification of significant events and moments in history. The nexus of both resides in hermeneutics and as we have seen, this is presided over by the agency of Esu, the ever-present interpreter-god and the world's first broadcaster. I have also noted that the poet as historian is a repository of oral forms ("domesticated" for the print medium), or engages the use of "para-oral" strategies which are reenacted as a storehouse for the future. The poems discussed in this chapter in no way exhaust the variegated nuances and forms of contemporary Nigerian poetry in the past four decades. It is hoped, however, that they *exemplify* the chosen theme of narration of nation within the purview of the para-traditional trope, in an eclectic project of the post-modern. The analysis dwells more on the intra-national than the international thematic preoccupation of poets and this, one hopes, explains the non-inclusion of para-traditionally troped monumental sequences such as *Ogun Abibimãn,* among others.[69]

NOTES

1. The period this chapter begins with falls within the second part of the tripartite periodization given by Dubem Okafor in *The Dance*

of Death: Nigerian History and Christopher Okigbo's Poetry, (NJ: AWP Inc., 1998).
2. Isidore Okpewho has advocated a separate poetics for oral performance in *The Epic in Africa: Towards a Poetics of the Oral Performance* (New York: Columbia University Press, 1979).
3. For a discussion of the concept of time in history, see G. W. Whitrow, *Time in History: Views of Time from Prehistory to the Present Day* (Oxford: Oxford University Press, 1988).
4. Extract from the 1965 Christopher Okigbo interview with Marjorie Whitelaw, in Donatus Ibe Nwoga (ed.), *Critical Perspectives on Christopher Okigbo* (Washington, D.C.: Three Continents Press, 1984).
5. Okafor, *The Dance of Death*, 22.
6. Nwoga, *Critical Perspectives*, 68.
7. Christopher Okigbo, *Labyrinths* (Ibadan: Heinemann, 1971), 3.
8. Ibid., 4.
9. Ibid., 28.
10. Ibid.
11. Ibid., 29.
12. Quoted in Okafor, *Dance of Death*, 143.
13. This is perhaps to underpin the difference in the concept of time in the African worldview and to juxtapose it to the regnant Western model normalized within regular historiography, as opposed to the poetic vision of time.
14. Wole Soyinka, *Idanre and Other Poems* (London: Methuen, 1967).
15. Nwoga, *Critical Perspectives*.
16. Soyinka, *Idanre*, 61.
17. Ibid.
18. See Isidore Okpewho, *Myth in Africa* (Cambridge: Cambridge University Press) 62.
19. Soyinka, *Idanre*, 57.
20. Okpewho, *Myth in Africa*, 104-106.
21. Soyinka, *Idanre*, 64. This elastic art of contemporaneity was reaffirmed in interviews with *Tell*, no. 27, July 5, 1999, and with *The News*, Sept. 2000. Also the idea of aeons was used to differentiate between the ancient dichotomy in timing between "aions", eternal time, and "chronos" the mundane time. For more on this, see Whitrow, *Time in History*.
22. Soyinka, *Idanre*. 64.

23. Wole Soyinka, *Myth, Literature and the African World* (Cambridge: Cambridge University Press, 1976), xii.
24. Soyinka, *Idanre,* 82-83.
25. Niyi Osundare, "Wole Soyinka and the Atúnda Ideal" in Adewale Maja-Pearce (ed.), *Wole Soyinka, An Appraisal* (Oxford: Heinemann, 1994).
26. Kwame Anthony Appiah, "Myth, Literature and the African World," in Maja-Pearce, *Wole Soyinka,* 112.
27. J.P. Clark, "Abiku," in E.K. Senanu and T. Vincent (ed.), *A Selection of African Poetry* (Essex: Longman, 1988), 205.
28. Ibid.
29. Ibid.
30. Ibid.
31. Ime Ikiddeh, "Iron, Thunder and Elephants: A Study of Okigbo's Path of Thunder," in Nwoga, *Critical Perspectives*, 185.
32. Okigbo, *Labyrinths,* 40.
33. Ibid.
34. For a detailed discussion of the stylistics of the epic poem, see Okpewho, *The Epic in Africa.*
35. Ibid., 93.
36. Quoted in Okafor, *Dance of Death*, 86.
37. Ibid.
38. Ibid., 67.
39. Ibid., 69.
40. See Omolara Leslie, "The Poetry of Christopher Okigbo: Its Evolution and Significance," in Nwoga, *Critical Perspectives,* 289.
41. Soyinka, *Idanre*, 54.
42. Ibid.
43. Wole Soyinka, *The Shuttle in the Crypt* (London: Rex Collins, 1972), 18.
44. Nnamdi Azikiwe, *Collected Poems* (Nsukka: African Book Co., 1976), 46.
45. Tanure Ojaide, *The Blood of Peace and Other Poems (*Ibadan: Heinemann, 1991).
46. Okigbo, *Labyrinths*, 71.
47. Ibid., 128.
48. Ibid.
49. Ibid., 62.
50. Ibid., 2.
51. Ibid.

52. Niyi Osundare, *Songs of the Marketplace* (Ibadan: New Horn Press, 1983).
53. Ibid., 3.
54. Ibid.
55. Ibid.
56. For an extensive examination of postmodernism, see, Charles Jencks (ed.), *The Post-Modern Reader* (London, Academy Editions, 1992), and Frederic Jameson, *Postmodernism, or, the Cultural Logic of Late Capitalism* (London: Verso, 1991).
57. Henry Louis Gates, Jr., *The Signifying Monkey: A Theory of African-American Literary Criticism* (Oxford: Oxford University Press, 1988).
58. Osundare, *Songs of the Marketplace*, 7.
59. Ibid.
60. Ibid.
61. Niyi Osundare, *Waiting Laughters* (Oxford: Malthouse Press Limited, 1990), 2.
62. For more on the use of the formula, see Okpewho, *The Epic in Africa*.
63. Osundare, *Waiting Laughters*, 3.
64. For more on the use of ideophones in African oral narratives, see Okpewho, *Myth in Africa*.
65. Osundare, *Waiting Laughters*, 4.
66. Ibid., 12.
67. Ibid., 22.
68. Ibid., 96-97.
69. Wole Soyinka, *Ogun Abibimãn* (London: Rex Collins, 1976).

20

FROM NIGERIA TO BENIN: INTRODUCING THE ÌDÀÁCHÀ DIALECT OF YORUBA

Désiré Baloubi

INTRODUCTION

This chapter introduces the Ìdàáchà people and their language as one of the most precious and tangible ties between Nigeria and Benin. In fact, Ìdaacha, a Yoruboid, is the mother tongue of a speech community whose forefathers migrated about six centuries ago from Nigeria to Dahomey, now the Republic of Benin. The Yoruboid languages are, "Yoruba, Igala, and Itsekiri (Isekiri) in Nigeria, Tsabe and Idaitsa in the Republic of Benin and Ana or Ife in Togo."[1] In this chapter, I focus on Ìdàáchà or Idaitsa, but commonly known as Ìdàáchà among the native speakers. I give some background information related to geographic location, the language, and the people. I underline the significance of this description, I discuss previous studies, and I summarize major aspects of the language.

BACKGROUND

This descriptive study targets a variety of Yoruba spoken by approximately 56,127 people in Benin.[2] Like most of the Yoruba dialects known as "ede"-languages in the Republic of Benin, Ìdàáchà has not been well described yet.[3] The speakers of the Ìdàáchà language live in the northern part of the former Zou Province, now called Département des Collines. They have very close ancestral relationships with the Yoruba of Nigeria as far as ethnicity is concerned. The literature abounds in information related to the presence of the Yoruba in Nigeria, Benin, Togo, Sierra Leone, Brazil, Haiti, Cuba, and the Caribbean islands in general. But what does "Yoruba" mean?

The term "Yoruba" is used in several ways, so it must be defined clearly here. First of all, one may consider "Yoruba" as a dialect cluster extending from Central Southern Nigeria into Benin. Capo has suggested that Yoruba can "be viewed as a lect within the cluster, a lect socially defined, which has its distinctive characteristics."[4] According to him, "in Togo and Benin, the Yoruboid people are better known as Anago and Ana, but they retain their specific names. In Sierra Leone, they were known as the Aku peoples."[5]

Referring to the *Commission Nationale de Linguistique*, Capo gives examples of Yoruboid dialects spoken in Benin: "Ije, Ketu, Tsabe, Mokole, Idaitsa, Ana or Ife, Itsa and Yoruba (urban variety)."[6] The term "Yoruba" is also used as the name of a standard language in Nigeria. The overall group, including the separate languages Itsekiri and Igala, is identified as Defoid.[7]

With regard to the origin of the Ìdàáchà communities, oral tradition indicates and a number of studies confirm that they were immigrants from western Nigeria. Smith, for example, says:

About thirty miles southwest from Ketu is the town known in French-speaking Dahomey as Dassa-Zoumé, capital of the former kingdom of the Dassa, or perhaps more accurately, Idassa. A list of twenty-six rulers has been compiled for this kingdom, beginning with Jagou Olofin, the founder of the Dynasty, who according to tradition came from Egbaland . . . .The twenty-six rulers in the list—which includes two women—are arranged in nine generations, and from this it has been calculated, on the basis of allowing thirty years to each generation, that the kingdom was founded about 1700.[8]

Smith has argued that there is some recollection among members of the dynasty of "pressure from Oyo, under a leader called in their tradition Adjinakou," which would confirm their Nigerian origin.[9] Smith also mentions John Duncan, a Scots member of the Niger Expedition of 1841 who passed through Dassa and described the people as Anagoos. This name is well known today as Anago or Nago. Specifically, the Ìdàácha today are believed to have come from what was then called the Oyo Empire. This included vast areas including Ife/Ile-Ife, Ilorin, Ibadan, Egba, Egbado, and Abeokuta, all of which represent mutually intelligible dialects of Yoruba.

Decalo defines Dassa as "[a] Yoruba ethnic group, arriving in Benin from Oyo but with an Egba royal dynasty. The clans settled in the vicinity of Dassa-Zoume."[10] Slavery, wars, and various conflicts between Dahomey, Yorubaland, and Benin led to declines, collapses, and subsequently to the rise of new states and empires. This is well documented by Webster, Boahen, and Tidy who report that:

> the victorious Ife and Ijebu armies swept into Egbaland turning the Egba into refugees . . . The wars and the refugee problem produced by them created bitterness and suspicion between the branches of the

Yoruba family, and prevented the Yoruba from uniting against external foes.[11]

Yacoubou also establishes the Yoruba origin of the Ìdàáchà, drawing on previous studies. She relies on oral tradition as an important source, using informants such as Tonoukouin, Abou, and Baba Egbe to elaborate on the folk etymology of the name "Idatcha" (hereafter "Ìdàáchà"). She claims that what is known today as Ìdàáchà was once created by immigrants who settled in a hilly environment similar to that of their homeland in Tado, Ile-Ife, Oyo, and Abeokuta: "Ces collines ont constitué des sites de refuges aux vagues successives des populations venues de Tado, d'Ile-Ife, d'Oyo pour former le peuplement du pays Idatcha."[12] According to Yacoubou's informants, "Ìdàáchà" is a combination of Ìda (princess) and "Itcha" (then a village), now the capital of Bante. Therefore, Ìdàáchà means "princess from Itcha." This princess was so popular that the people among whom she lived named their kingdom after her, that is, the Ìdàáchà kingdom whose capital was and still is called Igbo Ìdàáchà, meaning Ìdàáchà forest. The Fon invaders, mainly from Abomey, translated this name into their language and referred to this Yoruba area as Dassa-Zoume ("Dassa" for "Ìdàáchà" and "Zoume" for "Igbo").

Yacoubou also identifies the Ìdàáchà as Nagot or Yoruba from Nigeria:

> Les Idatcha qu'on appelle Nagot ou Yoruba du Moyen-Benin, ont leur origine au Nigeria. Enquittant le Nigeria pour des raisons diverses, ces derniers ont toujours gardé leur civilisation.[13]

Not only does Yacoubou's study agree that the Ìdàáchà came from Nigeria, but it also contends that they have preserved some Nigerian customs and cultural characteristics. Besides, it claims that the "Jagou" dynasty, from Egba in western Nigeria, were the founding fathers of Ìdàáchà kingdom in the early 1700s. This kingdom developed into a federation by absorbing early settlers and autonomous states ruled by the Yaka, Epo, and Ifita. The Ifita, from Ile-Ife, Oyoro, and Egba, founded their state between the 1400s and the 1500s, with the first king, Oba Sereku, from Ile-Ife.[14] Today Ìdàáchàland has two districts: Dassa-Zoumé (*Igbo*-Ìdàáchà) and Glazoué, also called Gbomina. Inhabited by 123,470 people, according to the latest census,[15] Ìdàáchàland is now divided into two districts: Dassa-Zoumé (64,065 inhabitants) and Glazoué (59,405 inhabitants). Glazoué, to the north, gained the status of district in the early eighties and comprises ten "communes" subdivided into forty-six villages. Dassa-Zoumé, to the south, is the capital town of ten "communes" comprising sixty-six villages. A "commune" is a local administrative entity that groups a variable number of villages together. A few "communes" are predominantly Mahi-speaking communities, related to the Fon, in the districts of Dassa-Zoumé and Glazoué: Gbaffo (3,411 inhabitants), Paouignan (18,075 inhabitants), and Soclogbo (7,357 inhabitants) in Dassa-Zoumé, with Aklamkpa (9,187 inhabitants), Assante (4,332 inhabitants), Ouedeme (6,794 inhabitants), and Thio (6,971 inhabitants) in Glazoué. For almost three-quarters of a circle, south, west, and north, the Ìdàácha territory is also bordered by vast lands inhabited by speakers of Fon and Mahi, neither of which is a Defoid language. To the east is the immense area of Yorubaland that spreads through southwestern Nigeria almost to the Niger River.

Besides Ìdàáchà, Standard Yoruba (SY) is used in a diglossic situation for religious purposes. Sermons are preached and bible studies are conducted in SY, while education is carried out in French. Most adults understand SY, but do not use it in ordinary conversations in the community. It may also be worthwhile pointing out that some Yoruba dialects, such as Icha and Ife, are closer to Ìdàáchà than are other varieties. But few of these Yoruba varieties have been extensively surveyed.

The place of Ìdàáchà may not be fully grasped without understanding the national linguistic environment in which it belongs. Based on the prevailing situation that predates the advent of national independence in Benin, Kitchen says:

> The many migrations and invasions that characterized Dahomey's turbulent early history have left three major Ethnic groups: the Fons, or Dahomans (about 700,000), who live in the south; the Adjas (220,000), who have settled along the Mono and Couffo rivers; and the Yorubas (160,000), who came from Nigeria and settled along the eastern border.[16]

The Fon speak Fon, a Kwa language widely used in the south and in Zou province or department. The Adja, 360,000, speak Aja, also a Kwa language, in Mono and "Atlantique" department, whereas Yoruba is a Benue-Congo language.

In fact, the people mentioned above (Fon, Adja, Bariba, and Yoruba) represent the ethnic majorities in Benin. They are very distinct from other groups. Best and de Blij describe the contrast in the following terms:

> The Fon, Adja and Yoruba form the largest ethnic groups in the south, and dominate most branches of government and the cash economy, while the less numerous Bariba, Peuls, and Sombas of the north claim they have been discriminated against.[17]

This account is consistent with Kitchen's description in reflecting a certain degree of ethnic diversity in Benin.[18] These diverse groups also speak diverse languages, and as O'Connor argues,

> Ethnic diversity produces great linguistic diversity in most African cities, and language plays a crucial part in determining the groups with which people

identify. It is language more than anything else which causes Ibo in Lagos or Luo in Nairobi to be labeled, and to label themselves, as such.[19]

As I indicate below, Greenberg's classification and Alexandre's description of Beninese languages as a part of a "large Congo-Kordofanian family, partially covering the 'Negro-African' family of Delafosse and the 'Negro' family of Westermann," have been updated.[20] Thus, what was known as Kwa has been reanalyzed. The new Kwa excludes Yoruba and just about every language east of Nigeria.

In Benin there are two major language categories: the Gur and the Kwa. Examples of such languages and their locations are specified below:

1. The Gur group—languages spoken in northern Benin such as Dendi, Baatonu/Bariba, Wama, Boko, and Foodo.[21]
2. The New Kwa group, in the south, also known as Gbe-languages in Benin, Togo, and Ghana.[22] These are a few examples: Aja-gbe (Benin and Togo); Ewe or Ewhe-Gbe (Togo and Ghana); Fon-Gbe (Benin); and Gen-Gbe (Benin and Togo).

As for Ìdààchà, it is a Yoruboid language included in the Benue-Congo group of Niger-Congo. It contains a significant number of loan words from Fon, a language located in an area adjacent to Idaacha territory. Katzner identifies Fon, Bariba, and Yoruba as major languages in Benin:

> Fon is the most important native language with about two million speakers in the southern half of the country. Bariba is spoken by about 500,000 people in the north, while Yoruba has a like number of speakers along the eastern border.[23]

Ìdàáchà, in particular, represents a western dialect of the Yoruba dialect cluster. This dialect cluster, in turn, belongs to Yoruboid. SY is also a Yoruba dialect. Therefore, I will use the term "Yoruba dialect cluster" to refer to this entire dialect group, "SY" for the Nigerian standard Yoruba language, and specific dialect names otherwise.

SIGNIFICANCE

In providing data and analysis of a not previously described variety of Yoruba, this chapter contributes to Yoruba studies in various ways. Indeed, Ìdàáchà has received little treatment in the linguistic literature, whereas numerous studies have been conducted on Yoruba dialects in western Nigeria. Pulleyblank and Ogunbowale rightly express the need for such a study to provide significant insights for research on SY.[24]

This study can also contribute to education. As a matter of fact, introducing native languages in academic curricula as early as the elementary school in Benin will be highly beneficial. The results of this work can serve as a reliable foundation for developing teaching materials for prospective instructors of the Ìdaacha language.

In general, this research has the potential to pave the way for more ambitious work on Yoruba dialects in Benin. When all of the dialects are surveyed in Benin, Togo, and Nigeria, there will be enough data for African linguists and Africanists to examine a number of important issues yet to be resolved in Yoruba linguistics. Courtenay expresses a similar viewpoint in saying that "no definitive study of Standard Yoruba can be made until more is known of the various dialects."[25]

LITERATURE REVIEW

This literature review will begin with a brief background review of the history of the Yoruba in general. It will then look at Yoruba dialectology, including major studies on the subject.

On the History of the Yoruba

Just a little will be said here about the origins of the Yoruba since no agreement has been established on that specific point in the literature. I will only focus on what is known about the Yoruba as sociocultural entities in recent centuries. Based on oral tradition passed down from one generation to another, the Yoruba in Benin believe that their ancestors were from western Nigeria. They also believe that from Nigeria to Benin and western Togo, the Yoruba cultural traits are very similar. The social structure, chieftaincy titles, deities, and basic customs, such as funeral rites and naming ceremonies, are very much alike. However, foreign observers and researchers do not consider this quasi-cultural uniformity to be evidence for the allegedly common Yoruba identity. For example, Lloyd remarks:

> The examination of the spread of such cultural traits provides an almost endless source of data for the historian but few easy solutions to his questions.[26]

He also alludes to cultural diversity and discrepancies throughout the Yoruba kingdoms, which may further complicate any historian's problems. In this regard, Lloyd argues:

> the structure of government in individual Yoruba kingdoms and communities is so diverse that one might . . . write a text book on African political structure drawing very many of one's examples from the Yoruba people.[27]

Nevertheless, the difficulties underlined above by no means negate the possibility of separating out the Yoruba from other ethnic groups. As a matter of fact, Lloyd and Johnson, among other researchers, agree upon the boundaries of the "Yoruba country" in Nigeria. They also divide the Yoruba into major ethnic groups in Kabba, Ekiti and Egba, Oyo/Ibadan, Ijesa, Ijebu, and Ondo.[28] Johnson claims that all these ethnic groups originate from Oduduwa and Ile-Ife.[29] But modern scholarship recognizes that this origin is purely legendary and mythical.[30] Law explains that "there exist among the Yoruba numerous origin legends which, while agreeing in tracing descent from Oduduwa and Ile-Ife do not refer to a migration from elsewhere."[31] In assessing accounts of the type that Johnson gives, Law adds this comment: "It should also be stressed that a myth of migration, even if accepted as fundamentally historical, cannot be assumed to refer to the whole people."[32]

It turns out that any historical account of periods before and during the nineteenth century should be taken with a grain of salt. As Biobaku puts it, "Much of what there is is not first hand, but hearsay."[33] One may therefore support the view expressed in the following terms: "For practical purposes the history of the Yoruba up to the nineteenth century is the history of a wholly non-literate people. The reconstruction of the history of such people, in the absence of the kind of written documentation on which conventional history depends, presents obvious problems."[34]

On the basis of the linguistic migration theory, however, the Yoruba can be deemed to have originated at least to the east or southeast of their present location, since Ekiti and Igbomina, two of the most divergent Yoruba dialects, are in the northeast, Igala, the most divergent Yoruboid dialect, is east of the Niger-Benue confluence, and Akoko, the most divergent of the Defoid group, is to the east as well. Furthermore, Yoruba is by far the westernmost of all of the Benue-Congo languages. Figure 1 indicates how these groups relate to one another.[35]

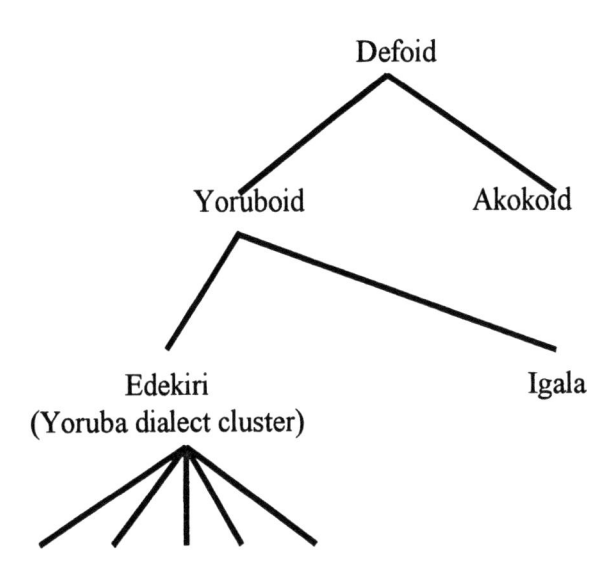

Figure 1: Defoid classification

```
            Defoid
           /      \
      Yoruboid   Akokoid
       /     \
   Edekiri    Igala
(Yoruba dialect cluster)
   /|\\\
```

Previous Studies

There are works, intended as literacy texts, by French missionaries and religious staff on Ìdàáchà. There are also some results of dispersed attempts to initiate adult literacy in Ìdàáchà, which was a national policy in the seventies in Benin. Such works must be retrieved from individuals and private archives. The contents are mostly historical facts, folktales, and healthcare and environmental issues, collected into leaflets by volunteers who have no training in linguistics. These materials, therefore, must be consulted with great caution and reservation.[36]

In short, previous studies on the Ìdàáchà dialect of Yoruba are very limited and may be grouped into two categories: (i) academic research and (ii) secondary works. The latter, briefly described above, are of little interest in this research. I will therefore deal with only the first category, identified as academic research.

Academic research in Ìdàáchà is very limited indeed. There are only two major studies to date, those of Tossou and Kouyomou.[37] The work of Tossou, a master's thesis at the Sorbonne University, is a list of Ìdàáchà proverbs. I consider this thesis an interesting and encouraging piece of work that sets the tone for further research in Ìdàáchà paremiology, but besides providing a specialized body of data, it is not of linguistic interest. The work of Kouyomou, a master's thesis in linguistics at the National University of Benin, is the first and the only major descriptive work on the phonology of the Ìdàáchà dialect. On the basis of his data collected in a few Ìdàáchà villages, Kouyomou basically presents an inventory of Ìdàáchà phonemes. His description is predominantly centered on articulatory phonetics, but he also touches on tones, vowel harmony, and syllable structure.[38]

The wide range of areas named above constitutes the strength of Kouyomou's study. One major weakness, however, is the lack of in-depth analysis in the work. Most importantly, there are no formal phonological rules and constraints to account for the results presented. In addition, there is no clearly stated theoretical framework within which the research is done. The author simply acknowledges that Martinet's methods and terminology[39] have influenced his writing to a very large extent:

> Nous nous sommes largement inspirés, lors de la rédaction de cette étude des méthodes et de la terminologie utilisées par A. Martinet.[40]

I will argue against the allophones Kouyomou suggests in the case of the following phonemes: /d/ (pp. 57-58), /l/ (pp. 64-66), and /t/ (p. 55). The palato-alveolar fricative he identifies, /sh/ or /S/, is a consonant in Standard Yoruba. This corresponds with the voiceless affricate /tS/ in Ìdàáchà, which I tend to reflect in my spelling of the name of the language itself.[41] Of course, orthography has no bearing on phonology but native speakers are most likely to spell words intuitively the way they pronounce them. This poses a problem that supports Capo's call for harmonization:

> in the area of orthography, one can talk of the 'Nigerian tradition' with dotted letters, and the 'Béninois trials' with special symbols, and obviously there is a need for harmonization."[42]

In contrast to this limited literature on Ìdàáchà, there are outstanding works on African linguistics in general and on Standard Yoruba as well as Yoruba dialectology in particular. Welmers's work, for example, is an encyclopedic study of African language families or groups that points out structural phenomena common to these languages, "but which are not necessarily typical of human language in the broadest sense."[43] Among other purposes, this work aims to describe examples of structural and phonological systems "in such a way that others can recognize or look for similar or significantly different systems in other languages." In that respect, I will look very closely at the Yoruba examples he provides, bearing in mind that

> Languages are not life forms that interbreed, transfigure or mutilate each other beyond recognition, or give birth to deformed as well as normal offspring. Languages are what people use in everyday life, and generation speaks to generation in each unbroken continuum.[44]

With regard to SY, there is an impressive amount of published research work. Early scholarship dates back to 1819, and Capo summarizes it as follows:

> Apart from the first vocabularies (Bowdich 1819; Kilham 1828; Claperton 1829; Raban 1830/32; Crowther 1943), there are a number of "descriptive

grammars" (Crowther 1852; Bouche 1880; Ward 1952; Bamgbose 1966; Awobuluyi 1977), two substantive dictionaries (CMS 1913; Abraham 1958), and a host of partial descriptions (Awobuluyi 1964; Adetugbo 1967; Courtenay 1968; Fresco 1970; Oyelaran 1971; Awoyale 1974; Akinlabi 1985, etc.[45]

Courtenay's descriptive work on Yoruba generative phonology examines these points: segment structure, sequence structure conditions, tone, phonological rules, and reduplication. The rules on the following are very interesting: nouns in association, vowel elision in nouns, possessive nouns, verb plus noun object, verb plus pronoun object, and verb aspect. This work also deals briefly with ideophones. It refers to previous studies on the subject.[46]

Also of major importance is "The Development of the Three-Way Tonal Contrast in Yoruba," a paper in which Stahlke says that "[t]he . . .observation frequently made is that the contrast between low and mid tone verbs is neutralized before a noun, where low tone verbs become mid."[47] He argues that this mid-low neutralization characterizes Yoruba at an earlier stage when the relationship between mid (M) and low (L) was allotonic. Stahlke does not disagree with Abraham, Bamgbose, Courtenay, and Delano, who describe the alternation as L becoming M before a noun. But he adds that it may also be historically true that mid-tone verbs become low except before nouns. It is also Stahlke's view that "the contrast between mid and low is not as general as that between high and non-high, since it is neutralized before nouns."[48]

Another important point is that the tone of an object clitic is polarized to the tone of the verb that goes with it. Stahlke therefore remarks that "this presupposes that the contrast between mid and low tone verbs is not relevant to the tone of pronouns."[49] Furthermore, Stahlke discusses what he calls "the grammatically conditioned change between mid and low tone found in the subject pronouns for the first and second persons." He comments that "the occurrence of low and mid tone is predictable morphologically, mid occurring in the preterit and certain other tenses and low before the tense markers **ń** (progressive) and **á** (future)."[50] Then he concludes that "because the distribution of mid and low tone in the subject pronoun is predictable, we can point to this as one further environment in which the contrast between mid and low is neutralized."[51]

Equally important is Stahlke's discussion of the forms of Yoruba pronouns (dependent and independent) in relation to tense and aspect. He argues that besides the future marker "yó," which may be analyzed, "[t]he morphology of the Yoruba tense/aspect system is at least as complex as that of the pronoun system, and any attempt at synchronic regularization is probably doomed from the outset."[52] Later on, Stahlke discusses prefixation in Yoruba, especially productive prefixes deriving nouns from verbs.[53] In this paper, Stahlke disagrees with Oyelaran and strongly supports Welmers's argument that all noun-initial vowels are indeed prefixes.[54]

With regard to dialectology, Adetugbo's work is quite illuminating. It is a comparative historical study of the Yoruba language across dialects. The Yoruba language, he argues, is a dialect continuum, and SY is "only a part of the Yoruba language; it is not the Yoruba language: the Yoruba language being an aggregate of all the dialects [including SY] spoken within the Yoruba linguistic area."[55] Adetugbo also classifies Yoruba dialects into three major groupings: Northwest Yoruba (NWY), Southeast Yoruba (SEY), and Central Yoruba (CY).

In an attempt to answer questions related to Yoruba origins and prehistory, Adetugbo's study focuses on specific areas such as pronominalization and phonological features. In so doing, it underlines the striking differences among the various dialects. For example, divergence in terms of pronoun and pronominal differentiation is described as follows:

a. coalescence of the terms for second and third person plural pronouns and pronominals in SEY as against their separation in both NWY and CY;

b. absence of the pronoun of respect in SEY *contra* its presence in the other dialects; the operation of vowel-harmony rules on the level of grammar in the singular pronouns of CY and its absence in both NWY and SEY; the polarization of positiveness and negativeness in the singular pronouns of CY and SEY; the use of pronoun as tense signaler in both CY and SEY as against the use of preverbs in NWY.[56]

As for phonological differences, taking into account a few features of consonants and vowels, Adetugbo states that "it is at this level [that is, phonology] that we find the most complex divergence among Yoruba dialects."[57] By way of illustration, Adetugbo provides examples of words in which SEY has preserved the Proto-Yoruba (PY) **gh*, a voiced velar fricative, whereas NWY has changed it to /w/, a bilabial semivowel, and CY has deleted it completely:

Table 1

SEY	NWY	CY	
oghó	owó	eó	"money"
àghò	àwò	aò	"skin, color"
èighò	èèwò	ee-ò	"taboo"
ghán	wón	ón	"costly, dear"
aghon	awun	aun	"tortoise"

A similar dialect study is the work in which Fresco reexamines a number of issues in Yoruba dialect phonology.[58] For example, he gives his own analysis of the phenomenon of vowel harmony in relation to the feature of Tense in a way that differs from previous work such as Ladefoged, Awobuluyi, and Courtenay.[59] Fresco argues that the motivation for the feature of Tense with regard to the constraints on vowel co-occurrence or sequence is inadequate in these studies. His detailed analysis of data from Central Yoruba or Standard Yoruba, Ketu (K),

Ondo (On), Ifaki (If), Okiti Kpukpa (Ok), Akure (Ak), Owo (Ow), and Oba (Ob) leads to the following conclusions: Harmony is a regressive process of tenseness assimilation based on a rule that "laxes all vowels to which it applies simultaneously and cyclically across the word boundary."[60] This rule is no longer active, at least not in all dialects, but one may formulate some generalization according to which 'obsolete' rules "can have a continuing effect on the grammar in the form of morpheme structure constraints."[61] The rule at an earlier stage must have applied to non-high vowels only, given "[t]he exclusion of i̱ and u̱ as prefix vowels from tenseness agreement in most dialects."[62]

Fresco also reassesses Stahlke's view that subject pronouns are derived and bimorphemic entities, "and that in their underlying form they are directly relatable to the corresponding independent pronoun set."[63] Fresco agrees on the derivability but objects to the direct relatabilty. Additionally, he reports that both he and Stahlke see the singular subject pronouns as having underlying forms that change their vowels to an o̱ under specific syntactic constructions. However, they have different opinions as to what this o̱ stands for: "This element Stahlke sees as an independent morpheme within the verbal auxiliary, and I see as the Subject Marker, whose base form is /ó/."[64]

Phonemic Inventory

I have identified thirty contrasting segments in Ìdàáchà, of which eighteen are consonants and twelve are vowels. I will use the binary features proposed by Halle, McCarthy, and Kenstowicz when referring to the phonological segments.[65] In drawing a feature tree, for example, Halle and McCarthy agree that [+cons, -cons] and [-son, +son] constitute the root. Obstruents will be identified as [+cons, -son], sonorant consonants will be [+cons, +son], while glides and vowels will be [-cons, +son]. Other features I will use in binary terms whenever applicable are: [round], [ant], [dist], [back], [high], [low], [nasal], [ATR], and [voiced].

I choose to use the Standard Yoruba orthography in this description. Therefore, I have adopted the conventional phonetic and phonemic transcriptions associated with SY. Besides what is well known of International Phonetic Alphabet (IPA), it is worthwhile underlining the peculiarities in Table 2 as far as Ìdàáchà and SY are concerned:

Table 2

Orthographic	Phonetic ([])	Phonemic (//)
ẹ	/ɛ/	[ɛ]
ọ	/ɔ/	[ɔ]
Vn	/Ṽ/ (if applicable)	[Ṽ]
P	/kp/	[kp]
gb (is one segment)	/gb/	[gb]
ṣ/ch	/ʃ/-/c/	[ʃ]-[c]
j	/ɟ/	[ɟ]

The Vowel System

The analysis of my data has led me to identify twelve vowels. The vowels ([-consonantal], [+sonorant]) are: i, e, ɛ, a, ɔ, o, u, ĩ, ẽ, ã, ɔ̃, ũ.. Seven of these are oral vowels and

Table 3

Oral vowels		Nasal vowels	
I	u	ĩ	ũ
e	o		
ɛ	ɔ	ɛ̃	ɔ̃
a		ã	

five are nasal vowels (See Table 3), which satisfies Ferguson's assumptions about nasal vowels,[66] especially Assumption XI which states that: "In a given language the number of Nvs is never greater than the number of non-nasal vowel phonemes." It is also important to note that Ìdàáchà has no long vowels.

Some of the vowels can also be found in Kouyomou's tables of vowels.[67] The vowels may be represented in terms of features as shown in Table 4.

Table 4

	I	ĩ	e	ɛ	ɛ̃	a	ã	ɔ	ɔ̃	o	u	ũ
high	+	+	-	-	-	-	-	-	-	-	+	+
low	-	-	-	-	-	+	+	-	+	-	-	-
back	-	-	-	-	-	+	+	+	+	+	+	+
ATR	+	+	+	-	-	-	-	-	-	+	+	+
round	-	-	-	-	-	-	-	+	+	+	+	+
nasal	-	+	-	-	+	-	+	-	+	-	-	+

The Phonemic Consonant Segments

Table 5: Consonant chart

	Stop	Fricative	Nasal	Liquid	glides
Bilabial	b		m		
Labio-dental		f			
Alveolar	t	s	n	I	
	d				
Palatal	c				j
	ɟ				
Velar	k				
	g				
Labio-velar	kp				w
	gb				
Glottal					h

These phonemes are specified as [+consonantal]. The following words illustrate the segments listed above. (See Table 6)

Table 6

Segment	Example in phonemic transcription	Ìdàáchà orthography	English gloss
b	/ibú/	ibú	dowñfall
m	/imú/	imú	nose
f	/ifá/	ifá	divination
t	/èta/	èta	tuber
d	/èdá/	èdá	creature
s	/isá/	isá	period/time
n	/iná/	iná	fire/light
l	/ilá/	ilá	okra
r	/ira/	irá	relative (s)
c	/acɔ/	achọ	cloth
ɉ	/aɉɔ/	ajọ	team/compannioship
j	/ɛjɔ/	ẹyọ	unit
k	/àká/	àká	granary
g	/àgá/	àgá	a type of yam
kp	/àkpà/	àpà	cut/wound
gb	/àgbà/	àgbà	mature/elder
w	/ìwà/	ìwà	character
h	/ìhà/	ìhà	mouse

CONCLUSION

This chapter focuses on the Ìdàáchà and their language, the Ìdàáchà dialect of Yoruba, as a historic human bond between Nigeria and the Republic of Benin. I have stated that

Yoruba dialects in Benin are yet to be surveyed; therefore, a description of this nature can be a useful starting point.

I have provided some background information about the Ìdàáchà-speaking community in terms of geographic location (present-day), origin, history, and relationships with the Yoruba in Nigeria. Indeed, on the basis of historical studies, some of which I have cited, the Ìdàáchà, like the Ife, Chaabe (Sabe), Icha (Itcha or Ica), inter alia, may be seen as communities speaking dialects descended from the same proto-language, Proto-Defoid.

NOTES

1. Hounkpati Capo, "Defoid," in John Bendor-Samuel (ed.), *The Niger-Congo Languages* (Lanham, Md.: University Press of America, 1989), 275.
2. See Institut National de la Statistique et de l'Analyse Economique (INSAE), "Deuxième recensement général de la population et de l'habitation, Février 1992," (Cotonou: Ministère du Plan et de la Restructuration Economique, 1994).
3. See Capo, "Defoid," for a complete list of "ede"-languages.
4. Ibid., 277.
5. Ibid.
6. Ibid., 276.
7. Bendor-Samuel (ed.), *The Niger-Congo Languages*.
8. Robert Sydney Smith, *Kingdoms of the Yoruba* (New York: Harper and Row, 1976). See also J. Toni, *Origines et fondation de Dassa* (Cotonou: Folio, 1957); A. Mondjannagni, and J. Plya, *Géographie du Dahomey* (Paris: Edition Armand Colin, 1963); Ogunsola J. Igue, "La civilisation agraire des populations Yoruba du Dahomey et du Moyen-Togo," thèse de doctorat 3è cycle de géographie, Université de Paris, 1971; and A. Biodun, "L'Etat d'Idaisa. La structure politique," *The Journal of the Structure and Administration of Precolonial Idaisa*, 1980, 72-82.
9. Smith, *Kingdoms of the Yoruba*, 84.
10. Samuel Decalo, *Historical Dictionary of Benin* (Metuchen, N.J. and London: The Scarecrow Press, 1987), 90.

11. J. B. Webster, Adu Boahen, and Michael Tidy, *The Revolutionary Years: West Africa since 1800* (London: Longman, 1980), 65.
12. Adama Yacoubou, *Techniques et rites agricoles traditionnels chez les Idatcha1801-1992,* mémoire de maîtrise d'histore, Université Nationale du Bénin, 1993, 11.
13. Ibid., 25.
14. Ibid., 28. See also Biodun, "L'Etat d'Idaisa," and Igue, "La civilisation."
15. INSAE, "Deuxième recensement," Nov. 1994.
16. H. Kitchen (ed.), *The Educated African: A Country-to-Country Survey of Educational Development in Africa* (New York: Praeger, 1962), 474.
17. A.C.G. Best, and H. J. de Blij, *African Survey* (Toronto: John Wiley and Sons, 1977), 215.
18. Kitchen (ed.), *The Educated African.*
19. O'Connor, *The African City* (London: Hutchinson & Co., 1983), 123.
20. P. Alexandre, *An Introduction to Languages and Language in Africa* (London:
    Heinemann, 1972), 69; Joseph H. Greenberg, *The Languages of Africa* (Bloomington: Indiana University Press, 1963); and Joseph H. Greenberg, *Studies in African Linguistic Classification* (New Haven, Conn.: Compass Publishing Company, 1955).
21. See the following studies on the Atakora language by André R. P. Prost: "Les langues de l'Atakora. I. Le wama," *Bulletin de l'IFAN* (BIFAN) 34, B.2, 1972, 299-392; "Les langues de l'Atakora. II. Le tayari," *BIFAN,* 34, B.3, 1972, 617-682; "Les langues de l'Atakora. III. Le bieri," *BIFAN,* 35, B.2, 1973, 444-511; "Les langues de l'Atakora. IV. Le ditammari," *BIFAN,* 35, B.3, 1973, 712-758; "Les langues de l'Atakora. V. Le yom," *BIFAN,* 35, B.4, 1973, 903-996; "Les langues de l'Atakora. VI. Le buli," *BIFAN,* 36, B.2, 1974, 323-413, "Les langues de l'Atakora. VII. Le nôtre," *BIFAN,* 36, B.3, 1974, 628-659; and "Vocabulaires comparés des langues de l'Atakora," *BIFAN,* 37, B.2, 1975, 412-448. See also Tony Naden, "Gur," in Bendor-Samuel (ed.), *The Niger-Congo languages,* 141-168.
22. See Hounkpati Capo, *A Comparative Phonology of Gbe* (Benin/ New York and Labo Gbe (INT) Garome, Benin: Foris Publications, 1991). For details of Kwa languages in general, see Green-

berg, *The Languages of Africa*, and John M. Stewart, "Kwa," in Bendor-Samuel (ed.), *The Niger-Congo languages*, 217-245.
23. Kenneth Katzner, *The Languages of the World* (New York: Routledge. 1995), 336.
24. Douglas Pulleyblank, "Yoruba," in Bernard Comrie, (ed.), *The World's Major Languages* (New York: Oxford University Press, 1987), 971-990; and, P. O. Ogunbowale, *The Essentials of the Yoruba Language* (New York: David McKay Company, 1970).
25. Karen Ruth Courtenay, "A Generative Phonology of Yoruba," unpublished doctoral dissertation, University of California, Los Angeles, 1968.
26. P.C Lloyd, "Political and Social Structure," in Saburi Biobaku (ed.), *Sources of Yoruba History* (London: Oxford university Press, 1973), 206.
27. Ibid.
28. Ibid.
29. Samuel Johnson, *The History of the Yorubas* (London: Routledge & Kegan Paul, 1921).
30. See R.C.C. Law, "Traditional History," in Biobaku (ed.), *Sources of Yoruba History*, 25-40.
31. Ibid., 30.
32. Ibid., 31.
33. Biobaku (ed.), *Sources of Yoruba History*, 3.
34. Ibid.
35. For more details, see Capo, "Defoid"; Kay Williamson, "The Classification of East-Congo," *JOLAN*, 1, 1982, 101-106; Kay Williamson "Niger-Congo Overview," in Bendor-Samuel (ed.), *The Niger-Congo Languages*, 3-45; Femi Akinkugbe, "An Internal Classification of the Yoruboid Group (Yoruba, Isekiri, Igala)," *Journal of West African Languages (JWAL)*, 11 (1-2), 1976, 1-19; and Femi Akinkugbe, "A Comparative Phonology of Yoruba Dialects, Isekiri, and Igala," Ph.D. dissertation, University of Ibadan, 1978.
36. Other works on similar themes include Lazare Edikou, "Les rois ou Djagoun de Dassa-Zoumé, manuscrit de la Sous-Préfecture de Dassa-Zoumé. Dassa-Zoumé, Benin, 1970 (unpublished); F. Faroud, "Chez les Dassa," *Echo des Missions Africaines de Lyon*, 67, Juin-Juillet 1929, and 8-9, Août-Septembre, 1929; Marti M. Palau, "*Notes sur les rois de Dassa*," Journal de la Société des Africanistes, 27, fascicule 2, 1957.

37. Marguérite Tossou, "Les proverbes Idatcha," mémoire de maîtrise, Université de la Sorbonne Nouvelle (Paris III), 1973; and Odoun Kouyomou, "Phonologie de la langue idaasha," mémoire de maîtrise de linguistique, Université Nationale du Bénin, 1986.
38. Kouyomou, "Phonologie de la langue idaasha."
39. A Martinet, *Eléments de linguistique générale* (Paris: Edition Armand Colin, 1970).
40. Kouyomou, "Phonologie de la langue idaasha," 8.
41. See Capo, "Defoid," 278-281, for these examples: Idaitsa, ede Idaitsa, Idaaca, ede Itsa, Ica, and ede Tsabe. See also Yacoubou , *Techniques et rites,* and others who prefer 'Idatcha'.
42. Capo, "Defoid," 287.
43. William E. Welmers, *African language structures,* Berkeley and Los Angeles: University of California Press, 1973), vii.
44. Ibid., 18.
45. Capo, "Defoid," 276.
46. Such studies include C. M. Doke, *Bantu Linguistic Terminology (London: Longmans. 1935); R. C. Abraham, Dictionary of Modern Yoruba* (London: University of London Press, 1958); and Ayo Bamgbose, "The Assimilated Low Tone in Yoruba," in *Lingua,* 16, 1966, 1-13.
47. Herbert Stahlke, "The Development of the Three-Way Tonal Contrast in Yoruba," paper presented at the Third Annual Conference on African Linguistics, Bloomington, Ind., April 6-8, 1972.
48. Ibid., 2.
49. Ibid., 3.
50. Ibid.
51. Ibid., 4.
52. Herbert Stahlke, "Pronouns and Islands in Yoruba," *Studies in African Linguistics,* 5 (2), 1974, 175.
53. Herbert Stahlke, "The Noun Prefix in Yoruba," *Studies in African Linguistics* (Supplement), 6, 1976, 243-253.
54. O. O. Oyelaran, "Yoruba Phonology," Ph.D. dissertation, Stanford University, 1971.
55. Abiodun Adetugbo, "The Yoruba Language in Yoruba History," in Biobaku (ed.), *Sources of Yoruba History,* 183.
56. Ibid., 186.
57. Ibid., 189.

58. Edward Max Fresco, *Topics in Yoruba Dialect Phonology*, (Los Angeles: University of California Press, 1970).
59. See Peter Ladefoged, *A phonetic Study of West African Languages* (Cambridge: Cambridge University Press, 1964); A. Oladele Awobuluyi,. "Vowel and Consonant Harmony in Yoruba: A Problem of Syntactic Analysis," *Journal of African Languages,* 6 (1), 1967, 1-8; and Courtenay, "A Generative Phonology of Yoruba."
60. Fresco, *Topics in Yoruba Dialect Phonology*, 54.
61. Ibid., 54.
62. Ibid.
63. Herbert Stahlke, "On the Morphology of the Yoruba Subject Pronoun," MS., University of Illinois, 1969, 5.
64. Ibid., 79.
65. Morris Halle, "Phonological Features," in W. Bright, (ed.), *International Encyclopedia of Linguistics* (Oxford: Oxford University Press, 1992), 207-12; John McCarthy, "Feature Geometry and Dependency," in *Phonetica*, 43, 1988, 84-108; and Michael Kenstowicz, *Phonology in Generative Grammar* (Cambridge: Blackwell, 1994).
66. Charles A Ferguson, "Assumptions about Nasals: A Sample Study in Phonological Universals," in Joseph H. Greenberg (ed.), *Universals of Language* (Cambridge: MIT Press, 1963), 42-47.
67. Kouyomou, "Phonologie de la Langue Idaasha," 102-113.

21

ORALITY AS SCRIPTURE: VERSES AND SUPPLICATIONS IN YORUBA RELIGION

Abdul-Rasheed Na'Allah

INTRODUCTION

A Yoruba proverb, a heterosporous web, is similar to agidigbo-drum's metanarrative. Local tradition says only *ologbon*–the wiser–can unravel this metanarrative, which is pertinent to this chapter. The local tradition states: "He/she who has not seen another person's farm claims there is no farm like his/her father's." My experiences[1] with religion and sacred textualities suit the argument in this adage. One easily and erroneously concludes that every world religion of substance must produce written scripture, a set of written commandments from God. Especially in this postprint age, we almost assume that religion cannot exist without a (holy) written text for its adherents to hold dear, regardless of whether such texts were compiled after the death[2] of that religion's proclaimer, as with the New Testament and the Holy Quran.

My points of discourse here include the many traditional African religions to which the concept of a holy written text is foreign and inconceivable, even within the world's markets of modernity and postmodernity. In this chapter, our sonorous gong throws its searching voice in the "oral scripture"[3] of traditional African society, with particular explications of oral textual elements from Yoruba religion. I intend to show that oral performance of traditional religious scripture is completely independent of print in an oral society. Oral performance of religious scripture is distant from the secondary orality of the reading and interpreting of the Bible and the Quran commonly used in a modern scriptural world. I shall maintain that the status of a written scripture as holy, as sacred, and as the "word of God" is similar to (never greater than) the status oral societies give to their oral scripture.[4]

SCRIPTURE AND THE CONCEPTS OF RELIGIOUSNESS AND HOLINESS

The term "scripture" has a reduced coloring in Western literate quarters, following its etymology. Its Latin interpretation is "writing," springing from the word "scriptura."[5] The Western notion of scripture is unfortunately an antithesis to oral tradition. Graham correctly contends: "Our current Western notions of 'holy writ' too easily take for granted the written text as the focus of piety and faith in scriptural communities."[6] The idea is that these written scriptures are the only "repository of divine, suprahuman knowledge or divine, heavenly decrees."[7] The word "scripture" narrowed and was then used only for the Christian Bible. Extending its connotations, it now signifies "sacred book" of many major religions, such as Christianity, Islam, Hinduism, Buddhism, Jainism, Sikhism, Zoroastrianism, Taoism, and so on.

Scholars who contributed to *Rethinking Scripture,*[8] such as Miriam Levering, Wilfred Smith, Thomas Colburn, William Graham, Kendall Folkert, and Barabra Holdrege, subject the notion of scripture to thorough scrutiny. The parameters identified for categorizing scripture in the West include divine origin, degree of respectability, and reverence by adherents. Others are normativeness, finality as canon, completeness, adaptability for religious and ritual contexts, and testimony to what is ultimate. Levering condemns some of these parameters as superfluous:

> These are intuitively appealing generalizations, yet they are curiously misleading. I suspect that those characterizations are so intuitively appealing [because] all but one of them belong to the widely shared common sense characterization of the Bible. But a fully informed comparative study casts considerable doubt on the universal applicability and fruitfulness of these characterizations.[9]

Levering says that though most of these statements are true about the Bible and the Quran, they are "far less significant . . . as statements about other scriptural texts."[10] This is actually referring to other written scriptures. Levering points out, however, that the Chinese do not necessarily regard their classics as complete. The Vedas are not looked upon as "a source of wisdom, knowledge or legal and ethical standards"[11] on every matter of life. Nichiren followers (in Japan) do not regard the Lotus Sutra, their scripture, as "a complete source from which to derive ethical or legal prescriptions or holy social institutions."[12] Folkert in "The 'Canons' of 'Scripture'" contends that the "scripture phenomenon" projects the image of the Protestant Bible. Identifying scripture with such other names as "holy word," "sacred literature," Bible, and canon, he insists:

> This reveals itself if one simply takes the time to consider how the several names of the scripture work out when applied with care to the Protestant Bible. To anticipate the result of some subsequent analysis, each name reveals and implies a significantly different dimension of the status of the Bible–or, at least, it should do so.[13]

The other names, according to Folkert, are actually applied "nearly interchangeably" to the Bible.[14] From the various discussions, scholars have established a common ground of "sacredness" and "holiness" and of scripture: the idea that it is a text of religious commandments and guidance.

However, the worship and guidance which scripture commands are not limited to Christianity and Islam, or any other scriptural religion. My understanding is that every religion has what it claims as a divine message and guidance admonitions. From this perspective one can say therefore that religions in oral societies are no less sacred than the "written faiths." Both have claims to divine texts. What I have seen of the religiosity of oral societies in Nigeria is sufficient for me to support the polemics on the rethinking of the term "scripture." Yet, I am not supporting the Levering-Folkert abandonist school, which wants to do away with the term all together. Neither do I agree with Thomas Coburn in his adoption of the term "the word" for the religious text of the oral traditional community of India.[15] After all, the terms, "text" and "literature," originally meant writing, yet they now connote both written and oral forms. In today's postmodern, postprint paradigm, the generalization of text, literature, and now scripture to account for both written and oral materials is polysystemically healthy. It is becoming fast outdated to condemn orality to the periphery of the written canon. It would be inappropriate to tag it as non-central, especially for the oral scholar. After all, "word" started as a unit of speech, yet today it also means a graphic representation of speech.[16]

ORAL SCRIPTURES AND THEIR EFFECTS AMONG THE YORUBA

The following samples of oral scriptures derive from Yoruba culture in Nigeria. There are over 400 deities among the Yorubas.[17] Bascom summarizes how Yoruba people worship their deities within the broader scope of Yoruba religion:

An individual normally worships the deity of his father, and some also worship their mother's deity as well. Many deities are identified within a particular clan in which case all members, male and female, are worshipers by virtue of birth to it. After marriage women return home for the annual festival of their own deity, but they assist in the performance of the annual festival of their husband's deity.[18]

However, people are free to worship any deity of their choice. Usually a babalawo, an Ifa priest, is consulted for guidance. The traditional Yorubas are very religious and worship all the time, everywhere. Bolaji Idowu adequately captures this in his book *Olodumare: God in Yoruba Belief.* Idowu writes:

In the life of the Yoruba, worship as an imperative factor stands out prominently. As a deeply religious people, worship for them begins, controls, and ends all the affairs of life. A Yoruba feels that he is the presence of divinity wherever he is and whatever he does. The active essence of his divinity is his controlling thought, whether that means for him a constant source of superstitious dread, or a sense of security which fills him with inward peace. In all undertakings, however trivial or vital, he puts his divinity first and calls upon him for blessing, support, and succor.[19]

We can see, therefore, that adherents of book religions are not necessarily more religious than others. Neither do they have greater reverence for deities or religious textualities.

The oral scriptures of the Yoruba religion are located in what Ogunjimi and Na'Allah have classified as religious poetry.[20] They are also found in proverbs, incantations, and epithets. The oral scriptures are realized in ritual performances, myths, legends, taboos and symbols. They are divine compositions rooted in Yoruba cosmology and cosmogony. Oral scriptures evolve with the society and change as the society changes.[21] Oral scriptures clearly show codes of behavior, processes, and modes of worship. They also form the bedrock of traditional literature. That is why it is not appropriate to describe African art as "art for art's sake." If anything, it is first an art for the sake of the gods.

Ifa is a good example of the many Yoruba deities. Its other names include "Orunmila" and "Agboniregun." It is said to have descended from heaven to the world. Ifa talks to its adherents through divination. Many of the worshipers of other deities approach Ifa in times of trouble.[22] The Ifa verses are very popular among the Yorubas. Because traditional religious verses are part of the society's popular traditions, every oral scripture is in the local dialect of the worshiper. So there are as many variants[23] of the "oral scripture" of a particular Yoruba deity as there are dialects among the Yoruba. While themes, history, and norms are central to all the scriptures, every verse portrays minor differences. The Ifa worshipers regularly evoke religious verse to thank gods and to worship them. The worshipers say,

Iba irun-male ojukotun;
Iba igba-male ojukosi;
iba ota-le-n-irun Irun-male
Ti o ja atari ona orun gbangba.

Worship to the four hundred divinities of the right hand;
Worship to the two hundred divinities of the left hand;
Worship to the four hundred and sixty divinities
Who actually line up the very road of heaven.[24]

The above verses share thematic and poetic qualities with the written texts of Islam and Christianity. They adore and pay homage to the metaphysical beings in elevated language. These characteristics parallel religious revelations. We can observe repetitions and lexical matching in the lines cited above.[25] The metaphors of "right" and "left" hands are particularly striking. The oral scripture lives in the verbal non-written state. Apart from scholarly research in modern institutions, it remains oral in words and actions: words are verses and actions are rituals and sacrifices. Traditional communities' symbols, movements, and cultural elements are important to an understanding of oral scripture. The worshipers have no problem interpreting oral scripture, because all its forms are rudiments of their lives.

Like most of the other Yoruba deities, Ifa is said to have settled on earth. He later decided to leave for heaven in annoyance when his last born son Olowo did not respect him. In the Ifa scripture, the following represents the god's anger and the consequent uneasy state between earth and people. The scripture describes this:

Aboyun o bi mo
Agan o towo ala bosun,
Okunrin o dide
Akaremodoo wewu irawe
Ato gbe mo omokunrin ni idi,
Obinrin o ri a see re mo.
Isu peyin o ta.
Agbado tape o gbo;
Eree yoju opolo.
Ojo paa paa paa kan sile,
Adie sa a mi.
A pon obe sile,
Ewure mu un je.

Pregnant women could not deliver their babies
Barren women remained barren.
Small rivers were covered up with fallen leaves
Semen dried up in men's testicles
Women no longer saw their menstruation.
Yams formed small but undeveloped tubers.
Corn grew small but unripened ears.
Well-sharpened razors were placed on the floor
And goats attempted to devour them.[26]

Similar verses showing God's wrath exist in written scriptures. A good example in the Quran is Suratul Lahab. It is a curse of Allah on Prophet Muhammed's uncle, Abu Lahabi, and his wife Imra'at for plotting against the holy prophet. Just like this and many other Quran verses, Ifa religious history expatiates on the circumstances behind the revelation. Similar to the incident involving the prophet's uncle, our example involves Ifa's own blood, his son. Muslims, however, see Muhammad as a messenger of God, and thus he is never treated as a god nor is he worshiped. However, Ifa worshipers see Ifa as a god and offer supplications to Ifa. These verses contain warnings of how gods may deal with erring humans. Repetition, irony, bluntness, powerful images, thesis and antithesis are among the literary devices employed in the above verses. The metaphors portray terrible destruction and disarray: "pregnant women could not deliver their babies" and "semen dried up in the men's testicles." Goats had to resort to eating "well-sharpened razors." All these elements help to represent helplessness, chaos, hunger, and destruction.

Another chapter in exultation of Ifa presents a poem of spectacular beauty:

Ifa lo loni,
Ifa lo lola;
Ifa lo lotunla pelu e.
Orunmila lo nijo oosa da'aye.

Ifa is the master of today,
Ifa is the master of tomorrow;
Ifa is the master of the day after tomorrow.
To Ifa belong all the four days created by divinities on earth.[27]

We can observe repetition, especially lexical matching, in the first three lines. These verses are similar to those in written scripture extolling God, as in Suratul Ikhalas, or the Chapter of Unity, from the glorious Quran. Here Allah describes Himself as One, Sustainer, Childless, and Inimitable.[28] This is similar to what the oral scripture accomplishes with Ifa.

There are 256 categories of poetry in the Ifa corpus.[29] These categories, called Odu in Yoruba, are regarded as revelations from Olodumare (the Supreme Being). Each Odu has 600 poems.[30] The following is a short chapter usually recited to appeal to Ifa for success:

Ogodo owu soke odo,
Payin kekeeke soloko;
A dia fun Alantaakun,
Omo asohungbogbo
Bi idan bi idan.
Ifa bi idan, bi idan
Ni o seree temi femi.
Ogodo owu soke odo,
Payin kekeeke soloko.

When the farmer looks at cotton wool on the other side of the river,
It seems to open its white teeth smiling joyfully.
Ifa divination was performed for the Spider,
Offspring of those who do all things
In a wonderful way.
Ifa, in your own wonderful way,
Bring all good things to me.
When the farmer looks at cotton wool on the other side of the river,
It seems to open its white teeth smiling joyfully.[31]

In this chapter, cotton wool and white teeth represent fertility, happiness, and achievement. The "other side of the river" alludes to the "other side" of poverty, which is plentiful. The Spider in Yoruba tradition is associated with industry, wealth, and good tidings. It is also an image of weakness, powerlessness, and lightness. The varying meanings of spider are archetypal. In Islam there is a story about how the spider wove a web around the hideout entrance of the prophet so that his enemies did not locate him. The above verses describe the Spider as strong, physically or metaphysically: "Offspring of those who do all things/ In a wonderful way." It is a supplication that expresses hope and expectations from Ifa.

The *ese ifa* quoted below is braided in even greater metaphors. The verses below are in local dialect. They employ images and metaphors from the indigenous culture, like shadow, leaf, and kolanut. The messages are not tough nuts for the villagers to crack:

Ojiji o beru ofin;
A dia fewe
Ti n lo lee gbobi niyawo.
Igba ti o ya,
Ewe ni oun o fe obi mo.
Lo ba ko obi iyawoo re sile.
Igba to obii lo tan,
Lo ba bere sii gbe.
Igba ti oran naa o wo mo,
Ni obii ba tun pada waa fe ewe,
Nagba naa ni o too wa bere sii ye e.
O ni ojiji o beru ofin;
A dia fewe
Ti nlo gbobi niyawo.
Ero Ipo,
Ero Ofa,
Igba obi loun o fewe mo,
Se bi gbigbe ni ngbe.

The shadow does not fear a deep pit.
Ifa divination was performed for Leaf
Who was going to marry kolanut.
After some time,
Kolanut said that she did not want to marry Leaf anymore.
She then divorced Leaf.
After kolanut had left Leaf,
She started to dry up.
When the matter became unbearable,
Kolanut returned to Leaf.
It was then that her life became good again.
She said, "The shadow does not fear a deep pit.
Ifa was performed for Leaf

Who was going to marry kolanut.
Travelers to the city of Ipo,
Travelers to the city of Ofa,
It was when kolanut divorced Leaf
That she started to dry up."[32]

While the passage above contains many images indigenous people would instantly identify, many foreign readers may jump to associations from their own cultures.

Leaf and the kolanut are gender metaphors. They represent the sustenance of the family, household, and community. The kolanut is central to Nigerian religious and secular life. A popular saying expresses its importance in people's lives: "He who brings kolanut brings life." In any social gathering, home, or market, the kolanut is passed around as a symbol of love, happiness, and togetherness. The kolanut is also a very important element in sacrifice and ritual among the Yorubas.[33] As important as it is, however, the above verses show that its survival is bound to Leaf, which provides it shelter and gives it shade from the scorching sun.

The meanings of these verses, like those of most written religions, are multifarious. However, they do not escape the understanding of indigenous people, whose cultural and linguistic traditions inform their composition. For example, the Yoruba woman knows that the Leaf metaphor not only signifies her husband, but more importantly, it signifies the home, the family, the community to which she is Mother. She does not hasten into a divorce. Divorce is exceptional among the Yorubas. The metaphorical "drying up" of the kolanut after she divorces Leaf in the above verses is ironic. It is the home and community that dry up. It is the children that "die." Leaf is haunted by these consequences of her divorce. She would rather stay in the home and fight within it. This passage employs repetition, direct speech, proverbs, and other indigenous techniques.

The oral scripture of primary oral societies projects the same purpose as the holy books of the scripted religions. Orality retains a sacred status in oral cultures where it is spontaneous and indigenous. Though Graham correctly claims greater orality for the Quran than the Bible, it is doubtful whether any written scripture can attain "the functional primacy of the oral text" that he vigorously suggests,[34] or whether readers are even interested in such a level of orality. Apart from the original revelation and memorization, the basis of the recitation of the holy Quran today is strictly the written text. Word for word, line for line, recitation follows the same written scripture all over the world, even where voices and recitation patterns differ. Moreover, orality of reading, recitation, and interpretation cannot be synonymous to the orality of spontaneous improvisation that is the hallmark of oral scriptures. Whatever its attainments, orality in written scripture remain a derived orality, and therefore secondary; while that of oral scripture is original, primary.

NOTES

1. I have lived and researched in a primary oral society. Ilorin (Nigeria), the city of my birth, can be described as a mixed society in the sense that it has some people who are literate in Arabic and English.
2. The issue of the death of Jesus is, however, controversial among the scriptured religions of Islam and Christianity. Muslims, for example, hold tenaciously to the belief that Jesus never died. The Quran, which was revealed to Muhammad (SAW), was compiled after his death.
3. After all, there is "oral literature" even though literature itself derives from the Latin's "littera" or letter, meaning "write" or "written."
4. Jill Geer, in "Written Scripture and Its Interpretations: Using a chapter of the Quran as an Example" unpublished manuscript, 1995, explores textual examples from the Holy Quran's Suratul Nisai (chapter on women), and demonstrates that orality in written scriptures cannot attain the primacy (effect) of the spontaneous performance in traditional oral religions.
5. W. A. Graham, *Beyond the Written Word: Oral Aspects of Scripture in the History of Religion* (Cambridge: Cambridge University Press, 1987), 53.
6. Ibid., ix.

7. Ibid., 51.
8. M. Levering, ed. *Rethinking Scripture: Essays from a Comparative Perspective* (New York: State University of New York Press, 1989).
9. Ibid., 8-9.
10. Ibid., 9.
11. Ibid.
12. Ibid.
13. K. W. Folkert, "The 'Canons' of 'Scripture,'" in Levering, *Rethinking Scripture,* 172.
14. Ibid.
15. See Thomas Coburn, "'Scripture' in India: Towards a Typology of the World in Hindu Life," in Levering, *Rethinking Scripture.* 102-128.
16. J. M. Foley, "Oral Literature Today," in M. A. Caws and C. Predergast, eds., *Harper Collins World Reader* (New York: Harper Collins College Publishers, 1994), 2592.
17. William Bascom, *The Yoruba of Southwest Nigeria* (New York: Holt, Rinehart and Winston, 1969), 77.
18. Ibid.
19. Bolaji Idowu, *Olodumare: God in Yoruba Belief* (London: Longman Group Ltd., 1962), 107-108.
20. B. Ogunjimi and A. Na'Allah, *Introduction to African Oral Literature* (Ilorin: University of Ilorin Press, 1994), 17-39.
21. Evidence has shown that such changes must, however, be from within. Despite the many centuries of writing in Africa south of the Sahara, it has not been able to influence oral scripture in form and state. To date, even literate adherents of traditional religions do not depend on written texts for worship and ritual performances. Whatever influence the written tradition may claim is entirely insignificant to the worshipers.
22. Bascom, *The Yoruba of Southwest Nigeria,* 80.
23. Apart from differences in dialects, oral scripture can also differ in words from performance to performance. The oral characteristic of improvisation makes no two performances identical. This dynamism of oral text makes it truly living text. Though content, words, and metaphors are largely retained from one performance to the next, their order of appearance in each line may be rearranged to suit the disposition and innovation of the performer/worshiper. This situation is definitely inconceivable in a written scripture.
24. Idowu, *Olodumare,* 67.

25. See W. J. Ong, *Orality and Literacy: The Technologizing of the World* (New York: Methuen, 1982), 31-46; and J. M. Foley, *Oral Formulaic Theory and Research: An Introduction and Annotated Bibliography* (New York: Garland Publishing, Inc., 1985), 11-22.
26. Wande Abimbola, *Ifa Divination Poetry* (New York: Nok Publishers, Ltd., 1977), 3.
27. Ibid., 15.
28. See the Quran, Chapter 112.
29. Abimbola, *Ifa Divination Poetry*, 15.
30. Ibid.
31. Ibid., 54-55.
32. Ibid., 142-143.
33. Idowu, *Olodumare*, 88, 108, 135, 142.
34. Graham, *Beyond the Written Word*, 110.

22

APPRENTICESHIP AND CONTINUITY IN TRADITIONAL YORUBA ART

Christopher O. Adejumo

INTRODUCTION

In recent times, literature in the domain of African art has been dominated by reflections on past artistic traditions on the continent. African art is often discussed in terms of an extinct phenomenon, lost to the primitivism of primordial tribes and cultures. This perception of African art, especially by Western scholars, has resulted in a lack of inquiry about the continuance of traditional art forms. Equally disturbing is the lack of broad-based intellectual discourse on the connectedness of traditional African art to contemporary art forms. Some of the questions that readily come to mind are: Did African cultures continue the production of superb traditional art works during and after the partitioning and colonization of most of the continent? Are there any relationships between traditional and contemporary African art forms?

This chapter will attempt to address the issues raised above, using Yoruba art as an example of African art. The chapter will explore how this art form has been practiced and sustained over several centuries. It will also examine its influence on more contemporary Yoruba art forms. For an indepth understanding of the Yoruba artistic culture, it is important to begin by briefly tracing the historical development of the Yoruba people.

THE YORUBA: HISTORICAL BACKGROUND

The Yoruba are predominantly found in Nigeria, a country of over one hundred million people. The Yoruba are one of several ethnic/linguistic groups in the country. "Yoruba" is the name for a distinct cultural group as well as the language spoken by that group. Etymologists have suggested that the name Yoruba originated from an outside culture that came in contact with indigenous people through trade.

Archaeological findings within some ancient Yoruba cities, such as Ife and Owo, indicate that Yoruba civilization dates back to around 900 A.D. As one of the most prominent ethnic groups in Nigeria, the Yoruba population is estimated at about twenty million. Spreading beyond the Nigerian borders, it is estimated that there are approximately fifteen million Yorubas in the rest of Africa, with most of them residing in the western part of the continent, especially in the People's Republic of Benin. As a result of the trans-Atlantic slave trade, a large part of the Yoruba population was relocated outside Africa. Yoruba settlements can be found in Europe, Asia, the Caribbean islands, and the mainland of the Americas, especially in Brazil where Yoruba culture has gained strong roots. The Yoruba population abroad is estimated at about thirty million, half of whom live in South and North America, including Canada. Despite their dispersal across the globe, the Yoruba people continue to share a common bond that is grounded in their ancestral origins, language, and beliefs.

An in-depth account of the origin of the Yorubas is a complex task that is beyond the scope of this chapter, for such an undertaking must examine various sources of information, such as oral and written history, myths, folk tales, legends, customs, traditional practices, norms, religion, and art. The need for a multiple approach is based on the fact that early Yoruba history is not available in a chronological body of literature. However, historians have focused on two major accounts of the origin of the Yoruba people. The first account entails several versions of a creation story. The Yorubas believe that they are descendants of one common ancestor, Oduduwa, who supposedly descended from heaven with a chain, bearing some earth, palm kernels, and a cock. He landed in Ife where these items were used to establish the earth and its agricultural resources.

The second account is the migration paradigm. Saburi Biobaku posits that the Yoruba people migrated from the area around Egypt in North Africa around 600 A.D. Other prominent Yoruba historians like Ade Obayemi, J. A. Atanda, and I. A. Akinjogbin have suggested that the Yorubas migrated between 500 A.D. and 1,000 A.D.,[1] from the Hausa-Fulani area of the Niger-Benue confluence, a region that is much closer to the current location of the Yoruba kingdoms. This theory is often supported by similarities in physical characteristics shared by both Yoruba and Fulani peoples, such as facial marks. Various accounts of Yoruba origins are still accepted by many people.

TRADITIONAL YORUBA ART

The rise of Yoruba kingdoms led to the establishment of sophisticated political systems and elaborate religious organizations and cults. These sociopolitical and religious developments led to an increased demand for art products. Yoruba artists fashioned exquisite works of art in wood, metal, terracotta, stone, and hand-woven fabric for domestic consumption and as paraphernalia for worship in the cults of a pantheon of *orisha* or gods. Some of the religious cults that patronize the artists are those of Shango, the god of thunder and lightning; Ibeji, the cult of twins; and Ifa, the god of divination. These cults often commission local artists to produce symbolic objects that are placed in shrines, used for ceremonial purposes, or worn as talismans for personal protection. Such objects include *ose Shango* (Shango staff); *ere Ibeji* (Ibeji twin figures); and *opon Ifa* (Ifa divination bowl).

The phrase "traditional Yoruba art" is used to describe many early art forms produced in the region. The corpus of traditional Yoruba art entails a broad range of items, such as jewelry, pottery, basketry, doors, and furniture. It is difficult to establish the exact dates when religious and secular art evolved in Yorubaland. However, some of the potsherds and sculptures excavated around Ife have been dated to around the twelfth century A.D. Also, Ijebu's textile industry was fully developed by the seventeenth century.[2]

Most Yoruba artists produce their works on a part-time basis to supplement subsistence agriculture. As a result, many of the artists maximize their art production during the dry season when they are less occupied with farm work. The type of art produced usually depends on demand and local availability of raw materials. For example, calabash decoration is prevalent in Oyo as a result of an ample supply of gourds, while the Ondo and Ekiti areas are known for producing outstanding pottery from their clayey soil. The establishment of trade contacts with other cultures in different geographical locations has made it possible for Yoruba artists to import and export materials and ideas. Through these contacts, the artists have been able to acquire resources that are not locally available. For example, Oyo is known for the production of superb leather goods and most of the raw materials used, such as cattle and goatskins, are imported from North Africa.

CONCEPTUAL AND STYLISTIC APPROACH

Traditional Yoruba artists often give considerable importance to the processes and inherent qualities of their works as opposed to seeking personal fame or recognition. The processes involved in Yoruba art productions are influenced by traditions that vary from one locality to another. However, the techniques used in some of the art forms are found in many locations. For example, the predominant approach to pottery in Yorubaland is the coil system. In this approach, clay is fortified with sand and shards of old pottery to reduce its plasticity and to keep it from cracking during firing. The mixed clay is rolled into long coils that are used to form various types of pottery. The pots are embellished with decorative patterns, glazed, sun-dried till they are leather-hard, and fired in locally constructed open-air kilns. The finished pots are used for different purposes, such as storing water, cooking, eating, and ritual use. Yoruba pots are used around their areas of production and are rarely traded, because of their volume and fragility. Products like Yoruba textiles are not only consumed locally but also exported to near and far away places.

Apart from the use of religious icons, traditional Yoruba art works are inspired by folklore, proverbs, adages, myths, and legends. The visual characteristics of the works draw upon forms and patterns that have been used for decades. Some of the visual characteristics of Yoruba art are bulging eyes, large noses with straight bridge, lips modeled in parallel bars, stylization of the hair with vertical and angular striations, rings around the neck, and disproportionately large heads.[3] Another consistent feature in Yoruba art is the elaborate embellishment of images with traditional patterns. Forms, tones, and textures in Yoruba art are expressions of the peoples' perception of the world around them. They are portrayals of their collective aesthetic preferences. For these reasons, Yoruba art conveys specific emotional experiences. For example, the human head is often represented twice as big as life-size. This is a way of communicating the significance of the head in relation to the other parts of the human anatomy. In the Yoruba belief-system, the human head embodies the spiritual essence of the individual. This is why reference is often made to one's *ori* or head in ways that denote transcendental or metaphysical import, as in the saying *ori eni longbe ire koni* ("one's good fortunes are initiated or bestowed by one's head").

The social and political structure of Yorubaland has under-gone various paradigmatic shifts since its early history. This is because the Yoruba have experienced protracted civil wars, secessions, incursion of foreign religions, slavery, and colonization by imperialist armies. Despite these crippling experiences, the traditional Yoruba aesthetic idiom has remained intact as described in this chapter. This may be credited to the well-established system of apprenticeship in traditional Yoruba art.

APPRENTICESHIP IN TRADITIONAL YORUBA ART

To impart skill is a popular practice among the Yoruba who believe strongly in tradition. Yoruba artistic traditions are often preserved through transfer of knowledge from an expert to a learner in a system of apprenticeship. Apprenticeship in Yoruba art entails partially formal and informal approaches. A partially formal apprenticeship usually involves a verbal agreement between (expert) artists and (novice) learners. This type of apprenticeship is sponsored by the learner's parents or through the combined efforts of extended family members. This type of apprenticeship is partially formal because the process of admission and the duration of training are usually not predetermined. In the formal approach, the duration and cost of apprenticeship and training procedures are meticulously deliberated upon during the admission proceedings. This is followed by a verbal or written agreement, sometimes made in the presence of witnesses. The apprentice is sometimes charged a certain instructional fee.

Apprenticeship in traditional Yoruba art usually begins at an early age. Many youngsters start their training when adults in their family consider them old enough to comprehend vital instruction. According to Archibald Callaway, a pioneer scholar of Nigeria's apprentice system, the ages of the apprentices range from 9 to 28 years, with nearly one-half between 16 and 19 years.[4] An art apprenticeship often begins at an early age because participants are rarely required to obtain any formal education prior to starting their training. However, some master artists make basic formal education (obtained through the primary school system) a requirement in considering candidates for apprenticeship because primary school education is believed to instill discipline and a sense of purpose in children. These are essential qualities for success in the apprentice system.

Apprentices in traditional Yoruba art usually work six days per week, averaging ten hours per workday. They learn by observing master artists at work and through intermittent formal instruction. The training period is often extensive because "freedom" or graduation symbolizes transition into adulthood. This newly acquired status entails numerous social and cultural responsibilities, including the maintenance of the artistic tradition. The process of determining an apprentice's preparedness for graduation may therefore extend beyond the work environment to include observation of behavior during social or cultural activities in the community.

The average period of apprenticeship in traditional Yoruba art is eight years. This is a relatively long period of time when compared to high school where students spend an average of five years studying multiple subjects. In explaining the reason for this long period of training, Callaway stated that it has to stretch into the productive period when the youth can pay for his training by serving the master.[5]

The type of work assigned to apprentices often depends on their age and years of experience. The younger ones run errands like fetching tools and keeping the work environment clean. When they are not doing these chores, their duties are to observe the master or other senior apprentices at work until they have been around long enough or have become old enough to manipulate the tools without much of a problem.

THE CONCEPT OF CONTINUITY IN TRADITIONAL YORUBA ART

The transfer of artistic skill from expert to novice among the Yoruba ensures continuity in the practice of traditional Yoruba art forms. The concept of continuity in Yoruba art is mostly based on a larger philosophical belief in transition or immortality of the soul. In Yoruba cosmogony, the soul of a dead person undergoes metaphysical transformation from the mode of physical existence on earth (*aiye*) to a spiritual plane (*orun*) located in the skies. These two modes of human existence are distinct in character but intricately connected in essence. The Yoruba believe that it is the responsibility of the living to maintain communication with the transformed souls of their ancestors, while the spirits of the dead are charged with guiding the lives of those that are on earth.

Communication between these two Yoruba worlds is conducted through religious or ceremonial rites. This mode of interaction often involves the use of religious symbols and cultural icons. These items are fashioned in various media by Yoruba artists whose patrons range from obas or kings to religious cults and private citizens. As a result of this pattern of patronage, the survival of traditional Yoruba art has depended to some extent on the continuance of Yoruba religious institutions and related cults. The development of Yoruba art to its highest potential may have been hampered by its reliance on traditional religions for patronage. This is because traditional Yoruba religious activities were disrupted by early Christian missionaries who depicted the native religions as idol worship and encouraged devotees to destroy their religious paraphernalia. However, the traditional religions have been able to survive in various Yoruba communities and this has sustained the continuity of the artistic tradition.

Yoruba artists approach their cultural and religious responsibilities with much care. Guilds and cooperatives are organized by local artists for the purpose of monitoring quality and sacred processes. The artists usually consult with their patrons at various stages in the production of commissioned works like religious icons. Such communication is helpful in working toward precise specifications. Certain religious objects may also require special rituals at various levels of production.

GENDER FACTORS IN THE APPRENTICESHIP SYSTEM

Gender often plays a role in the choice of occupation or distribution of tasks among the Yoruba. Philosophically, the Yoruba believe that males are genetically better endowed with physical and spiritual strength than females. Therefore, males are expected to work in occupations that are more physically and spiritually demanding. These gender-based assumptions are reflected in the type of media and tools used by the artists and their apprentices.

Female apprentices often train with female artists who specialize in arts that are designated as *ise obirin* or female occupations. These arts are perceived as less rigorous and they include fabric dyeing, pottery, sewing, and basketry. Female apprentices will eventually master these arts and transfer their knowledge to future female apprentices for the purpose of continuity.

Male artists and their apprentices usually work with media that are considered masculine in occupations (*ise okunrin* or male occupations) such as iron smelting, woodcarving, bronze casting, leatherwork, and stone carving. To practice some of these arts, male apprentices are required to be knowledgeable about certain Yoruba religious practices. For example, an apprentice blacksmith must be conversant with the rituals involved in the worship of *orisa Ogun* or the god of iron. Recently, female apprentices have sometimes been trained in male designated occupations in traditional Yoruba art.

CHANGES IN THE APPRENTICESHIP SYSTEM

The apprentice system has gone through some modifications in recent times. One of the changes is that the guilds are now making it mandatory for master artists or craftsmen to provide their apprentices with legally binding documents on conditions of admission and expected graduation date. This policy was instituted for the purpose of effecting high levels of competency.

Another important development in the apprenticeship system is the increasingly regular intervention by institutions of higher learning and independent members of Yoruba communities. For instance, in 1986 the Department of African Studies at the University of Ibadan organized a community sculpture and drawing workshop that attracted about eight apprentices. Commenting on this initiative, art scholar Ohioma Pogoson noted that the university was ethically bound to provide art supplies and an exhibition space for the youngsters on a regular basis.[6] Participants in such workshops were traditionally considered as outsiders within the apprenticeship system.

Another recent development is that some of the trainees who have received their freedom no longer feel compelled to work within their local communities. In the past, work in the local community was considered essential in order to help sustain the continuity of a trade by imparting knowledge to other learners. In fact, some artists who went through the system are not even practicing their trades within present day Nigeria. A prime example is Bintu Olaniyi, who did her apprenticeship in her husband's workshop in Oshogbo. Married to an internationally renowned artist popularly known as Twins Seven Seven, she relocated to the United States in the mid-1980s where she now produces batiks. Some of the major factors that lead to the relocation of artists like Olaniyi are availability of production materials and demand for their finished products. Although she resides in a foreign country, Olaniyi's works continue to show the strong influence of Oshogbo art. The conceptual and stylistic approach to her work reflects a strong grounding in the Oshogbo batik tradition that features animal figures, folklore, myths, and vibrant colors.

INFLUENCE ON CONTEMPORARY YORUBA ART

Traditional Yoruba art and the apprenticeship system that has sustained it have greatly influenced the more recent schools in Yoruba art. As Christopher Adejumo has noted:

> To thoroughly understand the aesthetics and depth of the contemporary [Yoruba] images ... it is necessary to have some knowledge about the link between traditional and modern [Yoruba] art in Nigeria.[7]

Contemporary Yoruba art consists of two modes. These are the transitional and transformational modes. Both of these modes are evolutionary in that they represent a convergence of various ideas with traditional art as their primary source of influence. These two art categories are not drastically different from each other.

The transitional phase draws on traditional art forms for content and style while introducing elements of abstraction that alter the forms in ways that are not beyond recognition. They utilize themes from everyday-life experiences within the Yoruba community. While they are informed by Yoruba aesthetic traditions, they are not limited by them in scope or possibilities.

The second category, transformational art, consists of works that are influenced by traditional Yoruba art but whose contents hardly indicate their sources of inspiration as a result of complete abstraction of forms. Contemporary Yoruba artists often find themselves going back and forth between these two modes of image production. Some of the most prominent Yoruba artists that work within this stylistic category are dele jegede, Moyo Okediji, and Jimoh Buraimoh. These artists often work in a broad range of media, engaging in printmaking, painting, drawing, and sculpture. Apart from their advanced Western-type education, these artists also interact extensively with traditional art institutions. For example, Buraimoh, who received a degree from Ahmadu Bello University, Zaria, also attended the Oshogbo art workshops organized by Ulli Beier in the 1960s. As a result of their affinity for traditional Yoruba art, these artists are still able to indicate the Yoruba identity in their works, despite their transmutations.

CONCLUSION

Produced with simple tools, traditional Yoruba works of art are globally regarded as some of the world's greatest treasures. Apart from their remarkable aesthetic qualities, art enthusiasts and collectors around the world perceive them as authentic representations of a great civilization.

The development of traditional Yoruba art has been linked to the development of Yoruba city-states and traditional religions. Yoruba art has flourished despite periods of near stagnation caused by political and religious attacks on the institutions that have supported the art forms. The art form's continued existence was also threatened by massive exportation of the raw materials that sustained their production activities, especially to Great Britain in the early nineteenth century. To compound this problem, the introduction of technology in the Yoruba economic system resulted in the proliferation of mechanized and mass production of goods, some of which were originally produced by the traditional art industry. The continuity of the art forms during these periods of drastic changes may be credited to the well-established system of apprenticeship.

For centuries, the apprenticeship system has functioned as a forum for the transfer of artistic knowledge from one generation of master artists to another. Works produced by these artists have been mostly patronized by traditional Yoruba religious institutions and their members. Devotees of various *orisas* or gods use the objects as religious icons for the communication of messages between the two cosmic spheres perceived by the Yoruba. The two Yoruba worlds are *aiye* (earth, domain of the living) and *orun* (habitat of Yoruba ancestors, *orisas*, and other spiritual entities located in outer space). As a result of this religious significance, the continuity of Yoruba art has largely depended on the patronage of traditional Yoruba religious institutions and their devotees.

Yoruba artists are loyal to their profession. As a result, they have adhered to long established (sometimes sacred) processes of production despite their access to mechanized tools. This commitment to preserving the aesthetic and spiritual import of Yoruba art is often kept at the expense of personal fame and commercial profit. Some of the artists might have gained better name recognition by using a unique stylistic approach while others might have profited monetarily by mass producing their works through mechanized processes. Critics have described the traditional Yoruba art production processes and the apprentice system as crude and lacking in sophistication. Ironically, it is the simplicity of these processes in relation to their elaborate outcomes that makes the works produced even more remarkable. Through their indigenous apprentice system and aesthetic philosophies, the Yoruba continue to perpetuate a superb artistic tradition for posterity.

NOTES

1. Biodun Adediran, "Yorubaland up to the Emergence of the States," in D. Ogunremi and Biodun Adediran (eds.), *Culture and Society in Yorubaland*. (Ibadan: Rex Charles Publication, 1998), 1-13.
2. H. J. Drewal; J. Pemberton III; & R. Abiodun. "*Yoruba: Nine Centuries of African Art and Thought.*" (New York: Harry N. Abrams Inc., 1989), 45-99.
3. Ibid., 121-203.
4. Archibald Callaway, "Nigeria's Indigenous Education: The Apprentice System," *ODU* 1 (1), 1964, 63-79.
5. Ibid.
6. Conversation with Pogoson on "Agbowo Community Art Center," Department of African Studies, University of Ibadan, 1986.
7. Christopher O. Adejumo. "Nigerian Artists: A Who's Who and Bibliography," in Abiola Irele (ed.), *Research in African Literatures*, 27 (3), 1996, 169-170.

NOTES ON CONTRIBUTORS

Akanmu G. Adebayo is Professor of History at Kennesaw State University. He obtained his Ph.D. from the University of Ife (now Obafemi Awolowo University), Nigeria, where he also taught for a number of years. He has also been Visiting Professor at York University, Canada. Professor Adebayo is widely published. He has co-authored (with Toyin Falola) *Culture, Politics and Money among the Yoruba* (New Brunswick, N.J.: Transaction Publishers, 2000).

Christopher O. Adejumo obtained his Ph.D. in Art Education from Ohio State University, Columbus. He is currently an Assistant Professor of Art at the University of Texas at Austin. He has held many art exhibitions in the United States and Nigeria, and has been awarded a number of research grants. He has published scholarly journal articles and is currently working on a book, *Contemporary African Art: Contents and Meaning in the Work of a Yoruba Artist*.

Julius O. Adekunle holds a Ph.D. degree from Dalhousie University, Halifax, Canada. He is currently an Assistant Professor of African and Caribbean History at Monmouth University, West Long Branch, New Jersey. He has published articles in *Anthropos, Ife: Annals of Cultural Studies* and *African Economic History*, and has contributed chapters to many books. He has won many academic awards, grants, and fellowships including the Judith M. Stanley Fellowship for Improvement of Teaching at Monmouth University. Dr. Adekunle has held teaching positions at Dalhousie and St. Mary's Universities in Halifax, and at Tennessee State University.

Adebambo Adewopo holds the LL.M. degree from both the University of Lagos and the Franklin Pierce Law Center, New Hampshire. He is a lecturer in Intellectual Property Law at Lagos State University. He has coedited *Reforms and Developments, Nigeria Commercial Laws* (Lagos, 1998), and has contributed articles to scholarly journals in Nigeria, Europe, and the United States, including the *International Review of Industrial Property and Copyright*. He has also contributed to intellectual property curriculum and law reform in Nigeria.

Funso Afolayan is an Associate Professor of African History and the African Diaspora at the University of New Hampshire, Durham. He holds a Ph.D. in African History from Obafemi Awolowo University in Nigeria. He has published widely in Africa, Europe, and the United States. He is coauthor of *Yoruba Sacred Kingship: A Power like That of the Gods* (Washington, D.C.: Smithsonian Institution Press, 1996). Dr. Afolayan has also held research and teaching positions at Obafemi Awolowo University, Amherst College, and Washington University at St. Louis.

Yinka Agbetuyi is a poet as well as a literary and cultural critic. He has worked for many years as a broadcast journalist in Ibadan, Nigeria. He has also taught English at the Department of Adult Education, University of Ibadan, and Newham College, London, United Kingdom. He now teaches English at Waltham Forest College, Middlesex University. He holds an M.A. in Cultural Studies, with a concentration in postmodernism, from the University of East London.

Michael Anda obtained his Ph.D. from the University of Wisconsin-Milwaukee. He is an Associate Professor and former Chair of the Department of Political Science at the University of Arkansas at Little Rock. His research interests include comparative politics and international relations with a regional focus on Africa. He is the author of *International Relations in Contemporary Africa* (New York: University Press of America, 2000); *Yoruba,* (New York: Rosen Publishers, 1996); and *Africa in the New World Order* (Little Rock, Ark.: DCI Publishers, 1996).

Désiré Baloubi is an applied linguist from the Benin Republic in West Africa where he was on the teaching staff of Benin Teachers Colleges and the National University of Benin. He was educated at the Ecole Normale Supérieure in Benin, Durham University in England, and Ball State University in Indiana, where he obtained a Ph.D. in Applied Linguistics. His areas of interest are African Linguistics with emphasis on Yoruba dialectology, cross-cultural pragmatics, and TESOL with emphasis on multicultural issues. He is currently an Assistant Professor in the Department of Multidisciplinary Studies, Shaw University.

Gloria I. Chuku received her Ph.D. in History from the University of Nigeria, Nsukka, where she worked on the changing role of women in the Igbo economy. She is currently an Assistant Professor of African History at South Carolina State University. She has previously taught at Imo State University, and held visiting positions at the Women's Studies Program, University of Arizona, the James Coleman African Studies Center at UCLA, and the University of Memphis. In 1995, she was a research scholar at CODESRIA, Dakar, Senegal. She has contributed essays to edited works and published articles in a number of journals including *Ufahamu,* the *Pakistan Journal of Rural Development and Administration*, and *African Economic History.*

J. I. Dibua is an Associate Professor of History at Morgan State University, Baltimore, Maryland. He has published articles on African history, politics, and economy in various international journals, and has contributed chapters to books.

Chima J. Korieh holds a first class degree in history from the University of Nigeria. He is currently completing a Ph.D. on agricultural sustainability, the state, and agricultural crisis in southeastern Nigeria, at the University of Toronto. He has published book chapters and journal articles, most recently in the *Canadian Journal of African Studies*.

O. B. Lawuyi has taught Anthropology at several African universities. Currently he is Professor and Head of the Department of Anthropology at the University of Transkei, South Africa. He has published extensively in the area of urban culture with specific emphasis on representation and consumption.

Abdul-Rasheed Na'Allah teaches African and African American Literature and Folklore at the Western Illinois University. He is an exponent of *Elaloro*, an indigenous African (Yoruba) discourse theory. His book, *People's Poet: Emerging Perspectives on Niyi Osundare* is being published by Africa World Press.

Ebere Nwaubani teaches in the History Department of the University of Colorado at Boulder. He has recently published *The United States and Decolonization in West Africa, 1950-1960* (Rochester: University of Rochester Press, 2001).

G. Ugo Nwokeji holds a Ph.D. degree from the University of Toronto, Canada. He is an Assistant Professor of History in the History Department and the Institute for African American Studies, University of Connecticut. He recently held a visiting fellowship at the Gilder Lehrman Center for the Study of Slavery, Resistance, and Abolition, Yale University, and a visiting scholarship at the Center for Modern Oriental Studies, Berlin, Germany. He has since March 1999 been a research associate at the W.E.B. DuBois Institute for Afro-American Research, Harvard University. Dr. Nwokeji is the author of several articles in scholarly journals such as *Comparative*

Studies in Society and History, the *Canadian Journal of African Studies*, and the *William and Mary Quarterly.*

Olatunji Ojo obtained his M.A. degree from the University of Ibadan, Nigeria. He has held a teaching position at Ibadan, and is currently a graduate student at York University, Toronto. He has contributed entries to the *Encyclopedia of Sub-Saharan Africa* (1997), and his articles have appeared in scholarly journals.

Onaiwu W. Ogbomo holds a Ph.D. degree from Dalhousie University, Halifax, Canada. He is Associate Professor of History and Director, African American Studies, at Eastern Illinois University in Charleston, Illinois. He is the author of many journal articles and a book, *When Men and Women Mattered: A History of Gender Relations among the Owan of Nigeria.* He has taught African and African American history courses in universities in Nigeria, Canada, and the United States.

Oyekan Owomoyela is the Ryan Professor of African Literature at the University of Nebraska, Lincoln. He was born and raised in Nigeria and took his bachelor's degree at the University of Ibadan.

Adebayo Oyebade obtained his Ph.D. in History from Temple University, Philadelphia. He has held teaching positions at various institutions including Ogun State University in Nigeria. He is currently an Assistant Professor of African History at Tennessee State University. He has authored many book chapters on African history and articles in scholarly journals such as *African Economic History* and the *Journal of Black Studies*. He is the coeditor of *Africa after the Cold War: The Changing Perspectives on Security* (Trenton, N.J.: Africa World Press, 1998). He is currently completing a book on the United States' strategic planning in West Africa during World War II. Dr. Oyebade has also been a recipient of Fulbright and Ford Foundation grants.

Uyilawa Usuanlele received his undergraduate education at the University of Ife (now Obafemi Awolowo University) and pursued graduate studies at Ahmadu Bello University, both in Nigeria. He is Assistant Chief Research Officer and the Head of the Edo Zonal Office of the Nigerian National Council for Arts and Culture in Benin City, Nigeria. He is also the Coordinator, Institute for Benin Studies, Benin City. He has published a number of articles in books and learned journals.

Olufemi Vaughan is an Associate Professor in the Department of Africana Studies and the Department of History at the State University of New York, Stony Brook. He obtained his Ph.D. from Oxford University in England. He has written extensively on the interaction between the state and grassroots forces in colonial and postcolonial Africa. He is the author of *Nigerian Chiefs: Traditional Power in Modern Politics, 1890s-1990s* (Rochester, N.Y.: University of Rochester Press, 2000), and coeditor of *Legitimacy and the State in Twentieth Century Africa* (Oxford: Macmillan Press, 1993).

Nimi Wariboko is an independent strategy and investment-banking consultant based in New York. He studied at Columbia University, and has since 1994 worked as a strategy advisor to leading investment banks. He also teaches at New York University and New York Institute of Finance as an adjunct faculty. Wariboko is the author of *The Mind of African Strategists* (1997); *Bank Analysis and Valuation* (1994); and *Financial Statement Analysis* (1993). He has also written extensively on business history and culture in journals including *African Economic History* and the *Nordic Journal of African Studies*.

INDEX

Aba Women's War, 369
Abacha, Sani, 114, 129, 130, 138, 161, 308, 338, 340, 421, 422, 423, 514
Abiola, M. K. O., 160, 421, 423
Abubakar, Abdusalami, 130, 138, 423
Abuja, 114, 282
Academic Staff Union of Universities, 157, 378
Achebe, Chinua, 489, 492, 498, 505
Adelabu, Adegoke, 441, 454
Adele II, 208
Adeyemi III, Lamidi, 446
Adeyemi, M. C., 24
AFRC. *See* Armed Forces Ruling Council
Agbekoya Rebellion, 444

Ahmaddiyya, 52
Ajayi, J. F. Ade, 6, 17, 23, 34, 35
Akenzua II, 59
Akintola, Samuel Ladoke, 88, 105, 338, 412, 419, 454
Armed Forces Ruling Council, 114
Association for Better Nigeria, 159
ASUU. *See* Academic Staff Union of Universities
Atooda myth, 539-540
Atúnda myth, 538-539
Awolowo, Obafemi, 83, 89, 95, 101, 105, 116, 118, 121, 338, 360, 412, 416, 417, 419, 420, 442, 443, 444, 445, 541

Azikiwe, Nnamdi, 88, 95, 96, 97, 121, 189, 360, 412, 417, 418, 545

Babangida, Ibrahim, 32, 129, 130, 138, 139, 140, 141, 142, 143, 144, 146, 147, 148, 149, 151, 152, 153, 154, 155, 156, 157, 158, 159, 160, 161, 262, 282, 283, 338, 339, 340, 347, 421, 514
Bada, Samuel Ojo, 24
Balewa, Abubakar Tafawa, 88, 89, 121, 338, 416, 418
Beier, Ulli, 610
Bekederemo-Clark, 540
See also John Peper Clark
Bello, Ahmadu, 413, 417, 543
Benue-Congo languages, 564, 565, 568
Better Life Program for Rural Women, 141, 142, 148
Biafra, 105, 250, 251, 252, 495, 545
Biobaku, Saburi, 5, 17
Buhari, Muhammadu, 139, 155, 156, 263, 337, 338, 347, 421, 514, 517

Campaign for Democracy, 159
Central Bank of Nigeria, 272, 273
Christian Association of Nigeria, 152
Church Missionary Society 15, 52, 61, 62,
Civil Liberties Organization, 159
Clark, John Pepper, 533
See also Bekederemo-Clark
CMS. *See* Church Missionary Society
Committee for the Defence of Human Rights, 159

Davies, H.O., 412, 415
DFRRI. See Directorate of Food, Road, and Rural Infrastructure
Dike, Kenneth Onwuka, 86, 87
Directorate of Food, Road, and Rural Infrastructure, 141, 148
Directorate of Social Mobilization for Social Justice, Self-Reliance, and Economic Recovery, 141, 148

Eastern Nigeria Marketing Boards, 233
Edo College, 60, 65

Egbe Omo Oduduwa, 95, 444
Enahoro, Anthony, 97, 100, 101
Eweka III, 65

Fajuyi, Adekunle, 443, 544, 545
Falae, Olu, 423
Fawehinmi, Gani, 160

Gates, Jr., Henry Louis, 549
General Agreement on Tariffs and Trade, 167-168
Giwa, Dele, 157
Gowon, Yakubu, 125, 127, 131, 132, 334, 335, 336, 337, 418, 420, 422,
Green Eagles, 512
Green Revolution, 341

Idiagbon, Tunde, 514, 517
Ifa corpus, 590, 591, 592, 594
Ife Humanities Society, 39
Ife-Modakeke Crisis, 21, 413, 422, 448
Ige, Bola, 445, 446, 448, 449, 453-454
Ighodaro, Samuel, 68
Ihonvbere, Julius, 29
Ikoli, Ernest, 414
IMF. *See* International Monetary Fund

Indirect Rule, 55, 81, 83, 98
Interim National Government, 138, 161
International Monetary Fund, 143, 262, 263, 264, 269, 277, 281, 282, 331, 347
Ironsi, Aguiyi, 124, 125, 419, 544
Ita, Eyo, 97

Jemibewon, David, 443
Johnson, Bishop James, 52, 61
Johnson, Samuel, 24

Kalu, Ogbu, 35
King's College, 55, 58, 59, 60, 65

Lovejoy, Paul, 11, 15, 35
Lugard, Frederick, 51, 55, 58, 75, 76, 77, 78, 104, 407, 414-415, 421

Macaulay, Herbert, 412
MAMSER. *See* Directorate of Social Mobilization for Social Justice, Self-Reliance, and Economic Recovery
Manufacturers Association of Nigeria, 273, 274, 276, 278, 282

Mbari Club, 533
Mohammed, Murtala, 335, 337, 339, 340, 420, 517
Morgan, Kemi, 24
Movement for the Survival of the Ogoni People, 151, 308

NADECO. *See* National Democratic Coalition
National Association of Nigerian Students, 156, 157
National Democratic Coalition, 129
National Directorate of Employment, 141, 142
National Electoral Commission, 139
National Electric Power Authority, 309, 310
National Security Organization, 155
National Youth Service Corps, 361
NDE. *See* National Directorate of Employment
Nigeria Medical Association, 156, 158
Nigerian Civil War, 149, 250, 333, 335, 414, 419, 429n, 437, 463, 476, 493
Nigerian Copyright Commission, 172

Nigerian Labor Congress, 158, 160
NSO. *See* National Security Organization
NYSC. *See* National Youth Service Corps
Nzeribe, Arthur, 159

Obasanjo, Olusegun, 133, 138, 147, 153, 334, 335, 337, 340, 344, 349, 363, 364, 372, 420, 421, 423, 425, 517
Oduduwa, 568, 601
Ogoni, 130, 150, 151, 308, 422
Ojaide, Tanure, 546, 547, 549,
Ojukwu, Odumegwu, 419-420
Okar, Gedion, 150, 158
Okigbo, Christopher, 533, 534, 535, 536, 537, 541, 542, 543, 544, 545, 546 548, 549
Okpara, M. I., 242
Olunloyo, Omololu, 446, 454
OPEC. *See* Organization of Petroleum Exporting Countries
Operation Feed the Nation, 341
Organization of Islamic Conference, 151, 152

Organization of Petroleum Exporting Countries, 343
Osogbo Art, 608, 609, 610
Osundare, Niyi, 539, 546, 548, 550, 551, 552,
Ovonramwen, 61

Pan-African Congress, 412
Pan-African Movement, 412
Phelps-Stokes Commission, 56

Ransome-Kuti, Beko, 160
Roman Catholic Mission, 52, 64, 65
Rotimi, Oluwole, 443
Royal Niger Company, 74, 192, 295, 306, 407

SAP. *See* Structural Adjustment Program
Saro-Wiwa, Ken, 130, 308, 422
Second-Tier Foreign Exchange Market, 144, 270, 272
Shagari, Shehu, 31, 32, 139, 262-263, 282, 334, 337, 341, 347, 363, 372, 420, 421
shari'a, 133, 134, 424,
Shonekan, Ernest, 421
Sijuwade, Okunade, 446
Soyinka, Wole, 484, 485, 486, 487, 488, 489, 492, 496, 497, 505, 506, 513, 514, 528, 533, 536, 537, 541, 545, 549, 550
Standard Yoruba (SY), 563, 566, 570, 571, 573, 576
State Security Service 156
Structural Adjustment Program, 143, 144, 145, 153, 159, 262, 263, 269, 270, 271, 272, 274, 275, 276, 279, 280, 283, 284, 338, 348, 525

Tofa, Bahir, 160, 421
Trade-Related Aspects of Intellectual Property Rights, 168, 177, 178
Trans-Atlantic Slave Trade, 600
TRIPs. See Intellectual Property Rights
Twins Seven Seven, 608

Vatsa, Mamman, 162n

War Against Indiscipline, 517
West African Frontier Force, 407
World Bank, 269, 277, 281, 309, 331, 347
World Trade Organization, 168

Zikist Movement, 189, 190, 191, 196, 197